Property Of:
The Graduate Institute
701 North Street
Milford, CT 06460

D0216931

Political Ideas
and Institutions
in Imperial Russia

POLITICAL IDEAS AND INSTITUTIONS IN IMPERIAL RUSSIA

Marc Raeff

Westview Press

BOULDER • SAN FRANCISCO • OXFORD

GI
DK
127
.R25
1994

All rights reserved. No part of this publication may be reproduced or transmitted in any form or by any means, electronic or mechanical, including photocopy, recording, or any information storage and retrieval system, without permission in writing from the publisher.

Copyright © 1994 by Westview Press, Inc.

Published in 1994 in the United States of America by Westview Press, Inc., 5500 Central Avenue, Boulder, Colorado 80301-2877, and in the United Kingdom by Westview Press, 36 Lonsdale Road, Summertown, Oxford OX2 7EW

Library of Congress Cataloging-in-Publication Data
Raeff, Marc.
  Political ideas and institutions in imperial Russia / Marc Raeff.
    p.   cm.
  Includes bibliographical references.
  ISBN 0-8133-1878-5
  1. Russia—Politics and government—1689-1801.   2. Russia—
Politics and government—1801-1917.   I. Title.
DK127.R25   1994
947—dc20   93-48117
                                                                                     CIP

Printed and bound in the United States of America

∞ The paper used in this publication meets the requirements
   of the American National Standard for Permanence of Paper
   for Printed Library Materials Z39.48-1984.

10   9   8   7   6   5   4   3   2   1

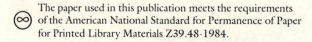

To Edward Kasinec and his fellow librarians,
whose enthusiasm and dedication
make scholarship not only possible but exciting

Contents

Acknowledgments

I wish to thank the publishers of the journals and volumes for permission to reprint the articles that originally appeared under their imprint. I am most thankful to Peter W. Kracht and Westview Press for undertaking the publication and to Connie Oehring and Ida May B. Norton for their meticulous supervising and editing in the process of publication. I am indebted to Molly Molloy of the Hoover Institution Library and Edward Kasinec and his staff at the New York Public Library for preparing and updating my bibliography.

Marc Raeff

Credits

Chapter 1: "Russia After the Emancipation: Views of a Gentleman-Farmer," *Slavonic and East European Review* 29(73) (July 1951): 470–485. Reprinted by permission.

Chapter 2: "A Reactionary Liberal: M. N. Katkov," *Russian Review* 11(3) (July 1952): 157–167. Reprinted by permission.

Chapter 3: "Some Reflections on Russian Liberalism," *Russian Review* 18(3) (July 1959): 218–230. Reprinted by permission.

Chapter 4: "Russian Youth on the Eve of Romanticism: Andrei I. Turgenev and His Circle," in Alexander and Janet Rabinowitch with Ladis K.D. Kristof, eds., *Revolution and Politics in Russia: Essays in Memory of B. I. Nicolaevsky* (Bloomington: University of Indiana Press, 1972), pp. 39–54. Reprinted by permission.

Chapter 5: "At the Origins of a Russian National Consciousness: Eighteenth Century Roots and Napoleonic Wars," *The History Teacher* 25(1) (November 1991): 7–18. Reprinted by permission.

Chapter 6: "The Russian Autocracy and Its Officials," in Hugh McLean, Martin E. Malia, and George Fischer, eds., *Harvard Slavic Studies, IV: Russian Thought and Politics* (Cambridge, Mass.: Harvard University Press, 1957), pp. 77–91. Reprinted by permission.

Chapter 7: "Introduction" in Marc Raeff, ed., *Plans for Political Reform in Imperial Russia, 1730–1905* (Englewood Cliffs, N.J.: Prentice-Hall, 1966), pp. 1–39.

Chapter 8: "Russia's Autocracy and Paradoxes of Modernization," in Gerhard Oberkofler and Eleonore Zlabinger, eds., *Ost-West-Begegnung in Österreich: Festschrift für Eduard Winter* (Köln: Böhlau Verlag SMBH, 1976), pp. 275–283. Reprinted by permission.

Chapter 9: "Patterns of Russian Imperial Policy Toward the Nationalities," in Edward Allworth, ed., *Soviet Nationality Problems* (New York: Columbia University Press, 1971), pp. 22–42. Reprinted by permission.

Chapter 10: "Uniformity, Diversity, and the Imperial Administration in the Reign of Catherine II," in Hans Lemberg, Peter Nitsche, and Erwin

Oberländer in cooperation with Manfred Alexander and Hans Hecker, eds., *Osteuropa in Geschichte und Gegenwart: Festschrift für G. Stökl* (Köln: Böhlau Verlag SMBH, 1977), pp. 97–113. Reprinted by permission.

Chapter 11: "In the Imperial Manner," originally published as "The Style of Russia's Imperial Policy and Prince G. A. Potemkin," in G. N. Grob, ed., *Statesmen and Statecraft of the Modern West: Essays in Honor of Dwight E. Lee and H. Donaldson Jordan* (Barre, Mass.: Barre Publishing Co., 1967), pp. 1–51. Reprinted by permission.

Chapter 12: "The Domestic Policies of Peter III and His Overthrow," *American Historical Review* 75(5) (June 1970): 1289–1310. Reprinted by permission.

Chapter 13: "The Empress and the Vinerian Professor: Catherine II's Projects of Government Reforms and Blackstone's *Commentaries*," *Oxford Slavonic Papers* 7 (New Series) (1976): 18–41. Reprinted by permission.

Chapter 14: "Pugachev's Rebellion," in Robert Forster and Jack P. Greene, eds., *Preconditions of Revolution in Early Modern Europe* (Baltimore and London: The Johns Hopkins University Press, 1970), pp. 161–202. Reprinted by permission.

Chapter 15: "State and Nobility in the Ideology of M. M. Shcherbatov," *American Slavic and East European Review* 19(3) (October 1960): 363–379. Reprinted by permission.

Chapter 16: "Muscovy Looks West," in Paul Dukes, ed., *Russia and Europe* (London: Collins and Brown, 1991), pp. 59–64. Originally published in *History Today* 36(8) (August 1986): 16–21. Reprinted by permission of *History Today*.

Chapter 17: "The Enlightenment in Russia and Russian Thought in the Enlightenment," in John G. Garrard, ed., *The Eighteenth Century in Russia* (Oxford: Clarendon Press, 1973), pp. 25–47. Reprinted by permission.

Chapter 18: "The Well-Ordered Police State and the Development of Modernity in Seventeenth- and Eighteenth-Century Europe: An Attempt at a Comparative Approach," *American Historical Review* 80(5) (December 1975): 1221–1243. Reprinted by permission.

Chapter 19: "Transfiguration and Modernization: The Paradoxes of Social Disciplining, Paedagogical Leadership, and the Enlightenment in 18th Century Russia," in Hans Erich Bödeker and Ernst Hinrichs, eds., *Alteuropa—Ancien Régime—Frühe Neuzeit: Probleme und Methoden der Forschung* (Stuttgart-Bad Cannstatt: Frommann-Holzboog, 1991), pp. 99–115.

Chapter 20: "Literacy, Education, and the State in 17th–18th Century Europe," transcription of a lecture given as the eighth annual Phi Alpha Theta distinguished lecture on history at the State University of New York at Albany on March 23, 1988 (brochure). Reprinted by permission of the Department of History, State University of New York at Albany.

Introduction

THROUGHOUT MY SCHOLARLY CAREER I have developed most of my ideas in essays and articles rather than monographs. I have preferred to roam over broad topics of Russian history and relate them to general European problems rather than to work on narrow themes in depth. In addition, during much of the first half of my active professional life, Russian archives and libraries were inaccessible, and later on when foreign researchers were given limited access, personal and practical considerations precluded long stays in the Soviet Union. To compensate for my scant work in the archives, I have stressed comparative aspects involving West European institutional and intellectual developments. I am convinced that it is in the realm of comparative history that Russian historians working abroad can make contributions, thanks to their broader perspective and greater familiarity with other experiences. This was (and still is) very much true of Russian historiography because its native practitioners were unable to travel and work abroad and had but limited acquaintance with Western historiography.

There may be some dilettantism in ranging over many aspects—and most periods—of imperial Russian history. But looking back over a lifetime's work, I detect some coherence and logic in my investigations of eighteenth- and nineteenth-century Russian history, as illustrated by the selections reprinted here. I have arranged the essays thematically rather than in chronological order, for some topics continued to hold my attention while I was working on new problems, and they would be reformulated or complemented in the light of subsequent interests. The collection thus reflects the meanderings of my ideas and interests as well as illuminates various problems that I deem crucial for a better understanding of imperial Russia's historical development. Because many of the articles reprinted here have appeared in hard-to-obtain collective volumes and Festschriften, it was felt worthwhile to collect them be-

tween two covers. They appear here with minor cuts and without updating
the notes and bibliographical apparatus, for in quite a few instances my efforts
have been further developed and illustrated—or qualified—by other scholars.

Before even starting my graduate studies, I had the good fortune of being
able to roam freely in the stacks of Widener Library at Harvard. There I discovered the works of Max Weber, Karl Mannheim, Otto Hintze, Carl
Schmitt, and major masters of modern Western historiography. In my graduate school days, also at Harvard, I became fascinated by the history of political
theory, in the way it was then taught by C. J. Friedrich and Louis Hartz. This
interest provided the impetus for doing independent research on the political
ideas—and their institutional context—of early sixteenth-century Muscovite
Russia. The paper that was the outcome of this effort was presented to a seminar on Renaissance political thought and practice, and it became my first
scholarly publication. It is not included here as it falls outside the chronological framework of the volume, but I mention it because it helped to define the
orientation I took in my subsequent work; naturally it was also important in
acquainting me with the pre-Petrine background of imperial Russia.

Archives and libraries in Soviet Russia were inaccessible in the late 1940s
and early 1950s; research thus had to be based almost exclusively on published and available documentation. There was also widespread and keen interest in the background and causes for the failures of the imperial regime and
for the ideas of the intelligentsia, in particular the latter's attitudes toward
peasant institutions—an important subject that neither pre-1917 nor émigré
(not to speak of Western) historians had adequately investigated. For this reason, I tried in my doctoral dissertation to find out in what ways the moderate
intelligentsia's ideological commitments changed in the light of new historical
circumstances. The first two items in this collection (originally chapters of my
dissertation that I decided not to publish) aim at illuminating the relationship
between basic intellectual premises and concrete institutional arrangements of
peasant life after the emancipation of the serfs in 1861. The moderate intelligentsia constituted the core of Russian political liberalism in the last decades
before the 1917 revolution, so that its views pointed to the direction reforms
had to take if a violent breakup were to be avoided.

Because the liberals had largely been neglected by the canonical Russian intellectual historians in the nineteenth century, it was necessary to define and explain the dilemmas and ambiguities of Russian liberalism in the pre-
revolutionary decades (Chapter 3). The lessons may still be applicable today
in spite of radically changed circumstances. In the course of this investigation,
it became clear to me that the ideas and practical projects propounded by the
liberals in the middle of the nineteenth century had their antecedents and
sociopsychological roots in the preceding generation. I was thus led directly
to research the ideas and reform policies advocated by the most distinguished
imperial official and statesman, M. M. Speransky.[1] The result was my only

comprehensive monograph, and it, in turn, led me to investigate—by then with recourse to archival sources in Russia—the generation of the early 1800s, originators of the psychology of the Russian progressive intelligentsia in the nineteenth century (Chapter 4). With the help of concepts borrowed from the sociology of knowledge and modern individual psychology, I aimed to sketch more sharply and in contemporary terms the dynamic role played by personal and social circumstances in shaping the mentality of the intelligentsia élite. In this manner I was pulled even farther back into the eighteenth century, a time when the life circumstances of Russia's educated élites laid the groundwork for the crisis they experienced in the first quarter of the nineteenth century.[2] It was a crisis that not only shaped the intelligentsia but also defined the character of Russian national consciousness—something I could explicitly describe only many years later (Chapter 5).

Any historian studying the problems involved in the reform and modernization (or better still, rationalization) of the imperial administration under the guidance of M. M. Speransky must confront the issue of the nature of the personnel destined to implement government policies. What traits characterized government personnel in the first half of the nineteenth century? The article written for the Festschrift to our professor at Harvard, M. M. Karpovich, called attention to some of their characteristic features that proved a stumbling block in implementing the more progressive and efficiency-oriented intentions of high officials (Chapter 6). The essay was perhaps first in a line of research that subsequently also made use of quantification and covered a longer chronological period.[3] A book of readings on the various plans of reform of government over a period of two centuries provided the occasion for singling out the basic issues and problems confronting reformers in government and for characterizing the ways in which the imperial establishment tried to deal with them. The essays helped clarify the paradox inherent in the government's long-term aim of making Russia into a modern (by contemporary West European standards) state with the help of inadequate or inappropriate institutional arrangements (Chapters 7 and 8).

The paradox highlighted a much-neglected aspect of Russian reality: the state's national heterogeneity and social and geographic diversity. The importance of this historiographically underplayed dimension became obvious in assessing the reforms introduced by Speransky in the administration of Siberia.[4] The article prepared for a symposium on the nationalities held at Columbia University endeavored to give an overview of the pattern Russia followed in becoming a multinational empire (Chapter 9). Subsequently I illustrated the application of this pattern in the reign of Catherine II (Chapter 10). The pattern has again become acutely relevant today as we witness the breakup of the Soviet empire and become aware of most Russians' unpreparedness in dealing with the nationalities.[5] An exemplary case of the complexity involved in the formation of the empire and of the personalized authority that promoted it was offered by the acquisition and integration of the southern territories stretching to the Black Sea (Chapter 11). Quite clearly, the events described are also at the root of today's Ukrainian national consciousness and territorial claims.

To understand the dynamics of the imperial administrative system, it is essential to have a clear notion of the governing élites and of their relationship to the ruler. The article on Peter III (Chapter 12) addresses this issue. Of the two essays dealing with the reign of Catherine II, one focuses on the empress's ideas for improving the effectiveness of her government, and the other on the people's reactions and relationship to the Petrine administration (Chapters 13 and 14). The particular conditions pertaining to frontier areas offer an illustration of how the imperial efforts at integrating them provoked the last widespread interregional outburst of popular opposition to uniformity, centralization, and bureaucratization (Chapter 14). As a counterpoint, from the opposite end of the social and political spectrum, an examination of the political ideas and projects of Prince M. M. Shcherbatov reveals the dialectics between traditional Muscovite and Western Petrine perspectives on Russia's character and needs (Chapter 15).

At this point it bears mentioning that my work on the nature of Russia's political system in the eighteenth century and of its relationship to Muscovite practices has been expanded and qualified by detailed studies of the composition of the ruling élites and of the character of the post-Petrine polity. Over the last decade or so, historians in the West and in Russia have significantly revised our understanding of the nature and dynamics of the imperial system in the eighteenth century. It may not be an exaggeration to say that the dogmatic rigidities of Soviet historiography were first breached in this area of historical scholarship.[6] In still another sense, this reorientation was applied to late nineteenth-century imperial institutions (and their staffs), and it has yielded significantly better understanding of the causes of their collapse in the twentieth century.

For those who, like me, believe that men's public actions are guided by their ideas and sociopsychological (i.e., cultural) values, it is natural to be concerned with the intellectual framework that shapes institutional practices and behavior. Paradoxically (but far from being uncommon in scholarship), highly ideologized and biased work may redirect a scholar's attention to problems that had been bypassed or ignored. In a review essay (written in French and not included here)[7] of works published in East Berlin by authors who formed a group under the direction of the political chameleon Eduard Winter, I pointed to the impact of German ideas on eighteenth-century Russia, a circumstance that also prepared the ground for Russian receptivity of German (including Austrian) legal and administrative practices in the early nineteenth century. This led to a reconsideration of the role of the Anglo-French Enlightenment in contrast to the German *Aufklärung*. The question was not so much that of direct borrowings from German writers and thinkers as of the gradual penetration of a complex way of thought that could be applied in devising the policies and practices of both Central European and Russian polities (Chapters 16 and 17).

The basic view was that traditional society (in the first place, the common people) had to be disciplined by a dynamic, modernizing government to accept the restructuring of its activities in a more "rational" (in Max Weber's sense) manner so as to enhance its productivity in all areas. The difficulty of the task stemmed from the fact that it required a new way of thinking about the nature of the universe and of its laws and about people's relationship to knowledge of these laws; consequently, there was also the need of developing new patterns of behavior. It was an all-European problem from the seventeenth century on, so that the issues of education, literacy, enlightenment, and modernization had to be approached from an all-Western perspective—a perspective of which the Russian situation was but a special case (Chapters 18, 19 and 20). The strains and disjunctions, especially between the people and the élites, that were the result present a new agenda for future historians.

This, in brief, was the scholarly odyssey that is illustrated by the essays reprinted here.[8] (I have not included articles in foreign languages and those written in direct preparation of my books. Nor did I deem this collection the place for reprinting review essays and articles of a publicistic [or polemical] nature.) Through the items included here, I have endeavored to raise and, it is hoped, to explain some basic features of Russia's historical experience—features that, I believe, are still at work in the travail resulting from the disintegration of the Soviet system and the breakup of the Soviet empire.

Notes

1. Marc Raeff, *Michael Speransky: Statesman of Imperial Russia, 1772–1839* (The Hague: Martinus Nijhoff, 1957; 2d ed. 1969).

2. Marc Raeff, *Origins of the Russian Intelligentsia: The Eighteenth-Century Nobility* (New York: Harcourt, Brace and World, 1966).

3. Walter McKenzie Pintner and Don Karl Rowney, eds., *Russian Officialdom: The Bureaucratization of Russian Society from the Seventeenth to the Twentieth Century* (Chapel Hill: University of North Carolina Press, 1980); P. A. Zaionchkovskii, *Pravitel'stvennyi apparat samoderzhavnoi Rossii v XIX v* (Moscow: Izdatel'stvo "Mysl'", 1978); and my review essay, Marc Raeff, "The Bureaucratic Phenomena of Imperial Russia, 1700–1905," *American Historical Review* 84, no. 2 (1979), pp. 399–411.

4. Marc Raeff, *Siberia and the Reforms of 1822* (Seattle: University of Washington Press, 1956).

5. Andreas Kappeler, *Russland als Vielvölkerreich: Entstehung, Geschichte, Zerfall* (Munich: C. H. Beck, 1992).

6. To mention but the most significant titles in English: David L. Ransel, *The Politics of Catherinian Russia: The Panin Party* (New Haven, Conn.: Yale University Press,

1975); Brenda Meehan-Waters, *Autocracy and Aristocracy: The Russian Service Elite of 1730* (New Brunswick, N.J.: Rutgers University Press, 1982); John P. Le Donne, *Ruling Russia: Politics and Administration in the Age of Absolutism 1762–1796* (Princeton, N.J.: Princeton University Press, 1984) and *Absolutism and Ruling Class: The Formation of the Russian Political Order, 1700–1825* (New York: Oxford University Press, 1991); and Isabel de Madariaga, *Russia in the Age of Catherine the Great* (New Haven, Conn.: Yale University Press, 1981).

7. Marc Raeff, "Les Slaves, les Allemands et les Lumières," *Canadian-American Slavic Studies* 1, no. 4 (1967), pp. 521–551.

8. The transliterations of the original articles have been retained in these reprinted versions.

ONE

Russia After
the Emancipation

Views of a Gentleman-Farmer

WE KNOW WELL THE RÔLE played by the slavophils in the preparation
and actual drafting of the Emancipation Act of 1861. The most prominent
representative of the so-called "young slavophils," Yury Samarin, a very active
and influential member of the Editorial Commission, has often been credited
with the preservation of the commune as the basic unit of peasant life.[1] But if
the views of the slavophils on emancipation and the commune in particular
have been studied for the period preceding the great reform, very little, if anything, has been said concerning their opinions of the working out of the
emancipation. Some of them lived long enough to evaluate the effects of the
survival of the village commune, an economic and political institution which
they had done so much to keep alive, or perhaps had even restored to life, if
we are to believe some of their critics. Did the hard test of daily life and of
"compromises with reality" in enforcing the emancipation settlement further
or destroy their principles?

An interesting answer to this question can be found in the opinions of A.
Koshelev. From his youth, he had been a very active and energetic member of
the Moscow slavophil circle, though he never could be counted among its
ideological and intellectual leaders. In the rather closely knit membership of
this circle, Koshelev had always been the "frondeur."[2] Not only was he the
most practical of them—at times even ruthlessly so—but he was also closer to
the west and more open to its examples and influences. A regular visitor to
Western Europe, he was a particularly eager and keen observer of the techni-

cal progress achieved there. Of very independent character, he did not easily accept the leadership of any one individual.[3]

Koshelev was far from the deep spirituality which animated Khomyakov and Samarin or the emotionality of an Ivan Aksakov. On the whole, he was the more worldly-wise member of the younger slavophil set. This brought him closer to the ordinary Russian country gentleman, the more so as he shared the latter's practical interests and concern for efficient farming conditions. Koshelev himself was a landowner, and with the exception of occasional participation in private and public economic projects, such as the development of railroad transportation, the management of his own estates took up most of his time and energy. Early interested in the problems of agrarian economics, he had soon realised the need for emancipation. To this effect he drew up plans for the abolition of serfdom on the basis of his observations abroad and experience on his own estates. The first plan he drafted provided for a very gradual and moderate emancipation. But even this modest proposal was rejected by Nicholas I who, however, allowed Koshelev to put it into effect on his own domain. With characteristic prudence when it came to his personal interests, Koshelev did not take advantage of this permission. When the right to discuss serfdom publicly was granted by Alexander II, Koshelev circulated another emancipation project which was considered most radical, because it provided for the freeing of the serfs with land at a moderate rate of redemption payments. At that time even Samarin was advocating mere palliative measures restricting the landlords' abuse of power. But Khomyakov insisted that Koshelev should send his plan to St. Petersburg, for the more radical the demands, the better the chances that something might be done. But events were moving rapidly then, and soon Koshelev's own project became too conservative for the makers of the reform.[4] Though active in peasant affairs for a long time, Koshelev was not called to participate in the work of the Editorial Commission. He was, however, appointed a member of the consultative body of noblemen who presented their views on the reform before its final approval by the Council of State and the Emperor. Apparently hurt in his pride, he opposed the final terms of the Emancipation Act, for they seemed to him too much the product of the St. Petersburg bureaucracy and not enough the result of a sharing of minds with the nobility;[5] a very characteristic and common attitude among the gentry at the time, even the more liberal among them. In applying the provisions of the Act of 19 February in his own domains, Koshelev was very careful to safeguard all his interests. The settlement with his peasants was among the least advantageous to the latter in his province.[6] Yet, he completely accepted the idea of emancipation and worked honestly to put it into effect. During the remaining twenty-odd years of his life, he was a most efficient gentleman-farmer, experimenting with technical novelties, trying to teach the peasants improved farming methods by his own example. He continued to write on agricultural and political subjects, basing his conclusions on the working out of the emancipation on his experience and practical knowledge of agrarian conditions.

Koshelev's views should therefore be interesting as a reflection of expert knowledge of the conditions in the villages and also as an indication of what a progressive-minded, but socially conservative member of the gentry felt the results of the emancipation to be. His opinions throw light on the desires of a sizable group of enlightened gentry who sought to make the most of the new opportunities which the emancipation and subsequent reforms had created. These noblemen understood that their new function was to lead Russia towards more modern and progressive economic and social conditions, and in so doing they furnished the technical and intellectual leadership for *zemstva* and judicial institutions. They perceived clearly that the abolition of serfdom was but a first step in a radical transformation of the country. Like all Russian intellectuals since the days of Novikov and Radishchev, the immediate as well as the main question they and Koshelev asked themselves concerned the political structure of the country. Would the emancipation bring to an end the absolutist and tyrannical police state and help to establish a *Rechtsstaat* (perhaps even with some representative institutions)? What would then be the rôle of the newly freed peasantry in this transformation? And would the commune remain an essential part of the peasant's life, enhancing his participation in administrative and political affairs? In a way, perhaps, even among these enlightened noblemen, Koshelev was more aware of the implications of the Emancipation Act. He saw that economic individualism was the "historical necessity" of the moment (a reflection of his early Hegelianism) and that it was further enhanced by the provisions of the emancipation. Its development would do more to change the character of Russian village life and of the peasant than all the laws drawn up by the intelligentsia. Any plan for political reform and transformation would have to take it into account and base itself on this new situation. Let us then turn to a consideration of Koshelev's findings and conclusions.

In good Hegelian tradition, but deviating from the more usual slavophil pattern, Koshelev's political and economic thinking was based on his views of the state. But in good slavophil tradition, for him too, the starting-point was the organic and indissoluble union of tsar and people. As in most romantic conceptions of this kind, the union was nothing more concrete than a spiritual bond similar to a father's relation to members of his family. He believed, however, that the St. Petersburg bureaucracy, "a Germanic importation," had erected a wall between the tsar and the people, so that the central government, i.e. the tsar, had no true idea of the people's wants and needs and that contrary to an erroneous, but frequently held opinion, the nobility was not responsible for this wall.[7] It was essential to eradicate this bureaucracy, for it corrupted every act of the state, however well intentioned. Speaking as an opponent of the Editorial Commission, Koshelev declared:

We saw in your complicated, petty, and strictly finite proposal an exhalation of bureaucracy, which would definitely kill the life of the people and the local significance of the landowners. And by replacing these two by regulations, the universally hated bureaucracy was only strengthened.[8]

In Koshelev's opinion, the only way of solving the great problems confronting the nation was to convoke a Zemskaya Duma in Moscow, the heart of Russia, far from its existing bureaucratic centre.[9] By eliminating the wall between people and tsar, the Duma would become the spokesman of the "land" before the throne. It would provide exhaustive information on the state of the nation and transmit to the throne the wishes of the people:

> If the government really wants to know the present opinion of the country and elicit useful advice, the only possible way is to let those people whose opinion one wishes to know elect representatives for this specific purpose. And why does the government fear these elections? ... Only those bureaucrats who want to continue to fish in troubled waters have to fear the election of new, capable, independent people.[10]

The practical and positive results of such a consultation would be to develop national talents and forces, contributing to their increase and strengthening. This in turn would considerably enhance the means of the state; and therefore a government, conscious of its rôle, confident in itself, should rejoice at this increase and foster it in all possible ways. Koshelev felt the government had already indirectly recognised that there was such a need. Alas, concretely and practically, little had as yet come of it. Before 1861, naturally, there had been no desire to share governmental and administrative powers, but the emancipation had produced different conditions:

> As long as millions of people were merely things which could be sold and bought, and thousands were their masters, there could be no question of local self-government or judicial reform based on any kind of justice. Even less could there be question of a participation of the nation in the legislative and higher administrative work of the state. Now that the possibility for these changes has been given, their necessity becomes apparent.[11]

As an institution, the concept of a Duma rested on old historical tradition "whose elective principle is older than Russia itself. For only the establishment of a bureaucracy sounded the death knell of consultative Dumas."[12] Yet the tsar's absolutism would not disappear even with a Duma:

> As Russia became an independent country and extended her borders and the power of the tsar grew stronger and even absolute, consultative assemblies were called from time to time. In these, representatives of the nation gave their opinion on matters submitted for their consideration by the government and informed the latter of the needs of the people. But the tsars made their decision according to their own will.[13]

These were the basic principles which clearly determined Koshelev's political demands. A union between tsar and people had existed in earlier times; the problem was to re-establish it. For this the bureaucracy had to be eliminated, or else made completely subservient to the will of the monarch. Quite obviously, such a change could not be carried out by the existing St. Petersburg administration which was entirely bureaucratic, yet to remain inactive could only lead to violent revolution and anarchy:

> The bureaucracy and the system it originated and now protects, cannot be changed gradually and piecemeal. One has to cut the evil at its roots. This can be done only by a bloody revolution or by means of a timely, sincere, and complete union of tsar and people.[14]

The latter could be achieved by proclaiming the reforms as an act of the tsar's will, his autocratic prerogative. Koshelev had to keep autocracy as the basis of Russian political life, for only it could bring about change without provoking anarchy:

> For us at the present time autocracy is essential [he wrote before the emancipation]. It alone could, in time and peacefully, destroy serfdom and make a land allotment to the peasants. It alone could solve the many problems vital to Russia from above and without disruption.[15]

The Act of 19 February had shown that this conviction was well-founded and it should serve as an example.

Koshelev shared the general slavophil belief in the dignity of the individual. The state and its agents would have to cease to treat the people like chattels:

> The principal cause of these pitiful conditions [of the country] resides in the fact that the government of Russia lives in isolation. We are something alien to it and in turn do not consider it part of ourselves. For the government consists of people who have been in service too long ... and who regard private persons like a herd of sheep or cows which can be shorn or milked, but whose opinion is a matter of indifference.[16]

A degraded people made for very bad subjects, and this in turn for a very poor country indeed. Such a treatment of people was demoralising to both ruled and rulers, just as previously serfdom had degraded serfs and owners alike. Therefore, in a political autocracy, where the wishes of the people would be known through a Duma, there should also be a complete guarantee of those individual rights which preserve and protect the status of the individual as a citizen. The more developed and prosperous the country, the more acute this need would become:

> Woe to those governments which still believe it possible to provide their subjects with the advantages and products of modern civilisation, making use of these in-

creased human forces yet without elevating them to the level of complete citizenship and without granting them that which alone makes true men.[17]

Koshelev felt sure that this view would receive eventual recognition, if not now, then in due time:

> Informed of the true needs of the country by a Zemskaya Duma, the tsar will give Russia a Basic Act (*Ustavnaya Gramota*) which will guarantee all those rights essential to a citizen. In other countries this was obtained after struggles and violence.[18]

In Russia there will be no need for violence if the government shows understanding and the people patience. And repeating previous slavophil arguments for free speech and opinion, Koshelev pointed out that the true state and wishes of the nation could not be conveyed to the tsar without freedom of expression.

But what was the peasant's rôle in this picture? After all he accounted for the most numerous group in Russia. To Koshelev, union between the tsar and the land (*zemlya*) meant above all a union of the tsar with the peasants, the backbone of the country. This union had existed in olden times, but the violent irruption of foreign elements under Peter the Great and his successors had torn this bond. Let us note, however, that the spiritual development of the peasant, even after the emancipation, had not yet matched his new civic rights. And though he had made great progress in the understanding of his prerogatives, it had not been the same with the understanding of his duties. And Koshelev continued:

> The peasants, though numerous and strong, will never be on the level of a first class in the state. Their relationship to the government must always remain indirect.

For this reason, they needed intermediaries.

> It [the people] has need of us [enlightened nobility]; it, more than we, is afraid of the bureaucrats; now we can become its guide.[19]

But class divisions were contrary to the Russian tradition; everything possible would have to be done to wipe out the corporate character of the nobility, this foreign intrusion brought in by Peter I and Catherine II.[20] Also, as an "organic" group in the Russian nation, the aristocracy had lost much of its claims. Demoralised by serfdom, spoiled by the bureaucratic spirit of St. Petersburg, spiritually separated from the people, it had suffered a severe economic and political blow in the emancipation. According to the very words of the Code of Laws itself, the nobility was no more than a name.[21]

"One method of solving the problem of the nobility definitely and to the satisfaction of all, is for it to act openly and in conjunction with the other classes of the state." For that, "we [nobles] must try to remain landowners, cherish this calling, look upon the soil as one of the most essential sources of our strength." Thus the landowners would naturally become the intermediaries between people and state. Access to the group would be free:

We shall not be a closed class. It is not by way of titles—a [hierarchical] ladder which the peasants believe inaccessible to them—that one can become a member, but by acquiring certain quantities of land.

The peasantry too—but only the better part—would have access to this class of intermediaries. And with France and England in mind, Koshelev found this better part of the peasantry among the rich private landowning farmers.

Their [peasants'] most natural, most convenient, and most friendly intermediaries can be the best men from among those living on the land, i.e. and landowners. These will not be only noblemen, i.e. a class completely alienated from the peasants' way of life, but people living in close relation with them, and maybe only yesterday's fellow members in the *mir*. ... The remainder of the village population will not be inimical but favourable to us (*meliores*), for among us there will be their kin in whom they have confidence and whom they respect. Moreover, each inhabitant, upon fulfilment of certain conditions, can take a seat among us.

Eventually, the largest contingent would be made up of peasants closely identified with the people's spiritual and cultural needs:

Admitting them into our ranks, we, the nobility, shall receive new and healthy forces from among the masses of rural population. Through them we shall unite with the people, we shall establish, maintain, and increase our ties with the strongest and least spoiled part of the nation.

As soon as a peasant (or anyone else for that matter) had acquired enough land in private property—the minimum to be set by statute—he would be automatically transferred into the class of "intermediaries."

In this manner, it is not we [nobles] who shall go into an alien society, but the people who will come to us. We shall not make ourselves small and humble, but those who join us will try to raise themselves and attain a higher position among us by acquiring landed property, knowledge, experience, etc. . . .[22]

If property became the only criterion, the arbitrary divisions of the population into classes would disappear by themselves. Anyone owning property in the city would become the "intermediary" there, a bourgeois in other words. Anyone owning land in the country would become a squire.[23] We can see how correctly Koshelev had perceived the basic element of 19th-century Europe's social development. He had also clearly sensed that, since the emancipation, Russia had been progressing in the same direction, towards a regrouping of society on the basis of property. His scheme was an attempt at making the process as painless as possible, while at the same time giving the nobility a chance to preserve its leading status.

And the commune? Would private ownership, the basis for the new dominant group, not make of the *mir* a useless institution? Koshelev did not think so. Even under these changed conditions the commune still had a function to fulfil. But we should note that already in 1848, unlike his fellow slavophils, Koshelev looked at the commune with great scepticism and pragmatism. In a letter to Khomyakov he wrote:

> [the principle of the commune] is a remnant of the childhood of our nation and precludes a future for educated society.[24]

Therefore, the commune was very good and necessary for understanding the present and dealing with it, but it should not become the guiding "beacon" for the future. Later on, Koshelev became converted to the idea of the commune, and we shall see in a moment on what conditions and for what purposes. But this statement of 1848 warns us that his assertions should be read not as the dogmatic pronouncements of an unshakable faith, but rather as precepts for practical action subject to modification in the light of a particular situation. Like some of his fellow slavophils, Koshelev implicitly recognised two types of arguments: the one deriving from history and psychological in nature, the other based on empirical reality and hence economic and practical.

The commune was the natural, existing order of the Russian peasant. But unlike the more chauvinistic slavophils, Koshelev did not see in it a "racial" Slavonic trait. It had become a Slavonic characteristic simply by force of circumstance, and had nothing to do with Orthodoxy as such.[25] But it did satisfy some of the spiritual and psychological needs of the Russian man:

> The egotistic predispositions of the peasants are mutually moderated, the intelligence of the one complements the other. And, standing on their own ground, their common decisions and behaviour are more intelligent than the opinion and action of one individual.[26]

The commune was also the embodiment of the peasant's conception of justice and law, by far not the same as the positive written law of the Code. For the peasant, this idea of justice and law was a matter of great practical importance in view of the Russian fiscal system:

> While the existence of the capitation (*podushnaya podat*) and the imperfect Russian administration continue, communal responsibility (*krugovaya poruka*) is essential for the collection of taxes.[27]

On this basis, too, the commune provided every man with the right to a minimum of land, guaranteeing both his subsistence and ability to pay his share of taxes. However, unlike most liberal intellectuals of the 50's, Koshelev did not use this fact as an argument to explain the absence of a proletariat in Russia. It was not the communal system, but the abundance of free land that had spared Russia this evil of Western Europe. He even went so far as to affirm that the commune held together best in rich villages, whereas it disintegrated wherever the population was poor.[28] This observation, not supported by enough factual evidence, was, to say the least, controversial. Yet, he did not deny that the commune gave moral and social security to Russia:

> Communes are essential. They are for our state what ballast is for a ship. They contain an intelligent conservatism, sparing us from the proletariat. They are a safe and ever-present refuge for an immense mass of the rural population.[29]

To insure this stability, the commune should always remain as subdivision of the state organisation. But it should not own the land and be responsible for the actions, in particular the misdemeanours of its members. The commune was at the source of any political and administrative organisation of Russia, but did not form its basis. At any rate, the true commune was not the one imagined by the slavophils, for the problem of its existence was a purely practical and not a philosophical matter.[30]

As time went on, experience showed Koshelev the economic working of the emancipation. He first noted a rise in the peasant's well-being:

> In some respects, the way of life of the peasants has improved since 19 February 1861. ... Opportunities for earning are apparently on the rise, and so noticeably is the peasant's initiative. In a word, in recent times the peasant's have considerably risen to the consciousness of their rights.

Continuing, he also noted a different set of factors, somewhat perplexing to a defender of the commune:

> The communal principle, formerly strong among the peasantry and the basic source of this class's social morality is apparently weakening. In its stead there is an increase of the most narrow self-love which, in the absence of education, is having murderous effects on the actions and standards of the people.[31]

As a successful farmer, Koshelev also saw that the commune was not the most efficient agricultural unit. Long before the emancipation he had warned Khomyakov against the evils of frequent redistribution of land.[32] Observations after 1861 confirmed his fears, especially as the habit of splitting up the holdings assumed alarming proportions. Only a few big family holdings had remained, all the others had been split up among members of the family. Another trouble was that the commune tied to the land many people who really did not want to (or could not) stay on it.[33]

From the economic point of view, individual initiative was obviously the most rewarding. But it implied a certain stability of possession. "Doubtlessly, I shall work my own land better than that which can be taken away from me." Therefore, ownership was better than possession, "and from the agricultural point of view, it is private land and not communal property that has undisputed advantages." Let us then give as much freedom as possible to the indi-

vidual. "For me society is an evil, but an essential evil ... the more perfect a society, the more limited it is in its demands, the more freedom personality has
for developing its forces and capacities."[34] If left free as a result of self-inter-
ested action, the energetic individual would also eventually become rich. Government supervision and incentive, needed in Russia to raise agricultural tech-
nique, should be given by local autonomous administrative bodies only. They
would know what was best in a given area and could provide the necessary
guidance and help without the stifling effect of bureaucratisation. For in Russia the central administration had always frustrated local attempts at self-improvement.[35] The combined efforts of local administrative units, consisting of
the noble landowner and the more prosperous commune members, could introduce new techniques and implements. In the effort, Koshelev himself
preached extensively by example. These techniques, of course, would have to
be taken from the West; technologically, Russia should learn from the West.[36]
And Koshelev was quite willing to accept the fact that European ideas and
even social organisation might also come with European tools and techniques. Only one need not be blinded by them.[37] In this same light he also
saw a much-needed development of Russian industry.

Left unhampered and given technological help, the more active, enterprising, and successful member of the commune would acquire his own land and
property. More and more he would become divorced from the interests of the
commune, for "strong, rich people cannot and should not remain in the commune. For they can become either despots or the victims of general hatred
and unkindness."[38] Unanimity in a diversified group could be of one kind
only: the enslavement of one side by the other. Either the commune's less
prosperous members would stifle and strangle the richer out of jealousy and
spite or else rich men would make bondsmen of the poor:

> We do not know of any example of a friendly fusion of wealth and poverty, educa-
> tion and ignorance, material force, etc. Usually, the one enslaves the other and
> conflict arises.[39]

Once he had reached a certain level of prosperity, the rich individual peasant
should automatically leave the communes and enter another agrarian class.
Under Koshelev's scheme, he would join the ranks of the individual landowners, the "intermediaries," whose present, but only temporary, bulk was
made up of former serf-owners. Rich peasant and former serf-owner formed
one group by virtue of their common economic and social interests. In this
way also, by the example of his personal success, the rich peasant would do
much more to further the technological and economic progress of the commune and the peasants than former serf-owners, and infinitely more than bureaucrats.[40] There was still too much suspicion on the part of the peasant towards the former master; Koshelev had felt it himself and spoke from experience.

In the last resort, though he himself never admitted it explicitly, the commune had become the refuge of the poor, unlucky, unenterprising members of the peasantry. If one followed Koshelev's reasoning to its logical conclusion, the commune should eventually disappear altogether. For one of two things would happen, as he had predicted to Khomyakov as early as 1848: the abolition of all property (desired by Western socialists but dreaded by him, a landowner); or the perpetuation of the division of the people into artificial classes. "But should society be organised for the benefit of the minority, the benefit of the poor?" His answer was that the commune should be organised for success and progress, not for petrification. One had to help the poor, but not prevent others from developing their forces and capacities. An indivisible commune was a stone that retarded progress.[41] Koshelev firmly believed that individualism and enterprise were essentially human traits, and that, given free rein, most peasants would become private landowners. No wonder he arrived at the conclusion, implicit in his writings, that the commune was merely the "social security fund" of the peasantry.

Koshelev's views were couched in slavophil language and reflected some of the more cherished slavophil beliefs. But we should not be misled by these appearances. In truth, behind this traditional slavophil terminology there was something new, more directly the reflection of the conditions created by the emancipation. It is this novel element, this change in tone and logic, which it is most interesting and important to note. Koshelev did not repeat the earlier slavophil arguments on the individual's "reconciliation" with the community. He saw Russia's future in a full and free development of the individual's economic activities. But this development was opposed to and destructive of the village commune which subjected the energetic and progressive peasant to the will and whims of the more backward majority. Seen from a purely practical point of view, without tearful sentimentality, the commune was only a refuge for the dead-weight of mediocrity. Only outside the *mir* could the progressive and successful peasant find satisfaction. And Koshelev's continued advocacy of the commune was purely humanitarian: he did not want to deprive the poorer and less successful peasantry of all land as a means of livelihood. As an observer of West European economic history, he did not want to see in Russia the misery and wretchedness of a landless peasantry flocking into the cities. He hoped that Russia would take the path of modern economic development at less cost.

But this solution of the agrarian problem through the development of the individual peasant's free activity and better technical knowledge was only one side of Koshelev's plans. As indicated previously, the solution of the peasant question was to him but the first stage in modernising and liberalising the country's social and political regime. Koshelev was interested in the creation of an agrarian middle class of small farmers, owning the land they cultivated and free to enrich themselves. These small individual farmers, like the French

peasants after 1789, would become the builders of a more stable and diversified economy, which in turn would lift Russia from its present backwardness
and semi-colonial status. In their economic and social interests, these peasants
would become one with the gentry; together they would, by right, assume the
leadership of the country. But progressive and economically successful men
could not be tyrannised and oppressed like slaves. Though maintaining the
tsar's absolutism in theory, the practical political proposals made by Koshelev
aimed at ushering in a mild form of constitutional and representative government, based on a large degree of local self government.

Of course there was a great deal of *naïveté* in Koshelev's views. It was utopian to count upon a harmony of interests between various groups in the village once free rein was given to individual initiative and competition. Also,
Koshelev had too high an opinion of the gentry's capacity of adaptation to its
new rôle. But perhaps the most idyllic was his picture of the tsar's autocratic
powers tempered by representative institutions. It was a reflection of the
idealised picture of the Middle Ages made popular by slavophil writers. This
wonderful union between tsar and land was certainly only a romantic illusion
similar to those current in Western Europe in the 1820's and 1830's. It was
significant for the intellectual climate of the period that a practical realist like
Koshelev, who moreover had the benefit of a knowledge of Russian history
and conditions, should have easily fallen victim to such a utopian hope. This
incurable romanticism, the costly heritage of slavophilism, rendered
Koshelev's political plans, and many others too, useless as a chart for the reform of the country.

Yet this political shortsightedness should not lead us to pass an entirely negative judgment on the significance of Koshelev's views and influence. On the
contrary, his example illustrated the new conclusions to which even traditional slavophil ideas could lead. It was significant that with the emancipation
the doctrinal slavophilism of the Kireyevsky or Khomyakov sort quite disappeared as a political and social ideology. It seemed to have fulfilled its historic
rôle. The set of political and social beliefs centring on the mystical qualities of
the Slavonic soul, on the peculiar historical and religious traditions of the Russian people, were well-nigh neglected after 1861. The new opportunities and
problems created by the emancipation confronted the Russian intelligentsia
with more practical issues. Yet even here slavophilism did make one important
contribution, and Koshelev exemplified it quite well in his own thinking. This
contribution was the insistence on the dignity of the individual and the necessity of letting him develop all his potentialities. Applied to economic and political problems, it affirmed the need of allowing the individual to pursue his
economic interests as he liked. It gave him liberty of opportunity in the economic field in a basically competitive society. To this end the peasant, too, had
to be given full equality and freedom like all other Russians. This attitude indicates clearly that the slavophils themselves had accepted the fact that a com-

munal, closed system of society was incompatible with modern economic conditions. Preservation of the village commune was merely an expedient for the alleviation of what they hoped would be temporary economic and social ills. It was an important landmark in Russian political and economic thinking, profoundly affecting the politically active members of Russian officialdom and society.

In quite different terms, but for similar reasons, economic and social individualism also became the programme of the progressive liberals in the *zemstva* and other local institutions. The government, however, realised and understood it only at the beginning of the 20th century when it was perhaps too late. A similar attitude was later adopted, in quite different forms and with different aims, to be sure, by the liberal bourgeois groups (*Cadets*). Of course, it would be an exaggeration to call Koshelev the spiritual father of these diverse trends. But as an influential spokesman for the enlightened gentry in the first decades after emancipation, his views commanded a large audience. His keen understanding of the new forces shaping Russia proved a useful guide to newly appointed *zemstva* officials. Unfortunately the imperial regime, much to its own detriment, neglected to make use of this insight. Koshelev's failure in political leadership was less a reflection of the shortcomings of his own plans and theories than a sad commentary on the tsarist government's inability to draw the conclusions from its own actions.

Notes

1. Cf. Nikolay P. Semyonov, *Osvobozhdeniye krest'yan v tsarstvovaniye imperatora Aleksandra II*, 3 vols in 4, St. Petersburg, 1889–1892; Baron B. E. Nolde, *Yury Samarin i yego vremya*, Paris, 1926; Robert Stupperich, *Die Anfänge der Bauernbefreiung in Russland* (*Neue Deutsche Forschungen*—Abt. Slawische Philologie und Kulturgeschichte), Bd. 208, Berlin, 1939.

2. Cf. *Zapiski*, 78, 80, 141, and also Appendix No. 3 (On London International Exhibition, 1852). For biographical material on Koshelev, cf.: A. I. Koshelev, *Zapiski A. I. Kosheleva 1812–1883*, Berlin, 1884; I. S. Aksakov, "Nekrolog Kosheleva," *Rus'*, 1883; S. Yur'yev, "A. I. Koshelev," *Russkaya Mysl'*, 1883–XII; N. Kolyupanov, *Biografiya A. I. Kosheleva*, Moscow, 1892; V. Stroyev, "A. I. Koshelev," *Russkiy biograficheskiy slovar'*, vol. 9. Unless otherwise indicated, all references are to writings in Koshelev.

3. "I value very much the opinions of our late friend (A. S. Khomyakov)," he wrote, "but I try to live according to my own opinions as they are worked out and changed under the impact of time and circumstances." Letter to I. Aksakov, 2.iv.80 in *O minuvshem* (St. Petersburg, 1909), p. 406.

4. Cf. Semevsky, V. I., *Krest'yanskiy vopros v Rossii v 18-om i pervoy polovine 19 vv.* St. Petersburg, 1888, Vol. 2, pp. 409–10.

5. Cf. N. Semyonov, *op. cit.*, II, pp. 933ff., in particular Appendix No. 5 and *Zapiski*, 103–05, and Appendix No. 6.

6. Semevsky, *op. cit.*, pp. 411–12.

7. Koshelev, *Kakoy iskhod diya Rossii iz nyneshnego polozheniya?* (1862), p. 10.

8. Princess O. Trubetskaya, *Knyaz' V. A. Cherkassy i yego uchastiye v razreshenii krest'yanskogo voprosa—Materialy dlya biografii,* Moscow, 1901, vol. I, p. 140 (Letter to I. Samarin, dated 1 February 1860).

9. *Kakoy iskhod dlya ...,* p. 38.

10. Koscheleff, *Unsere Lage* (Berlin, 1875), p. 22.

11. *Unsere Lage,* pp. 13, 20.

12. *Kakoy iskhod ...,* p. 39.

13. *Unsere Lage,* p. 16.

14. *Kakoy iskhod ...,* pp. 36–37.

15. *Kakoy iskhod ...,* p. 38. Cf. "Wir sind fest überzeugt, dass derjenige, welcher zur rechten Zeit die Leibeigenschaft aufhob, auch das grosse Werk der Befreiung Russlands vollenden und uns zu wirklichen Staatsbürgern machen wird." *Unsere Lage,* p. 24.

16. *Ibid.,* p. 77.

17. *Ibid.,* p. 19.

18. *Kakoy iskhod ...,* p. 39.

19, Koshelev, "O nyneshnem polozhenii krest'yan i o merakh k ulushcheniyu ikh byta," *Golos iz Zemstva,* I, Moscow, 1869, pp. 82–83; Koshelev, "Chto takoye russkoye dvoryanstvo i chem ono byt' dolzhno," *Golos iz Zemstva,* I, p. 62; *Kakoy iskhod ...,* p. 16.

20. *Kakoy iskhod ...,* p. 16.

21. Koshelev, "O dvoryanstve i zemledel'tsakh," *Golos iz Zemstva,* p. 68.

22. "Chto takoye russkoye dvoryanstvo ...," *op. cit.,* pp. 57–62 *passim; Kakoy iskhod ...,* p. 20.

23. "O dvoryanstve i zemledel'tsakh," *op. cit.,* p. 68.

24. N. Kolyupanov, *op. cit.,* ol.2, Appendices, p. 103 (Letter to Khomyakov, 16.iii.48).

25. "Otvet Khomyakovu" (no date), *ibid.,* pp. 106–07.

26. "Chto takoye russkoye dvoryanstvo ...," *op. cit.,* p. 62.

27. Koshelev, "O zemskikh sobraniyakh," *Golos iz Zemstva,* 1; "O prusskikh podatyakh," *Beseda,* 1871, II, p. 277.

28. "Otvet Khomyakovu," *op. cit.,* p. 108; Letter to Khomyakov, Kolyupanov, *op. cit.,* p. 104.

29. "Chto takoye russkoye dvoryanstvo ...," *op. cit.,* p. 58.

30. Letter to Khomyakov, *op. cit.,* p. 104; "Otvet Khomyakovu," *op. cit.,* p. 107.

31. "O nyneshnem polozhenii krest'yan ...," *op. cit.,* pp. 75, 77.

32. "Otvet Khomyakovu," *op. cit.,* p. 106.

33. "O nyneshnem polozhenii krest'yan ...," p. 76; *Unsere Lage,* p. 75.

34. Letter to Khomyakov, *op. cit.,* pp. 104–05; "Otvet Khomyakovu," *op. cit.,* p. 108.

35. *Unsere Lage,* p. 76.

36. Cf. *Zapiski,*p p. 78, 80, 141, and also Appendix No. 3 (On London International Exhibition, 1852). Koshelev makes a curious comparison between agrarian conditions in Russia and the U.S.: "After England, the U.S. holds the first rank in agriculture, and for us, Russians, its economy is hardly less interesting than the farms of Great Britain ... America is closer to us. The conditions under which agriculture is develop-

ing and perfecting itself there are more like our own. The soil, climate, overabundance of land coupled with a lack of labour, and many other conditions, are more or less common to both the U.S. and Russia. For long time already I am nourishing the hope of visiting that country and to study on the spot those problems which we too shall have to solve and which have already been solved there (or which approach their final solution). It is with particular curiosity that I visited the American section of agricultural implements ...," *Zapiski*, Appendix No. 3, pp. 22–23.

37. *Unsere Lage*, p. 107.
38. "Chto takoye russkoye dvoryanstvo ...," *op. cit.*, p. 58.
39. "O dvoryanstve i zemledel'tsakh," *op. cit.*, pp. 56, 57.
40. "Chto takoye russkoye dvoryanstvo ...," *op. cit.*, p. 58.
41. Letter to Khomyakov, *op. cit.*, p. 105.

TWO

A Reactionary Liberal

M. N. Katkov

THE OPPRESSIVE CENSORSHIP exercised by the Tsarist régime throughout the nineteenth century did not prevent the publication of many journals of the most varied shades of opinion. Naturally, the editors of and contributors to these journals were most important figures in Russian society; and one of the most interesting and influential among them was Michael N. Katkov. The *enfant terrible* of Russian political journalism, Katkov held the center of the journalistic stage for over a quarter of a century, the most praised and the most vilified of Russian newspapermen. No doubt his voice was among the most popular and it made him influential in moulding public opinion. Oddly enough, however, there is no adequate study as yet of this interesting and important figure. In the general histories of the period we have only a few rather vague statements, mostly from the pen of his political enemies. The few biographical sketches available are post-mortem eulogies by his friends and admirers and they are as uncritical as the vilifications of his opponents. They have little value except as catalogues of factual detail.[1]

Abroad, Katkov is perhaps best known for his chauvinist and Pan-Slavist propaganda. His rôle in arousing Russian public opinion during the Polish Rebellion of 1863 and the Balkan crisis of 1875–1878 has been frequently commented upon by historians.[2] Yet, a closer examination of the period of Alexander II shows very clearly that his influence extended far beyond the narrow circle of the rabid chauvinists and Pan-Slavists of the 1870's. From the middle 1860's on, he was a powerful figure in government circles, and not only in matters of Russian "national honor" and international position.[3] And though by no means very progressive or radical, he advocated policies which could have initiated a moderate and controlled liberalism in Russian economic and social life.

Two periods in the life and activity of Katkov, the beginning and the very end of his career, have been emphasized, although they were not the most characteristic for his over-all political views and rôle. In the 1840's, when he was a student, Katkov belonged to the "liberal" intellectual circles, in which, however, he never became very prominent. He was closer to the Westerners than to the Slavophiles, whose dreamy historical idealism he scorned. He studied in Berlin where he listened to Schelling and came under his influence. When he returned to Russia, he became the leading exponent of Schelling's philosophy and embarked upon a promising academic career with a study of the Russian grammar and a lectureship at the University of Moscow. But this first, academic, stage closed when he took over the journal of the University of Moscow (*Russkii Vestnik*) in 1856 and almost immediately showed his gifts as a journalistic polemist. And the newspaper he founded in 1863 (*Moskovskie Vedomosti*) rapidly became one of the most widely read and vocal dailies in Russia.

In the last years of his life, shocked by the assassination of Alexander II (March 1, 1881), Katkov used the influential position he had gained through his paper to undo the work of reform accomplished under Alexander II, reforms he at first had supported sincerely, though with reservations. In this anti-liberal and reactionary furor he forgot all restraint and reasonableness. It was also during these years that he gave free rein to his virulent and narrow nationalism, pursuing with implacable hatred the national minorities of the Russian Empire and advocating a racial and religious chauvinism unparalleled in Russia before. Unfortunately, these policies were followed by Pobedonostsev and Alexander III. In this way Katkov inspired the fateful attempt at setting back the clock of history and restoring at the close of the nineteenth century conditions which had prevailed in the eighteenth. But in so doing he lost his popularity with the public, and his influence became limited to a handful of inveterate reactionaries, the forerunners of the Union of the Russian People and the Black Hundred.

Between these two periods, for about twenty-five years, he was the perceptive echo of every event and the sounding board for many of the most vital and interesting ideas that agitated the Russian public. The study of this quarter of a century of his career helps us to understand more fully the implications and rich potentialities of the reform period of Alexander II, a period, it seems pretty clear today, which might have planted the seeds of a truly western and progressive Russia. Therefore, it is fruitful to examine the political ideas of Katkov as an example of the attitudes of someone who was important in shaping public opinion in that period.

The scope of the present analysis is, of necessity, very limited. Chronologically we shall deal only with this productive and influential period of Katkov's career, i.e., from 1863 to 1881. But even there we must limit ourselves. Keenly aware of all happenings in Russia, Katkov in his writings covered a very wide range. He recorded every movement in Russian public opinion, whether he approved of it or not, like a sensitive seismograph. He had something to say on almost every aspect of Russian public life—Emancipation, economic conditions, administrative changes, foreign affairs, intellectual and artistic trends. And on these he spoke out in a pungent, acid, and emotional manner in his daily editorials for the *Moskovskie Vedomosti*. To describe and analyse his views on all these subjects would take a volume. Inasmuch as the Emancipation had not solved the agrarian question, leaving the fate of the peasant as Russia's central issue, Katkov's attitude towards the rural problem is perhaps a most convenient issue on which to focus an exposition of his political and economic attitudes. One more word of warning: Katkov was a journalist, reacting rapidly and acutely to every event. He did not have the time or genuine desire to think through the theoretical implications of his opinions; therefore, in his case we cannot expect a logical and perfectly consistent ideology. Yet, behind his emotional outbursts and in spite of his contradictions, one can discern a pattern of attitudes towards Russia's political, economic, and social problems.

In spite of his Russian nationalism, Katkov always looked towards England for guidance in economic and political matters; his Anglomania was proverbial among his contemporaries. In politics, his model was pre-Reform England, before its rapid evolution towards more liberal, democratic forms. Unlike young Disraeli (with whose ideas he had much in common), Katkov did not understand the direction and the flexibility of English historical developments in the nineteenth century. As with the British conservatives of the first quarter of the nineteenth century, the starting point of his political thinking was respect for existing institutions, a recognition of the right of prescription. "Russia cannot wish for improvised and manufactured institutions. ... Everything manufactured, everything that does not derive directly from the desires and needs of life itself does more harm than good. To begin the study of the desires and needs of the country there is no need to create some new institutions *ad hoc*. We can begin with what already is."[4] In the second place, applying Schelling's concepts and following Slavophile teachings, Katkov desired a harmony between the classes of the nation and the throne. There should be no conflicts and divisions between classes, for each had its own rôle which should be sufficient ground for social harmony. "Nothing pleases us more," he wrote, "than the signs of friendly relations and solidarity of interests among peasants and noble landowners—and this in spite of their confused accounts."[5] For this reason Katkov opposed the proposal that the Zemstva institutions be sub-divided according to estates.[6] A kindly mediator and fatherly protector of all, the Tsar should be above these classes and harmonious groups. "The throne has been raised so that the differences between estates, guilds, groups, and classes are levelled beneath it. ... A single power and none other in the land, a people of 100 millions obedient to this power alone, such is a true Empire."[7] Thus, the Tsar was the personification of the unity of the fatherland.

In Katkov's opinion, classes were not closed castes; they should be open to everyone. "But when at the wave of the Liberator's hand the chains of serfdom fell, everything which had separated the nobility from the people also disappeared. Now, the nobles merely march in the first rank of the nation."[8] "The nobility still exists as a separate organization," he continued, "but it is open to entry by new elements. ..."[9] As soon as anyone would show, by his work and achievement, that he belonged to another class than his own, he ought to be admitted to it. As in England, the aristocracy should be open to merit and achievement.

But even with social mobility assured, there should be no political privileges on the basis of class distinction. Members of all classes ought to participate in the public life of the country; they should all be responsible citizens and civically alert. However, Katkov spoke primarily of civic duties, and he was far from advocating elected representation. Representative self-government meant a state within a state and led to the disintegration of authority.[10] Katkov assigned no policy-making rôle to the classes of society, for he conceived their rôle as pre-eminently an advisory one, at most administrative on the lowest local level (for economic matters in the Zemstva). But, this was in part negated by his hatred of the bureaucracy, a hatred which he shared with all progressive groups of society (even including some government members).[11] One is somewhat at a loss to see what Katkov really wanted. How could a strong state power be exercised by a fatherly Tsar with the help of an advisory public opinion but without any bureaucracy? Even in later years he merely reaffirmed the necessity of a strong, non-bureaucratic, non-representative government. How that was to be accomplished remained a secret.

The basis for class distinction was private ownership of property. Everybody was equal from the legal and civic points of view. Since 1861, even the nobility was only a *primus inter pares*, exclusively by virtue of its vaster economic resources. Obviously, private property should also be the criterion for participation in political—or rather civic and administrative—life. "Universal experience shows," he wrote, "that the affairs of the land must rest in the hands of the owners, so situated that they can be representative of all estates."[12] Again using England as an example, Katkov believed that only those who had something to preserve and take care of were fit to participate in governing the destiny of the community. "The main basis for local organization should be the possession of land, and, in general, the character of the property held."[13] In rural areas, ownership of land was to be the criterion of participation in the local institutions which provided the bond between the nation and the throne. These property owners ought to be entrusted with local justice and administration, like the Justices of the Peace in England. However, this did not have to lead to the introduction of the elective principle. "Self-government has the desirable characteristic if it is an organ of the same state power which also acts through the bureaucracy. That is why self-government can do without the elective principle, as we see in England where the Justices of the Peace are appointed by the Crown."[14]

As a corollary to this position, Katkov wanted administrative services performed by property owners without compensation, again like the English Justices of the Peace. "We do not take upon ourselves the impossible task of foretelling what will become of the Zemstva institutions. But there cannot be the slightest doubt that they will enjoy general respect only to the extent that their services will not be compensated."[15] Absence of compensation was not only a condition for good local self-government, but also for the self-preservation of the educated classes in the coming struggle for political existence. Uncompensated Zemstvo service, Katkov repeated, was the landowner's principal weapon against the triumph of wild and blind democracy in local administrative institutions, a triumph which would subvert the very foundations of civilized society.[16]

The peasants, the most numerous group in Russia, must be full-fledged members of society; they must be free. The Emancipation in 1861 did not quite free them. They could not be truly free unless they owned property, and the Emancipation settlement subjected the peasant's land to the dominant control of the village commune, the *mir.* Incidentally, the terms of the Emancipation also impaired the civic equality of the peasant. The inalienability of land allotments, in conjunction with communal ownership, might still prove a harsher form of control than serfdom.[17] Naturally, on this point, Katkov ran against heavy opposition from many quarters, for the illusions about the commune's function had not yet dissipated. In heated argument he accused the very architects of the Emancipation of pro-servile tendencies. He denounced progressives like Iurii Samarin, who "... are happy to enslave the peasants forever in communal land ownings, collective responsibility for taxes (*krugovaya poruka*), under the despotism of the mir assemblies and the so-called peasant self-government."[18] The peasants had to obey the decisions of the majority of the mir, and it was well known that a small group of rowdies and hoodlums could impose its will on an entire commune. Such practices endangered the very foundations of the mir, and could lead to the intervention of the bureaucracy, and the final settlement between landowners and peasants would come under the direct control of the provincial authorities. This, under Russian conditions, would hardly be a blessing. Moreover, one might add, the mir was not a universally Slavic, or even an all-Russian institution; it was primarily a local phenomenon and thus could hardly provide a basis for the economic and social structure of the whole Russian Empire.[19]

Only individual enterprise and complete freedom to dispose of the fruits of one's labor could become the foundation for constructive and useful work.

"Prince Vassilchikov is a thousand times right when he says that the main and most substantial gauge of all success in agriculture consists in the *personal work of the landowners themselves*" (Katkov's italics).[20] As long as the peasant in the commune did not own his land but possessed it only temporarily, his efficiency and individual enterprise would not be stimulated. Indeed, Katkov thought that the commune was the main cause for the peasant's inability to improve his economic and moral status and to participate fully in the administration and consultative functions of public opinion. Tied hand and foot by his dependency on the village authorities, the peasant, willy-nilly, had to live from day to day, deprived even of those advantages which Emancipation should have given him. "When the peasant tills the plot allotted to him, it is not for himself that he labors, but it is for the commune, which at the next redistribution will take away this plot worked by the sweat of his brow and give it to another, while he receives the strips another peasant has made useless."[21] The peasant loses interest in his own future and goes to drown his sorrows in the tavern. Thus the latent energies and potentialities of the Russian peasant are dissipated.[22] "Only dreamers who like to walk in half darkness ... can pin their hopes on a compulsory introduction of communal plowing as a way of easing the burden of communal responsibility. Actually, this would have the reverse effect. Communal responsibility for taxes is unjust. It holds back progress ... by preventing that 'free racing game' which is a necessary condition for success, not alone in the sciences and arts, but also in any industry."[23] The whole of Russia suffers from the evil consequences of the peasant's inability to better his lot, thus precluding the full development of the country's resources and energies.

It has been argued that the commune was a protection for the weak and unlucky. With this, however, Katkov disagreed violently; there was no room in the world for the weak and unlucky. Indeed, a whole nation or even a group, should not be retarded for the sake of a minority of weaklings. In the commune, the power was in the hands of the idlers and drunkards who merely wanted to profit from the labor of others.[24] Only energy and hard work could make a man and those who could not succeed were not worthy of living on dole. This was crude social Darwinism; the fittest survived and they alone were entitled to survive. If a peasant could not find a place in his village, he ought to be able to leave it and seek useful employment elsewhere; possibly he could go to the cities where the need for labor in the rising industries was great. Moreover, the government should foster resettlement and colonization, in order to bring into use the vast unproductive areas of the Russian Empire; this too would help increase Russia's economic wealth and make her independent of Europe.[25]

Thus, only the active, energetic, successful, and willing would remain to work the land. For these alone, a group skilled and vitally interested in their craft, could play a productive rôle in the nation's economy. Katkov's incorri-

gible Anglomania again drew lessons from England's example: "The superiority of the agrarian system of England [a superiority which was already questioned in his time—M. R.] has its roots in the almost general custom of
landowners to lease their lands to farmers. ... Sooner or later, we too shall
have to take this road; i.e., it will be necessary to break up the big estates into
plots and lease them out to people who will choose agriculture as their trade
and will not speculate on a wasteful exploitation of the soil."[26] In other
words, put agriculture on the same rational and efficient basis as capitalistic
enterprises in industry and commerce.[27]

The reforms of 1861, Katkov felt, had been steps in the right direction. The
task of the future was to implement them and carry them to their logical conclusions. The Emancipation Act included provisions for the full liberation of
the peasant, his exit from the commune which should not be hampered. The
redemption payments must be understood as the peasant's purchase of the
right to dispose of his land freely, independently from the mir. By the same token, this would also give the peasantry an incentive to save, an incentive which
was sadly lacking and without which an improvement of Russian agriculture
could not be achieved.[28] Though still true to Schelling's concept of organic
development, Katkov did not want to speed up the process artificially; he insisted upon removing the fetters placed on individual ownership by the Act of
1861. If we recall that the property owner was the foundation of society and
of the political system, we can easily see the similarity between Katkov's views
and Stolypin's famous "wager on the strong peasant" in 1906. True enough,
after 1881 Katkov grasped at every straw to maintain the *status quo,* which he
considered to be in imminent peril at the hands of the revolutionaries. And he
showed some velleity of preserving the commune as a pillar of autocracy.
However, even then, Katkov's defense of the commune was on purely political grounds and did not affect his basic premise that individual initiative and
property were the only foundations of society.[29]

We have seen that Katkov was a convinced individualist for whom social
progress depended entirely on the energy and creative ability of man. "Only
the movement which leads to the triumph of personal liberty can be considered progressive for the peasant's way of life ..." he wrote in 1868.[30] This was
best manifested in man's economic life; therefore, completely ruthless individualism (or in the American phrase—rugged individualism) ought to reign
in it. Competition and the desire for improvements were excluded by the mir,
hence the necessity of abolishing it. The argument that the abolition of the
mir would create a landless proletariat with revolutionary leanings did not disturb Katkov too much. "The main barrier to the establishment of economic
freedom in Russian agrarian society ... is the fear of a proletariat. But in Russia, with our boundless area, this fear, we dare say, makes not the slightest
sense. ... However, it is true that in our rural way of life there is no elbow
room for the good farmer who cannot get richer while remaining a peasant

and continuing to till the soil."[31] Therefore, the use of hired labor should be fostered, even in rural areas. And to bolster this point, Katkov used a typically capitalist argument in its favor: "The more hired labor is used in the economy, the better the conditions of agricultural laborers, on the basis of the general economic rule that the introduction of any new capital in agriculture has its effects on the raising of wages for farm labor."[32] All this was prevented by the commune where unenergetic and unambitious peasants were holding back progress. Like swimmers in a whirlpool or fast current, the strong must pull loose from the weak, otherwise both will perish.

Katkov envisioned the rather easy abolition of the commune by a change in the fiscal system which bolstered it artificially. Once this outside compulsion was removed by a modern taxation system, the strong peasants would automatically seize control of the mir and bring about the "liquidation" of the commune.[33] He considered that the break-up of the commune was but one aspect of the change taking place in the economic structure of the country. As the Western European states had done earlier, Russia was entering the path of industrialization and capitalism. This fact had to be accepted and the necessary implications drawn from it. There was no use in sentimentalizing a past that could not be revived or maintained against the stronger natural forces of an organic development.

Thus we see that Katkov wanted a modern, "liberal" (in the Manchesterian sense of the word) economic and social basis for Russia. Yet, as we have shown earlier, the political structure of the country was to remain quite "medieval"; in particular, the Tsar's autocratic power was not to be touched. Katkov's economic views, progressive for his time and country, could not be squared with his conservative and even reactionary political plans. Like so many of his Russian contemporaries, he did not see that his economic and social system, based on free enterprise and individualism, required an equivalent in the political realm (at least a *Rechtsstaat*). The liberation of the peasantry from the commune would not be complete as long as the police and the local nobility retained their political and social privileges.

Katkov was eager to get away from the old Moscovite concept of the service state, in which all individuals and classes of society existed only by virtue of the services they render to the state. He wanted to establish the Russian state, as in England, on the principle of individual activity and free enterprise. The state—in the person of the Tsar—would then play but a passive rôle in reconciling and circumscribing the areas between individual interests. Such a program would have resulted in West European political and economic liberalism. Yet, Katkov, fascinated by the historical rôle of the Russian state, an obsession in Russian political thought, refused to lessen the power and rôle of the Tsar. This made a reorganization of the government on an entirely new basis well-nigh impossible.

By these contradictory attitudes, Katkov exemplifies the tragic paradox of Russian political thinking in the nineteenth century. The advocates of liberty and individualism in the economic and social realms were, on the whole, defenders of a conservative and obsolescent political régime. On the other hand, the liberals and radicals in politics were, by and large, defenders of social collectivism and antiquated sentimental views in economics. The failure to correlate the political and economic concepts of their thinking led both radicals and conservatives into blind alleys from which the only issue seemed to be an elemental revolution.

Notes

1. For biographical material on Katkov see: S. A-v, "M. N. Katkov," *Russkii biograficheskii slovar,* vol. 8. D. Ilovaisky, "M. N. Katkov—istoricheskaya pominka," *Russkii Arkhiv,* 1897, No. 1. "Katkov—dokumenty k ego biografii," *Russkii Arkhiv,* 1909, No. 10. "M. N. Katkov kak redaktor *Moskovskikh Vedomostei* i vozobnovitel *Russkogo Vestnika,*" *Russkaya Starina,* 1897, Nos. 11 and 12. A. Lyubimov, *M. N. Katkov i ego istoricheskaya zasluga, po dokumentam i lichnym vospominaniyam,* Moscow, 1889. First published in *Russkii Vestnik,* 1888–1889. Nevedensky (J. Shcheglovitov), *Katkov i ego vremya,* St. Petersburg, 1888. "Pamyati M. N. Katkova, 1887—20 July—1897," *Russkii Vestnik,* 1897, No. 8. V. Rozanov, "Katkov kak gosudarstvennyi chelovek," *Literaturnye ocherki,* St. Petersburg, 1899 (not available to this writer). R. I. Sementkovsky, *Katkov, ego zhizn i literaturnaya deyatelnost,* St. Petersburg, 1892. P. Shchegolev, "Katkov, Valuev i Timashev," *Golos Minuvshego,* 1914, No. 4. D. D. Yazykov, "*Obzor zhizni i trudov umershikh russkikh pisatelei,*" vyp. 7 of *Bibliograficheskie zapiski,* 1892, No. 2.

2. Cf. for example B. H. Sumner, *Russia and the Balkans,* Oxford, 1937; Irene Gruening, *Die russische öffentliche Meinung und ihre Stellung zu den Grossmächten 1878–1894,* Osteuropäische Forschungen, Neue Folge Band 3, Berlin and Königsberg in Preussen, 1929.

3. See General D. A. Miliutin's bitter resentment at Katkov's influence in *Dnevnik D. A. Miliutina, 1873–1875,* vol. I. Moscow, 1947, pp. 110ff.

4. M. N. Katkov, *Sobranie peredovykh statei Moskovskikh Vedomostei 1863–1887,* 24 vols., Moscow, 1898 (hereafter referred to as *K.*), 1863, No. 200, p. 539.

5. *K.,* 1864, No. 51, p. 138.

6. *K.,* 1863, No. 219, p. 590.

7. *K.,* 1881, No. 114B, p. 205.

8. *K.,* 1874, No. 217.

9. *K.,* 1874, No. 9A, p. 31.

10. Cf. *K.,* 1881, No. 119, p. 213 and 1882, No. 130, p. 234.

11. Cf. *K.,* 1874, No. 9A, p. 31 and Katkov's letter to P. A. Valuev, 2 Dec. 1863, in "Pisma M. N. Katkova k P. A. Valuevu" (A. Kizevetter, editor), *Russkii Istoricheskii Arkhiv,* Sbornik 1, Prague, 1929, p. 295.

12. *K.,* 1863, No. 82, pp. 173–74.

13. *K.,* 1863, No. 218, pp. 588–89.

14. *K.,* 1864, No. 70-A, pp. 186–187.

15. *K.,* 1865, No. 37, pp. 96–7.

16. K., 1865, No. 62.

17. K., 1865, No. 28, p. 74.

18. K., 1864, No. 51, pp. 137–8.

19. K., 1864, No. 56, pp. 150–51; 1863, No. 220, p. 592.

20. K., 1869, No. 153, p. 447.

21. K., 1875, No. 176, p. 361.

22. K., 1875, No. 176, p. 362.

23. K., 1868, No. 189, p. 501.

24. "As in the case of drunkenness, [communal] resolutions on this question [rare and definite periods of redistribution] met serious opposition from bad farmers and idlers who at repartition time wish to receive good strips, fertilized by someone else's labor." K., 1874, No. 30, p. 80.

25. K., 1881, No. 111B, p. 199. We learn from his biographers that Katkov had very numerous and widespread interests in various important industrial, commercial, and financial enterprises. Some contemporaries even claim that he was not averse to bribes from prominent captains of finance and industry to advocate their plans of economic policy in his papers. These allegations could not be checked by us, but they are so persistent as to make us believe that they may have some foundation.

26. K., 1869, No. 254, p. 758.

27. Only in truly extraordinary circumstances could charity become a form of individual help, as for example in the case of the Pavlovo village which burned to the ground accidentally. K., 1872, No. 186, pp. 476–77; 1872, No. 201, pp. 511–12.

28. K., 1865, No. 20, p. 53.

29. K., 1881, No. 15B, pp. 35; 1881, No. 142.

30. K., 1868, No. 189, p. 502.

31. K., 1865, No. 18, p. 47.

32. K., 1865, No. 18, p. 48.

33. K., 1871, No. 201, p. 606; 1865, No. 41, pp. 105–06; 1870, No. 220, p. 650; 1871, No. 139, p. 426; 1871, No. 201, p. 605.

THREE

Some Reflections
on Russian Liberalism

TWO THEMES HAVE DOMINATED Russian historiography in the West during the last two decades: the origins of the Revolutions of 1917 and the alternatives to them. First in chronology and first in importance were the search for the roots of the revolutions and tracing the sources of Bolshevik ideology. Concern with origins raised the question "what alternatives were there to the revolutionary solution?," for only through an understanding of the nature of the alternatives could the triumph of Bolshevism become fully intelligible. There was, of course, another reason as well: rehabilitate the "vanquished," because the picture of Russia before 1917 would not be complete if the "losers" (ideologically and socially) were omitted. After all, before they became the "losers" they were at times more prominent and significant than their then unknown Bolshevik conquerors. Thus during the last decade, largely under the stimulation and guidance of Professor M. Karpovich at Harvard, much attention and effort has been devoted to the study of Russian liberalism.[1] Yet, in spite of these efforts in clarifying, illustrating, and explaining specific events, personalities, and problems, no satisfactory overall picture or history of Russian liberalism has emerged thus far. The student of Russia's past has not received a satisfactory (or even partial) answer to the questions: was liberalism a really viable alternative to revolution, and if so, why did it display so little resistance to both reactionary and radical pressures? In the following pages I wish to clarify somewhat the state of our knowledge of Russian liberalism and suggest some reasons for the subordinate role it played in the intellectual, political, and social history of Imperial Russia during the nineteenth and early twentieth centuries.[2]

Soviet historiography does not recognize alternative paths of historical development, it is not interested in the "vanquished." To the extent that it has dealt with "liberalism" (and for that matter conservatism, too)—as it had to for a full history of Russian revolutionary movements and ideas—it has treated liberalism as a set of isolated ideas or events which never combined into a meaningful pattern or trend. Such limited one-sidedness could not satisfy Western historiography as it implied a *vae victis* mentality alien to its humanistic search for truth and historical understanding.[3] This circumstance has contributed in determining an essential characteristic of recent work in the West on Russian liberalism: liberalism was a possible alternative to revolutionary radicalism. Hence, most efforts have been directed at distinguishing liberalism from radicalism, at drawing a sharp and meaningful boundary so that liberalism could not be confused with revolutionary extremism or radicalism. But in their effort at distinguishing liberalism from the "left," historians have neglected the equally important task of setting it off from the "right," from conservatism.[4] If individuals and ideologies are to be categorized it should be on the basis of rather clear and universally acceptable criteria. I am perfectly well aware that this is not an easy matter. While in the nineteenth century—in Russia as well as in the West—the term liberal had a very specific connotation in contrast to reaction, the distinction has become blurred in our days as a result of our experience with "totalitarian democracy." Whereas the boundaries between liberalism and radicalism had been shadowy and mobile in the nineteenth century, those between conservatism and liberalism were drawn sharply and rigidly. But today the reverse is true. A very sharp distinction is now made between traditional liberalism and the revolutionary radicalism which emerged from late eighteenth century enlightenment and utopianism.[5] It is no accident that in recent decades the study of liberal thought has led to a positive reappraisal of conservatism and stressing of liberalism's indebtedness to the juridical and spiritual tradition of the *Ständestaat*.[6] This popularity of conservatism in Western historiography is matched nowadays by the great interest in conservative figures and movements among Russian historians in the United States, England, and Germany.[7]

At least two definitions of liberalism (or any other of the major *isms*, for that matter) can be used by the Russian historian. First, we have an absolute definition which would set forth very clearly and precisely the specific, unchangeable, and essential components and characteristics of an ideology or political movement (this can be readily done for Marxism, Communism, and Socialism, though there will be several variants of each). Liberalism (like conservatism) is, however, difficult to define in this way. That is why another approach might be to use a "relativistic," "historicist," and pragmatic definition. Under such a flexible "historicist" definition, liberalism would have different components and a different meaning depending on the time and place.[8] Still, as long as the same term is used in all instances we have in view some specific

common principles or concepts. In Russia, however, even this flexible and relativistic definition has not proven adequate. To begin with, borrowing most
of their political notions from the West, the Russians—as was only natural—
tended to simplify them and, more important still, immediately turned them
into directives for action.[9] As a result, in popular Russian terminology (and
thinking) liberalism obtained the meaning of opposition to the government,
or rejection of state authority. Until the last decades of the nineteenth century, little distinction was made between the terms liberal and revolutionary
or radical. Liberal was anything that meant or led to a decrease in state power.
hence the opposition was not so much between liberalism and radicalism or
even liberalism and conservatism (as witness, e.g. the existence of "slavophile
liberals"), as between liberalism and authority in the name of freedom from
autocracy and bureaucracy. As a consequence, there was no real understanding, let alone sympathy, for the position of "liberal conservatives or conservative liberals" such as Pushkin, Mordvinov, and later Prince S. Trubetskoi and
Maklakov.[10]

The situation was made worse by the concentration on the negative aspect
of liberalism. Liberalism was advocated to achieve an escape *from* governmental authority, under all circumstances, regardless of the means used or the proposed alternative program. In this simplifying negativism lay the roots of
many misunderstandings and mislabelings. Because an official or public opinion leader was against autocracy or the tyranny of the bureaucrat he was automatically labeled "liberal." It did not matter what specific ideas and programs
he advocated or by what means he wanted to attain a "liberalization" of the
system. On the basis of such an oversimplification Alexander I, Speransky,
Kiselev, and Loris-Melikov, for instance, were labeled liberals. On the other
hand, anyone who defended the authority of the state, of political power, and
the traditional concept of a paternalistic monarchy was branded a reactionary;
again without regard to the context or the concrete contents of the ideology
or program. In some cases those pilloried as conservatives or even reactionaries were in a sense more truly "liberals" than their denunciators, especially if
liberalism is to be taken as the defense of the individual and his personal freedom and dignity against *all* attacks (e.g. Dostoevsky, Maklakov, Struve). Finally, Russian history can do little with a relativistic, historicist definition as it
would deprive the concept of any definite meaning; liberal would then be always whatever decreases the power of the state at a given moment. This may
be a useful approach for political polemics, but it is hardly adequate for historical analysis.

Discarding the relativistic, historicist definitions of liberalism, some writers
define liberalism in terms of legality, the juridical guarantee of individual and
property rights. Here, liberalism is equated with the establishment and preservation of a *Rechtsstaat*. As a starting point for an analysis of Russian liberalism
this approach has great merit and can be very valuable.[11] Yet it also raises seri-

ous difficulties. The legalistic notion of liberalism as developed in the West (at least since Montesquieu's time), implies the preservation, reinvigoration, or expansion of a certain set of accepted and well-established norms and legal practices. Legalistic liberalism (to coin a phrase) made sense in a traditional political framework that accepted *a priori,* or on historical grounds, such fundamental legal norms as respect of individual rights, sanctity of property, etc. It was, fundamentally, an extension—and adjustment to the economic and social conditions created by the scientific and industrial revolutions—of traditional medieval legal notions of *proprietas* and *potestas,* of feudal concepts of contract and authority, of Christian justice and kingship.[12] But what sense could such notions make in Russia? The Russian reality and historical heritage were those of arbitrary autocracy and bureaucratic tyranny; introduction of real legality could only mean the overthrow of the existing regime, the abolition of traditional state power and political authority. Advocacy of such a course right away led to the blurring of the line between radicalism and liberalism, while a refusal to follow such an extreme course implied the preservation of the existing order, hence conservatism (however much it might be tempered by administrative reforms).[13] How difficult it was to remain a consistent legalistic liberal without being drawn into radical opposition to a government that refused to give way to a true *Rechtsstaat* can be seen from the career of V. A. Maklakov, the sincerest as well as most far-sighted spokesman for legalistic liberalism.[14]

In the domain of economic policy, legalistic liberalism meant the guarantee of individual property rights, the freedom of economic activity. V. Leontovitsch is quite right in devoting so much attention to this important facet of liberalism in Russia.[15] But his own analysis and description show the almost hopelessly difficult task faced by those who wanted to introduce this form of liberalism into Russia. First of all, it went against the grain of the juridical traditions and norms of the vast majority of the Russian peasantry. This tradition might have been overcome gradually if the proper political, economic, and educational measures had been taken and followed through consistently after the Emancipation. Leontovitsch shows why this was not done; the main reason was again the insuperable barrier of the political order and the radicalism of the potential liberal leaders. When "liberation" from the traditional fetters did finally come and Stolypin introduced juridical liberalism into the domain of land tenure and peasant rights, it was too late; World War I stopped short the process of growth and development of these innovations. In other words, while there was a potentially fertile soil for the establishment and expansion of the economic aspects of legalistic liberalism the latter could not sink solid roots because of the survival of the political and administrative regimes. Again, the primacy of the political factor proved to be the source of Russian misfortunes.

The difficulty, if not outright impossibility, of separating economic-social legalistic liberalism from an active, radical political program plagued the Russian intellectual leadership as well. Harmony between the economic and political facets of liberal demands could easily be achieved in the West in the eighteenth and early nineteenth centuries, as they complemented each other and involved the same social classes and economic groups. Not so in Russia where the need of modernizing the economy, of rapidly raising the material and cultural level of the people were essential tasks which did not readily harmonize with a gradual legalistic political program.[16] The combination of political gradualism and the advocacy of active economic individual freedom led, under Russian conditions, to ideological contradictions and paradoxical political programs which terminated in a dead end or in paralysis. This proved to be the tragedy of those "liberals" of the 1860's and 1870's who tried to devote all their attention to economic and social issues. As a result, later in the century, having learned the hard lesson of Russian political reality, the liberals were all too easily drawn into radicalism.[17]

Liberalism has never been a very precise and clearly defined ideology or philosophic concept, even in the West. Rather, it has been a *method* of political action and a broad view of society and the relationship between individuals and institutions. Historically, it has been associated with the triumph of individualism and the consequent application of individualism to all fields of social and political organization, with the economic and social interests of the bourgeoise, with the birth of national self consciousness. In the context of these historic circumstances, liberalism has advocated the elimination of "feudal" traditions, concepts, norms. To the extent that liberalism was a method of social and political action it required for its very existence at least some of those social forces, economic conditions, institutional frameworks, and political needs which assured its victory in the West. Did they exist in nineteenth century Russia? Certainly, Russia did have plenty of political needs and demands, but it had neither the economic conditions nor the social forces, at least not until the last quarter of the nineteenth century. We are able, as many historians have been, to discover the existence, analyze the nature, and trace the development of individual specific theoretical elements of liberalism (individualism, natural law, economic theories); but their existence did not make for liberalism as a political and social program. After all, what matters is not the individual concept or idea but the dynamic relationship in which it finds itself to other ideas and its historical environment.[18] It is my belief that in Russia, at least until the 1880's, the relationship between liberal concepts and historical circumstances was an inert one; liberalism could not attain a dynamic function in the process of the country's transformation.

After the 1860's, more particularly after 1881 (to use a convenient, though admittedly arbitrary date) economic and social circumstances began to change in favor of a positive and dynamic function of liberalism. But even then it encountered special difficulties. First of all there was always the autocratic state which stood in the way of any meaningful liberal approach and program. It had to be done away with, a necessity which forced even conservative liberals into a radical path.[19] As a result, authority and leadership passed to the more active and radical personalities; thus, Miliukov became the spokesman for the liberals, and according to most observers, he was more of a radical than a true liberal in temperament and outlook.[20] In view of Russian conditions, it seems to me, the more radically-minded liberals were also the more realistic politicians. They could not have forseen the dangers of totalitarian democracy as inherent in revolutionary radicalism. The pessimistic and hazy forebodings of Struve, Maklakov, Trubetskoi could not impress a generation that had not known the first World War or 1917. Correctly, I feel, they believed that the first obstacle to be removed was the autocracy. But could this be done without radicalism?[21] After all, it was not until 1905 that truly objective conditions for liberalism were created, and even then the political conditions remained much less satisfactory than the economic and social ones. Nothing but the strongest pressure could have changed the imperial regime.[22]

In accounting for the weakness of liberalism even after 1905 we must take into consideration the relation of the liberals to the peasantry. It would appear that the liberals did not think in terms of the peasantry as such; of its specific economic, social, and legal needs, rather they preferred to think of the Russian people as a whole.[23] In his biography of Struve, Frank observes that the Russian liberal (or intellectual) remained under the spell of populist myths, even when he rejected specific populist notions and programs. Liberals thought and spoke in terms of the Russian people, they hoped to preserve its spiritual and moral integrity (or so they believed) against evil outside influences. But all too often they forgot the peasant, the member of a special group with very specific immediate economic and social needs. To the last, in their agrarian programs, in their relation to Stolypin's policies, the liberals proved inadequate to the political and historical task that should have been theirs.[24]

Besides the various reasons of an economic, social, and political nature suggested above for the weakness of Russian liberalism, there was also another very important factor. The Russian liberals, of whatever hue, belonged to the intelligentsia.[25] Now, the characteristic trait of the Russian intelligentsia was that it conceived of its role as one of service to the people (*sluzhenie narodu*). I cannot here go into the reasons for this situation, let me only state the hypothesis that it was closely related to the fact that the intelligentsia's original membership was drawn from the service nobility. However that may be, there is a vast difference between the ideal of *service* and that of *defense* of the interests of a specific group or even of an entire nation. Issued from aristocratic and corporative traditions, Western liberalism developed in defense of particular social and cultural interests and needs. Not being an "interest group" (which makes its moral glory, of course), the Russian intelligentsia could not accept the full implications of the liberal creed and its socio-economic expressions in the West.[26] Furthermore, the intelligentsia arose in response to a feeling of moral indignation at Russian conditions. It took up "service" for the sake of changing these conditions, of abolishing the oral indignity and injustice which afflicted the Russian people. This resulted in its being always drawn, by avocation, to an activist and—under Russian conditions of the nineteenth century—radical position. Political ideals and concepts, aesthetic and moral values were transmuted into bases for social and political action.[27] This was unavoidable because in order to change the conditions and rectify the social and moral injustices, the political and social orders had to be destroyed. The members of the intelligentsia thus conceived of themselves as charismatic leaders of the people, and in the eyes of public opinion (i.e. the educated), they were truly the "knights" of a crusading order that was to bring justice and freedom to Russia.[28] For similar reasons, too, their Westernism could never be absolute. Western ideas and scientific and philosophic achievements were not so many avenues to truth, as guides for action on the Russian political (and social) stage.[29] Complete Westerners, i.e. individuals who were interested in Western ideas for their scientific and philosophic or aesthetic truth value were either narrow professional scientists or very rare exceptions among the intelligentsia (B. Chicherin, P. Struve). Western ideas were transmuted into action-oriented eschatological programs.[30] Of all Western political notions, liberalism was the least adaptable to such a transformation, as it was in its very essence a negation of abstraction, eschatology, utopia. Liberalism could therefore hardly satisfy most of the members of the intelligentsia, and except for individual notions taken out of context, liberalism remained relatively unpopular and uninfluencial during the formative period of Russia's ideologies.

True, the picture began to change after 1905 under the influence of the revolution and the disappearance of the worse aspects of autocracy, with the growth of an individualistic free enterprise economy,and the spiritual crisis of Russia's "silver age." But the forms of thought and the attitudes developed for more than a century by the best of Russian minds could not be discarded or changed overnight. They lingered on and hindered a gradual and harmonious evolution. Even more important in snuffing out whatever beginnings there were, was the outbreak of World War I. "Un beau mourir toute la vie embellit," and the beautiful and noble decline and death of the Russian intelligentsia and humanistic ideals after 1917 will serve, let us fervently hope, to redeem the errors and weaknesses of Russia's liberalism and its leaders. As an historic force liberalism had failed, but as a spiritual value it may yet have its rebirth.[31] This alone is more than adequate ground to study it with sympathy and understanding.

Notes

1. Independently, but related to this interest, there have been published numerous and important sources of Russian liberalism, mainly in the form of memoirs, cf. the catalogue of the Chekhov Publishing House of the East European Fund, Inc., and the file of *Novyi Zhurnal*, 1942 to date.

2. I make no pretence at bibliographical completeness. I only wish to raise some questions on the basis of recent literature that has come to my attention.

3. "Certainly, *vae victis* is not a principle for historians to follow!" M. Karpovich, "Two Types of Russian Liberalism: Maklakov and Miliukov" in E. J. Simmons ed., *Continuity and Change in Russian and Soviet Thought*, 1955, p. 130.

4. This is the major failing of Victor Leontovitsch's important study, *Geschichte des Liberalismus in Russland*, Frankfurt/Main, 1957, especially in its first part. By the same token, incidentally, the desire to set off conservatism from "reaction" has led to the blurring of the "left" boundaries of conservatism with the result that we find the same names among the heroes of both liberalism and conservatism for pretty much the same reasons. E.g. Karamzin, classed as a liberal by Leontovitsch (*op. cit.* pp. 73–89) and a conservative by R. E. Pipes, "Karamzin's Conception of Monarchy," *Harvard Slavic Studies*, IV (1957), pp. 35–58.

5. J. L. Talmon, *The Origins of Totalitarian Democracy*, London, 1952, pp. 1–16 *passim*. This is also the burden of Sir Isaiah Berlin's interpretation of Herzen in his introduction to *From the Other Shore and The Russian People and Socialism*, London, 1956. Berlin's discussion of Herzen as the Russian "libéral par excellence" is extremely interesting and suggestive. Unfortunately, it is too personal an approach to be very useful in an analysis of "liberalism" as a movement or ideology.

6. This is illustrated by the popularity of A. de Tocqueville and the "reception" in Anglo-Saxon countries of Otto Gierke's work on medieval and early modern law. See also L. Krieger, *The German Idea of Freedom*, 1956; G. Ritter, *Die Dämonie der Macht*, München, 1948; O. Brunner, *Adeliges Landleben und Europäischer Geist*, Salzburg, 1949.

7. Most of the work is still in progress, but *Vorarbeiten* on various conservative themes can be found in *Harvard Slavic Studies* IV; *Forschungen zur Osteuropäischen Geschichte*, II, VI.

8. This was the approach of G. de Ruggiero in his classic *Storia del Liberalismo Europeo*, 1949.

9. See the stimulating essay by Robert E. MacMaster, "In the Russian Manner: Thought as Incipient Action," *Harvard Slavic Studies*, IV, pp. 263–280.

10. S. L. Frank, "Pushkin kak politicheskii myslitel," *Etiudy o Pushkine*, Munich, 1957, especially pp. 43–57 and the same, *Biografiia P. B. Struve*, New York, Chekhov Publishing House, 1956, pp. 213–14.

11. This is the core of Leontovitsch's analysis, see *op. cit.* pp. 1–18.

12. Cf. O. Brunner, *op. cit.;* D. Gerhard, "Regionalismus und ständisches Wesen als ein Grundthema Europäischer Geschichte" *Historische Zeitschrift*, 174 (1852) pp. 307–337; E. H. Kantorowicz, *The King's Two Bodies*, 1957; H. Rosenberg, *Bureau-*

cracy, Aristocracy, and Autocracy; The Prussian Experience, 1660–1815, 1958, especially Introduction and ch. 2.

13. If I may be permitted, at this point, to make a plea *pro domo mea:* my view of Speransky as a conservative (though enlightened) bureaucrat is based on the belief that he would not and could not have introduced a sufficient degree of legalistic liberalism to change the essential nature of the Russian government. True, some of his plans contained individual abstract liberal notions, but their *dynamic* relation to his total proposals was not at all "liberal" in any essential sense. M. Raeff, *Michael Speransky—Statesman of Imperial Russia,* The Hague, 1957.

14. V. A. Maklakov, *Iz vospominanii,* New York, Chekhov Publishing House, 1954; M. Karpovich, "Two Types of Russian Liberalism: Maklakov and Miliukov," *loc. cit.;* Leontovitsch, *op. cit.,* part III. The same was true of P. Struve after 1905, cf. S. Frank, *Biografiia P. B. Struve.*

15. Leontovitsch, *op. cit.,* part II.

16. See the interesting remarks of A. Gershenkron, "The Problem of Economic Development in Russian Intellectual History of the 19th century," *Continuity and Change in Russian and Soviet Thought,* pp. 11–39.

17. This is one of the main themes of G. Fischer, *Russian Liberalism: From Gentry to Intelligentsia,* 1958. Cf. also M. Raeff, *The Peasant Commune in the Political Thinking of Russian Publicists: Laissez-faire Liberalism in the Reign of Alexander II* (unpubl. dissertation, Harvard University, 1950); same, "Russia after the Emancipation: Views of a Gentleman Farmer," *Slavonic and East European Review,* XXIX, No. 73 (June 1951), pp. 470–485 [Chapter 1 of this volume], and "Georges Samarin et la commune paysanne après 1861," *Revue des Etudes Slaves,* XXIX, 1952, pp. 71–81. There are also some curiously interesting remarks on the "staying power" of the bureaucracy in the face of economic pressure in Karl A. Wittfogel, *Oriental Despotism,* 1957, pp. 179–181.

18. Ernst Cassirer, "Some Remarks on the Question of the Originality of the Renaissance," *Journal of the History of Ideas,* IV-1, January, 1943, p. 55.

19. Some tried to resist, but even the strongest were not always very successful in their resistance to the blandishments of radicalism on the one hand and the hopeless ossification of autocracy on the other. V. A. Maklakov, *Iz vospominanii;* Kn. O. Trubetskaia, *Kniaz' S. N. Trubetskoi—vospominaniia sestry,* New York, Chekhov Publishing House, 1953.

20. M. Karpovich, *op. cit.;* also G. Fischer, V. Leontovitsch, S. Frank (*Biografiia P. Struve*) as well as the memoirs of V. Maklakov and P. N. Miliukov published by the Chekhov Publishing House.

21. See the very correct analysis G. Fischer gives of the radicalization of the zemstvo leadership (G. Fischer, *op. cit.* chs. 4 and 5).

22. S. Frank in his biography of Struve reminds us that modern nationalism is an integral part of the liberal creed of the West. He further points out that the Russian intelligentsia was unusually devoid of a true understanding of modern nationalism (he even goes so far as to question the very existence of patriotism among the large mass of the intelligentsia—but this is going too far, I think). He is raising a very interesting and important question. Unfortunately, it can not be dealt with here, mainly because the history of nationalism in Russia—as a sentiment and an ideology—has received very scant attention. It is a subject that should engage the attention of Russian historians; a virgin

field, it has, however, a large amount of sources and materials that can be readily exploited.

23. See the stimulating discussion given by Leontovitsch of the liberals' failure to face the peasant problem realistically and honestly.

24. A similar criticism, alas, can also be often leveled against liberal attitudes to the needs of the growing urban proletariat. S. V. Panina, "Na peterburgskoi okraine," *Novyi Zhurnal*, 48 (1957).

25. This was also true of those who started out as practical *zemstvo* leaders in a program of "small deeds"; cf. G. Fischer, *Russian Liberalism* and "The Russian Intelligentsia and Liberalism," *Harvard Slavic Studies*, IV, pp. 317–336.

26. We have only to think of Herzen's violent and emotional rejection of the "bourgeois" order in France (see I. Berlin's introduction referred to in footnote 4 above). Incidentally, Western individualism was developed through a dynamic process of struggle against "tribal," "feudal," and "ecclesiastic" communalism and authority. The individualism of the Russian intelligentsia, on the other hand, was rather the "passive" result of their cultural and social isolation in the country. Thus, the Russians' individualism was at the same time more complete and less secure than that of the Western intellectuals. Is that not at least a partial explanation of the yearning of so many Russian intellectuals for communalist ideologies?

27. Martin E. Malia, "Schiller and the Early Russian Left," *Harvard Slavic Studies*, IV, pp. 169–200, R. E. MacMaster, "In the Russian Manner," *loc. cit.*

28. G. P. Fedotov, *Novyi grad—sbornik statei*, New York, Chekhov Publishing House, 1952, p. 13. For the implications of these traits of modern "professional intelligentsias" in underdeveloped countries, see G. Fischer, *op. cit.* and Edward Shils, "The Concentration and Dispersion of Charisma: Their Bearing on Economic Policy in Underdeveloped Countries," *World Politics*, XI-1, October 1958, pp. 1–19.

29. P. Scheibert, *Von Bakunin zu Lenin—Geschichte der russichen revolutionären Ideologien 1840–1895*, Bd. I. Leiden, 1956, states this idea on p. 20 and develops it throughout his book. For our purposes the chapters dealing with the first expressions of nihilism and realism are most relevant.

30. In spite of many exaggerations and all too sweeping generalizations one can find many interesting and informative facts and comments on this situation in E. Sarkisyanz, *Russand und der Messianismus des Orients*, Tübingen, 1955, part I.

31. Could Pasternak's work not be a token of this hope?

FOUR

Russian Youth on the Eve of Romanticism

Andrei I. Turgenev and His Circle

Ibo ne redko v izobrazheniiakh umershago naidesh cherty v zhivykh eshche sushchago. [For often you will find in the representation of a dead person the traits of the living.]
A. Radishchev, *Zhitie Fedora Vasilevicha Ushakova.*

THE ACCESSION OF ALEXANDER I not only overlapped very nearly with the beginning of a new century, it also coincided with the coming of age of a new generation in Russia's intellectual life. The new youth differed more sharply than is usually the case from the ways and traditions of their parents. Within the closed framework of seminal and dynamic small groups (or secret organizations), they gave currency and first rank importance to those cultural and ideological elements which, as a rule, are contrasted to the rationalism of the Enlightenment and associated with Romanticism. In the following pages we shall try to come to grips with this phenomenon with the help of the evidence provided by the activities and ideas of Andrei Ivanovich Turgenev and the circle of his close friends in the *Druzheskoe literaturnoe obshchestvo* (Friendly Literary Society).[1]

Andrei Turgenev's life was extremely short—he died suddenly from a chill and fever at the age of twenty-two—and in fact quite unremarkable, its outward events differing little from the existence of other young members of the Russian nobility. He was exceptional, however, in his discerning literary taste, his genuine (albeit minor) poetic talent, and the intensity of his friendships. For these reasons his brief existence throws much light on the social and cultural dimensions of the emotional and intellectual development of educated Russians at the dawn of the nineteenth century.[2]

Turgenev was born in 1781 to Ivan Petrovich Turgenev, a friend and associate of N. Novikov, V. Lopukhin, and other prominent freemasons and mystics in the reign of Catherine II. The elder Turgenev had had an ordinary, lusterless career in the military and civil services.[3] In 1792, in connection with Catherine's closing of the masonic lodges and persecution of their leaders, he was exiled to his estate. In 1796 Paul I allowed him to return to Moscow where he became Director of the University. Thus, part of Andrei Turgenev's formative years was spent on the family estate near Simbirsk, in close contact with and under the supervision of his father, a situation that was far from typical of the eighteenth century pattern of noble upbringing. He later entered the University of Moscow (1799), where he found himself close to such major figures of Russia's cultural life as the writers Karamzin, Dmitriev, and Izmailov. After a few years' study at the University Andrei entered state service in the College of Foreign Affairs, and "worked" first at the College's archives in Moscow. In 1801 he became a translator and junior secretary at the College's chancellery in St. Petersburg. He served as courier to Vienna where he spent several months in the winter of 1802–1803. He died in St. Petersburg in early spring, 1803, soon after returning from his Viennese mission. Even if allowance is made for the earlier maturation of young people a century and a half ago, the short life of Andrei Turgenev could hardly have been more than a token of what he might have done and become. To his friends and contemporaries his short existence seemed exemplary of their own aspirations and dreams, and thus for young Muscovites, he became both symbol and legend of the unfulfilled promise of the first decade of the nineteenth century. Hence, it is important to consider the details of his emotional and intellectual development. Fortunately we are in a position to do this, since his papers—diaries, drafts, letters—have been largely preserved.[4]

In fashion characteristic of a member of the educated nobility, Andrei Turgenev was raised with the conviction that he had a task to perform on earth. To this end he received a careful and well-supervised western education, first at home, then at the Noblemen's Pension, and later at the University of Moscow. More important still was his own feeling that his life had to be meaningful, by assisting others to rise to a higher moral and cultural level. This consciousness of a duty to lead a socially useful active life went hand in hand with an equally strong sense of personal accomplishment. Realizing that his interests and ability lay in the realm of literature, he wanted to make his contribution as writer, critic, and poet.[5] This striving, the ambition to leave a mark on contemporaries and posterity, was perhaps the paramount avowed concern of all the young men around him.[6]

What were the driving forces behind this attitude? The old-fashioned orientation toward state service helped create the psychological and mental climate in which the educated and progressive nobility grew up in the eighteenth century. The Turgenev family stressed, as did families of nobility, social utility as the goal of education.[7] The children's readings and first writing exercises were full of didactic tirades on duty and work, on the obligation to devote one's life to the service of others,[8] and particularly on the ethical values implicit in these precepts. Injustice, misery, and evil caused by man to man were not only to be condemned completely but also to be redressed through charity and philanthropy. Horror seized Andrei Turgenev at the sight of brutality and abuse of authority. How much he would have liked to have helped remedy the evil, console the afflicted and the wronged! But awareness of moral and physical evil seemed to paralyze his energies and he could only express sympathy in the form of literary reminiscences.[9]

At the same time Andrei Turgenev's philanthropic attitude and moral concern involved a curious paradox; his commitment to serve was not only an end of the *vita activa*, it was also an instrument of the *vita contemplativa*. Indeed, like the freemasons of his father's generation, Andrei believed that it was his duty to give maximum development to his inner moral sense. Thus, the improvement of each individual's mind and soul demanded constant dedicated effort. Such purpose, however, implies quite a strong streak of selfishness. At the least clash with an outer barrier, the cultivation of the "inner garden" could easily turn into the cultivation of one's own garden *tout court*, an escape from personal sacrifice and a withdrawal into the private sphere. Andrei Turgenev and his friends asserted that to be merely a good *pater familias* also meant to be a good citizen and a worthy individual.[10] To be sure, the warm family atmosphere prevailing in the Turgenev household was in inspiration. But withdrawal into private family happiness meant giving up striving and accepting oneself and one's present condition. But could one? Did one even know oneself? Fulfillment of the ideal set forth by Andrei's educated young friends meant finding the person whom one was sure of and with whom one could contentedly share one's condition. This required a decision to cease the pursuit of unfulfilled expectations and to accept the daily drudgery of "small deeds" and responsibility. For such an act of will Andrei Turgenev lacked courage.[11] He feared that present actuality was but a mirage of what was possible; would not the realization of the possible be foreclosed if the present were seriously and fully accepted? He was not unaware of the weakness of character that this hesitation implied, but his complaints and regrets about it were self-pitying and not devoid of a touch of narcissism. In a sense Turgenev was escaping the finality of the present and fleeing into the safety of the "open" future. This was quite an understandable reaction, since his moral premise was the selfish enhancement of his own spiritual and moral being, without recourse to any transcendental values or hierarchies. Hence his hesitations, the alternations of desires and expectations, and the fear of fulfillment.[12] The result was a romantic stance of unremitting grief about lost possibilities, the regret of past time, and the ever recurring accent on future hope.[13]

The history of Andrei Turgenev's one love, Catherine Sokovnin, is characteristically revealing in this respect. It was a rather banal story of infatuation and sentimental correspondence, ending in his withdrawal. It would not deserve particular mention were it not for the insight it provides into his character. The romantic involvement, quite short lived, may be told in a few words:[14] Andrei Turgenev met the sisters Sokovnin at a theater party in the Noblemen's Pension. His younger brother Alexander was in love with one of the sisters. Anna Mikhailovna, and at first Andrei fell in love with her too. In the beginning he felt a little guilty vis-à-vis his brother, but then consoled himself with the hope for a kind of *ménage à trois*. But finally, after some hesitation, he turned his attention to another sister, Catherine. The involvement grew deeper, although it always was hesitant and filled with much sentimental daydreaming and regret, spiced with appropriate reminiscences of *La Nouvelle Héloise* and *Werther*. When Andrei left for St. Petersburg the connection continued by mail. At this point Catherine openly declared her love for Andrei and pledged to be his alone. Catherine's avowal frightened him; he trembled for his liberty and for the future of his literary hopes and career. He withdrew, albeit hesitatingly and without breaking the relationship; but when he left for Vienna, his letters became rare and finally stopped altogether.

In letters to his brother Alexander and his friend Andrei S. Kaisarov, both in Goettingen, he was full of regrets, sentimental *épanchements*, and self-justificatory tirades.[15] The next time we hear of his amours, it is a passing affair in Vienna, but this was a purely physical involvement which left his emotions free and unaffected.[16]

In view of Turgenev's pretensions at moral elevation and purity, the selfishness of the rationalizations that he proffers to justify his shying away from genuine personal commitment is revealing. He makes two points which deserve brief mention. He says that he is not worthy of Catherine Sokovnin's pure, devoted, self-abnegating love. Objectively, of course, he was not; but the point is that it was not only an excuse for escaping but an expression of his genuine conviction that he was spiritually and intellectually still incomplete, that he had achieved nothing to give him a sense of genuine identity; this was the course of the malaise experienced by Andrei Turgenev and his generation. The other point emphasized by Turgenev in the letters to his friends is the fear of losing his liberty. To be sure, it is a fear common among men, especially those still close to adolescence, when faced with the finality that the marriage commitment (church sanctioned, of course) entails. But it is also the fear of jeopardizing one's ability to strike out in new directions, to be creative, and actively to pursue the ideal of the *vita contemplativa*. In this sense the fear of losing one's liberty is but another aspect of the feeling of not yet having found one's identity. The struggle for identity was hard on Andrei Turgenev's generation and personal emotions were made to pay the price.

Why was this search for identity, especially in the intellectual and spiritual realms, so difficult? Why did it present special problems to the young men in Moscow around 1800? This question leads us to ask also why did Andrei Turgenev and his friends feel so different or "alienated" from their elders. In view of the fact that Andrei Turgenev and his circle shared the characteristic traits of the early *Sturm und Drang* forms of Romanticism, we may further ask why the acute sense of a break with the older generation and the search for identity were such powerful forces in this Russian generation (as they had been in its German prototypes personified by Schiller's dramatic heroes)?

It seems to us that the answer is to be sought in a fundamental contradiction in the system of values and ideas of the generation of Andrei Turgenev's parents.[17] By the last quarter of the eighteenth century, educated Russians had fully assimilated the basic notions of Enlightenment thought. They had acquired a secular view of progress, especially with respect to the economic, social, and cultural welfare of the nation. They had accepted and internalized the Petrine belief that the goals and norms of the state took precedence over all, and that, by virtue of their leadership function, the monarch and the government brought glory and modernity to Russia. They had also developed a virtually "Protestant" bourgeois sense of duty and service to society. In other words, the transcendental values and goals of medieval society had given way to secular and rational interests and concerns. The Russian Church, captive of the state since the establishment of the Holy Synod, had declined as a source of moral authority, inspiration, and spiritual guidance and had shriveled to the mere policing of ritual conformity. It is true that these aspects of secularism were accompanied by a revival of personal religious life and a genuine concern for the moral and spiritual welfare of the people. It was "philanthropy" (but not Christian charity!) in the best meaning of the word that was associated with the activities of Novikov. But the interesting thing about philanthropy, whatever its spiritual and religious fount, is that it aims at the improvement of the condition of man in *this* world, not at preparing his salvation in the hereafter. In short, the emphasis is on the material and intellectual progress of the individual, in terms of rational judgment, rather than on a transcendental system of values justified *sub specie aeternitatis* with reference to the historical drama of salvation. It was this orientation that found repeated expression in the didactic and juvenile literature which Andrei Turgenev and his friends read and absorbed in their childhood.[18]

At the same time, and in conflict with this secular, rational and individualistic outlook, the traditional insistence on complete submission and obedience to authority—the monarch and parents—was not abandoned. Both the ruler and the family-head were endowed with a God-given aura of authority, borrowed heavily from Lutheran precepts and behavior, that made their orders and directives the object of unquestionable obedience.[19] What had been easy to accept in a traditional society became a source of unresolved conflicts in values in a rationalistic and welfare-oriented civilization. If the goals of human activity were to be based on nothing but rational and utilitarian considerations, why then insist on unquestioned obedience not even justified by a transcendental view of history and society? As long as the ruler (or parent) fulfilled a visible function of leadership in the country's (or family's) cultural progress and modernization, his authority could be accepted. But by the end of the eighteenth century this ceased to be the case.[20] Particularly striking to Andrei Turgenev's generation was the fact that most of their elders served only *pro forma* and did little, if anything, to justify the obedience that they demanded.[21] It is little wonder that Turgenev and his friends felt that they were being asked to act contrary to the social and intellectual values of their culture when unquestioned submission to authority was demanded of them.

The value conflict helped to shape the young generation's relationship to their parents and to their service obligations. Andrei Turgenev, like all young nobles of his day, entered state service as a matter of course. But it did not take much experience to realize how insignificant his service obligations were. It is clear from many remarks scattered throughout his papers that his official work was neither absorbing nor meaningful. The young men's knowledge and talents, in languages for example, were not put to good use. It was merely a way to pass time; obviously the important tasks were performed either by experienced clerks or a very few high dignitaries. In some ways the offices to which they were attached served as a kind of "post-graduate" educational institution.[22]

In the literature on Andrei Turgenev and his brothers much stress is laid on the warm and genuinely good atmosphere that prevailed in their family. Credit for this is usually given to the mildness and kindness of their father, Ivan Petrovich, to his genuinely humane interest in his children as well as to his religious and philanthropic concerns. From all the evidence, Ivan Petrovich was indeed a benevolent, kind, affectionate man whose sincere love for his children (and for mankind in general) cannot be doubted. Yet this same man was a serf owner, who apparently allowed his wife and stewards to treat the domestics harshly, and who also constantly preached complete submission and obedience, even to evil. In part this reflected his timidity, for he was not a courageous or forceful individual and did all he could to avoid clashes with authority. When he did get into trouble with Catherine II for his masonic activities, he not only submitted to his fate but plaintively tried to deny any responsibility for his actions.[23] As Director of the University he was a gentle and understanding but nor forceful supervisor; one has the impression that he performed his duties conscientiously, but without much energy or display of initiative.

Not surprisingly, therefore, his son's attitude to him was somewhat mixed. He had learned to obey him and there is little doubt of the genuine feeling he had for his father. Ivan Petrovich returned Andrei's affection in full. Yet

Andrei's does not seem to have been an affection based on genuine respect. Andrei felt sorry for his father, he loved him, but he did not identify with him.[24] It is very reminiscent of the relationship which Karl Moor, in Schiller's *Die Räuber,* had to his own father, and not the least reason for the enthusiasm of Andrei Turgenev's generation for Schiller's early works. Perhaps Andrei also saw a good illustration of this unfulfilled yearning for identification with his father in Goethe's poem *Mahomets Gesang* which he tried to translate.[25] We note manifestations of this ambivalence when, in his middle teens, Andrei was faced with the choice of obeying his father or following his inclination to be with his good friend A. S. Kaisarov. He obeyed, but his obedience did not come from within, it was not derived from a felt sense of right or a recognition of his father's moral or intellectual superiority.[26] We see similar instances of ambivalence later in connection with his service and questions of his health and personal future.[27]

Naturally, the mother's personality, too, played an important role in the relationship between a son and his family. As was true in the case of A. Kaisarov (and there are many more examples to be found in this period) the mother was stronger and more domineering than the father. Yet she was barely literate and did not share her husband's and children's cultural interests. She was concerned only about her sons' prospects in service, and the management of the family estate, and she was not easy to please. She was also a person of great temper, strong willed and irascible, which in the context of serfdom easily led to capricious and cruel treatment of servants and serfs. Obedience to such a woman was hard to justify on rational or moral grounds; it could only be a matter of injunction and outward submission.[28] Characteristically, Andrei's letters home sound contrived and formal in their expressions of obedience and respect; they reveal little of the interests which he willingly shared with his friends.

The young men of Andrei's generation, as has been noted earlier, were educated to obey, but not told why; they were also taught to rely on reason, to think in terms of social utility, and to promote their own spiritual growth and intellectual independence. Submission or revolt seemed the only alternatives, the former implying the acceptance of a vegetating life. This was an impossible choice, if only because their service-oriented upbringing had been directed at a constructively active life and career. But for this Russian reality offered little scope; activity in service seemed artificial, useless, unrewarding, and ill-directed. They were forced to escape into literature and intellectualism. All this created an all-pervading feeling of discontent and a sense of futility.[29] They were dreaming of what they could and should accomplish, of what might happen in the future or could have occurred in the past. Hope and regret were the leitmotifs of their existence—and they were forever failing to cope with the present. But identification in terms of a distorted past or a future hoped for meant an identification forever incomplete; they remained perpetual adolescents.

The first overt goal of the friendship that linked Andrei Turgenev and the members of his circle was to help them to further their individual development and become useful to society. Clearly the bonds of friendship were much stronger and tighter than those resting merely on personal sympathy; each partner expected to gain in spiritual stature from the friendship. We also note the extremely heightened emotional tone of these friendships. A friend exists and is chosen, they felt, to make one better, to help in one's moral growth and spiritual development. Quite naturally the friendship, or association, was formed to study together, to discover new mental horizons, to become acquainted with new books and writers, to help each other in drawing out the full meaning of these discoveries.[30]

The emotional quality of their friendship was so strong that it is best described by the French phrase, *amitié amoureuse*. It is unlikely that it had overt homosexual aspects, but we may not be quite certain in view of that generation's great reticence about matters sexual.[31] Naturally, there is an element of unfulfillment—sexually speaking—in this kind of relationship. As we shall have occasion to observe, this feature fits in with the major intellectual and spiritual characteristics of this generation. It was a passionate involvement that required constant presence, or at least daily epistolary contact; it also had to be confirmed and strengthened by tangible evidences which we associate with sentimental girlish crushes.[32] It is also very noteworthy that this kind of friendship imposed an obligation on both partners to be better, to improve morally so as to prove worthy of the affection of the friend. It was a stroke of luck to gain a friend, it created a moral and spiritual debt that could not easily be paid.[33] As a result, the relationship was fraught with tensions, with constant questioning of one's own worthiness. It was in a sense a substitute for the lack of an older object of identification as well as a manifestation of an inadequate sense of identity, of a lack of certitude with respect to one's own worth and role in life.[34] We also detect an urge to remain pure vis-à-vis one's friends, a purity that was interpreted not only in spiritual and moral, but in physical and sexual terms as well, underlining the amorous element and latent homosexuality of the bond. Sexual promiscuity and emotional experiences that lacked purity and ethereal idealism were seen as a betrayal and a sullying of one's friends.[35]

A friend was either someone to look up to, to identify with, or someone for whose sake one had to be particularly good and worthy. This might also explain why goodness, a good heart (*dobryi, dobroe serdtse*), was the most valued trait.[36] It implied the ability to feel for the friend, to be understanding and, what is more, to be forgiving. Hence the interest in small instances of benefaction and charity, the happiness produced by cases of simple and heartfelt piety.[37] It was not so much sentimental admiration for the alleged simple virtues of the people, as had been the case with Karamzin and his imitators, but rather a genuine personal involvement in the fate of specific individuals. To be sure, some amount of sentimental idealization was not lacking, but instead of leading to lachrymose moralizing it provoked an urge to do something about redressing the wrong. Literary models for their standards of judgment were readily available. Schiller's dramas gave their feelings the additional dimension of universality and also supplied the young men with a comprehensive ethical and psychological outlook.[38]

We have seen that the older generation did not provide adequate objects for identification or models for emulation. It was, therefore, the friend and the circle of friends that had to serve as the framework for the process of identification. There was no possibility of breaking away, since it was this youthful generation that had "created" the identity of its members for the remainder of their lives; it is little wonder that there was always a touch of adolescence in the Russian intelligentsia. One left this group and its ethos only at the price of suicide or surrender to the Establishment. The lesson had been made clear by their great literary hero, Karl Moor. In order to be himself, he had to identify with his brigand friends and sacrifice to them his personal love and happiness. As they had "made" him (and he them) he could not turn from them except through death. Sacrifice to friends and friendship became a binding cement, and it is quite easy to see how the fate of those who had left the circle early and young could be interpreted in sacrificial terms. It was not an accident that the source of inspiration and the model to be emulated should have been those who had been torn away from the circle, either through early death, like Andrei Turgenev or N. Stankevich, or through arrest and imprisonment, as was to be the case of later generations.

Not only did friendship play a major part in the personal lives of Russian youth in the 1800s, it was the setting for their literary and cultural activities as well.[39]

In 1801, Andrei Turgenev and his friends A. F. Merzliakov and A. S. Kaisarov, along with Andrei's younger brother Alexander and V. Zhukovskii, who were still pupils at the Noblemen's Pension, decided to organize their own literary circle. Unlike the associations founded by their fathers' generation, their society—*Druzheskoe literaturnoe obshchestvo*—did not have a public purpose. It was a friendly society for the promotion of the literary culture and taste of its members. True, literature was defined broadly and, as we shall see, was considered in its relation to other general topics. Essentially, it was as a study group, based on a cult of friendship, whose members wanted to be better individuals and more worthwhile citizens. To be useful to the fatherland and to be friends, such was their purpose.[40]

The society proved to be shortlived. It met for only about half a year, in the course of which twenty-three papers were read at its sessions.[41] The public impact of its activities at the time was practically nil. But memory of it was profound in the minds of its surviving members and this secured it a seminal place in the intellectual history of nineteenth century Russia. Scholars have tried in recent years to situate the group with reference to the literary factions of the time and to draw ideological implications for its role in the pre-history of the Decembrist movement. But it seems to us that this is stretching the evidence. The speeches read at the society's meetings are rather formalized statements of general ideas for purposes of discussion. Let us examine some of these ideas and their implications for the members of the group, so as to obtain a clearer picture of the mental and emotional climate in which this generation came to maturity.

Quite naturally, the theme of friendship occurred repeatedly in the speeches addressed to the group. In an early speech which he delivered in January, 1801, A. F. Merzliakov (the society's main organizational figure) stressed the role of the bonds of friendship for the moral and intellectual development of each member; he also remarked that thanks to these bonds they could cope with the harsh cold world outside.[42] But, Merzliakov maintained, friendship had a still higher function, namely that of endowing the sciences and arts with an emotional quality, making them reflect the life of the heart. Under the impact of friendship and the emotional side of life, science would no longer be cold pseudo-knowledge but a truth relevant to man. That was also the reason that the friendly society was a good preparation for its members' future public role as true sons of the fatherland. This basic point was repeated by V. Zhukovskii in a later speech.[43] But Zhukovskii also stressed the importance of those qualities of the heart that made a friend more worthwhile to others and to himself. In short, what we noted earlier in Andrei Turgenev's correspondence is now repeated n the group more comprehensively and within a broader context. The primary historical contribution of the friendly society was to have emphasized the intimate connection between the emotional bonds uniting several individuals and their potential public utility. No wonder that Schiller's *An die Freude* was their ever recurring source of inspiration!

The role assigned to emotional involvement and friendship in an individual's progress was closely related to the views of psychology and epistemology held by Turgenev's circle. Mikhail Kaisarov postulated the innate quality of basic moral reactions and values[44] although he admitted that they might become conscious only through man's ability to make comparative and analogical judgments. Thus he departed from eighteenth century Lockean empiricism, even though he accepted the utilitarian teleology of the Enlightenment. This could be further proven, argued his brother Andrei Kaisarov,[45] by recognizing that even misanthropy had at its origin the innate good heart of man. Finally, Alexander Turgenev insisted that the world is the way we look at it.[46] Our predisposition and will, he maintained, form our perception and experiences, Zhukovskii echoed these beliefs by saying that our happiness and unhappiness are exclusively within us. In typical rejection of eighteenth century optimism, he added that both are necessary if we want to experience happiness, for we know it only by contrast.[47] All in all, we have here the elements of the "romantic" view of man and of his relation to the outside world. This was not a novel discovery, to be sure—Pascal's writings alone testify to the prior existence of the "romantic" outlook. But this insight had been pushed into the background in the eighteenth century, especially in Russia, where there had been much stress on the rationality and uniformity of human cognition and behavior in order to bridge the gap that still separated the Russians from their Western European models.

We find again an affirmation of the individual aspect of dignity and liberty in the curious encomium to Peter III pronounced by A. F. Voeikov.[48] In praising Peter III for freeing the nobles from compulsory state service, Voeikov gives an unexpected twist to the most fundamental belief held by his entire generation, that the educated individual must be free spiritually and allowed to do his duty voluntarily. Peter III is further praised for freeing millions of serfs from the darkness of Church rule (more precisely from the monasteries), by transferring them to the status of state peasants. Besides the obvious political implications (which, however, Voeikov's subsequent life and career would belie), one may note the emphasis on the necessity for individual enlightenment and culture.

It was not only the desire to keep up with and imitate the most recent developments in Western Europe that accounted for the circle's enthusiasm for German literature.[49] In the writers of the *Sturm und Drang* (later also in early English romanticism and in Shakespeare) they found expressions of personal liberation, of the ambivalent relationship to their elders, of the human emotions, basically simple, yet complicated in their manifestations, which corresponded best to their own needs and moods. Although they had been nurtured on sentimental literature—and they went on reading and even translating it—they were not carried away by it in the way their fathers had been. Their own preference went to the moralizing dramas and stories of writers like August von Kotzebue. In them they found nourishment for their sense of outrage at the sight of moral wrongs and of pity for the poor and downtrodden. Of course, the subject matter of some of these works reminded them directly of Russian social reality (and of their ambiguous position in it), for example Kotzebue's *Die Negersclaven*, which Andrei Turgenev and A. S. Kaisarov set out to translate.[50] *Werther*, naturally, was a *livre de chevet*; the hero's hopeless and unfulfilled love seemed to them an accurate image of genuine love, which existed only as a remote ideal. In the long run this highly charged emotional diet proved to be unsatisfying, and our young critics and *littérateurs* perceived the need for greater formal discipline and tougher intellectual fare. They turned again to the French classics, especially Racine, whom they rediscovered as a truly great master. Here again, however, it was the poet of individual experience and of the fatal consequences of emotion which appealed to them.[51]

This is not the place to analyze in detail Andrei Turgenev's literary criticism. But a few words should be said about two of his speeches to the society in which he dealt with the state and task of Russian literature.[52] In essence he made two major points. He attacked the misuse of literature and he deplored the absence of a truly national literature in Russia. The work of Karamzin had become the main focus of literary debate in the early nineteenth century and, not surprisingly, Andrei Turgenev turned his argument to Karamzin's role in Russian literature. He had, we know, liked and respected Karamzin mainly as editor of the children's readings on which he had been raised, and also as a friend of his family. In his speech, he further acknowledged Karamzin's contribution in introducing Western sentimentalism; this had helped to turn the Russian reader's attention to the inner life, to the moral and spiritual qualities of the common people. Karamzin thus widened the horizon of Russian spiritual experience. But this positive contribution had to be balanced against one important negative consequence of Karamzin's writings. Sentimentalism, especially in the hands of Karamzin's many imitators, had resulted in shallowness of feeling, the drowning of genuine psychological and emotional traits beneath an accumulation of vapid sentimentality. Thus the moral and emotional value of literature had been debased. It was, of course, taken for granted by Andrei Turgenev and his friends that literature had a moral function, that it served to improve man, society, and culture. By lowering the demand he made on his readers, Karamzin had diverted Russian literature into the by-ways of mere entertainment for the semieducated. Quite consistent with his elevated view of literature, Turgenev leveled a similar criticism at Lomonosov. Besides his incontestable merits as the founder of modern Russian literature, this "Peter the Great" of the modern Russian language had also done much to debase literature by writing verse on command for every imperial anniversary, birthday, and court occasion. To laud great men of the past, and on occasion even the living ruler, was perfectly consonant with the high calling of the poet. But to lavish indiscriminate and extravagant praise on sundry members of the imperial house was to betray the high calling of literature. In the eyes of Andrei Turgenev and his generation, literature no longer had the didactic cultural function it had had for eighteenth century writers; a high moral and national role had been conferred on it.[53]

His ideas on the exalted function of literature were related to Turgenev's second point, namely that Russian literature was not as yet a truly national one. This was because it did not portray real Russian characters and heroes, but only foreigners with Russian names or costumes. Even those works that claimed to follow the Russian popular and epic tradition were nothing more than imitations of Western European prototypes with pseudo-national trappings. This criticism was quite valid, as a perusal of contemporary journals and popular literature will readily show. The demand for a truly national, folk-inspired literature was not merely a parroting of western romanticism and historicism; it had Russian roots going back at least to the second half of the eighteenth century. But the generation we are describing had been raised in the ideas of cosmopolitanism. Their early ideal had been not only to become Russians but to merge in a broader family of nations, become truly European, cosmopolitan citizens.[54] Of course, this had also been their fathers' aim. Now, however, in the first decade of the nineteenth century, educated youth felt that cosmopolitanism was a mere construct of the mind, that it had no emotional, historical, or social reality.

To the young men of the 1800s, to be consciously Russian meant to acquire an identity of their own, different from that of their parents and related to their nation. They did not feel that they were complete individuals as long as they were floating in mid-air, outside the human context of Russia. This was their way of overcoming the sense of alienation from land and people that had been characteristic of the Russian educated nobility in the previous century. Their fathers and grandfathers had tried to overcome their alienation by identifying with the West, something outside themselves, and by attempting to create a new type of Russian man who was an European. But already Radishchev and Novikov had shown this way to be sterile, leading only to further oppression of the serfs and a drawing away from the people. It was natural, therefore, to return to a reassertion of the national element. It was less a feeling, or even a consciousness (to borrow Hans Rogger's term) of nationalism than a genuine and fully conscious patriotism. It was love of the fatherland, *otechestvo*, in the direct physical sense of love of one's land, as Karamzin had understood it; but it was also a means of self-fulfillment in the service of a wider community, of dedication to the welfare of one's country and nation.[55] This was the kind of patriotism that found its fullest expression during the Napoleonic wars: "we are ourselves, we are Russians and we need not be ashamed of it, on the contrary!" This is what Alexander Turgenev noted in Goettingen upon hearing Schloezer's praise of Russian history and comparing his own national consciousness to the bored indifference of his German fellow students.[56] This was how Andrei Turgenev felt when, on his trip to Vienna, he attended a play about Peter the Great and visited a Czech scholar (whose efforts to promote national literature he approved with quite a touch of patronizing superiority and condescension).[57] It was this very sentiment that made A. S. Kaisarov volunteer for military service and meet his early death in battle near Görlitz in May, 1813. Love of country and sacrifice for the common good was the legacy of the Turgenev circle which inspired the Decembrists as well.

It is not only the personalities and ideas of Andrei Turgenev and his friends that are of interest to us. Equally important is the historical memory of the circle and of its young hero and *spiritus rector*, for this memory provides a link to the first generation of the Russian intelligentsia, *sensu stricto,* and foreshadows some features of its subsequent "organization" in circles.

The Friendly Literary Society existed for only a few months; Andrei Turgenev died barely twenty-two years old. Other members of the circle not only survived but participated actively in the cultural life of the two capitals. A. F. Merzliakov moved to St. Petersburg and became a known *littérateur* and professor of rhetoric; he also joined another important literary-cultural society, *Vol'noe obshchestvo liubitelei slovesnosti, nauk i khudozhestv,* where the new "romantic" mood combined with enlightenment traditions. Many members of this society were later closely associated with the Decembrists.[58] A. F. Voeikov, too, became associated with this society. A. S. Kaisarov made a name for himself in scholarship and became professor of Russian literature and language at the University of Dorpat. During the campaign of 1812–13, he organized and directed the publication of proclamations and political pamphlets in Kutuzov's headquarters, thus helping to give an ideological and intellectual dimension to the war against Napoleon. His personal contacts in the army and his brother Paisii's (also a friend of Andrei Turgenev) command of partisan units point to connections with the future Decembrists.[59]

Historically and literarily, the most influential member of the group turned out to be V. A. Zhukovskii. He was the mainstay of the prominent literary society *Arzamas* (where young Pushkin was a shining light). Even though he was close to the imperial court, Zhukovskii kept up a friendship with the Decembrists, as well as with all prominent personalities in mid-century intellectual and literary life for whom he often acted as petitioner. Finally, Alexander Turgenev (also a member of *Arzamas*) kept in close touch with all things cultural despite his own literary and scholarly sterility, official position, and lengthy absences from Russia. He was the *colporteur* of literary and philosophical news, a collector of books and documents pertaining to Russian history, and a petitioner for his fellow *littérateurs.* All these men kept alive the memory and interests of the Friendly Literary Society with which they had been associated in their youth.

But these are only tenuous personal links. More significant is the fact that the *kruzhok* (circle) became and remained the framework for the development and education of every generation of the intelligentsia and, later, revolutionary youth. Indeed, only the *kruzhok* provided the means to still the craving for the kind of vital "existential" knowledge not to be obtained either at home or in the universities. The young people thus turned to each other for guidance in their reading and discussion of the ideas discovered. The Friendly Literary Society and Turgenev's circle of friends were prototypes whose example was followed throughout the nineteenth century.

The psychological and intellectual success of the *kruzhok* depended very much on its members' finding a figure to follow and emulate, someone who would inspire and guide them, someone with whom to identify. Under the conditions prevailing in nineteenth century Russia, the older generation was excluded from this role; nor could the object of identification be men of recognized accomplishment. Indeed, the very fact of a successful career (or public reputation) meant acceptance of the Establishment and, by implication, betrayal of the hopes, ideals,and aspirations of their youth. The hero of the circle had to be someone whose promise had remained unfulfilled—be it because of early death or political persecution. It also had to be someone capable of inspiring enthusiasm and worship by his character and example. Finally, the hero had to be a "whole" (*tsel'nyi*) personality, that is, someone whose identity was perceived strongly enough to be the source of unquestionable moral authority. In other words, it had to be someone who was convinced of possessing the moral truth, yet kind enough to overlook the weaknesses of his friends and to help them obtain the same insight. Such was the light in which N. Stankevich was seen by the intelligentsia of the 1830s and 1840s, and he is often cited as the model hero of the *kruzhok*;[60] no doubt he best personified these traits. But he was far from being first or alone in this role in the history of the Russian intelligentsia. We may mention D. Venevitinov, N. Ogarev, and M. Butashevich-Petrashevskii. This is the role in which Andrei Turgenev was cast by his friends.

The "canonization" of Andrei Turgenev started immediately upon his unexpected death—here was a classical case of unfulfilled promise. His brother Alexander Turgenev and his close friends A. Kaisarov and V. Zhukovskii were most active in creating the "myth" of his life and role.[61] Like everyone who holds the memory of someone dear, they overlooked the blemishes and remembered only the good. Andrei, as we have seen, was far from perfect and far from truly having found his identity at the time of his death. His friends turned his expectation of identification into actuality, and thus the promise of his existence became the myth of his life.

Another element in the process of mythologizing the inspirational leader of a *kruzhok* was the glorification of his role in introducing new ideas, styles, and philosophical interests. In this respect Andrei Turgenev's contribution was quite characteristic and very significant. He played a major part in introducing the literature and ideas of the German *Sturm und Drang* and in paving the way for the powerful impact of Schiller on Russian intellectual history. He thus helped lay the ground for the reception of German philosophic idealism. It is not altogether accidental that the "heroes" of later *kruzhki* also were carriers of new philosophic and aesthetic revelations: Venevitinov propagandized Schelling's *Naturphilosophie;* Stankevich, Hegel's metaphysics; Ogarev, Christian socialism; Petrashevskii, Fourierism. It is important to repeat that mere literary and philosophical contributions—such as they were—were not enough to confer the aura of spiritual leadership in the *kruzhok*. What was needed was an emotional and moral commitment that could serve as inspiration. This is what Andrei Turgenev offered his friends, and what Odoevskii or Khomiakov or Herzen did not.

Were there no antecedents for this phenomenon of the *kruzhok* hero? What about the "circle" of Radishchev and his fellow students in Leipzig and the "myth" about their friend Fedor Ushakov? In reading Radishchev's life of Ushakov (characteristically called *zhitie*, i.e., life of a saint), we are struck first of all by the fact that Ushakov was actually the senior, energetic, practical leader of a group whose members had come together accidentally, at imperial command, and who found themselves disoriented in a foreign environment, at the mercy of their supervisor. In the second place, Radishchev and his friends seem to have had no problem about identification. They clearly belonged to Russian society, they had a concrete task to perform, and their future existence was both clearly mapped out and accepted by them. Radishchev's subsequent writing of the *Journey from St. Petersburg to Moscow* was occasioned by a *crise de conscience*, not a crisis of identity. I would suggest that Radishchev's generation had no more than the universal adolescent problem of identity; consequently the societies and associations that they founded had quite a different character and function from those of the early 1800s.

The features we have noted in Turgenev's circle stemmed from a feeling of disorientation, largely motivated by a sense of uselessness, futility, and alienation from a social and political world that was spiritually and morally unacceptable, and by the strong urge to discover new truths for themselves. The fateful thing was that the basic condition which engendered this feeling among Russia's youth did not change materially to the end of the nineteenth century, and even to the eve of the 1917 Revolution.[62] That is why the *kruzhok*—with its blend of intellectual and psychological traits, emotional needs, and moral demands—remained the institutional framework for the intellectual, moral, and ideological development of every generation of the Russian intelligentsia. For similar reasons, the *kruzhok* also played a seminal role in the history of the revolutionary movement. It is not surprising that the revolutionary study and propaganda circles owed many of their basic traits to the experience and tradition which had originated in the circle of Andrei I. Turgenev.

Boris Nicolaevsky, whose memory we honor in the present volume, was in many ways—albeit under the special conditions of his time and life—a representative of this tradition, a tradition which has contributed so much to the glories, as well as the sorrows, of modern Russia's cultural and political history.

Notes

1. Serious study of the Society was started only after the archives of the Turgenev family (in Paris until the first years of the twentieth century, when they were turned over to the Russian Academy of Sciences) were made available to scholars. The first de-

tailed account was in A. N. Veselovskii, *V. A. Zhukovskii (Poeziia chuvstra i "ser-dechnogo voobrazheniia")* (St. Petersburg, 1904). See also M. Sukhomlinov, "A. S. Kaisarov i ego literaturnye druz'ia," *Otdelenie russkogo iazyka i slovesnosti Akademii Nauk, Sbornik,* 65, No. 5 (1897), 1–33; A. Fomin, "Andrei Iv. Turgenev i Andrei Serg. Kaisarov—novye dannye o nikh po dokumentam arkhiva P. N. Turgeneva," *Russkii bibliofil,* January, 1912, pp. 7–39; "Andrei Sergeevich Kaisarov (Novye materialy dlia biografii i dlia kharakteristiki ego literaturnoi deiatel'nosti iz arkhiva P. N. Turgeneva)," ibid., April, 1912, pp. 5–33. In the two decades preceding and following the Russian Revolution, V. M. Istrin made an extensive study of the Turgenev archives in preparation for their publication. See V. M. Istrin, *Zhurnal Ministerstva narodnogo prosveshcheniia* (cited hereafter as *ZMNP*), n.s., 26 (March, 1910), 1–36; 28 (July, 1910), 80–145; 28 (August, 1910), 273–307; 32 (April, 1911), 205–37; 44 (March, 1913), 1–15. Istrin gave an overall account and interpretation of the Turgenev circle in the long introduction to *Pis'ma i dnevnik Aleksandra Ivanovicha Turgeneva gettingenskogo perioda (1802–1084) i pis'ma ego k S. A. Kaisarovu i brat'iam v Gettingene (1805–1811), Arkhiv brat'ev Turgenevykh,* vypusk 2 (St. Petersburg, 1911). The same source was summarized by V. I. Rezanov, *Iz razyskanii o sochineniiakh V. A. Zhukovskogo,* vyp. 2 (Petrograd, 1916). During the next two and one-half decades there were no further sources or monographs published on the Turgenev circle. A revival of interest in it occurred in the 1950s as reflected in e.g. Iu. M. Lotman, "Andrei Sergeevich Kaisarov i literaturno-obshchestvennaia bor'ba ego vremeni," *Uchenye Zapiski Tartuskogo gosudarstvennogo Universiteta* [Tartu Riikliku Ülikooli Toimetised], vyp. 63 (Tartu, 1958), and in his *Puti razvitiia preddekabristkoi obshchestvenno-politicheskoi mysli,* Diss. 1961 (Leningrad University). Although some material quoted below is cited in works referred to in this note, we shall give references to the originals because our viewpoint and interest differ in many ways from that of previous scholars and the excerpts quoted do not quite overlap.

2. The fullest account of Turgenev's life is in Istrin, *Arkhiv brat'ev Turgenevykh,* vyp. 2.

3. E. I. Tarasov, "Kistorii russkogo obshchestva vtoroi poloviny XVIII st.-mason I. P. Turgenev," *ZMNP,* n.s., 51 (June, 1914), 129–75.

4. Akademiia Nauk, Institut istorii russkoi literatury (Pushkinskii Dom), Leningrad, Arkhiv Turgenevykh, fond 309 (hereafter cited as F 309). Additional materials are to be found in the Rukopisnyi otdel, Gosudarstvennaia publichnaia biblioteka imeni Saltykova-Shchedrina, Leningrad, Arkhiv V. A. Zhukovskogo, F 286. Individual items may also be found in the *fondy* of the main participant literary figures such as Voeikov, Merzliakov.

5. F 309, No. 271, Journal entry 22.XI.1799, p. 10 ("Do good according to your ability, do your duty, act for the good of others and your own, exhaust yourself in activity …"); No. 272, Journal entry 14.III.1802, p. 40 ("To what purpose is now the main striving of my spirit: to be known in literature?"). Also his letter to Zhukovskii, 19.VIII.1799, quoted by Veselovskii, *V. A. Zhukovskii,* p. 64, and the last lines of his poem, "I vetkhomu poddevicheskomu domu A. F. V[oeiko]va," in Iu. M. Lotman, ed., *Poety nachala XIX veka,* Biblioteka poeta, malaia seriia, izdanie tret'e (Leningrad, 1961), p. 261 (hereafter cited as *Poety nachala*).

6. F 309, No. 1239, Journal entry 16/28.IX.1802, p. 13 ("Activity, it seems, is higher than liberty. For what else is liberty? Activity endows it with all its value. … Put

chains on man and leave him a free spirit and a clean conscience, he will not stop being active in his mind. ... Activity is the stairway to perfection."); F 309, No. 840, Letter to Andrei S. Kaisarov, no pl., n.d. (from Vienna?), ("If *idealisieren* means to make oneself ideals for future life, i.e., make plans, and if one is not to expect their fulfillment, then man has also another goal, the most virtuous and useful for him and for others: he can be active, he must be active. For what is the use of sleep without tiredness and of entertainment without work? As for contemplation that has no influence on the activity of life, it is nothing but an empty condition of the soul—it brings neither labor nor tiredness. Look how philosophical I have gotten!")

7. For example, *Utrenniaia zaria (Trudy vospitannikov Universitetskogo blagorodnogo Pansiona)*, Bk. 1 (1800), 193–211 (Rech' o liubvi k otechestvu); Bk. 2 (1803), 235–50 (Rech' o tom kakov dolzhen byt' blagorodnyi vospitannik); Bk. 3 (1805) (Rech' o istinnykh dostoinstvakh blagovospitannogo cheloveka); Bk. 5 (1807), 5–81 (O vospitanii); P. S. Zheleznikov, ed., *Sokrashchennaia biblioteka v pol'zu gospodam vospitannikam pervogo kadetskogo korpusa*, 2 (St. Petersburg, 1802), 241 ff; 3 (1804), 381.

8. F 309, No. 542, Letter of I. P. Turgenev to Andrei Turgenev, 1.X.1793 ("... a dedicated striving to please God and serve men will open the world to you ..."); also a curious book given as a present to Nicholas Turgenev by his father for good progress in studies: *L'Ami de l'Enfance ou Contes moraux à la portée des enfants et des adolescents de l'un et l'autre sexe*, Du Laurent (Paris, 1795), F 309, No. 54, Cf. also first writing exercise of Alexander Turgenev, March-May, 1790, Gosudarstvennaia publichnaia biblioteka im. Saltykova-Shchedrina, otdel rukopisei, Bumagi V. A. Zhukovskogo, F 286, No. 316 (hereafter cited as Zhukovskii, F 286).

9. F 309, No. 271, Journal entry 9.XI.1799, pp. 5, 7 (sight of peasant woman and three children); entry of 3.XII.1799, pp. 23–24 (sight of soldiers dragging away drunk man); No. 745 (Nekotorye chuvstva i mneniia moi), entry 28.VIII.1799, p. 5 (sight of old procuress and young prostitute); F 309, No. 271, entry for 3.XII.1799 tells the story of a non-commissioned officer whose wife was seduced by an officer and who had to accept this outrage, which reminds him of the plot of *Kabale und Liebe* ("This flaming, sensitive heart—crushed and tortured by the hand of despotism—deprived of all rights! ... Oh, if I could only express all that moves my heart. If I could only describe this silence!").

10. F 309, No. 271, entry 15.II.1800, p. 36 (Daydreams about living alone, independent, with modest income without having to serve); No. 272, entry of 14.III.1802, p. 40 (daydreaming about family bliss on voyage to Vienna). We are reminded of Alexander I's daydreaming that he would retire on the banks of the Rhine in quiet private family bliss.

11. F 309, No. 272, entry 25.I.1802, p. 38; entry 14.III.1802, p. 40 ("With such lively feelings [of love for Catherine Sokovnin] I will not be able to occupy myself with literature and poetry"); entry 10.V.1801, p. 6 ("I shall live in the past, I shall weep over the past, I shall revive [the past] with renewed strength in my memory."); No. 840, Letter to A. S. Kaisarov 26.XII.[1802] 7.I.1803.

12. The mood is well summarized in his poem "I v dvatsat' let uzh ia dovol'no ispytal," *Poetry nachala*, p. 263. Characteristic of this mood is the design of Andrei Turgenev's seal: a flower on a short leafy stalk with the motto: "jusqu'à son retour." F 309, No. 276, entry for September, 1799, p. 33; entry for June, 1797, p. 59–60 (draft

of a poem: "I net otrady mne ni v chem"); entry for 15.VIII.1797, p. 73 ("Liubvi minuta est' nagrada / Za god unyniia i slez"); No. 272, entry for 10.V.1801, p. 5. See also the poems "Uma ty svetom ozaren" and "Moi drug! Kol' mog ty za-bluzhdat'sia," *Poety machala*, pp. 262, 274; journal entries of Zhukovskii, Zhukovskii, F 286, I No. 1 b, p. 5 ("Ach, das *dort* ist niemals hier!").

13. The theme is given poetic form in his Elegy, the most significant of his literary efforts, *Poety nachala*, pp. 267–70; also F 309, No. 272, pp. 41–42.

14. F 309, No. 272, pp. 16–37 (dated 13.XII.1801) contains copies of letters of Catherine, the following pages contain many references to the affair, expressions of re-gret, hesitations, etc. The affair is summarized (with a different interpretation) by Istrin in *Arkhiv brat'ev Turgenevykh*, vyp. 2; see also the interesting parallel to Evgenii Onegin's Tatiana drawn by Veselovskii, *V. A. Zhukovskii*, p. 82.

15. Catherine died unmarried in 1809.

16. F 309, No. 840, Letter to A. S. Kaisarov from Vienna, no date, and No. 1239, entry for 10/22.I.1803.

17. And which, *mutatis mutandis*, would also hold true of the German scene about two generations earlier, when the traditional Protestant and authoritarian framework was called into question.

18. For example the literary works on which Andrei Turgenev's generation was reared, *Detskoe chtenie dlia serdtsa i razuma* (Moscow, 1785–89); *Detskii sovetnik prepodaiushchii iunoshestvu Pravila, kak blagorazumno v svete postupat'*, Ia. Beliavskii, ed. (St. Petersburg, 1789); *Sokrashchennaia biblioteka*, 3 (1804), 370–81.

19. *Detskoe chtenie dlia serdtsa i razuma*, 1 (1785), 8 ff ("Povest' o Seleme i Ksamire"), 3 (1785), 8–16 ("O podrazhanii roditeliam"). The theme is strongly em-phasized in Ivan P. Turgenev's own book, *Kto mozhet byt' dobrym grazhdaninom i vernym poddannym* (Moscow, 1796), pp. 1–28 *passim*.

20. Was this not the burden of the lesson which Radishchev drew from his experi-ences and which impelled him to write his *Journey*?

21. It had also become clear that the nobility did not (or perhaps could not) take ad-vantage of the opportunities for useful local life as paved by the acts of 1775 and 1785. This also explains the bitter sarcasm with which the average provincial nobleman and his way of life were satirized by this generation. The irony is more cutting than the smiling ridicule of eighteenth century satire; it presages Griboedov, the gloomy picture of Gogol', and the angry outbursts of Saltykov-Shchedrin, cf. examples in E. G. Ermakova-Bitner, ed., *Poetry satiriki kontsa XVIII—nachala XIX v.* (Leningrad, 1959) and A. Fomin's attribution of "Brakosochetanie Karamzina" to A. S. Kaisarov (*Russkii bibliofil*, January, 1912, pp. 30–39). There were exceptions, of course, but they were few, which explains the admiration which was heaped on a man like I. V. Lopukhin.

22. See Andrei Turgenev's diary in Vienna, F 309, No. 1239 with his plans for study and excerpts from historical books, also his letters to parents from St. Petersburg and Vienna, F 309, Nos. 1231, 1238 *passim*, in which he announces his new objects of study (English, reviewing of Latin, etc.) No doubt, a similar point of view accounts for the orientation towards technical training as preparation for *meaningful* service which we note in Alexander and Nicholas Turgenev's letters and diaries from Goettingen.

23. F 309, No. 544, Letter to his friend Vasilii Stepanovich (?) 9.XI.1794, from Selo Turgenevo.

24. F 309, No. 840, Letter from 7.IX.1799. On the reaction to Andrei's death see the full documentation by V. Istrin, "Smert' Andreia Iv. Turgeneva," *ZMNP,* 26 (March, 1910), 1–36.

25. F 309, No. 271, entry for 1.XII.1799. The most significant stanzas in this context are: "... Bruder!/ Bruder, nimm die Brüder mit,/ Mit zu deinem alten Vater,/ Zu dem ewgen Ozean,/ Der mit ausgespannten Armen,/ Unser wartet,/ Die sich, ach! vergebens öffnen,/ Seine sehnenden zu fassen ..." and "Und so trägt er seine Brüder,/ Seine Schätze, seine Kinder/ dem erwartenden Erzeuger/ Freudebrausend an das Herz."

26. F 309, No. 840, Letter 1.X.1799. See also the allusively revealing remark by Catherine Sokovnin in a letter, 26.XII.1801: "Il ne faut pas se sacrifier tout à fait aux autres, mais nous leur devons des ménagements. Osobenno vy vashemu batiushke. Il a des droits bien forts sur vous." (F 309, No. 272, p. 32). Cf. also his long description of the relationship between Prince Kozlovskii and his father, from whose clutches he wants to free him, F 309, No. 1231, letter of 25.XII.1801.

27. We need only compare F 309, Nos. 840 (to Kaisarov) and 1231, 1238, 1237 (to parents).

28. See the curiously revealing entry in Turgenev's Diary, 8.IV.1802 (F 309, No. 272, p. 46): "My mother's character has a great deal of influence on mine, on my morality, and on my happiness. She confines my soul. How frequently did she not permit the development of some joyful, elevated feeling; how often she smothered that which already was there. If it had not been for her, my soul would have been freer, more joyful, more enterprising, and consequently better, nobler. ..."

29. The expressions of a sense of incompleteness and futility pervade all the writings of Andrei Turgenev and his friends. His poetry is the best introduction for it. Most frequently in diary for the Vienna period, F 309, No. 1239. Andrei's youngest brother, Sergei explained more fully the social-political dimensions of this feeling of futility in his diary for 1814: "Denn ich zweifle sehr ob das Vaterland oder der Mensch Nummer eins ist. Das höchste Ziel des Menschen ist sein Glück, der Staat ist ein Mittel zur Erreichung desselben; und das Vaterland scheint nur eine Folge des Staates zu sein [... illegible] haben kein Staat und kein Vaterland. Und was bekümmert mich ein Staat wo ich kein Bürger bin, und ein Vaterland welchem ich nicht dienen kann ohne sich [illegible] manches gefallen zu lassen, was der Würde des Menschen zuwider ist ..." (No. 16, pp. 75–76).

30. There are no elaborate descriptions of friendship in general terms in Andrei Turgenev's papers. The sentiment is reflected in his poetry. A more general definition is given by Zhukovskii in a letter to Alexander Turgenev, remembering the early circle of friends (quoted by Sukhomlinov, *Sbornik,* 65, No. 5 [1897], 1–2): "Our friendship, yours, mine, Merzliakov's, Kaisarov's, was based on imagination. ... Brothers, let us be friends; we'll *do* much more. ... Even now I am not very active, but at any rate I see the necessity of being higher, higher: for this I demand the help of my friends. Brothers, together, together let us go to everything that is good! It is not an enthusiast, childish and fiery, who speaks this, but cold reflection. ... We must be inspired by one thing, supported by one thing! In a word, our life must be *cause commune.*" An elegiac expression of the same feeling was given by Andrei Turgenev in a letter to Zhukovskii (Fomin, *Russkii bibliofil,* January, 1912, p. 12 note): "... I would wish that on the festive days [of our Society]—1 or 7 April, the other I don't remember—each one of us

would celebrate it, wherever he may be. This would be pleasant to many of us; others might do it out of consideration to the others. Imagine that one of us would be in Paris, the other in London, the third in Sweden, the fourth in Moscow, the fifth in St. Petersburg, and that on these days they are together in spirit. Each one will know that ... every one of his spiritual friends is thinking of him. This thought is worth something." A. F. Merzliakov gave a comprehensive and accurate expression to this conception of friendship in several of his poems, *Stikhotvoreniia,* Iu. M. Lotman, ed. (Leningrad, 1958), pp. 198, 229.

31. The entire correspondence between Andrei Turgenev and Andrei Kaisarov illustrates this, F 309, Nos. 840, 50. The only clear reference to a homosexual attachment among members of this generation encountered by this writer is the case of A. Kh. Vostokov. Cf. "Zametki A. Kh. Vostokova o ego zhizni," *Sbornik statei chitannykh v otdelenii russkogo iazyka i slovesnosti Akademii Nauk,* 70 (St. Petersburg, 1901).

32. F 309, No. 840, Letter 15.VI.1797(?); "I found on the road wonderful forget-me-nots, your favorite flower. I picked them and put them in my pocket, and as soon as I saw them I remembered you, and then later also S[andunova?]." Also No. 50 (5.V.1802).

33. Cf. the frequent reference to the lines from Schiller's *An die Freude:* "Wem der grosse Wurf gelungen,/ Eines Freundes Freund zu sein."

34. F 309, No. 840, 15.VI.1797(?); ibid. from Moscow, New Year's eve, 1800. Even more dramatic are the self-doubts of Kaisarov, who waits with trepidation for Andrei's letters as a sign that he still loves him, without him he is "an orphan" (F 309, No. 50).

35. The revealing confession of their friend I. F. Zhuravlev that he slept with a prostitute (or courtesan) in Vilno, F 309, No. 1213, 31.VII.1798.

36. F 309, No. 840, Letter to A. Kaisarov, 2.IX.1799. ("For example, I determined that you have a good heart, tender and kind, which makes those whom it loves happy, and that it loves me.")

37. F 309, No. 50, Letter of A. Kaisarov to Andrei Turgenev, 8.V.1802. No. 276, entry for 14.VIII.1799, p.34.

38. For example, *Kabale und Liebe* and *Die Verschwörung von Fiesko.*

39. The practice of organizing societies for the pursuit of cultural and social goals (largely to make up for the inadequacies of educational, religious, and government institutions) became popular in the second half of the eighteenth century, particularly as a result of the efforts of the freemasons. A Prokopovich-Antonskii sponsored the organization of a society for literary and cultural pursuits among the pupils under his care at the Noblemen's Pension of the University of Moscow. Of course, the Corps of Cadets had set a precedent for this kind of activity in a private school for children of the nobility. But Prokopovich-Antonskii's foundation had a much more purposeful moral and didactic orientation, consonant with the sentimental religiosity and philanthropy of the late eighteenth century. It helped give a new institutional framework to Russian cultural life, which conveniently replaced the traditional associations based on family, church, and class solidarities.

40. The works of Istrin, Lotman, and Rezanov are the best introduction to the history of the society. See also Iu. M. Lotman, "Stikhotvorenie Andreia Turgeneva 'K otechestvu' i ego rech' v 'Druzheskom literaturnom obshchestve'," *Literaturnoe nasledstvo,* 60, pt. 1 (Moscow, 1956), 323–38. The members were as follows: A. F. Merzliakov, A. I. Turgenev, M.S., A. S., and P. S. Kaisarov, V. A. Zhukovskii, Alexan-

der I. Turgenev. S. E. Rodzianko and A. Ofrosimov joined the group later. The rules of the Society have been published by N. Tikhonravov, "Zakony Druzheskogo literaturnogo obshchestva," *Sbornik obshchestva liubitelei rossiiskoi slovesnosti na 1891 g.* (Moscow, 1891), pp. 1–14.

41. F 309, No. 618, "Rechi druzheskogo obshchestva 1801" (hereafter cited as "Rechi"). This is not a transcript but a copy (incomplete) of the speeches (probably from the final drafts submitted by the authors). Not all speeches have titles.

42. "Rechi," 19.I.1801, pp. 11–24.

43. Ibid., 27.II.1801; with stress on the closeness of friendship to love, a theme that he repeated in his speech, "On Passions," 12.IV.1801(?), 75–77. Also note the significant statement of Andrei Turgenev: "Even a criminal can fall in love. But to feel friendship, this only a virtuous heart can do." F 309, No. 271 (entry for 30.VII.1800, p. 63).

44. "Rechi," 15.III.1801(?), "O tom, chto esli by chelovek s samogo rozhdeniia ostavlen byl na neobitaemom ostrove; to mog li by on otlichat' v posleduiushchee vremia porok ot dobrodeteli?" pp. 60–63.

45. Ibid., 1.VI.1801, "O tom, chto mizantropov nespravedlivo pochitaiut bezchelovechnymi."

46. Ibid., "O tom, chto liudi po bol'shei chasti sami vinovniki svoikh neschastii i neudovol'stvii sluchaiushchikhsia v zhizni," pp. 115–18.

47. Ibid., 22.IV.1801, pp. 83–89, echoed by M. Kaisarov, 26.I.1801, "O tom, chto voobrazhenie dostavliaet nam bol'she udovol'stvii nezheli sushchestvennost'," pp. 31–35.

48. Ibid., 26–30, not dated. The most recent scholar on the subject, Iu. M. Lotman, has argued strongly that the speech was a direct allusion to the reign of Paul I (by contrast) on the basis of the hypothetical date of January 19 on which it may have been delivered. True or not, the point is of no essential consequence.

49. The language best known in the Turgenev circle was German. Andrei Turgenev refers to his readings of German literature from the earliest diary entries. (See also E. Bobrov, *Literatura i prosveshchenie v Rossii v XIX v. [Materialy issledovanniia i zametki],* 2 [Kazan', 1902], p. 120 [letter of G. P. Kameneva, Nov. 26, 1800, relating visit with I. P. Turgenev].) He played the major role in introducing Schiller to the group, and his and his friends' writings are filled with references or quotations (often incorrect and not very varied) from Schiller. What M. Malia says about the appeal of Schiller for the generation of the 1830s could apply also to the Turgenev circle, perhaps even more so. It seems to us that Malia is underestimating the dynamic role of the early vogue for Schiller ("Schiller and the Early Russian Left," *Russian Thought and Politics,* H. McLean, M. E. Malia, and G. Fischer, eds., *Harvard Slavic Studies,* 4 [1957], pp. 169–200; cf. also Hans-Bernd Harder, *Schiller in Russland—Materialien zu einer Wirkungsgeschichte (1789–1814).* Frankfurter Beiträge zur Germanistik 4, Bad Homburg-Berlin-Zürich, 1969.

50. Zhukovskii, F 286, 2, No. 327.

51. F 309, No. 272, entry for 24.V.1802; No. 840, letter to Kaisarov, 27.III.1803.

52. "Rechi," 5.IV.1801(?), "O poezii i o zloupotreblenii onoi," pp. 71–74; 19.IV.1801, "O russkoi literature," pp. 78–82.

53. Note the parallelism to Schiller, although I could find no evidence of their being acquainted with his philosophic and aesthetic essays. For a recent study of Schiller which brings out very well those aspects of the poet's work that would appeal to Andrei

Turgenev and his generation, see Emil Staiger, *Friedrich Schiller* (Zurich, 1967), especially the chapters, "Fremde des Lebens" and "Freiheit."

54. Andrei Turgenev noted, for instance, in his diary, 15.VIII.1797 (F 309, No. 276), p. 75: "Il n'y a plus aujourd'hui de Français, d'Allemands, d'Espagnols, d'Anglais même, quoiqu'on en dise, il n'y a que des Européens."

55. See Andrei Turgenev's draft of a speech on patriotism, *Literaturnoe nasledstvo*, 60, pt. 1 (1956), 334–36. It may be worth pointing out that in the language of the time, reference was to *otechestvo* (neuter, derived from *otets*, father) when speaking of the country Russia. The current term *rodina* (feminine) was used only with reference to the specific place or region of birth. The hunt for psychoanalytical interpreters is open!

56. *Arkhiv brat'ev Turgenevykh*, vyp. 2, p. 198 and *passim*.

57. F 309, No. 1238, letters of 8/20.VI.1802 (the play was *Das Mädchen von Marienburg*) and 29.VI.1802 (the name of the Czech scholar is torn off): "I spoke to him as it behooves a Russian to speak about the Russians, praised to him our epic poems, mentioned Derzhavin and [illegible] poets, did not forget also Karamzin, Dmitriev and mentioned Izmailov, finally I promised to send him Russian tea and took my leave. ... "

58. The most readily available introductions to this society are V. Orlov, *Russkie prosvetiteli 1790–1800kh godov* (Moscow, 1950), and V. Bazanov, *Uchenaia respublika* (Moscow-Leningrad, 1964).

59. See Lotman's biography of A. S. Kaisarov mentioned in note 1 above; also Iu. M. Lotman, "Pokhodnaia tipografiia shtaba Kutuzova i ee deiatel'nost'," in *1812 god—K stopiatidesiatiletiiu Otechestvennoi voiny* (Moscow, 1962), pp. 215–32, and R. E. Al'tshuller and A. G. Tartakovskii, eds., *Listovki Otechestvennoi voiny 1812 goda, Sbornik dokumentov* (Moscow, 1962).

60. Edward J. Brown, *Stankevich and His Moscow Circle 1830–1840* (Stanford, 1966). Incidentally, the *kruzhok* is one form of "adolescent society" as we know it in the West today, and the two have a similar causal dynamics, i.e., the problem of identification with the father. See Kenneth Keniston, *The Uncommitted-Alienated Youth in American Society* (New York, 1960), and, more generally, the theoretical discussion of the need to take into account the particular historical and total social contexts in Erik H. Erikson, *Identity—Youth and Crisis* (New York, 1968).

61. See Veselovskii, *V. A. Zhukovskii*, p. 95; the vast amount of evidence in Istrin, *ZMNP*, n.s., 26 (March, 1910), pp. 1–36, and this confession of Alexander Turgenev: "I am becoming an empty man. The more I reflect on the fate of my brother, the more cause I find to envy him. He died at the very moment of life when we stop being enthusiastic, enjoying life, and when there approaches that emptiness which unavoidably must fill the second half of our life." (F 309, No. 1210, letter of 25(?).VI.1805 to Sergei A. Kaisarov). Still later, Kaisarov was to write to Sergei Turgenv, 8.VII.1810 (F 309, No. 386, p. 4): "Sometimes he [Andrei Turgenev] would lighten my ills by his affectionate kindness, but now I am completely alone ... and it seems as if I am condemned to spend the whole life alone, far from everything that is dear to me and loving."

62. On Russia's "pedocracy" see the very suggestive, albeit overly critical, remarks of A. S. Izgoev, "Ob intelligentnoi molodezhi—Zametki ob ee byte i nastroeniiakh," *Vekhi, Sbornik statei o russkoi intelligentsii*, 3rd ed. (Moscow, 1909), pp. 97–124.

FIVE

At the Origins of a Russian National Consciousness

Eighteenth Century Roots and Napoleonic Wars

ALMOST EVERY DAY NEWSPAPERS and magazines relate stories of problems connected with national, cultural, or ethnic identity. If in the Western world these questions are no longer connected exclusively with the state, in the Third and ex-Soviet worlds issues of national identity are intimately bound up with state (re)building. As national claims by non-Russians move into the center of the state in the Soviet Union, one should also pay attention to the nature of Russian national consciousness. Is there anything in the history of Russian national identity that may explain its peculiar forms of expression and clarify the attitudes the Russians bring to non-Russians within the boundaries of the Russian Empire or the Soviet Union? To answer this question, as well as for the light it may shed on the nature of modern Russian culture, a sketch of the formative period of the Russian sense of nationality may be of interest. But before proceeding several preliminary observations are in order.

Modern nationalism, or the sense of national identity, is a phenomenon whose birth can be pretty exactly traced to the time of the French Revolution and the Napoleonic wars. In contrast to other senses of identity—religious, local, or estate bound—that are documented for *ancien régime* Europe (and that are still at play in many parts of the non-Western world), modern nationalism is not only associated with the notion of a national state, but also sets itself a goal or task that the nation is to fulfill—be it linguistic unity, recuperation of ethnic territory, ideological mission, or cultural leadership. Of course, even before the end of the eighteenth century, people who lived in a definable territory had a sense of belonging to larger groups than family or clan. But it was rather an awareness of specific forms of existence rather than a project to be realized in the future. Religion, of course, was one of the major criteria of distinction on the frontiers of Christendom, or wherever two or more denominations came into contact (e.g., the Germanies, Poland). Language might have played that role, too, but its concrete manifestations have not been adequately investigated as yet. Such forms of identification survived among the peasantry in Europe down to the second half of the nineteenth century, or even later—as long as the rural world remained relatively self-contained. They broke down only with the penetration of modern means of transportation and communication, and the uniformizing role of school and administration, a process that has been brilliantly illuminated by Eugene Weber in his *Peasants into Frenchmen.*

For the area that interests us here, a graphic illustration of the pre-modern, amorphous and fluid sense of group identity was given in an English diplomatic report during the Civil War in the Ukraine in May 1918:

> The peasants speak the Little Russian dialect; a small group of nationalist intelligentsia now professes a Ukranian identity distinct from that of the Great Russians. Whether such a nationality exists is usually discussed in terms in which the question can receive no answer. Were one to ask the average peasant in the Ukraine his nationality, he would answer that he is Greek Orthodox; if pressed to say whether he is a Great Russian, a Pole, or a Ukrainian, he would probably reply that he is a peasant; and if one insisted on knowing what language he spoke he would say that he talked the "local tongue." One might perhaps get him to call himself by a proper national name and say that he is "russkii" [Russian], but this declaration would hardly prejudge the question of a Ukrainian relationship; he simply does not think of nationality in the terms familiar to the intelligentsia. Again, if one tried to find out to what State he desires to belong—whether he wanted to be ruled by an All-Russian or a separate Ukrainian Government—one would find that in his opinion all Governments alike are a nuisance, and that it would be best if the "Christian peasant-folk" were left to themselves.[1]

To articulate the specific characteristics and goals of a "nation," the intellectual or ideological leadership of an educated elite was necessary. It was such an elite that provided an intellectual validation, or ideology if you will, rooted in the Enlightenment belief of permanent progress and a Romantic faith in the existence of a people's (*Volk*) character and destiny. For this reason the spiritual leadership had to come from the ranks of the educated—of whatever social origin. Consequently, it was the professionals, the academics, the clerics, as well as noble and bourgeois leaders who became the spokesmen and advocates of a nationalism that, in the long run, also served their selfish interests by providing new opportunities for social advancement, recognition of social status, and bureaucratic employment. Moreover, only an organized, centralized political sovereignty could implement a "rationally constructivis," future-oriented policy. Such a role had been adumbrated by the "Well Ordered Police State" of the late seventeenth and eighteenth centuries as it had laid the foundations of an activist administration and professional staff.

As we learn from psychologists, linguists and anthropologists, the sense of identity is very often defined and sharpened by the discovery of an "Other" against which to compare or measure oneself. Thus, the discovery of America not only led to a new knowledge of an "Other," but also refined and enhanced the Spaniards' or Christians' sense of identity. And so it was also that the first form of a national Russian consciousness took shape in opposition to the image of Russia and its history that foreign (particularly German) scholars had projected in the eighteenth century, as has been beautifully shown by Hans Rogger in his classic book, *National Consciousness in Eighteenth Century Russia* (1960). This consciousness was the work of an educated elite and it took place in the eighteenth century, which endowed the process with specific characteristic traits which the present article will endeavor to define.

Throughout the eighteenth century the Russian elites strained all their energies to fulfill Peter I's (the Great's) project and become "Europeanized." They had succeeded, we may say, by the end of the reign of Catherine II (1762–1796). From then on we can speak of a "civil society of the educated," i.e., of those educated to partake of the cultural and intellectual life of Western and Central Europe. This "Europeanization," however, had a number of specific traits that are often overlooked because of an overemphasis on the influence of the French *philosophes*. In the process of internalizing the European models, Russia's educated elites had come to stress not so much the cerebral as the affective aspects. They found themselves closer to the German *Aufklärung* than to the French *lumières*, and we should speak of an "enlightenment of the heart" as their most characteristic ingredient. This gave a more emotional tinge to the ethical goals they pursued in their efforts at a "Transfiguration" (*Preobrazhenie*) of Russia and of its people. We cannot help but be reminded of the French revolutionary project to "regenerate man" according to the rather ambiguous prescriptions of the *philosophes* (cf M. Ozouf, *L'homme régénéré—Essais sur la Révolution française*, 1989).

Indeed, a revival of religious and spiritual concerns was a significant aspect of the Europeanization of the Russian elites. Ever since the late seventeenth century, the Russian elites had been exposed to German Protestant spiritualist and hermetic literature that served to compensate for the inadequate spiritual fare offered by the official Orthodox Church after Peter's reforms. The Pietists found a particularly favorable reception, for not only did they teach the ways to a richer personal religious life, but they combined it with an energetic furtherance of society's material progress. They were eager to help realize Peter I's project of transforming Russia into an energetic and productive country, so as to enhance the military and political power of the State. In this way the model of *pietatis praxis* (ways of piety) could receive a social ethical dimension: in helping fellow men to improve their material circumstances one also enabled them to lead a proper Christian life in preparation for the hereafter. To combine the furtherance of the individual's spirituality with the active service to the community for the sake of society's moral perfection as well as material progress—such was the aim of the masonic lodges that attracted the educated elites in the reign of Catherine II, as witnessed by the career of N. I. Novikov, pioneer publisher and philanthropist. By the end of Catherine's reign we may speak of a "civil society of the educated" that aspired to an autonomous existence, independent from state service, and full freedom to contribute to cultural and material progress, their own, as well as that of the country at large. Catherine's panicky response to the French revolution (more precisely to the execution of Louis XVI) and Paul's militaristic tyranny brought about the closing of philanthropic organizations, such as the masonic lodges and of printing presses, and the persecution of prominent cultural leaders (N. I. Novikov, A. N. Radishchev), as well as the imposition of a restrictive censorship. Such a policy did not destroy the elite's emotional commitment to its ethical ideals, but it enhanced the sense of frustration and uselessness of the younger generation.

Among the less illustrious victims of Catherine's anti-masonic measures at the end of her reign was Ivan Turgenev, Director of the University of Moscow's Boarding School, who was exiled to his estate in Simbirsk province. His four sons came to be in many ways paradigmatic for their generation—a generation that reached maturity in the years following the Jacobin dictatorship in France and the rise of Napoleon Bonaparte. Under their father's guidance the four sons were introduced to German culture—belles lettres (Schiller in particular) and philosophy (Kant and the earlier *Aufklärer*)—that came to have a more powerful impact on them than the French enlightenment. Of note, too, is the fact that, contrary to expectation, the main events and legislative accomplishments of the French revolution did not arrest their attention. In this respect they only followed the example of the writer Nicholas M. Karamzin, a friend of the family. Karamzin (1766–1826) had been associated in his youth with Novikov's publishing activities (as editor of the first Russian journal for the young, *Detskoe chtenie dlia serdtsa i razuma, 1785–1789*); he experienced the influence of German authors of the *Aufklärung* (Gottsched, Wieland) and of the budding sentimentalism in England (Gray, Sterne). He gained recognition and celebrity with his sentimental novel, *Bednaia Liza* (Poor Lisa), showing the moral worth of the simple folk, and with his *Letters of a Russian Traveler* that illustrated how much an eighteenth century educated Russian was at home in the culture of the West, especially in Germany.

The reign of Paul I (1796–1801) demonstrated to Karamzin and the young Turgenevs the deleterious effects that a capricious and tyrannical sovereign could have on the development of a free and creative personality, not only by stymieing his actions, but also by threatening the very survival of a sensitive heart and an exacting moral conscience. Paul's rule convincingly showed how fetters binding the individual spirit and conscience prevented active and useful involvement in society, and in so doing, contributed to the perpetuation of the Russian people's backwardness and misery.

Upon accession to his father's throne, Alexander I (1801–1825) promised to "reign in the spirit of my grandmother," Catherine II. The proclamation revived the educated elite's hopes that the movement towards ever greater Europeanization and socio-economic progress would be resumed. The first decade of the reign seemed to justify these expectations. The central administration was reformed and its procedures rationalized and economic and social progress was promoted by government legislation. In addition, Alexander I furthered education and culture by founding new universities and granting them a large degree of academic freedom and internal autonomy; censorship was relaxed so that informative and critical journals could be published, while the government also encouraged and subsidized the translation of the most important progressive Western writers in political economy and jurisprudence (Smith, Bentham). Rumor had it that these measures would be topped by a constitution; Alexander did nothing to discountenance this talk, quite the contrary, he himself spoke of the need "to rebuild (*perestroit*) the dilapidated structure of government." The "civil society of the educated" that had come into being in the reign of Catherine II, only to be choked by Paul I, revived and optimistically set about to resume its creative spurt.

A key element in the "Europeanization" of Russia (as it was to be elsewhere at other times) was the development of a language capable of handling the technical and cultural terminology demanded by European ideas and ways. As the process of Europeanization seemed completed for the educated elite, it was also necessary to bring to completion the development of a modern literary Russian language; this task was of primary concern to the literary and aesthetic circle founded by the oldest of the Turgenev brothers, Andrei. His circle was the first to create the heady mixture that combined aesthetic and emotional commitment to the moral and spiritual development of friends with a mounting interest in, and concern for, the welfare of the nation. It was to inspire subsequent generations of young members of educated civil society—the intelligentsia—who would not, under conditions of autocracy, find a meaningful and creative role for themselves in Russian society.

The task of developing an adequate modern Russian language, along with the challenges presented by Russia's active involvement in the political events on the international scene, led the young generation of the 1800s to become interested in the history of Russia. The eighteenth century belief that modern Russia had its source exclusively in the reign of Peter I was no longer tenable. Russia's success in fulfilling Peter's project of becoming a major power could not be explained in such a simple way. Furthermore, the concepts of history and historical development formulated in the eighteenth century by *philosophes* and *érudits* had penetrated into Russia and they had been reinforced by a growing feeling that Russia's difference from Europe had to be preserved along with the conscious efforts at imitating the latter. The scholarship of European academics invited to Russia and the urge to disprove those European authors who only saw barbarity and despotism in Russia, further stimulated the study of history. With Alexander's benign approval and support, an increasing number of Russians studied in universities abroad, most particularly Göttingen, then the capital of cameralist and historical scholarship. Along the same vein, Alexander created the position of official historiographer to which he appointed N. M. Karamzin. As we have noted, Karamzin was not only close to the Turgenev family but had been strongly influenced by the religious and ethical notions of the *Aufklärung*.

It is, however, the experience of 1812 that proved particularly seminal. It is neither surprising, nor a novel observation, that Napoleon's invasion of Russia released a wave of patriotic feeling among the elites; and the common people were also swept up by it once they realized that the invader would not bring any beneficial social or economic changes. It is also a cliché of most Russian (and Western) historiography that the defeat of the French heightened national pride. But as the recently discovered and published diary of the young noble militia officer, Alexander Chicherin (an ancestor of the Soviet Union's first Commissar of Foreign Affairs, Boris N. Chicherin) makes clear, the more significant feature of the experience of 1812 was a double "discovery" made by the educated participants in the struggle against Napoleonic France (*Dnevnik Aleksandra Chicherina 1812–1813*, ed. by S. G. Engel' and M. I. Perper: Moscow, 1966).

The first "discovery" made by young Chicherin was that he was not alone in being interested in the life of the spirit and of the muses (in his case, poetry and music). He found among fellow militia officers like-minded spirits of similar educational and cultural background who thirsted for a chance to be useful to their country. Useful not only by expelling the invader from Russian soil, but also by devoting their knowledge and energies to further their people's well-being and their country's progress. The common bond of similar education and aspiration created a subgroup of civil society that eagerly awaited the chance to prove itself. The second "discovery" was perhaps more surprising and significant: this was that the common people of Russia—the peasants conscripted to fight the French invader—were as capable as the well born of loyalty, initiative, dependability and devotion to the common weal of the country. In *War and Peace* Leo Tolstoi may have idealized the figure of Platon Karataev, but he did make of him a fair example of the common people discovered by many a young educated nobleman who joined the army as a junior officer. Of course, the young nobles in the army and militia had known the Russian peasant even before entering service; most likely they had been raised on the family estate in close contact with the peasants and their children. Therefore, it should be noted here that even in the course of the eighteenth century, the image of the peasant in the minds of the cultivated elites had already undergone a change: seen at first mainly as a brute, potentially dangerous (and serf revolts seemed to confirm it), under the influence of the Enlightenment and of Sentimentalism, the peasant was increasingly seen as a "child of nature," capable of education to civilization and self discipline. Karamzin's early writings illustrated this transformation.

On the estate the peasants were only passive participants in the noblemen's life, however, performers of routine tasks in the field and in the house; they were hardly seen as personalities in their own right endowed with a sense of dignity and devotion to the common good. The discovery in war of "another peasantry" led the young nobles to the conviction that the soldiers should receive adequate rewards for their sacrifices in the form of positive steps to solve the serf question and to raise the people's moral and material condition. This discovery heightened the young officers' awareness of their duty and responsibility as an educated elite towards the people. It confirmed them in their conviction that their task would not be finished with the expulsion of the invader, but that a still more important task awaited them, namely active participation in reforming the nation's institutions and improving the economic and spiritual life of the people. Clearly the generation of the 1800s had internalized the eighteenth century Pietist project of an inner improvement and personal spiritual enhancement to accompany the reconstitution of society, so as to prepare it for the ultimate synergism (i.e., melding with the Divine through active oral, social, and spiritual purification).

A similar constellation of intellectual elements was at work at the same time in the Germanies. Not only was a modern nationalism rapidly gripping the emotions and intellectual efforts, but the tradition of Protestant spiritualism and service was enlisted in the cause of the nation's liberation and renovation. We should not ignore the religious elements—spiritual, moral, eschatological—present both in the *Tugendbund* and in the affective and ideological makeup of Romantic nationalism. While Freiherr vom Stein and Scharnhorst represented the rational and practical political side of the struggle against France, "Turnvater" Jahn, the poets Uhland and Körner, and academic philosophers like Fichte, proclaimed its spiritual and emotional ethical character. Quite naturally, the Russians who fought alongside the Germans and participated in the administration and policies pursued during the campaigns of 1813–1815, fully experienced the impact of this highly charged atmosphere. Among these Russians were members of the Turgenevs' circle, such as A. Kaisarov and V. Vostokov, who played an important role in what we today call psychological warfare; and the oldest Turgenev, Nicholas, held a high position on the staff of Freiherr vom Stein and the Russian military administration in Germany.

The members of the younger generation who had actively taken part in the wars against Napoleonic France had every reason to expect and hope for an active involvement in shaping the destinies of their country upon the return of peace. They were prepared and eager to assume leadership roles in reforming the administrative institutions, eliminating abuses, and in taking radical steps to improve the conditions of the peasantry. To this end they needed greater freedom of expression (*glasnost'*—a term used even then), the possibility of meeting openly with each other and in organizing public associations. Most important of all, they wanted to have an active role in the public life of the empire.

They well realized that to be fully effective they had to complete their education, which had been interrupted by the war. This need for self-development and self-improvement led many a member of this generation to gain admission to masonic lodges (reopened with Alexander's permission) and to join religious groups and associations dedicated to the same goals as those pursued by their fathers in the preceding century. Examples of these were the group gathered around the Labzin couple and its journal, *Sionskii vestnik* (Courier of Zion) and the Russian branches of the Bible Society. In addition, they became active in a variety of philanthropic endeavors in such fields as popular education or prison reform. It was still another instance of the eighteenth century Pietist heritage of combining individual spiritual enhancement with social reform. This time, however, in contrast to eighteenth century precedents, the stress was not so much on the enhancement of the inner individual as on broader social concerns—the betterment of the spiritual and material circumstances of the whole people. It both reflected and manifested the heightened sense of national identity and pride generated by the war of 1812 and its aftermath.

All this activated a variety of privately financed public enterprises that reached a growing number of people and served to structure the "civil society of the educated": public lectures, schools and institutions of higher learning and professional training, journals of larger circulation offering serious, semi-professional as well as literary fare, societies for the promotion of good causes (soldiers' education, prison reform, etc.), and religious communities. Members of civil society actively engaged in these institutions demanded and expected greater latitude and freedom of action, a higher degree of autonomy and independence from tutelage by the government. In this hope, however, they were sadly disappointed. The government, the Emperor in the lead, were not willing to grant the kind of autonomy and freedom of action that were expected. On the contrary, Alexander I and his advisors felt that the relaxation produced by war and exposure to foreign countries had to be countered by the imposition of stricter supervision, controls, and guidance on Russian society, especially on its younger educated members. How reminiscent of the Stalin–Zhdanov repressive measures against intellectuals and artistic production after 1945!

Under the circumstances, conflict between society and government was a foregone conclusion. Civil society, in the person of its more energetic and creative young members, withdrew into a virtually underground existence. It reconstituted literary and artistic circles as in prewar years, but this time with an added political aim, to press for change in imperial policy so as to bring about reforms and a constitution. Ultimately, in the early 1820s, there also arose secret societies for which political action and ideology-formation were in the forefront of attention. Conceived at first as coordinating centers for the public activities of civil society, the secret societies turned into proto-revolutionary organizations in response to the conservative, nay reactionary, course of the government. Seizing the opportunity offered by the death of Alexander I, and the confusion over his succession, the secret societies attempted to stage a revolutionary coup in what came to be known as the Decembrist revolt (14 December 1825). The story of the revolt need not detain us. It suffices to note that it illustrated the politicization of civil society's aesthetic and cultural concerns and the spiritual-ethical ingredients of its commitment to the service of the people. The emotionally charged spiritual-religious aspect (often played down in the historiography) is well documented in the correspondence of the Decembrists and exemplified by their cultural and pedagogical activities in their Siberian exile.

While the developments and events we have just summarized were taking place in the public life of Russia, Karamzin had been carrying on his task of official historiographer. Indeed, the first volume of his History of the Russian State (*Istoriia gosudarstva rossiiskogo*)—note the significant title—appeared in 1818. It was an instant success (new printings and editions were published in rapid succession), and subsequent volumes were eagerly awaited and avidly read upon their appearance. Such a response shows that there was a great need for a serious and readable history of Russia. Indeed, there had existed no satisfactory history of the country, and the intense patriotism and pride produced by the war of 1812 had to be satisfied. Karamzin's literary skill explains a great deal of his history's popularity. But he also wrote in the "pragmatic" tradition of eighteenth century historiography, giving biographical, psychological sketches of rulers that lend themselves to moralistic interpretations. For this reason, too, in reaction to the desiccated and ideologized Communist Party-approved histories, Karamzin is having a genuine renaissance in the Soviet Union today—the History has been reprinted and serialized, and the first scholarly edition is in preparation.

Karamzin's history converged with, and fed on, the spiritualist and socioethical aspects of modern Russian culture that Peter I's project of Europeanization had firmly entrenched among the educated elites. Karamzin's political orientation was a conservative one—not only had he been frightened by the brutal chaos of the French Revolution he had personally witnessed, but he had also been deeply disturbed by the innovative experiments with rationally constructed institutional reforms in the first decade of Alexander I's reign. His interpretation of Russia's past, besides bringing out its glory, emphasized the beneficial role of autocracy and of the nobility's paternalistic authority over their serfs; it also underlined the threat to social stability and peace that weak and corrupt rulers and landowners brought in their wake. In short, in his history and publicistic writings (most specially in the *Memoir on Ancient and Modern Russia* he circulated in 1811) Karamzin advocated monarchical patriotism and sang paeans to a powerful state and a glorious empire. The Decembrists, on the other hand, displayed a form of nationalism committed to the furtherance of the greatest welfare, prosperity and felicity of the Russian people.

One may say that this polarity contained all the future of Russian nationalism. On the one hand we find the "chauvinistic" identification with the state that relied on the ruler's enlightened morality and leadership. Its major spokesman was to be the Minister of Education of Nicholas I, Count S. S. Uvarov (who had also been associated with some of the progressive circles in the reign of Alexander I). On the other hand we find a patriotism primarily concerned with the social progress of the nation through intense didactic activity, a concern that could easily be extended to the non-Russian peoples in the empire who, in the opinion of these populist nationalists, had to be taken into the orbit of the "higher" modern (i.e., Europeanized) Russian culture. This latter form of nationalism was to be exemplified by the writings of the Slavophiles and radical populists, and it was also adopted and adapted by the Marxist revolutionaries in the twentieth century.

Each pole, however, owed much of its thrust and energy to a religious and moral ingredient that imparted to it a heightened emotional tone and transformed it into an ideology. In either case, too, the "paternalistic" notion of *Kulturträgertum* implied the elites' leadership in the Transfiguration (*Preobrazhenie*) of people (Westernization) and the renovation of institutions (socio-economic and political programs). And it was advocated without adequate empirical knowledge and tolerance, with a sense of cultural superiority that aimed at transforming non-Russians into Russians in order to bestow upon them the full benefit of eventual Europeanization and a "rational organization" of society and culture. In each case, too, we detect the eighteenth century heritage that found expression in the intellectual environment of the first quarter of the nineteenth century and a new emotional tone in the experience of the war against Napoleon's invasion of Russia.

These comments do not pretend to give a complete solution to a major historical problem—that of Russian nationalism—in the last two centuries, but they do throw an interesting light on it. Let us remember, however, the admonition of Fustel de Coulanges, "L'histoire ne résout pas les questions, elle nous apprend à les examiner" (history does not resolve questions, it teaches us [merely] to examine them).

Notes

1. I owe this quotation to the kindness of Prof. David Saunders from the University of Newcastle-upon-Tyne.

Select Bibliography

On the 18th century background: Franco Venturi, *Settecento reformatore, vol. III, La prima crisi dell' Antico Regime, 1768–1776* (Torino: Giulio Einaudi, 1979); Eduard Winter, *Halle als Ausgangspunkt der deutschen Russlandkunde im 18. Jahrhundert* (Berlin: Akademie Verlag, 1953); Marc Raeff, "Les Slaves, les Allemands et les 'Lumières',"" *Canadian American Slavic Studies*, 1:4 (winter, 1967), 521–551; *Viaggio [di Radiscev] da Pietroburgo a Mosca—con un saggio introductivo di Franco Venturi* (Bari: De Donato editore, 1972); Isabel de Madariaga, *Russia in the Age of Catherine the Great* (New Haven: Yale University Press, 1981).

On Karamzin, besides the numerous histories of Russian literature: J. L. Black, *Nicholas Karamzin and Russian Society in the Nineteenth Century* (Toronto: University of Toronto Press, 1975); J. L. Black, ed., *Essays on Karamzin: Russian Man-of-Letters, Political Thinker, Historian, 1766–1826* (The Hague & Paris: Mouton, 1975); Richard Pipes, *Karamzin's Memoir on Ancient and Modern Russia, A Translation and Analysis* (Cambridge: Harvard University Press, 1959).

The transition to the 19th century and the early years of Alexander I are treated by Allen McConnell, *Tsar Alexander I: Paternalistic Reformer* (New York: Thomas Y. Crowell, 1970) and Marc Raeff, *Comprendre l'Ancien régime russe: Etat et société en Russia impériale* (Paris: Le Seuil, 1982) translated as *Understanding Imperial Russia* (New York: Columbia University Press, 1984).

Literary circles and the spiritual atmosphere in the reign of Alexander I are best approached through Marc Raeff, "Le jeunesse russe à l'aube du XIXe siècle: André Turgenev et ses amis," *Cahiers du monde russe et soviétique*, 8:4 (October-December, 1967), 560–586 [see Chapter 4 of this volume for English version]; the introductory material in *Poety nachala XIX veka,* ed. by Iu. M. Lotman (Leningrad: Sovetskii pisatel', 1961); and Markus Wischnitzer, *Die Universität Göttingen und die Entwicklung der liberalen Ideen in Russland im ersten Viertel des 19. Jahrhunderts* (Historische Studien, Heft LVIII, Berlin, 1907; reprint Vaduz: Kraus Reprint Ltd., 1967).

On the impact of the war of 1812 see: *Dnevnik Aleksandra Chicherina, 1812–1813* (Moscow: izd. "Nauka," 1966), and, of course, Leo Tolstoi's *War and Peace.*

The literature on the Decembrists and on the political, intellectual and social background of their movement is immense. For a handy introduction see Marc Raeff, *The Decembrist Movement* (Englewood Cliffs, NJ: Prentice-Hall, 1966); Franco Venturi, *Il moto decabrista e a fratelli Poggio* (Torino: Giulio Einaudi, 1956); and Anatole G. Mazour, *The First Russian Revolution, 1825: The Decembrist Movement: Its Origins, Development, and Significance* (Berekeley, University of California Press, 1937; reprinted, Stanford: Stanford University Press, 1962).

SIX

The Russian Autocracy
and Its Officials[1]

1

THE UNDERGRADUATE STUDYING for his final examination in Russian domestic history no doubt often feels that it consisted merely of a series of futile attempts at reforming the political and social structure of the Empire.[2] Successive rulers and their ministers appear to have devoted the best of their time and energies to devising measures which, they fondly hoped, would bring some order to the "chaotic structure of the Empire" (in the words of Alexander I). So much effort was spent on drafting and implementing various reforms that no time seems to have been left for a systematic study of the country's condition and for the working out of long-range policies. And how often does the historian put down the records of the deliberations of administrative bodies or the memoirs and letters of officials with a feeling of the complete absence of any purposefulness or continuity in the actions of the Imperial government? And while this original feeling may be qualified somewhat by subsequent analysis and research, the basic impression of the lack of direction in the tsar's administration will not be eradicated. The origin of this state of affairs is not hard to see.

By saddling the government with new tasks and problems, Peter the Great radically changed the traditional foundation of the Russian state. The Muscovite concept that Russia was a patrimony (*votčina*) of the tsar, to be administered and exploited like a private domain, made way for the notion of the *state* as a political and social institution, separate from the person of the ruler, with tasks and problems of its own. But in effecting this change, Peter the Great failed to provide the "new" state with an administration capable of insuring its smooth operation. To use a modern industrial simile, Peter I set up a new type of production, while neglecting to hire the technical personnel capable of running and adjusting the new machinery. For a century and a half, the energies of the government were largely spent in coping with this situation and in trying out various improvements of the unwieldy administrative machine bequeathed by the Tsar Reformer.

Peter created the modern Russian state. In this respect he did only what Louis XIV, the Great Elector, or Elizabeth I had done earlier in their own countries. In Western Europe, though, the tasks and functions of the modern state had been performed with relative efficiency and success almost from the beginning, because of a parallel development in the methods and personnel of government. As new tasks and requirements arose, new institutions were devised; and as new institutions were created, the men to staff them were found among a numerous class of politically mature and experienced nobles and bourgeois. Eventually, men and institutions were effectively and harmoniously welded together by a complex pattern of firm rules and traditions: the Western monarchical state became predominantly bureaucratic.

In Russia, however, the situation was different. Peter the Great and his successors set up many new political and administrative institutions. But they could not find the proper "labor force" to make them work. At the opening of the nineteenth century, the political framework erected by Peter the Great—and expanded by his successors—had become stabilized. The "state" had assumed the burden of many novel functions: it was the leader and promoter of Russia's social and economic development, and it wished to expand its role further by becoming the nation's guide on the road to moral and spiritual progress. The government personnel, however, was not equal to these tasks. For this reason, the reform plans in the first decade of the nineteenth century—especially those of Speranskij[3]—were not so much concerned with the creation of new political institutions as with the renovation of the administrative personnel, with the creation of a true bureaucracy on the model of Prussia or Napoleonic France.

Speranskij and other contemporary reformers failed, and Russia's administration remained largely unchanged until the Emancipation of the Serfs in 1861. Only then did some significant changes come about. But as they came too late and proved too limited, many features of the older administration survived until the end of the old regime.

For an understanding of the political evolution of Russia in the nineteenth century it is therefore important to have a clear idea of the nature of the body of men who assisted the autocrat in formulating policies and supervised the implementation of his decisions.

2

A striking, and at first glance paradoxical, feature of the government of imperial Russia was its lack of a homogeneous, effective, and powerful bureaucracy.[4] At the local level of the administrative pyramid we find two groups of administrators. In first place, by virtue of the Statute of 1775,[5] were officials elected by and among the nobility of the province. They acted as local police officers and supervised various public services. They performed these functions almost without any regularly trained clerical help. In a sense, their power was an extension of the patrimonial power exercised by the noble landowner (*pomeščik*) on his own estates. By the reform of 1861, the elected noble officials were deprived of their social foundation and eventually yielded to the professionally trained functionaries of the zemstvo.

The real official hierarchy began with the personnel of provincial and district government bureaus, the second group of local administrators. The incredibly large amount of routine paper work in these offices[6] was performed by lowly clerks, the sons of completely impoverished local gentry, merchants, or village priests. There was no regular procedure for recruiting these clerks that would insure some degree of uniformity in the staffing of local offices. Nobody expected them to have a standardized or uniform level of education. Whatever knowledge was needed they received on the job, an apprenticeship which did not make for a widening of their intellectual horizon. They were an underpaid, demoralized lot, open to corruption and the worst kind of graft.[7] Possessing neither education nor ambition, they were utterly incapable of giving useful advice to their superiors. At best, they could apply blindly the prescriptions handed down from St. Petersburg. Any innovation in procedure meant readjustment or learning, neither of which these clerks were willing or able to do. Thus they made it exceedingly difficult for the authorities in the capital to implement far-reaching administrative changes on the local level.

At the top, in St. Petersburg offices, the run-of-the-mill scribes, the minor officials, were every bit like their confrères in the provinces. Like their colleagues, the vast majority of clerks in the capital had but the bare minimum of education and received no special training; they too learned their limited duties by experience alone. As the majority remained in the same department or bureau throughout their careers, they mechanically learned only a few routine operations. And so it was that the lowly clerks in the capital had as much difficulty in accepting and adjusting to innovations as their counterparts in the provincial offices.

The hosts of clerks were officered, as it were, by relatively few dignitaries and high-ranking officials who advised the emperor on policies and supervised their implementation. As in all absolute monarchies, this group consisted of leading regular high officials (individual senators, councillors of state, principal ministers) on the one hand, and of personal friends and confidants of the monarch, on the other. It should be added that it was not a clear-cut division; individuals often belonged to both categories, and the personal friends of the emperor usually had also some specific administrative positions. The top officials and the influential courtiers together administered the Empire, subject to imperial approval, of course. It will be instructive to take a closer look at the composition and political nature of this grouping in the first half of the nineteenth century.

It was to be expected in an autocracy that the sovereign would often appoint his personal favorites and friends to the highest administrative functions. Not infrequently, though, the nominees had neither preparation nor inclination for the post for which the emperor had selected them. Nobody could have been more surprised than Prince Aleksej I. Golicyn—an avowed Voltairean skeptic—when Alexander I insisted that he become Procurator General of the Holy Synod. And what should we say of the appointment of Prince Adam Czartoryski, a staunch Polish patriot, as Acting Minister of Foreign Affairs of the very same empire that was holding his homeland in bondage?

Along the same lines, members of the imperial family frequently played a most significant role, not only as intimate confidants and advisers (Grand Duchess Catherine to Alexander I, for instance, or Grand Duchess Helen in the reign of Alexander II), but also at the head of important government offices. While most grand dukes held only military commands, Grand Duke Constantine, brother of Alexander II, played a very active role in framing the policies of the 1860's. The vast range of his duties and activities is illustrated by some of his official titles: Admiral General of the Fleet, Minister of the Navy, Viceroy of Poland, President of the Council of State, and membership in countless committees and commissions. Even distant relatives of the ruler were at times entrusted with administrative duties as in the case of Duke George of Oldenburg, brother-in-law of Alexander I, who was appointed Chief of Highways and Transportation and Governor General of three important provinces. However, we should not insist too much on this aspect of the selection of high officials; it was the natural by-product of autocratic absolutism.

As a primary feature of bureaucratic organization, Max Weber has listed the functional division of duties among its members and the specialization of its personnel. It is difficult, though, to detect technical specialization and a functional use of talent and experience in the Russian administration during the first half of the nineteenth century. As in the early stages of the model French or Prussian bureaucracies, officials moved freely from one area of government to another. Count Viktor P. Kočubej made his political début as a diplomat, and it was not until much later in life that he became the leading expert on domestic affairs. Another member of the Unofficial Committee, Count Nikolaj

N. Novosil'cev, occupied diplomatic posts, then turned to domestic concerns, and eventually ended as the principal delegate of Alexander I in Poland.

Remarkable too was the facility with which officials moved from military to civilian functions, and vice versa.[8] Military personalities entrusted with important civilian concerns formed a numerous and prominent group in the administrative hierarchy of the Empire. Thus General Count Aleksej A. Arakčeev occupied key administrative positions in the reign of Alexander I, first in his own special military field, but gradually branching out into various areas of domestic policy until he became the principal minister. A naval officer, Admiral Nikolaj S. Mordvinov, developed into Russia's top economic expert, and in recognition of his contributions in that domain, Alexander I appointed him to the presidency of the section on State economy of the Council of State. To replace Speranskij as *rédacteur* of imperial decrees and manifestoes, Emperor Alexander I appointed Admiral Aleksandr S. Šiškov—a prominent littérateur, but without government experience. Nicholas I followed his brother's practice. A successful general in the Danubian campaign against Turkey, Count Pavel D. Kiselev, was called upon to govern the state peasants and to reform their status. A military careerist, General-Adjutant I. V. Vasil'čikov found himself at the head of the Council of State, the highest administrative and political body of the Empire. The key positions in the all-important Third Section of His Imperial Majesty's Own Chancery (secret police) were held by military personalities. Nor did Alexander II abandon the tradition of his father and uncle. At the outset of his reign, he put his friend General Jakov I. Rostovcev in charge of the Editorial Committee that prepared the Emancipation Decree of 1861. And at the end of his life, tracked and almost trapped by revolutionary terrorists, the Tsar Liberator entrusted the "dictatorship of the heart" to Count Mikhail T. Loris-Melikov, a general who had distinguished himself in the Caucasus.

For the performance of particularly important tasks or for supervising vital "sectors" of the government, the emperor had recourse to members of his military household. It is easy to understand why the monarch turned to his *aides-de-camp* or *flügel' adjutanty*. In the first place, constantly surrounded by them, he knew their qualities, talents, and experience best. In the second place, both Alexander I and Nicholas I were firm believers in the virtues instilled by military training and life. Themselves educated as officers, they trusted their comrades-in-arms much more than civilians. Reliance on the imperial military household reached its high point in the reign of Nicholas I, who endeavored to extend the "army ways" to the entire field of government. Little wonder that he selected his most influential assistants and advisers from among his adjutants and military aides: Count Aleksandr Kh. Benkendorf, General Leontij V. Dubel't, Count Aleksandr I. Černyšev, General V. Levašev, Count Aleksej F. Orlov, General-Adjutant I. V. Vasil'čikov, General-Adjutant Aleksej S. Men'šikov, *e tutti quanti*.

Still more significant was the custom of appointing military commanders to the vital post of provincial governor. It might have been argued that men accustomed to command and administer troops would make good provincial administrators, especially as there was a great dearth of experienced leadership on the local level. This might have been true had the appointments been made on a long-term basis, but such was not the case. No sooner had the new governor become superficially acquainted with his task than he was transferred back to the capital or to the army. Such a practice made neither for continuity nor effectiveness in local administration.

Of course, friends and relatives of the emperor and soldiers alone could not satisfy all the technical needs of the imperial government. The Russian monarchs also needed real specialists in some fields, in particular political economy, commerce, industry, and law. Eminent experts in these fields, however, either did not exist in Russia, or had to be recruited outside the regular officialdom. Appeal was therefore made to Russian or foreign scholars at academic institutions. The Carpatho-Russian political scientist, Mikhail A. Balug'janskij, was called from his chair at what became the University of St. Petersburg to advise the government of Alexander I on economic and legal questions. He returned to the government and rose to very high posts (chairmanship of the Second Section of H.I.M.'s Own Chancery in charge of codification, membership in the Council of State). Count Egor Kankrin, a trained mining engineer and industrial administrator became the Minister of Finance of Alexander I and Nicholas I. Just beyond our chronological confines we find in the career of Konstantin P. Pobedonoscev the most interesting example of an academic person's rise to political power in Imperial Russia. Introduced to the inner circle of the court as tutor to the heir presumptive, this outstanding specialist and professor of civil law became Procurator General of the Holy Synod and the most influential figure in the governments of Alexander III and the first decade of the reign of Nicholas II. His was an exceptional case, but it was not out of character. On a more modest level, as technical advisers, we can list the names of such prominent scholars as K. A. Nevolin, A. V. Kunicyn, K. D. Kavelin, Fr. von Adelung, Heinrich Storch—to restrict ourselves to the first half of the century.

Best known abroad—and often much exaggerated—was the great number of foreigners in the military and political service of Russia. Some of these foreigners were used as experts on a temporary basis, others settled and made their careers in Russia. During the period that interests us, many *émigrés,* especially French and Prussian, served in the government of the tsars. Best remembered is Duc Armand Emmanuel de Richelieu, Governor of New Russia and founder of Odessa. He was not alone, though; witness the names of the Marquis de Traversay, Comte Andrault de Langeron, Count "de" Laval, and a host of minor officials. At a time when diplomacy was still a truly cosmopolitan craft, it was not unusual to see scions of foreign aristocratic families among ambassadors, ministers, and special envoys. The Russian diplomatic corps, too, counted many foreign noblemen in its ranks. We have already referred to the Polish Prince Adam Czartoryski; we may add the names of Karl Robert Graf von Nesselrode, Carlo Andrea conte Pozzo di Borgo, Ioannis Count Kapodistrias, Baron Alexander von Rennenkampf, and Peter Oubril; and A. Gervais and Beck, among the lesser employees of the Ministry of Foreign Affairs.

Of all the ministers and advisers of Alexander I and Nicholas I, the name of Mikhail M. Speranskij is no doubt known best of all. The son of a village priest, his rise to influence and fame might at first glance seem an anomaly in an autocracy based on the nobility. Yet his career, while most dramatic and successful, was by no means an isolated instance. Since the last years of the reign of Catherine II, there had arisen a great demand for educated men to fill responsible intermediary positions of an administration that was becoming increasingly complex and specialized. Many sons of the clergy, upon graduation from the ecclesiastic seminaries—the only regular "free" secondary schools—obtained their transfer to government service. Better educated, more ambitious than the run-of-the-mill clerk, these *popoviči* made good in the administration and attained high positions. Two of Speranskij's own friends from the Aleksandro-Nevskij seminary could be mentioned in this connection: Ivan I. Martynov, a well-known translator and littérateur-publisher, rose to high rank in the Ministry of Public Instruction; Demjan V. Illičevskij became civilian governor of Tomsk. Other classmates became public servants too, but did not rise so far—for instance, the Siberian writer and educator, Petr Slovcov. Another priest's son, N. I. Treskin, rose from subaltern clerk in the Postal Department to the governorship of Irkutsk and virtual dictatorship of Siberia. Successful careers like these became increasingly rarer in the reign of Nicholas I. But the number of officials from the ranks of the clergy and the merchant class kept growing throughout the remainder of the century. And while it remains true that the upper ranks of the administration were staffed predominantly by nobles, representatives of other social classes were not altogether unknown.

Finally, at the very end of the period that concerns us here, in the first years of the reign of Alexander II, the new policies of reform were worked out with the advice and participation of well-known civic leaders and publicists. The "private representatives of society" (sometimes with past administrative experience), Jurij F. Samarin, Aleksandr I. Košelev, Prince Vladimir A. Čerkaskij, were active in the preparation and implementation of the Emancipation, and the prominent lawyer Sergej I. Zarudnyj was an active leader in the judiciary reforms.

3

The preceding illustrations have suggested something of the variety of background that was to be found among the high officials of the imperial administration. The high-ranking officials could hardly be said to have formed a homogeneous class. Government service was not a career in which one rose step by step through the ranks within the area of one's specialization, acquiring the feeling of solidarity and the traditions of the service. There was too much mobility; furthermore, almost none of the top officials had started at the bottom of the hierarchy. Even "career officials," like M. Speranskij or Nikolaj A. Miljutin, had begun at a relatively high level in the central offices of the capital, and their entire careers were spent in making policy and supervision of subordinate bureaus.

It could be asked, however, if a common cultural and educational tradition did not offset the diversity in social origin and service experience. To some extent, it is true, during the first quarter of the nineteenth century, most officials shared the intellectual and spiritual life of Russia's educated "society." But this was more a matter of common interest in literature and philosophic ideas and had—unfortunately—little impact on their behavior as administrators. If we define education more strictly as formal schooling, the top administrators of Russia had no common educational tradition. Some had received their secondary education at home from private (often foreign) tutors, others in private boarding schools attached to the universities. After its opening, the *lycée* at Carskoe Selo attracted the sons of the socially prominent nobility. Only few high dignitaries and officials had studied at the university level, and when they had, it was at foreign universities (as did, for instance, the famous Turgenev brothers, Nikolaj and Aleksandr). The majority of nobles, unable to afford either private tutors or boarding schools, sent their sons to military institutes and corps of cadets.

The quality of the schooling dispensed at these many sources varied a great deal, and there was hardly even a common body of knowledge. But more significant still, in our context, was the fact that this education did not aim at preparing the student for a professional career in the government. Only the military schools gave specialized training and developed the feeling of professional group solidarity. But theirs was not the kind of preparation that was most useful to the future civilian official. Even the *lycée* at Carskoe Selo, among whose alumni we find many diplomats and high officials, gave only a good general education. It would be superfluous to belabor the point that the officials of lower-class origin, having attended ecclesiastical or city schools, had little common educational background with the graduates of the private and special state schools. Significantly enough, Russia—unlike the bureaucratic states of Western Europe—had no special educational facilities devoted to the training of its officials.

The variegated and somewhat haphazard composition and background of the uppermost ranks of the administration explain the lack of ideological solidarity among the advisors to the tsar. Unlike the royal councils of Western Europe, Russian political institutions contained a surprisingly large variety of philosophical and political points of view. To illustrate this observation it is enough to recall the names of the influential members of the government of Alexander I in the first years of his reign: Baron von der Pahlen, Count Nikita P. Panin, Senator Gavriil R. Deržavin, the brothers Semën and Aleksej R. Voroncov, Count Pavel A. Stroganov, Count Nikolaj N. Novosil'cev, Count Viktor P. Kočubej, Prince Adam Czartoryski. A sampling of the "inner circle" on the eve of the French invasion reveals a similar disparity: Prince Aleksej I. Golicyn, Speranskij, Count A. Arakčeev, Count Dmitrij A. Gur'ev. Count Nikolaj P. Rumjancev, Admiral Nikolaj S. Mordvinov, Marquis de Traversay, Duke George of Oldenburg, Count Armfelt, Grand Duchess Catherine. Nor did the methodical and logical Nicholas I select his advisers with any greater regard for ideological uniformity, as the list of his principal aides in the 1830's attests: Benkendorf, Kankrin, Kiselev, Speranskij, S. S. Uvarov, Nesselrode.

As implied in the discussion of the lower echelons of the administration, a deep gulf separated the high officials from the vast army of subordinate secretaries and clerks. This gulf was not just a matter of social origin. More important was the fact that it could not be bridged, since there was no way of advancing from a minor clerkship to a position of influence. An Akakij Akakievič could never dream of becoming the head of his section. For someone without good aristocratic connections, the only way to the higher ranks was through a private secretaryship to a high dignitary. This had been the path of Speranskij, who, as personal secretary to the Procurator of the Senate, Prince Aleksej B. Kurakin, joined the government hierarchy at the respectably high level of chief of chancery in the Senate.

Administration on the lower level had degenerated into a mere processing of papers according to well worn formulas. For the ordinary clerk, administration consisted only in the "movement" of papers: filling out of forms, copying reports, and forwarding them to another office—for what purpose and to what advantage remained a mystery to him. Yet the lower ranks wanted to preserve this state of affairs, for they feared that any innovation—whether "liberal" or "conservative," it did not matter—would burden them with tasks for which they were not prepared and which they either could not or would not learn. They looked with misgivings at all high officials who tried to reform the administration and opposed them with a mute but highly effective passive resistance. Conversely, practically all progressive dignitaries and reform-minded officials had nothing but distrust and contempt for their subordinates.[9]

The task of making policy and of giving direction lay in the hands of high officials who could not count on advice and support from those who were to implement their policies. A newly appointed official, more likely than not, stepped into a position which lacked any clear political tradition and even lacked its own pattern of action, except for the routines of filling out and "moving" papers to another office. Frequently he himself was a newcomer to the area, and he found no responsible assistants with requisite training, experience, and sufficient prestige to orient and advise him, or even to understand his ideas and goals. Not that such handicaps did not occur in better organized bureaucratic governments, and it may be even plausibly argued that lack of rigid tradition is a blessing in disguise. In Russia, though, the lack of tradition, combined with an inheritance of conflicting political attitudes stemming from Peter the Great, resulted in disorder and immobility. Furthermore, the newly appointed high official very likely had no common background, no common goals, or even similar educational tradition, with his colleagues. While he himself might be a civilian, an experienced financial or judicial administrator, the colleagues on whose coöperation and understanding he had to depend might be military officers, courtiers, or diplomats who could not—or would not—understand his problems. Nor were his chances of proving the worth of his policies on the local level very good, for there, too, his decisions were perhaps carried out without understanding, and perverted, by governors of military background without experience in civilian affairs. Finally, as there was no ministerial solidarity, policies could not be coördinated, and ministers acted at cross purpose or even in open opposition to one another.

In spite of their nominal power, the high-ranking officials were extremely insecure, both in their tenure of office and in the support they could expect for their policies. To follow through a consistent line, the official had not only to forestall opposition from his own colleagues in the administration; he also had to contend against the influential counsel of the personal friends of the monarch, men without official status or responsibility in the government. And while the personal counselors might at times exercise a beneficial influence on the ruler (as did the members of the Unofficial Committee, for instance), their interference with, or opposition to, the ordinary process of administration did not necessarily make for better government. That is why an effective administrator—as measured by his ability to accomplish worthwhile changes—was not so much the regular member of the administrative hierarchy as the imperial favorite appointed for a special task (Generals Kiselev or Rostovcev, for instance). Incidentally, this situation lay at the core of the relatively small influence wielded by the oldest permanent administrative institution of imperial Russia—the Senate. Only as individuals did a few Senators, personally well-liked by the monarch (as was the poet Gavriil R. Deržavin in the beginning of the reign of Alexander I), manage to play an influential role.

Under the conditions we have described, every would-be reformer felt that success lay only in the support of the monarch. The reformer's task, therefore, was to "secure" the adherence of the monarch to his views and programs, disregarding the question of wider support among his colleagues. Only the emperor's autocratic power could break through the existing system and enforce reform. As a result, "liberal" reformers—whether of Western orientation like Speranskij, Kiselev, and Dmitrij A. Miljutin, or of Slavophile persuasion like

Samarin, Košelev, and Čerkaskij—agreed with the rabid conservatives Uvarov, D. Tolstoj and Pobedonoscev on the need of preserving the autocracy intact. The truly "liberal" reformer found himself in the most paradoxical position of all: he had to accept, and even bolster by making it more efficient, the autocrat's administration in order to eliminate the evils which had been bred by the very same autocratic system. It is not surprising that, in the final analysis, they proved rather ineffectual. In this regard, at least, the true conservative had the advantage of consistency.

Conversely, it became easy for the monarch to preserve his autocratic power without compromise and to maintain full control over all phases of government. He did this by appointing men of varying opinions to the inner council, by balancing the influence of the regular officials with the authority he vested in the hands of his friends and *aides-de-camps*, by delegating some civilian matters to the military, and by having outsiders implement the policies drafted by his ministers. The variety of their interests and backgrounds prevented the emperor's topmost advisors and administrators from forming a solid and enduring coalition.

And so we reach the somewhat odd and at first glance paradoxical conclusion that autocracy in Russia remained strong and rigidly conservative throughout the nineteenth century because there was no true bureaucracy. And while Russia had a host of minor executive clerks busily writing papers they never fully understood, it had no homogeneous, efficient, alert, and politically conscious policy-making bureaucracy, comparable to the Prussian, French, or even Austrian. The Russian "bureaucracy" was unable to create a *Rechtsstaat,* the *sine qua non* of orderly bureaucratic government, and as a result, the arbitrary and capricious personal power of the Russian autocrat remained undiminished until 1905.

The peculiar make-up and nature of Russia's administrative personnel explain why it was well-nigh impossible to work out and put into effect any comprehensive program of governmental (and social) reorganization. Only Peter the Great—coming at an opportune time—had had the vision and will-power to impose a machine of government; later sovereigns could do nothing more than make minor repairs and adjustments. To its own misfortune, as well as Russia's, the character of its administrative personnel prevented the Imperial regime from bringing the political machine into consonance with the intellectual, social, and economic evolution of the country.

Notes

1. The present essay is in the nature of a synthesis and suggested interpretation of a rather broad aspect of imperial Russia's political life. Based on the author's readings, previous research, and reflection, the arguments developed in it cannot be readily substantiated by references to specific sources. Most of the illustrations adduced here can be found in the general histories of Russia in the first half of the nineteenth century, the

standard biographies of rulers and statesmen, the published private archives of individual families, and the official histories of government institutions. The curious reader, though, will find further interesting information and hints in the following specialized works:

1. Andreevskij, *O namestnikakh, voevodakh i gubernatorakh* (St. Petersburg, 1864); I. Blinov, *Gubernatory—istoriko–juridičeskij očerk* (St. Petersburg, 1905); N. F. Dubrovin, "Russkaja žizn' v načale XIX v.," *Russkaja Starina,* XCVI–XCIX (Dec. 1898–Aug. 1899); A. D. Gradovskij, "Istoričeskij očerk učreždenija general-gubernatorstv v Rossii," *Russkij Vestnik* (Nov.-Dec., 1869); I. M. Kataev, *Doreformennaja Bjurokracija* (St. Petersburg, n.d.); D. F. Kobeko, *Imperatorskij Carskosel'skij licej* (St. Petersburg, 1911); S. A. Korf, *Dvorjanstvo i ego soslovnoe upravlenie za stoletie 1762–1855 gg.* (St. Petersburg, 1906); S. M. Seredonin, *Istoričeskij obzor dejatel'nosti Komiteta Ministrov,* 4 vols (St. Petersburg, 1902); V. G. Ščeglov, *Gosudarstvennyj Sovet v Rossii, v osobennosti v carstvovanii Aleksandra I* (Jaroslavl', 1892–1896); H. Storch, *Russland unter Alexander I* (St. Petersburg–Leipzig, 1804–1808); B. V. Titlinov, *Duhovnye školy v XIX st.* (Vil'na, 1908–1909); P. Znamenskij, *Duhovnye školy v Rossii do reformy 1808 g.* (Kazan', 1881).

2. A similar feeling of hopeless bewilderment was nicely expressed in Count Aleksej K. Tolstoj's poem, "Russkaja istorija ot Gostomysla s IX po XIX vek" (in *Polnoe Sobranie Sočinenij,* St. Petersburg, 1907, I, 465–477).

3. As was illustrated by the two laws on government service he sponsored: "Decree on the *Kamergery,*" *Polnoe Sobranie Zakonov Rossijskoj Imperii* (abbrev. PSZ), No. 23, 559, April 3, 1809, and "Decree on examinations for promotion to the 8th and 5th ranks (*čin*)," PSZ No. 23, 771, August 6, 1809.

4. The term bureaucracy, as referred to in this essay, is based on the "ideal type" formulated by Max Weber (*Wirtschaft und Gesellschaft,* Part III, chap. 6); English translation in H. H. Gert and C. Wright Mills, *From Max Weber: Essays in Sociology* (New York, 1946), pp, 196–204.

5. "Statute on the Provinces [*gubernija*]," PSZ No. 14,392, November 7, 1775.

6. In the 1840's, for example, the governor had to sign 270 papers daily (i.e., 100,000 a year!) which would have taken him 4- ½ hours at one minute per paper. In addition, he had to attend 17 meetings of committees and bureaus every day. We can easily imagine the amount of paper involved. See I. Blinov, *Gubernatory—istoriko–juridičeskij očerk* (St. Petersburg, 1905), p. 161.

7. Speranskij described the clerks as "a mob of 'office boys,' semi-literate and poor as beggars" in "Zamečanija o gubernskikh učreždenijakh," *Arkhiv istoričeskikh i praktičeskikh svedenij otnosjaščikhsja do Rossii* (1859), No. 4, p. 96.

8. There was an equivalence of ranks (*čin*), in the military and civilian branches of government, which facilitated transfer without loss of rank or seniority.

9. It was this state of affairs, incidentally, which gave in Russia a somewhat narrow and special meaning to the concept of *Rechtsstaat:* guarantee against the autonomous exercise of power by the officialdom.

SEVEN

Introduction

to Plans for Political Reform
in Imperial Russia, 1730–1905

AS A NATION OR SOCIETY undergoes change, its institutions, too, have to be transformed to adjust to new conditions and needs. Failing this, there develop strains and stresses which, if allowed to go on, may result in the sudden and violent upheavals we call revolutions. As a society and polity, Russia was launched onto the path of rapid and extensive transformations by Peter the Great. Of course, there had been change before Peter, but such transformations had been very gradual and limited in scope. Since Peter's times the elite, at any rate, had endeavored to make Russia the equal of the Western European states and to have it participate actively in what we call modern Western civilization. Yet some of Russia's basic institutions failed to adjust adequately to the new orientation, to the urge for change. Hence the strains and stresses that eventually led to the collapse of Imperial Russia, a collapse that took place in two stages—in 1905 and 1917.

Naturally, the process of inadequate adjustment and ultimate breakdown did not go unchallenged. At various times efforts were made by individuals or groups to bring about reforms to decrease the strains on the Russian polity and exorcise the threat of upheaval and revolution. These efforts were directed at a variety of institutions and conditions that needed correction: serfdom and then the agrarian crisis, administration and justice, education and cultural life. Throughout the entire period, however, the condition and nature of the state was the center of attention; it was the one institution that influenced, if it did not actually dictate and create, all the other conditions that needed correction. Furthermore, the Russian state, whatever its weaknesses, retained to the last the power to assist or prevent the realization of the proposals and reforms that were advanced. Naturally, therefore, the state itself ultimately became the principal object of reform proposals.

The extremely powerful and influential Russian state was an autocracy. Any reform had perforce to aim at the very center of the institution, that is, the position and role of the autocrat and those organs of government directly associated with him. All other government institutions, whatever their direct impact on the population, were always, and quite correctly, seen as reflections of the central organs in St. Petersburg. The thoughtful Russian was convinced (and historical experience validated his belief) that no partial or local reform had much chance of success without some radical change in the attitudes and practices of the central authorities as well. For this reason, the most important projects of general political reform were concerned primarily with the central governmental institutions in St. Petersburg and the role of autocracy. ...

From the death of Peter the Great to about 1825, the members of Russia's educated elite remained basically loyal to the system created by the first Emperor. This was not true, of course, of the common people, whose revolts were directed as much against the Petrine system as against individual landlords or specific abuses. After 1825 the situation changed, and there developed among the upper classes widespread and vociferous opposition to the very principles of the Russian polity. Many of these opponents of the regime advocated extensive changes aimed at creating a new society as well as another political system. Yet there were also many who believed and hoped that the political structure might be reformed from inside, without provoking sharp breaks and violent social upheavals whose ultimate consequences could not be foreseen. Members of the Establishment itself frequently and insistently clamored for reform in the basic structure of Russia's political and administrative institutions in order to forestall revolutionary upheavals.

The programs of revolutionary groups were directed to the future, when the imperial regime would be a thing of the past. The reform proposals, on the other hand, were directed to the present; they were, therefore, of more immediate relevance in determining the country's development. Their failure proved as important as the revolutionary movements themselves in bringing about the collapse of the regime.

*   *   *

Whatever their roots in the past of Muscovy, the reforms of Peter the Great marked the beginning of a new era in Russia's public life. It is hardly an exaggeration to speak of Peter the Great as the founder of the modern Russian state who set the framework of its institutional development for the entire course of the eighteenth and nineteenth centuries. Obviously, Peter did not build on empty ground; the very nature of Russia's past and the characteristic features of Muscovite society enabled the first Emperor to give a radically novel form to the institutional pattern, but at the same time imposed limitations on their later development.

Muscovy had evolved a pattern of institutional and political life that clearly distinguished it from both Eastern and Western European medieval traditions and practices. Disregarding many qualifications of detail, we might say that the Muscovite polity had displayed the following basic traits since the middle of the sixteenth century: First, the power of the Tsar over all his subjects and all facets of national life was absolute and virtually unchallenged. All policy decisions of any consequence were made only by the Tsar, with the assistance of his close advisers. Second, and, of course, deriving from the first, was the virtual absence of corporations and political or social estates, and thus the extreme insecurity and limited rights which characterized even the so-called privileged classes. Of course, in view of the vastness of the realm and the limited technological means at the disposal of the government in the sixteenth and seventeenth centuries, Moscow could not take over all functions of local administration. Although a trend toward restricting local administrative and judicial autonomies had become manifest since the end of the Times of Troubles in the early seventeenth century, it had not yet eliminated some elective local institutions, more particularly in the north-eastern regions of the realm. Moreover, Moscow interfered little in the daily routine of villages and peasant communes.

Although exalted to nearly divine status and surrounded by a complicated ceremonial of Byzantine origin which set him off from common mortals, the Tsar manifested his power in essentially patriarchal forms. The Tsardom of Muscovy was considered the patrimony (*votchina*) of the Tsar, and its inhabitants were entrusted to his paternal care. In other words, political authority was still expressed very much in personal terms: in all important matters, and even in many trifling ones, the Tsar's personal command was final, and it was to the Tsar himself that his subjects always turned in case of need. Officials of the government were viewed only as the personal representatives of the ruler; in the performance of their duties they merely carried out the "errands" (*posylka*) of the Tsar; they were his "servants" (*kholopy*) and had no authority of their own. In principle, at least, their actions were based on tradition and custom, and the Tsar was the guardian of these hallowed practices. Of course, this was the theory; the practice was departing from it increasingly. Yet even in their breach the old theory and tradition continued to play a considerable role. In the mind of the seventeenth-century Russian, whether nobleman or peasant, the Tsar's personal concern and actions helped to temper the harshness of his rule. Nor should we forget the essential fact that the function of government was conceived largely in negative terms. The Tsar was the protector of his people: defender against external enemies, guardian of the Orthodox faith and of those principles and customs which made for the good life of his God-fearing subjects. He was the just ruler who righted wrongs, succored the poor and orphaned, and by his own exemplary life and deeds helped to maintain his Orthodox Christian people in the grace of God. It was the typical medieval Christian view of kingship, and if in Moscow such an outlook did not conflict with the fact that the government played an active role in certain areas of public life (especially the economic), it was due to the weakness of the state structure and the absence of autonomous centers of power.

Some of these characteristic features of Muscovite society had been modified in the course of the seventeenth century, and new elements had come to the fore. The expansion of the territory, increasingly more frequent and extensive military and commercial involvements with Western Europe, and the growing complexity of national life had all contributed to a decline of the patrimonial, functionally undifferentiated character of government. We note the government's growing concern with matters which heretofore had been outside its ken, such as the establishment of industrial enterprises and various new cultural activities, including theaters and schools. The continuing process of centralization and functional organization of the administration weakened further the already feeble elements of regional and group solidarity and loyalty. Finally, the roles of tradition and birthright were waning, as illustrated by the rise of professional army units, the abolition of the *mestnichestvo*, the disappearance of the *Zemskii Sobor,* and the decline of the *Boiar Duma.*

In spite of these changes, the basic structure and character of Muscovite public life remained almost unaffected, because the transformations occurred very gradually, ... They were barely perceptible to the contemporary observer; their potential contribution to the shaping of a new society was not realized. Most important of all, there had been no break in the continuity of Russian culture and no consciousness, therefore, of being confronted by an alien spirit and a new system of values. Thus, the subjects of Tsar Theodore had no reason to feel or believe that their situation was in any appreciable way different from that of their grandparents in the reign of Michael. Into this unawareness burst Peter the Great, with his ruthless energy and seemingly revolutionary program of innovation. Historians who, like S. Platonov, have stressed the basic continuity of Russian history and played down the revolutionary impact of Peter's reforms have underestimated this aspect of the situation.[1] Fastening only on the apparent formal or technical similarity in Russian institutions before and after Peter, these historians have concluded that the first Emperor did not really innovate much. But the fact remains—and in itself it is of historical significance—that contemporaries disregarded these similarities and were primarily conscious of having experienced a radical break, and it is this awareness of a change that they transmitted to their children and children's children.

It is possible, for our purposes, to disregard the complicated structural detail of Peter's institutions, as well as the twists and turns of his legislation. We may summarize the eventual results of his reforms as follows: The ruler's person was separated from the government; henceforth the ruler viewed himself, and came to be considered by many of his subjects, as the servant of the interests and welfare of the *state*—a new concept, which in reality covered a congeries of institutions. The areas of governmental concern were extended to cover nearly all aspects of national life and many phases of personal life. Through its administrative institutions and its officials the state frequently took the initiative in establishing and promoting new fields of public and private endeavor, so that for several generations it became the principal industrial and commercial entrepreneur, the chief educator, and even a leader in the country's cultural and social life. Such an extension of governmental concern led to the creation of many new administrative and cultural institutions of all types, a tremendous increase in the number of government officials, and the elaboration of rules to guide the actions of both institutions and officials. These rules were drafted either in imitation of available Western European models or on the basis of rational and theoretical considerations. There could no longer be an appeal to tradition or old custom ("as done in olden times"); the new rules could be justified only by appealing to some abstract concept or value—hence the rationalist and universalist character of Russian legislation in the eighteenth and early nineteenth centuries. It is easy to see how the army could serve as the most readily available and most easily understood model for the civil administration to emulate, and it inspired not only Peter I, whose prime concerns during most of his reign were the needs of war, but his successors as well. The obvious danger was that form would outweigh content in administrative practice. Rationalist, abstract, formalistic legislation and administrative procedures tended to remove government from the realities of national life; it led officials to see their tasks in terms of shuffling papers and to forget the concrete human or particular local circumstances. Even after the appeal to rational concepts and foreign models (rather than to divine law and tradition) had lost its force in the course of the eighteenth century, the new administrative practices introduced by Peter could never build a bridge to the traditional political and moral consciousness of the common people.

The necessity of organizing new institutions and of adapting to "rational" (in Max Weber's sense) procedures and rules of administration put the ruling elite under great pressure. Throughout the first three quarters of the eighteenth century, policies and institutions were in constant flux, in search of a harmonious adaptation of the new norms to existing conditions and in search of stability in the face of frequent changes of rulers and favorites. This is why the codification of existing legislation became such a vital problem. Codification was necessary not only to eliminate laws reflecting outworn traditions and precedents but also to reconcile conflicting norms and procedures which *ad hoc* measures were constantly introducing. Not until the reign of Alexander I did the administrative organization initiated by Peter receive its more or less permanent shape, and not until Nicholas I was codification brought to a successful conclusion.

The main obstacle to a satisfactory adjustment of Peter's institutional innovations to Russian life was the nature of the people who staffed these institutions and acted according to the new rational principles of administration and legislation. In all fairness it must be said, though, that the barrier became an insuperable one largely because of the character of the society itself. At times one has the feeling that the gap between the Emperor's officials and his subjects was never bridged. No sooner had the officials learned how to deal with one type of problem than society's evolution had transformed their work and created new attitudes and forces which could not be solved by those very policies that, only recently, seemed to have been so successful. The lag between government and society was a result, as well as a cause, of the state's inability to bring about conditions of order and relative permanence which might have permitted social change without a radical transformation of the basic relationship between government and society. ...

The new administrative institutions created by Peter the Great and his immediate successors and the new legislation promulgated to direct the work of these institutions required officials capable of acting on the basis of formal, general, rational regulations within the framework of a highly organized bureaucratic hierarchy. This meant a radical departure from the more traditional and personal methods of earlier times. Essentially, the issue faced by the elite immediately after Peter's death (and in a way the problem remained a live one until the end of the imperial regime) was whether to follow the personal or the formal, bureaucratic approach in dealing with the population. It is quite striking to note how slowly the elements of personal relationship disappeared from Russian public life. Naturally, the very fact that the sovereign ruled as an absolute autocrat helped to perpetuate the personal element in government. Indeed, as long as appeal to the Emperor for his personal decision or judgment was possible, the exercise of political power retained something of its earlier patriarchal character, and the subordinate officials were seen, or considered themselves, as personal delegates of the monarch.[2] It was difficult to give up this view of authority. In the first place, there was a rather simple political and sociological reason: the personal appeal to the ruler or his delegate provided the only protection against or redress from injustice, abuse of power, or persecution by subordinate officials who acted on the basis of vague or poorly understood regulations. And it was easy for the officials to take advantage of the monarch's remoteness and of the ignorance, poverty, and weakness of those they were supposed to govern, but in fact oppressed. In addition, the sovereign was the embodiment of ethical and religious values, which remained powerful among the people and which at times found expression among the educated classes in times of public crisis or personal tragedy.[3] Of course, parallels to the personal character of political authority so nicely illustrated by Pushkin at the end of *The Captain's Daughter* could be found in the chronicles of all monarchies, but in Russia it retained greater force much longer, as witnessed, for example, in the behavior of many Decembrists or the aura which surrounded Alexander II.

With the westernization and modernization of the Russian state, such a personal relationship between rulers and ruled could not, of course, remain the foundation of administration and policy decisions. Bureaucratic norms and procedures had to be worked out, and, as always happens in such a case, they became the object of bitter resentment and hatred. Procedures seemed to have become mechanical, rules were frequently deemed arbitrary and injust, the attitudes of clerks and officials were felt to be callous or capricious. How could one secure "justice" (*pravda*) under such circumstances? And yet it was firmly believed by the people that the defense and enforcement of justice were the most important functions of political power.[4] Thus the officials, the bureaucracy, came to be seen as an insuperable barrier separating an understanding and compassionate Tsar from his people. It is irrelevant in our context that such a feeling might have been an illusion, a myth, or an unwarranted, retrospective idealization of a relationship that had never existed in this form even before Peter the Great. What matters is the survival of the ideal and the expectation that authorities ought to act in accordance with it. Paradoxically, perhaps, Nicholas I tried in his own way to give practical and institutional form to this political psychology. But the circumstances of Russian society had changed, while the means Nicholas used (the Third Section of his Chancellery and the Corps of Gendarmes) actually led to a contrary result by giving yet greater scope to arbitrariness and corruption.[5] The autocratic character of the Emperor's power contributed to the survival of the belief that all things flowed from him and that he could at any moment set all wrongs aright. This belief stayed alive down to the Bloody Sunday of January, 1905, when it was finally shattered in the minds of the common people as well. But as long as it lived it bred a sense of frustration and grievance that had its source in the dichotomy between personal (charismatic) and rational (bureaucratic) norms of political action. This in itself did not make the task of government and administration easy, even had the institutions themselves been more workable and the officials more efficient.

The conflict between personal and bureaucratic orientation was largely determined, and heightened, by the nature of Russia's administrative personnel. In a sense, the officials themselves prevented the formation of a genuine bureaucracy on the Western model. Not until late in the nineteenth century, and only in the upper ranks of the hierarchy at that, did there develop anything like a sense of professional responsibility, technical competence, an *esprit de corps,* and a set of ethical norms reflecting the social responsibilities of the bureaucracy. Of course, the maintenance of the autocracy was in itself the primary cause of the situation, for it robbed the officials of genuine responsibility and prevented them from feeling that they could give definitive solution to any matter of consequence, as the final decision depending on the autocrat, or his personal favorites.

It is difficult to speak of Russian officials as if they were a unitary, well-defined, and relatively homogeneous group.[6] To begin with, we can distinguish two separate categories of government servants: The first consisted of the officials in the strict sense, who possessed a definite place and function according to the Table of Ranks and who, in principle at least, could rise in the hierarchy to positions of influence and control. The second category comprised the copyists and clerks and secretaries. These were outside and below the Table of Ranks, poorly paid and badly educated. Scorned by their superiors and by society, they were demoralized and easy prey to drink and graft. They were caught in a dull routine of copying and processing paper which they did not always understand and for whose contents they were neither responsible nor concerned. Russia's tragedy was that, because of the vastness of the Empire and the ubiquity of the administration, a great role devolved on an officialdom that counted too few well-educated and adequately prepared individuals in its ranks. As a result, the lowly clerk wielded much more influence than was warranted by either his position or his personal qualifications. As the routine of processing papers was at the heart of the administrative machinery, the clerk played a vital role, and by standing, so to speak, at the entrance to every level of the administrative and judiciary hierarchy, he was able to forward papers rapidly or hold them up for a long time. He therefore acted as a barrier between the population and the upper rungs of the administrative ladder, and prevented the high officials from learning the true conditions of the people. The failings of this lower stratum of the bureaucracy helped to undermine the government's effectiveness and prevented the regime from reforming itself. The clerk's low level of education, professional competence, and morality precluded the introduction of any progressive and sophisticated improvements in administrative practices and norms. Finally, these features of the lower administrative personnel stymied all intentions and attempts at giving greater responsibility and wider scope for independent action to administrative institutions on the local level.

On the upper levels of the administrative apparatus the situation was different, of course, but in some ways no more satisfactory. Throughout most of the imperial period there was little opportunity for obtaining technical training for the tasks of administration. The official who came from the nobility received a very broad and rather superficial general education, with a strong admixture of eighteenth-century rationalist concepts and a somewhat naïve and mechanistic outlook on questions of social and administrative policy. He was little versed either in the history of his own country or in the traditions of its administration or legal system. The situation changed appreciably for the better in the last third of the nineteenth century, but even then a large proportion of the higher officials had only this unsatisfactory educational background. At least until the middle of the nineteenth century (but still to be found in the reign of Nicholas II), many high officials began their career in the military branches of the state service and were educated in military schools. Shifting to the civilian branch because of reverses in their service fortunes, by the direct command of the monarch, or out of personal considerations, they were ill-prepared for their new duties. They were inclined to apply to the problems of administration, social policy, and justice the attitudes, norms, and conceptions of the military. This led to an overemphasis on external good order, strict obedience, and hierarchical subordination, and the tendency to refer all complicated matters to superiors. When the high official, who usually was also a ranking officer, acted as the direct representative of the Emperor, he tended to exercise his authority on a personal basis, disregarding established rules and procedures and disrupting the regular course of business. It became difficult to avoid the pitfalls of arbitrary and dictatorial decisions, even when they were taken in a good cause. Such personal representatives of the Emperor, although less likely to succumb to corruption and bribery (unless they were on a grand scale), were still very much at the mercy of the will of court factions and prey to court intrigues.

Many highly placed officials not of noble origin were the children of clergymen. After successful studies in the ecclesiastical schools they rose through the ranks of the administrative hierarchy, often after a head start as a private secretary or tutor in the household of an influential dignitary. To the same category belonged the individuals (increasingly more numerous toward the end of the nineteenth century) with professional training and experience who entered government service and rose to occupy positions of responsibility and policy-making importance.[7] The education received by these men, whether in ecclesiastical or professional schools, while excellent for the purpose of mastering the techniques of analysis, rhetoric, and written presentation, did not give much understanding of or contact with actual social conditions. Lowly birth, as well as the submissiveness acquired in ecclesiastical schools, could hardly instill a spirit of enterprise, initiative, and independence. Moreover, the habit, acquired in the course of their schooling, of thinking primarily in terms of abstractions, theories, and universal categories tended to blind them to the variety and complexity of Russian society. Lastly, as they owed everything to the system of promotions, the Table of Ranks, the benevolence of their superiors, and—ultimately—the Emperor, they relied on that system and believed that autocracy was the only satisfactory way to govern a country like Russia. Even those who had spent their childhood close to the people and should have been familiar with their miseries and needs were in fact separated from the lower classes by their schooling and careers; they, too, became a barrier rather than a link between the government and the population.

There were, naturally, many individuals who were not typical of the bureaucracy to which they belonged. At some periods—for example, in the early years of the nineteenth century and during the heyday of Alexander II's reforms—exceptional men were numerous and quite influential. Yet, the overall picture remained by and large characteristic until the disintegration of the regime, and it contributed to the very conditions of Russian public life which reform projects strove to correct.

It should also be kept in mind that in an autocracy the Emperor is always surrounded by courtiers and court factions. A weak sovereign may easily become the prisoner of such factions. By their nature, court factions are interested only in securing immediate personal benefits for their members. The same may be said of the individual favorite, who may exercise great political influence, but still primarily for his own selfish ends. The harm done by court factions and favorites lies not so much in their selfish grabbing, for a rich country may be able to afford some amount of graft if it makes for smoother operation of the government. The greatest threat to a harmonious and beneficent relationship between the ruler and his people stems from the fact that such favorites monopolize access to the ruler's ear. Only the information they are willing to transmit, and in the form they transmit it, can come to the monarch's attention; thus, only one side of a case may ever be known to the ruler. The opportunities for arbitrary, capricious, and unjust decisions are great, and so is the lack of continuity and permanence and the insecurity that such a situation generates. Most reform projects in the eighteenth and early nineteenth centuries aimed at eliminating this interference of favorites and factions and substituting for it regularity of procedure; that is, sought to replace the personal element by the bureaucratic.

Implied in our discussion so far has been the existence of what was perhaps the basic problem of Russian political and administrative life throughout the eighteenth and nineteenth centuries: the inadequacy of the channels of communication between the government and the nation. The central offices and policy-making officials in St. Petersburg depended entirely on the written reports of their subordinates. In view of the quality of this personnel, these reports were highly unreliable as well as incomplete. The Emperor's subjects were normally unable to obtain a hearing by relatively high officials, except by accident, through the intervention of well-placed friends, or with the help of bribery. Equally serious was the government's inability to inform the population of its true intentions and of the purpose of its decisions and legislation. Peter the Great had used legislation for civic education, to inform his subjects of his aims, and to impart to the people notions of rational government. His successors did not follow his practice, and in any event it is doubtful that even Peter had been very successful in his efforts. Cut off from direct contact with the country at large, imbued with only vague and general theoretical notions of government, high officials in St. Petersburg rarely conceived that it would be desirable to communicate with the people or allow the people to communicate with them. Many decrees, laws, and statutes were issued in such a way as to remain unknown (if not actually hidden) to the majority of the population concerned, including the educated classes. Even the lower officials were not always adequately informed of the legislation or regulations they might have to enforce.

A second serious problem for the Russian government, largely the product of the features we have just discussed, was the need for better coordination of decisions and policies. In principle, the sovereign was the source of all law and the final instance of appeal for all matters of administration and justice. But he could not possibly coordinate all facets of public life himself. This was especially the case when the ruler was not quite equal to his task, as happened all too frequently. Much legislation was of an *ad hoc* nature to cover specific cases and was not always known even to all the officials who might be concerned. Codification was not achieved until 1835, and even then the former practice of *ad hoc* decrees and rulings kept cluttering the books without being brought into harmony with the provisions of the code.

Perhaps of greater significance than lack of harmony in the laws was the absence of coordination in the administration itself. There was no single institution specifically entrusted with this function. Peter the Great had intended the Senate to play this role, but after his death the Senate's authority declined, and it eventually became primarily a supervisory body and high administrative tribunal. There were brief periods during which the Senate acted as the agent of centralization for the administration (but not as coordinator of legislative policy), as under Elizabeth and to some extent also under Catherine II. Throughout the eighteenth century and in the first years of the reign of Alexander I efforts were made to restore to the Senate this function of coordination. But it was believed in high government circles that delegating functions of policy coordination to the Senate could give it an authority and power that might enable it to exercise some measure of control, and in so doing put a limit to the autocratic absolutism of the monarch. Thus, this solution was never accepted. Similar considerations in the nineteenth century prevented the Committee of Ministers from exercising functions of legislative coordination. Attempts were also made to secure greater coherence and consistency of policy by means of special councils that would assist the ruler while being completely under his control. Yet, again and again, universal fear of the rule or influence of an oligarchy prevented such plans from being implemented in full.

In a paradoxical way, perhaps, the lack of adequate coordination of legislation and administration made it possible to preserve the power of autocracy intact into the twentieth century. As the ruler's decisions was required in so many matters, he was able to issue *ad hoc* legislation at will. No group of men could challenge the autocracy's supremacy by virtue of their regular administrative functions. Yet at the same time inadequate policy coordination paralyzed the monarch's autocratic power on a day-to-day level. Indeed, his will could easily be betrayed by subordinate officials, who were in a position to act arbitrarily according to their own whim without being called to account, as there was no effective system of coordination and control.[8] While the situation improved immeasurably in the second half of the nineteenth century with respect to social and economic policies, lack of policy coordination continued to have a disastrous effect on the strictly administrative and political aspects of Russia's public life until the outbreak of the revolution.

The rulers of Muscovy had succeeded in preventing the development of social classes into estates, and the population of Russia had been "atomized" quite early in its history. The absolute power of the autocrat had destroyed whatever feeble manifestations of an estate structure had struck roots among the nobility. The reforms and modernization of Peter the Great eliminated the last remnants of a decaying pattern. The elements of regional and class solidarity had never been strong among the peasant population because of the great mobility of its members. The feeble expressions of such solidarities were nipped in the bud by the spread of serfdom and completely destroyed by the poll tax, which turned the peasant into the property of an individual owner who could easily and arbitrarily disrupt at any time his serfs' attachments to a village or region. The clergy had never enjoyed the privileged status of its counterpart in the West. What did bind together members of the same class or group were family relationships (or tribal and clan loyalties, if we follow the terminology popular in Russian historiography in the nineteenth century). But for political purposes, ties and solidarities based on family connections are not so strong as the bonds between members of an estate. In a sense, family loyalties separate or oppose individual families quite as much as they bind together the members of the same family. In Russia individual families (or clans), particularly among the nobility, rose and fell as the Tsar's favor was bestowed or withdrawn from their members, but these families were not able to act in unison to secure rights and privileges of benefit to each and all of them. It would be impossible at this point to go into detail about the reasons for and origins of this situation. Suffice it to note that the two opposed principles of birthright and service achievement helped to keep the nobility divided: nobles who advocated special status on the basis of individual service merits came into conflict with those who claimed status on grounds of birthright. Peter the Great's Table of Ranks gave the conflict a new form, but preserved the nobility's basic lack of cohesion. As rank was strictly personal and not transmissible to others in the family, it could not survive as a basis for estate solidarities and privileges and was even contrary to them. Even the Charter of 1785 did not succeed in transforming the Russian nobility into a genuine estate. The paramount role of rank kept the nobility an open and divided class. Quite naturally, the sovereign was only too happy to preserve a situation that worked to his own advantage. The cities and their burghers were few, economically weak, and very much dependent on the sovereign's favors, and thus could not be the mainstay of a strong third estate as in France.

Consequently, the individual Russian, including the members of the upper classes, faced the autocrat and the apparatus of the state alone. Naturally, he could not have a strong sense of security, with respect either to his person or to his property and status. Needless to say, the situation was twice as bad for the peasant, who stood in the same isolated and insecure position with respect to his master. Even after 1861, he did not obtain full security, as he remained under the control of his commune as well as of the agents of the government.

Three basic elements, therefore, determined the efforts at government reform which we observe in the eighteenth and nineteenth centuries: (1) the desire to establish regular channels of communication between the government and the population; (2) the need to coordinate and harmonize more effectively the policies of the government; and (3) the wish to invest the relationship between the government and the governed with security of person, property, and status to the latter. The greater attention paid at various times to one or another of these three elements allows us to distinguish several major periods in the efforts at reform over a span of almost two centuries.

*   *   *

One may liken Peter the Great to a man who is trying to erect a house while hurricane winds are blowing overhead. Part of the structure collapses almost immediately under the next gust of wind, and while repairs are made to it, there is no time to complete the other parts or to lay solid foundations. The government edifice Peter left at his death in 1725 resembled a cluster of more or less completed, more or less well-built structures, poorly integrated both among themselves and in relation to the landscape. Peter had rushed to complete as much as he could, breaking up a great deal of the old edifice, and in so doing completely disregarding the needs of individuals. He had driven everyone hard, no matter what the consequences; the pace had been furious, and the nation was exhausted. Not surprisingly, therefore, the first concern of the service noblemen Peter had helped to bring into being by means of the Table of Ranks was to catch their breath, consolidate their gains, and acquire some sense of security and stability.

The first years after the death of Peter were quite confusing; emperors and empresses followed one after another in rapid succession, and their powerful favorites were more short-lived still. The sense of insecurity was at a peak, for every change in the power constellation at court or in government affected deeply the fortunes of many service noblemen. Loss of favor, moreover, meant not only removal from a position of influence but frequently loss of personal liberty and confiscation of property as well. An additional reason for profound insecurity stemmed from the fact that, while the old, traditional order of social relations, especially with regard to the upper classes, had been shattered or even completely destroyed by Peter's reforms, the new rules and relationships had not yet taken hold. In the absence of a feeling of stability, permanence, or coherence, individual members of Russia's nobility felt very much disoriented, socially as well as personally.

The first opportunity to vent these feelings publicly and to suggest ways for dealing with them came in 1730 on the accession of Empress Anne. ... Yet the crisis was ended with Anne's resumption of absolute and unlimited autocratic power without a satisfactory solution for the basic problems of stability and security. *In the long run,* members of the nobility were given a measure of satisfaction on some of their aspirations, such as greater freedom in disposing of their property, more opportunities for the education of their children, liberalization of the rules of service. But they did not obtain the "right" to security for their person and property. As a matter of fact, Anne's reign was quite tyrannical and arbitrary; the individual privileged service nobleman remained as much the sovereign's *kholop* as his ancestors had been. His property, his life, and his status were entirely at the mercy of the monarch's whims and subject to the tyranny of high officials and favorites.

One of the reasons for this state of affairs was the fact that Russia did not have an up-to-date, comprehensive code of laws. The last code had been drawn up in 1649, and its provisions had to a great extent been rendered obsolete by the profound transformations in Russian government and society wrought by Peter the Great. In the absence of a comprehensive modern code, the conflicts between old and new juridical norms and social values, between the demands of reason and will and those of tradition, could not be settled or reconciled. Peter had recognized the necessity of bringing the elements of historical tradition into harmony with those imported from the West. To this end he had called together the first commission on codification, but it did not do the job, nor did the many that followed it in the eighteenth century or in the first quarter of the nineteenth century (codification was finally carried out by Speransky in 1833). Yet by their very existence, the commissions on codification (some of which were made up of elected or appointed representatives of the upper classes) had at least two effects: they helped to introduce and popularize notions of modern law, in particular natural law; and they were instrumental in making the Russian elite conscious of the fact that their security— both as individuals and as a group—could be safeguarded only by fundamental and stable laws. Codification, therefore, became a symbol of progress and reform, just as much as a constitution or administrative reorganization. At the same time, though, it fostered the belief that all the problems of Russia could be solved by an acceptable code and thus abetted the almost natural propensity of the westernized educated elite for theoretical, "radical," and universal solutions, and their tendency to see basic political problems solely in juridical terms. To put it differently, it fostered the elite's tendency to think in terms of the ends of government rather than of the means. ...

Even though she rejected the reform suggestions made in 1730, Anne had to establish some coordinating center. Her solution was the Cabinet of Ministers, whose leading spirits, A. Osterman, A. Cherkasskii, and A. Volynskii, were able men who could do an effective job. Unfortunately, as with everything else in those years, the Ministers were also entirely dependent on the support and good will of Anne's personal favorites, especially Biron. The Conference of Ministers established in the reign of Elizabeth had basically the same character as Anne's Cabinet; in addition, it dealt almost exclusively with matters of foreign policy.

N. Panin's project was the most important of the many efforts made at that time to give the sovereign's council a stable membership, clearly defined functions, and a full role in coordinating, supervising, and stabilizing policies. Panin and others clearly saw that such a council or institution would in fact share in the sovereign's legislative burden, for, in the final analysis, it would have to prepare, present, discuss, and decide on essential legislation with all the evidence and information at hand. Many who counted solely on the ruler's personal favoritism interpreted the extensive role of such a council as the first step toward the surrender of the monarch's unity of sovereignty and authority. The fear of oligarchy, which had been so influential in bringing to naught D. M. Golitsyn's plans of 1730, derived its strength from the memory of the events of 1610–13 and the period of appanages in medieval Russia, and its impact was so pervasive that every council of some autonomy, permanence, and stability seemed, to the minds of contemporaries, to harbor a threat to the unity of the Russian state.

In a sense, Panin's failure ended the first period of reform efforts. These were immature and naïve in many ways; they were directed at lightening the noblemen's burdens of service and attaining some degree of security and permanence. Unable, perhaps, to see their demands in a broader framework, the service noblemen contented themselves with the maintenance of autocracy in the hope that the sovereign, on the basis of his personal relationship to his subjects, would give them satisfaction on an individual basis. Overconcern with the preservation of the unity of sovereignty (natural after periods of civil war or upheaval, as in France after the Wars of Religion or in England in the mid-seventeenth century) led to a defense of absolutism, for complete unity of sovereignty could be secured only by one absolute ruler.[9]

In the course of the eighteenth century, Russian society, especially the upper class, underwent a profound transformation. This became manifest not so much in the structure and basic social character of the class as in the cultural outlook and activities of its members. In brief, Russian noblemen as a group (including newly created nobles and a few professionals) had come of age: they were now individualized and westernized. The nobleman was individualized in the sense that he had broken out of the closed framework of family and clan solidarities; each member was now on his own, and his position in society depended primarily on his personal achievements within the framework of governmental service. At the same time he had adopted Western customs and was beginning to acquire Western modes of thought. With respect to the latter, it is true, progress was rather slow, especially in the provinces, where the vast majority of the petty gentry was still quite uncouth and uncivilized from a Western European point of view. But the leaders, the men who lived in the capitals and served in commanding positions in the army or administration, had become thoroughly westernized. In our context the most important result was that for the elite westernization meant acquiring a sense of self-respect, worth, and dignity. When Catherine II finally prohibited the use of derogatory diminutives and humiliating epithets in official petitions to the ruler, she was wiping away an anachronism. The average educated nobleman no longer thought of himself as a slave (*rab*) or servant (*kholop*) of the ruler; he considered himself a loyal subject and, more important still, a "true son of the fatherland." Naturally, he expected to be treated accordingly, to be secure in his person and property, and to be given public recognition for his class's cultural accomplishments. In short, the Russian nobleman had finally become conscious of his "nobility"; he yearned for the public consideration enjoyed by his Western European counterpart; he was convinced that he ought to have special rights and privileges which could guarantee his status and worth as the cultural and moral leader of the nation.

The acts of 1762 (Freedom from State Service), 1775 (Statute on the Provinces), and especially the Charter of 1785 mark the steps which the government took in recognition of the nobility's new position. A reading of the Charter to the Nobility of 1785 would make it appear that the Russian nobility had obtained the status of a privileged corporation, of an estate, whose members were guaranteed security of person and property as well as a dominant role in the government and in the country. The reality, however, was somewhat different. First of all, the security which the nobility believed they had attained was of a very unstable sort. The nobleman in fact remained at the mercy of the autocrat and his officials. Catherine II made this amply clear by repressive measures against members of the masonic lodges, for example, in the last years of her reign, while her sons' disregard of the Charter led to a new height in the capricious and arbitrary treatment of members of the service nobility.[10] Thus, at the beginning of the nineteenth century, the upper classes found themselves once again at the mercy of the personal caprices of the Emperor and his favorites.

The deeper cause for the failure of Catherine's legislation with respect to the nobility's corporate rights and privileges lay not so much in the personality of the ruler as in the emergence of an officialdom separated from the nobility and, at times, even opposed to it. Until the middle of the eighteenth century there had been no clear separation between officials and the rank and file of the nobility in service. As long as the nobility's obligation—and only occupation—was to serve the state, its membership coincided with that of officialdom, even though some officials were not noblemen by birth but had merged into the nobility on reaching a specified rank in the Table of Ranks. The situation began to change by the middle of the eighteenth century. The act of 19 February 1762, "freeing" the nobility from compulsory service, should be seen as the state's declaration of independence form the nobility on the one hand, and, on the other, as an attempt by high and wealthy dignitaries to direct the members of the nobility into new activities. Indeed, as far as can be ascertained, the act of 1762 was "hatched" and prepared by men like the Vorontsovs who wished to see in Russia an aristocracy, an estate of privileged individuals whose main source of power, influence, and status in society would derive from their role as owners of land and serfs. The service nobility was to become independent of state service and to be transformed (on the English model) into an economically active and enterprising landowning "gentry" with a dominant role in local self-government.[11] Be that as it may, with the granting of freedom from state service it became possible for noblemen to have other interests and occupations. True, state service remained the principal activity and norm by which membership in the nobility was gauged. But it was no longer life-long, and for many a nobleman, especially after retirement, other activities began to be of greater interest. Such noblemen gradually dissociated themselves from the government and its officials. As their new economic and cultural interests diverged from the principles and policies of the government, the identity between state and nobility that had dominated Russian public life for well-nigh two centuries gradually disintegrated. This did not yet necessarily imply conflict, but it did mean that the traditional relationship between "society"[12] and government would undergo fundamental changes. The problem of communication mentioned earlier thus took on a new aspect and required a solution in terms of the new, emerging relationships between the ruler and the elite of his subjects.

At the same time the intellectual westernization of the Russian elite was beginning to bear fruit. Under the impact of the philanthropic and enlightened ideas of eighteenth-century Western thought, introduced by members of masonic lodges and a few outstanding individuals like Novikov, the conviction grew that government was for the welfare and prosperity of the people and that good government must be based on the rule of law. It reflected, of course, the Enlightenment's belief in the active and positive role of a good code of laws based on just principles. The more progressive and enlightened members of the Russian nobility had absorbed the basic concepts of natural law (in its eighteenth-century enlightened and secular form), as well as belief in the role of positive governmental action for the happiness of the nation, and they increasingly felt that any kind of reform had to redefine the relationships between monarch and subjects of all classes, not excluding even the serfs.

Such attitudes led to the conclusion that Russia had to become an *autocracy based on law,* or, in other words, ruled by an autocrat respectful of the limitations of self-imposed laws. What at first glance seems to be a paradoxical formulation (which had a precedent in Roman Law) turns out to be less so if we recall that for eighteenth-century Russians autocracy connoted primarily absolute sovereignty, that is, the independent and unitary character of the Russian state. There was no reason, therefore, why autocracy could not be combined with a *Rechtsstaat*—a state based on the automatic and beneficent action of stable, permanent, and fundamental laws designed to secure the nation's welfare.

The real question was how this desirable end—an end on which both the "government" and "society," with Paul's reign vividly in mind, would readily agree—could best be attained. Two major schools of thought became manifest, each advocating a specific approach in the quest for security and the rule of law, on the one hand, and in planning state policy for the solution of Russia's major social, economic, and administrative problems, on the other.

There were, first, those who put security of person and property above everything else in the firm belief that all other problems of Russia's public life would find their solution once this security had been achieved. In a sense they implicitly agreed that the best government was that which governed least, limiting itself to negative functions such as protection of law and order at home and defense against external enemies. In Russia, they argued, autocracy was essential if these functions were to be performed well, for only the autocratic sovereign could preserve the unity of the state and personally insure just treatment under law for all. It should be kept in mind, of course, that the defenders of this approach accounted only for those subjects who might be said to constitute the *pays légal* of the time, that is, the nobility and those from other social groups (such as townspeople, merchants, clergy, foreigners) who were personally free and able to engage in economic and professional activities in their own name.

The aim of this first school of Russian public opinion was to secure fundamental and inalienable rights for the Russian nation; these might vary from one group or class to another, but they would be immutable and absolute. In a sense, the aim was to promote the emergence of genuine estates (in the late medieval, European meaning of the term), or, to put it in somewhat different words, to create social classes, each with its clearly defined juridical character. One of the principal features of the proposals made along these lines was the establishment of some institutional framework to safeguard fundamental rights granted by the Emperor. To this end two different methods were put forward. First was the suggestion that the elective offices established by the Charter of 1785 and the Statute on the Provinces of 1775 serve as the source for some body (or bodies) that would have the right to bring to the attention of the government any abuse of power and violation of basic rights and privileges. In the second place—and on the whole it was the more popular as well as the more realistic approach—were the proposals to invest the Senate with the authority to safeguard basic rights and to supervise the officials with respect to the lawful performance of their duties. Some projects went on to suggest that the membership of the Senate might include some elected or appointed representatives from provincial assemblies of the nobility and municipal assemblies of major towns. The basis for assigning individuals to a particular class was never debated in full, and no consensus emerged. Yet in the last years of the eighteenth century and the first years of the nineteenth, the belief grew that achievement in the economic domain should be given consideration along with birthright and service-acquired status. In any event, the fruits of man's acquisitive activities were to be as secure against administrative arbitrariness and abuse as the person and status of the service nobleman.

The pattern of political reform just outlined has often been branded reactionary or conservative. The first epithet is, of course, grossly inaccurate, for the aim of such reform was different from anything Russia had known before. In terms of Russia's historical tradition and experience, the proposals of those who have often been called the Senatorial party (because of their reliance on a reorganized Senate as the lynchpin of the new order) had no real antecedents.[13] But their proposals certainly were conservative, in the Burkean sense: they provided for some change, or more precisely, for the creation of a basis for gradual evolution along novel lines, but not a radical departure from trends that might have been noticed by careful observers in the last years of the eighteenth century. Nor were these proposals uninfluenced by foreign models which had been studied, examined, and debated by prominent representatives of eighteenth-century Russian public opinion. The most influential model was, of course, England, with whom some leaders of the Senatorial party had close connections. The examples, closer to home, of Prussia, Austria, or Sweden and Poland did not attract much attention at the time.

To introduce genuine estates implied favoring a gradual evolution and slow transformation. Observing that the *Ständestaat* is capable of evolving into either enlightened absolutism or parliamentary monarchy, Otto Hintze noted that in both cases there is a dispersion of power among well-established and secure legal groups of social classes.[14] Although Europe has experienced only the two alternative developments noted by Hintze, we cannot say, of course, into what other forms the *Ständestaat* might have evolved under different political, social, and economic circumstances. This "open endedness"—its unpredictability and reliance on gradual and undirected change—made the *Ständestaat* unpopular with eighteenth-century reformers, whether from the camp of the *philosophes* or of the royal bureaucrats. As Roscoe Pound has observed, it was peculiarly ill-adapted to a society or cultural climate which had an optimistic faith in human reason and was eager to use its creative will to transform social and political relationships in the light of a clearly perceived goal.[15] This explains why the *Ständestaat* broke down in the West in the eighteenth century and also why it failed to strike roots in Russia.

Intent on preserving the role of reason and will, in the tradition of Peter the Great, many wished to reserve exclusively for the government the right and power to shape the country by positive and creative action. They wanted to endow governmental policies with the conscious awareness of specific goals to work for. Security of person and property against arbitrary and tyrannical action of officials had to be guaranteed, of course. But to attain the specific goals (to increase Russia's power and secure the people's welfare) it was essential to coordinate effectively the government's legislative and administrative policies. Hence the idea of streamlining the government's *organization* to provide for both security and coordination. Implied also was the hope that institutional reorganization would result in better communication between the autocrat and his subjects, not through representatives of estates, but through an administrative setup that would make it possible to bring any problem and injury to the attention of regularly established, competent authorities. Clearly, such an organizational reform could be best accomplished, without undermining the autocrat's power, through sovereign command. The ruler himself could only welcome such an approach and such a goal, for they would facilitate the task of government through a better division and distribution of functions.

After the approach proposed by the Senatorial party had been rejected by Alexander I as a danger to the autocracy, those who advocated what might be called the "bureaucratic" approach were invited to submit concrete projects of reform. For about a quarter of a century experiments were made with quite a large number of projects and proposals; some were discussed by the closest advisers of the Emperor, a few received partial application, but none was ever adopted and carried through in its entirety. These projects shared one essential characteristic: they were all concerned with the mechanics of coordinating administrative policies and, to a lesser degree, with setting up a mechanism by which the government would be better informed of what was happening in the country.

One of the institutional innovations was the creation of ministries to replace the old colleges that had already begun to disappear. But the problem of adequate coordination was not solved thereby. Indeed, Emperor Alexander I and all his successors were adamant in their refusal to bring together the heads of the ministries into a "cabinet" to develop coordinated policies and offer their collective advice and counsel to the monarch. The Committee of Ministers was merely an occasional meeting of several ministers; it had no policy-making role and only limited administrative authority. Another attempt to coordinate imperial legislation was the establishment of the Council of State, as proposed in Speransky's Plan of 1809. It was to have some of the functions envisaged by Panin for his imperial council, but in addition it was to enjoy an autonomous and rather broad advisory role within the framework of the other institutional reforms proposed by Speransky. But when the Council of State was set up, the remainder of the Plan was "sent to the archives"; torn from its context and its main architect disgraced, the Council of State rapidly sank to the role of a mere editorial board for drafting new legislative acts. As such it survived to the revolution of 1905; no doubt it performed a useful function, but it had no role in directing or coordinating policy.[16]

So far our discussion has been based on the implicit view that the Russian Empire was a unitary, centralized state, administered as if it were made of one piece, with little or no regard to the great variety in its geographic and human makeup and the still greater variety of its regional historical traditions. After the wars against Napoleon some attention was at last paid to the Empire's multinational character. This new interest and concern was probably in large part the result of the incorporation of the Grand Duchy of Finland and the personal union that bound the constitutional Kingdom of Poland and the Russian monarch. In addition, it was becoming obvious, even to conservative officials, that the growing complexity of social and economic problems and the resulting need for better coordination between local and central administrative authorities required some reform action. More effective supervision of local institutions was necessary because the quality of the lower clerical personnel had not improved much over the last century: it had not kept pace with the greater needs and sophistication of an ever-growing proportion of the population. If the government wanted to exercise effective leadership in bringing about economic and social progress, it had to direct local institutions into taking account of specific variations in the physical and human environment.

Several proposals were made to take care of this need. Two approaches may be distinguished: The first was to create lieutenancies or governor-generalships by combining several provinces, so that their combined appointed chief, the governor-general, could act as the personal representative of the monarch. The governor-general was not supposed to participate directly in day-to-day administration, but he was expected to coordinate and supervise the actions of local authorities, seeing to it that laws and rights were respected and regulations applied in the spirit in which they had been issued by the sovereign and his ministers. The other approach, in a way less bureaucratic, was to give fairly extended rights of self-government to more or less representative bodies within each of the larger subdivisions of the Empire. The most elaborate, as well as the most radical, of such proposals was drafted in 1820 by N. N. Novosiltsev. His major source of inspiration was clearly the constitution of the Republic of Poland before its partition. The obvious fact that his proposal led to the dispersal of the Emperor's authority, if not actual division of his sovereignty, made it quite unacceptable, and no part of it was ever implemented. The experiment of a "federal" solution was not renewed, and all later projects of reform treated the Empire as a single unit with little regard to the special character of its constituent parts. Naturally, such disregard only increased the lack of communication and understanding between the Emperor and the central government, on the one hand, and those of his subjects who differed in language, custom, religion, and culture from the Russians, on the other.

Efforts at mechanical adjustments and improvements of the administration lasted, in a sense, into the reign of Nicholas I. Only the outbreak of the revolutions of 1848 in the West put a halt to all discussion of reform. None of the secret committees set up by Nicholas I to formulate administrative and social reform helped to bring about better understanding or communication between the nation and the government. Quite the contrary; as they were secret, their discussions remained unknown to the people, and they could not seek the cooperation of influential leaders of public opinion.

Nicholas I was extremely suspicious of Russian educated society and cut it off completely from the government. He also was aware, however, of the government's need for better information on what was going on in the Empire. In the absence of trustworthy officials, efficient institutions, or representative bodies, supervision of the administration and redress of its wrongdoings had to be the task of the ruler himself. To this end he created the Third Section of His Own Chancellery and the Crops of Gendarmes. Their failure and perversion of their mission into a kind of secret and ubiquitous political police must have made it obvious to all that even in Russia genuinely effective personal and patriarchal kingship was not possible any more.[17]

The reforms of Alexander II, above all the emancipation of the serfs, helped to usher in extensive changes in Russian society. These changes were bound, of course, to affect the country's public institutions and the pattern of its administration; the resulting transformation might be described as an acceleration of the process of modernization or of the establishment of a modern industrial society in Russia. In the context of our discussion, we might say more specifically that the reforms of Alexander II—in particular the emancipation, the *zemstvo* organization, and the reorganization of the judiciary—led to an expansion of the role of administration. The role of governmental institutions was expanded because of the ever-increasing complexity of Russian life, particularly of economic life, in which the government took a lively interest by participating in the development of industry and transportation. Industrialization and its accompanying social and economic problems required the government's active involvement in matters related to public health, social legislation, urban control, and the like. Furthermore, the government had to meet new responsibilities and face greater challenges in connection with the establishment of the *zemstvo* institutions and the reformed judiciary. The greater professionalization of life led to deeper governmental involvement in controlling and supervising education, cultural activities, and the press. If, as had been its wont since Peter the Great, the Russian state wished to preserve its leadership and keep under strict control most facets of public life, it had to expand its functions, which meant increasing the number of officials and providing them with greater technical competence.

The institutional structure inherited from the past (its basic organization was not to change appreciably in the half century preceding the revolution of 1905) had difficulties in adapting and keeping pace with the emerging new social and economic realities. The unwieldy machine creaked and puffed, yet somehow it did hold together and managed to perform. This was not so much the result of its flexibility as of the emergence of many new institutions capable of performing public functions without actually being part of the government. As a result, a greater number of professionally trained people became available to staff both private and public institutions; new blood could be pumped into the bureaucracy. The officials whose characterization was discussed earlier were gradually giving way to a regular, genuine bureaucracy, a body of men trained for their tasks, acting according to set rules, possessing a degree of professionalism and continuity as a body. These new officials had a genuine sense of civic responsibility (within the limits set by the existing political regime, of course); they were not altogether blind to nor uncritical of the evils of the political system, and they desired to improve it.

Unfortunately, this change in the character of Russia's administrative personnel was taking place only on the higher-middle level of the hierarchy. In other words, the clerks remained much the same as their predecessors of the eighteenth and early nineteenth centuries: ill-prepared, incompetent, demoralized, as well as open to graft and corruption; the compensatory mechanism of their petty tyranny still weighed most heavily on the lower classes of the population. Nor was there any change at the very top of the pyramid. In the absence of a responsible and coherent ministry and effective institutions of administrative coordination and supervision, the absolute ruler depended on his courtiers, personal friends, and advisers picked up by chance. The most trusted top advisers of the last three Emperors were a very mixed group. Some were efficient and remarkable professionals or experts (for example, Pobedonostsev, Bunge, Witte). Some others had had brilliant careers in the military or civil administration (Miliutin, Valuev, Stolypin). Yet at the same time great influence—at times the dominant one—was exercised by courtiers and members of the imperial family. In some cases these personal favorites worked well (Rostovtsev, Lanskoi, Grand Duke Constantine), but in many more they worked very badly indeed. Personal favorites, as in the eighteenth century, still could play a major role, as witness the genesis of the Russo-Japanese War or, on the eve of the imperial regime's final collapse, the incredible influence of Rasputin. The Emperor worked with each dignitary separately, and in addition he listened to the advice of courtiers and personal aides and favorites. Little wonder that there was no stability, coherence, and continuity in policy decisions. After conferring with the Emperor and securing his assent to a proposal, even the most influential and important minister or councilor could not be sure that he would obtain permission to implement his project. Every minister tried to be the last to see the Emperor to prevent unfavorable advice from reaching the Emperor before signature of his reports. The ruler was not unaware of the situation, but he permitted it, for it allowed him to retain control of the government, something the weaker monarchs were always worried about.

Thus, petty tyranny, corruption, and arbitrariness reigned at the bottom level of the administration, oppressing and exploiting the small people. On the middle-level, highly competent and more responsible officials displayed a genuine desire to respond adequately to the country's needs and problems; they tried their best to bring legality and order into the administration. On the very top, autocratic absolutism continued its arbitrary and capricious rule. The existence of these three levels explains the long survival of the regime as well as its basic weakness and eventual total collapse. The revolution of 1905 postponed the ultimate reckoning by giving greater scope and strength to the middle-level officials and by starting the improvement of the lower. But even it proved incapable of genuinely transforming the character of the top level of Russia's government. The consequence was 1917.

The reforms of the 1860's and 1870's had their greatest impact on institutions and activities not directly dependent on the government. In spite of many onerous restrictions, the peasant was now free to pursue his economic self-interest. In addition, peasant institutions, especially the commune, had more numerous and significant functions than ever before. After the emancipation we witness the reform of local government and the establishment of the *zemstvos*. As is well known, the *zemstvos* took on important functions in the realms of education, welfare, public health, and economic and social protection. In addition they provided men and women with an opportunity of doing socially useful and responsible work without becoming part of the official bureaucracy. The same might be said of the judiciary; although judges and procurators were still government officials, the new system gave rise to an influential and well-trained class of lawyers.

Equally significant was the fact that new social groups and classes—entrepreneurs, merchants, traders, financiers, workers, engineers, managers, accountants—were establishing private organizations and associations to promote their particular interests and concerns. They were thereby laying the groundwork for a pluralistic society.[18] This development found further expression in the growing role of the press and those organizations which provided education and a place for public exchanges of ideas—for example, schools, universities, and learned societies. These new institutions naturally demanded that their lawful activities be free and secure from arbitrary administrative interference; they wanted the right to expand and maximize their contribution to the welfare, prosperity, and cultural growth of the Russian people.

A new dilemma thus made its appearance in Russian public life, new at least in its scope and intensity: government guidance and control or free initiative of private associations and professional groupings. While the old tradition of state leadership and control maintained itself on the very top of Russia's governmental structure, Russian society had been striking out more and more on its own and at a much more rapid pace than the government was willing to admit. Paradoxically, perhaps, as the work of Peter the Great came to fruition, it destroyed that very basis of a community of interests between government and society that had been its aim. Indeed, Peter the Great had viewed the state's role of leadership as a *means* for bringing out the economic and spiritual potential inherent in the nation and for raising Russia to the level of Western Europe. Once this was accomplished, Peter believed, the interests of the state and of the individual members of society would merge to further the greatness and glory of Russia. By the second half of the nineteenth century the government had done its job relatively well, and it had helped to bring into being new forces and sources of power for the Russian nation. But these forces then began to demand greater freedom of action and more scope for their growth, while the government found it impossible to abandon its leadership and control of society. The effort made in the reign of Alexander I to lay the foundation for a new relationship by giving private endeavor a larger role and greater freedom was stifled by the bureaucratic approach to institutional reform and the decision to preserve autocracy intact.

The more enlightened members of the government realized that without the participation and help of "public opinion" (as represented b leading circles of Russia's educated classes) it would be impossible to carry out peacefully the great transformation of Russian society implicit in the emancipation of the serfs. Thus, work on the emancipation itself was carried on with the help and advice of selected individuals or groups of the enlightened elite. In the years immediately following, the same approach was taken in working out the *zemstvo* legislation and judicial reform. Russia's elite thus came to hope that it would continue to be asked to collaborate with the administration; such a collaboration had been made easy by the creation of an appropriate institutional framework through the *zemstvos,* universities, technical commissions, and professional associations. But, as is well known, the government betrayed this hope and turned a deaf ear to the pleas of public opinion. In the eyes of the administration the growth of the revolutionary movement and its increasing violence justified repressive policies and efforts at maintaining strict controls over most aspects of public life. Thus, the expected collaboration between government and public opinion did not materialize, and, worse still, the government lost the confidence and support of even the moderates, who began to protect and finance revolutionary agitation. Clearly, the break of communication between society and the state was at its most serious. An unfortunate byproduct of this break was the government's increasing inability to secure adequate information on what was really going on in the country. Officials believed that the representatives of public opinion had no business suggesting anything pertaining to matters of administration and treated critical information and complaints alike as expressions of subversive sentiment. The catastrophic effect of the famine of 1892 was in large part due to this breakdown in communication.

The more intelligent and enlightened officials realized the danger this situation presented to the country's political and social structure, and they bent their efforts at breaching the gap. Their proposals of reform aimed at establishing the means to keep open regular and good communication between society and government. The difficulty was to bring about this communication without permitting the representatives of public opinion to participate in the actual process of legislation or government. One way of circumscribing the role of advisory representatives of society was to limit strictly the circle of potential participants. In other words, the *pays légal* (those permitted to elect and be elected) was to be kept very small by all kinds of restrictions, mainly property qualifications. It was not only a matter of property, however, but also of class status; preference was given to the landed nobility in the belief that they would be the most loyal and moderate. One glaring weakness of these projects was the scant respect paid to the multinational character of the Russian Empire. Border regions and most non-Russian minorities were in fact given inferior status and not permitted to participate on an equal basis with the Great Russian population. Such a short-sighted policy was fraught with great dangers for the future, in view of the ever-growing strength of national consciousness and the economic and cultural development of most nationalities within the Russian Empire.

In the final analysis, the imperial regime failed to reform itself from within. Unwilling to abandon the traditions and attitudes developed in the course of the eighteenth century, unable to adjust rapidly enough to the economic, cultural, and social transformation of Russian society, distrusting the free initiative and participation in public affairs of its subjects, the regime could not cope with the growing complexities of the situation it had helped to create. Poorly served by its officials, it lacked the necessary flexibility and courage; incapable of bending, the regime cracked and eventually disintegrated. Yet, not everything is to be blamed on the nature of the imperial government; other factors in Russian society contributed to the final crackup and collapse. In our context the most important of these factors was a failure to develop centers of authority and power outside the framework of government; that is, the absence of strong corporations or estates endowed with privileges, rights, and autonomy of action within their domain.

Russia never became a *Ständestaat,* and the imperial government prevented the creation of a dynamic and flexible *Rechtsstaat.* In spite of all efforts and improvements, the imperial regime could not withstand the stress of modernization and contact with the West. But the very reasons that made it vulnerable also explain why it survived so long: there was no readily available alternative, at least not until a pluralistic society had begun to emerge in the second half of the nineteenth century. ...

Notes

1. S. F. Platonov, *Lektsii po russkoi istorii,* I. Blinov, ed. (St. Petersburg: 1904), especially pp. 367–78 and 457–60; the same, "Boiarskaia duma—predshestvennitsa Senata," *Stat'i po russkoi istorii (1883–1912),* 2d ed. (St. Pedtersburg: 1912), pp. 444-94.

2. Peter the Great himself contributed to the perpetuation of the personal element through the acts on single inheritance and on succession to the Russian throne. By these acts both the private landowner (also serf owner) and the ruling monarch were given the right to designate their successors and heirs freely, thereby strengthening the absolute patrimonial character of their authority. The acts in question are in PSZ, No. 3893 (5 February 1722, Statute on Succession to the Throne) and No. 2789 (23 March 1714, On Inheritence of Real and Movable Property).

3. On the notions of true kingship in Russia see M. Cherniavsky, *Tsar and People— Studies in Russian Myths* (New Haven and London: Yale University Press, 1961).

4. This view was also expressed by some influential and high-minded officials at the end of the eighteenth century. Cf. the memoris of G. Derzhavin and Prince N. Lopukhin: *Zapiski Gavriila Romanovicha Derzhavina (1743–1812)* (Moscow: 1860); "Zapiski nekotorykh obstoiatel'stv zhizni i sluzhby d.t.s. senatora N. V. Lopukhina, sochinennye im samim," *Chteniia v imperatorskom obshchestve istorii i drevnostei rossiiskikh pri Moskovskom universitete* (1860), Bks. II and III.

5. S. Monas, *The Third Section: Police and Society in Russia under Nicholas I* (Cambridge, Mass.: Harvard University Press, 1961). For rich and revealing illustrations of the realities of Nicholas's ideal see *Memoiren von Jacob Iwanowitsch de Sanglen 1776– 1831* (Stuttgart: 1894); A. V. Nikitenko, *Dnevnik,* 3 vols. (Moscow: 1955–56); and, of course, Herzen's *My Past and Thoughts.*

6. M. Raeff, "The Russian Autocracy and its Officials," *Harvard Slavic Studies,* IV (1957), pp. 77–91; the same, "L'état, le gouvernement et la tradition politique en Russie impériale avant 1861," *Revue d'Histoire Moderne et Contemporaine* (Oct.- Dec., 1962), pp. 296–305.

7. Among high officials of clerical origin were M. M. Speransky and I. I. Martynov in the reign of Alexander I. K. Pobedonostsev, K. Bunge, S. Witte are examples of professonals and technicians who became ministers. Until the last decades of the nineteenth century, most professionals had been educated in ecclesiastical schools.

8. The best-known and most glaring example of such an abuse of authority was the governorship of I. B. Pestel in Siberia (1805–19).

9. Carl Schmitt, "Soziologie des Souveränitätsbegriffes und politische Theologie," in M. Palyi, ed., *Erinnerungsgabe für Max Weber* (München-Leipzig: 1923), Bk. II, pp. 1–35.

10. It is true that Paul I at times made a show of magnanimity and generous understanding; it is possible that he had the welfare of his people at heart (as in his legislation to limit the obligations of the serfs). But he was also most disrespectful of the rights of his subjects. Paul wanted to be benevolent, but he refused to recognize the *rights* of anyone; in other words, the notion of the sanctity and respect of laws was quite alien to him. See also M. V. Klochkov, *Ocherki pravitel'stvennoi deiatel'nosti vremeni Pavla I,* Zapiski istoriko-filologicheskogo fakul'teta imperatorskogo Petrogradskogo universiteta, vol. CXXXII (Petrograd: 1916).

11. A. N. Filippov, "K voprosu o pervoistochnikakh 'zhalovannoi gramoty dvorianstvu'," *Izvestiia Akademii Nauk SSSR,* 6th series, 1926, vol. XX, Nos. 5–6 and 7–8; A. N. Kulomzin, "Pervyi pristup v tsarstvovanii Ekateriny II k sostavleniiu Vysochaishei gramoty dvorianstvu Rossiiskomu," in N. Kalachov, ed. *Materialy dlia istorii russkogo dvorianstva,* fascicle 2 (St. Petersburg: 1885); G. V. Vernadskii, "Manifest Petra III o vol'nosti dvorianskoi i zakonodatel'naia komissiia 1754–1766 gg," *Istoricheskoe Obozrenie,* XX (1915), pp. 51–59.

12. The Russian term *obshchestvo,* as used in historical literature, connotes the educated elite, the public opinion of the enlightened and cultured classes of the nation.

13. It would be possible, though perhaps a little far-fetched, to link the arguments and plans of the Senatorial party with the notions of Prince Kurbskii, the "sworn charter" exacted from Basile Shuiskii, and the "conditions" of the Supreme Privy Council in 1730.

14. O. Hintze, "Typologie der ständischen Verfassungen des Abendlandes," "Weltgeschichtliche Bedingungen der Repräsentativverfassung," *Staat und Verfassung* (Leipzig: 1941).

15. R. Pound, *Interpretations of Legal History* ("Cambridge Studies in English Legal History," Cambridge: 1930).

16. All other projects of the period bore primarily on limited technical aspects of Russia's administration and suggested merely mechanical improvements.

17. In one respect, however, the "technological" approach to administrative reform yielded positive results. The compilation of the Code in 1833, under the chairmanship of Speransky, made it possible at last for the rule of law to prevail in ordinary civil affairs, although it was not until the reforms of the 1860's that an independent and honest judiciary came into being. For a sympathetic summary of the administration of Nicholas I, see N. V. Riasanovsky, *Nicholas I and Official Nationality in Russia, 1825–1855* (University of California Press: 1959), and for a perceptive sketch of Nicholas I as man and ruler (too favorable to its subject, perhaps), see C. de Grunwald, *La vie de Nicolas Ier* (Paris: 1946).

18. Useful information may be found on these associations in J. Walkin, *The Rise of Democracy in Pre-Revolutionary Russia (Political and Social Institutions under the Last Three Czars)* (New York: Frederick A. Praeger, 1962).

EIGHT

Russia's Autocracy and Paradoxes of Modernization

TRADITIONALLY, WESTERNIZATION or modernization is equated with the development of a pluralistic social structure and a widening scope for individual activity based on security of person and property. This view clearly has its roots in the experience of England (and to a lesser extent Holland) and its extensions beyond the seas, especially as it was interpreted by liberal historiography in the 19th century. *Mutatis mutandis* the experience was also shared, so it was believed, by France, though the Ancien Régime and Napoléon had assigned a greater role to the state. And it was hoped that the same pattern might hold true of Italy and the Germanies, though the results were disappointing in the short run. Not surprisingly, Russian liberal historiography, too, argued that Russia's "europeanization" (as it preferred to call the process of westernization or modernization) would lead to social pluralism and political liberalization. As this result failed to materialize, Russia's historical path was perceived as "unnatural" and outward forces were held responsible for impeding a "natural" course.

Was, however, the historical course perceived by liberal historiography so natural after all? Could not the reverse have been equally "natural"? For one need not be mesmerized by an England conceived as *the* natural model. Looked at from another perspective, "europeanization" or "westernization" and "modernization" may themselves prevent the structuring of society and enhance political and cultural repression. What is here suggested is that in Russia the very process of "westernization" helped preserve autocracy and repression. The culturally and politically repressive policies of the imperial system in turn gave rise to the tensions that not only led to revolution, but also created favorable conditions for dictatorship and the perpetuation of the paradox under new forms.

Before proceeding further it is essential to clarify terms. For heuristic purposes, the essence of modernity may be defined as the belief that natural and human resources are well-nigh inexhaustible (are we therefore coming to the end of the "modern" age now?) and that the purpose of social and political institutions is to maximize the creative potential of man so as to enable him to expand forever society's material and spiritual wellbeing. This belief rests on the philosophic presuppositions of the regularity (lawfulness) of all phenomena in nature and that this regularity can be known by man through rational (i. e. scientific) inquiry. On the basis of this rational knowledge, and by exercise of his will, man is able to carry through programs of action that will result in maximizing his creative potential and material resources. Quite obviously these attitudes and beliefs had their roots in the Renaissance and Reformation; in a more immediate sense, however, they achieved such preeminence as to determine the thoughts and actions of European élites in the second half of the 17th century. In the 18th century, an "amendment" was added by the Enlightenment to the effect that the individual's own happiness, as well as his society's welfare, could be increased indefinitely in this manner. In addition, such an increase in material capacity was to be viewed not only as a means for the pursuit and realization of the good life, but it was to become an end in itself. In short, after the 18th century, modernization was completely secularized, without a trace of the spiritual ends that still played a significant role in the 17th and early in the 18th centuries (e. g. Pietism) and "productivity" came to be valued for its own sake (it was the major merit of Socialist thought in the 19th century to reverse this trend and reinstate ulterior spiritual—moral and psychological—ends to the process of material acquisition).

It is important to remember that Russia (i. e. its "Establishment") consciously embarked on the path of westernization, that is modernization, at precisely the time of the triumph of these attitudes in the administrative theories and practices of Cameralism and absolutism, roughly at the end of the 17th century (though there had been earlier attempts in the 16th and more significant efforts from the middle of the 17th century). The significance of this chronology is that the means at the disposal of the Russian polity to implement the goals of modernization were both limited and strongly affected by traditional patterns. Moreover, the techniques of modernization were most effectively elaborated not so much in the Holland and England that had initiated the process, but within the framework of the political and social institutions of the absolute monarchies of continental Europe. In particular it was the German states which provided the institutional and ideological models most directly relevant to the emerging power and ambition of the Tsar. These models may be subsumed under the conception of the well regulated police state, *wohl geordneter Polizeistaat*.

The most striking characteristic of this conception is its reliance on the ruler's (and his assistants') will and therefore on the directive and controlling functions of legislation and administrative institutions. Since the ruler's will—based on his clear conception of the social goal and a rational understanding of the laws of nature—was the driving motor, the system implied direction and coercion in organization and policy. To carry out the ruler's insights and will necessitated the creation of a technically trained and politically devoted corps of officials, and the establishment of orderly and hierarchic bureaucratic institutions acting on the basis of coherent prescriptive laws and regulations. The regulatory and coercive character of the system was qualified only by the political establishment's ability to make use of existing social structures (estates and corporations) and to enlist the creative elements of society for the purposes of its own goals. The system was, therefore, highly constricting wherever the social matrix did not readily permit cooptation, and it could, on the contrary, be stimulating wherever productive elements could be readily enlisted and tapped. This should not surprise us, for the *Polizeistaat* approach contained a built-in paradox or contradiction: its goal was to stimulate and develop the productive potential of society, that is, of the subjects, and this meant emphasising and rewarding the creative energies of individuals. On the other hand, this goal was to be achieved through royal (i. e. state) initiative, bureaucratic direction, and legislative controls, and it was not to upset social stability and political balance. In short, dictation and controls were to stimulate initiative and creativity, while individual productive activity was to be held in check so as not to subvert existing social structures and the harmony and balance of the institutional framework. In the cultural realm the same contradiction may be detected: reliance on reason and science in discovering the mechanisms and laws of nature while insisting on a cultural and religious conformity that were predicted on a belief in the uniformity of human nature and an identity of way of life. In the long run these contradictions spelled the failure of the *Polizeistaat* in achieving its goals, while its very efforts helped develop the forces that led to its subversion and more or less violent replacement by pluralistic and libertarian societies in the 19th century.

It is universally agreed that whatever the antecedents, Peter the Great's reign was the "take-off" period of Russia's westernization or modernization (europeanization as the Russians call it). It is also true, as contemporary scholarship has confirmed, that in his domestic policies Peter applied the notions and techniques of the well ordered police state, and thus also introduced the basic paradoxes of the system. The repressive aspects of his reign are well known and they have found their masterful graphic illustration in Russian art and literature. Unable to coopt existing social structures and traditional institutions and beliefs, Peter set out to destroy them and to replace them with new rational and bureaucratic ones. In so doing he created the modern administrative apparatus of the empire that had to lead society onto the path of full modernization. Yet at the same time he subjected the forces of independent initiative and thought to intolerable controls that stifled their productive potential and creative energies.

Two aspects of Peter's reign deserve brief mention here. To make up for the lack of trained personnel to carry out his innovative policies Peter had to create new cadres. He did so, as is well known, by forcing the nobility (as well as some others, e. g. children of soldiers, clergy, and urban dwellers) into service and subjecting them to a process of intensive cultural westernization. He thus unwittingly planted the seeds of the Russian intelligentsia—the offspring of the Petrine service nobility imbued with Western education and cultural values and dedicated to the service of the community's welfare. These values and dedication were to become the source of a great creative potential, but a potential that was not to be circumscribed and restrained for long by the interests and needs of the state. While in Peter's own times cultural and intellectual dissent originated in traditionalist circles, soon after his death, criticism came from the new intelligentsia whose members chafed at the bit and would not be satisfied with the limits imposed on free rational thought and discourse and the implementation of moral judgments. Eventually, unable to determine the state's policies in favor of their moral concerns, the intelligentsia was driven to an oppositionist stance. Thus the repressive apparatus designed by Peter to cope with the opposition of the traditionalists was turned against the one-time agents of the state and the intellectual spokesmen of modernity. The story is too well known to bear repetition here—let it be merely hinted at through a recitation of its symbolic landmarks: Kantemir, Kheraskov, Novikov and Radishchev, the Decembrists, the "remarkable generation" of the 1840s, the Nihilists, the revolutionaries and the Movement of Liberation.

The other aspect of Peter's reign is perhaps still more significant in our context, even though it is related to the first. The shortage of qualified personnel forced Peter not only to create new cadres of servitors but also to resort to the traditional method of impressing members of various social groups into government service. We may leave out of account here, though in terms of their numbers and the price they paid in human lives they provide the most dramatic instance, the impressment of peasants to build the new capital, to man the new navy and army, and fight the long and costly wars. That this was not accomplished without the use of brutal repressive force on a lavish scale is well known—we only need to recall the savage persecution of the Old Believers who rejected the claims of Peter's state on their loyalty, labor, and resources. More important still was the drafting into state service of other creative and useful groups, especially the clergy and significant segments of the urban population. As a consequence of Peter's use of the Church, the clergy became a closed estate whose traditional functions declined to such a point that it ceased to be a cultural and spiritual force. This led, by the end of the 18th century, to an increase in sectarianism which, because of its socio-political dissident overtones, was to be severely repressed. The clergy's failure to provide cultural leadership resulted in various spiritualists currents attaining great popularity among the élites whose members were thereby still further alienated from the Establishment (e. g. the cases of mysticism and free masonry as exemplified in the career and fate of Novikov, or the reception of romantic *Weltanschauungen* by the generation of the 1840s).

In the case of the urban classes, the service and fiscal obligations imposed by the state resulted in a stifling of their spirit of enterprise and contributed to the undermining of strong institutional or corporate structures ("pouvoirs intermédiares" they might have been) that could have provided a framework for the dynamics of modernization which the government aimed at. The weakness or absence of such structures, by precluding the development of the pluralistic and libertarian aspects of modernization, also permitted the autocracy to outlive its usefulness. In short, the very cameralist techniques and solutions by means of the *Polizeistaat* precluded the development of creative groups and dynamic structures capable of truly maximizing the potential of resources of the vast empire. It also meant an intensification of state controls and repression of society with the usual consequences of cultural dissent and political conflict. Naturally, these tensions had also an important socio-economic dimension, specifically because of the new character of serfdom. The many and various manifestations of this dimension need not be detailed here. Serfdom not only held back Russia's economic and institutional development, it also widened the rift between the educated élites and the state, paving the way to the ultimate clash between "society" (*obshchestvo*) and "régime" (*pravitel'stvo*).

Peter's notions and techniques, modelled on the European absolutist *Polizeistaat*, also proved of great significance with respect to his successors' approach to the multinational character of the Russian empire. Rooted in the intellectual presuppositions of cameralism, the belief in the uniformity of human nature (and its determined social evolution through stages of ways of life) implied a disregard of the specific cultural diversities and traditional peculiarities of the non-Russian peoples in the empire. The aim of government was to russify by imposing an uniform way of life through legal and administrative measures. Naturally this did not go without resistances, so that the imperial administration resorted to repression and physical force. This paved the way for serious conflicts between the national cultural élites and the imperial establishment, which in turn intensified the repressive character of imperial policy, not only in police and administrative matters, but in the domains of language and religion as well. In the 19th century, more particularly in its second half, the repressive policies towards the nationalities not only hampered the success of modernization on an imperial scale, but also exacerbated social and political antagonisms. These put a drain on the administrative and police capacities of the imperial polity, as well as precluding the development of the non-Russian nationalities' creative potential within the framework of their own social and institutional structures.

If the preceding observations have validity, they provide an explanation for the inherent—*System immanent*, as contemporary German social scientists would put it—limitations on all reform efforts by the imperial régime. They may also offer a key to the antinomies, or paradoxes, of the dynamic pattern of the empire's public life, from the middle of the 18th century onwards to its final demise in 1917. And beyond this date, I would argue, they also contributed to the peculiar history and evolution of the subsequent revolutionary régimes.

We are confronted by a double set of paradoxes: First, the personal authority of the ruler (and his helpmates), essential to the voluntaristic aspect of the process of modernization, conflicts with the equally strong necessity of routinizing political authority so as to secure the regular (*zakonomernye*) and rational aspects of modernization as an ongoing process. The second paradox is that the state and its repressive apparatus are used both to promote and to set limits to the development of groups, classes, or estates that provide security of person and property to the creative elements of society. We have mentioned earlier the cultural dimension of this paradox and we need not repeat or elaborate on it here. Thus the ultimate consequence of the conscious efforts at modernization, or europeanization, which became the dominant theme of Russian public life and state policy, was a self-limiting situation: in order to go forward with modernization the autocracy had to be maintained, and this in turn prevented the development of those very social and institutional structures that were the *sine qua non* of progress. Let us briefly illustrate these general observations by a few salient aspects of Russian history, beginning with the reign of Catherine II when the basic policy orientations became more conscious and the contradictions of the development more obvious.

The second paradox may be more easily treated first. Peter I had already realized the necessity of guaranteeing the individual and corporate security of the productive elements of society. His efforts included not only the granting of property privileges to select groups and individuals, but above all attempts at creating a self-policing and economically secure urban estate. He failed in the latter endeavor, for not only was the urban population itself inadequately prepared for such a role, but the state would not free it from the service obligations it had imposed. As Kizevetter has conclusively shown (whatever the other weaknesses of his argument), these service obligations prevented the development of an energetic and autonomous urban entrepreneurial class. As to the nobility, even though its members slowly acquired a greater degree of autonomy and protection of person and property after the death of the Tsar Reformer, they too failed to overcome the limitations of their bondage to the state.

The disadvantages of this state of affairs to the process of modernization became quite obvious to the Russian élites by the middle of the 18th century. The government of Catherine II, therefore, undertook to sponsor through legislation the formation of genuine estates in Russia. In the opinion of the empress and her advisors, this would provide the necessary security of person and property to all creative elements of Russian society, while preserving its static equilibrium. The legislative effort along these lines culminated in the issuance of the charters of the Nobility and to the Towns in 1785, and the drafting of a Charter to the State Peasantry which, however, remained in the government's archives. The significant fact, however, is that in the final analysis, the local and corporate autonomies implied in the Charters did not develop into genuine self-administration and corporate identity. On the contrary, both in the towns and in the country, the actual police and executive powers—not to mention the judicial—remained in the hands of the imperial bureaucracy and the personal representatives of the autocrat. Although it was granted some administrative functions on the district and "county" levels, even the nobility did not develop the structures of genuine local self-government. In part this was due to the nobles' service traditions and state orientation, as well as to their gravitating to the cities where they could enjoy the cultural benefits of europeanization. But to a still larger measure it was due to the government's refusal to let the local "noble societies" mature, and to its limiting the authority of the elected administrators while luring the best local elements into the central bureaucracy.

A similar pattern may be detected as the government bestirred itself, in the reign of Alexander II, to foster the development of classes in the contemporary sense. The fate of the zemstvo institutions (as one aspect of this process) are too well known to be commented upon here. A class of genuinely independent peasants was both fostered and impeded in its growth by the act of emancipation of 1861, since the preservation of the commune and of a discriminatory legal status precluded the development of the peasant class that had been initiated by the statute of 19 February. The situation was no different with respect to the urban classes, in particular the proletariat: the consequences of both the state's protection and limitations defined the pattern of events in the cities at the turn of the 19th century. In a similar vein the development of professional groups and corporations was at the same time encouraged by the government and circumscribed within very narrow limits. Such was the case of the legal profession after the 1860s. Still more dramatic and pregnant with serious sociopolitical consequences were the frustrations engendered by the contradictory policies with respect to the universities, the rights of faculty and students, throughout the 19th century. The same ambivalence may be observed in the political sphere. Even the modest efforts to enlist the participation of society in informing the government of the country's condition and needs were ultimately negated by centralized supervision and control. Most important of all, it made impossible the substitution of the autonomous application of law for the personal supervision and interference of bureaucrats. A *Rechtsstaat,* however limited its liberalism, was precluded in Russia, and thus the legal guarantee of continuing and full modernization was never realized.

The preceding illustrations of the second paradox we have stated earlier are also explanatory elements of our first paradox. If indeed the approach of the cameralist *Polizeistaat* prevented the full development of autonomous and self administering estates, classes, corporations or professional groups, then it becomes understandable that the position of the autocracy was preserved intact almost to the end. The pursuit of a maximizing of the polity's creative potential and resources is viewed as an act of will and deliberate planning; as such it is best initiated by him who has both an understanding and knowledge of the rational laws of development and the energy (i. e. force or authority) to secure their proper working. Such a person is the *roi philosophe* (and his assistants), or in Russia, modelling himself on Peter the Great, the sovereign emperor—the autocrat who implements this approach by virtue of the personal character of his absolute political authority. Indeed, the traditional personalized role of authority was eminently suited to bring about modernization in the face of the reluctance and opposition of vested interests, ignorance, prejudice and obscurantism. And so it was that throughout the 18th and 19th centuries in Russia practically all innovation and westernization was carried through the leadership and initiative of the autocrat (and his immediate aides). Naturally this too implied repression of dissent and opposition.

Of course, the autocrat could not carry out his purpose without the help of officials or a bureaucracy. But this bureaucracy was conceived as an extension of the ruler, not as the institutionalization of means to implement rationality and regularity, as was the case in the ideal *Rechtsstaat.* To secure and maintain such regularity, society had to be structured in such way that its constituent parts behave according to predictable and rational patterns. In other words, it presupposed autonomous and self-administering groups that, as we have seen, were not allowed to develop in Russia. Using the personal character of political authority as the framework for its *modus operandi,* the bureaucracy prevented the free working of laws and rules, and in so doing, perpetuated the abuses and arbitrariness that necessarily gave rise to repressive policies. Intensified modernization—as proven again by the experience of the 1860s—became possible only because of the initiative and leadership assumed by the autocracy and its loyal bureaucracy. Such leadership in turn implied repression of all opposition and the maintenance of full control and supervision by the state which worked at cross purposes with the trends initiated by the reforms themselves. This pattern, rather than the ensuing economic difficulties, explains to my mind the limited nature of the reforms and the unforeseen dilemmas brought about by their implementation.

The progressive elements in society and bureaucracy understood the situation perfectly well. They always turned to and relied upon the autocrat to bring about the improvements and reforms they believed necessary for further modernization. The Miliutin brothers exemplified this orientation, using the Tsar to carry through the "great reforms" of the 1860s. And so did Witte and Stolypin, who both believed that the survival of a strong autocracy was a prerequisite for successful modernization. Of course, under the circumstances they were willing also to resort to force to break resistance, from whatever quarter, to compel "society" to accept the consequences of their innovations.

What escaped the attention and understanding of these statesmen—who were following in the path of Peter I and imperial advisors of the 18th and early 19th centuries—was that their appeal to the personal authority of the ruler itself set limits to the success of their enterprise. Not only did the use of force to repress opposition provoke violent discontent among the more articulate members of society, foreclosing their cooperation; it also ran counter to the cultural goals of modernization. More important yet, in the long run, was the limitation set to the development of a structured society and its active involvement in public life. This political myopia is best illustrated by S. Witte's well known dislike of the zemstvos which, after all, were the most amenable and potentially most effective supporters of his ultimate goal of Russia's economic and social modernization. Seen in this light, his ambivalent behavior in 1905–1906 comes as no surprise. Stolypin's behavior points in the same direction. Like Witte and so many reformers before him, he, too, thought that the autocrat's support and power alone would carry through his grand design of restructuring Russian society. He did not realize that even the most conservative social and economic forces, once organized, would want to play an autonomous role and might not be controlled. That is, unless he resorted to force and put them down, thus destroying them after encouraging their emergence. The polarity or antagonism between society and autocracy (e. g. the state) could not be resolved, for the Petrine model of westernization could not be abandoned, and it prevented the development of social and institutional structures that could underpin the state's willful drive for modernity. Finally, the dynamics of successful modernization precluded the preservation of the role of the *roi philosphe*, a fact that had been experienced in the West earlier.

The conclusion we reach is that revolution was inescapable since the opposite forces of state and society could not be reconciled—in the final analysis, they worked at cross purposes. But the revolution, which indeed occurred in 1917, acquired its particular physiognomy for having been so long delayed. Paradoxically, it was a consequence of the autocracy's success in initiating and carrying through the first stages of modernization and its effectiveness in preventing the development of a pluralistic structuring of society. When the imperial Establishment was swept away (it literally vanished overnight) there was revealed an inadequately structured and economically underdeveloped society which needed yet to be shaped. To my mind, this largely accounts for the failure of the February Revolution and the Bolsheviks' success in seizing power in October 1917.

Nor surprisingly the new regime, too, found itself confronted by the traditional dilemma which Peter had first experienced and tried to resolve. Modernization from above meant the coercive setting of limits to the development and structuring of social forces and institutions. The limits and paradoxes of this situation, in a contemporary revolutionary context, became glaringly apparent in the course of the New Economic Policy. No wonder that a "second revolution" was deemed necessary—and this revolution, carried out by Stalin, reproduced many of the traits and dynamics of earlier problems and solutions. Nor has the basic problem disappeared as yet. As modernization is successfully promoted by the state, and the implications of its cultural and social dynamics become apparent, the political arm intervenes to set bounds and preserve a static equilibrium. This again entails dissidence and revival of repression. *Eppur si muove?*

NINE

Patterns of Russian
Imperial Policy Toward
the Nationalities

RUSSIA WAS A MULTINATIONAL empire. That seems obvious to us now, but it was not always so apparent either to the imperial government or to its subjects. Not until Peter the Great introduced it was the official adjective *rossiiskii* used by the government in referring to the "Russian" Empire. *Rossiiskii*, as distinguished from the traditional *russkii*, was derived from the Latin and was supposed to point to the fact that the state fashioned by Peter I was not exclusively Great Russian in composition.

We tend to view the "question of nationalities,"—the relationship of national minorities to the larger unit and its authorities—in terms of our twentieth-century vantage point; that is, through a mental set which is a legacy of what may be called the revolution of national consciousness. We thus run great danger of making an anachronistic analysis of the conditions and attitudes that antedated this revolution.

If the multinational character of the Russian Empire is to be properly understood in its historical perspective,[1] several aspects of the situation must be taken into consideration. These remarks will concentrate upon the period during which basic attitudes and policies toward the nationalities were formed—from about the late sixteenth to the middle of the nineteenth centuries. After this, there was still one more Russian expansion, into Central Asia, but it came along with rapidly growing industrialization and social modernization and partook rather of the Western style of new colonialism.

The first difficulty confronting a historian who wishes to analyze the evolution of attitudes and policies toward the nationalities in the Empire before the middle of the nineteenth century is the paucity of both historiography and published sources. Russian historiography is overwhelmingly "Great Russian" in orientation and barely takes into account the multinational character of the political entity with whose history it deals. Even one of Russia's foremost historians—V. O. Kliuchevskii—hardly acknowledged the fact that Russia comprised a multinational imperial polity. He did speak, it is true, of the early Slavic conquest and assimilation of Finnish tribes, but this is almost prehistory.[2] The historiographies of most nationalities are very recent, if we exclude medieval chronicles or epics, and have their obvious limitations in narrowness of focus. Understandably a product of the revolution of national consciousness we spoke of earlier, they often are so extremely chauvinistic as to be of little use. Finally, histories written in the Soviet period, although valuable for much factual detail, present historiographical and critical problems that are heightened by the ideological and political touchiness of the subject.[3] With respect to the publication of relevant sources, some progress has been made in recent decades; but there is still a shortage of documentation concerning political aspects of the problem.[4] Besides this, many recent source collections issued by the academies of sciences of the Soviet republics have been published only in the nationality languages.

A major factor in determining policies and attitudes of the officials toward nationalities is the time of the conquest or incorporation of non-Russian territory and the circumstances of the non-Russian populations. The imperial expansion of the Muscovite state began in the sixteenth century when one might have thought of differences both inside and outside it in religion, in family structure, in way of life, but not of nationalities. Neither Muscovites nor others were conscious of nationality in any sense that comes close to our modern usage. Moreover, the means of control available to the government of the czars were quite different from those of a modern state: conquest merely meant the extension of the sovereignty which the ruler exercised through his household or court (*dvor*). He depended on a small number of military servitors to keep control over the new territory. For this reason he used existing institutions—particularly family structures—to exercise and maintain his authority, resorting to direct interference only in case of necessity. Conquest in the sixteenth century meant only the end of independent international status, but it did not necessarily entail a noticeable change in the social and economic organization of the conquered people. Unlike the lands that were forming the Habsburg Empire, for example, at approximately the same time, the territories conquered by Muscovy were little more than weak, loose political associations of traditional clans and families, bound merely by a common way of life. Moreover, in contrast to western Europe, there was no strong feudal tradition either in Muscovy or the newly acquired territories and, consequently, little respect for political autonomy, juridical separateness, and regionalism, those very elements so essential to the constitution of the monarchies and empires of the sixteenth and seventeenth centuries in the

West. France, Spain, Burgundy, and Austria had expanded their boundaries by extending their monarch's suzerainty over principalities and lands that retained their own rulers, laws, and customs; this path was not available to Moscow. Even the absorption of the appanage principalities (*udely*) had been based on the tradition of common family authority and succession. This explains the almost immediate integration of the appanage lords into the retinue and household of the Grand Duke of Muscovy and the disappearance of the political distinctiveness of the principality.

There was also the quite obvious factor of geography. The beginnings of imperial expansion, meaning the bringing of non-Russian, even more of non-Slavic and non-Christian people, under the sway of Moscow, took place on a territory that was "open" and on which the sparse population had at all times been quite mobile. It was the stage of the perennial confrontation between the world of the nomadic cattle raiser and that of agricultural settlers. Many features of the conquest, as well as of the pattern of eventual absorption, have their roots in this basic geographic and social circumstance.

Conquest, for instance, was frequently only the continuing process of expanding settlement carried on by peasants or military colonists interested in acquiring more land and in securing their safety from raids launched by the nomads of the open steppe.[5] Undoubtedly there was a certain hypocritical sophistry in Prince Alexander M. Gorchakov's note of 1864, in which he explains why Russia had to push further into Central Asia: the settled communities of peasants have to be defended against the nomads; in so doing, control is imposed upon the neighboring nomadic tribe; but then one is confronted with the next nomadic people, who have to be subdued in order to provide security, and so on. This was obviously a poor justification for Russian colonial expansion into Central Asia. But it contained an important grain of truth if taken as describing the pattern of expansion accomplished in earlier periods.

Two major dimensions of the process of imperial expansion and of the incorporation of national minorities should be clearly kept in mind for purposes of analysis, even though they were frequently inextricably intertwined in reality: one is territorial and political, the other socioeconomic and cultural.

Beginning with the territorial and political dimension, it is evident at the start that the building of the empire was an almost unnoticed follow-up to the so-called gathering of Russian lands under the dominion of the Grand Duke of Moscow. In a sense, perhaps, the "gathering" itself may be described as a process of expansion, certainly so with respect to the northwestern territories such as Novgorod and Pskov. The line between the "gathering" in of lands that had once belonged together and were then dispersed and this "imperial expansion" is a rather thin one. The significant step beyond a "gathering of Russian lands" was made by the first czar, Ivan IV, with the conquest of the khanates of Kazan and Astrakhan, which secured the entire course of the Volga and allowed the czar to push beyond it. With Ivan's blessing and permission, the Stroganovs, salt and fur merchants, hired mercenary cossacks to secure passage across the Urals and begin the conquest of Siberia.

The push beyond the Volga found its natural conclusion when, in the middle of the seventeenth century, the vastness of Siberia had been crossed from the Ural Mountains to the Pacific Ocean. At about the same time (1654) we witness the incorporation of the Ukraine, first as a protectorate and then as a rapidly integrated entity in the Czardom of Muscovy. This was followed by a more limited advance, albeit of great political and military consequence, in the Baltic provinces during the reign of Peter the Great, an advance that took place according to the prevailing rules of military and diplomatic acquisition. A very sizeable extension of the empire's territory occurred in the late eighteenth and early nineteenth centuries with the conquest of the shores of the Black Sea and the Crimea, the partitions of Poland, the incorporation of Finland, and the beginning of a penetration into the Caucasus. Finally, the colonial acquisition of Central Asia took place in the second half of the nineteenth century.

Let us turn to the methods of acquisition and incorporation, first leaving aside the modern military and diplomatic means which were relevant only for the Baltic provinces, Finland, and the partitions of Poland. The traditional way in which areas were acquired and integrated seemed to be of prime importance in setting the framework for the nationality problems in Imperial Russia. In this process, conquest or acquisition was the first step, incorporation the second, and assimilation the final goal. Traditional patterns developed in the early sixteenth century remained operative throughout the succeeding centuries through the so-called modernizing revolution of Peter the Great, and even into the nineteenth century. For the first step—acquisition— the most significant and characteristic of the several ways used may be called that of social and political pressure (which did not exclude the use of military force, either directly or as a threat). Not always quite consciously, sometimes at the invitation of one of the parties concerned, Moscow would attempt to enroll the services and loyalty of an influential segment of the non-Russian society. This could be done by suggesting that they move away to new lands where they would be granted privileges and estates such as the "Czardom" of Kasimov; or individuals would be attracted into the service of Moscow by appropriate promises of rewards. Even after moving away, these people retained ties to their original society and could be of use in undermining it like a fifth column. In itself, their departure weakened their homeland, especially since they frequently constituted the more active, ambitious, and energetic military leadership. The eventual conquest of the territory then became a foregone conclusion. It may be noted that this pattern had been developed by Moscow in the course of its "gathering" of appanage lands. Such was largely the case of Kazan and Astrakhan, whose resistance had been undermined, not only by internal factional disputes, but also by the departure of military leaders and servitors in the reigns of Ivan III and Basil III, long before Ivan IV undertook the final conquest.[6] The practice of luring away military personnel prevailed in the sixteenth and seventeenth centuries, but it persisted into the post-Petrine period and was used to good advantage with respect to some Siberian groups and in Central Asia.[7] By then, of course, the power of Russia was so overwhelming that luring elites into its fold was not difficult, and it is hard to think of it as a repetition of the same method that had been employed in the early sixteenth century.

But military groups alone were not the object of such a lure. In the eighteenth and nineteenth centuries the Russian government's ability to persuade economically influential groups to move away from home undermined the local power of resistance and turned the take-over into a military promenade. This was the case of the Crimea in the 1780s. The government of Catherine II persuaded Greeks, Armenians, Georgians, and other Christians, who played a key role in Crimean trade and agriculture, to emigrate from the peninsula to the newly conquered shores of the Black Sea. This sapped the social as well as economic stability of the Crimean Tatar khanate that had been set up by the peace of Kuchuk Kainarji; the take-over followed automatically and easily.[8] In the Caucasus too, the government of St. Petersburg manipulated social groups that were in conflict with one another for religious as well as economic reasons and thereby softened any power of resistance to the conquest.[9]

Pressures of a political character, backing one contender to the throne against another, playing off one faction or clan against another, are commonly found in all forms of colonial conquests. The Russians used them whenever feasible, on their own initiative or at the request of one of the warring parties. Sometimes the initiative would come from political leadership trying to escape domination by another neighbor (one wonders how free such an initiative then was). This was why the Ukrainian cossacks turned to Moscow to save themselves from Poland. Protection might be asked, or offered, to assist a small Christian land against a threatening non-Christian neighbor, as it frequently was in the Caucasus. Finally, cultural pressures could take political form: appeal to religious solidarity—in the case of the Ukraine for protection against Polish Roman Catholicism, or in the Armenian lands against Persians and Turks. This act of selecting one means over the other, and taking advantage of one opportunity as against another, preconditioned the manner of the take-over and the initial relationship between the newly incorporated people and the imperial government.

But what was the purpose of expansion? An answer to this question, too, may offer a clue to the nature of the take-over and the resulting relationships. There was first the desire for more agricultural land. It led to peasant settlement beyond the state's borders, either with or without the consent of the government. At times the government moved reluctantly to protect Russian peasants who settled on or beyond the border; at other times the state's military initiative in securing a frontier led peasants to flock into the area. Because peasants do not leave records, and as this side of the Russian state's activity is poorly illuminated by our sources, it is difficult to know exactly when the peasants were used by the government and when, on the contrary, the farmers forced the officials' hand. It has been convincingly shown that both took place, at times almost simultaneously and interchangeably.[10] This was certainly rue of the territory between the Volga and Kama rivers and in the Urals, and frequently also in the south and in Siberia.

Obviously, considerations of security frequently motivated expansion. On the open steppe frontier, military security, by whatever means, was considered of paramount concern. It was at the origins of the expansion into the southern steppe and the Caucasus, and it played not an insignificant role in the advance into the steppes bordering on the Caspian Sea and on southern Siberia that paved the way to the conquest of Central Asia. Rarely, however, do we find the expectation of gain from commerce and the security of trade as a major factor in expanding the territorial boundaries of the Empire. Sometimes the lure of mineral wealth would lead to conquest, or at least penetration, as in the Urals and Siberia.

Much was written, especially in the nineteenth century, about the desire to protect or spread Russian Orthodoxy as a factor of imperial expansion. Naturally, this could also have its defensive side, too (in the Caucasus, for example), although to a modern ear the notion sounds rather hollow. There is practically no evidence of religious missionary zeal as the direct purpose of expansion, although protection of Russian clergy did produce intervention in a few cases which in turn might lead to conquest, as in the Caucasus and Central Asia. There was no attempt before conquest on the part of the Russian imperial government to spread Orthodoxy or to assist its missionary enterprises. This does not mean, of course, that religion was not used for purposes of diplomacy, but this is another story. The government was even reluctant to take advantage of opportunities offered by religious affinity to expand the state's boundaries. Hence, the hesitations before extending protection to the Ukrainian cossacks or in responding to the appeals of Armenians and Georgians. But of course, the religious factor is not to be disregarded altogether, especially since it offered opportunities to local governors and commanders to extend their authority, notwithstanding the absence of direct instructions from St. Petersburg. Catherine II used the argument of her duty to protect coreligionaries in creating the conditions that led to the partitions of Poland.

What were the consequences deriving from these methods and purposes of expansion? In the first place, there was little or no awareness—especially in the earlier periods—of Russia's imperial extension. Because expansion had taken place gradually and had largely been accompanied by the agricultural settlement of Russian peasants, Russian society remained unaware of the state's having become a multinational empire. The impression was created that it had taken place elementally, naturally, through people's movements and not through conscious policy on the part of the government. Thus, the crucial period was not that of conquest but that of incorporation, of absorption into the fabric of Russia's policy. Having established their political suzerainty, the Russians believed that this was not enough, that the new territory had to become part and parcel of the Russian land and that the new populations must live according to the same social and economic pattern as did the Russian people. In the absence of a strong tradition of localism and of administrative and political separateness or autonomy even for territories inhabited by Russians (consider the brutal and rapid extinction of the particularism of Tver and Novgorod in the fifteenth and sixteenth centuries), there was a strong urge to impose administrative unity on the new territory. There was no tradition—as there was in the West—of coalescing different historical units and politico-juridical systems without destroying their particularism: the kind of feudal or protofeudal "federalism" that had helped to create Burgundy, France, Spain, Austria. Once a territory was under effective control, the almost automatic reaction of Russian administrators was to extend to it the social and administrative arrangements prevailing in the Russian provinces. This was often done without any regard for the conditions which might make such an extension undesirable or even feasible. For example, when in 1775 Catherine II promulgated a new statute for provincial administration which included the participation of elective officials from among the local nobility, she automatically extended it to Siberia (allowing a few years for transition) without reflecting that Siberia had no nobility. Clearly, one of the essential elements of the reform could not be implemented there.

The frequent coincidence of conquest and the expansion of Russian peasant settlement and administration resulted in a great deal of ethnic and administrative confusion. Indigenous groups mingled with the Russians that had moved in, and transfers of population resulted in linguistic and cultural mixtures within the same administrative unit. This applied primarily to conditions of expansion eastward to Kazan, Siberia, the Urals, and the southeastern steppes. There were some variations on this pattern which, however, did not change the picture too much. For instance, in the Ukraine the Cossack Host managed to preserve its autonomy and organization at least until 1709, and it even lingered on in a limited way until 1775. In 1709, as a consequence of Hetman Mazepa's siding with Charles XII at Poltava, the autonomy of the Dnieper Cossack Host was drastically curtailed. In 1775—following the Pugachev rebellion—Catherine II abolished the Zaporozhian *Sich* altogether. But here too, though slower, the process was similar, in that it aimed for and resulted in eventual absorption of the conquered people into and sociocultural integration with central Russia.[11]

In the Caucasus, linguistic and religious antagonisms had been part of the process of conquest, so that the government had to take them into account;

and, in the first stages at least, the local population was allowed greater autonomy than those elsewhere in preserving its peculiarities. But this policy did
not aim at preserving differences; rather, it acted merely as a political expedient to speed up the conquest and eventual incorporation by dealing first with
the local non-Russian leadership on political terms. A similar pattern was to
prevail in the conquest of Central Asia in the latter half of the nineteenth century.

Very different, of course, were the conquest and incorporation of the Baltic
provinces, Finland, and Poland. Because the original acquisition had been accomplished through military conquest ratified by international treaty, the imperial government began by guaranteeing a special status to the newly conquered lands and by promising to respect the autonomy and privileges of the
local ruling classes. This was the case in the Baltic provinces and in Finland.[12]
The policy was less clear in Poland, where the occupation occurred in several
stages. The first partition of Poland (1772) gave to Russia territories which
were claimed to be "Russian," and which Moscow had been prevented from
"gathering in" in the sixteenth century. Therefore, the Russian administration and juridical system were introduced here quite rapidly, allowing only for
a very brief period of adjustment. But the Baltic and Finnish model were followed in the so-called Congress Kingdom of Poland, established under a personal royal union by the treaty of Vienna in 1815, until the revolts of 1830
and 1863 led to the abolition of all special statutes and privileges.

The acquisition of such totally alien territories under promise of respect toward traditional privileges and autonomies created a serious problem for the
imperial government. It undermined the concept of the unitary nature of the
Russian state and also raised questions as to the character of the sovereign,
who, indeed, was a constitutional Grand Duke of Finland and King of Poland
while remaining the autocratic Emperor of All Russia. The government,
therefore, explicitly denied the existence of the problem, for to recognize it
might have led to envisioning a federal structure for the empire. This, however, was anathema for historical as well as political reasons—and not only to
the ruler and his officials, but also to a large part of Russian "public opinion"—because the specter of a return to the appanage divisions seems to have
been an ever-haunting theme. As if this were not complicated enough, the
preservation of special statuses and privileges raised the question of identifying the genuine historical tradition of those lands that should be preserved.
After all, here was a peasantry (Latvian, Estonia, Finnish) ruled by foreign
nobilities: German in the Baltic provinces, Swedish in Finland. Preserving the
privileges of these nobilities meant perpetuating the conquest of long-de-
feated or vanished powers and their descendants' subjection of the peasantry.
Would it not be more advantageous for the Russian state to secure the loyalty
of indigenous populations, who would benefit by being drawn into the orbit
of often higher Russian culture and greater material prosperity at the expense

of the privileges held by the foreign nobility dominating them? This is what the Russian government tried to accomplish in the second half of the nineteenth century, not without success in the Baltic provinces, but with little luck in Finland. In acting in this manner and disregarding the "psychological" dimension of national consciousness while taking into consideration only legal forms, the imperial rulers unwittingly helped to promote nationalism among the non-Russian peasantry, adding to the explosiveness of the nationality question in the twentieth century.

While our sources permit the reconstruction of the steps by which the empire was created and territories integrated into the Russian administrative framework, it is not so easy to trace the process of cultural and social integration. Available documentation is spotty, and many of the sources simply do not provide the answers to the kind of questions we are interested in. Yet, an attempt must be made, even if only a few general remarks on the dynamics of the process may be hazarded at this point.

The imperial expansion of Russia started in the middle of the sixteenth century and first moved east and southward. From its beginnings it involved the conquest of non-Christian, nomadic societies and people who were socially and economically less complex than contemporary Russia, less developed not only in terms of a western European standard but also in terms of contemporary Muscovy. The difference, to be sure, was rather slight in some cases. Thus, it has been suggested that, with respect to the khanates of Kazan and Astrakhan, Muscovy was only continuing the tradition and practices of the "political system of the steppe" as one of the successor states of the Golden Horde.[13] Of course, some of the people or societies conquered by Muscovy may, like Central Asia in the Middle Ages, have had a very high and brilliant culture in the remote past. What is at issue here is their condition at the time of conquest. Therefore, feelings of religious and cultural superiority on the part of the Russians were unmistakable, and quite strong as early as the sixteenth and seventeenth centuries. This sense of superiority, giving rise to self-righteous justifications of the conquest, though historical, legal, and religious arguments were advanced too, was reinforced by what often seemed a supine acquiescence on the part of people who were absorbed. Such passivity also made it possible to take advantage of the split between the upper and lower classes within the alien populations. The upper classes, heads of clans, families, former military leaders of the khans, were wooed by the Russians and converted into instruments of Moscow's administrative and judicial control. This happened in Kazan, Siberia, and the Caucasus. It is also fair to say that these indigenous leaders were attracted by the superior wealth of the czar, as well as by the opportunities that incorporation into the Russian ruling class might offer. The example of those of their compatriots who had been lured away before the conquest also served as an incentive.

The Russian social and political system made it possible to translate that wooing and attraction into concrete material and social, as well as political, benefits in favor of the wooed. The Russian nobility constituted a service class whose ranks were relatively open to newcomers. Anyone from the upper levels of the conquered societies, by taking up service, could acquire the rank (*chin*) which would put him on a footing of equality, or at least provide this opportunity for his children, with his Russian counterpart within the framework of the dominant "Establishment." This might be accomplished by merely carrying on the traditional leadership role within the clan or tribe, but only as an agent of the Russian administration. Social and cultural Russification provided an additional avenue for acquiring a status of equality with the Russian service class. Thus, the alien leaders sent their children to Russian schools, paving the way for their eventual Russification, acquisition of ranks, estates and even serfs. In so doing these leaders became virtually assimilated, in style of life and economic interest, with the Russian service nobility. This was true not only of the descendants of the ruling families of Tatar and Caucasian principalities, but also of their retainers, as well as of the chieftains of many a Siberian tribe or people.[14]

This process helps to explain in turn the greater difficulty experienced by the Russian "Establishment" in absorbing those elites that were not inferior to the Russians, possibly even superior to them, by contemporary standards. This was, for instance, the case of the German nobility and bourgeoisie in the Baltic provinces. Their integration—such as it was—followed a somewhat different pattern. Since their educational level was distinctly superior to that of the average Russian in government service in the eighteenth century, they could do well in the Russian military and civil services, rising to high positions. Having done so, such aliens became a part of the cosmopolitan milieu of the court. They were considered members of the Russian elite even though they retained their own culture, language, and religion, as well as their traditional role of local leadership in their province of origin. Their political loyalty, however, belonged unquestionably to the Russian Empire. They were truly a bilingual and bicultural segment of the imperial political, military, and intellectual elite.[15] Another illustration, showing opposite results, is supplied by the Jews. Incorporated into the empire at the partition of Poland, they did not feel, and were not, culturally inferior to the Russians. But to join the Russian governing elite would have required them to abandon their traditional way of life, their religion—and they could not abandon their separateness. The Jewish policy of the imperial government before the 1870s, when it became openly discriminatory and oppressive, reflected its ambivalence and bewilderment at such a situation. The government wanted to attract the Jews into Russian society, allowing them to retain their religion. But only on condition that the Jews abandon their way of life, their customs, everything that in a secular sense differentiated and separated them from Russian society. But the

Jews would not accept this, since to do so was to desert their religion. The government was incapable of appreciating the close connection between religion and the way of life—Alexander I's attempts at liberal "emancipation" and acceptance of them into Russian society failed. In disgust, Nicholas I embarked on forced Russification and brutal repression.[16]

Economic conflicts that existed or developed between the Russian people and the outsiders also hampered the latter's social integration into the empire. Obviously the major instance of such economic conflict was provided by the struggle for land between cattle-raising nomads and Russian peasant settlers. The imperial government, too, was anxious to have the nomads settle down and till the soil, since, in its opinion, settled agriculture was the hallmark of a higher level of civilization. This was a common eighteenth-century Enlightenment notion based on the belief in a universal pattern of cultural progress leading upward from hunter and fisherman to nomad cattle raiser, and finally to the settled agriculturalist and trader. The government considered it important to assist in this evolution. All those who were not yet peasants or otherwise settled should be helped to adopt this higher, better way of life. We have here a conscious policy of assimilation and Russification by way of promoting a uniform way of life throughout the empire. Reports of local governors in the Volga and Ural areas, as well as in Siberia, confirm that they conceived it their duty to Russify the tribesmen by transforming hunters and nomads into settled peasants. The same effort would also facilitate administration, since the system of laws and regulations applicable to Russian peasants would then automatically be extended to the non-Russians who had taken up agricultural pursuits. Even in the course of writing down the traditional oral law of the tribes (for instance, during the codification of Siberian local customary law in the 1820s and 1830s), Russian officials would introduce new concepts which Russified such law and made it into an instrument of social and economic transformation along the lines we have been considering here.[17]

In this instance, too, the traditional leaders and the rich were the first to be persuaded to adopt the Russian pattern and then help to bring their fellow nomads along. To this end the tribal elite were offered rewards of money, land, medals, even ranks, and they were confirmed by the government in their position of authority. In cases like that of the Buryats the policy worked. But once a nomadic population had settled down, Russian law and administration were extended to it, and it found itself absorbed into the dominant Russian world, albeit in a lower status. The poor, who could not easily change their way of life, were disregarded by Russian officials; retaining the old patterns of beliefs and traditions, they came thus to be separated from their own natural leadership as well as from the Russian establishment. Little wonder that when a new leadership arose from their ranks it not only spoke up for their old traditions but also rejected completely the system that had resulted in the isolation, poverty, and backwardness of their fellows. The emerging leaders confronted the imperial government, and its Russified elite, with the demand that it recognize their "national" identity—a demand for which the establishment was psychologically unprepared and with which it could not cope.

In the early years of the nineteenth century romantic notions of historicism, respect for tradition, and the uniqueness of every culture and society led to a recognition in Russia that the transition from one way of life to another may follow different patterns. The goal remained the same—administrative and social homogeneity throughout the empire—but the methods became more flexible, gradualistic, and took into consideration local conditions and traditions. Mikhail Speransky, when a government official, tried to strike a practical compromise which balanced the recognition of separateness with the ultimate aim of uniformity. He was moderately successful with the Siberian tribes, whose organization was simple, numbers small, and economy poor. It proved almost impossible to apply this policy consistently among the more complex, advanced areas of the Caucasus, Finland, and Central Asia.

The goal of social, economic, and political uniformity remained constant in the policy of the imperial government with respect to non-Russian lands and people throughout the pre-1917 period. At no point was it conscious or aware of the dynamic force of nationalism and nationality. Yet, the Russian government did not aim at eradicating or destroying nations and nationalities.[18] It simply felt that their way of life should change in a process of natural evolution which their membership in the empire could speed up and help along. That this might at the same time lead to the destruction of traditional customs, language, or sense of identity which people held very dear did not seem to enter into governmental expectations.

True, some of the people in Siberia, in some areas of the Caucasus, and along the upper Volga valley had no clear sense of nationality or what could be called a genuine national consciousness. Their passive acquiescence to Russian domination rendered the government even more impervious to the claims and opposition of those people that did have a strong sense of national identity and who were not willing to give up their traditional ways and values. As long as it was only a question of changing ways of life there was some hope of enlisting the support of the upper classes. But once national consciousness had begun to spread and take firm hold, this limited goal, too, became impracticable. Faced by the rejection of its drive for uniformity in way of life, the government turned to an active policy of Russification in the second half of the nineteenth century, just at the time when self-awareness was beginning to take hold of the nationalities. The stubbornness and myopia expressed in this policy paved the way for the mass disaffection of the nationalities that proved a very strong element in the collapse of the imperial regime.

Of the major factors which determined the patterns of Russian imperial policy, time—chronology—is the first to be kept in mind. In the earlier stages of expansion (sixteenth and seventeenth centuries), traditional means were used to conquer and integrate the new territories into the Russian polity. This was a continuation of the "gathering in" of lands claimed by the Grand Duke and Czar of Moscow as rightfully his own.[19] The process of incorporation, too, followed methods suggested by the patrimonial (*votchinnyi*) conception of authority, and it was intimately bound up with the elemental expansion of Russian peasant settlement. This was also the pattern that prevailed subsequently along the eastern borders of the empire—into Siberia and the southeastern steppes—perpetuated as it was by the offensively defensive tactics of the Cossack hosts. Both at the beginning of this process in the sixteenth century and at its end in the second half of the nineteenth, territorial consolidation for the sake of security was hardly to be distinguished from outright expansion and seizure of sparsely settled lands held by nomadic people on a lower (from the Russian point of view, of course) level of cultural and economic development.

The military and diplomatic acquisitions of non-Russian territory in the eighteenth and at the beginning of the nineteenth centuries involved old, established social and political structures of a western European type in the Baltic provinces, Finland, and Poland. Russian conquest had to make allowance for this fact, and it started on the basis of a federal type of relationship. The privileges and traditional rights of the local ruling elites were respected at first. Gradually, however, by virtue of the growing modernization of Russia's culture and socioeconomic makeup, these privileges and rights became anachronistic, not to speak of their being antithetical to prevailing political and ideological conceptions. The government in St. Petersburg proceeded to erode and eventually abolish the privileged status of these areas, especially the traditional rights of their ruling classes. This was accomplished by acquiescing in the local economic and social relationships and the elite's cultural uniqueness, while enforcing political and institutional unification.

Finally, alongside the imposition of political and economic control by the central government, there took place a gradual but relentless process of social Russification. It introduced uniform institutions and power structures, and this automatically led to administrative Russification as well. In its drive for uniformity in the way of life of all its subjects, the imperial government ended up by actively promoting *de facto* institutional and political Russification, which in the case of the weaker nationalities brought with it cultural Russification. This had been the experience of the Ukrainians and the cossacks in particular, and in the eighteenth and nineteenth centuries it was also experienced by the people involved in more recent acquisitions in the south and east. With varying means, at different rates, Russian imperial policy toward the non-Russian people within the borders of the state was one of social and administrative assimilation, which in the nineteenth century was bound to carry in its wake strong suggestions of cultural Russification as well.

Notes

No attempt will be made to provide a comprehensive coverage of the literature that may be relevant to the problem of nationalities in pre-1917 Russia. The titles cited below are those that the present author has found most helpful and that also contain useful suggestions about further literature, preference being given to those in Western languages.

1. The legal aspect of the unitary or federal nature of the empire is discussed by Boris E. Nol'de, *Ocherki russkago gosudarstvennago prava* (St. Petersburg: "Pravda," 1911); N. M. Korkunov, *Russkoe gosudarstvennoe pravo,* vol. I, 4th ed. (St. Petersburg: Tipografiia M. M. Stasiulevicha), (particularly, Obshchaia chast', otdel l, glava I).

2. A laudable departure from the Kliuchevskii tradition appears in the recent syntheses by George Vernadsky, *Russia at the Dawn of the Modern Age* (New Haven: Yale University Press, 1959), and *The Tsardom of Muscovy* (New Haven: Yale University Press, 1969, 2 vols). Hugh Seton-Watson also allocates more space to the non-Russian territories of the empire than do run-of-the-mill textbooks in his *The Russian Empire, 1801–1917* (Oxford: Oxford University Press, 1967). The ideological and intellectual aspect of the problem is treated in the essays of Georg von Rauch, *Russland: Staatliche Einheit und nationale Vielfalt (Föderalistische Kräfte und Ideen in der russischen Geschichte)* (Munich: Veröffent lichungen des Osteuropa-Institutes München, 1953, Bd. 5).

3. Practically all general histories of the USSR contain separate chapters dealing with non-Russian territories and peoples. Naturally, the emphasis stresses the conquest, the economic exploitation, and the revolutionary movements. But much useful information may be gleaned from this literature: B. D. Grekov, S. V. Bakhrushin, V. I. Lebedev, *Istoriia SSSR,* 2 vols., 2d ed. (Moscow: Gospolitizdat, 1947–1949); *Istoriia SSSR s drevneishikh vremen do nashikh dnei, v dvukh seriiakh v dvenadtsati tomakh* (Moscow: Izdanie Akademii Nauk, Institut Istorii, 1966), especially vols. 2–4 of the first series; *Ocherki istorii SSSR* (Moscow: 1953–1957). Naturally, the histories of the various constituent republics and territories of the USSR provide useful information and relevant documents.

4. In recent years the major Soviet republics have been publishing source collections on the period of conquest and incorporation into the empire.

5. One case study, superficial but informative, is *The Russian Conquest of Bashkiria 1552–1740, A Case Study in Imperialism* by Alton S. Donnelly (New Haven: Yale University Press, 1968).

6. Boris Nolde, *La Formation de l'Empire russe—Etudes, Notes et Documents I* (Paris: Collection historique de l'Institut d'Etudes slaves, vol. XV, 1952).

7. Seymour Becker, *Russia's Protectorates in Central Asia: Bukhara and Khiva, 1865–1924* (Cambridge: Harvard University Press, 1968; Russian Research Center Studies no. 54).

8. Marc Raeff, "The Style of Russia's Imperial Policy and Prince G. A. Potemkin" [Chapter 11 of this volume], in Gerald N. Grob, ed., *Statesmen and Statecraft of the Modern West: Essays in Honor of Dwight E. Lee and H. Donaldson Jordan* (Barre, Massachusetts: Barre Publishers, 1967, pp. 1–51; Nolde, *La Formation ...,* II (Paris, 1953), part IV; Alan W. Fisher, *The Russian Annexation of the Crimea, 1772–1783* (Cambridge: Cambridge University Press, 1970).

9. David M. Lang, *The Last Days of the Georgian Monarchy, 1658–1832* (New York: Columbia University Press, 1957).

10. Nolde, *La Formation.* ... vol. I.

11. Venedikt A. Miakotin, *Ocherki sotsial'noi istorii Ukrainy v XVII–XVIII vv.* (Prague: 1924–1926): H. Auerbach, *Die Besiedelung der Südukraine in den Jahren 1774–1787* (Wiesbaden: Veröffentlichungen des Osteuropa-Institutes München, 1965, Bd. 25).

12. For the Baltic provinces' institutional incorporation in the course of the eighteenth century, see Ia. Zutis, *Ostzeiskii vopros v XVIII veke* (Riga: VAPP, 1946). The literature about Finland and Poland is too vast to be cited here and properly takes up an important sector in the respective national historiographies of these countries. For Poland, there is a convenient introduction in *The Cambridge History of Poland* (Cambridge: Cambridge University Press, 1951). For Finland, see John H. Wuorinen, *Nationalism in Modern Finland* (New York: Columbia University Press, 1931); Peter Scheibert, "Die Anfänge der finnischen Staatswerdung unter Alexander I," *Jahrbücher für Geschichte Osteuropas,* IV (1939), Nos. 3/4.

13. Edward L. Keenan, Jr., "Moscovy and Kazan, 1445–1552: A Study in Steppe Politics" (Cambridge: Harvard University, unpublished dissertation, 1966).

14. Marc Raeff, *Siberia and the Reforms of 1822* (Seattle: University of Washington Press, 1956).

15. Reinhard Wittram, *Drei Generationen, Deutschland–Livland–Russland 1830–1914* (Göttingen: Deurerlichsche Verlagsbuchhandlang, 1949); Friederich von Schubert, *Unter dem Doppeladler (Erinnerungen eines Deutschen in russischem Offizieersdienst 1789–1814)* (Stuttgart: K. F. Koehler Verlag, 1962).

16. S. M. Dubnow, *History of the Jews in Russia and Poland from the Earliest Times until the Present Day,* vols. 1 and 2 particularly (Philadelphia: Jewish Publication Society of American, 1916–1918, reprinted 1946).

17. For the Siberian case, see Marc Raeff, *Siberia and the Reforms of 1822,* ch. VI. Also, Aleksndr E. Nol'de, *Ocherki istorii kodifikatsii mestnykh grazhdanskikh zakonov pri grafe Speranskom,* 2 vols. (St. Petersburg: Senatskaia Tipografiia 1906–1914); Evgenii Iakushkin. *Obychnoe pravo—materialy dlia bibliografii* (Moscow: Universitetskaia Tipografiia, 1908).

18. A case study concerning the Volga Tatars in Alan W. Fisher, "Enlightened Despotism and Islam under Catherine II," *Slavic Review,* vol. XXVII, No. 4 (December 1968), pp. 542–53.

19. For a comprehensive description of Muscovite claims to eastern territories in the sixteenth century, see Jaroslaw Pelenski, "Muscovite Imperial Claims to the Kazan Khanate: A Case Study in The Emergence Of Imperial Ideology" (New York: Columbia University, unpublished doctoral dissertation, 1968).

TEN

Uniformity, Diversity, and the Imperial Administration in the Reign of Catherine II

SINCE THE BEGINNINGS of its history Russia was—and still is—a vastly diversified and multi-ethnic polity. Yet, its historiography has barely reflected this fact, leaving not only a gap in our knowledge but also influencing the views and actions of the ruling élites. It is, therefore, both of interest and importance to see how the cultural-human diversity and the physical size were dealt with administratively by the imperial government. In the present article I shall focus my attention on the reign of Catherine II which was a significant period in this respect, as in so many others.

An important factor in the ways newly acquired territories and their peoples were dealt with by the central authorities, in Moscow or St. Petersburg, was the time and manner of their acquisition. As I have argued elsewhere,[1] the fact that the first conscious and significant "imperial" expansion occurred in the 16th century, as if continuing the so-called "gathering of Russian lands," played a no mean role in the elaboration of the outlook and methods of Russian administrators. Some new elements were introduced with the "modern" incorporation of the Baltic provinces by Peter the Great; but even these innovations were implemented in the spirit and with the means that had been developed by previous generations under different circumstances. In dealing with the period of Catherine II we should, therefore, remember that basic attitudes and many practices had a long history. But her reign did witness the development among the governing élites of an awareness of the basic issues involved in the empire's diversity. This heightened consciousness stemmed from the greater cultural and political sophistication developed by the Russian élites, but also from Russia's integration into the Western world, so that con-

temporary European ideas and practices were purposefully applied to the solution of administrative and political problems.

First, let us briefly consider the intellectual framework within which Catherine II and her advisors operated. The underlying conceptual and method-
ological assumptions were derived from cameralist theory and practice of
Western and Central Europe of the late 17th and early 18th centuries. We may
recall that Catherine II herself received her first education in the cameralist
environment of a petty German court in the first half of the 18th century,[2] and
that whatever secular education was imparted formally or informally to the
leading personalities of Russia was patterned on the prevailing European
models.[3] Furthermore, the Russian administration was generously sprinkled
with officials of foreign background and training, either specially hired by the
state or issued from the Westernized élites of the Baltic and Western provinces.

The prevailing political and administrative notions of continental Europe in
the late 17th and the first half of the 18th century were what we call, in short
hand fashion, cameralism and mercantilism. We need not differentiate between the two, for in essence they were only two facets of one system.[4] Developed in the world of petty German territorial principalities following the
Thirty Years War (although its roots go back to the theologians and political
practitioners of the Reformation), cameralism views the state as a single and
self-contained unit. The ruler and his administration are the driving force of
an active and interventionist policy covering all facets of public life within the
territorial limits of the state, whether large or small. The dynamic quality of
the regime derives from a voluntaristic conception of the political function: to
maximize society's economic and cultural potential, so as to expand its wealth
and power to maintain independence and extend its influence within a system
of equally sovereign, autarkic, and dynamic states. Little wonder that these regimes' main concern was fiscal, and that their principal administrative goal
was to increase the productive capacity and resources of the nation.[5]

Applied to administration proper, this political conception resulted in the
so-called "well ordered police state," whose working principle and goal has
been well stated by J.H.G. von Justi in a popular and influential treatise which
Catherine II read early in her career:

> Der Endzweck der Policey ist demnach, durch gute innerliche Verfassungen die
> Erhaltung und Vermehrung des allgemeinen Vermögens des Staates zu bewirken;
> und gleichwie das allgemeine Vermögen des Staats nicht allein alle, der gesam-
> mten Republik und allen Mitgliedern derselben zuständige, Güter, sondern auch
> die Geschicklichkeiten und Fähigkeiten aller, zu der Republik gehörigen, Per-
> sonen unter sich begreift; so muss die Policey beständig bemühet seyn, den al-
> lgemeinen Zusammenhang aller dieser verschiedenen Güter vor Augen zu
> haben, und eine jede Art derselben zu Beförderung der gemeinschaftlichen
> Glückseligkeit immer dienlicher und brauchbarer zu machen.[6]

Of course such an orientation paved the way for the administration's involvement in the supervision, control, direction, and promotion of all facets of public—and frequently also of private—life as they seemed to affect the goal of expanding welfare and progress. As it was described in a memorandum prepared for Maria Theresia and passed on to Catherine II:

> La police ... renferme l'universalité des soins relatifs à l'administration du bien public, le choix et l'emploi des moyens propres à le procurer, à l'accroître, à le perfectionner. Elle est, on peut le dire, la science de gouverner les hommes et de leur faire du bien, la manière de les rendre autant qu'il est possible ce qu'ils doivent être pour l'intérêt général de la société.[7]

It also resulted in the state's active and energetic involvement in educational and cultural policy. The ruler's, or state's, task was to maximize the potential for greater prosperity and happiness by eliminating conflicts and frictions through a firm anchoring of security of person and property, and by seeing to it that each estate, class, or group in society make its proper contribution.

*   *   *

The practical effectiveness of the system rested on the preservation of existing social structures, for the corporate bodies, estates, and classes had to be used as instruments in achieving the goals we have described. To be sure, these traditional bodies were not sufficient and the positive role of the state could be performed adequately only with the help of a body of officials organized along bureaucratic lines as the willing instruments of the ruler.[8] But the two went hand in hand, and in the successful cameralist absolutisms the ruler's bureaucracy cooperated effectively with the traditional leadership (with which it frequently had common social roots) in the pursuit of new policy goals which, in fact, transmuted the original social structure in favor of a dynamic, modern one. Significantly, social change and social mobility were to be kept within bounds and the traditional framework was to be preserved; but not too rigidly, perhaps, so as to permit select individuals, who by their capacity and dynamic enterprise had contributed to the overall purpose, to rise in status and eventually merge with the ruling élites of the polity.[9]

The basic assumption of political and economic harmony, and of social and cultural uniformity, points to some paradoxes or contradictions in the cameralist approach to administration and state policy.

There is a contradiction between reliance on positive state direction and controls and the maximizing of the productive (creative) potential of individuals and groups. We also observe an antinomy between expanding wealth, welfare, and happiness and the preservation of social stability. Finally there is scope for conflict in the reliance on the activity of autonomous groups and estates, the free role of "*pouvoirs intermédiaires*" on the one hand, and the *dirigisme* of the central state bureaucracy, on the other.

In a sense these contradictions were immanent to the philosophical and anthropological preconceptions of 17th and 18th century cameralist administrators. The absolutist *Polizeistaat* was based squarely on Cartesian rationalism which—besides its mechanistic conception of nature—posits the uniformity of human nature operating within a stable universe.[10] Thus laws and other human arrangements should basically be the same everywhere since man's nature is uniform. Differences are differences in developmental level and are thus the object of guidance and informed action by the state that aims at overcoming them. Yet it was precisely in the 16th and 17th centuries that the Europeans discovered cultural relativism; a realization that men are different in their ways and ideals entered the consciousness of the educated European and were beginning to be taken into account, however inadequately, by administrators of colonial empires.[11] The apparent discrepancy between the two insights about man—uniformity of nature and variety of culture—were reconciled in the notion of levels (stages) of development within a general uniform pattern of evolution and progress in man's way of life. A people's way of life becomes the criterion of achievement on the developmental scale; and the necessary transformation in a way of life can be fostered, helped along, or in some cases even imposed, by the intervention of the paternalistic state through "police" legislation.

*   *   *

These general considerations should be kept in mind as we turn to an examination of the concrete policies pursued in the reign of Catherine II with respect to the empire's economic, ethnic, cultural diversity. The view that the empire was a single economic unit had been given legislative form by Elizabeth when she abolished internal tariffs. The final sanction came in the first years of the reign of Catherine II. The incorporation of the provinces acquired at the first partition of Poland gave rise to the advocacy of an expansion of the empire's economic borders by abolishing custom posts between the Ukraine, Russia proper and the former Polish lands.[12] Contemporaries noticed, on the model of the West, that trade itself could also be a means for furthering and expanding political control and increasing the potential of the empire. This was especially true if this became the preliminary for agrarian settlement.[13]

With the promotion of agricultural settlement, and especially the furtherance of agriculture, we are in the realm of classical cameralist concerns and the problem of handling ethnic and cultural variety. The state's furtherance of agriculture through foreign settlements and internal migration corresponded exactly to the basic cameralist goal of maximizing society's resources to make the state self-sufficient and foster population growth.[14] This consideration led

Catherine II to support and promote the settlement of the southern steppe regions, especially after the elimination of Turkish and Crimean threats to the area's security. The policy had, of course, also diplomatic and territorial impe-rialistic aspects which only reinforced the state's direct concern and interven-tion. But what is more interesting and important for us here is to note the manner in which Catherine and her main advisor, Potemkin, dealt with the problem of ethnic and cultural variety the settlement policy fostered.

First was the belief, based on the notion implicit in 17th century rational-ism, that the highest stage of human socio-economic development was settled agriculture combined with active trade (and some manufacturing). To pro-mote agricultural settlement, therefore, was to extend the area of this high stage of social development. And in so doing the state was setting an example and preparing the ground for those populations that had not yet reached this stage.[15] The government would help with various incentives, but these incen-tives were predicated on the other equally important aspect of the policy: the standard used to gauge the level of development and which also provided the institutional framework was the Great Russian peasant, or those foreigners—i.e. Germans—who had the same high level and even higher institutional forms. Thus the administration endeavored to draw in non-settled natives into the orbit of the Russian agricultural population. This aim was pursued with special energy in the newer frontier regions—i.e. Siberia, East of Astra-khan—where the help of the native élites was actively enlisted to this end. The success was mixed, and on the whole not significant, in the absence of an ade-quate density of Russian agricultural settlement to provide a model and invite emulation through more or less amicable persuasion. The best documented instance, besides the earlier expansion of Russian peasant settlement beyond the Volga and into the South, was the case of the Buriat region in Siberia at the end of the 18th century and in the early years of the 19th.[16] It goes with-out saying that such a policy helped to disrupt and even change traditional patterns, which in turn produced those very conflicts which the government aimed at avoiding. In any event, the policy's thrust was clear: to bring about uniformity and full integration by eliminating social and economic differences and by bringing all subjects to share a similar way of life—a way of life which 18th century enlightened rationalism considered the height of social develop-ment.

Most important for the imperial administration, the settlers and their ad-vanced institutions offered the basis for the extension to the new frontiers the legal and administrative ways and norms of the central core lands. That this was indeed the intention of the imperial administrators is made clear in the fis-cal and administrative provisions for different treatment of these regions: all advantages were to be strictly temporary, to be eliminated gradually as the re-gion's population became more and more alike to that of the central provinces in its way of life.[17]

The *Gleichschaltung* went beyond the fiscal domain, for the final step was to come when the native population were to be equalized with the Russian peasantry with respect to recruiting duties and obligations.[18]

The implicit belief in economic and social uniformity meant that the imperial administration would endeavor as much as possible to develop and promote manufacturing and trade, not only out of purely cameralist considerations of maximizing resources and securing autarky for military requirements, but also to promote lateral social mobility. Indeed, the cameralist conception implied a belief in the social division of labor along estate lines, each estate—or corporate entity—having its specific function in the polity.[19] The balance and harmony of functions assured the state's wealth and power while promoting the subjects' welfare, progress, and prosperity. Therefore, in the absence of such estates or corporate groups it behooved the state, i.e. the administration, to foster their development. Thus Catherine endeavored to promote European style estate structures for the Russian population, in particular to foster the middle class of merchants, tradesmen, and small manufacturers that was still lacking inspite of the efforts of Peter I.[20] This the imperial government did not only within the confines of traditional Russia, but also in the frontier regions where the native populations had a very different social makeup and institutional traditions. Here, too, the purpose was to generate the basic social uniformity that was considered necessary for harmony and to assure security and stability.

More significant still, and more successful, was imperial policy in fostering the integration of the non-Russian economic élites into the all-Russian imperial framework. Wherever there was a class of native traders efforts were made first to guarantee them security of person and property, along their traditional customs, and to give them a stable role in the pattern of economic and social relations in their home areas. This was to be achieved by laws that maintained traditional behavior and organizations while separating these economically active élites from the masses of their fellow subjects. The privileged position of these élites paved the way for their integration into the Russian pattern: gradually the special privileges were eroded as they were forced to give way to Russian norms when native and local élite organizations were assimilated to the Russian estate institutions. Thus the pressure for the full integration and russification of the native economic élites increased.[21]

From an administrative—or rather political—point of view, the empire was considered as an unit.[22] Of course its enormous expanse, especially in view of contemporary techniques of transportation and communication, created the need for regional or local deconcentration, i.e. the delegation of some functions to local level institutions. But in the Russian case we encounter even in this respect a basic uniformity which is striking when compared with contemporary France and Prussia, not to speak of the Habsburg monarchy. This high degree of uniformity had its roots in the very process of the "gathering of

Russian lands" and it had received renewed impetus in the mechanistic and rational approach of Peter the Great. Functions could be delegated, but only on the assumption that the government was paternalistic and performed a didactic role, so that functions of administration were the same everywhere, that they would be implemented in a socio-cultural uniform environment, and that the means available for their implementation would also be basically identical. This implied making use of uniform bureaucratic techniques, for variations affected only superficial differences which would, in most cases, be temporary, until the economic and social forces of integration and assimilation we have mentioned earlier had produced their effect.

Since Peter I's measures on local government, we can trace a consistent and conscious policy of eliminating traditional, historically conditioned administrative units in favor of a pyramidal structure of identical subdivisions.[23] The policy reached a first stage of fulfillment in the reign of Catherine II.[24] The old, large *guberniias* were split up and reshuffled and the empire was divided into new provinces based on a roughly identical number of population (between 200,000 and 300,000), with little regard for geography, historic social bonds, or effective economic connections. In order to provide the necessary administrative centers, new "cities" were created by *fiat* out of villages, though some lip service was given to their potential economic functions as trade centers.[25] But this economic potential was evaluated from the point of view of imperial connections, not on the basis of local and regional patterns of trade. The large provincial units in turn were subdivided into a number of districts (*uezdy*) also on the basis of population, with distances to the provincial centers playing a subordinate role, and they were endowed with uniform institutions.[26] With this went uniform administrative procedures and personnel. Of course, distinctions between regions could not be fully ignored; but Catherine acknowledged only such broad distinctions as north, center, south, east. The local officials, both elected and appointed, were given identical uniforms with only different color uniforms corresponding to these regions based on the directions of the sky.[27]

The perennial Russian shortage of qualified personnel to take care of the new local institutions forced the government to rely on local participation. But it made sure that this participation be uniform in terms of forms and procedures, and especially in terms of recruitment from comparable social groups. Wherever local forces were absent or inadequate, the administration continued to rely on the regular bureaucracy. In case of need, personnel was sent from the capitals and an effort was made to create new bureaucratic cadres locally. These new cadres were recruited from the traditional strata of Russian society so as to ensure their continued predominance in the empire. For instance, an effort was made to recruit subaltern officials and clerks from the clerical estate (*dukhovnyi chin*) whose Great Russian tradition was firmly rooted in an uniform education and culture.[28]

At the same time the government also endeavored to create or develop the local forces that its institutions required. This was accomplished by means of the integration of native local élites through cultural and political russification.[29] The process received renewed impetus from the legislations of 1775 (Statute on the Provinces) and 1785 (Charters to the Nobility and to the Towns): in an apparent paradox, while promoting greater reliance on local forces and extending the areas of administrative deconcentration, the statutes also intensified the pressures for russification on the part of the native élites and their integration into the all-Russian estate structure.[30] In the end, the policy suffered failure because opposition and difficulties were dealt with through harsh centralization and forcible integration—but this was to be the story of the 19th century which brought about insuperable strains and open conflict.

The goal of integration and uniformity which was implied in the cameralist belief in the uniformity of human nature and an universal pattern of social progress was never achieved with respect to the Old Believers, especially the extreme sects whose members were persecuted and kept out of public regular institutions. A policy of active discrimination against religious extremism was pursued in the reign of Catherine II who considered all forms of religious exaltation (including Free Masonry and mysticism) dangerous to government and society—which only resulted in their retreating to the borders of the empire (e.g. Dukhobors in Transcaucasia).[31] But in other cases religion proved a convenient vehicle for the achievement of cultural and social integration. Russian Orthodoxy was favored, of course, as the state religion.[32] Efforts were made to attract new members, although missionary activity was normally not encouraged by the state.[33] More important, recognized minority churches and denominations were put under state administrative control similar to that of the Russian church, while their governing bodies were at times removed physically to be nearer to the central authorities.[34]

In line with the hallowed experience that family bonds were one of the most effective means to fasten ties and secure loyalties, the imperial government endeavored to foster such family alliances among the local élites as would integrate them more easily into the Great Russian nation. On the other hand the state's administrative apparatus and influence were brought to bear to discourage family ties with non-Russians. It was an old policy, for *mutatis mutandis* it had been followed with respect to Tartar élites in the 16th century, and it had not been forgotten when it came to integrate the Crimea and the Southern steppe regions.[35] An even more blatant instance may be found in the Ukraine where the local élite experienced the strong cultural pull of neighboring Poland, a pull that St. Petersburg felt imperative to break. In the reign of Anne already a secret instruction had been issued to influence marriages.[36] Catherine pursued a similar policy with respect to education, especially after the first partition of Poland, to steer the élites into local or Russian schools and prevent them from going to Polish, particularly Jesuit, institutions of learning.[37] Not quite so openly, because of the need for their skills, was the effort to orient the Baltic noble élites towards Russia and to reduce their studying in Germany. Eventually it led to the reopening of a German university at Dorpat (Derpt, Iur'ev) in the early 19th century and making it a tool of Russian cultural integration.[38]

Another traditional method to cope with ethnic and cultural variety was to "russify" the élites in the hope that they would lead or drag their fellow subjects to integration into Russian culture and society. For the achievement of this goal the imperial government had a particular effective tool at its disposal: the Table of Ranks. Indeed, the Table permitted to reward all services to the state with ranks that could lead to ennoblement and assimilation to the Russian ruling élite. Reward with ranks was particularly effective in creating a single imperial ruling élite, for it conferred equal rights and privileges with respect to ownership of serfs, control of mineral resources on the private estate, security of person and property. The system had been used with good results in the case of the Ukrainian élite, especially the Cossack *starshyna*, culminating in the integration of the Cossack Hosts after the destruction of the *Sich* in 1775.[39] Of course, other forms of official reward and distinction might lead to similar benefits, for example bestowal of military and civil orders. Characteristically, the imperial government was prepared to make allowance for native cultural and religious traditions to enable their leaders to accept these awards: for instance, a special form of the order of St. George was designed for Tartars, so as not to hurt their religious susceptibilities.[40] The cooptation of local leaders for subaltern administrative services and offices led to their integration into the bureaucratic hierarchy whose forms and procedures had to be followed; and this in turn might lead to award of ranks and foster their social and cultural russification. These methods proved particularly effective in the Crimea and later on the Southeastern frontier and in Sibera.[41]

In view of the "modernizing," goal-directed, active nature of the cameralist state, its élite and bureaucracy had also to share a common outlook, values, and language, which resulted in assigning a leading role to education. At issue was a westernized education, but an education that was carried on in a Russian form and it, therefore, also implied integration into the emerging imperial Russian culture. We need not belabor the frequently amusing or pathetic existential aspects of the process which are to be found in numerous memoirs.[42] The result is well known: a modern Russian culture open to all members of the educated classes, from whatever background, and which served as the foundation and matrix for the astoundingly creative and vital literary, artistic, and scientific achievements of the 19th century, achievements that in turn served as a pole of attraction to the new leadership from both the lower classes and non-Russian peoples. The educational process resulted in a cultural and linguistic uniformity which became the royal road of access to the leading positions in Russia, attracting thereby the ambitious élites of the subject peoples in the empire. It served to weaken, if not actually erode, the cultural identity of these élites and thus undermined their people's ability to resist russification. Early and effective results along this line had become apparent among the Ukrainian leadership.[43] These élites became largely russified and were coopted into the imperial bureaucracy. It was to require the newcomers from the lower classes to revive effectively the national and cultural traditions of the Ukraine. In the case of politically and culturally strong ethnic groups the result was a bi-cultural and bi-lingual élite as illustrated by the German-Russian society of the capital which made signal contributions to both the administrative and scientific lives of the empire in the 19th century.[44] On a more modest scale we observe a similar development among the Greek and Armenian communities whose settlement in newly acquired Southern Russia, especially in the Crimea and Odessa, was actively promoted by Catherine II.[45]

Special arrangements and privileges granted to individual groups to cope with particular local problems and conditions were never regarded as permanent within the framework of an empire that would respect local differences and socio-cultural variety. The imperial government viewed them strictly as temporary and transitional to facilitate the way to full integration, in fact to what we must call, for want of a better term, full russification. The intention as well as the cameralist form of the process were made explicit in Catherine's well known secret instruction to Count Rumiantsev upon his appointment to the governor-generalship of the Ukraine.[46]

A similar observation may be made about all special provisions to respect native legal traditions; they were temporary and served to smoothen the path to eventual integration—social, economic, and cultural. Not only were customs always to be superseded by Russian law whenever a Russian was one of the parties to a legal dispute, but also Russian legal norms were to be applied in all cases not specifically covered by customary law.[47] The application of Russian norms, however, entailed the introduction, however gradual or indirect, of Russian institutional and organizational patterns. This was good cameralist, *Polizeistaat* tradition which, basing itself in the priority of abstract reason, also gave precedence to royal edicts and law over custom.[48] Another step was taken in Russia as well; the customary law was collected and codified, and in the process subjected to further russification in substance, if not always in form. If there was acceptance of cultures and norms considered high on the Enlightenment scale of values, for example in the Baltic provinces, it was only in the expectation of assimilating them, too, into the imperial fabric once economic progress, education, and culture had raised Russia proper to conform to the higher level of development. The other peoples deemed to be at an inferior stage had to be integrated by transforming their way of life to conform to the higher level of the Russians. There was rather little effective resistance to this policy since the material advantages were great, Russian power overwhelming, and the national consciousness of the non-Russian, as well as Russian, populations still far from developed. In such a situation the state could find ample scope for its didactic and leading role and it did not fail to take advantage of it.

The pattern, therefore, was clear: temporary recognition of local and cultural differences but only as a step in the process of integration; integration was to lead to uniformity, first administrative and economic, then institutional and social, and finally cultural. In fact, the goal may be termed institutional russification, though it was not seen as such by contemporaries: the local and cultural entities did not fully perceive it, partly because of their low sophistication, partly because its effects had not become apparent. The Russian government and administrative élites did not perceive it because modification and "modernization" involved no compulsory change in language and religion. As a matter of fact, to the political writers and practitioners of the day, issues of language and religion were secondary matters, and they were surprised when they triggered violent discontent or general national opposition.[49] To a cosmopolitan élite language was but a convenient instrument and they were ready to accept another if it seemed more effective or desirable. If the Russian élites were prepared to acquire German or French for this reason, why should not other peoples in the empire switch to another language as a better instrument of communication and cultured way of life? The imperial government was blind to the problems of cultural autonomy and identity and their relationship to administrative, economic, and social uniformity. Catherine's ideal was that of the rationalist cameralist autocrat whose duty it was to bring enlightened progress to all his peoples. She expressed this attitude clearly, not without playfulness as was her wont, on the occasion of her visit to Kazan' in a letter to Voltaire:

> Il y a dans cette ville [Cazan] vingt peuples divers, qui ne se ressemblent point du tout. Il faut pourtant leur faire un habit qui leur soit propre à tous. Ils peuvent se bien trouver des principes généraux, mais les détails? Et quels détails! J'allais dire—c'est presque un monde à créer, à unir, à conserver, etc. Je n'en finirai pas et en voilà cependant beaucoup trop de toutes façons.[50]

In conclusion we should take note and emphasize—as it is in contrast to what was to happen inside Russia and outside from the middle of the 19th century on—the great flexibility in the means resorted to by Russian administrators in the 18th century in paving the way for integration and uniformity. Emphasis was on gradualism, and generally mild tolerance, so as to preserve stability and peace.[51] But precisely this emphasis on—and belief in—maintaining harmony and stability blinded the Russian officials to the contradictions and the potential dangers inherent in their policies. It was difficult to square social stability based on estates and corporate bodies with the dynamic expansion and maximizing of the productive potential of society. Fraught with greater hazards still proved to be the myopia of 18th century enlightened cameralist rationalism for the religious, cultural, and socio-psychological dimensions of men's sense of identity. These blind spots came to haunt the government of St. Petersburg in the 1860s and they endowed the emerging Russian and national intelligentsias with much of their strength.

Notes

1. "Patterns of Russian Imperial Policy Toward the Nationalities" [Chapter 9 of this volume] in E. Allworth ed., Soviet Nationality Problems, Columbia University Press 1971, pp. 22–42.

2. B. v. Bilbassoff, Geschichte Katharinas II, Bd. I, Berlin 1891 and the curious information contained in W. Hosäus, C.F. Gellerts Briefe an die Fürstin Johanna Elisabeth von Anhalt Zerbst, in: Mittheilungen des Vereins für anhaltische Geschichte und Alterthumskunde, Bd. IV, Heft 5 (1885), pp. 268–86.

3. Most convenient introduction in A. Vucinich, Science in Russian Culture. A History to 1860, Stanford University Press 1963. See also M.J. Okenfuss, The Jesuit Origins of Petrine Education, in: J. Garrard ed., The Eighteenth Century in Russia, Oxford 1973, pp. 106–130 as well as the classical monographs of M. Vladimirskii-Budanov and S. Rozhdestvenskii.

4. A. Tautscher, Staatswirtschaftslehre des Kameralismus, Bern 1947 and the collection of articles in D. C. Coleman, ed., Revisions in Mercantilism, London 1969.

5. J.B. v. Rohr, Einleitung zur Staats-Klugheit ... Leipzig 1718, p. 838.

6. J.H.G. von Justi, Grundsätze der Policeywissenschaft, 3. Ausg., Göttingen 1782, p. 8 (reprint Frankfurt a.M. 1969).

7. J.-B. C. LeMaire, La Police de Paris en 1770, in: Mémoires de la société de l'histoire de Paris et de l'Ile de France, V, 1878, pp. 27–28. Cf. also R.A. Dorwart, The Prussian Welfare State before 1740, Harvard University Press 1971.

8. H.C. Johnson, The concept of Bureaucracy in Cameralism, in: Political Science Quarterly 79 (1964), 378–402; J.M. Seuffert, Von dem Verhältnisse des Staates und der Diener des Staats gegeneinander im rechtlichen und politischen Verstande, Würzburg 1793.

9. von Rohr, p. 778 advocates a "table of ranks" and 792–93 where he argues for personal ennoblement for service. J.M. Seuffert, advocates professionalization of judicial and administrative offices. For the social implications see the admittedly late statement of P.A.F. von Münchhausen, Ueber Lehnsherrn und Dienstmann, Leipzig 1793.

10. Chr. Wolff, Le Philosophe-Roi et le Roi-Philosophe, Berlin 1740, pp. 113, 121. Cf. also N. de LaMare, Traité de Police (Paris 1722, 2. verm. Aufl. Amsterdam 1729, I, p. 240 and the well known opinion of Frederick II, "Dissertation sur les raisons d'établir ou d'abroger les lois," in: Oeuvres, VII, 1790, p. 105.

11. R. Etiemble, L'Orient philosophique au XVIIIe siècle, Paris (Les Cours de Sorbonne) 1956–1968. J.H. Elliott, The Old World and the New, 1492–1650, Cambridge University Press 1970.

12. "Remarques sur quelques points de la représentation de M. le Procureur-général, 30 Mai 1774 par le Comte Münnich," LOII, fond 36, No. 451 ff. 152–175.

13. "Mneniia R.L. Voronstsova v Senate, 1761?" LOII, fond 36, kniga 1067, ff. 44 (verso).

14. There was an obvious and ready model in the settlement-policies of Brandenburg-Prussia.

15. On the colonization of the South cf. E.I. Druzhinina, Severnoe prichernomor'e, v 1775–1780gg, Moscow 1959; H. Auerbach, Die Besiedelung der Südukraine in den Jahren 1774–1787, Wiesbaden 1965 and R. Bartlett, Foreign Settlement in Russia under Catherine II, in: New Zealand Slavonic Journal, 1974, No. 1, pp 1–22.

16. B. Nolde, La Formation de l'empire russe—Etudes, notes et documents, 2 vols., Paris 1952–53; Fr.-X. Coquin, La Sibérie. Peuplement et immigration paysanne au XIXe siècle, Paris 1969, especially ch. 1.

17. For ex. with respect to Kondrov Tartars, Arkhiv Gosudarstvennogo Soveta, I, part 2, St. Pbg. 1869, pp. 363–64; on the autonomous institutions of Armenians and Tartars in Astrakhan cf. report on Nikita Beketov, 26 Nov. 1764, TsGADA, fond 16, No. 606, ff 2–5 and opinion of N. Panin, ff 6–15.

18. "Predlozhenie R.L. Vorontsova o rekrutskom nabore, 5 Oct. 1761" LOII, fond 36, No. 1067, f.58 (verso) to f.72 (verso) passim.

19. V.L. von Seckendorff, Teutscher Fürstenstaat, Jena 1737 especially part II, ch. 8, (reprint Aalen 1972).

20. D. Geyer, Staatsaubau und Sozialverfassung—Probleme des russischen Absolutismus am Ende des 18. Jahrhunderts, in: Cahiers du monde russe et soviétique, VII-3, 1966, pp. 366–77; ders. Gesellschaft als staatliche Veranstaltung, in: Jahrbücher f. Geschichte Osteuropas, XIV-1, März 1966, pp. 21–50; also with particular reference to the Ustav blagochiniia my ... study, The Role of the Well-Ordered Police State in the Development of Modernity in 17th and 18th Century Europe [Chapter 18 of this volume].

21. Arkhiv Gosudarstvennogo Soveta, I-2, pp. 263, 274, 365.

22. B. Nol'de, "Edinstvo i nerazdel'nost' Rossii," in his Ocherki russkogo gosudarstvennogo prava, St. Pbg. 1911, pp. 223–554 and suggestions in G. von Rauch, Russland: Staatliche Einheit und nationale Vielfalt, München 1953.

23. See the classic M. Bogoslovskii, Oblastnaia reforma Petra Velikogo. Provintsiia 1719–1727 gg., Moscow 1902 and Iu. V. Got'e, Istoriia oblastnogo upravleniia v Rossii ot Petra I do Ekateriny II, Moscow 1913–1941, 2 vols.

24. R.E. Jones, The Emancipation of the Russian Nobility 1762–1785, Princeton University Press 1973. [The administrative chain of command, not always too clearly, culminated in the Senate in the reign of Catherine II. It was only in the reign of Alexander I that a functionally clear pyramidal structure culminating in the Ministries was established.] For some apposite and challenging remarks see the otherwise not quite satisfactory discussion in G.L. Yaney, The Systematization of Russian Government. Social Evolution in the Domestic Administration of Imperial Russia, 1711–1905, University of Illinois Press 1973.

25. For ex. discussion in Senate of proposal of Count Sievers to establish new towns, TsGADA, fond 248, kniga 3823 and the application of Siever's example by A. Mel'gunov, "Doneseniia gen. gub. Aleksei Mel'gunova o Iaroslavskoi, Vologodskoi i Kostromskoi guberniiakh, 1777–1784," in: TsGADA, fond 16, No. 1012, part I. Also see Iu. R. Klokman, Ocherki sotsial'no-ekonomicheskoi istorii gorodov severo-zapada Rossii v seredine XVIII veka, Moscow 1960.

26. For ex. Donesenie gen. gub. grafa Romana Vorontsova, TsGADA, razriad XVI, No. 636, ff 16–17 (1778) and order of A.A. Viazemskii, 13 Sept. 1784 on uniform procedures, TsGADA fond 248, No. 6570, ff 8–12 and following. Also the proposal of kn. M.N. Volkonskii, LOII, fond 36, No. 398, ff 476–88 (7 Febr. 1775) and in Sbornik IRIO, V (1870), pp. 125–28.

27. V.A. Grigor'ev, Reformy oblastnogo upravleniia pri Ekaterine II, St. Pbg. 1910, p. 208. One may wonder whether this classification according to the directions of the sky is not so much a reminiscence of Mongol customs as an illustration of the new fad for things Chinese.

28. For ex. memorandum to Catherine II of Namestnik of Vladimir and Kostroma, Graf I. Saltykov, 10 July 1786, TsGADA, fond 16, No. 639, ff 62–64 or the report without date (1782) TsGADA, fond 16, No. 777 part 2, ff 186–187. For the suggestion to settle clergy as clerks in new offices to be opened in Novorossiia cf. Raeff, The Style of Russia's Imperial Policy and Prince G.A. Potemkin [Chapter 11 of this volume], in: G.N. Grob ed., Statesmen and Statecraft of the Modern West. Essays in Honor of Dwight E. Lee and H. Donaldson Jordan, Barre, Mass. 1967, p. 23.

29. For the Crimea see Raeff, The Style pp. 14–16 and for Siberia, at a later date, Raeff, Siberia and the Reforms of 1822, University of Washington Press 1956. Numerous other instances may be gleaned in the collections of published documents about the Caucasus, Bashkiriia, the South Eastern steppes.

30. Cf. the memorandum of a Count Panin suggesting the creation of two types of nobility—provincial and imperial. The former to be held by hereditary local *optimes,* the latter only as reward for state service. Lenin Library, Moscow. Manuscript division. Fond 16, No. XVI-a, part 2, f. 4–5. Also the provision for two types of nobility in Siberia, Raeff, Siberia and the Reforms of 1822, and the census and review of Crimean titles of nobility by commission in 1795, Istoricheskaia spravka ob obrazovanii v Tavricheskoi gubernii tatarskikh dvorianskikh rodov, in: Zapiski odesskogo obshchestva istorii i drevnostei, XXIII, 1901, pp. 41–43.

31. P. Brock, Vasya Pozdnyakov's Dukhobor Narrative, in: Slavonic and East European Review, XLVIII, Nos. 100–101. The role of religious dissenters in the Pugachev revolt is well known, cf. D. Peters, Politische und gesellschaftliche Vorstellungen in der Aufstandsbewegung unter Pugacev, in: Forschungen zur osteuropäischen Geschichte, Bd. 17, 1973 and V.V. Mavrodin, ed., Krest'ianskai voina v Rossii v 1773–1775 godakh, III, Leningrad 1970.

32. For instance the incident with Prince Arenberg, Arkhiv Gosudarstvennogo Soveta, I-2, pp. 383–84 (1 March 1792).

33. A. W. Fisher, Enlightened Despotism and Islam under Catherine II, Slavic Review, XXVII-4, Dec 1968, pp. 542–53.

34. For ex. the proposal to transfer administration of the Protestant Church to St. Petersburg and attach it to the Protestant parish of the capital directly under the Senate, Arkhiv Gosudarstvennogo Soveta, I-2, pp. 18–19.

35. Raeff, The Style, passim.

36. Bumagi Komiteta Ministrov, in: Sbornik IRIO, Bd. 108, p. 26 (31 Jan 1734).

37. For the problems created, see S.P. Pisarev, ed., Instruktsiia o vospitanii, in: Russkaia Starina, XXXI, 1881, pp. 660–661.

38. For Catherine's opposition to study abroad in the latter part of her reign, see for ex. her letter to Bezborodko, April 1791, in Sbornik IRIO, XLII, p. 153. The russifica-

tion role of Derpt is illustrated in the career of A.S. Kaisarov as first professor of Slavic philology, V.M. Istrin, A.S. Kaisarov, professor russkoi slovesnosti, in: Zhurnal Ministerstva narodnogo prosveshcheniia, n. s. LXIV, July 1916, pp. 102–31 and Iu. M. Lotman, Andrei Sergeevich Kaisarov i literaturno-obshchestvennaia bor'ba ego vremeni, in: Tartu Riikliku Ülikooli Toimetised, 63, 1958.

39. Raeff, The Style, and the literature cited therein.

40. Arkhiv Gosudarstvennogo Soveta, I-2, pp. 5–8 (24 Sept 1789).

41. For ex. Iakut chieftains, Arkhiv Gosudarstvennogo Soveta, I-2, pp. 257–60 (1 Oct 1789), and for later instances, Raeff, Siberia and the Reforms of 1822.

42. For the avatars of the Greek school of cadets, cf Raeff, The Style, p. 25 and the argument in an anonymous French mémoire of 1766 to use Corps of Cadets to form an imperial "national character," LOII, fond 16, No. 398, ff 200–231.

43. Of course, identity of religion and closeness to language, as well as common anti-catholic traditions helped to speed the process.

44. F. von Schubert, Unter dem Doppeladler, Erinnerungen eines Deutschen in russischem Offiziersdienst 1789–1814, Stuttgart 1962 and the valuable studies of Professor Erik Amburger on Russo-German personalities.

45. Raeff, The Style, and the references cited there.

46. Nov. 1764, Sbornik IRIO, VII (1871), pp. 376–91.

47. Polnoe Sobranie Zakonov, 1st series, No. 12 307 (13 Jan 1765) and the curious change in Finnish criminal law, PSZ, No. 11 936 (25 Sept 1763). Also, Arkhiv Gosud. Soveta, I-2, p. 263.

48. "La raison et la Loy sont au-dessus de la coutume … ," de la Mare, I, p. 242.

49. This was the predicament of Joseph II in both the Low Countries and Hungary. A curious statement of the 18th century approach to integration in a multinational empire is the anonymous mémoire, 15 July 1766 "Quelques moyens pour lier et attacher de plus en plus les Provinces conquises à l'Empire de Russie," LOII, f. 36, No. 398, ff 200–231.

50. Letter of 29 May 1767, Sbornik IRIO, X (1872), p. 204.

51. Of course, the *Pugachevshchina* was a recent and salutary warning.

ELEVEN

In the Imperial Manner

IF ONE WERE TO SINGLE OUT the periods of Russia's greatest expansion the choice would no doubt fall on the reigns of Ivan IV (1533–1584) and Catherine II (1762–1796). In the sixteenth century, Russia broke down the barriers restraining the movement of its population to the east by gaining control of the entire course of the Volga and by pushing on into Siberia. In the eighteenth century Russia secured its southern border by the acquisition of the northern shore of the Black Sea and, by eliminating the troublesome neighbors in the southwest and west, prepared the ground for the settlement and rapid economic development of the Ukraine.[1] It is easy in retrospect to view these events as a working out of conscious designs, ideological tenets, and consistently purposeful actions. But such a view is too much of an *ex post facto* rationalization and it harbors the danger of anachronistic judgment. The uncontrolled and spontaneous movements of population, the search for adventure and wealth, the longing for effective protection against incursions by unruly neighbors, the historical memory of past political and spiritual unity, the expectation of a great political and economic international role, the desire to contribute to the spread of Christianity and to the liberation of brethren in religion from impious domination, the seizing of unexpected opportunities— these are some of the elements which, woven into an inextricable web, account for Russia's expansion into a Eurasian empire. …

How can we give a meaningful and historically accurate account of the "imperial" policies of Catherine II? A perusal of the decrees and laws promulgated by the Empress during the thirty-four years of her reign (and their general tenor was adumbrated in the notes she jotted down for herself when she was only the wife of the heir presumptive)[2] points to one concern that, for whatever reason, was ever present in her mind: develop the economic resources and potential of the empire, help to bring into play all the economically creative forces of the population. It is true that this had to be done without touching at the foundation of Russian society—serfdom. This strikes us as being so completely incompatible that we readily dismiss her major aim as mere sham; but in so doing we forget that neither she, nor most contemporaries, felt it as such. This was the goal behind Catherine's laws giving full security to the private property of the nobility, including the right to exploit at will whatever was to be found on their estates, on the surface or beneath it.[3] The same motive underlay the legislation abolishing internal duties, restrictions on private industrial and commercial enterprise, as well as the measures promoting the modernization and expanding the productivity of agriculture.[4] Finally, in spite of their inadequacy or ambiguity, the statutes giving some measure of corporate organization to the nobility and the towns population also helped to promote this same goal.[5] Naturally, economic growth and a higher level of prosperity would also benefit the government and give to the Empress and her courtiers greater means for indulging their love of luxury. This selfish aspect, however, in no way negates the genuineness and consistency of purpose of Catherine's economic legislation.

*   *   *

Russia's expansion to the south and southwest could further these same ends. It is doubtful that the expansion was determined by the needs of Russian trade or incipient extensive agriculture, as Soviet historians like to believe. But quite clearly the expansion, it was felt, would promote them once they became a realistic possibility. The term "expansion" is somewhat misleading in this context, for it was not so much the political control over new territory that was significant for economic development, but rather the settlement of people and the promotion of agriculture and trade on the underpopulated lands of the south that had been under Russian sovereignty for several generations. Yet, clearly, in order to be of economic benefit, these territories had to be safe from foreign incursions and possess adequate access to waterways.

The quest for security in the south determined Catherine's policy toward Turkey and led her to fight two wars for the establishment of Russian control over the northern shores of the Black Sea. Similar considerations explain the more aggressive penetration into the Caucasus, as well as the annexation of the Crimea. It would be more difficult to establish a connection between these trends and the blatantly imperialistic plans and moves of Catherine II, e.g., the notorious "Greek project."[6] Most likely this ambitious (and unrealistic) scheme was only a move in the diplomatic game as it was played at the time. In the eighteenth century much of political and even military life was carried on within a framework of play, as manifested not only in the rules and forms of diplomacy and warfare, but also in their aims.

Of all of Catherine's moves in foreign affairs, the partition of Poland made the deepest impression abroad and, incidentally, saddled Russia with a heavy psychological and political burden for generations to come. But from the point of view of Russia's internal affairs, as well as in terms of its style of imperial policy, it was not Poland but the push to the south that was most characteristic and significant. This push enabled Russia to settle and develop the fertile plains of the Ukraine, which in turn led to the formation of an exportable surplus and made of the Ukraine an international breadbasket. The acquisition of the Crimea proved less significant economically, although it was essential for defense and the development of Russian shipping on the Black Sea.

Unlike the conquest and settlement of Siberia, but like the first eastward advance in the sixteenth century, the expansion into the south was intimately connected with international military and diplomatic events. The Russians had first to wrest control from the Turks and their Tatar vassals, and then secure the grudging assent of the powers by treaty in order to maintain their domination. Consequently the policies of settlement and economic development of empty territories could not be dissociated from military policy; nay, military and naval considerations frequently dictated both form and goal of administrative and economic measures. The establishment of fortresses and harbors, and the organization and maintenance of garrisons to protect the area went hand in hand with colonization and the foundation of towns that would promote economic activity. As the distances over the newly acquired lands were great and the means of transportation scant, the military establishment had to procure the necessities of life on the spot. This increased the demands on agriculture and the need for settling an economically active population. Military and economic purposes could not, therefore, be separated and the colonization of the south always had a double aspect: military and agricultural. In this sense the steppes and shore of the Black Sea played a role similar to the old Roman *limes* and their Byzantine and Near Eastern successors.[7] Those organizing Russian authority in this part of the world had to be both military and administrative leaders. For this reason, too, Catherine's most dynamic and influential military adviser, Grigorii Aleksandrovich Potemkin, also took the lead in the economic and agricultural development of the region. He was truly a builder of empire and may in all fairness be counted among the great colonizers of modern times. Our main task will be to examine the ways by which he pursued his purpose, so as to be able to draw some conclusions about the style of his statesmanship and make some observations on the pattern and methods of Russian imperial policy in the eighteenth century.

*   *   *

The highlights of Potemkin's meteoric career can be given in a few words.[8] The future Prince of Tauris (i.e., Crimea) was born in Byelorussia in 1739, the son of a somewhat eccentric retired officer of middling wealth. His father died when he was six years old and the boy was raised in Moscow under the supervision of his godfather. He attended the gymnasium attached to the newly founded University of Moscow and received several distinctions for outstanding performance. He was particularly interested and proficient in theology and Greek, and at one point he even seems to have contemplated entering the Church. He did not maintain his good academic standing and was dismissed in 1760. He then joined the regiment of the Horse Guards in Saint Petersburg. During the hectic days in June 1762 when Catherine overthrew her much disliked and incompetent husband, Peter III, Potemkin was in her entourage and apparently made himself useful to the new sovereign. His reward, however, was modest and at the time he did not achieve the prominence he ambitioned. He secured, however, an appointment to the chancery of the Holy Synod; he became the executive secretary of the Ober Prokurator, a rather important and responsible position for a man of his age and which shows that his earlier theological interests and studies did not go unwasted.[9]

Potemkin did not remain long in the ecclesiastical administration, however, and returned to the Horse Guards in Saint Petersburg. He was admitted to court and his attractive physique and good humor were noticed by Catherine II. After the outbreak of the first Turkish war in 1768 Potemkin joined the army on the Danube. If the Empress had no occasion to learn of any high feats of his, she did notice his absence and thought of the dangers to which he was exposed. She wrote him that she had not forgotten him and asked him not to endanger his health or life. The hint was clear. Potemkin arranged to be sent with news of victory to Saint Petersburg; there he promptly became Catherine's lover and favorite. From then on, his rise was dazzling. By 1775 he had been created count, appointed vice-president of the College of War, and put in charge of all military forces and administrative authority in the southern provinces and territories. He later became fieldmarshal, president of the College of War, which gave him control over the entire military establishment of the empire.

Even after he had ceased to be the Empress' lover he kept his great influence over her mind and remained her most trusted and influential counselor in all matters political and administrative. He took on responsibility for developing the regions acquired by terms of the Treaty of Kuchuk-Kainardji and as governor of New Russia he became the satrap of the empire's south. He engineered the seizure of the Crimea; entrusted with the protection of the Caucasian frontier he helped to further Russia's penetration and extend its protectorate over the princelings of Abkhazia and Kabardinia. The last important act of his life was the capture of Ochakov which paved the way for the victorious end of the second Turkish war, and end he did not live to see. He died in characteristically theatrical fashion in the open air, on an Oriental rug laid out in the steppe in October 1791.

* * *

Since the sixteenth century the Cossacks had been in the forefront of the unplanned, gradual advance of the Russian people into the open steppe lands of the south and east.[10] Part adventurers, part soldiers, always ready to pick a good fight, especially if it promised booty, tillers of the soil and fishermen when they were not fighting, the Cossacks had developed a social organization of their own. Theirs was a kind of "military democracy" which attracted all those who wanted to escape the yoke of serfdom and the shackles of the law, be it in Poland or Muscovy. At first the Cossacks had appeared on the banks of the lower Dnieper where by the late sixteenth and early seventeenth centuries they had created a respectably strong political and military organization with headquarters at the Dnieper rapids (the so-called Zaporozhian *sich'*, or *sech'*). Eventually they had to accept the overlordship of Muscovy. From then on their social system, political organization, and even economic and cultural way of life underwent erosion at a rapidly increasing pace. Basically the pattern of this process was the following: the officers and headmen (*starshina*) secured increasing wealth and power; they associated themselves with the Russian government, obtaining rewards, estates, and ranks. Gradually this led also to their social and cultural russification in the eighteenth century and to their forgetting the traditions, way of life, and values of "military democracy"; in fact they had betrayed the "Cossack liberties." The rank and file, on the other hand, were rapidly sinking to the level of peasant bondsmen. The process was accelerated after Hetman Mazeppa's siding with Charles XII of Sweden against Peter the Great and the flight of his followers to Turkey. In retaliation, the Russian government proceeded to abolish all Cossack privileges and traditions systematically. The final blow fell in 1775 when Catherine II destroyed the last stronghold of the Dnieper Cossack liberties, the Zaporozhian *sich'*.[11]

But already in the late sixteenth century many Cossacks from the Dnieper had decided to move eastward, where they hoped to find more scope for both their warlike energies and agricultural endeavors. The Russian government had favored this movement as it helped to protect the southeastern frontier of the state.[12] Thus a Cossack Host and political organization had emerged on the banks of the Don River. But as had been the case of the Dnieper Cossacks, the Don community became rent with inner dissensions as the wealthy officers endeavored to entrench themselves in their leading position on a hereditary basis, while the rank and file opposed them in the name of traditional Cossack equality and liberties. These dissensions, and the ensuing discontent, led many Don Cossacks to join the Pugachev rebellion that swept across eastern Russia in 1772–1775 and threatened to shake the very social and political foundations of the empire. For the central government the problem was, therefore, to retain the Cossacks as a valuable military organization, ready to be called upon to do garrison duty on the frontier, to fight in case of war or internal disturbance, while at the same time preserving their economic role as free peasants, capable of providing for their own livelihood and equipment. It fell upon Potemkin, as commander in chief of all irregular troops, to work out a solution.

The simple solution was to take advantage of the social and economic rift existing in the Cossack corps in order to reform and control it for Russia's imperial purposes. The Host's ataman (chief commander) had in the past wielded almost absolute power, although he was in principle elected by the entire Host. This had enabled him to pursue any policy he wished. Like their counterparts on the Dnieper earlier, witness Mazeppa, the atamans of the Don Cossacks were of doubtful loyalty. They were bent upon making themselves hereditary masters of the Host and well nigh independent rulers of the Don Cossack territory.[13] Although the Cossacks would have liked to preserve complete independence from any power, they were not willing to submit to the ataman's autocratic rule, the more since he was in fact elected by a small minority of wealthy officers. It was therefore natural and easy for the Russian government to play on this dissatisfaction to abolish the elective character and autonomous power of the ataman.

As commander in chief of all Cossack forces in the empire, Potemkin in 1775 transformed the office of ataman of the Don Cossacks into an appointive position. He himself appointed the new ataman, A. I. Ilovaiskii, whom he knew to be devoted and loyal to the empire.[14] Preserving the ataman's power in matters of military discipline, Potemkin split the traditional unity of the military and political organization of the Host by establishing the "Host's Civil Administration." This administration was directly under the governor-general of New Russia as part of the Azov province.[15] It consisted of the appointive ataman, two counselors appointed by the governor-general, and two counselors elected by the general assembly of the Host. In this manner the control of the central government and of the regular hierarchy of local administration was secured over the Host, at the same time a measure of participation and autonomy was left to the Cossacks themselves. The degree of autonomy was still greater in judiciary matters and with respect to village life. Justice was administered by a panel of five judges of which four were elected. Customary law prevailed for minor cases, but the law of the empire took precedence in cases on appeal.[16]

Most important, however, was the decision to equate the Cossack officer ranks with those of the Russian regular army, and thereby give the Cossack leadership group access to the status of Russian nobility with all its privileges.[17] This gave official sanction to the social process of differentiation that had been going on among the Cossack hierarchy in the same way as it had among the Dnieper Cossacks. In this manner the Cossack ruling group was deprived of any need to oppose the imperial government. Gradually, though quite fast, Cossack officers were assimilated into the Russian élite and abandoned their claims to special treatment and rights. As for the rank and file, they were satisfied not to be at the mercy of the ataman and his henchmen, of enjoying the security of imperial law, while preserving their traditional ways in local matters. In addition they could retain the illusion, or hope, that through a successful service career they had the possibility of joining the ranks of the nobility, of acquiring serfs, and of playing an active role in the life of the country.

There were further compensations of an economic nature. The wealthier officer group, by becoming part of the Russian nobility, could now acquire populated lands and they also obtained the right to purchase serfs in Russia proper and settle them on their personal estates.[18] The rank and file Cossacks retained their personal freedom, their rights to the communal lands, and experienced an alleviation of their service obligations, in particular with respect to garrison duty in border fortresses. With the decline of the threats to the security of the area, the military obligations decreased still further. Eventually, the Cossacks became a militia called upon only during time of war.[19] Furthermore, they received preferential treatment if they settled in newly acquired territories in the foothills of the Caucasus and on the Kuban, where eventually a new Host was formed along the same lines as on the Don.[20]

*   *   *

The reorganization of the Don Cossack Host was essentially a matter of domestic policy. The annexation and assimilation of territories which had belonged to the Ottoman Empire was a different matter. There was, in the first place, plain military conquest, or cession by treaty. But more interesting in our context was the procedure followed in the case of the Crimea, a former possession of the Ottoman Empire which had become an independent state by the Treaty of Kuchuk-Kainardji, and which was annexed by the Russians in 1783. We shall leave aside the international aspect, the complicated intrigues of two contending factions of the Crimean ruling family, the Gireis, as well as the relations with the bordering Nogai hordes.[21] We shall only be concerned with the way in which the Russians—under Potemkin's direction—prepared the ground for the bloodless annexation of the rich and attractive peninsula.

The population of the Crimea consisted of several distinct national, linguistic, and religious groups. The Tatars, Moslems speaking a Turkic language, were the majority and had been the dominant group since medieval times. Next there were sizable Christian minorities, Greeks, Armenians, and Georgians. The latter two were the leading fruit growers and owned most vineyards, while the former—because of their far-flung connections—played a particularly important commercial role. Potemkin proposed to lure to Russia these valuable minorities. He had two main considerations in mind for so doing: in the first place, he correctly suspected that the migration of these elements would fatally weaken the Crimean state, making it ripe for easy absorption into the empire. Secondly, and here Potemkin was to be proven only partly correct, he thought that by settling in Russia, these minorities would play the same beneficial role for the economic development of the southern territories of the empire as they had in the Crimea.

At the direction of Potemkin, the military commander at the Perekop isthmus, Prince A. A. Prozorovskii, approached the religious leaders of the Greeks, Armenians, and Georgians and, playing on their traditional fear and hatred of the Moslems, persuaded them to organize a mass migration of these national groups.[22] Two additional considerations helped, no doubt, in persuading the Greeks and Armenians to go to Russia: the promise of economic benefits and privileges to be conferred upon them by the Russian government and the expectation that with the help of Russia they could work for the independence of their mother lands.[23] About 20,000 Greeks left their homes in the harbors and trading centers of the Crimea. A large number, not exactly known, of Armenians did likewise. As the Georgian group was quite small, no further information has been preserved about it beyond the fact of its migration.

As was to be expected, the migration of such a large number of people did not proceed too smoothly. The Russians could not always make good on their promises to provide adequate food, shelter, and transportation. The whole movement was arranged rather precipitously; those involved had to sell their possessions at ridiculously low prices, their plight brought about much abuse; disease set in on the road to fill the cup of bitterness to the brim. The mortality rate was very high and discontent intense.[24] But there was no turning back. As the Greeks were not used to work on farms, they eventually were allowed to settle in towns, e.g., Taganrog and Mariupol, which, in a sense, were founded especially for them.[25] The Armenians and Georgians, on the other hand, resettled on the land; not all of them, however, remained in the proximity of the Crimea and quite a few moved farther west, to the banks of the Dnieper and Dniester. Eventually, those who survived assimilated and became accustomed to their new environment. The Greeks, in particular, whose ranks were swollen by their compatriots from the islands, came to play a prominent role in the economic as well as cultural life of the whole region, particularly of Odessa and Sebastopol. The Armenians do not seem to have been as successful, for they have left few traces of their contribution to the development of the Black Sea shore in the eighteenth century.

The primary objective of the mass migration, namely the sapping of the Crimean polity, was accomplished. Within a few years the Crimea could be annexed by Russia without any difficulty or resistance. The whole episode is quite interesting from the point of view of the methods used. It is reminiscent of a pattern—albeit in modernized form—that had prevailed in the sixteenth century. When after two centuries of Mongol-Tatar domination, the Russians took the offensive against the successor states of the Golden Horde—the khanates of Kazan' and Astrakhan'—they first undermined the latter's power of resistance by luring away their most active and useful subjects: noble servicemen, junior members of the ruling families. These Tatar nobles and princes were given estates and rewards, they joined the ranks of the Grand Duke's military establishment; in some cases—e.g., the Kasimov princes— they founded vassal principalities along the fluid boundaries between the khanates and the Grand Duchy of Muscovy. Eventually they converted to Christianity, became russified, and were absorbed into the Russian service nobility.[26] The Greeks, Armenians, and Georgians played a similar role in regard to the Crimea. But conditions had changed since the sixteenth century. Instead of undermining the military service class, the Russians were luring away those most active and productive in the economic life of their potential victim. But as in earlier times, the newcomers bolstered the strength of Russia and pumped new blood into its economic lifestream.[27]

*　　*　　*

The policy we have just described helped to undermine the Crimea and facilitated its annexation, but it did not solve the problems involved in organizing the administration of the newly acquired territory. Unlike most other territories conquered or absorbed by the Russian Empire so far, the Crimea had neither been contiguous (except for a few short years after Kuchuk-Kainardji, and even then the boundary ran through almost empty lands) nor populated by people sharing with the Russians a common language, historical tradition, religion, or culture.

The Russians endeavored at first to disturb the existing social and political order as little as possible. Only the sovereign power of the Khan was superseded by a Russian governor, who combined military command and administrative authority. This governor, a lieutenant of Potemkin, was directly responsible to him and received instructions from his chancellery; in the final analysis, of course, he was responsible to the Empress, but in view of Potemkin's powers this was purely a formality. The troops moving into the Crimea were instructed to be on their good behavior and not to harm or offend the local population.[28] As usual, unfortunately, this order was frequently disobeyed, as witness the episodes related in our sources. The fact that special injunctions had to be given not to tamper with property and to remind soldiers and officers that the Crimea was not to be considered conquered enemy territory tells us what the normal situation was in fact.[29] Also, the local population were permitted to leave the Crimea to go to Turkey if they so chose.[30] Quite a number took advantage of this opportunity, sold their possessions and abandoned their estates. This resulted in a dislocation of the local economy which hastened further the decline initiated by the migration of Greeks, Armenians, and Georgians. As at the time there was no one who could buy these lands and keep them in production, the annexation of the Crimea led to the impoverishment and ruin of the province. Only generations later did Russian landowners and new settlers manage—at great cost—to restore the Crimea to its rank of the empire's garden and orchard.

One may wonder why Potemkin allowed this to happen. The explanation must be sought in the fact that eighteenth-century Russian administrators did not believe that people might abandon their homes when they felt threatened in their survival as a religious, linguistic, or cultural entity. In fact the Russian authorities were determined not only to let the local population carry on its traditional way of life, but also to draw them into the new local institutions. The Russian military commanders heading the administration of the province were to act so as not to hurt local customs and prejudices. Russian law, for example, was to be introduced very gradually and only in cases involving Russians. The administration was to secure its information about local conditions—particularly on the distribution of real estate and population—only through local inhabitants.[31] In strictly local and personal matters elected elders or traditional chieftains were to have the decisive voice.[32]

The local *optimes* could receive recognition as nobles and be assimilated to the Russian nobility. This is what happened in very numerous instances. With the introduction in the Crimea of the institutions provided by the Charter of the Nobility of 1785 the Tatar nobles automatically became members of the Tauric Assembly of the Nobility. Of course, the validation of a Tatar claim to nobility was not always an easy matter, although the Russian administration accepted the traditional local criteria. A special commission was set up to disentangle the complicated and often cumbersome details involved in the claims to noble status. Characteristically, this commission consisted of the local mufti, seven Tatar nobles, four native officials, and two Greeks who had been ennobled in Russian service.[33] Under the circumstances it did not prove difficult to introduce eventually the local administrative institutions provided by the Statute on the Provinces of 1775. This took place step by step, but rather fast.[34]

The native élite, treated like the nobles in Russia, were allowed to hold assemblies, elect some officials, and participate in local affairs along with their Russian counterparts. But, from a strictly nationalistic point of view (which probably did not occur to Potemkin and his contemporaries), here was the rub: to be assimilated to the nobility of the empire, to be able to participate in local affairs within the framework of the acts of 1775 and 1785 put a special premium on russification. Indeed, rapidly a large number of the Tatar upper class did become russified. This meant, however, that those who could not or would not be russified slipped in the social scale, sinking to the sad lot of peasant. It moreover created a new gap between the traditional native leadership and the local population—a cultural gap even more profound than the one which separated the Westernized Russian nobleman from his serfs. Little wonder that the feeling of national identity and cultural consciousness of the Crimean Tatars in the nineteenth century came to be closely associated with Islam and their Turkish past.

The Crimea had been annexed in the expectation of the expanded economic opportunities as well as strategic and political benefits it would bring to the empire. In this sense it was a colonial acquisition. Russian officers and officials, first of all Potemkin, of course, were granted land holdings either from empty lands or from estates that had been abandoned at the time of the Russian annexation. A new class of Crimean landowners thus came into being. Together with the russified native élite the Russian landowners became the most influential group on the peninsula. They, too, were most aggressive in exploiting the local peasant labor, importing serfs from Russia and setting up orchards and vineyards on a large commercial scale. The Russians also brought with them more "modern" and Western notions as to what constituted "civilized" activities and the most desirable way of life. In particular, they held sedentary agriculture in highest esteem and scorned cattle raising which was associated in their minds with dangerous, unruly, and primitive nomadic tribes. They therefore promoted an agricultural development which was determined by their own preconceived notions, interests, and traditions, disregarding Tatar preferences and customs, in spite of their alleged claim to work for the common good. Such a trend could only multiply the areas of friction between Russians and natives.[35]

If we look at the methods and approaches used in the incorporation of the Crimea and analyze their rationale—implict or explicit—we are struck by their resemblance to the sixteenth century pattern in the case of the conquest and absorption of the khanates of Kazan' and Astrakhan' (to some extent of western Siberia as well). Things and circumstances had changed, of course: Russia's economy was different, the military balance overwhelmingly in favor of Russia, the religious-cultural sophistication of the Russian leadership greater. Yet, in truth, the parallel is quite close. The results, too, were similar in their ambiguity: incorporation into the Russian empire brought distinct benefits to the conquered states: e.g., eventual economic "modernization," participation in Russian culture for the élite, domestic peace and military security. But they were accompanied by the disadvantages of Russian bureaucratic centralization, and had to be bought at too high a price in economic and psychological terms, a price which many of the new subjects were unwilling or unable to pay.

* * *

Closely related to the annexation of the Crimea was a set of measures which brought foreign colonists to the shores of the Black and Azov seas. After the annexation of the peninsula foreign colonists were settled there too. We have mentioned the role played by the migration of Greeks, Armenians, and Georgians from the Crimea proper. In addition, colonists from the Mediterranean were brought in to set up garrisons and relieve the regular Russian troops by protecting the newly settled territories against the nomads of the adjoining steppes.

First came the so-called Albanians, mainly Greeks from the islands and from the Adriatic and Ionian coasts, who had followed the appeal issued by Count Alexis Orlov to assist the Russian fleet during the Mediterranean campaign and who feared Turkish vengeance. They settled in military townships, in Kerch and Enikale, and the regular army units into which they were organized retained their identity into the middle of the nineteenth century.[36] In passing it may be noted that Catherine II allowed them to retain their national costume as part of their military uniforms.[37] The "Albanians" were joined by a few Italians, Corsicans, and other Mediterranean peoples, primarily from the islands.[38] Their numbers stayed small and, with rare exceptions, they did not remain on the lands originally set up for them. As soon as urban life revived on the shores of the Black Sea they moved to the towns (Odessa, for example) where their presence contributed to the formation of an active economy, and cosmopolitan intellectual atmosphere. In any event, they helped a great deal to establish a *présence "russe"* on the contested shores and to spearhead the development of a modern society there. They were also active in helping to organize the administration of the Crimea and to integrate its economy into that of the empire.

In connection with these colonists and their settlement (which was actively advertised and encouraged by the Russian authorities in St. Petersburg as well as locally) the question arises, of course, whether the real purpose was to introduce them as an active yeast in the newly acquired lands, or whether ulterior political motives played the decisive role. The latter, involving the future of the Ottoman Empire, may have continued to be an element in Catherine's thinking, even after Russia had asserted its preeminence in the Black Sea. If the Greek project was to be more than a diplomatic maneuver or the pipe dream of a few enthusiasts, these settlers could be of service in advancing political claims in the Mediterranean and in interfering in the affairs of the Porte. It was in this light that the Turks viewed these colonization moves. For our part, we are rather inclined to think that in St. Petersburg the main consideration was a desire to develop better and faster the resources of the newly acquired areas. Naturally, should the occasion present itself, the Russian government would not hesitate to make political use of the foreigners settled there. But the occasion did not present itself, except in an indirect and minor way at the time of the Greek War of Independence, and by that time the original settlers had been well integrated into the empire.[39] In any event, there is no doubt that Catherine and Potemkin thought of these settlers above all in terms of the needs of an imperial domestic policy. Clearly, the empire of the tsars had by this time ceased to be isolated politically and culturally; on the contrary, it was a cosmopolitan meeting ground on which the modern Russian culture and polity were making their appearance.

*   *   *

Attracting and settling foreigners was not a new policy. It had a precedent in the settling of foreigners along military lines in the Ukraine proper. But Potemkin put the finishing touches to it and brought to a successful conclusion a trend initiated in the preceding reign—although it should be said that Potemkin's success was made possible by a combination of several factors that had not been simultaneously present in the past.

The complexities of the Ukrainian situation stemmed from the fact that it lay at the intersection of several cultural and political cross currents. It also was a region where the Dnieper Cossack Host had developed and maintained over a long period its peculiar social and political institutions. Lastly, it was relatively unpopulated and, therefore, attracted settlers from everywhere. All these elements had helped to shape the notions of the separateness and particular social identity of the Ukraine. But with the incorporation (1654) of the Cossack Host under Moscow's sovereignty the officers began to be russified; eventually they merged with the nobility and joined the military and civil service of the empire. At the same time, the loyalty of the leadership that had not become russified had been put into question, as we have seen, by Mazeppa's defection and the subsequent flight of the Zaporozhian Cossacks into Turkey.

To forestall the possibility of future desertions and to foster the social and economic trends that were undermining the traditional Cossack ways, the government of Empress Elizabeth embarked on a policy of settling auxiliary troops that would be completely dependent on St. Petersburg. As a majority of these settlers were recruited among the Orthodox and Slavic-speaking peoples of East Central Europe they were called "Serbians," although most came from the Habsburg Empire. Even though they could maintain their customs and language, their leaders at any rate were soon assimilated to the Russian nobility. This was not surprising, for by virtue of their military duties and ranks, and their possession of granted estates, the "Serbian" officers came to have the same way of life and values as the Russian noble servicemen. We need not go into the details of this colonization here; it has been the subject of several detailed studies in Western languages.[40] Suffice it to note that in this instance the Russian government was following the Muscovite system of granting estates (*pomestie*) in return for military service, a system that had reached its high point in the second half of the sixteenth and first half of the seventeenth centuries and had been abandoned by Peter the Great.[41]

From the very beginning of her reign, Catherine II pursued a double policy with respect to the complex multinational Ukraine (we shall leave aside the implications with regard to Russia's relations to Poland and Turkey). In the first place, like her predecessors,[42] she dismissed all claims for recognition of the distinctiveness of Ukrainian language, religion, customs, and the like. She firmly believed that the Ukraine was part and parcel of the Russian lands and that its people were fundamentally Russians—a belief, incidentally, which found validation in the assimilation of the Ukrainian élite to the Russian nobility and the undeveloped national consciousness of the common people at the time. The obvious differences in customs, legal system, attitudes, and the resulting administrative or political distinctiveness, were quite superficial, due only—the Empress thought—to historical accidents. As for Cossack particularism, it was based on the uncivilized ways of a gang of unruly ruffians who had to be disbanded for the sake of the peace and security of the region as well as of the empire. This was accomplished, as we know, when the Zaporozhian *sich'* was destroyed in 1775. The external differences between the Ukraine and Russia proper had to be eliminated gradually and the region (along with some other areas of the empire) assimilated to the pattern of the central provinces. It could be done gently, through appropriate gradual administrative russification. This was the policy Catherine laid down as a guideline for the central and local institutions in her instructions to Prince A. A. Viazemskii upon his appointment as procurator-general of the Senate.[43] In the second place, she was very much concerned to have the potentially rich Ukraine contribute its full share to the general economy of the empire. Instead, she noted, it was a drain on the government's resources, for the scheme of foreign military settlements had proven quite costly and failed to develop the local resources. This was the burden of her directives to Count Peter Rumiantsev at the time of his appointment as governor-general of Little Russia (i.e., right bank Ukraine).[44] From 1775 on, Potemkin's activities in the Ukraine were to bring to successful fruition Catherine's double-faceted policy: complete administrative uniformity and making the region economically and politically profitable to the empire.

After the Hetmanate had been abolished and the *sich'* destroyed, the administrative uniformity with Central Russia was completed by the creation of the governor-generalships of Little Russia under Rumiantsev and of New Russia under Potemkin. The latter included, in fact, more than the Ukraine in the strict sense (for example the Kuban' and Don areas, and later the Crimea), but it extended over most of the southern steppe and frontier areas with similar social and economic conditions. It is not necessary for us at this point to delve into the intricacies of the administrative arrangements, their subdivisions, and frequent changes of detail.[45] Two things, however, deserve to be noted: first, that the power wielded by Potemkin was well nigh absolute and that he had complete control over the vast areas yet to be developed. We shall return to this point later when discussing the character of Potemkin's authority. Secondly, we note that the administrative institutions followed closely the pattern and model of the governor-generalships (or vicegerencies) introduced in Russia proper at the time. In this manner they helped to bring about a uniformity of structure between these new territories and the core lands. The main task of these institutions was to fill up the area with people and to develop its economy; in so doing the new administration destroyed most of the significant elements of autonomous—Cossack or other—traditions and public ways of life that had survived.

The imposition on New Russia of an administrative uniformity with Russia proper cannot be divorced from the government's promoting those social processes that tended to make the social structures of the two areas of the empire alike. We can touch on this aspect only very briefly and superficially; it was very complex and extends beyond the chronological framework of this essay. The foreign settlers brought in under Elizabeth were rapidly assimilated to the normal Russian pattern. This meant that the rich officer class was acquiring estates on the same terms as the Russian nobles and was using more and more the labor of the native peasants. The latter were rapidly turning into the landowner's bondsmen. The step to full enserfment then was a short one, and it was taken before the reign of Catherine II was over.[46] As the military value of the original "Serbian" colonies had proven to be a doubtful proposition, the government did nothing to maintain or preserve their distinct regiments, so that their personnel was gradually absorbed into the regular Russian military establishment and their officers, as we have noted, drawn into the service and culture of the empire.

Potemkin tried at first to continue the old policy of attracting new military colonists. Entrepreneurs who would bring to South Russia a number of settlers would be rewarded with ranks in proportion to the number of people they persuaded to settle, ranks which carried with them the award of a specific amount of land. In this manner there came more settlers from Modavia, Bulgaria, Hungary, Poland, Habsburg, and Turkish possessions, as well as some Swedes, Mennonites, and German peasants from the Baltic. But their number was so small that they could not keep their own military units and had to be merged with existing regiments.[47]

To free the government from the costly expedient of bringing in foreigners—who had to be given special financial incentives, large land grants, and promised the respect of their customs, language and religion—and to further the other facet of Catherine's policy, that of economic development, Potemkin urged the settlement of Russians.[48] The possibilities in this respect were limited in view of Russia's chronic manpower shortage; the central provinces could not be depleted in favor of the new lands in the south. Several special social groups, however, could be tapped for this purpose. In the first place were the many Old Believers who had fled to Poland to escape the persecution of the governments of Tsar Alexis and Peter the Great. An energetic effort was now undertaken to lure them back into Russia. Old Believers were promised that local bishops would permit them to follow their ritual and consecrate their priests. In addition, they were given generous economic inducements in form of land grants, exemptions from taxation for long periods, and relief from the discriminatory capitation tax rate. They were also allowed to settle on the same terms as the military colonists, which automatically would exempt them from furnishing recruits. In return, they would have to hold themselves ready to answer calls to active duty in time of war.[49] The policy had some success, although not as much as expected, in part because of the reluctance on the part of the Church hierarchy and the loss of interest in the scheme on the part of Catherine's successors.

Another group that might be tapped were the children of the Orthodox parish clergy. As the sons of priests automatically belonged to the clerical estate, and as there were fewer parishes than sons of priests, the latter were threatening to become a semi-educated clerical "proletariat." Potemkin suggested that supernumerary sextons and sons of priests be attracted to South Russia. There they could settle in agricultural pursuits, combined with some military obligations along the same lines as the Old Believers. If they preferred, however, they could enter the civil service and provide educated personnel for the much understaffed local administrative institutions, while at the same time fostering the russification of the region. In reward, the expectation was held out to them that, in view of the dearth of good administrative personnel, they might rise rapidly in the service, secure high ranks, which in turn would enable them to acquire estates and even the title of nobility with the right to own serfs. A number of children of the clergy took advantage of this opportunity and the administrative offices in the south were staffed by many from their ranks; a few eventually made very good careers in the imperial government.[50]

Finally, one should mention that the various officers and officials from Russia could bring to their newly acquired estates in the south serfs from the central provinces.[51] This was a potentially double-edged measure which did not go without some complications. Indeed, the danger was that serfs would be lured away or that owners in the central provinces would traffic in serfs to provide for the labor needs of the south. Such traffic was forbidden and landowners could transport and resettle only their own serf families.[52] How well these rules were obeyed is hard to say. However this may have been, two things are clear: first, many serfs were moved to southern Russia, contributing to the ethnic russification of the local population (thus confusing still further the national picture for later generations). Secondly, serfdom was introduced into the Ukraine, an area that had heretofore been spared this evil.[53] The

growing similarity of the social structures in the southern and central provinces enabled the russification and total assimilation of the Ukraine to make
rapid strides.

*   *   *

The administrative organization and the social transformation fostered by
Potemkin and the St. Petersburg government served to integrate the Ukraine
into the economic structure of the empire. This structure, which was beginning to emerge at the end of the eighteenth century, consisted in its international aspect of a shift from the export of naval stores, industrial raw materials,
and semi-manufactured products (pig iron, for example) to that of agricultural products, mainly grain. It is in this development that the Ukraine, or
more generally speaking all of southern Russia, was to play the major role. Indeed, the steadily increasing number of large estates belonging to noble
servicemen and high officials, the transformation of many local peasants into
serfs, and the settlement of many more from the central provinces, were
changing the Ukraine into a region of extensive agriculture for the export
market. The foundation and development of commercial ports—first Kherson, later Odessa—served both as illustration and stimulant of this new
trend.[54] This transformation conformed to what were Catherine's and
Potemkin's ulterior goals, which they may only have half-consciously groped
for, but which—with the benefit of hindsight—appear quite clearly. These
goals reflected the basic policy concerns of Catherine which we have noted at
the beginning of this essay; they may be subsumed under the fashionable
terms of "modernization" and "rationalization" of Russian life in general,
and of the social and economic structure of the newly acquired regions in particular. Let us consider briefly some of these goals and the way in which they
began to be realized.

In the first place we might cite urbanism, that is the foundation and development of towns and cities. This fitted well into the Enlightenment's preference for urban civilization and its infatuation with town planning and archi-
tectural design, expressive of utopian rationalism.[55] Loving the grandiose and
given to flashy display, Potemkin found in town planning and building a particularly satisfying outlet for his energies and ambition. He first devoted his attention to Kherson which he destined to become the political and cultural
center of the newly gained lands and the dockyard for the Black Sea fleet.[56]
Later he allowed the town to decline (where it remained until Soviet times)
and its place was taken in Potemkins' heart by Nikolaev which was located
closer to the open sea. Symbolically, Potemkin hastened his own death by his
desire to return to Nikolaev when his forces gave way at Iassy.[57] Taganrog and
Mariupol' were two other creations of his, a byproduct, as we have seen, of
the settlement of Greeks from the islands and the Crimea. Lastly, Potemkin

selected Ekaterinoslav as the capital of the vicegerency of New Russia and gave it his particular attention and care. He hoped to make it into the "Athens" of the Ukraine. He laid out the town in grand manner, started the building of a cathedral that was to exceed St. Peter's of Rome in size, and—on paper—established a university for which he hired several faculty members, including a professor of music and of fine arts.[58] In contrast to this utopian urge to create *ex nihilo* and to build "Athens," complete with university and academy in what was still economic and social frontier country, was the resort to traditional and archaic means. For example, to speed along his building plans, Potemkin instructed his subordinates to purchase serf masons in central Russia and to bring them to Kherson. He also ordered the compulsory training of recruits in various crafts, purchased unfree craftsmen, and had them enrolled into military units where they had to work at their trade whenever ordered to do so by their superiors or local authorities.[59]

The harebrained plan to set up a university in an incompleted city amidst barely populated steppes was not the only manifestation of Potemkin's concern for education in the region under his rule. In a more realistic vein, whose effects proved to be lasting, Potemkin took the lead in establishing secondary schools. At the time of the Russian naval expedition to the Mediterranean, young Greeks had been brought to Russia; a school, along the lines of the Corps of Cadets, was opened for them in 1774 in Oranienbaum, near St. Petersburg. Other foreign Orthodox pupils were also admitted to it. In 1783 this school was transferred to Kherson where it served as the nucleus of a very successful secondary school, not so much for the non-Russian children as for the children of the local administrators and officers. In Nikolaev a Corps of Cadets for 300 pupils was planned; in Kremenchug a secondary school for girls was opened and supported from state funds.[60]

Closely related to these efforts at education, Potemkin helped to develop book publishing in South Russia. The mobile printing press attached to his headquarters served as the foundation of local printing presses equipped to print in several languages (Greek, Latin, French, and Russian). These presses were used not so much to print official orders and regulations, as had been intended at first, as books of general educational interest. Curiously enough, most of the books so produced were either popular Western classics or else had a theological content. They helped to spread the common storehouse of Western culture alongside with ecclesiastic learning and religious concerns among the settlers of the new region.[61]

Potemkin's recommendations for appointments to newly established dioceses are also indicative of his cultural concerns. Thus Evgenii Bulgaris, a leading scholar and active figure in the neo-hellenic movement, was made bishop of Ekaterinoslav and Kremenchug. He distinguished himself more by his efforts at establishing educational institutions than as a shepherd of his flock (whose language he barely spoke).[62] As can be readily seen, there was more than one purpose in such a choice: not only did Bishop Bulgaris promote learning and culture in New Russia, but his position in the neo-hellenic movement could become politically useful as an instrument against the Turks.

In a more sportive mood, perhaps, Potemkin endeavored to bring about diversity in agriculture and beautification of the landscape. Attempts were made to introduce new cultures, such as sericulture, and to improve and expand existing ones, vineyards and tropical-fruit growing, for instance, in the Crimea. To beautify the region, groves were planted, parks created in the new cities, the estates and residences of the high dignitaries and administrators of the region embellished by fancy gardens and alleys of exotic trees. Potemkin contracted with several leading agronomists and gardeners to draw up and work out these projects, albeit the results were mixed and, on the whole, indifferent.[63] Lastly, obvious military needs led to the active building and expansion of fortresses and harbors, thus laying the foundation for the economic and historical roles of Sebastopol, Taganrog, and Odessa.

In all of these activities there is an unmistakable element of "play," in Huizinga's sense, of course. While Potemkin pursued fundamental long-range Russian imperial and national interests (or so it appears to us in retrospect), in the forefront of his own mind there was only the desire to enhance the glory of his sovereign, to demonstrate his own talents and power, and to indulge in his passion for luxury and magnificent display. The military context in which he acted gave him a wide stage and endowed many of his activities with an element of orderly rationality that was not devoid of aesthetic appeal. It also provided Potemkin and his aides with the physical means and manpower to carry out the most ambitious schemes. The style of Potemkin's military, administrative, economic, and building activities in the south is strongly reminiscent of the efforts made—on a more modest scale—by many Russian noblemen to introduce a rational and "civilized" way of life into their residences and on their estates.[64] In both cases the essential elements of "modernity" were vitiated by the sad fact of Russian life in the eighteenth century: that they had to be introduced by autocratic fiat and given reality by servile labor. This is perhaps the basic reason why so many of these ventures proved to be stillborn and why the grandiose, but potentially useful, projects of the Prince of Tauris turned into so many "Potemkin villages."

*   *   *

Despite its limitations and failures, from a long-range point of view, the last quarter of the eighteenth century proved to have been a period of great accomplishments in terms of the incorporation and development of the newly acquired south. This was the result not only of an almost traditional process of expansion and colonization, but also very much of the conscious policy of

Catherine II and her main assistant and counselor, Prince G. A. Potemkin of Tauris. Let us examine the methods he used and the means at his disposal; perhaps it will enable us to explain his relatively dramatic success, contrasted to the much slower and less significant accomplishments earlier.[65] Unquestionably Potemkin has few peers in the history of modern Russia in terms of the scope and significance of his work for the empire, as well as of his success; only Count Muraviev-Amurskii, in the mid-nineteenth century, comes readily to mind as a figure of comparable stature. The other architects of the Russian Empire—Speransky as administrative reformer in Siberia, General Kaufman as colonial conqueror in Central Asia, and the principals of the conquest of the Caucasus (General Ermolov, Vorontsov, Prince Bariatinskii)—great as were their merits, can hardly compare to the brilliant favorite of Catherine II.

The all-powerful satrap of southern Russia exercised his authority at a distance. Potemkin either resided at the court in St. Petersburg or was to be found at his headquarters in the theater of operations. There never was a town that might have been called his administrative residence, although at first Kremenchug and later Ekaterinoslav was officially the capital of New Russia. Yet he exercised absolute control at all times. His official correspondence and reports which have been published (only a fraction of an astoundingly large amount) show that he kept an eye on every facet of the life of the regions under his administration and took a hand in deciding even the most trivial details. For this purpose he had his own private chancery, an organization of about fifty competent bureaucrats of all ranks, headed by his trusted factotum V. S. Popov, who held the rank of lieutenant-general. It was a completely personal staff, not subject to any imperial institution or dignitary, selected and maintained by Potemkin alone. This staff processed, digested, prepared the vast amount of factual information that was forwarded for Potemkin's consideration and decision. In Potemkin's name the chancery issued orders and directives to all institutions and subordinate authorities in South Russia. The degree of functional specialization among these personal officials of Potemkin's may be gauged from the fact that one of them, R. M. Tsebrikov, had been a classmate of Radishchev's at the University of Leipzig and was assigned to Potemkin's headquarters exclusively to take care of the Prince's French correspondence.[66]

V. S. Popov, who acted as a kind of chief minister, enjoyed the unbounded confidence of Potemkin, so that most matters went through his hands. To increase the channels of information at the Prince's disposal without burdening him with undue detail, Popov had the chief local officials and regional governors write to him regularly on an informal—at times quite chatty—basis. These letters give an insight into the day-to-day life of the region, the activities, problems, and concerns of its officials. They also show how devoted and eager the authorities were to please Potemkin in matters both official and private. One has the impression that Potemkin is the actual sovereign and Catherine II only the far-away "god" to whom they all owe devotion, but who is a remote and almost abstract symbol for most; and this in spite of Catherine's very personal style of government. The local officials communicated directly only with Popov and Potemkin, not with the central institutions of the empire—the Senate or the Colleges—to which they were formally subordinated. As a result Potemkin not only exercised firm control, but also obtained information which was usually not vouchsafed a high dignitary. The same system served also to keep a close watch over happenings in St. Petersburg during his absences (a vital element in his long-lasting political influence). He had a highly placed business agent, General Garnovskii, who took care of all his private affairs—which were extensive and involved dealing with the highest dignitaries of the empire. Besides reporting on Potemkin's private business and the execution of his manifold instructions, Garnovskii kept Popov informed of all court and diplomatic gossip and events in an uninterrupted flow of letters of which a representative sample has been preserved and published.[67] We can see how Potemkin, even at a distance, could react to practically everything that might affect his position and activities, including the choice and success of Catherine's *amant en titre*.

The fact that Potemkin combined in his person both military and civilian authority explains why he wielded such great power over so many officials and institutions. As the territories under his control had but recently been acquired and were still on a military footing (not to mention areas which lay directly in the zone of operations during the second Turkish war), his position as commander in chief and as president of the College of War gave him an uncontested power of decision. His military office permitted him to bypass the very complicated and overlapping jurisdictions and hierarchies of the civilian establishment. On a lower level the same was true of the governors subordinated to him who also were local military commanders. In all matters they referred to Potemkin and his chancery with which they had both formally and practically the right to communicate directly, disregarding all other hierarchies and echelons of command. One last observation may be in order at this point. Because so many policies and decisions were dictated, or could be justified, by military necessities—such as defense, preparation for war, or the conduct of military and naval operations—they were left to the discretion of local commanders and carried out in a military manner by subordinate officers. No civilian authority or central institution, the Senate for example, could make its considerations or arguments count decisively under the circumstances.

Naturally, much of Potemkin's style of administration had a distinctly militaristic character. Instructions and directives had to be executed like a military command by the personnel of local military units; their implementation was supervised by the military and any delay or opposition dealt with in a peremptory manner. More important still was the seemingly utter disregard of a reasonable ratio between cost and result that is so characteristic of the militaristic mentality. Provided that the expected result was reached, whether in battle or in administration, any price and any means were deemed justified. An order had to be blindly executed, regardless of cost or difficulties, without taking into account local complexities and circumstances. Of course, Potemkin and his aides were quite aware of local conditions—we have seen how they were put to good advantage to further imperial interests—yet as one reads their correspondence, one senses that this awareness was rather superficial and did not extend to a genuine realization of local needs. Local conditions were, at best, treated as limiting factors, never as possible positive features to be furthered for their own sake or for the advantage their preservation might have for the empire subsequently. Like a staff officer who takes into account the relief of the terrain to direct artillery fire and troop movements, but thinks in essentially non-local terms, Potemkin made sweeping plans to achieve an overall goal without much regard for local circumstances and requirements.

In this respect Potemkin's task was facilitated by the fact that he had unlimited imperial confidence. We shall deal with his relationship to Catherine II later. But by virtue of this relationship Potemkin had almost limitless financial means at his disposal; what is more, he did not have to give a detailed account of the way he spent the sums given to him. In fact he disposed at will of countless millions of rubles that the Empress made available to him. Because of Potemkin's own habits of spending, his conception of the total and personal nature of his authority he—like an autocratic ruler—did not differentiate between personal and public expenses. His lavish entertainments were paid out of the same monies as the settlement of foreigners or the building of a new man-of-war. It proved so difficult to unscramble these accounts that, eventually, Alexander I had to write off the Prince's expenditures as part of the public debt left by Catherine II. Even the trusted Popov—perhaps for good reasons of his own—could not give an itemized account of large sums received by his chief, as is made abundantly clear by his report of the audit he made after Potemkin's death. ...[68]

In another way, too, Potemkin showed that he was practically a monarch in South Russia. While the grandiloquent display of titles was common practice in the eighteenth century everywhere in Europe, no less than in Russia, Potemkin's manner in this respect is noteworthy. His official communications—for example to the Cossack Host informing them of his nomination as commander in chief of all irregular forces and of the appointment of their new ataman, his proclamations on the occasion of the annexation of the Crimea—were introduced by an enumeration of his titles, ranks, offices, and orders of chivalry that closely resembled royal titles. The fact that he spoke in the name of his Gracious Sovereign was obliterated by this endless enumeration of his own qualities. Not unexpectedly under the circumstances, persons addressing themselves to Potemkin in official communications used formulas that came quite close to those reserved for the monarch.[69] These may seem to be trifling details, to be ascribed to an excessive degree of personal vanity on Potemkin's part, but there was substance behind this form.

Potemkin had wide powers of direct appointment, not only indirectly through his influence on Catherine II. He thus selected and appointed in his own name the ataman of the Don Cossack Host, Ilovaiskii. He conferred military offices and titles at the highest level. More significant still was the fact that he conferred ranks (*chin*), which in Russia were the principal criterion of status and privilege. And in the manner of the Russian rulers themselves he also gave estates as reward for meritorious services, as in the case of the prince of Nassau-Siegen. It is superfluous to mention that he also awarded decorations for bravery and outstanding deeds. In one case he even conferred to a noble family the right to a specially designed coat of arms in recognition of an exploit of great bravery by a member of this family under his command.[70]

These ways and deeds made Potemkin appear rather like a monarch, a viceroy at the very least, than an extraordinarily powerful governor-general or commander-in-chief. And in a way that was characteristic of the traditional Russian concept of sovereign power, Potemkin had a personal concern for the well-being of his "subjects." It was not merely the concern which any good chief has for his subordinates, or a patron who knows that the loyalty of his clients depends on his interest in them. In fact he scorned the opinions of others and disregarded their sensibilities; his arrogance could be quite monumental, as indignantly noted by the French diplomats and émigrés who were used to the polite ways of Versailles, especially on the part of the monarch.[71] But Potemkin felt a sense of responsibility to the common people which is strongly reminiscent of the medieval idea of just kingship. He had almost none of this sense toward his officers and high officials. On the contrary, like the unrestrained and coarse Russian despots of the eighteenth century, he reputedly slapped officers and high officials, insulted them publicly by his words and his behavior, not to speak of taking advantage of their wives and daughters, if it suited his lust.[72] Toward the common folk, especially the soldiers, he was quite different. He considered himself their father and felt directly responsible for their well-being. Indeed, he strongly believed that the health, comfort, good cheer of the soldiers were his concern, in a human, as well as military sense. By his orders the Russian soldier was freed (alas, for a time only) from the excruciating headdress and uniforms that Peter III had introduced in imitation of Prussia. Potemkin had uniforms designed for comfort and to suit the climate of Russia.[73] In his instructions to his subordinates he warned that soldiers should be treated with leniency and trained only for the sake of their military performance on the battlefield, and not for show at parades.[74] Finally, the soldiers' health was an object of his constant care, as witness his numerous instructions for sanitary measures and the means he put at the disposal of hospitals and quartermasters.[75]

In short, Potemkin's success—such as it was—in the huge and complicated task of organizing and administering the vast territory of South Russia was made possible by the combination of unusually great financial and political means at his disposal and of the way he looked at the responsibilities of his position in human terms. He was a sovereign in fact, if not in name, and he accepted the traditional Russian notions of the responsibilities and burdens of kingship.[76] His behavior illustrates the price he paid in psychological terms for this acceptance. Today we no doubt would diagnose Potemkin as a neurotic individual, subject to periods of depression during which he could do nothing but loll on his couch, a prisoner of feelings of surfeit and anxiety.[77] Historians have explained this moodiness, Potemkin's frenzied activity and extravagant dissipation alternating with gloomy apathy by the extraordinary rapidity and ease with which he attained the heights of power and riches, by the fact—as he himself confessed—that he was too lucky.

Everyone agrees, and documentary evidence confirms it, that he was a thorough "Russian"—in the sense of sharing his people's traditions, values, and even prejudices—individual. Living at the cosmopolitan court of Catherine II he seems barely to have been touched by the fashionable European culture of his day. He knew French, of course, he read and spoke it; but he did not live in its cultural realm as most courtiers did. At first sight, his intellectual interests were strange for a man of his position: mainly theology and religious questions in the traditional dogmatic framework of orthodoxy. There was little that he liked better than a good theological disputation, at which he was quite adept, citing freely and accurately the Eastern Church Fathers and their commentators.[78] We have mentioned that in his youth he had contemplated taking holy orders; he remained—amidst the skeptical court of Catherine II—a deeply believing individual, although his moral conduct was far from being above reproach, by even the most latitudinarian standards. His moodiness, therefore, may also be ascribed to a burning awareness of his great sinfulness. But we think it is also fair to argue that he genuinely believed that his vast power, by leading him to sin on a grand scale, also burdened him with guilt and conferred a particular responsibility. In the Russian tradition power is evil by definition, and should be accepted by no one but the God-annointed tsar, who shares thereby responsibility for his subjects' sins. The tsar's lot is to be pitied and his commands obeyed in a spirit of compassion and forgiveness. This is why the ruler is seen as a Christlike figure, for like Christ he has accepted the burden of power (or existence) to help men to the good life and guide them toward redemption.

But why should we recall this web of beliefs and attitudes when reflecting on the career of Potemkin? Why do such reflections not come to mind in the case of other influential and successful administrators or military commanders? One obvious answer is too simple-minded to be satisfactory: Potemkin was a "large personality"; he dominated wherever he was, in whatever he did.

He had the outward appearance of the great role he played in fact; his mental equipment was outstanding: a quick and sharp mind, broad and realistic intelligence, excellent memory, a capacity for dreaming high dreams and bold adventures; he had, to an unusual degree, the ability to please, to make himself beloved and respected, as well as hated. But all of these qualities would have availed him little without Catherine II. In the final analysis, Potemkin became what he was because he was the favorite of the Empress.

But it was not only in the obvious and ordinary sense that he was a favorite. Catherine II kept a male harem and the list of her lovers—declared or secret, long-lasting or for a night—is impressively long. Potemkin, however, was alone in also becoming a political personality in his own right (the last favorite, Platon Zubov, also wielded political influence over the aged but still sensuous Catherine, but he never exercised even the shadow of the power Potemkin did). There is some evidence for the belief that Potemkin was Catherine's morganatic husband; but true or not, this is of little importance. What is significant is that Catherine accepted him as a counselor on equal terms with herself, trusted him completely to the end of his life, leaned on him. This is why she gave him full authority and such vast means to act in the way he did in South Russia. The letters of Catherine to Potemkin show that he enjoyed the highest degree of intimacy and affection, of genuine respect and trust, even after he had ceased to be her lover.[79] For fourteen years he was really her "husband" in the sense that he shared her responsibilities, plans, hopes, and work, whether he shared her bed or not. The contemporaries, the high-born and lowly commoners alike, understood or sensed this relationship (which neither Catherine nor Potemkin did much to hide).[80] He was, therefore, seen almost as a co-ruler and his ways only confirmed the public in this opinion. This situation lent to Potemkin's actions a force and authority that no one else in the empire could muster.

*   *   *

Our description and analysis point to one obvious observation: the fundamental ambivalence of the style of Russian imperial policy in the eighteenth century, an ambivalence which the career of the main executor of this policy, Prince Potemkin, so well illustrates. This ambivalence may be expressed by the two sets of words: old and new goals, traditional and rational ways. As a matter of fact, the whole history of Russia in the eighteenth century may be described by this double antithesis. Indeed, it was truly a transitional period in the course of which the Muscovite past was jettisoned and the groundwork laid for a modern polity and culture. While the latter—in the form of literature, music, science—achieved a triumphant success in the nineteenth century, the former—i.e., political and public life—did not overcome the ambivalence of the eighteenth century. This ambivalent political heritage of the eighteenth century survived—albeit in somewhat changed forms—until the end of the imperial regime and has even bedevilled the Soviet rulers who overthrew it. ...

*   *   *

Surely in every state and society, in every period, the new coexists with much of the old, although in a state of dialectical tension. Eventually this tension is resolved as the traditional gives way and as the new adjusts to realities; a new pattern emerges.[81] But it is a striking feature of what we have chosen to call the Russian style of imperial policy in the eighteenth century, as exemplified by the activities of Potemkin, that there was no dialectical tension; that the opposition remained unresolved between the traditional and rational approach on the one hand, and between the old and the new goals on the other. The two facets of the style seemed to coexist without any one appreciably impinging on the other, or of being able to displace it completely. In other words, the Russian state pursued ambivalent goals with ambivalent methods and did not evolve a synthesis which would overcome the ambivalence. The results of its activities also bore the stamp of ambivalence and proved—in the final analysis—to be inadequate and unstable. ...

... The pursuit of imperial expansion was crowned by glorious success: the empire's territory greatly expanded, in several directions Russia reached what may be called its "natural boundaries." The military power of the empire increased so that Russia could effectively play the role of a leading world power. The rational and active exploitation of the economic resources of the country was given strong impetus and reached a high level (comparatively speaking). In human terms, too, the policy seemed to be successful at first glance: new nations were annexed to the empire without much difficulty, their élites were absorbed into the mainstream of Russia's social and cultural life.

Yet this apparently successful result was vitiated at the core: it was incapable of organic life or development. The imperial polity that had been created proved capable neither of adjusting to novel situations nor of devising workable solutions to unforeseen problems. Indeed, the russification of the native élites only paved the way for a most painful emergence of the national question, it helped to spread the deep gulf between the common people and the educated classes to all the nationalities of the empire. Far from being undermined by the "rationalization" of the empire, the dreadful and harmful system of serfdom was temporarily strengthened and exported into the new territories. Lastly, uniform centralization and militarism froze the vital forces that were most needed to further progress and adaptability to the problems of genuine "modernization": local initiative and individual entrepreneurship, the energies and liberties for the development of new foci of power and authority capable of assisting in the creation of an increasingly varied and complex polity, of giving meaningful expression and support to the personalized authority of the autocratic tsar, and of providing workable substitutes for the rigid centralized bureaucracy.

Potemkin's career dramatically shows that in Russia authority derived from the personal and dynamic (charismatic in Max Weber's terminology) character of political power. It was in flagrant contradiction to the static bureaucratic framework that it had imposed on the country. When it became clear that personal authority was inadequate to the tasks set by modern imperial policy there was nothing that could complement or replace it effectively. Potemkin—like Peter the Great—had succeeded in using both traditional and rational methods in a policy that aimed at building a new empire which, by bringing to conclusion old political trends, would also initiate a modern dynamic social and economic development. But he had been able to do it not so much because of his great talent as by virtue of his special relationship to Catherine. It is this relationship that endowed his authority with the traditional personal character and made it acceptable to, and obeyed by large segments of the population. No one else in Russia could duplicate this combination later and thereby repeat his performance. Prince Grigorii Aleksandrovich Potemkin thus proved to have been not only Russia's greatest imperial statesman, but also the last.

Notes

1. Throughout this essay, unless otherwise qualified, we use the name Ukraine in its modern connotation, i.e., to refer to the entire south of European Russia, between the lower Don and the lower Dniester.

2. Sbornik imperatorskogo russkogo istoricheskogo obshchestva (Sbornik IRIO), VII (1871), 82–109.

3. Polnoe sobranie zakonov rossiiskoi imperii (PSZ), 12474 (September 19, 1765), 15447 (June 28, 1782); Sbornik IRIO, XXVII (1880), 68, 186. It was a break with the policy of Peter the Great who had reserved to the state the monopoly over all minerals and ores and the control over the exploitation of such resources as timber.

4. For ex. PSZ 14275 (March 17, 1775); cf. P. I. Liashchenko, *Istoriia narodnogo khoziaistva SSSR*, I (Moscow, 1947), 418–424.

5. The so-called Charters to the Nobility (PSZ 16187, April 21, 1785) and to the Towns (PSZ 16188, April 21, 1785).

6. Recently, historians have come to the conclusion that the project was drafted by A. A. Bezborodko and that it does not seem to have been taken seriously by anyone else, except as a gambit in the tortuous relations between Russia and Austria. See O. P. Markova, "O proiskhozhdenii tak nazyvaemogo grecheskogo proekta (8oe gody XXVIII v.)," *Istoriia SSSR*, 1958, No. 4, pp. 52–78; and E. Hösch, "Das sogenannte 'griechische Projekt' Katharinas II," *Jahrbücher für Geschichte Osteuropas*, N. F. XII (1964), 168–206.

7. For this aspect of the history of the southeastern European plain, see W. H. McNeill, *Europe's Steppe Frontier, 1500–1800: A Study of the Eastward Movement in Europe* (University of Chicago, 1964).

8. The biographical data are drawn from A. Loviagin, "Potemkin, G. A.," *Russkii biograficheskii slovar'* (Plavil'shchikov-Primo) (St. Petersburg, 1905), cols. 549–670; Th. Adamczyk, *Fürst G. A. Potemkin: Untersuchungen zu seiner Lebensgeschichte* (Emsdetten, 1936); the only modern biography in English, G. Soloveytchik, *Potemkin: Soldier, Statesman, Lover and Consort of Catherine of Russia* (New York, 1947), is unfortunately useless to the historian. A number of legends are connected with the dazzling career of Potemkin; most of them have been shown to be derived from one or two malevolent contemporary Western pamphlets, cf. V. Bil'bassov, *Katharina II. Kaiserin von Russland im Urtheile der Weltliteratur*, 2 vols. (Berlin, 1897).

9. Sbornik IRIO, VII, 316–318; Zapiski odesskogo obshchestva istorii i drevnostei, ZOOID, XIII (1883), 187–188.

10. The best account is G. Stökl, *Die Entstehung des Kosakentums* (München: Veröffentlichunges des Osteuropa-Institutes, 1953); the most recent comprehensive Soviet history is V. A. Golobutskii, *Zaporozhskoe kazachestvo* (Kiev, 1957).

11. PSZ 14354 (August 3, 1775); N. F. Dubrovin, *Bumagi kniazia Grigoria Aleksandrovicha Potemkina-Tavricheskogo* 1774–1788 gg. (St. Petersburg: Sbornik voenno-istoricheskikh materialov, vyp. VI, 1893), nos. 36, pp. 36–37, and 47, pp. 46–52. Hereafter this source will be cited as *Bumagi Potemkina*.

12. Cf. S. G. Svatikov, *Rossiia i Don 1549–1917 (Issledovanie po istorii gosudarstvennogo i administrativnogo prava i politicheskikh dvizhenii na Donu)*, (Belgrade, 1924); V. A. Golobutskii, *Chernomorskoe kazachestvo* (Kiev, 1956).

13. The instructive example of Ataman S. Efremov was vividly present in Catherine's mind, cf. Svatikov, pp. 210–216, 223.

14. *Bumagi Potemkina*, Nos. 22, pp. 17–18, and 24, pp. 20–21.

15. PSZ 14251 (February 14, 1775), 14252 (February 14, 1775); *Bumagi Potemkina*, No. 23, pp. 18–20.

16. Sbornik IRIO, XXVII, 63.

17. *Bumagi Potemkina*, No. 23, p. 19.

18. *Bumagi Potemkina*, No. 81, p. 89.

19. Their use as military police—especially during strikes, riots, and pogroms—which gave the Cossacks their ill-famed notoriety on the eve of the Revolution did not come about until the end of the nineteenth century.

20. I. I. Dmitrenko (ed.), *Sbornik istoricheskikh materialov po istorii Kubanskogo kazacheskogo voiska I*, 1737–1801, gg. (St. Petersburg, 1896); and Golobutskii, *Chernomorskoe kazachestvo*, passim.

21. For Catherine's considerations, see Sbornik IRIO, XXVII, 221–225 for general treatment and background, B. Nolde, *La Formation de l'Empire russe (Etudes, Notes et Documents)*, II (Paris: Collection historique de l'Institut d'Etudes slaves, XV-2, 1953), Chaps. IX and X. Also Alan W. Fisher, *The Russian Annexation of the Crimea, 1772–1783* (New York: Cambridge University Press, 1970).

22. N. Dubrovin (ed.), *Prisoedinenie Kryma k Rossii (Reskripty, pis'ma, reliatsii, doneseniia)*, Vols. I–IV (St. Petersburg, 1885–1889), in particular see II (No. 114), 318–319 and (No. 117), 320–321. Hereafter cited as *Prisoedinenie Kryma*.

23. The charter to the Greeks is in PSZ 14879 (May 21, 1779) and to the Armenians PSZ 14942 (November 14, 1779); cf. also ZOOID, II (1848–1850), 660.

24. Report of Gen. Suvorov, *Prisoedinenie Kryma*, II (No. 314), 752–753.

25. ZOOID, I, 197–204 and IV (1860), 359–362.

26. Best summary in B. Nolde, Vol. I (Paris: 1952), Chaps, I–III.

27. One may also note in passing the greater role played by religion and language in the eighteenth century in bringing about the separation between different national groups that had lived in the same territory.

28. ZOOID, XII (1881), No. 38, p. 265, and No. 101, p. 286.

29. For numerous illustrations see the memoirs of a member of the Russian administration D. B. Mertvago, "Zapiski Dmitriia Borisovicha Mertvago 1760–1824," Appendix to *Russki Arkhiv,* 1867, especially pp. 177–178.

30. ZOOID, VI (1867) 604; XIV (1886), 149–150; XXXI (1913) 79.

31. ZOOID, XIV, 149–150, 153.

32. Sbornik IRIO, XXVII, 245–246; ZOOID, XXXI, 62–63; PSZ 15988 (April 24, 1784).

33. ZOOID, XXIII (1901), 41–43.

34. PSZ 15920 (February 2, 1784), 15925 (February 8, 1784), 15988 (April 24, 1784).

35. ZOOID, XV (1889), 678–680.

36. *Bumagi Potemkina,* No. 43, p. 43; No. 48, pp. 52–53; No. 84, pp. 90–92; No. 85, pp. 92–94; ZOOID, I, 205–226.

37. Sbornik IRIO, XLII, No. 406, p. 383.

38. ZOOID, VI, 604; XI (1879), 330–331.

39. J. Nicolopoulos, "Père et fils dans l'Aufklärung néohellénique: Les Paniagiodor-Nikovul," Ο ΕΡΑΝΙΣΤΗΣ (Athens, 1964), XII, 254–279.

40. N. D. Polons'ka-Vasylenko, *The Settlement of the Southern Ukraine* (1750–1775), The Annals of the Ukrainian Academy of Arts and Sciences in the U. S., Vol. IV–V, No. 4 (14)—I (15), Summer-Fall 1955; H. Auerbach, *Die Besiedelung der Südukraine in den Jahren 1774–1787* (Wiesbaden, 1965), (Veröffentlichungen des Osteuropa-Institutes, München, Band 25).

41. Polons'ka-Vasylenko, p. 220; cf. also E. I. Druzhinina, *Severnoe prichernomor'e v 1775–1780 gg.* (Moscow, 1959).

42. See the curious secret instructions of Empress Anne on promoting russification through a governmental matrimonial policy, Sbornik IRIO, CVIII, 26.

43. See § 9 of this instruction, Sbornik IRIO, VII, 348.

44. Sbornik IRIO, VII, 376–391.

45. The best summary is E. A. Zagorovskii, "Organizatsiia upravleniia Novorossii pri Potemkine," ZOOID, XXXI, 52–82; see also relevant chapters in Auerbach and Druzhinina, cited above.

46. Cf. ZOOID, XXIX (1911), Part II, 59–81.

47. ZOOID, XII, 127–131; II, 662–663, 665–666; Sbornik IRIO, XXVII, 350. The basic legislation and administrative framework for foreign colonists in Russia was the decree of July 22, 1763, PSZ 11879, which set up the so-called Chancery for the Tutelage of Foreign Colonists.

48. The problems involved in tracing the history of the unofficial migration of Russian settlers to the south are briefly discussed by A. Florovskii, "Neskol'ko faktov iz istorii russkoi kolonizatsii Novorossii v nachale XIX v.," ZOOID, XXXIII (1919), 25–40.

49. *Bumagi Potemkina*, No. 117, p. 120 (§2); No. 188, pp. 192–193; Sbornik IRIO, XXVII, 468; ZOOID, IX (1875), 285–288; VIII (1872) 212; Auerbach, p. 102.

50. ZOOID, VIII, 212; XV (1889), 613; Sbornik IRIO, XLII, 416; *Bumagi Potemkina*, No. 117, p. 129 (§1); No. 310, pp. 268–269.

51. Although this permission must be balanced by Potemkin's purchases of serfs from private estates in the Ukraine for settlement in military units. Thereby these serfs were converted into state peasants whose lot was by and large, much better than that of private serfs. Druzhinina, pp. 188–189 and PSZ 16605 (Jan. 14, 1788).

52. The plot of Gogol's *Dead Souls* is, of course, based on this situation.

53. Auerbch, pp. 108–110. It is true that for a while the strictness of serfdom was mitigated in the south by the need for labor which made the owners chary of introducing the harsh patterns that prevailed in the central provinces.

54. For the "prehistory" of this development, see D. Gerhard, *England und der Aufstieg Russlands* (München-Berlin, 1933); the three studies of H. Halm under the general title of *Oesterreich und Neurussland* give the best account and fullest documentation of the development of Russian trade in the Black Sea. They clearly point to the conclusion that the expansion of trade followed the political and administrative changes in the area and did not contribute much to bring them about. H. Halm, *Donauschiffahrt und -handel nach dem Südosten, 1718–1780* (Breslau, 1943); *Habsburgischer Osthandel im 18. Jahrhundert, Donauhandel und Seeschiffahrt, 1781–1787* (München, 1954) (Veröffentlichungen des Osteuropa-Institutes, München, Bd. VII); Jan Reychman, "Le commerce polonais en Mer Noire au XVIIIe siècle par le port de Kherson," *Cahiers du Monde russe et soviétique*, VII, No. 2 (Avril-Juin 1966), 234–238.

55. See the suggestive proceedings of an international symposium held in Nancy, P. Francastel (ed.), *Utopie et institutions au XVIIIe siècle (Le pragmatisme des Lumières)* (Paris-LaHaye, 1936). Of course, J.-J. Rousseau fought against this trend, but his impact was not felt until the very end of the century, and even at that it did not prevent the continuing interest in town planning and building.

56. See Potemkin's instructions to his agent there, M. I. Faleev, ZOOID, XI, 324–377 and also XIII, 184–187; IV, 362–373.

57. Graf. A. N. Samoilov, "Zhizn' i deianiia general-fel'dmarshala kniazia Grigoriia Aleksandrovicha Potemkina-Tavricheskogo," *Russkii Arkhiv*, V (1867), cols. 1557–1560.

58. ZOOID, IV, 375, 377; II, 332; XV, 616.

59. ZOOID, XIII, 185, 186.

60. Sbornik IRIO, XXVII, 5, 230–231; ZOOID, IV, 374, 376; XIII, 184. The medico-surgical school in Simferopol, established in the 1790's, owes its origins to Potemkin's educational policy, cf. ZOOID, II, 331, 333.

61. ZOOID, IV, 470–472; II, 211–219. Also Georges Haupt, "La Russie et les principautés danubiennes en 1790—Le Prince Potemkin Tavričeskij et le *Courrier de Moldavie*," *Cahiers du Monde russe et soviétique*, VII, No. 1 (Janvier-Mars 1966), 58–62.

62. ZOOID, II, 330–356; see also A. Lebedev, "Evgenii Bulgaris, arkhiepiskop slavenskii i khersonskii," *Drevniaia i novaia Rossiia*, 1876, No. 31, 209–223.

63. Sbornik IRIO, XXVII, 357, 360; ZOOID, IX, 254–255; XIII, 186; XV, 668.

64. On a truly imperial scale Potemkin behaved in much the same way as the middling nobleman, A. T. Bolotov, whose activities we know particularly well from his voluminous memoirs, did on his own estate and as steward of an imperial domain south of Moscow. *Zhizn' i prikliucheniia Andreia Bolotova opisannye im samim dlia svoikh potomkov*, 1738–1793, Vols. I–IV (St. Petersburg, 1871–1873).

65. The following represents a synthesis of the observations we were able to make in the course of our work on the documents and sources of Potemkin's activities, in particular the correspondence of his main lieutenants, V. V. Kakhovskii and I. M. Sinel'nikov, in ZOOID, X and XV, and elsewhere. A systematic summary of some of the main aspects is to be found in Zagorovskii, *loc. cit.*, and Adamczyk.

66. "Vokrug Ochakova—1788 (Dnevnik ochevidtsa)," *Russkaia Starina*, 84 (September 1895), 147–211; cf. also ZOOID, XI, 506–508.

67. M. Garnovskii, "Zapiski Mikhaila Garnovskogo 1786–1790," *Russkaia Starina*, XV (1876), 9–38, 237–265, 471–499, 687–720; XVI (1876), 1–32, 207–238, 399–440.

68. ZOOID, IX, 219–227; VIII, 225–227.

69. ZOOID, XIX (1896), 105–106; XX (1897), 53–54; *Arkhiv grafa Vorontsova*, XXIV (St. Petersburg, 1880), 291–293.

70. "Vokrug Ochakova," p. 156; V. A. Bil'bassov, "Prints Nassau-Zigen v Rossii, 1786–1796," *Istoricheskie monografii*, IV (St. Petersburg, 1901), 523–592 passim; see also ZOOID, XXII (1900), 24.

71. A. G. Brikner, "Kniaz' G. A. Potemkin (po zapiskam grafa Lanzherona, khraniaschchimisia v Parizhskom arkhive)," *Istoricheskii Vestnik*, LXII, 1895, 822; *Mémoires ou souvenirs et anecdotes*, par M. le Comte de Ségur, II (Paris, 1826).

72. Brikner, "Kniaz' G. A. Potemkin," p. 824, and the more popular biographies of Potemkin, Soloveytchik's (see note 8) for example.

73. "Mnenie kn. Potemkina ob obmundirovanii voisk (1783)," *Russkii Arkhiv* (November 1888), pp. 364–367; *Bumagi Potemkina*, No. 38, p. 38; Sbornik IRIO, XXVII, 238–239. The biographies of Adamczyk and Loviagin cited in note 8 make this point forcefully and give illustrations.

74. "Vokrug Ochakova," p. 172; *Bumagi Potemkina*, No. 11, p. 8.

75. ZOOID, XI, 346–347, also Adamczyk, Chap. III. Folklore is, of course, an unreliable source of historical information if it cannot be checked against documents. But it may be worth mentioning that the popular or soldiers' songs about Potemkin that have come down to the nineteenth century show him in the posture of the fatherly military hero at the siege of Ochakov and use the traditional epic form (*byliny*) to do so. Potemkin is compared—as was the Kievan prince Vladimir—to the "beautiful sun." P. A. Bezsonov (ed.), *Pesni sobrannye P. V. Kireevskim, izdannye obshchestvom liubitelei rossiiskoi slovesnosti*, vyp. 9 (Moscow, 1872), pp. 309–313; D. A. Rovinskii, *Russkie narodnye kartinki*, kn. II (St. Petersburg, 1881), 129–133 and IV, 411.

76. Cf. M. Cherniavsky, *Tsar and People: Studies in Russian Myths* (Yale University Press, 1961); H. Fleischhacker, *Russland Zwischen zwei Dynastien: 1598–1613* (Wien, 1933); Studien zur osteuropäischen Geschichte, N. F. I., especially "Voraussetzungen: Herrscher- und Gesellschaftsbegriff," pp. 15–39.

77. See the suggestive portrait drawn by S. V. Eshevskii, "Ocherk tsarstvovaniia Elizavety Petrovny," *Sochineniia po russkoi istorii* (Moscow, 1900), p. 9.

78. Ségur, II, 287.

79. For example, her addressing him as "Papa," Sbornik IRIO, XLII, 410; see also "Ekaternia i Potemkin (Podlinnaia ikh perepiska) 1782–1791," *Russkaia Starina,* XVI (1876), 33–58, 239–262, 441–478, 571–590; what Potemkin meant to her, Catherine made abundantly clear in her letters to Baron Melchior Grimm, Sbornik IRIO, XXIII. All of Potemkin's biographers cite her expression of despair on learning of Potemkin's death.

80. The official court poets of the day used for Potemkin neoclassical vocabulary identical to the images applied to the monarch since Peter the Great's time (Cherniavsky, Chap. 3). Some samples are to be found in S. A. Vengerov, *Russkaia poezia,* I (St. Petersburg, 1897), pp. 358–359, 388, 402–403, 790–791; Appendix, pp. 353, 354, 356. A similar observation may be made apropos Potemkin's monument in Nikolaev.

81. This scheme quite clearly does not apply to genuine revolutions—its absence is precisely what makes the revolution, turns men to violence, and exacts a heavy price for the new order that eventually emerges.

TWELVE

The Domestic Policies
of Peter III
and His Overthrow

HISTORIANS OF RUSSIA have been kind to neither the reign nor the personality of Peter III. The descriptions of Peter as a man are usually based on the portrait sketched by his wife, Catherine II, who had good reason to make him appear as ridiculous and unappealing as possible. The reign, which lasted only from Christmas Day 1761 to June 28, 1762, is usually dismissed in a few sentences, with notice taken only of the end of compulsory service for the nobility and of Peter's fawning admiration of Frederick II and all things Prussian, a mania that robbed Russia of the fruits of her spectacular victories in the Seven Years' War. If we add the dissatisfaction of the Guards regiments with their new Prussian-style uniforms and the threat of their transfer from the capital to fight for the emperor's interests in his native Holstein, we have exhausted the common explanation for his dethronement and violent death at the hands of Catherine's favorites.[1]

The historian of peasant attitudes N. N. Firsov has pointed out, however, that while Peter III aroused the bitter enmity of the Guards, the court, and the Church, he was popular with the masses on account of several measures he took during his brief reign.[2] Historical reputations are notoriously based on myths; yet myths are historical data that should not be disregarded altogether. What are we to say of the popularity of Peter III among the common people, as witnessed by the appearance after his death of a dozen pretenders (Pugachev being only the best known and most successful) claiming to be Peter III, pretenders who received the support of large masses of Russia's common folk?[3] Nor were illiterate peasants alone in their devotion to Peter III. In 1801 a young, well-educated member of the nobility delivered before his friends a panegyric to Peter III in which he argued that Peter III had begun the liberation of the individual in Russia; noblemen were freed from compulsory state service while hundreds of thousands of peasants were rescued from the obscurantism and oppression of the Church.[4] It is also striking to recall that not one of the nobles—for whom the act of February 18, 1762, is alleged to have been the fulfillment of long-cherished hopes and demands—lifted a finger in defense of the ruler who "freed" them. It is true, too, that Catherine II continued Peter's major policies, including even the Prussian alliance that is supposed to have aroused the patriotic ire of the capital.

Such inconsistencies between interpretations and facts suggest that it is time for a new look at what Peter's government tried to accomplish and how it went about doing it. Foreign policy may be left out of the present account, as it has been well summarized by P. Shchebal'skii, S. M. Solov'ev, and, more recently, by H. Fleishhacker.[5] I shall try to summarize and analyze the most important measures of domestic policy on the basis of unpublished records of the senate and the few remnants of Peter's official correspondence.[6] These findings may help, furthermore, to explain Peter's overthrow and at the same time reveal more clearly the mainsprings of the system of government of Imperial Russia. Obviously, Peter III did not personally make the major policy decisions, nor did he even define the pattern or determine the ultimate direction of the legislation issued in his name. I shall, therefore, endeavor to determine the nature of the group that formed the effective government. For convenience as well as brevity, I shall use the name of the monarch as synonymous with his government, with the clear understanding that I by no means believe that Peter played a paramount role.

The best known of all of Peter III's legislative acts was the so-called "Manifesto on the Freedom of the Nobility," dated February 18, 1762,[7] which put an end to the compulsory nature of the nobility's state service, without, however, encouraging noblemen to take advantage of their new "freedom." Traditionally this act is seen as the culmination of the efforts of the nobility to escape the harsh service obligations imposed by Peter the Great; it therefore appears as a triumph for the nobility who were able to take advantage of the incompetence and weakness of Peter III. Yet contemporaries report that the manifesto came as a shock, disorienting many of its beneficiaries. The contemporary belief that the act was accidental, that it was issued without serious preparation or discussion, is illustrated by the well-known anecdote about its actual drafting. To hide his spending the night with someone else, the story goes, Peter III told his *maîtresse en titre* that he would be busy with state affairs. He then ordered Privy Secretary D. Volkov to draft some legislation and locked him up in a room. The manifesto was the result of Volkov's involuntary house arrest.[8]

But Professor G. Vernadsky, in one of his early articles, has correctly pointed out that, far from being accidental, the manifesto was the deliberate

work of an influential group within the government.[9] He ascribed its author-
ship to A. I. Glebov, procurator-general of the senate, and saw it as part of the
efforts of those dignitaries—the brothers Michael, Roman, and Ivan
Vorontsov, and N. Panin, for example—who wanted to erect the legal framework and lay the social and economic groundwork for a genuine aristocracy in
Russia. In the opinion of these dignitaries freedom from service would enable
the Russian nobility, in particular its richer, better educated, and energetic
members, to turn their attention to economic enterprise and the improvement of their estates. This in turn would have the effect of making them a
genuine social, economic, and cultural elite with a political role similar to that
of the contemporary English aristocracy. The Soviet historian N. L.
Rubinshtein has carried this analysis a step further.[10] He has shown that the
text of the manifesto is closely linked to the discussions about the rights of estates in the Codification Commission of 1754–66. In contradistinction to the
approach taken by the Vorontsov faction, the notion of universal exemption
from service was opposed by P. and A. Shuvalov, the influential advisers of Peter's predecessor, Empress Elizabeth, who wanted to divide the nobility into a
"service gentry" and a monopolistic, entrepreneurial oligarchy. After the
death of Elizabeth, Rubinshtein argues, the idea of freedom from service was
separated for tactical reasons from the Shuvalovs' proposed general statute on
the rights and privileges of the nobility. Promoted by Roman Vorontsov, the
manifesto aimed at reorienting the nobility's attention to greater concern for
the economic exploitation of their estates.

Neither Vernadsky nor Rubinshtein paid much attention to the manner in
which the manifesto was first suggested to the senate. In the minutes for the
session of January 17, 1762, a session that Peter attended (although he came
late), we read:

> Out of His high mercy towards his loyal subjects, [He] graciously deigned to or-
> der the nobles to continue their service according to their [own] wish for as long
> and wherever they want to; and in wartime they would have to present themselves
> [for duty]; and draft a form [project] on the same basis as it is done with the no-
> bles from Livland and submit it with all circumstances for the signature of His
> Imperial Majesty.[11]

There is no record of any further discussion, debate, or even of any consideration of this imperial command.[12] The minutes for February 19, 1762, record
merely the bland and routine order that the Manifesto of February 18, 1762,
be printed and distributed.[13]

These records are meager, laconic, and quite inconclusive. The most tanta-
lizing element in the minutes is the reference to the situation prevailing in
Livland, a reference that may also suggest that the idea stemmed from the
German-Baltic entourage of the emperor. If acted upon, it would have implied introducing into Russia the whole nexus of genuine "feudal" rights and

privileges, most significantly those of local self-government and police, rights and privileges that the Baltic nobles had retained even after the Swedish and Russian conquests. But neither the manifesto itself nor any later legislation pursued these implications. The act of February 18 remained silent on those rights and functions that would have offered the nobility an alternative to the service obligation that had been their very raison d'être. Seen in this light, the manifesto can hardly be considered to have expressed the point of view of the Vorontsov group, who wanted to give noblemen a greater stake in private and local concerns. But D. V. Volkov, Peter's private secretary and mainspring in the administration, who probably drafted the manifesto, may have expressed the thinking of P. Shuvalov, whose protégé he had been. Shuvalov believed that a small, closed oligarchy should control Russia's economic life by means of monopolies and regalias with rank-and-file nobles continuing to provide most of the military and bureaucratic career personnel.

Soviet historians, Rubinshtein in particular, rightly argue that the manifesto should not be taken in isolation, even though the act appears curiously unconnected to anything else. There is no documentary evidence to show that it was a direct response to the demands of the nobility as a whole or even of an important segment of the "ruling classes." Nor do the sources that have come to light so far allow us to draw firm conclusions based on a "class analysis" of the manifesto, that is, that the nobility as the ruling class forced the government to legislate exclusively in favor of the economic interests of the nobles as owners of land and serfs. This, in our opinion, oversimplifies the nature of the Russian nobility and its relationship to the Petrine state. The logical jump from what the sources say to interpretation of what they say in terms of the putative class interests of the nobility is too great for anyone but the most convinced orthodox Marxist to make.[14] But it is possible to relate the act of "freedom of the nobility" to a series of measures in Peter III's own reign dealing with the organization and structure of the machinery of government.

Several decrees indicate the government's desire to regularize the service of civilian officials, to create the basis for what might eventually become a "bureaucracy." Implicit in these decrees is a desire to create an officialdom in place of the old form of "gentry service" that had developed in the seventeenth century and that later had been regularized according to a modern military pattern by Peter the Great. Thus, on April 19, 1762, the senate expressed its intention of drawing up a table of equivalency between the civilian and military branches of the service, so that civilians would cease to be inferior in questions of salaries and preferment. To encourage the professionalization of the civilian branch, the senate plan provided that an officer would suffer no loss in salary if he transferred from the military to the civilian branch on a permanent basis. The senate also intended to re-establish court ranks, as an additional and self-contained branch of the government service.[15] The desire to create a corps of officials not necessarily based on noble status was also evidenced in the senate's proposal that meritorious clerks be promoted to secretaryships, even if it should entail ennobling a commoner. Peter III confirmed the proposal.[16]

Naturally the success of this policy required the availability of a pool of trained men from which officials could be drawn. Following a practice advocated by Peter the Great, but neglected in the reign of Elizabeth, the senate now encouraged the recruitment of officials among the graduates of schools, especially the University of Moscow, even if they were not nobles. The importance the senators attached to this practice is indicated by the fact that they reserved to themselves the selection and assignment of promising graduates.[17]

In the reign of Peter III, then, consistent efforts were made to form a professional corps of officials and to transmute the non-serving nobility into a class of landed gentlemen of leisure who would be merely *honnêtes hommes*. It was decided that one corps of cadets was adequate for the education of *honnêtes hommes*. The several cadet schools were, therefore, combined and consolidated under the direction of I. Shuvalov; they were given more money and the curriculum was reorganized to emphasize "general education" at the expense of narrowly technical fields.[18] This reorganization adumbrates the more comprehensive pedagogical reforms, openly designed for cultured gentlemen, that were introduced by I. I. Betskoi in the reign of Catherine II.[19] At the same time, new technical schools were opened for the professional training of subalterns. A gymnasium that would be attached to the Corps of Cadets was established for the purpose of preparing a civilian service, and the senate's *iunker* corps was re-established. Originally introduced by Peter the Great, the *iunker* corps combined an internship in the senate chancery with schooling.[20]

Seen against the background of these measures on service and education, the Manifesto of February 18, 1762, appears as another illustration of the government's desire to dispense with the unwilling services of those nobles who might prefer to mind their estates or to lead a life of cultured leisure. Was Peter III not, in effect, saying to the nobility "der Mohr hat seine Schuldigkeit getan, der Mohr kann gehen"? For men who thought primarily in terms of their role in the state and whose economic independence was questionable to say the least, it was a policy that could lead to a sense of frustration and rejection. At the same time the government's policy forced many nobles to go back to their estates and to participate actively in the policing of the provinces.[21] But the owner's presence and greater involvement in the management of his estate could, and at times did, lead to stricter control over and greater demands on his serfs, provoking resentment and, not infrequently, rebellion among them.[22]

*   *   *

The implementation of such a policy made it possible for the government to dispense with the inadequately trained, inefficient, overage personnel. Similar considerations lay behind Peter III's measures concerning the Church. In that area Peter III's own attitude toward the Russian Church and religion no doubt played an important part. Born and brought up a Lutheran, he never fully accepted Russian Orthodoxy, to which he was forced to convert when his aunt Elizabeth selected him as heir to the throne. There are many anecdotes about his practical jokes, teasing, and crude impropriety during church services. It is not impossible that he wished to refashion Russian church life and organization along Lutheran lines. Be that as it may, his government promulgated a series of laws relating to the Church that unquestionably affected Russian life directly.

Various restrictions and disabilities that previous rulers had imposed on the non-Orthodox were relaxed by decree.[23] Most significant among these decrees was the general invitation extended to all Old Believers who had fled abroad, mainly to Poland, to return and settle on free lands in the southeast, in particular in the Irgiz river valley.[24] One of the stipulations of the resettlement provisions was that the Old Believers could use their own books of worship and were to be protected against abuses by local authorities.[25] To a senate report of February 19, 1762, Peter III added a paragraph on March 22, 1762, that prohibited Russian and Ukrainian monasteries from admitting monks from abroad, a measure taken in part to guard against the influx of possible agents from the Ottoman and Habsburg empires and in part in imitation of a policy begun by Peter the Great to restrict further the number of monasteries.[26] Similarly, to control the unsupervised proliferation of churches, an *ukaz* prohibited the existence of most chapels that had been established by wealthy noblemen and merchants in private houses in the two capitals.[27] More generally, Peter's tone with the Holy Synod was quite brusque and sharp, underlining his dislike of all Russian ecclesiastical institutions and practices.

More significant than the measures affecting the externals of religious life was the legislation that directly impinged on the economic and social situation of the population under Church jurisdiction. This legislation concerned the secularization of land belonging to ecclesiastical institutions, primarily monasteries, and the fate of peasant serfs living there. Seizure by the Russian state of lands and peasants owned by the Church goes back to the sixteenth century, and further significant and radical steps had been taken by Peter the Great. Even the pious Elizabeth had tentatively approved a measure that would have transferred to state control most of the settled lands belonging to episcopal sees and monasteries, to assure greater equity and to stem the abuses and exactions to which their serfs were subject. This step would naturally benefit the state, since a better administration of the peasantry would make for better taxpayers while also increasing the amount of land available for distribution to officials and courtiers. But it is interesting to note the rationale offered by Peter III for the legislative acts concerning monasteries and their property, a rationale directly related to his own Protestant sympathies on the one hand and to eighteenth-century secular humanitarianism on the other. The argument justifying the upkeep and wealth of monasteries as asylums for the old, veterans, and orphans is dismissed as spurious, since the monasteries do not adequately care for those entrusted to their ministrations. Moreover, in the form in which they had developed in early Christian times, monasteries were seen as truly parasitical institutions and as a perversion of the original teachings of Christ. The state, therefore, should assume the social functions of monasteries—the state should, for instance, build insane asylums and remove the unfortunate from monasteries—by converting the latter into institutions where true anchorites might retire, institutions which, consequently, would not need much property. He argued, further, that such provisions would be in line with practices in Western Europe, where it had been discovered that this important function had to be exercised by the state; insane people are ill and cannot be left to their own devices or to the hazards of private and religious benevolence.[28]

On March 21, 1762, Peter III issued an *ukaz* concerning monastic lands and peasants.[29] Thereafter the serfs on monastery lands would be subject to an annual capitation of one ruble, enjoy the usufruct of the land they worked, and be administered directly by the College of Economy. The state, that is, the officials of the college, would collect the peasants' dues and finance those church activities that were recognized as necessary or useful. State subsidies to monasteries were to remain on the low level set in the reign of Peter the Great, without even taking into account the inflation, estimated at thirteen per cent, that had taken place since that time. Under the terms of Elizabeth's legislation, dues from peasants under the college's jurisdiction were to have been collected on a commission basis by local persons, retired officers, or tax farmers. This practice had unavoidably led to considerable abuse and discontent among the peasants. Peter's decree provided that the College of Economy would establish local offices and on the *uezd* and *guberniia* levels it would have its own officials who would be responsible for the collection of dues and the administration of these peasants.[30] These officials would be appointed from among former prisoners of war or officers no longer fit for field duty.[31] This measure, creating an important outlet for the many superannuated and under-educated government servants who were no longer useful in the central administration or the active army, would also lead to an increase in the number of local officials, whose inadequacy and scarcity had been a major cause of the abuses and failures of the provincial administration. The law fitted well into the government's long-standing preoccupation with improving controls and administration on a local level.[32] In any case, at a stroke of the pen, the decree of March 21, 1762, removed hundreds of thousands of peasants from the jurisdiction of the Church and turned them into state peasants; in a sense this meant that they were to enjoy wide autonomy, even if they had not been given full freedom.[33]

It goes without saying that this legislation incensed the Church. But in view of its institutional weakness and the supineness of its hierarchy, this discontent could be easily disregarded. More serious was the fact that application of the law stirred up the peasantry. The peasants thought that the decree had actually granted them full freedom and that it was only the first step toward a general emancipation. They frequently refused to obey local officials charged with implementing the act, and in many instances they revolted. A senatorial clarification spelling out the limitations of the decree only poured oil on the flames.[34] Eventually, in the fall of 1762, Catherine II was forced to cancel the act and to start new secularization procedures in 1764 in a more orderly and conservative fashion.

*   *   *

It is difficult to speak of the steps taken by the government of Peter III with respect to social and economic policy without viewing them against the background of plans and measures that go back to earlier reigns. Yet there are still too many gaps in our knowledge of the economic evolution of the Empire to allow a definitive assessment of its main dynamics.[35] For our purposes, however, it may suffice to list the most important measures undertaken by Peter III and to evaluate their overall character. In a general way, there is no break with the preceding reign; on the contrary, one may even speak of deliberate continuity, a continuity personified by the role of Peter's right-hand man, D. V. Volkov, who had risen under the patronage of the Shuvalovs in the reign of Elizabeth.[36]

Naturally, the interests of the first class of the realm, the nobility, were uppermost in the minds of the government. The economic needs of noblemen were to receive special attention; efforts were to be made to develop the nobility's resources. In line with the serfs' total subjection to their masters, and with a view toward opening new territories to agriculture and removing surplus population from the central provinces, the decree of January 29, 1762, gave to the nobles the right to transfer serfs without prior permission from the Treasury College.[37] Thereafter it would be sufficient to register the transfer with the appropriate local authorities, thereby strengthening the trend toward administrative devolution and encouraging life on the local level. At the same time, in a reaffirmation of earlier legislation and a tightening of the fetters of peasant bondage, serfs were forbidden to file complaints against their masters.[38] Nobles benefited further from a liberal loan policy that allowed them to borrow money for ten years without interest on the newly minted copper coinage.[39] In a sense this represented a first step toward direct government financial subsidy to the landed nobility, a policy that culminated in the establishment of land banks for nobles in the reign of Catherine II.

Conversely, nothing was done to alleviate the condition of the private serfs. The proposal of procurator-general of the senate. A. I. Glebov, on January 18, 1762, that the capitation should be collected by the serf owners or their bailiffs instead of special officials, was justified in terms of the benefits that would accrue to the peasants freed from the burdens and exactions of periodic expeditions of tax collectors.[40] Yet the act can as well be considered to have further expanded the landlord's rights and to have tightened controls over his serfs. It is true that some effort was made to protect the peasants from the rapacity of merchants, though such protection would benefit the landlords just as much. Peasants were forbidden to give promissory notes to merchants without the approval of either their lord or the entire commune, and the notes had to be drawn up in prescribed form at specified government offices.[41] Notes issued in violation of this rule could not be collected. That this might also be a handicap to a more active expansion of trade and to the formation of a market economy did not seem to worry the government.

On the other hand it was made easier for a peasant under Church and monastery control to join the ranks of the merchant class. It would suffice to pay five hundred rubles for himself and one thousand rubles for his family.[42] True, the sum was very high for the times; but it was thought that some peasants would indeed be able to find that amount of money, an opinion that says much about the potential wealth buried in the Russian village. It is questionable that the merchants considered the measure to be in their own interest; we know from the *nakazy* and debates at the Commission on Codification of 1767 that the Russian merchantry advocated closed social estates (*Stände*). Another act of Peter III may be interpreted as restricting the merchant class while at the same time raising the hopes of the peasantry. The decree of February 22, 1762, put a temporary halt, allegedly until a final decision was taken on the rights and duties of every estate by the Commission on Codification, to the purchase of villages and serfs for factories.[43]

The adjudication of an interesting lawsuit seems to indicate that the government wanted to promote what might be called individual property rights to benefit capitalist development. A major handicap in the formation of private capital in Russia was the tradition, sanctified by law, of equal inheritance rights. It led to a constant subdividing and splintering of estates and property, decreasing their economic potential from one generation to the next. An even greater danger threatened factories and mining enterprises because it was impossible to divide up a factory or mine among several heirs without actually destroying it. This was the basic issue raised by a lawsuit involving the fate of several factories in the Urals that had been owned by Baron Alexander Stroganov. The matter had been discussed at various times in the senate before the accession of Peter III. In December 1761 the senate had held that in the case of factories or mines, splintering or dividing up should not be permitted; one person would inherit the entire establishment and compensate the other heirs in cash. The ruling, reminiscent of Peter the Great's law of 1714 on single inheritance, was made general, extended to salt production as well, and given legislative sanction in the decree of April 22, 1762.[44]

The decision reached in the case of Alexander Stroganov's inheritance points to the government's efforts to mobilize the natural and human resources of the country; in so doing the government continued the policy of the previous reign and prepared the ground for the more systematic approach of Catherine II. In this connection it is worth noting that the government was well aware of the advantages of free labor, as compared to compulsory labor and serf work services in kind (*zemskaia povinnost'*). The senate ordered that, whenever possible, free hired labor be employed in repairing and maintaining the Volkhov waterway, in digging new canals, and in the upkeep of the highway between St. Petersburg and Moscow. In the final analysis, the senators argued, the cost would be less than if serf labor were used and the peasants torn away from their regular agricultural tasks.[45] Nor should the labor potential of retired non-commissioned and commissioned officers go to waste. Their settlement along the Lower Volga, in Astrakhan' *guberniia*, was encouraged.[46]

Of greater and more permanent significance was further relaxation of controls over trade. In the reign of Elizabeth internal duties had been abolished, but the peasants still had to present passports and to register with gate-keepers upon entering Moscow and other big cities, even if they came only for the day's market. Passports had to be obtained from the lord or the commune, not always an easy or costless procedure; and then the peasants had to fight their way through bottlenecks at the town gates, so that many preferred not to come to urban markets. These restrictions were now eased to permit peasants to come for trade to Moscow, where they could even stay overnight, without having to register.[47] But given the commonly held notion that laborers were dangerous and unreliable, hired hands continued to be registered with the police and had to be strictly accounted for, especially in the large cities and the two capitals.[48] The measure may have had a much greater impact than it would appear to have had at first glance. The fortunes and entrepreneurial activities of peasant industrialists in the early nineteenth century seem often to have begun with grandfathers who plied their commerce between countryside and towns after their access to the latter had been liberalized under Peter III.

A liberalizing policy was pursued with respect to foreign trade, too; it aimed particularly at loosening the fetters of monopoly concessions granted under Elizabeth. Without abandoning mercantilist policies on imports, policies that in general benefited an underdeveloped country like Russia, Peter III encouraged free export of Russian raw materials through all ports and highways of

the Empire. Ending the monopoly position enjoyed by Riga and St. Petersburg, the grain trade was allowed to move through the ports of the Black Sea
and on overland routes in the Ukraine. The same was true for the export of
salted meat across the Ukrainian border. Finally, encouragement was given to
trade with Persia and protection offered it by the establishment of Russian
consulates in the towns bordering on the Shah's domains.[49] While the collection of custom receipts was again farmed out to a few persons,[50] the trend toward greater freedom of domestic and foreign trade was unmistakable; Catherine II was merely to expand it.

   In connection with the efforts to expand and liberalize trade with Persia, we
may mention a project of Count Roman I. Vorontsov that was submitted to
the senate and discussed at the very end of Peter's reign.[51] Vorontsov advocated the energetic promotion of Russia's Asiatic trade and, in a sense, the reorientation of the Empire's pattern of trade and economic development eastward. The count bolstered his proposal with the argument that Russia's
future and mission lay in the East much more than in the West. While no concrete decision was reached under Peter III, we know that Catherine continued to exhibit a keen interest in the development of Russian trade and agricultural expansion in the East, although her foreign policy definitely favored the
West.[52] One cannot help being reminded of the alternative that confronted
Muscovy two centuries earlier when Ivan IV and his *Izbrannaia Rada* had to
decide whether to expand on the conquests of Kazan' and Astrakhan' or to
turn to the Baltic.

   It is well known that, after signing an armistice with Prussia, Peter III concluded a treaty of friendship with Frederick II. On the eve of his overthrow he
planned to embroil Russia in another war, this time on the side of Prussia, in
defense of his Holstein family interests. Then as now, expenditures and
preparations for war meant the retrenchment of domestic programs. Earlier
efforts to develop the economic potential of Russia were thus partly negated,
so that Catherine II's decision to shun diplomatic entanglements and
preparations for war was eagerly welcomed by her subjects. Of all the programs that fell victim to the economy drive in support of military
preparations, none had more serious implications for the country's general
welfare than the slowing down of the general land survey that had been
started under Elizabeth. By a decree of May 17, 1762, surveying operations
were restricted because of a shortage of manpower—the officers who carried
out the operations had had to rejoin their units for active duty—and were limited to the province of Moscow where they could be carried on by retired officers from the College of Economy.[53] If we remember that the nobility, state
peasants, and *odnodvortsy*[54] depended on a definitive land survey for the security of their holdings, Peter III's decision appears a serious backward step that
easily could have undone his well-intentioned economic measures. Yet it does
not seem that the full effects of this measure were appreciated at the time; in

any event, the overthrow, which came so soon thereafter, can hardly be accounted for by the dissatisfaction of the nobility with this action.

What then can we conclude about the character of Peter's domestic policy? Quite obviously, he did not slight the interests of the nobility and did not lift a finger to remedy the wretched conditions of the serf peasantry. One may ask, however, whether his efforts at separating the nobility more sharply into career officials in the bureaucracy and a leisured group of economically active serf-owners met with the approval of all nobles. Some, like the well-known memoirist A. T. Bolotov, were quite happy to devote themselves exclusively to private pursuits. But on Bolotov's own testimony, he was in the minority; most of his friends and neighbors continued to live and think in terms of state service. The same may be said for the peasantry, for Pugachev's "program" definitely emphasized the liturgical character of the Russian polity grounded on universal service. We see, therefore, no new departure in economic policy, but only an extension of trends in the reign of Elizabeth. The main goal was to foster the maximum development of the potential resources of the Empire and its population. Nor was the drive toward secularization and functional institutional organization new. Peter III merely followed the path of all his predecessors since Peter the Great. But, in view of the bad reputation that his reign has been given by Catherine II and later historians, it is worthy of note that the government of Peter III could boast of some accomplishments. Its legislation anchored more securely the evolution toward "modernity," secularization, and increased economic activity, as well as "bureaucratization."[55] In no sense was the legislation radical, nor did it introduce any notions and practices that were alien to the Russian polity of the eighteenth century. If, in some specific cases, one group of the nobility was favored over another, it is difficult, on balance, to see why Peter's social and economic policies should have resulted in his violent overthrow. Leaving aside the matter of personality and personal conflict with Catherine II (not that this is a negligible matter), was there anything in the methods of government that may yield a clue to the events of June 28, 1762?

*   *   *

The first acts of Peter III signaled a departure from custom and hinted at a distrust of the natural line of imperial succession. The manifesto of accession omitted mention of Grand Duke Paul, Peter's only son and presumptive heir, and so did the oath of loyalty required of all subjects except private serfs.[56] The bad impression this created was indirectly confirmed when Catherine II made a point of including the name of Grand Duke Paul in both her manifesto of accession and the oath.[57] Even more curious is the order to bring the great imperial crown from Moscow to St. Petersburg, clear evidence that the tsar intended to hold his coronation in the new capital on the Neva.[58] This would have been a radical departure from a tradition that even Peter the Great's successors had not violated. In contrast, immediately upon overthrowing Peter III, Catherine II stated emphatically that she would be crowned in Moscow.[59] More important was the contrast offered by Peter III to the "maternal" image of Elizabeth, an image that Catherine II so assiduously cultivated later. Indeed, the emperor made himself as inaccessible as possible to his subjects. Peter the Great, who did not want to be bothered by petitions that properly fell under the jurisdiction of regularly established institutions, nonetheless remained easily accessible. Peter III, on the contrary, held himself aloof from the nation and threatened with dire penalties anyone who dared to petition for redress of grievances or for rewards; an exception was made only for those officers who were not satisfied with the decisions of their commanders.[60]

Still more significant than these matters of ceremonial and etiquette was the change in the ruling group. Understandably, the accession of a new ruler in an autocracy brings about a change in the inner circle of those who surround the monarch and help him to govern. Immediately upon his accession, Peter III removed Elizabeth's adviser, Alexander Shuvalov,[61] as well as the recently appointed procurator-general of the senate, Prince Ia. Shakhovskoi, one of the most experienced officials of the previous reign. In place of Shakhovskoi another expert in the bureaucratic routine, General Quartermaster Alexander I. Glebov, was appointed procurator-general of the senate.[62] But unlike his predecessor, Glebov was not destined to play a major policy-making role. That role fell to Dmitrii V. Volkov, for whom the new position of privy-secretary to the emperor was created on January 31, 1762.[63] This made him the virtual head of the entire administrative machinery, for everything submitted to or coming from the sovereign had to pass through his hands. A member of the senate as well, Volkov became in fact if not in name the chief minister.

Volkov's position was further enhanced by the abolition on January 29, 1762, of the Special Conference at the Imperial Court, the body that had acted as a kind of war cabinet, coordinating and planning all policies in the last years of Elizabeth's reign. As Peter's trusted factotum, Volkov could decide on who and what was to be brought to the monarch's attention or decision; he could also influence decisions, but by himself he could not coordinate and plan long-range policies, then particularly complicated by Russia's diplomatic and military reorientation.[64] Count Mikhail I. Vorontsov advised the creation of a new "conference" to coordinate and plan policy, a move Nikita Panin was to suggest later to Catherine II, with the same negative result.[65] The Vorontsov suggestion was not acceptable to Peter III and his circle. It looked too much like a return to the practices of the previous reign and was interpreted as a restriction of the freedom of action of the new sovereign (or his advisers). Yet there was a desperate need for such an institution, for communications even between various subordinate agencies and commanders were completely disrupted after the disbanding of the conference.[66] The limited problem of proper channels of communication with his monarch that faced the Russian commander in the field was easily taken care of when a special conference for military matters was appointed in March 1762. The conference consisted of a cousin, Duke Ludwig of Holstein, Prince Georg von Holstein-Beck, the emperor's uncle, Generals N. Trubetskoi, A. Villebois (Vil'boa), I. Glebov, and A. Mel'gunov, and Adjutant Baron Ungarn.[67] This committee, however, was an informal body; it did not have its own staff or chancery, and it was limited to Peter III's personal concern, military affairs. The perennial need of the imperial government for a regular institution to channel information, discuss proposals, and make long-range plans that would not at the same time impinge on the autocratic authority of the ruler grew more pressing in the case of a sovereign whose understanding of and interest in domestic affairs was, to say the least, limited.

A solution was found in the creation of a new body, similar to the Conference at the Imperial Court of Elizabeth, but its members were not the usual high dignitaries. The *ukaz* of May 18, 1762, that set it up did not even give it an official name; it merely stated that daily meetings of persons closest to the emperor were to be held to make decisions on the basis of reports submitted by Privy-Secretary Volkov.[68] The persons were Duke Holstein-Beck, Prince Georg von Holstein, Marshal B. Münnich, Prince N. Trubetskoi, Chancellor M. Vorontsov, Generals A. Villebois, Volkonsky, and A. Mel'gunov (when available), and Volkov. There was much overlap with the membership of the military committee; one-third of the members were Germans; and the crucial role devolved upon Volkov, whose position is reminiscent of that held by State Secretary M. Speransky in the reign of Alexander I. The new council was given its own staff, so that it truly could become a governing body.

In short, Peter III made significant changes in the composition of his principal advisers. These changes meant the predominance of the Holstein relatives and of the military. The civilian dignitaries N. Trubetskoi and M. Vorontsov had remained during a period in which there were many changes at court and had hardly any coloring of their own—they were typical and perennial, and in N. Trubetskoi's case superannuated, bureaucrats. The most active and important civilian official was Volkov, an able executive, who, however, unlike the famous Artemii Volynskii who had held a similar position during the sway of Biron (Bühren) and Löwenwolde in the reign of Anne,[69] lacked a political physiognomy of his own. This ruling group reached their decision in closed session, in the chambers of Peter III; their relationship to existing government institutions was not at all defined. It was a "kitchen cabinet," made up of Holsteinians, generals, and Volkov. It bore a strong resemblance to the Supreme Privy Council (*Verkhovnyi tainyi sovet*) in the reign of Catherine I and to the Cabinet of Ministers under Anne. But in the case of the two earlier bodies, there had been a clearer definition of their place within the regular structure of state institutions; Elizabeth's conference had been in the nature of a committee of prominent officials rather than of personal favorites. It is true that the Holstein princes were also given official appointments, but their appointments were exclusively in the military establishment,[70] a step that only served to underline the very personal basis of their power.

All autocracies need a centralized and efficient police. Russia, both before and after Peter the Great, was no exception. The police organization of Imperial Russia had its beginnings in the Preobrazhenskii Prikaz, established by Peter I. In the eighteenth century it relied heavily on denunciations (*slovo i delo gosudarevo*) as an effective weapon of wide-ranging terror.[71] Under various names, but employing the same methods, the political police continued to be a mainstay of government under the successors of Peter the Great; in the reign of Elizabeth they were called the Secret Investigating Chancery (*Tainaia rozysknaia kantseliariia*). Like any political police, this chancery was the most dreaded and unpopular institution, especially among the Old Believers, who were persecuted under Elizabeth. In February 1762 Peter III abolished this chancery in a popular move for which he received plaudits from both high and low quarters.[72] The decree abolishing the Secret Investigating Chancery stressed the personal character of kingship, contrasting it to the remoteness of a ruler separated by a bureaucratic hierarchy. In view of Peter's own aloofness, one may question the sincerity of the decree; on the other hand the *ukaz* tried to convey a "medieval" image of the monarch, emphasizing his desire to rule primarily through moral suasion and attention to the major task of a sovereign, that of chief justicer. A personalized conception of authority had been pushed into the background by what Max Weber called the "routinization" of power since Peter the Great; successive autocrats tried to resuscitate the earlier personal character of rulership, the notorious Third Department of Nicholas I being neither the least nor the last effort in this direction.

Still, the police administration underwent an interesting transformation in the brief reign of Peter III. Discussions of a more efficient and "modern" police to replace the *slovo i delo* denunciations had been initiated in the reign of Elizabeth. Discussions focused on increasing the functions and responsibilities of the policemaster of St. Petersburg, who dealt with all matters of welfare as well as with problems of political and social security, and who also controlled the policemaster of Moscow.[73] The senate suggested complete separation of the two police offices and equalization of their status. The senate recommended further that city policemasters be appointed by and subordinated to the authority of the local administration, that is, the *gubernskie*, provincial, and *voevodskie* chanceries. In short, the senators thought that policemasters who had to deal with day-to-day housekeeping problems of urban centers should be well integrated into the regular administrative pyramid and that therefore they should ultimately come under the senate. Soon thereafter, in the reign of Peter III, Privy Councilor Iv. I. Divov was appointed policemaster-general of Moscow, but subordinated to the policemaster-general of St. Petersburg, the chancery of the *guberniia* of Moscow, and the senate. This arrangement, however, was not put into effect.[74]

In March 1762 the new trend in police administration became apparent with the issuance of directives to the policemasters in provincial cities. General Baron Nicholas A. Korf, chief of the Main Police Administration, policemaster of St. Petersburg, and a personal favorite of Peter III, was authorized to install policemasters in those towns and cities he believed needed them. The investigative functions of these officials were to come under the superior jurisdiction of the policemaster-general of St. Petersburg. Moreover, in all matters concerning police, the governors, too, were to come under the jurisdiction of General Korf's office; his staff was also greatly increased.[75] Quite clearly, a comprehensive police network was being established throughout the Empire under the personal control of General Korf and removed from direct supervision by the senate. While to some extent this move resulted in a deconcentration of administrative authority and possibly in an increase in the power of the provincial governors—who were usually personal appointees of the monarch—it meant, above all, tighter police control by the men around Peter III.

The policy as we have outlined it, clearly aimed at replacing the administrative chain of command that traditionally culminated in the senate with the personal authority of the monarch's new men. As early as January 1762, for example, it was decreed that the sovereign's verbal orders, if transmitted by an individual senator, the procurator-general (A. Glebov, one of the *homines novi*), or the presidents of the first three colleges (war, navy, foreign affairs), would have force of law without being referred to the full senate for recording let alone sanctioning. The implications of the policy for the position of the senate, and more specifically of the thirteen senators, were profound.[76] Under Elizabeth they had constituted the highest governing (*pravitel'stvuiushchii*) body of the state, a role that even the Conference at the Imperial Court had not completely undermined, since the latter consisted of regular officials and concerned itself primarily with the conduct of war.[77]

Let us trace the several steps that led to a radical decline in the authority of the senate. A decree of January stipulated that all petitions were to be considered in special departments created within the senate, the College of Justice, and the Estates College (*Votchinnaia kollegiia*),[78] an action that undercut the power of the *reketmeister,* who was a functionary of the senate. An order issued in the same month—and expanded in April—stipulated that matters concerning promotions be referred to the relevant functional institutions rather than to the senate, where they had previously gone.[79] Even before this, on January 10, 1762, all promotion files were to be removed from the docket of the senate and turned over to the Office of the Heraldry. The latter was actually a division of the senate, so that while the step was not as radical as those mentioned earlier, it certainly indicated the direction in which the wind was blowing.[80]

But the most significant measure, in my opinion, was the *ukaz* of June 1, 1762, which read: "We, by the Grace of God ... most highly command that from now on the Senate issue to the public no decree with force of law, or [which] even serves to interpret previous laws, without submitting it to Us and obtaining Our approval for it."[81]

Characteristically, the decree was signed by all the members of the inner council. One further step was taken with the decree of June 5, 1762, only three weeks before Catherine staged her coup. The decree provided that no reports be submitted to the senate on matters not directly related to its current work.[82] In short, the paramount role of the senate in government had been whittled down and its political authority well-nigh eliminated. In the light of this development it is significant that at the time of her coup d'état, on June 28, Catherine delegated the care of the Empire to the senate. Furthermore, after her success, she decreed on July 2, 1762, that for matters of current concern, orders signed by only four members of the senate would have force of law. Her first step as autocrat was, then, to restore the senate to its former position.[83]

*   *   *

The burden of the argument in the preceding pages has been that the demotion of the senate helped to bring about the overthrow of Peter III. The senators whom Peter inherited from his aunt represented the "in-group" that had been in control since the time of Peter the Great.[84] They were closely connected with the court and, consequently, with the Guards (and Catherine) as well. Of course, there had been other reasons for dissatisfaction with Peter III—his manners, his scorn for Orthodoxy and for everything Russian, his admiration of Prussia and Frederick II and the threat to send the Guards to fight in Germany, and, finally, his open clash with Catherine. But most of these elements of discontent were personal and to be expected in an autocracy; they could be offset by groupings favorable to the ruler and his style. We have seen, moreover, that in domestic legislation the regime of Peter III offered no serious reasons for complaint or opposition.

The demotion of the senate, however, could have far-reaching political implications, as it touched on a tender spot in the Russian polity. Indeed, to contemporary Russians, Peter III's method of government meant the establishment of a personal regime, personal not only in the sense that any autocracy is personal but in the sense of a small coterie of favorites gaining control over both sovereign and machinery of the state and imposing its will outside the framework of regular institutional order.

The modern Russian state, as shaped by the forceful personality of Peter I, was an autocracy; but by 1762 its routine operations had to a large degree become regularized, well ordered, and grounded in laws and regulations enforced by institutions, not by the ruler's personal whim (although his arbitrary will was still decisive in specific cases). Between 1725 and 1762 a see-saw struggle had taken place between personal regimes of favorites and an orderly administrative system resting on regulations and laws. The latter, triumphing under Elizabeth, appeared under the banner of the senate, in opposition to oligarchies of "accidental people."

Peter III dramatically reversed Elizabeth's system. He set about creating a personal regime, in which foreigners and the military played the dominant role, and he secured control of the Empire by an effective police administration headed by a personal favorite. Modern and efficient as it was in its conception, the police network threatened to undercut the regular institutions and to transform orderly administration into the dictatorship of a coterie. Most important of all, the new regime appeared to undermine the personalism of autocracy by interposing an effective barrier of favorites between ruler and subjects. And was not the promotion of professionalism in the civilian corps of officials a way of isolating those officials from the source of all power and of cutting them off from a broad social base? Fear was abroad that Russia was witnessing the return of the rule of the Supreme Privy Council under Peter the Great's minion, Prince A. D. Menshikov (1725–27), or the dictatorship of Biron and the Germans of Empress Anne, of cliques of "accidental people" who were neither an aristocratic oligarchy nor the representatives of the Russian service nobility. This fear outweighed the benefits of Peter's social and economic policies favoring the dominant social class as well as of those measures that helped the country as a whole. Peter III managed to alienate not only the Guards regiments representing the nobility but the high officials and courtiers as well.

* * *

More generally, the question of the methods of government favored by Peter III and his entourage focuses our attention on a basic and constant problem in the political history of Imperial Russia, the relationship between autocracy and nobility. We noted that in the course of the eighteenth century there was a trend to regularize the pattern of institutions, to endow them with some degree of autonomy of action in their daily routine, while always carefully preserving the ultimate authority and control of the autocrat. On the face of it, this seemed an adequate compromise between personalization and routinization of sovereign power—and two centuries of Russian history from the time of Peter the Great validated it. It reflected the ambivalent interests of the nobility, or, more precisely, the two aspects of their interests. There was, first, the desire to free the nobleman from the state, to make him a truly autonomous and independent private individual, to allow him to concentrate his energies and attention on running his estate and to lead in the cultural development of the nation, while at the same time assuming a share in the maintenance of law, order, and security on the local level. This aspect implied acceptance of routinized political power or of well-ordered institutions whose officials would be guided by precise regulations as well as restricted by the existence of broad areas of autonomous private activity. But equally important and vital to the nobles—especially in view of their economic weakness and dependence on serfdom—was the preservation of their service role. This accounts for their ambivalence and disorientation in the face of the formation of a regular bureaucracy and their "liberation" from service in 1762. To safeguard this aspect of their interests and self-image the nobility also had to rely on the personal elements of political authority, on a strong autocracy. The autocrat was, indeed, seen as the only protector of the economic and social position of the nobility, especially of its lower and middle ranks. He was the safeguard against the threat of a pluralistic and open society that was growing stronger as cultural and economic "modernization" progressed.

The conflict of interest between the nobles' service role and their private activities could find accommodation in the sort of compromise we have described. The door was left open for direct appeal to the autocrat to intervene in their behalf. Still the nobles were threatened by a personal regime of favorites or by an oligarchy. Indeed, such regimes meant the loss of political influence for large numbers of the rank-and-file nobility and a challenge to their economic and social security by putting them at the mercy of grasping, selfish favorites. At the same time, these regimes cut off the ordinary nobleman from direct access to the monarch on whom he depended for favors, protection, and the hopes of a rise in status through service.

"Successful" rulers—Catherine II, Alexander I, Nicholas I, Alexander II— were fully aware of this situation and acted accordingly. In so doing they perpetuated autocracy and prevented, or at least did not encourage, the transformation of the service-oriented nobility into a "gentry" on the English model. As a result, when outside pressures resulting from the economic and cultural transformation that followed the Emancipation of 1861 became too great, neither autocracy nor nobility were prepared to face it and to devise a new equilibrium of political and socioeconomic power that would prove more responsive to changed circumstances. They were both destroyed. The reign and fall of Peter III provide us with a concrete, almost clinical, example of this pattern; they reveal both the nature of the issue and the character of the basic compromise that dominated the institutional organization of Imperial Russia.

Notes

1. S. M. Solov'ev, *Istoriia Rossii s drevneishikh vremen* (Moscow, 1959–66), XIII, Bk. 25 (1965), Chap. I, 7–102; Robert Nisbet Bain, *Peter III, Emperor of Russia* (London, 1902). A recent attempt at a "rehabilitation" that is not too convincing is H. Fleischhacker, "Porträt Peters III," *Jahrbücher für Geschichte Osteuropas,* Neue Folge V (1957), 127–89.

2. N. N. Firsov, "Peter III i Ekaterina II—Pervye gody ee tsarstvovaniia," *Istoricheskie ocherki i eskizy* (Kazan', 1922), II, 43–109.

3. K. V. Sivkov, "Samozvanstvo v Rossii v poslednei tret'i XVIII v.," *Istoricheskie Zapiski,* XXXI (1950), 88–135.

4. Akademiia Nauk SSSR, Institut istorii russkoi literatury (Pushkinskii dom), Leningrad; Arkhiv Turgenevykh, Fond 309, No. 618, ff. 26–30.

5. P. Shchebal'skii, *Politicheskaia sistema Petra III* (Moscow, 1870); Solov'ev, *Istoriia Rossi,* Fleischhacker, "Porträt Peters III."

6. Unless otherwise indicated, unpublished documents referred to in this article are located in the Central State Archives for Ancient Charters, Moscow (Tsentral'nyi gosudarstvennyi arkhiv drevnikh aktov). They will be cited by Fond (File), No. (*edinitsa khraneniia*), date (if available), and folio pagination.

7. *Polnoe sobranie zakonov Rossüskoi imperii,* 1st Ser. (St. Petersburg, 1830), XV, No. 11.444 (hereafter *PSZ* with number of law or decree). All dates in the present article conform to the Julian calendar, that is, the dates are eleven days behind the corresponding days in the Gregorian calendar for the eighteenth century.

8. Prince M. M. Shcherbatov, *On the Corruption of Morals in Russia,* ed. and trans. A. Lentin (Cambridge, 1969), 232, 233.

9. G. V. Vernadskii, "Manifest Petra III o vol'nosti dvorianskoi i zakonodatel'naia komissiia 1754–1766 gg.," *Istoricheskoe Obozrenie,* XX (1915), 51–59.

10. N. L. Rubinshtein, "Ulozhennaia komissiia 1754–1766 gg i ee proekt novogo ulozheniia 'O sostoianii poddannykh voobshche' (K istorii sotsial'noi politiki 50kh–nachala 60kh godov XVIII v.)," *Istoricheskie Zapiski,* XXXVIII (1951), 208–52.

11. Fond 248, No. 3426, 17 Jan. 1762, f. 283 (§24). Note elliptic and incorrect syntax.

12. The only exception is the terse notation, *ibid.,* 18 Jan. 1762, f. 316, that Procurator-General A. Glebov suggested the erection of a golden statue of Peter III in gratitude for his concern for the nobility. There is no record of action taken on this proposal.

13. Fond 248, No. 3427, 18 Feb. 1762, ff. 134–38, 19 Feb. 1762, f. 171.

14. Rubinshtein has used the minutes of the Committee on the Freedom of the Nobility of the Commission of Codification, Fond 16, No. 235. His argument rests on the linking of individual dignitaries and high officials to specific interest groups within the nobility. For the latter the evidence is very indirect and at best highly circumstantial.

15. Fond 248, No. 3429, 19 Apr. 1762, ff. 175, 177–78. See also Peter the Great's Table of Ranks, *PSZ* 3890.

16. Fond 248, No. 3428, 14 Mar. 1762, f. 444, No. 3429, 23 Apr. 1762, f. 219.

17. Fond 248, No. 3426, 10 Jan. 1762, ff. 94–97, concerning the promotion of Ia. Kozitskii and the staffing of the Codification Commission; No. 3429, 30 Apr. 1762, f. 413; No. 3431, 12 June 1762, f. 138, concerning the promotion of V. Ruban.

18. I. Shuvalov had already suggested the idea in May 1761. See Leningradskoe otdelenie Instituta istorii Akademii Nauk SSSR (L.O.I.I.), Fond 36, Bk. 398, ff. 182–92. *PSZ* 11.474 (14 Mar. 1762), which refers to the Manifesto of 18 Feb. 1762; *PSZ* 11.515 (24 Apr. 1762); Fond 248, No. 3430, 14 May 1762, ff. 226–33, permitting an increase in staff and budget. Thirty-five thousand rubles were to be levied especially for this purpose from state peasants.

19. Betzky [I. I. Betskoi], *Les Plans et les Statuts des différents établissements ordonnés par Sa Majesté Impériale Catherine II pour l'Education de la jeunesse et l'utilité générale de son Empire,* trans. Mr. Clerc (Amsterdam, 1775); *PSZ* 12.741.

20. *PSZ* 11.515 (24 Apr. 1762); Fond 248, No. 3430, 14 May 1762, ff. 251–52, concerning the implementation of these measures.

21. This function was clearly delegated to them only by the Act on the Provincial Administration of 1775 and the Charter to the Nobility of 1785.

22. As was demonstrated by the Pugachev rebellion, 1773–74.

23. 23. *PSZ* 11.434 (1 Jan. 1762), stopping investigation of cases of self immolation and assuring Old Believers that they would not be prosecuted for their beliefs.

24. *Opis' vysochaishim ukazam i poveleniiam khraniashchimsia v Sankt-Peterburgskom Senatskom Arkhive,* ed. P. I. Baranov (St. Petersburg, 1872–78), III (1740–62), 1878, No. 11.979 (29 Jan. 1762); *PSZ* 11.420 (29 Jan. 1762). Pugachev took advantage of this decree to legalize his status after escaping from prison in Kazan'.

25. Fond 248, No. 3427, 7 Feb. 1762, ff. 53–61; *PSZ* 11.435 (7 Feb. 1762).

26. Fond 248, No. 3428, 22 Mar. 1762, ff. 558–79.

27. Fond 203, No. 1, 8 Mar. 1762, ff. 6–7; *PSZ* 11.460 (5 Mar. 1762).

28. See Fond 248, No. 3429, 23 Apr. 1762, ff. 205–06, for the case of the insane brothers Kozlovskii; *ibid.,* 24 Apr. 1762, ff. 237–38; *PSZ* 11.509 (20 Apr. 1762).

29. Although the decree referred to the report submitted by the senate to Elizabeth, it spelled out the Protestant-like condemnation of monasteries. Contenting himself with pointing out the abuses, not even Peter the Great had gone this far.

30. *PSZ* 11.481 (21 Mar. 1762). Note that the senate report that served as the basis for the law was dated 19 Feb. 1762, a data that may indicate some connection with the Manifesto on the Freedom of the Nobility. Fond 248, No. 3428, 22 Mar. 1762, ff. 558–79.

31. *PSZ* 11.525 (4 May 1762), 11.572 (14 June 1762); see also Fond 248, No. 3431, 5 June 1762, f. 68, concerning a petition of former prisoner-of-war Major Jacob Semichov.

32. Catherine II shared this preoccupation. One of her earliest measures was to ask Prince Ia. Shakhovskoi, the former procurator-general of the senate under Elizabeth, to make a study of this problem and present recommendations. Although adopted by the senate with only minor changes, Shakhovskoi's recommendations were not implemented at the time. They did, however, serve as an important element in drafting the Statute on Provincial Administration of 1775. Fond 370, Nos. 21, 22 ("Vsepoddaneishii doklad Senata s predstavleniem mneniia d.t.s. kn. Shakhovskogo o preobrazovanii grazhdanskikh shtatov, kotorye Vysochaishimi imennymi ukazami 1762 g. iulia 23 i avgusta 9 poveleno bylo rassmotret' pravitel'stvuiushchemu Senatu"); see also Iu. V. Got'e, *Istoriia oblastnogo upravleniia Rossii ot Petra I do Ekateriny II* (Moscow-Leningrad, 1913–41), II (1941), 165–69.

33. The latest calculations put Economy peasants—those peasants who formerly belonged to monasteries and episcopal sees—at 1,050,000 male souls in 1767. See M. T. Beliavskii, *Krest'ianskii vopros v Rossii nakanune vosstaniia E. I. Pugacheva* (Moscow, 1965), 82.

34. Fond 248, No. 3431, 17 June 1762, ff. 161–62.

35. The bulk of Soviet historical literature deals with the burdens of serfdom. What is needed is a modern economic analysis of available statistical material. Some hopeful signs that such analyses will be pursued can be seen in the works of A. Kahan, of the University of Chicago, M. Confino, of the Hebrew University, and Soviet historians S. Troitskii and I. Koval'chenko.

36. Dmitrii Vsail'evich Volkov, 1718–85, had been secretary of the Conference at the Imperial Court under Elizabeth. A later memorandum summarizes his general outlook on economic matters fairly well. See his letter to G. G. Orlov, in *Russkaia Starina*, XI (1874), 484–85. Biographical material can be found in "Dmitrii Vas. Volkov. Materialy k ego biografii 1718–1785," *ibid.*, 478–96; *ibid.*, XVIII (1877), 372, 576, 744.

37. *PSZ* 11.423 (29 Jan. 1762).

38. Fond 248, No. 3431, 14 June 1762, f. 154. Although the necessity to repeat this kind of legislation frequently during the eighteenth century suggests that it was not effectively enforced.

39. Fond 248, No. 3428, 1 Mar. 1762. f. 5.

40. Fond 248, No. 3426, 18 Jan. 1762, ff. 349–50; *PSZ* 11.429 (31 Jan. 1762).

41. Fond 248, No. 3428, 4 Mar. 1762, f. 101. The purpose of the act was to prevent the exploitation of peasants by merchants who took advantage of the notorious instability and low yields of harvests. On selling grain to the peasants during times of scarcity, merchants bound the peasants for long periods of time. Generally the legislation reflected an opposition to merchants that was shared by nobles and peasants alike.

42. Fond 248, No. 3426, 10 Jan. 1762, ff. 108–14.

43. Fond 248, No. 3428, 22 Mar. 1762, f. 552 (§8), ff. 613–14; *PSZ* 11.490 (29 Mar. 1762).

44. Fond 248, No. 3364, 4 Dec. 1761, ff. 21–22, No. 3428, 6 Mar. 1762, ff. 157–59, No. 3429, 23 Apr. 1762, ff. 207–08; *PSZ* 11.511 (20 Apr. 1762); Fond 248, No. 3397, ff. 166–67.

45. Fond 248, No. 3426, 17 Jan. 1762, ff. 286–92, No. 3427, 30 Jan., 19 Feb. 1762, ff. 197–98, No. 3429, 19 Apr. 1762, f. 156; *PSZ* 11.455 (28 Feb. 1762), 11.495 (5 Apr. 1762), 11.520 (26 Apr. 1762).

46. Fond 248, No. 3430, 4 Mar., 8 May 1762, ff. 168–70; *PSZ* 11.556 (30 June 1762); see P. Liubomirov, "O zaselenii Astrakhanskoi gubernii v XVIII veke," *Nash krai*, No. 4 (Apr. 1926) (Astrakhan'), 1–24 (available in offprint only).

47. Fond 248, No. 3427, 7 Feb. 1762, ff. 73–74; *PSZ* 11.446 (21 Feb. 1762). By implication the rule was extended to other towns, in Siberia, for example. *PSZ* 11.545 (22 May 1762).

48. Fond 248, No. 3429, 5 Nov. 1761, 4 Mar. 1762, 19 Apr. 1762, ff. 153–55.

49. *PSZ* 11.489 (28 Mar. 1762), 11.557 (1 June 1762).

50. Fond 248, No. 3430, 17 May 1762, ff. 273–76.

51. L.O.I.I., Fond 36, Bk. 1067, ff. 17–55 (dated 21 June 1762).

52. For a general survey of the problems of Russian eastern trade see Clifford M. Foust, *Muscovite and Mandarin: Russia's Trade with China and Its Setting, 1727–1805* (Chapel Hill, N. C., 1969).

53. Fond 248, No. 3430, 17 May 1762, ff. 277–79.

54. Literally "single homesteaders"—a class of free peasants who, in the sixteenth and seventeenth centuries, originally had been settled on the frontiers of the state as military servicemen. See T. Esper, "The Odnodvortsy and the Russian Nobility," *Slavonic and East European Review*, XLV No. 104 (Jan. 1967), 124–34.

55. At the end of the reign orders were given that government institutions draw up more precise budgets for future needs and review staff requirements. Catherine II only acted on these orders when, on July 23, 1762, she ordered a general survey of the Empire's economic resources.

56. *PSZ* 11.390, 11.391 (25 Dec. 1761).

57. *PSZ* 11.582 (28 June 1762); Fond 248, No. 3377, 1 July 1762, f. 569. It is true that Catherine II may have believed it more politic to bow to the pressure of those who, Like Count N. I. Panin, expected her to act merely as regent until Grand Duke Paul came of age.

58. Fond 248, No. 3364, 26 Dec. 1761, f. 257.

59. *PSZ* 11.582 (28 June 1762); Fond 248, No. 3377, [5] July 1762, ff. 629–30, 6 July 1762, ff. 632–38, 647. The latter reproduces the extended version of Catherine's manifesto of accession which, curiously enough, was not included in the *PSZ*.

60. Fond 248, No. 3428, 1 Mar. 1762, ff. 31–34; *PSZ* 11.459; *Opis' vysochaishim ukazam*, ed. Baranov, No. 12.019 (28 Feb. 1762).

61. Fond 248, No. 3364, 26 Dec. 1761, f. 261; see also *Opis' vysochaishim ukazam*, ed. Baranov, No. 11.910 (26 Dec. 1762). Shuvalov—who died soon thereafter—had been forbidden to attend the senate except in the presence of the emperor. Since Peter III rarely came to senate sessions, this meant that Shuvalov could virtually never attend.

62. Fond 248, No. 3364, 25 Dec. 1762, f. 253.

63. *Ibid.*, No. 3426, 31 Jan. 1762, f. 618; *Opis' vysochaishim ukazam*, ed. Baranov, No. 11.981 (30 Jan. 1762).

64. Fond 248, No. 3426, 29 Jan. 1762, f. 542. See also H. Kaplan *Russia and the Outbreak of the Seven Years War* (Berkeley, 1968), 47–48. It is only fair to say that while Volkov was an able official he was no real statesman. Later, as governor-general of Orenburg, his performance was less than distinguished.

65. *Arkhiv kn. Vorontsova*, ed. P. Bartenev (Moscow, 1870–95), XXV, 251–54.

66. Fond II, No. 839, 13 Feb. 1762, f. 3 (letter of General Peter I. Panin to Volkov from Königsberg), No. 753 (letter from Panin to Count M. I. Vorontsov, 16 Mar. 1762, from Königsberg).

67. *Opis' vysochaishim ukazam*, ed. Baranov, No. 12.031 (6 Mar. 1762).

68. Fond 248, No. 3430, 20 May 1762, ff. 307–09; *Opis' vysochaishim ukazam*, ed. Baranov. No. 12.162 (18 May 1762). The final text, in *PSZ* 11.538 (18 May 1762), contains a list of members and reads in part: "to work under Our Own direction ... to gather every day at Court and in Our apartments. ... Decrees issued from this place [body] We shall sign in Our Own hand; but matters of lesser importance they will sign, also in Our name [and send] to all places, and therefore, they are to be executed as our

own decrees; and reports on this to be written simply by memorandum to our name, addressing the envelope to our Privy State Councilor Volkov."

69. For Volynskii see D. A. Korsakov, "A. P. Volynskii i ego 'konfidenty' 1689–1740," *Russkaia Starina,* XLVIII (1885), 17–54, *Iz zhizni russkikh deiatelei* (Kazan', 1891), 283–330, "A. P. Volynskii," *Drevniaia i novaia Rossiia,* II (No. 6, 1877).

70. While Hostein-Beck was also appointed governor-general of St. Petersburg this, too, was primarily a military office.

71. The best and most recent introduction to this subject is N. B. Golikova, *Politicheskie protsessy pri Petre I* (Moscow, 1957), where references to earlier monographic literature can easily be found. For a briefer survey, see N. B. Golikova, "Organy politicheskogo syska i ikh razvitie v XVII–XVIII vv.," in *Absoliutizm v Rossii (XVII–XVIII vv.), Sbornik statei k semidesiatiletiiu so dnia rozhdeniia i sorokapiatiletiiu nauchnoi i pedagogicheskoi deitel'nosti B. B. Kafengauza* (Moscow, 1964), 243–80.

72. Fond 248, No. 3427, 7 Feb. 1762, f. 60 (§24); *Opis' vysochaishim ukazam,* ed. Baranov, No. 11.997 (16 Feb. 1762); *PSZ* 11.445 (21 Feb. 1762).

73. Fond 248, No. 3426, 24 Aug. 1761, 7 Jan. 1762, ff. 39–40. The term police is used here as it was used in Russia at the time, in its eighteenth-century French and German connotation, as in *Polizeiordnung.*

74. *PSZ* 11.401 (9 Jan. 1762); Fond 248, No. 3426, 10 Jan. 1762, ff. 119, 120.

75. Fond 248, No. 3428, 22 Mar. 1762, f. 553 (§3), ff. 613–14; *PSZ* 11.477 (21 Mar. 1762) and 11.478 (21 Mar. 1762).

76. Fond 248, No. 3426, 22 Jan. 1762, ff. 373–74; *Opis' vysochaishim ukazam,* ed. Baranov, No. 11.969 (22 Jan. 1762); *PSZ* 11.411 (22 Jan. 1762). The thirteen senators were Mikhail I. Vorontsov, Roman I. Vorontsov, kn. Nikita Iur. Trubetskoi, kn. Petr Nikit. Trubetskoi, Mikh. Mikh. Golitsyn, Aleksei Dm. Golitsyn, Aleksandr I. Shuvalov, Ivan Vas. Odoevskii, Ivan Iv. Nepliuev, Aleksandr Bor. Buturlin, Aleksandr Grig. Zherebtsov, Ivan Iv. Kostiurin. Note the exclusively "Russian" composition and the high proportion of old distinguished service families.

77. See Kaplan, *Russia and the Outbreak of the Seven Years War, passim,* and *Istoriia Pravitel'stvuiushchego Senata za 200 let 1711–1911,* ed. S. F. Platonov (St. Petersburg, 1911), I, *passim.* Kaplan rates the role of the conference higher, but admits it was a "regular" governmental institution.

78. Fond 248, No. 3426, 29 Jan. 1762, ff. 499–500; *PSZ* 11.422 (29 Jan. 1762).

79. *PSZ* 11.409 (18 Jan. 1762); Fond 248, No. 3429, 23 Apr. 1762, f. 219.

80. Also *PSZ* 11.561 (5 June 1762).

81. Fond 248, No. 3377, 1 June 1762, f. 556; *PSZ* 11.558 (1 June 1762); Fond IX, No. 44 (*opis'* No. 5), ff. 22 (1 June 1762), which is the draft of the act, perhaps in Volkov's hand.

82. *PSZ* 11.563 (5 June 1762).

83. Pravitel'stvuiushchii Senat, *Senatskii Arkhiv* (St. Petersburg, 1888–1913), XII (1907), 178; Fond 248, No. 3384, 2 July 1762, f. 395. The senate remained the highest government institution, even if not the main policy-making body. But its procurator-general, Prince A. A. Viazemskii, was for a quarter of a century Catherine II's main minister, so that through his mediation the senate preserved its primary administrative role.

84. As a matter of fact, this ruling circle was largely recruited from the same big "clans" (*rod*) that had occupied the major offices in the Tsardom of Muscovy. In the

absence of a genuine Third Estate, there were few alternative sources from which the Russian ruler could draw his military and civilian servants. On this little studied and important question in Muscovite times, see the revolutionary posthumous monograph of S. B. Veselovskii, *Issledovaniia po istorii klassa sluzhilykh zemlevladel'tsev* (Moscow, 1969), especially 7–36, 465–85.

THIRTEEN

The Empress and the Vinerian Professor

Catherine II's Projects of Government Reforms and Blackstone's Commentaries

ON 4 AUGUST 1776 CATHERINE II wrote from Tsarskoe Selo to her faithful correspondent in Paris, Baron Grimm:

> Sir Blackstone qui ne m'a point envoyé ses commentaires, jouit seul de l'honneur d'être lu par S. M. depuis deux ans; oh, ses commentaires et moi, nous sommes inséparables; c'est un fournisseur de choses et d'idées inépuisable; je ne fais rien de ce qui'il y a dans son livre, mais c'est mon [un?] fil que je dévide à ma façon.[1]

In saying this the Empress was giving a good description of her working habits with respect to legislation and administration. She read voraciously and widely, and she always read with pen in hand. Not only did she make extensive excerpts and summaries of what she was reading, but she also noted her own reactions and ideas as she went along.

In the case of *Commentaries on the Laws of England* by William Blackstone (Vinerian Professor of Law in the University of Oxford, 1758–62) we are fortunate in having the full text of the notes Catherine took while reading the French translation of this classic of English jurisprudence.[2] These notes were used by her as she worked on plans for judicial reform and on drafts for new codes of civil law and procedures.[3] Together the notes and drafts allow us to glimpse the Empress at work and to gain an insight into her plans for the central government and for Russian society. The purpose of the present essay is to present the highlights of these plans and to offer some comments on the character of Catherine's views on the internal problems of Russia in the second half of her reign.

From the outset Catherine makes it clear that she is not going to study foreign law—in this case England's—in order to transfer it directly to Russia, 'Il est plus utile d'étudier les lois de sa patrie que les lois des pays étrangers', she paraphrases Blackstone.[4] But the English jurist provides her with the necessary stimulus and inspiration. In the footsteps of Blackstone, and following her own practice of using history and 'philology' for national glorification, Catherine endeavours to find in Russia historical precedents and parallels for the early English legal and institutional forms described in the *Commentaries*.[5] She assumes a connection between the Saxons and the Slavs, so that to her mind all Saxon traditions are in fact also Slavonic ones.[6] To prove her point she engages in some rather fanciful popular etymology with the intention of enhancing the native Russian tradition and placing it in the mainstream of European development.[7] In passing it may also be noted that in several instances where Blackstone emphasizes English historical antecedents, Catherine not only omits the specific English example but phrases her notes in such a way as to imply a universal historical trend.[8] Furthermore, possibly because of her German background and early upbringing, she stresses the northern European affinities, contrasting the traditions of freedom of the 'liberty-loving' Germanic and Slavonic peoples with the slavery and tyranny of the Romans as displayed in Roman law.[9]

If Catherine's historicism exemplifies her traditional Enlightenment attitudes, it may seem rather surprising that in her notes on Blackstone she invariably omits the references he makes to natural law.[10] The reason for the omission might be that these ideas were accepted as a matter of course. But it seems more plausible to suppose that the omissions are deliberate and reflect the Empress's reluctance to base practice on doctrinaire juridical ideologies at the expense of the empirical and the pragmatic.

Catherine is nothing if not empirical, constantly on the look-out for the possibility of anchoring both her thoughts and actions on Russian reality, history, and practice. As she reads Blackstone she reminds herself to check on relevant Russian legislation or precedents, especially if they have a bearing on an eighteenth-century problem.[11] She duly notes similarities and especially comparisons favourable to her own administrative arrangements or legislative measures. In her draft codes she is even more explicit in reminding herself to check the existing legislation and to seek information on earlier practices and relevant legal traditions.[12] In short, these notes on her reading and on her plans for codification reveal her as completely undogmatic, with a clear sense of the practical and the possible, and with an insatiable appetite for information and stimulation from any source.[13] The Empress obviously has a bent towards syncretism—perhaps not always the most desirable intellectual orientation, but quite useful in a ruler and more effective in the long run than rigid ideological or theoretical dogmatism. Furthermore—and this is not the least important observation that our sources allow us to make—Catherine took her *métier de roi* very seriously, displaying tremendous application and industry, and doing her utmost to fulfil the role of monarch as she understood it. The time and care she devoted to reading and digesting Blackstone and to writing innumerable drafts for legislation and codification, are most impressive, especially if we recall the amount of time she spent on public and court functions, love-affairs, and cultural interests.

As Catherine read the wide-ranging description of English social organization and legal life which Blackstone gives in his *Commentaries,* she could not fail to be reminded of the social and administrative problems which plagued her empire. She recorded some of her reflections in marginal notes or in comments *à propos* of what Blackstone wrote about England. Not surprisingly she took the existing official social structure of Russia (as defined in her own laws) for granted as something not requiring fundamental change.[14] That is why she pays no specific attention to the bourgeois, urban aspects of English society and refers to the status of the British nobility (and gentry) only when she equates feudal (knightly) tenure with *pomest'e.* It is clear that Catherine fully accepts the basic hereditary and privileged character of the nobility, but with respect to the Russian nobility she is also very conscious of their service status.[15] Most of the significant privileges that the nobility enjoy are the result of its members' position as servants of the state. She makes a curious remark about the class being divided into six groups or categories—obviously on the basis of their service status.[16] But she is very concerned about the shaky economic position of the nobility; she knows and worries about the impoverishment of families as a result of the fragmentation of the inheritance with each successive generation. In order to restrict the deleterious consequences of this practice, Catherine proposes two measures. In the first place, real estate holdings of fewer than fifteen or twenty households should not be divided, but pass intact to one legal heir, while movable property might be split up among all heirs.[17] In the second place—obviously imitating the feudal practice of primogeniture and entail—Catherine proposes the creation of entailed estates for families with large properties—one son (presumably the eldest) inheriting the whole estate undivided, while his siblings share in the movables.[18] The family remains prosperous while many of its members are freed for activities useful to the state or to society. Of course, as Catherine is well aware, the idea had occurred to Peter the Great, who in 1714 tried to introduce single inheritance; but, as was also well known, it did not work and Catherine hopes that her efforts might be more successful since Russian society had matured and her legislation had secured the nobility's economic interests.

The Empress pays only slight attention to the needs and problems of the clergy, who—characteristically—are not considered as an estate of the realm, although they were a closed and hereditary *chin* or *soslovie.* This is not surprising, for Catherine had secularized church lands and was little inclined to give preferential treatment to a class that, in her opinion, played no major useful role in the state. But, in keeping with her desire to regularize all estate (class) organizations, she promoted the even distribution of competent parish clergy and regularized their appointment by village communities and estate owners. Inspired perhaps by Blackstone's description of ecclesiastical benefices, she proposes to give local landowners—if they are so inclined and have suitable candidates—the power of nomination to parish livings, subject to confirmation by the bishops who would vouch for the theological and ecclesiastical suitability of the candidates.[19] She also suggests that for the sake of equalization and greater efficiency dioceses should coincide territorially with provinces (*gubernii*) and receive a uniform monetary allowance sufficient for their upkeep.[20] Catherine insists that the clergy should be well trained, and also proposes that the communities of state peasants should play a part in supervising the economy of the parish and have a say in the selection of their clergy.[21] Although Catherine did little to improve the ecclesiastical administration and schools, the second half of her reign witnessed a steady growth in the number of better-trained clergymen and a significant rise in their cultural level—developments that paved the way for the more active role played by children of the clergy in the Russian bureaucracy and in cultural life in the nineteenth century.[22]

Not unnaturally, the condition of the state peasantry caused the Empress to give serious consideration to their situation, and she makes some interesting proposals for the reshaping of their communal relationships. Unlike the private serfs (and similar groups) who were entirely under the control and in the care of the nobility, a situation that Catherine had no wish to change, the state peasants—about half of the peasant population—were very much the concern of the government. Although Catherine and her advisers never expressed it explicitly, it may be fairly assumed that they were well aware that any organizational and economic change in the situation of the state peasants would not only affect the condition of all serfs but also have a direct influence on the future economic development of the empire. Catherine worked out a scheme for administering the state peasants as part of the general provincial administration. This scheme was largely implemented in the *guberniya* of Ekaterinoslav in 1787 and resulted in a greater degree of order and self-government in the state peasant communities.[23] But as usual, the administrative apparatus was too cumbersome and bureaucratic for the low level of the peasants' economic development; in the event it proved unworkable, though some of its features were later incorporated in the projected reforms of the administration of state peasants put forward in the reigns of Alexander I and Nicholas I.[24]

Catherine's proposals for the rural estate, made in connection with Blackstone's discussion of tenures and titles by inheritance and of alienation by special customs, provide for a fairly comprehensive scheme of economic organization for the state peasantry. The scheme relates to one of Catherine's fundamental concerns: the encouragement of economic enterprise by protecting the property of those who are economically productive. In Catherine's project the peasant communities distribute the land in such fashion that provided a peasant works his land satisfactorily, he cannot be deprived of it.[25] The industrious and successful peasant may even bequeath his allotment to his widow and sons, with the same proviso as in the case of the nobility, namely that very small holdings should not be divided.[26] If, however, the peasant neglects his land and duties, he will, upon proper certification by the community, be deprived of his allotment, which will be apportioned to more deserving villagers.[27] The peasant communities constitute units whose members are responsible for each other, but whose assemblies and elected elders enjoy a fair amount of independence of action.[28] The basic administrative and judicial framework, however, was that of the Instructions to the Economic Administration (or *ekonomicheskii ustav*) which suffered from the usual Russian imperial disease: over-bureaucratization and mistrust of local authorities.[29] There is little question that had it been implemented, Catherine's plan would have organized the state peasantry as a rural estate, paralleling in many ways the basic safeguards of property and the limited degree of corporate self-government enjoyed by the nobility and the townspeople under the Charters of 1785. It was no doubt due to Catherine's indecisiveness and caution that none of the economic provisions were included in the 1787 draft of an administrative 'charter' for the state peasants.[30]

It was natural that Blackstone's *Commentaries,* the first modern complete and systematic exposition of the common law, should concentrate on civil law since this was the field of law most relevant to the expanding economy and social transformation of eighteenth-century England. This aspect of law attracted Catherine's attention too, but her notes and comments reveal a greater understanding of questions of administrative and social structure than of civil and procedural law; the Empress had neither the training nor the knowledge to make expert judgements on legal technicalities. Furthermore, the English model appeared to open up some new horizons for Catherine— the legal forms of capitalist economic relationships, such as torts, contracts, bankruptcy—and she was tempted simply to copy it. This probably explains why in reading Book II 'Of the Rights of Things' and Books III and IV on private and public wrongs affecting property, she merely follows closely Blackstone's text, without making any comment (except for frequent 'NBs') or excursuses of her own.[31]

On matters of civil law most of her attention is directed towards the rules of inheritance and the types of titles to property.[32] In trying to apply Blackstone's ideas she is handicapped by her obviously vague understanding of the distinctions made by English and Russian legal definitions. She distinguishes only movable and immovable property, while Blackstone speaks of personal and real property and of corporeal and incorporeal hereditaments.[33] The whole question of incorporeal hereditaments—perhaps of little importance in such an underdeveloped economy as Russia's—is left out of consideration by Catherine. In line with Russian legal practice she distinguishes clearly between inherited and acquired real property. She plans to maintain this distinction even after transfer to another generation, which means treating inherited patrimony differently from all other acquired property.[34] If enacted, this principle would naturally tend to favour fixed property relationships and discourage fluidity and the 'mobilization' of real estate for purposes of economic development. In fact one notices throughout Catherine's notes and drafts a constant tension between the need to secure permanently the economic base of the landowning population (primarily the nobility, of course, but the state peasantry would also have benefited from her proposals) and the desire to mobilize all resources for purposes of expansion. This is well illustrated by her attitude towards wills. She strongly condemns what she understands as the latitude given by English law to testamentary dispositions at the expense of the 'automatic' effect of traditional laws of inheritance.[35] This is a development she wants to prevent in Russia; but to do so means restricting the free disposal of potential assets in the form of land or some other property. Yet, perhaps not altogether consistently, she does not want the state to be in control of the disposition and ultimate fate of landed estates either. Thus she suggests that instead of an estate escheating, as it did in Russian law, on extinction of the fourth generation in direct line, it should pass on to a collateral line.[36] This would help impoverished branches of prominent families and also increase the number of moderately prosperous persons, who are the more desirable and active elements in the population.[37]

Catherine was also concerned about those aspects of legal procedure that guaranteed titles, secured property rights, and provided for speedy and equitable settlements of disputes. But in her notes she advances few concrete proposals of her own and contents herself with detailed and accurate summaries from Blackstone's chapters dealing with torts and bankruptcy procedures. In her draft codes she copies these excerpts word for word. To facilitate speedy settlements and rapid checking of titles she suggests decentralizing the procedures of registration and record keeping. Most records of transactions affecting property and contracts should be kept in provincial centres and claims should be made within reasonable time.[38] Of course, because of Russia's size, longer periods must be allowed for claims and contestations than in England where everything can be done through London and within a short time.[39]

In criminal matters she repeats her opposition to torture[40] and also suggests more flexible and generous provisions for bail and sureties so as not to keep defendants in jail needlessly.[41] One may say that this would only benefit members of the propertied classes, since only they were able to put up bail or find relatives or friends willing and able to act as surety for their appearance in court.

Finally, it should be mentioned that Catherine is strongly opposed to the interpretation of laws on the basis of court precedents and judicial opinions.[42] Here the Empress departs from her English model and finds herself at one with the juridical thought and practice of central Europe. She also relies on abstract reason rather than on human nature. This she makes clear *à propos* of torture when she insists on the primacy of reason in reaching judicial decisions or in obtaining a confession or conviction.[43] Strict, reasonable and uniform rules of law are more reliable, permanent, and hence fairer than individuals, however well motivated and worthy they might be. We can hear the echo of the perennial cry of Russian reformers: rule by institutions and laws, not by men—although it sounds paradoxical coming from a monarch so strongly committed to the principle of autocratic power.

It is in the area of state administration, however, that our sources provide the most interesting, and previously unnoticed, ideas and suggestions. Taken together they offer the foundation for a new approach to the political organization of the Russian empire. They also show that even in the second half of Catherine's reign, which is often presented as a period of retrenchment and conservatism, the Empress continued to be interested in basic structural change pointing towards the nineteenth century rather than in merely renovating an old machine.

Naturally enough, Catherine upholds clearly and steadfastly the autocratic nature of sovereign power in Russia.[44] At the apex of the state hierarchy stands the sovereign autocratic emperor of all the Russias.[45] He and he alone is the single source of all sovereignty, and therefore of all creative legislation.[46] In her summaries and excerpts from Blackstone she consistently translates or rephrases 'sovereign power' by 'imperial majesty' and 'imperial majesty's power'. She is therefore not very interested in what Blackstone has to say about the nature of English kingship, of the role and relationship of the king to Parliament, etc. These sections of the *Commentaries* are either omitted altogether or summarized briefly, superficially, and not always very accurately.[47] The autocrat's sovereign power is indivisible and inalienable.[48] Officials and institutions have only advisory power and their opinions are never binding on the ruler. In spite of this peremptory assertion of the inviolable character of autocracy, Catherine offers certain ideas and suggestions which to some extent qualify or subtly change its nature.

In the first place, though it is of little but historical significance and simply echoes the Bill of Exclusion, it is emphasized that a ruler of Russia must be of the Greek Orthodox faith.[49] And if the consort of a reigning empress is non-Orthodox or a foreigner, he has no say in the government and no military commitment may be undertaken to defend his foreign interests.[50] In the second place, foreshadowing the legislation of Paul I which finally resolved (at least in principle) the question of succession left open since the time of Peter the Great, the line of succession is established to and through the first-born male, to his descendants, and then to collateral lines, preference being given to male issue over female.[51] In the third place, if the heir is a minor or mentally or physically handicapped, a regency is instituted under a 'successor' (*preemnik*) or regent (*pravitel'*).[52] The regent would presumably be a close relative of the heir, but his appointment is to be ratified by the Senate and an assembly (sometimes called the 'Chief Executive Chamber') consisting of elected delegates from each province, one for each of the three estates of the realm: nobility, townspeople, and peasants (*sel'skie zhiteli*).[53] Passing reference is made to the power of this assembly to elect or nominate a ruler or regent in the case of the total extinction of the reigning dynasty, but the matter is not further explored. It is, however, stated that the provincial delegates should be present at every coronation.[54] The regent or 'successor' cannot act on the most important matters without consulting the Senate and possibly the Chief Executive Chamber. Upon the ruler's reaching majority, the regent retires to membership of the Imperial Council.[55]

Further provisions are also made for the status of the spouse of the reigning ruler and of the dowager empress.[56] These provisions are of little interest, they are copied from Blackstone's discussion of similar matters in English practice, and they were to receive legislative sanction along similar lines in Paul I's Statute on the Imperial Family (1797). Historically and psychologically it is interesting to note that Catherine's plans were drawn up in direct response to the case of Peter III and were designed to preclude any repetition of her own seizure of power. In other words, the possibility of another Peter III would be ruled out, but so also would a *coup* such as Catherine's of 28 June 1762, which would be completely illegal.

With respect to the empire Catherine merely restates and stresses the inalienability of its territory and the preclusion of the creation of appanages for any member of the imperial family. For administrative purposes the empire is divided into uniform provinces grouped by regions.[57] The overall scheme also establishes a pyramid of central and subordinate local institutions in a uniform and logical order.[58] The whole territory of the empire is treated alike, though at one point Catherine does state that provinces possessing any special privileges would be confirmed in them.[59] A significant feature is the provision that each emperor, upon accession, should take an oath to maintain the inalienability of the empire as well as to respect the order of succession.[60] This in itself might lead to a restriction of the autocratic character of supreme power in Russia.

For the higher institutions of the administration Catherine II has nothing of interest and significance to propose. It is noteworthy, though, that she emphasizes the advisory role of the Senate—divided into departments—and of the first three or four colleges (which are also subdivided into departments).[61]

In addition, following the description given by Blackstone of the Privy Council, she envisages an imperial council of advisers, selected by the ruler from holders of the three highest service ranks and including the heads of the principal colleges.[62] The council's function and place in the political hierarchy are not specified—probably intentionally, since its main task is to advise on whatever the ruler submits to its consideration. Inasmuch as the Imperial Council had not yet received permanent status and organization, Catherine's notes foreshadow the institution of the *Nepremennyi sovet* in the last years of her reign and its further evolution in the early nineteenth century into its final form as the Council of State in 1810. We might also note that the Council, in a manner not clearly indicated, participates with the Senate in the legislative process. All major acts have to be submitted to the Council for consideration, so that it can give its opinion and advise on the final version.

The most interesting and potentially most significant institutional innovation, which Catherine considered over a long time and in several forms, was the Chief Executive Chamber (*Glavnaya raspravnaya palata*), mentioned earlier in connection with the imperial succession.[63] The idea of a Chief Executive Chamber is put forward quite early in the notes while reading Blackstone. From the context in which it appears, though it is not closely connected with the notes on the *Commentaries,* the idea of a Chief Executive Chamber may have been suggested by Blackstone's discussion of the character and role of Parliament. The first description Catherine gives of the Chief Executive Chamber is, however, quite elaborate, so that it seems probable that she had given it some previous thought. The frequency with which allusions and descriptions of the Chamber appear in the notes on Blackstone, as well as the prominence given to the institution (with modified function, as we shall see) in the drafts on codification, are telling evidence of its central position in the thinking and planning of the Empress.

The Chief Executive Chamber is to consist of three departments:[64] the first with legislative functions which will be discussed below; the second concerned with criminal justice; and the third acting as a high court of equity. In one version there is an incomplete description of a fourth department, the function of which appears to have been to give opinions on the general utility (in economic terms?) of proposed legislation.[65] Leaving aside this fourth department, the character and function of which were not elaborated, we have two judicial boards or courts with review functions in matters criminal and civil, plus the first department. The latter affords a particularly interesting and important insight into Catherine's thinking and the tendency of her ideas on the structural reform of the central government. Except for brief references to the second and third departments (the criminal bench and high court of equity, which obviously parallel the King's Bench and Equity Courts), our description and analysis will concentrate on the first department which, in the Empress's mind, *was* the Chief Executive Chamber.

The most striking feature of the institution planned by Catherine is its membership. Each of the departments would consist of a president (appointed from among the officials in the top three ranks of the official hierarchy), a small number of councillors, and a varying number of assessors. These assessors—or full members in the case of the first department—would be drawn from a body of representatives elected by each *guberniya*. Each of the *gubernii* would have three delegates, one for the nobility, one for the townspeople, and one for the rural estate (i.e. the state peasants).[66] Nowhere is the method of election described, but elections would take place every three years. Ten *guberniya* representatives from each estate are assigned as assessors to each of the two judicial departments; in every case under adjudication the members of the criminal bench or the high court of equity are to be joined by elected representatives from the estate to which the defendants and/or plaintiffs belong. In addition, according to one version of the plan for the Chief Executive Chamber, a representative from the university (i.e. of Moscow) is appointed to sit in the fourth department.[67] Finally, a special school is to be attached to the Chamber, the students of which will receive practical training in administrative and judicial matters.[68] They are presumably to be drawn from university students or young noblemen preparing for a career in the civil service.

What were the functions envisaged for this novel institution with representation from the *pays légal* of the provinces? It is always to be remembered that in Catherine's scheme the Chief Executive Chamber—including its first department—is subordinate to the Senate, which stands directly under the autocrat at the top of the governmental pyramid. At times Catherine put the Chamber on the same level as the first three colleges, at others above them, but at no time was it to preempt any function of the Senate. It shares, however, one role with the Senate, namely that of local inspection. In some of the later versions of her plan for the Chief Executive Chamber Catherine proposes regular inspections of the provinces to be carried out by a joint inspectorate drawn from the Senate and the Chamber.[69] Representatives of the latter would have the specific obligation of reviewing the local judiciary, with power to settle pending cases and to clear the courts' dockets, subject to appeal by the parties concerned to the first department of the Chief Executive Chamber in full session and ultimately to the Senate. It would thus appear that the main task of the representatives of the Chamber would be to supervise the proper administration of justice, rather than to make decisions on specific issues of law.

In her notes on Blackstone Catherine gives the first department of the Chief Executive Chamber extensive and important legislative functions. Important and far-reaching legislative acts may be initiated in the Chamber and all such acts are anyway presented for its consideration.[70] The results of its discussions, and the decision reached by the Chief Executive Chamber, are passed on to the Senate for further discussion and thence to the ruler for approval. In case of disagreement with the Senate, the legislation is returned to the Chamber for further consideration; its final conclusions, together with the minutes of the discussion, are then submitted to the sovereign for his decision.[71] A major task of the Chief Executive Chamber is to ensure that new legislation is consonant with existing law and does not infringe the basic laws of the Russian empire.[72] But Catherine makes it quite clear that the Chief Executive Chamber has no independent legislative power, for the sole source of legislation in the empire is the sovereign, and he alone.[73] Yet there is no doubt that, if introduced, the Chief Executive Chamber with its consultative legislative role (one is reminded of the *droits de remonstrance et d'enregistrement* of the French *parlements*) would have been a potentially significant innovation.

At some point, too, Catherine conceived of a supervisory or controlling role for the Chief Executive Chamber. Complaints can be addressed to it and it can sit in judgement on high officials—e.g. governors (*gubernatory*)—suspected of misdemeanour by constituting itself into a special high court.[74] The probity of the members of the Chamber would be guaranteed, it was believed, by prohibiting anyone who had business dealings with the state (tax farmers in particular) from sitting in the Chief Executive Chamber.[75] On the model of the English Parliament, the Chief Executive Chamber is to have supervision over all corporate bodies, granting their charters and reviewing and inspecting their activities.[76] It has responsibility not only for private and semi-administrative bodies such as the *prikazy obshchestvennogo prizreniya* (boards of social welfare), but also for public educational establishments—schools, universities, and academies.[77] Finally, in its judicial capacity, the Chamber participates in the appointment of procurators and in the supervision of 'colleges of lawyers' (bar associations).[78] Taken together, Catherine's remarks on the constitution and functions of the Chief Executive Chamber scattered through her notes on Blackstone's *Commentaries* suggest that the Empress had in mind the establishment in Russia of a high administrative, legislative, and judicial institution, a partly representative body with delegates elected by the different estates from all the provinces of the empire. Presumably non-Russian populations would be excluded from representation, particularly in those areas that had not yet received the uniform provincial organization provided by the act of 1775.

On the face of it, Catherine's notes concerning the Chief Executive Chamber imply the reshaping of the empire's body politic by the creation of a permanent advisory representative institution. As we have seen, this institution would also play a role at the accession of a new ruler, especially in the case of a regency and the extinction of the ruling dynasty. We have also observed that the coronation oath requested of the monarch would include the promise to preserve this institution as one of the legal bases of the empire. But as some of the preceding references have also indicated, Catherine's drafts for codification preserved in the Central State Archives of Ancient Charters placed chief emphasis on the judicial functions of the Chief Executive Chamber she planned to create—functions that were mentioned in her notes on the *Commentaries*, but not developed there in any significant detail. From what we can infer about the chronology of the two sources the drafts for codification are of later date than the notes on Blackstone. The Empress seems, therefore, to have changed her mind so as to limit the significance and the innovatory, not to say revolutionary, character of the proposed institution.[79] But it still may be fairly argued that had even the more limited form of the Chief Executive Chamber been fully implemented, the Russian empire would have been given a solid *Rechtsstaat* foundation that might have served to promote the gradual and smooth modernization of its society and economy in the nineteenth century.

Catherine had alluded to a primarily judicial role for the Chief Executive Chamber in the notes on the *Commentaries* when she spoke of the president of its first department as the 'guardian of justice'.[80] It was a function that seems to have been suggested to her by the duties of the Chancellor in the English (and perhaps also the French) monarchy as she understood them.[81] In fact, the Guardian of Justice was more like an ombudsman in the later Scandinavian tradition—a role which logically and historically fitted better into the framework of the autocracy. Indeed, the task of the Guardian of Justice (or of the Law) was to receive complaints about miscarriages of justice, to right wrongs, and to extend a helping hand to the victims of maladministration.[82] He was to be but an extension of the ruler himself.[83] The personal aspect of political authority was thus fully preserved, while checking any possible abuse of power by the impersonal bureaucracy.

In addition to its function as ombudsman, the Chief Executive Chamber, especially its first department, was to exercise general supervision of the administration of justice. As we have seen, Catherine—at one with most of the enlightened despots of her day—firmly opposed 'judge-made' law. She wanted no part of the English practice of precedent which would lead to decisions and interpretations of law being made by the courts or by other institutions.[84] She even went as far as to prohibit the publication of court decisions on the ground that such publication would make possible the interpretation of the laws, a function which, in her opinion, belonged only to the sovereign as the sole legislative power.[85] It is, therefore, not surprising that Catherine's prime concern was to ensure the smooth operation of the mechanism of judicial administration, since it alone guaranteed a correct application of the existing laws.[86] Here the Chief Executive Chamber had to play an important role, not only by exercising its right of periodic inspection but also by *ad hoc* reviews.[87] Finally, the Chamber could be asked to pass judgement on the correctness of procedures followed in any given case, along the lines of the *Cour de cassation* to be established by Napoleon in post-revolutionary France.[88]

Also, as mentioned earlier, the second and third departments of the Chamber could act as the highest courts of appeal in criminal and equity cases. In these instances the regular staff was joined by assessors drawn from the elected representatives of the provinces according to the estate of the parties concerned. As supreme guardian of legality and supervisor of correct judicial procedures, the Chief Executive Chamber might have played a very significant role indeed, since this was the area of greatest administrative inefficiency, corruption, and abuse. But the path traced by Catherine was not followed either by herself or by her successors, although it is true that the transformation of the Senate into a primarily judicial body, supervising the administration of justice and, after 1864, acting as a *Cour de cassation,* may be seen as in line with the functions suggested for the Chief Executive Chamber. It may also be noted that the 'explanatory' (providing *razyasneniya*) role played by the cassation department of the Senate in the last decades of the imperial regime was precisely what Catherine had in mind for the Chamber once she had abandoned the idea of a consultative representative assembly for legislation and administration.

At first glance the scheme for a Chief Executive Chamber, whether a legislative or a judicial institution or both, seems such an innovation that one looks for models that might have inspired Catherine—for she was rarely very original. Obviously, she was inspired by English institutions of which she was reading in Blackstone at the time she noted her ideas for social and institutional reorganization. But as our presentation has made clear, in fact the English model was not followed at all closely. As Catherine herself put it in her letters to Grimm, she unravelled the thread in her own fashion. She had no intention of introducing any kind of parliament, judicial independence, or legal interpretation. Yet the fact remains that she did have the idea of a legislative consultation, the role of the King's Bench, and the basic principle of equity courts in mind when she was thinking about the Chief Executive Chamber. What she did not seem to realize quite clearly—perhaps she even hid it from herself— was that the English system rested on a social structure that was quite different from that of Russia. In matters of civil law she could hope that her new codification might initiate a trend that would move Russia in the direction of a British-type society; but this obviously would be a very long process and one may well wonder whether it could ever have come to pass as long as serfdom remained the condition of the greater part of the population.

The Chamber's administrative and legislative roles also give it a family resemblance with the newly established Austrian *Reichsrat* (1760) which, as we know, included a few select representatives of the estates from the major provinces of the Habsburg monarchy. There is no evidence in the sources that Catherine had this model consciously in mind. She no doubt knew about the *Reichsrat,* since she was interested in and well-informed about what was going on in Europe; and she also had direct opportunity of gaining information from Joseph II. Austria was a natural source of inspiration, for its administration had been recently reformed, its laws codified, and it too was a large and multinational empire with a social structure akin to Russia's.

But could there not also be Russian origins for some of the suggestions for a Chief Executive Chamber? We may think of Nikita Panin's proposal for an advisory imperial council which was advanced in 1762 but not implemented.[89] But Panin's proposal could have suggested only minor aspects of the Chamber scheme which differs from it in some fundamental respects. As we look closer at the Chief Executive Chamber, however, some interesting antecedents to its provisions come to mind, though it must be emphasized that we have no documentary proof that Catherine was in fact inspired by them. The similarities—such as they are—are functional rather than structural, which makes these parallels even more interesting. Chronologically, the closest 'model' may be found in the proposals of the upper ranks of officials (*generalitet*) and the nobility at the time of the succession crisis of 1730.[90] The reform of the Senate proposed by the *generalitet* would have turned it into a restricted representative body entrusted with the guardianship and supervision of justice. If given life, this institution would have also transmitted information on local conditions and needs, and advised on new legislation. Even more interesting is the parallel provided by the Chief Executive Chamber as a limited consultative representative body with the old Muscovite *zemskie sobory*, especially in their later form of the second half of the seventeenth century. The *sobory*, too, were convened to give information and to advise on proposed major legislation. It is true, of course, that the *sobory* were called irregularly and for special purposes only; also they usually included representation only from those groups of the population that were directly concerned with the particular issue at hand. Naturally, the parallels should not be pushed too far, for in a sense they all stem from one common root: the estate assemblies of medieval and early modern Europe.

Be that as it may, Catherine's suggestions not only had precedents both inside and outside Russia, they also had an 'after life'. We have already mentioned certain similarities of the Chief Executive Chamber to the Council of State as shaped by Speransky. More instructive for the historian concerned with the nature and problems of the imperial system is the striking similarity that the Chief Executive Chamber bears to the reform projects of the second half of the nineteenth century. The main objective of these projects was to adjoin to the highest organ of the imperial administration, the Council of State (which had inherited most of the political function of the old Senate), a body representing the population of the provinces. There were differences in the extent of representation proposed, in the manner of election, and in the weighting in favour of one or another social class, but there was no difference in the basic character of the proposed institution: representatives of the empire's population were to be directly consulted in drafting new legislation and in supervising the execution of existing laws and regulations. Moreover the representatives could convey to the highest organ of government information and expressions of needs without submitting them to the sifting and 'censorship' of the bureaucracy. These representatives were to be elected (or selected) on the basis of a narrow franchise and they were merely to inform and advise without any power to bind the autocratic government. Such proposals were made by Grand Duke Constantine, the Minister of the Interior Valuev, and Loris-Melikov. In its most developed form this approach served as the basis for the so-called Bulygin Duma of 1905.

The perennial revival of proposals for this type of reform illustrates the central government's need to establish better communication with the population at a local level, by-passing some of the barriers thrown up by the bureaucracy, and its determination that such communication should pass through existing social organisms (the estates, the *zemstva*). In addition care was always taken that the full sovereign power and responsibility of the ruler should never be seriously questioned or infringed. It bespeaks the difficulty of governing a huge multinational empire solely on a personal basis as well as the need to secure reliable information outside the regular bureaucratic channels and to control its own officials. In retrospect it may seem that these efforts were doomed to failure from the outset since they neither restricted the autocracy nor provided for an active and genuinely representative assembly. But one may ask whether the failure was foreordained in the eighteenth century. Would not the creation of an open, two-way channel of communication between the autocrat and his free subjects and an organ of effective judicial control have improved the administration and made subsequent developments much easier? With hindsight it may be plausibly maintained that the establishment of the Chief Executive Chamber would have prevented the radical, dramatic, and violent split between the autocracy—i.e. the state—and the best educated and active elements of the ruling class and would thus have forestalled the formation of the intelligentsia as a distinct force. And in the absence of a radically inclined intelligentsia the historical destiny of Russia in the nineteenth century (and beyond?) would certainly have been quite different.

Besides opening such avenues for speculating on possible alternative ways of development for Russia, the sources used for the present study also shed interesting light on Catherine's method of work. As was pointed out at the beginning, the manuscript notes of the Empress testify to her industry and attention to detail, to her great curiosity and her knowledge of both foreign literature and Russian practice. Moreover, she enjoyed this legislative work, as she confessed to Baron Grimm:

> ... sachez et soyez persuadé aussi que chacun a son lot et que le mien est de devenir législomane: régulièrement tous les ans à certaine saison je sens des redoublements qui vont en augmentant; celle de cette année est plus persévérante

que celle d'aucune autre, et Dieu merci nous critiquons et nous en savons en plusieurs occasions plus et autant que Blackstone lui-même.[91]

We have also noted her pragmatic and simplificatory bent of mind as well as her concern to introduce innovations into a well-established framework.[92] Unlike Peter I, she was not prepared to discard an institution or break an existing mould in order to introduce something novel. Even when she decided to innovate she proceeded slowly, with constant reference to and reliance on existing conditions and Russian traditions or precedents. Reading foreign literature and listening to others to obtain information and ideas served also to stimulate her own independent thinking.[93] She was also quite conscious of the peculiar, and what today would be called 'backward', nature of her empire, compared to the more dynamic and progressive states of the west, especially France and England. For this reason she felt it necessary first to bring Russia to the level of the contemporary great powers and only then to advance further.

The models she had before her[94] were those of enlightened despotism, i.e. strong centralized states with absolute monarchs ruling over societies organized along estate lines. These estates, with a firm legal and historical basis, provided the framework for ever more active and dynamic socio-economic developments. As Catherine saw it, the task of her government was to create the legal, social, and economic framework in which the individual members of the estates could pursue their most productive and creative activities. A prime requirement was to give security of property and person to members of these estates.[95] This was best achieved by means of good laws, fair and efficient administration of justice, and the establishment of adequate channels of communication which would enable the autocracy and central government to redress wrongs immediately and to be accurately informed of the country's needs and wishes. The serfs were excluded from this scheme, since they were considered and treated as the children, the 'wards' of their lords.[96] Seen in this perspective, Catherine was not so much trying to create the *bürgerliche Gesellschaft* in Hegel's (and Marx's) nineteenth-century sense, but rather the polity—civil society—that Frederick II and Kant wrote about. But in Russia, which did not yet possess the legal and institutional framework of such a polity, the first task was to create estates, give them a firm legal foundation, and extend protection and security for their members' activities in pursuing their lawful economic and cultural interests. This is what codification was all about, and this is what Catherine hoped to achieve by setting up the Chief Executive Chamber.

If such indeed were her long-term intentions, then taking into consideration her careful pragmatism and socio-political timidity, we should be less surprised that she accomplished little than that she accomplished anything at all. When all is said and done, she did leave Russia with a stronger institutional and legal framework, with a more rational and better-ordered—and hence more efficient—central administration and, most important perhaps, with the elements of corporate self-government for the upper classes and the idea of directed social and economic development, a development which would be led by the most dynamic and successful members of the recognized estates of the realm.

The Empress herself had no illusions and possessed too clear a sense of her political possibilities to see her reign as an unmitigated success and the crowning achievement of the process of Russia's westernization. Her chastening realism is best expressed in an interesting note she wrote to herself:

> Use the winter of 1787 and the beginning of 1788 to compose the chapters on the Senate and the Senate's procedures and instruction, do this with application and honest industry, if however the information [received] and criticism reveal barriers and annoying (*skuchnye*) or cunning (*lukavye*) difficulties, then put the whole work away (*v dolgii yashchik*), for we do not see (?) for whose sake I labour and will not my labours, care and warm concern for the good of the empire be in vain, for I do see that I cannot make my frame of mind (*umopolozhenie*) hereditary.[97]

Did she think only of Grand Duke Paul when she mused on the impossibility of transmitting her attitudes? Or did she also consider the relative backwardness of Russian society for whom many of her plans and expectations might seem premature? We do not know. But what we do know is that this was not just the passing mood of a tired, old, and disenchanted woman. Throughout her life she had displayed a similar attitude and followed this line of conduct, so that her reign—and her legislative activities—constitute an organic unity. It was this unity of outlook and approach that played a major role in setting the course for the subsequent evolution of Russia. Perhaps the best and most accurate epitaph we can write in conclusion is that Catherine's plans, aims, efforts, and partial success created the framework for the transformation of society in the first quarter of the nineteenth century and, at one remove, the *sine qua non* for the reforms of the 1860s. Paradoxically her legislative achievement provided both the foundation for the emergence of modern Russian society and the cause of the empire's institutional rigidity.

Notes

1. 'Pis'ma Ekateriny II k Grimmu', ed. Ya. Grot, no. 34, *Sbornik Imperatorskogo Russkogo istoricheskogo obshchestva (SIRIO)*, xxiii (1878), 52.

2. Manuscript Division, Lenin State Library, Moscow, *fond* 222, *karton* xvii, no. 1—hereafter cited as 'Notes'.

3. Central State Archives of Ancient Charters (TsGADA), *razryad* x, *delo* 17—hereafter 'Drafts'.

4. Notes, f. 1ᵛ. Cf. *Commentaires*, i (Discours préliminaire), 5–6 and 4th Oxford ed. (1770) of the *Commentaries*, i, 5–6. Quotations from the Notes and Drafts in this arti-

cle are given in French where Catherine used French and in English translation where the original text is in Russian. The spelling of the French and of transliterated Russian words has, where necessary, been corrected and modernized.

5. On this intellectual stance in eighteenth-century Russia, see H. Rogger, *National Consciousness in Eighteenth-Century Russia* (Cambridge, Mass., 1960), especially ch. iii.

6. For example: 'Le Saxon descendait des Slavons, les manoirs sont aussi anciens que *usad'by, gospodskii dom, gospodskii dvor, gospodskie lyudi'* (Notes, f. 35). And 'NB The origin of the word baron seems to be taken from the word *bary* or *boyary*. England was settled and conquered by the Saxons who are of the race (*rod*) of Slavs' (ibid. f. 107). Cf. also Notes, f. 22^v and Drafts, ff. 386, 464.

7. 'In Mexico, Peru, Chile there is a large number of Slavonic words in the names of towns and settlements, such as, for example, the town of Cuzco (Kusko), the town of Guatemala (Gatimalo), etc., and perhaps England and America itself had the Slavs as their lawgivers, hence the similarity of institutions' (Notes, f. 108). See also Notes, ff. 32, 34, 109, and 217^v.

8. e.g. Notes, f. 66^v.

9. In connection with a description of the practices of Admiralty Courts (*Commentaires*, iv, 173): 'NB Taken from Roman law and similar to its [Rome's] customs rather than to Anglo-Saxon, wherein the spirit of freedom is more noticeable than in Roman ones, [the latter] serving to enslavement and debasement'; and with reference to the Loi d'Oléron: 'NB This is a Norman right and smells of the Slavonic North' (Notes, f. 135^v). Cf. also Drafts, f. 386 ('slavery is a Tartar gift') and Notes f. 120^v.

10. The one specific reference to natural law is not taken from Blackstone: 'Natural rights [*sic*] are not subject to elimination or weakening either by time or by regulations' (Notes, f. 14). If this expresses Catherine's sincere opinion it would put her squarely in the camp of enlightened thinkers, but she may have been merely expressing a *lieu commun* without thinking of its implications.

11. Notes, f. 27 ('NB Consulter les Loix de Russie sur tout cela'), 34^v, 218, 352 ('NG Il faudrait comparer les loix d'Henri I Roi d'Angleterre avec celles de Iaroslav').

12. Drafts, f. 480^v ('NB See *Ustav blagochiniya* and project of new criminal code and printed *ukaz* of Aleksey Mikhailovich to forgive those who show contrition and *Tainaya ekspeditsiya* [acts]'.)

13. Letter to Grimm from Tsarskoe Selo, 28 August 1776: 'Je me suis toujours senti [*sic*] beaucoup de penchant à me laisser mener par les gens qui en savent plus que moi, pourvu qu'ils ne me fassent pas sentir qu'ils en ont l'envie ou la prétention, car alors je m'enfuis à toutes jambes' ('Pis'ma Ekateriny ...' (n. 1), 57). This may explain the failure of Diderot and Mercier de la Rivière to be taken seriously by Catherine.

14. Drafts, f. 226–226^v; Notes ff. 21^v, 22.

15. Notes, f. 33.

16. Ibid. f. 21^v ('K chinam privyazana dolzhnost'') and Drafts, f. 226.

17. Notes, ff. 27^v, 42^v, 46^v—a similar rule was to apply to state peasants (ibid. f. 47^v).

18. With reference to *Commentaires*, iii, 27, she notes: 'The first [in a family] to be distinguished by a title has permission—for the upkeep of the title—to separate out a patrimony of 500 to 700 households which will remain in the family undivided for the oldest in the family' (Notes, f. 44).

19. Notes, ff. 7, 21^V; Drafts, f. 225^V. In so doing she is reverting to seventeenth-century practice.

20. She suggests allocating 22,000 roubles for every *guberniya* of 300,000 to 400,000 souls. See Notes, f. 21 and Drafts, f. 225^V.

21. Notes, f. 21.

22. See G. L. Freeze, 'The Russian Parish Clergy: Vladimir Province in the 18th Century' (dissertation, Columbia University, 1972).

23. Notes, f. 19–19^V; *Polnoe sobranie zakonov Rossiiskoi imperii*, xxii (Spb., 1830), no. 16,603 (December 1787).

24. See N. M. Druzhinin, *Gosudarstvennye krest'yane i reforma P. D. Kiseleva*, I (M.-L., 1946), ch. ii.

25. Notes, ff. 47^V, 61.

26. Ibid. ff. 35^V, 61–61^V.

27. Ibid. ff. 35^V–36. The peasant household and allotments are to consist of the following seven categories: tilled land, meadow-land and hay, cattle, buildings, forests, water, people.

28. Ibid. ff. 38, 61.

29. *Polnoe sobranie zakonov Rossiiskoi imperii*, xix (Spb., 1830), no. 13,590 (4 April 1771); largely repeated in no. 16,603 (see n. 23).

30. 'Proekt imperatritsy Ekateriny II ob ustroistve svobodnykh sel'skikh obyvatelei', *SIRIO*, xx (1877), 447–98.

31. e.g. with respect to *Commentaires*, iv, ch. viii in Notes, ff. 137–47, where the French text of pp. 220–3 is literally copied with 'NBs' on every line.

32. Catherine excerpts very carefully Book III, ch. xxx, xxxi.

33. Notes, f. 30^V with reference to Blackstone, Book II, ch. ii ('Corporeal Hereditaments'), and ibid. f. 154 for the expression of her confusion.

34. Ibid. f. 36^V.

35. Ibid. f. 164^V ('NB England is in such a situation now that, as a result of the unlimited will of testators, succession laws [rights] have been completely eradicated ...'). The same sentence is repeated as a marginal comment in Drafts, f. 414^V.

36. Notes, f. 164.

37. But she definitely gives preference to social utility over absolute property rights of individuals. For example, her treatment of the case adduced by Blackstone (*Commentaires*, iv, 355–6) on the duplication of a ferry across the river if it violates the private interest of the first ferry-owner or franchise (Notes. f. 172).

38. Notes, ff. 60^V, 221 (with special allowance for those on state service).

39. Ibid. ff. 115^V, 188^V.

40. Ibid. f. 8.

41. Ibid. f. 216.

42. Ibid. f. 116^V.

43. Ibid. f. 307.

44. Notes, ff. 10, 13^V.

45. 'La Majesté Impériale est une personne seule, dont la volonté est uniforme et ferme et dont la personne n'a point d'égale dans l'Empire de Russie, Elle est Supérieure en dignité et en pouvoir à tout autre et jouit d'une existence séparée, toujours capable d'agir dans tous les temps et en tout lieu' (Notes, f. 10^V). Cf. also ibid. f. 14^V.

46. Notes, f. 16–16^v and f. 183 for personal responsibility to redress wrongs.

47. Catherine omits the end of Book I, ch. vii and viii ('Of the King's Prerogatives', 'Of the King's Revenue').

48. Notes, f. 12.

49. Ibid. Cf. the influence of the Bill of Exclusion in Blackstone, _Commentaires_, i, 302.

50. Ibid. ff. 6^v and 14^v.

51. Ibid. 44^v.

52. Ibid. ff. 11–12.

53. Ibid. ff. 9^v, 14.

54. 'Les provinces réunies seront representées à chaque couronnement du souverain par leurs députés savoir trois de chaque gouvernement, un de la Noblesse un des Villes un des Communes' (ibid. f. 6).

55. Ibid. f. 14–14^v.

56. Ibid. f. 12–12^v.

57. Ibid. f. 6–6^v.

58. Scheme in Notes, f. 18^v—but it may perhaps be a summary of the institutions established in 1775.

59. Notes, ff. 6 and 289^v (the latter guarantees freedom of worship to all recognized creeds).

60. 'Chaque successeur est prié de confirmer et ratifier cet Acte de sa signature et d'y apposer son sceau' (Notes, f. 6^v).

61. Ibid. ff. 12^v, 14, 17.

62. Ibid. ff. 12^v–13.

63. Our analysis and discussion of this proposed institution is based primarily on Catherine's Notes, but in some instances we shall draw on the Drafts as well, for they help to clarify the Empress's intentions.

64. The fullest description is given in Notes, f. 9–9^v and Drafts, f. 200.

65. Drafts, f. 200^v.

66. Notes, ff. 6^v, 9, and Drafts, f. 200–200^v.

67. Drafts, f. 205.

68. Ibid. f. 381.

69. Drafts, f. 512. The joint team consists of three branches (_kolena_): 1. 'Law and order'. 2. 'Listens and investigates'. 3. 'Accuses and exonerates'. See also ibid. ff. 446^v and 449.

70. Notes, ff. 6^v, 9.

71. Drafts, ff. 200^v–201.

72. Notes, f. 5; for civil cases, Drafts, f. 470.

73. Notes, f. 5^v.

74. Ibid. f. 9^v; Drafts, f. 383^v, and generally with respect to malfeasance in office, Drafts, ff. 188–9.

75. Notes, f. 9^v.

76. Ibid. f. 29^v and Drafts, f. 382.

77. Notes, ff. 3^v, 29; Drafts, f. 387^v.

78. 'NB Collèges des jurisconsultes is under the supervision of the Chief Executive Chamber and may be set up and supervised' (Notes, f. 106^v). See also Drafts, ff. 376^v–

377 concerning students attached to the Chamber as *stryapchie* and *khodatai*, and concerning law schools to be set up also under the supervision of the Chamber.

79. A comprehensive description of the new structure envisaged is given in Drafts, f. 172–172^v.

80. '*Khranitel' prav*' (Notes, f. 29^v).

81. See Notes, ff. 1, 43^v, for obscure references to 'chancelier'.

82. Drafts, ff. 188–188^v, 383.

83. Ibid. f. 175, where he is also referred to as *zakonodavets*.

84. 'NB To this date I am of the opinion that one should not permit the interpretation of laws and any commentaries on them—except [as performed] by the legislative [i.e. sovereign] power' (Notes, f. 210).

85. 'Les décisions des tribunaux ne doivent jamais être imprimées. Les décisions [des] Tribunaux imprimées et les commentaires sur les lois étouffent la loi' (Drafts, f. 320).

86. Ibid. f. 513.

87. Ibid. ff. 447^v, 449.

88. Ibid. ff. 178–9, 486^v.

89. Cf. D. Ransel, 'Nikita Panin's Imperial Council Project and the Struggle of Hierarchy Groups at the Court of Catherine II', *Canadian Slavic Studies*, iv (1970), 443–63, and idem, 'Nikita Panin's Role in Russian Court Politics of the Seventeen Sixties: a Critique of the Gentry Opposition Thesis' (dissertation, Yale University, 1969).

90. If Prince Dmitry Golitsyn had indeed a constitutional plan of settlement in hand, it too bore some faint resemblance to the Chief Executive Chamber as a legislative advisory council. For an introduction to the problem of the crisis of 1730 (and excerpts of documentation), see M. Raeff, *Plans for Political Reform in Imperial Russia* (Englewood Cliffs, N.J., 1966), especially ch. i and the Bibliography (p. 158).

91. Letter of 15 November 1779, 'Pis'ma Ekateriny II ...' (n. 1), 159.

92. Drafts, ff. 316 et seq., 480^v; Notes, f. 159^v.

93. See n. 13.

94. The events of 1789 only served to confirm Catherine in her preference for the Ancien Régime and to convince her of the dangers both of revolutionary social changes and of the destruction of the estates and 'pouvoirs constitués'.

95. Drafts, f. 198^v.

96. J.-L. Van Regemorter, 'Deux images idéales de la paysannerie russe à la fin du XVIIIe s.', *Cahiers du Monde russe et soviétique*, ix (1968), 5–19, and M. Confino, 'La politique de tutelle des seigneurs russes envers leurs paysans vers la fin du XVIIIe siècle', *Revue des études slaves*, xxxvii (1960), 39–69, and idem, 'Le paysan russe jugé par la noblesse au XVIIIe siècle', ibid. xxxviii (1961), 51–63.

97. Drafts, f. 296 (original punctuation retained).

FOURTEEN

Pugachev's Rebellion

IN THE EIGHTEENTH CENTURY Russia was undergoing a rapid transformation, albeit its rate varied from one aspect of the country's political, social, and economic life to another. ...

The pace of change in Russia was most noticeable in the military and diplomatic fields, where larger expenditures of money and manpower were entailed, as well as in the area of administration, where the primary task was to mobilize the country's resources for political and military action. A glance at the share of the state's expenditures devoted to military and administrative purposes between 1725 and 1767 readily illustrates the point. Total expenditures for the military establishment rose from 6.5 million rubles to 9.6 million, even though they fluctuated, dropping below the 1725 level in 1767, only to jump rather steeply after the outbreak of the first Turkish war in 1768. The relative importance of administration and court costs, rose consistently in the same period, from 31.1 per cent to 41. 5 per cent for general and fiscal administrative purposes and from 4.4 per cent to 10.9 per cent for the court.[1] At the same time, the expansion of the military establishment increased the burdens of conscription, borne exclusively by the peasantry, as after 23 August 1773 the call rose from 1 conscript for every 150 male "souls" to 1 for every 100.[2] It is true that part of the increase in taxation was absorbed by the rapid growth of the population. But the accompanying expansion of the empire's borders imposed more and greater administrative and military tasks on the government, and these in turn pushed up expenditures.[3]

It is rather difficult to assess adequately the rise in economic potential, which might have rendered the increased burdens more bearable. The industrial development introduced by Peter the Great did not maintain itself on the same level after his death but during the reign of Elizabeth its pace quickened. This time it took place under the sign of individual enterprise, in the form of

234

monopoly privileges granted to select individuals of Elizabeth's entourage, in particular the Shuvalovs. The pace of economic development was further stimulated by the abolition of internal duties in the 1750s and of *octroi* rights in 1762.[4] These measures also helped to involve the peasantry in local trade by encouraging them to take their goods to nearby town markets. After the death of Elizabeth the government fostered competitive entrepreneurial activity, especially on the part of the nobility, by abolishing the monopoly concessions granted in the previous reign and by giving to the owners complete discretion in disposing of the products grown or found on their estates as well as the products of their peasants' labor.[5] Carried out with the help of foreigners, especially settlers in the south and east, this promotion of economic activity increased the complexity of administration and opened the gates to many social, ethnic, and religious conflicts between the indigenous population and foreign newcomers.

With respect to the dynamics of social structure we observe a double phenomenon: On the one hand, the nobility was coming closer to being a genuine estate (*Stand*), enjoying all cultural and social, as well as economic, advantages. The nobles were gradually, albeit incompletely, changing from a class of state servants into a privileged estate of leisured and landowning individuals who were free to pursue their private interests. On the other hand, the peasantry had become almost a closed caste whose members were no longer bound to the land, but tied to the person of their owner—in fact, mere chattel. In addition, they were barred from access to the source of political authority. The connecting links that had existed, albeit in diminishing form, between the peasant community and the czar were broken by the interposition of the serf owners—be they private lords or agents of the Church or state. The return of more and more nobles to their estates (after 1762) meant that individual serf owners could effectively impose their tyrannical whims on the peasants, controlling in minute and annoying fashion their daily routine and interfering in their personal lives. The lord's presence made recourse to any state agent or institution well nigh impossible. The peasants felt abandoned by the modern state. This transformation of their relationship to state and landlord had been in the making since before Peter the Great. Gradual as it had been, it bore the earmarks of inevitability, and the peasant masses, although far from reconciled, bowed to it as they bowed to the rigors of their natural environment.[6] More specific facts and conditions, however, helped to fashion the background of the Pugachev revolt.

In Western Europe the increase in fiscal burden played a major role in paving the ground, or providing the spark, for popular revolts. We have mentioned that in Russia the total expenditures of the state rose sharply in the eighteenth century; consequently, taxation increased also. The basic item of direct taxation was the capitation (*podushnaia podat'*) introduced by Peter the Great, which applied to every adult male soul of the taxable population (i.e., mainly peasants, although other small social groups also were subject to it). Curiously, the rate of capitation did not increase dramatically in the course of the half-century preceding Pugachev's rebellion. Total receipts increased, but this was partly because of the population growth already mentioned.[7]

Was this relative stability of the rate of capitation evidence of the marginal character of Russian agriculture, or was it rather the result of the government's reluctance to burden the property of the nobility and thereby in fact reduce the serfs' contribution to their masters' revenue? To date, the available evidence has not provided a clear answer. In any event, the increase in the state's requirements was largely met by a sharp rise in indirect taxes, which naturally fell most heavily on the ordinary consumer—the peasant. Between 1724 and 1769 the share of direct taxes in the total revenue of the state dropped by 11.6 per cent, while that of indirect taxes rose by 10.6 per cent and of regalia by 1.4 per cent.[8] The tax burden of every male soul increased by 181 per cent between 1724 and 1769, and direct taxes rose by 146 per cent; indirect taxes rose by 242 per cent. Most indicative of the growing burden imposed on the common folk is the fact that revenue from such essential products as salt rose by 190 per cent and from vodka by 345 per cent, while *octroi* receipts (affecting local consumption) increased by 188 per cent.[9] In addition, a strong inflationary trend resulted in higher prices on all goods. The value of money dropped by an estimated 13 per cent between 1725 and 1767; it fell even more sharply after the start of the Turkish war in 1768 and eventually led to the introduction of paper *assignats* and still greater inflation in the second half of Catherine's reign.

Naturally, the increase in prices affected grain trade as well. In the west, rising grain prices had often precipitated popular unrest and revolts, mainly in the cities. Soviet scholars make much of the rise in grain prices as evidence of increasing feudal exploitation and deepening crisis in the feudal economy. I confess that this reasoning does not strike me as convincing. Of greater significance, I think, are certain basic features of eighteenth-century Russian agriculture which are only indirectly tied to the price fluctuations of grain. In the first place, the marginal character of agricultural production throughout most of the empire should not be overlooked. A yield of three times the seed planted was considered a good average, and a yield of from four to five per unit of seed was considered very good and fortunate indeed. If we take into account the necessity of preserving seed for the next planting, for reserves, and for feeding an ever-increasing population, we discover the precariousness of the peasant's condition.[10] The low yield was accompanied by capricious and sharp seasonal and geographical fluctuations. Grain prices also fluctuated greatly because the peasants were forced to buy grain for food and seed in times of penury. Prices rose sharply in the 1760s and 1780s.[11] It should be noted, however, that the lion's share of high grain prices lay in the cost of transportation, which limited the possibility of shipping grain over long distances and prevented relief from reaching areas stricken by bad harvests, if they were remote from areas yielding good crops.

The needs and interests of the nobility may help to explain the great concern for high grain prices evinced in the second half of the eighteenth century. Indeed, before the great expansion of grain production in the Ukraine and its easy shipment to domestic and foreign markets, the nobles purchased grain for their own needs, for a rather large number of unproductive domestic serfs, and on occasion to help their own peasants. Paradoxically, therefore, the landowning nobles (in service and away from their estates) were consumers and buyers of grain rather than its producers and sellers. At the same time, as an increasing number of peasants left the estates to work in cities or non-agricultural occupations on a permanent basis (*otkhod*), their lords gained the impression that the number of productive hands working the land was decreasing while the number of mouths dependent upon purchased grain was growing.[12] The latter stimulated the need for marketable grain, holding out hopes for more income from greater agricultural production. These hopes seemed particularly attractive because serfs who paid only quitrent (*obrok*)—the value of which was relatively low and stable—provided an inadequate and quite inflexible source of revenue. Interest in agriculture as the main source of wealth was in part stimulated by the popularization of fashionable western economic ideas (e.g., physiocracy) and the government's educational propaganda (competitions sponsored by the Free Economic Society). We can therefore readily understand that a psychological and cultural climate favorable to agriculture developed in the second half of the century and encouraged the nobility to seek an increase in their share of agricultural production.[13] The successful raising of quitrent payments above the inflationary decline of the currency's purchasing power seemed to demonstrate the peasantry's greater ability to pay and, by implication, offered more scope for the exploitation of serf labor.[14]

These factors explain what M. Confino has called the "rediscovery" of *corvée* (*barshchina*) on the part of the serf-owning nobles.[15] They account for the spread of *corvée* not only on large estates but also to smaller ones and, of particular significance for our topic, to those estates in the east and southeast which heretofore had been relatively immune to this form of servitude. The *corvée* was more burdensome than the quitrent, not so much in terms of economic accounting as in human terms, which were immediately perceived by the serfs: stricter control and a regularization of peasant activities on the estate and a reduction of the land available to the serf for his own use. Little wonder that the system was resented and that its spread (or return) to new estates aroused those peasants who had become accustomed to greater leeway in their routine activities. It is of some significance that, in the rich agricultural region of Voronezh Province affected by the Pugachev rebellion, 384 of the

393 estates that fell victim to the rebels were on *corvée,* only 2 per cent being on quitrent.[16]

The 1760s and early 1770s showed greater concern for a livelier pace of economic activity, fuller exploitation of all available human and natural resources in the empire, and a gradual shift to a market orientation. The truly dramatic change, however, would come only in the 1780s and later, with the opening up of the agricultural potential of the south. But the discussions at the Codification Commission of 1767 and the competitions sponsored by the Free Economic Society gave expression to the growing realization that the old ways of economic life had to go and that new ones were needed.[17] This realization served to create a mixed atmosphere of hope and disarray among the nobles and peasants. The latter expressed their confusion in a restlessness and pervading discontent, a proneness to rumor and rebelliousness.

What aggravated the situation in Russia before 1773 was the persistence of a few conditions which had been sources of irritation and conflict since the beginning of the century. As the repeated complaints of deputies to the Codification Commission of 1767 testify, security and protection of property and person were woefully inadequate in the Russian empire. The complaints came mostly from nobles who had been spoliated and browbeaten by richer and influential neighbors, attacked by brigands, and cheated by unscrupulous merchants. But anything that worsened the condition of these nobles also directly affected their peasant serfs, who in the final analysis had to make up for their masters' losses and who bore the brunt of the brutality directed at their owners.[18]

A major source of lawlessness and dissension was the frequent lack of set and recognized boundaries between estates, peasant allotments, Church property, and state lands. Hence the general demand for a comprehensive land survey. After a false start under Elizabeth, it really got under way with the issuance of revised instructions in 1765.[19] As badly needed as it was, however, the survey did have undesirable consequences for some groups of the population. Indeed, Catherine's instructions of 1765 directed that the surveyors register and validate all existing boundaries unless they were being contested in court by the parties concerned. These instructions meant in effect that the state acquiesced to previous seizures of state lands and empty tracts, and ratified the spoliations of free peasants and petty serf owners by rich and influential nobles.[20] Among the main victims were the *odnodvortsy* (owners of one homestead), about whom more will be said in connection with the Pugachev revolt itself. Along the same lines, the third general census, begun in 1762, not only counted and registered the taxable population but also immobilized it. As it had done since the sixteenth century, the process of counting drove to flight those who did not wish to be tied down permanently.

To round out the picture of disarray and insecurity which contributed to the peasantry's forebodings of the traditional world's crumbling and of worse times to come, we should note the frequent recurrence of crop failures, plagues, and epidemics. Among the latter the most dramatic was the 1771 epidemic in Moscow, which brought to the surface all the unconscious and unfocused fears and panics of the populace.[21] In a way, it was a prelude and dress rehearsal for the Pugachev revolt. That is why, on the eve of the rebellion, the report of drought in the Ural area sounded ominous indeed.[22]

Government policies with respect to Church matters further contributed to the unsettling atmosphere which permeated the Russian body social in the early 1770s. Since the sixteenth century the Muscovite state had followed a policy which aimed at putting under secular control all lands owned by the Church (monasteries, dioceses). Peter the Great pursued the same goal, but shifted the focus of attention to the political and fiscal control of the Church hierarchy. The latter was saddled with new obligations, while its administration was assimilated to a department of the secular state. But the Church's resources—or the means of collection—were inadequate to meet the new obligations imposed on it. As a consequence, its serfs were among the most exploited and poorly administered of the peasantry. Little wonder that discontent and unrest were endemic among Church peasants, so much so that Catherine II estimated that about fifty thousand were in open revolt at the time of her accession. Elizabeth had laid the ground for a new administrative setup by transferring Church (primarily monastic) peasants from the direct control of ecclesiastic institutions to that of local noblemen and tax farmers. However, this arrangement did not prove very successful either, because the tax farmers and local nobles used their new function to their exclusive personal advantage.

The legislation of Peter III with respect to the Church aroused some of those rumors and hopes which played no small part in the Pugachev uprising. Following perhaps his personal anti-Orthodox inclinations, as well as his unreflecting impetuosity, Peter decreed on 16 February and 22 March 1762 that all Economy Peasants (i.e., serfs on monastic and diocesan lands) be removed from the direct administration of the College of Economy and, in return for the payment of a yearly quitrent of one ruble per soul, have the free use of all the land they worked.[23] This act was naturally interpreted as a freeing of the Church peasants and as the first step toward a general emancipation of all serfs.[24] The peasants "interpreted" the decrees to mean that they were free to discontinue their payments and obligations to church authorities, and the government had to intervene with clarifications restricting the implications of the law.

To assuage the Church hierarchy, as well as to provide a firm basis for new legislation, Catherine II annulled the act of Peter III upon her accession. This annulment aroused the peasants' suspicion of her as an evil, illegitimate ruler enthroned to cheat them of the freedom granted by their "true" czar. Eventually, Catherine promulgated her own, more moderate act of secularization in 1764, which eliminated any hopes for general emancipation the peasants may have entertained.[25] The confusion and tergiversations of the government in this matter led to rumors and disturbances, all of which came into the open during the Pugachev uprising, when many Church peasants revolted in support of their own "true" emperor, who had given them freedom, a freedom of which the evil nobles and unlawful empress had robbed them.

Peter III had also made himself quite popular with the Old Believers and other dissenters through a series of measures which improved their status, permitted freer exercise of their rites, and encouraged those who had fled beyond the borders of the empire to return to Russia. The resettling of Old Believers from Poland in the eastern provinces—e.g., the valley of the Irgiz—made of Peter III's name a virtual password into the ranks of that peculiar freemasonry which was the Old Believers and of which Pugachev made good use in the earlier stages of his career.[26]

Often we read in general histories that Peter III's granting freedom from service to the nobility led the peasants to expect a similar act freeing them from serfdom; and the failure of such an act to materialize was ascribed to the conspiracy of the nobility to which Peter himself fell victim. This interpretation is hard to document, and it is doubtful that such reasoning, if it did occur, played a decisive role in the *Pugachevshchina*. But, to the extent that Peter's manifesto of 18 February 1762 made it possible for many nobles to leave service and return to their estates, it resulted in increasingly closer supervision and greater exploitation of the serfs. The fact that this was indeed sometimes the case and a direct cause of peasant discontent and rebellion is well documented in our sources.[27]

With the peasants agitated by various rumors of freedom relating to the short reign and mysterious demise of Peter III, it is little wonder that the people believed he had not died, that he would return to complete the emancipation of his people. Hence the dozen or so pretenders—*samozvantsy*, familiar company in times of trouble in Russia—who are known to have appeared between 1762 and 1774.[28] Without going into the fascinating story of this phenomenon it may suffice to note here that the legendary pretender, *samozvanets*, appears as the suffering and wandering czar or prince-redeemer, the savior; the false Peter III also appeared in this saintly form.[29] In the case of the Old Believers the myth was reinforced by their mystical conceptions of the Second Coming of Christ. Thus the founder of the Skoptsy sect (castrators), Kondratii Selivanov, claimed to be both Christ and Peter III.[30] Nor was it an accident that Pugachev's claim to be Peter III was suggested to him and promoted by Old Believer hermits in the Iaik region.[31]

In summary, Russia was undergoing the travails and disarray that accompanied its adaptation to the innovations introduced by Peter the Great earlier in the century. With respect to social structure, the nobility and the peasantry had undergone a transformation that had changed their mutual relationship as well as the relation of each to the state; but their estate character still needed to be defined more clearly by legislation. The legislation had been promised but had not yet been fulfilled.[32]

To the population the role of the state appeared particularly ambiguous. On the one hand, it had spread its grip geographically and administratively: many areas and activities that earlier had been left to communal and individual action were now within its direct purview. On the other hand, the state aimed at promoting novel trends in the economy and society which would make for entrepreneurial modernity. At the same time it had also taken the seemingly paradoxical step of eliminating direct connection with the people by allowing the serf-owning nobles to become a barrier between peasantry and ruler. The decree of 1767, which completely prohibited direct petitions to the empress from the peasantry, was only the final act of a trend that had shattered the traditional concept of the sovereign held by the people.[33]

* . * . *

Let us now turn to an examination of the specific conditions that prevailed in the region where the Pugachev revolt took place—i.e., the middle Volga valley (the area between the Volga and the Ural watershed) and the open plains between the southern slopes of the Ural Mountains and the Caspian Sea. The mere enumeration of these constituent parts gives an idea of the area's variety, a variety of landscapes and economic resources which was reflected in the social makeup of the region. We shall therefore describe and discuss the specific regional circumstances that formed the background of the rebellion, and were sometimes a direct cause of it, in terms of groups and classes of inhabitants.

In the absence of reliable detailed local studies, it is difficult to generalize about the conditions of Russian peasants in the areas of agricultural settlement, i.e., the provinces of Penza, Perm, Saratov, and the eastern fringe of Voronezh. Yet, on the basis of studies that treat this area roughly as a unit, the dominant impression is that the peasant was better off in this eastern frontier than in the central provinces around Moscow. An area of relatively recent settlement and development, the peasants' land allotments were not only adequate but even plentiful, although in truth much of it was not used to the full.[34] Balanced against these positive aspects was the fact that because of the recent date of their settlement the peasants were not quite attuned to the local geographical and climatic conditions, so that we observe greater fluctuations in harvest yields than occurred in the old central provinces.[35]

But, in the eighteenth century, land had not yet become the scarce commodity and sore spot of the peasants' economy which it was to be in the late nineteenth century. More vital to their prosperity were the serfs' dues and obligations to their masters and to the state. The quitrent payments had risen considerably in the course of the eighteenth century; yet from all evidence they had remained lower in the east than in the central agricultural regions of Russia.[36] On the basis of our present knowledge it is more difficult to determine the extent of conversions to *corvée*, which we have noted as one of the significant trends, during the second half of the eighteenth century. There are indications that it took significant proportions in the Province of Penza, which more and more produced for export beyond its own confines, taking advantage of transportation facilities offered by the waterways of the Volga system. A similar trend is to be observed in Saratov Province. As mentioned earlier, a change to *corvée* was perceived as a new, rigid, and particularly burdensome form of "exploitation"—even though in strict economic terms the *corvée* was not necessarily worse than the *obrok*. This feeling was especially strong in "new" areas of settlement, where the peasants had generally enjoyed greater leeway than their counterparts in the central regions.

The extent of the steady increase in hired help on noble and peasant lands and of social stratification within the village, emphasized by Soviet historians as a factor in rural ferment, is difficult to determine. The mere presence of landless agrarian workers naturally contributed to the lack of cohesion in the village and may have made for acute conflicts, but it need not have resulted in open revolt. Quite clearly, however, with its peasant organization and life resting on traditional forms and fixed customs, the village would react strongly to any sudden change, and such a reaction could take the form of disobedience, open revolt, and anarchy. For instance, a change in ownership might trigger a revolt if the new owner attempted to change—not to mention increase—the dues and obligations of the peasants. While not confined to Russia, such a situation was more frequent there in the eighteenth century—and the effects more dramatic—because the inheritance laws and customs led to a considerable redistribution and splintering of estates which radically transformed their character.[37]

All in all, the condition of the serfs and the state of agriculture in the areas of Russian settlement were no worse in the east than in the center; as a matter of fact, all things considered (including the greater likelihood of the landlord being far away in the capitals), it was probably better. Although it was no doubt idealized, the picture traced by S. Aksakov of his grandfather's estate on the Kama was not too far off the mark. But the circumstances of the other social groups reveal a few important differences from those of the Russian peasantry.

The Volga valley had for a long time been the haven for escaped serfs from the central provinces. Although gradually superseded by regions farther east (and south), in the eighteenth century the middle course of the "Mother River" still attracted many loose-footed elements of the Russian people.[38] These escapees (*beglye*) either established their own villages or joined existing households and estates. Most of them were runaways from state lands in the central provinces; only a minority had escaped from privately owned estates, because individual owners, or their agents, apparently managed to control their serfs better than did state officials. Beginning in the 1730s, however, a new trend may be discerned in the pattern of settlement of these escapees from the center. In the first quarter of the eighteenth century most of the peasants who had fled settled down in their own households, forming new villages of their own. After the 1730s they tended to become landless, hired agricultural help on the estates of local nobles (or Cossack elders) or in other peasants' households.[39] Obviously, this development meant that the more restless, as well as impoverished, element was on the increase in the region. The escaped peasants settling along the middle Volga were the object of a double squeeze. The free land they worked as squatters was coveted by estate-owning nobles (*pomeshchiki*) moving from the north and northwest who were grabbing all the land they could lay their hands on, by means fair or foul—state grants, purchase, or outright seizure. On the lands they acquired these nobles settled their own serfs, whom they moved from the old estates in central Russia, or they took in the landless laborers mentioned above and virtually turned them into their bondsmen. A similar squeeze was exercised from the south. The Cossack elders (*starshina*, i.e., officers) from the Don Cossack Host had become landowners (an act in 1775 was to equate them in status with the Russian service nobility) and were expanding their holdings beyond the territory of the Host, where their opportunities were restricted by the privileges of the Cossack Host and the absence of serf peasants. They, too, settled their new estates with serfs moved from the central provinces or with landless *beglye*, whom they attached to the land. Thus from both north and south the formerly free "frontier" of the Volga valley was nibbled away by the advance of the estate (*pomestie*) using serf labor.

In the westernmost part of the region swept by the Pugachev rebellion, the right bank of the middle Volga (administratively part of the Voronezh *guberniia*), were a number of *odnodvortsy* (single homesteaders).[40] These were the descendents of petty military servicemen who had settled on what in the sixteenth and early seventeenth centuries had been the military frontier (*liniia*) protecting Moscow from Crimean Tartars and Ottoman Turks. With the end of their military function, they had declined to the status of small, but free, peasants who tilled their own lands, in some cases with one serf family to help them out. A high proportion of them also were Old Believers, so that they felt particularly alienated from the state established by Peter the Great—an alienation which an extra heavy fiscal burden did nothing to relieve. Having lost their military *raison d'être*, the *odnodvortsy* were no longer subject to the state's concern and protection. As they occupied lands that lay directly athwart the path of the nobility's agricultural expansion into the fertile black-soil steppe, they were hard-pressed by landowners from the central provinces who by hook or by crook were acquiring land and settling their serfs on it.[41]

Impoverished as they were, the *odnodvortsy* were defenseless against the encroachments of nobles who had connections in the capitals and the means to bribe officials. The poorest among them lost their land and sank to the level of hired laborers and sometimes even became serfs.[42] At the same time, they continued to claim privileged status, their right, as servicemen and freemen, to own serfs themselves. Because of their own economic weakness they resisted and mistrusted everything that tended to modernize the economy and to change the traditional pattern of self-sufficiency into production for a market. Their loss of economic and social status paralleled somewhat the fate of the small imperial knights in Germany at the time of the Reformation. As the knights had done in the fifteenth and sixteenth centuries, the *odnodvortsy* reacted to their sense of loss and alienation from the new trends by pinning their hopes on the providential leader or ruler who would bring them salvation by restoring them to their former function and status. It is from their ranks that several of the pretenders arose; and Pugachev, who claimed to be Peter III the czar-savior and restorer, found ready support among the *odnodvortsy* of Voronezh *guberniia*.[43]

If the *odnodvortsy* represented a native social group that had lost its traditional military, political, and economic functions, the foreign colonists who had been settled on the Volga in the reign of Elizabeth were a new and alien element.[44] The foreigners were not too numerous, about 23,000 souls, but they occupied lands on the lower middle course of the Volga, neighboring on the Kalmyk and Don Cossack territories, where the last act of the Pugachev rebellion was to take place. Although one might expect their situation to have been better than that of the Russian peasantry, it was not. In the first place, not all foreign colonists had the same legal status or were treated alike. Indeed, about half of them had been brought there by individual recruiters and were obliged to turn over to the latter one-tenth of all their produce, as well as to submit to their authority in all administrative and police matters. The recruiters' power, however, was more arbitrary and direct than that of the regular provincial administration. Many of the colonists had been recruited hastily, only to satisfy the greed of the recruiters, and they were not prepared for agricultural work—at any rate, not under Russian conditions. The yield of their labor was therefore quite small, for they suffered profoundly from crop failures and famine.[45] In addition, they were much exposed to raids and incursions by their nomadic neighbors, which added physical insecurity to their hardships.[46] In 1764 new regulations improved their status by placing them under the special supervision of regular state organs. But this compromise did not satisfy the settlers, because they wanted to be state peasants and completely free of control by their recruiters or special officials.[47]

Northeast European Russia traditionally had been a region of large Church landholdings. Between the Volga and the northern massif of the Urals there were several large monasteries with huge amounts of land and

numerous peasant serfs attached to them. It was to be expected that the confusion which resulted from the fitful attempts at secularization—Catherine's
retreat from Peter III's legislation and then her own compromise settlement—would excite the peasants, whose hopes for freedom had been raised
high only to be belied by subsequent events. The remoteness of the area from
the capital and the nearest episcopal sees (Kazan and Nizhni Novgorod) prevented the local authorities from adequately coping with peasant discontent;
by the 1760s thousands of peasants belonging to monasteries were in open
rebellion.[48]

The longest and most dramatic revolt was at the Dalmatovo Monastery in
the Urals, the so-called *dubinshchina* in 1762–64. General A. Bibikov (future
commander of the forces against Pugachev) and Prince A. Viazemskii (future
procurator-general of the Senate) were dispatched to investigate the causes of
the revolt, put it down, and suggest reforms to prevent its repetition.[49] Obviously, these high officials succeeded in coping with only the outward manifestations of discontent, for we find the peasants of the Dalmatovo Monastery at
the center of the Pugachev rebellion in the Urals in 1773–74.

Besides the regular monasteries there were also numerous small monasteries and hermitages (*skity*) of Old Believers in the region east of the Volga.
They constituted another element that was receptive to Pugachev's appeals.
As a matter of fact, the network of Old Believer *startsy* ("holy men") and hermitages served to propagandize the appearance of Peter III—Pugachev—and
his successes, and they also helped him recruit his first followers from among
the Old Believer Cossack of the Iaik.[50]

In the middle of the eighteenth century the Urals were Russia's major mining and industrial region. The area had developed at a rapid pace since Peter
the Great had allowed factory and mine owners to attach and ascribe
(*pripisat'*) serfs to their enterprises. Serfs so ascribed were compelled to work
in the mines and factories at those times when they were not needed in the
fields. In fact, their obligations were particularly burdensome and intolerable
because the time spent in traveling to and from the factory or mine (sometimes as far away as several hundred miles) was lost. Naturally, the serfs' aspiration was to return to their villages for good and be freed from the horrible
work in the factories and mines. In the course of the century it had become
evident that such compulsory labor was quite unsatisfactory. A decree of Peter III,[51] which prohibited the further ascription of villages and peasants to
factories until such time as a new code of laws would settle their status definitely, had raised the expectation among ascribed peasants that their freedom
was near and that they would be allowed to return to their homes. The appearance of Pugachev (whom they also believed to be Peter III) was naturally
interpreted by them as a signal to rise, leave the factories and mines, and return to their native villages.[52]

In the 1770s, however, the mainstay of the Ural labor force was the workers who belonged to the factories—industrial serfs, we might call them (*possessionnye krest'iane*).[53] As everywhere in Europe at the time, such labor was the lowest of the low, at the bottom rung of society and the economy. Needless to say, the working conditions, with heavy reliance on child and female labor, were appalling by any standards. In addition, the workers had to carry a heavy burden of taxation and various dues. Their quitrent payments rose from one ruble to one ruble seventy kopecks in the middle of the eighteenth century, but their wages did not increase. By the middle of the eighteenth century many of the factory hands and miners were children of the original factory serfs and frequently held the status of hired laborers, who were paid wages. But the pay scale was very low, and working conditions were not good in their case either.[54] Because they no longer tilled the soil they were particularly hard hit by the rise in prices on such vital commodities as salt and grain.

The situation of many workers worsened when in the reign of Elizabeth a number of state-owned factories were turned over to private owners (in fact given away to such favorites as the Shuvalov brothers). The new owners, interested only in obtaining high benefits rapidly, intensified the exploitation of their labor force (and plant facilities) without regard for the future. At the same time, like landowners with respect to the serfs, they stood as a solid barrier between their workers and the government, precluding appeals to, and intervention by, the state for improvement of conditions. With the loss of Russia's competitive advantage on the world market (due mainly to high transportation costs and technological rigidity) the production of the Ural mines and iron-smelting factories declined, hitting hardest the workers who had no other place to go or no other skill to market.[55] Quite clearly, then, there was enough material to support rebellion against the system. By and large the factories supported Pugachev, some voluntarily continuing to produce artillery and ammunition for the rebels (a significant factor in Pugachev's success).[56]

The workers' support of Pugachev frequently had another motive as well: their need of protection against Bashkir raids on factories in the southern Urals. (In the north, where this danger was minimal, the factories were more divided in their loyalties.) The Bashkirs had been pushed from their traditional winter camps and summer grazing lands as dams were built, flooding encampments and pastures, and forests were cut down to meet the needs of the expanding mining and industrial enterprises. The Bashkirs had to yield their lands, grazing grounds, and fishing places under duress and at derisive prices, much like the American Indians selling Manhattan Island. Not surprisingly, they hated the factories and took their revenge whenever possible by raiding them or attacking their workers.[57] That is why some factories appealed to Pugachev, whom the Bashkirs supported, for protective charters (*okhrannye gramoty*) and in return worked for him.[58]

The conflict between the factory population and the Bashkirs highlighted the fact that the region affected by the Pugachev revolt comprised many non-Russian, non-Christian native peoples. Such a heterogeneous population created special problems for the government, and it provided opportunities for those opposing the state and seeking support among the discontented, as yet unassimilated natives. Instead of considering separately each one of the many non-Russian peoples caught up in the revolt, let us look at three major "problem areas," as contemporary jargon has it, that were the sources of discontent and opposition to the central Russian government and its agents.[59]

In those areas which had been under Russian control for a long time and whose native population was primarily sedentary, the major problem was conversion to Orthodox Christianity. This was the case in the upper valley of the Volga and its northeastern tributaries, a territory dependent upon the archdiocese of Kazan, the native population of which consisted of Tatar Muslims and primitive groups of hunters, fishermen, and tillers such as the Cheremys, Mordvinians, and Chuvash. Initiated by Empress Anne and continued under Elizabeth, an active program of conversion had been promoted under the aggressive aegis of the archbishops of Kazan.[60] With respect to the Tatar Muslims the results had been disappointing, and the conversion campaign only resulted in the destruction of many mosques, the digging up of cemeteries, and various economic and social hardships determined by the whims of local officials and landowners. In any event, it seems that the Tatar Muslims did not play an active part in the Pugachev uprising, even though large numbers of them lived in and around Kazan.[61]

But the peoples and tribes which practiced various forms of paganism, shamanism, and animism offered much less resistance to conversion. Allured by promises of tax advantages (e.g., exemption from capitation for three years) and quick to bow to the pressure of local authorities, they converted—at least formally—in large numbers in the eighteenth century. But the act of conversion itself became the source of further exactions and a shameless abuse of their trust. With the full support and active participation of provincial officials, local clergies collected "gifts" and the tribute in kind (*iasak*) under various pretexts; noticing (or deliberately planning) evidence of inadequate fulfillment of ritual and dietary prescriptions on the part of the newly converted, they would impose heavy fines or exact bribes. Confused and impoverished by such illegal collections and exactions, the natives became restless. They tried to bring their plight to the attention of the central government; elections of deputies and the meetings of the Codification Commission of 1767 afforded them the long-sought opportunity to voice their grievances.[62] But their last hopes were shattered when their petitions were turned back, their access to the sovereign being impeded by local officials. They were ready to join a movement of discontent or rebellion.

While conversion was not a major issue for the natives farther east—Muslim and Buddhist nomads in the open steppes beyond the Volga—the advance of agricultural settlement brought in its wake serious and far-reaching conflicts. Throughout the eighteenth century the imperial government consistently pursued a policy which aimed at changing the nomads' way of life by transforming the cattle raisers into sedentary tillers of the soil (which in the long run would bring about their cultural and social Russification as well). The successful outcome of such a policy would make it possible for greater numbers of Russians to move onto new arable lands without fear of raids from neighboring nomads.[63] Thus the grazing lands of the Bashkirs and Kirghiz were relentlessly whittled away. The Kirghiz were hard pressed on the lower Volga and the Irgiz, while the Bashkirs were gradually dispossessed of their summer grazing spots on the southern slopes of the Urals. At the same time, the nomads were pressured into abandoning their traditional ways and taking up sedentary agricultural pursuits.

The Bashkirs were the main target of this conversion effort: their elders and tribal chiefs were promised rewards of rank, money, gifts, and medals if they would lead their people into social and economic change.[64] The effort was not fruitless, for some chieftains and their clans began to settle down and till the land. Not surprisingly, however, this development caused considerable tension within Bashkir society, and the breakup of traditional links and solidarities resulted in friction and unrest.[65] In addition, the turn to agriculture frequently required the settlement of a new, alien element—non-Russians of various origin, known as *tepteri,* who provided a landless agricultural labor force for the richer, settled Bashkirs. Friction was great between these exploited and scorned *tepteri* and the Bashkirs among whom they lived, so that when the latter rose in revolt the *tepteri* remained loyal to the Russian government, in whom they saw a protector. The Russian state was also using fiscal policy to tighten its control over the Bashkirs and to push them onto a new path of social and economic development. Indeed, the basis of taxation was changed from the tribute in kind, normally levied on all non-Christian peoples of the east, to compulsory purchases of salt in state-owned stores at fixed prices. Eventually the Bashkirs were put on the *obrok,* albeit at a low rate. All these measures tended to introduce the elements of a market and money economy by government fiat, and they were bound to upset the traditional equilibrium.[66]

There was, of course, also the usual conflict between nomadic peoples and their settled neighbors, a conflict heightened by national, religious, as well as political, rivalries. The Cossacks on the Don clashed with Kalmyk and Kirghiz nomads, and the foreign colonists were frequently the object of ruinous raids by Kirghiz tribes. We have commented on the conflict that pitted Bashkirs against factory workers; in addition, there were clashes between Bashkirs and Russian agricultural settlers branching out from the regional center, Orenburg. Finally, old rivalries between nomadic peoples (Kalmyks versus Kirghiz, Kirghiz versus Bashkirs) were cleverly exploited by the Russians (especially by I. I. Nepliuev, the governor-general of Orenburg from 1742 to 1758). All of these developments kept the region seething with discontent, and pretexts for defection from the central government were never lacking.[67]

The third and final aspect of what in modern parlance would be called the nationality question involved the relationship between the natives and the central government. This relationship was no longer a live issue along the banks of the Volga, because the central government was well in command there and the administrative setup followed the usual Russian pattern. Where central control was a more recent development, however, the areas of friction were numerous. The establishment of Orenburg had been viewed by the Bashkirs as a symbol of the physical presence and control of the Russians, and this view was confirmed by the colonization drive and the protection given to Russian settlers by the governors of Orenburg. (Pugachev's promise to abolish the *guberniia* of Orenburg was designed to arouse the Bashkirs, who indeed would join him enthusiastically in besieging the hated city.)[68] But the Russians had not only built the fortress of Orenburg and settled and administered its territory, they had also imposed service obligations (frontier guards, auxiliary troops against the Turks) on the Bashkirs and had levied large numbers of horses for their own military needs. These policies provoked bitter and long-lasting revolts (1735–41, 1755–57) that required a great military effort before they were quelled; but each repression was followed by heavy levies of horses, fines, and more stringent service obligations.[69] Undaunted, in 1773 the Bashkirs were once more ready to shake off the most burdensome aspects of Russian rule, and they listened with favor to Pugachev's promise to restore to them the right to "be [free] like steppe animals."[70] Their antagonism toward the government explains why they joined the revolt, in spite of their own quarrels with the Iaik Cossacks and their profound aversion to everything Russian. They would provide Pugachev with some of his best and most loyal lieutenants.[71]

Several times in the preceding pages passing reference was made to the Cossacks. It is time now to turn our attention to them, because they triggered the revolt and provided the mainstay of Pugachev's military power to the very end of the uprising. Since the middle of the seventeenth century (when the Zaporog and Don Cossacks came under Moscow's sovereignty), Cossack societies had been undergoing a dual process of transformation.[72] Their social organization, political autonomy, and military function steadily yielded to pressures from the central government in Moscow and St. Petersburg, and by the middle of the eighteenth century the latter was asserting complete and direct control.[73] The Cossacks' right to elect their chiefs (*ataman* and *starshina*) and to follow their "democratic" traditions was steadily eroded and restricted. In the case of the Don Cossacks, from whose midst Pugachev had come, *Ataman* S. Efremov tried in the 1760s to stem the tide and obtain a loosening of controls by St. Petersburg. His attempt failed (1772), and the way was opened for the complete incorporation of the Don Cossack Host into the regular framework of the military organization of the empire, which was completed in 1775 by G. Potemkin.[74] Other aspects of St. Petersburg's growing control were the increases in the number of Cossacks obliged to serve on the border and the formation of new Cossack regiments to be held in constant readiness. In this way the Volga Cossack Host was formed in 1732. In 1770 a special regiment, *Mozdovskii Polk,* was detached from this Host and sent to the Kuban frontier for permanent military duty.[75] In short, the fear was ever present that the loose and traditional Cossack organization would be changed to the rigid regimentation of the regular army (*reguliarstvo*). It was a constant cause of agitation that easily turned into open rebellion.

But the traditional Cossack pattern was also eroded from within. Indeed, a process of economic and social differentiation was taking place: the *starshina* (elders, i.e., "officer" group) was becoming more prosperous, more influential, and it increasingly identified with the way of life, ideals, and aspirations of the regular Russian elite.[76] The Cossack elders were accumulating land, estates on which they settled serfs (or used their poorer fellow Cossacks like virtual bond labor). They petitioned for and received ranks from the central government which gave them the status of regular noblemen and at times secured for them political advantages as well. Obviously, such developments in the midst of what at one time had been a "military democracy" brought friction and discontent in their wake. The ever-present antagonism between the government-oriented *starshina* and the rank and file erupted into open conflict at the slightest provocation.[77] Only shortly before the appearance of Pugachev, the Dnieper Cossacks had been shaken by a rebellion of the lower and footloose elements, the *koliivshchina.*[78]

Of the several Cossack hosts in existence in the eighteenth century, that of the Iaik was most directly and completely involved in the Pugachev revolt.[79] This particular Cossack society was an offshoot of the Don Host: most of its members were Old Believers who had settled along the Iaik (now Ural) River, from its estuary at Gurev to the upper course, where the main center, *Iaitskii gorodok,* was located. They guarded the empire's borders primarily against the Kirghiz nomads that roamed the steppes beyond the Iaik; on occasion they were also called to participate in other temporary operations, particularly against the Turks. Their main occupation and source of revenue was fishing in the plentiful Iaik River. In the reign of Peter the Great the fishing rights had been farmed out to the Cossacks, the Host having to pay a fixed annual sum. The collection of this payment was the responsibility of the *ataman.*

In the person of M. Borodin the *ataman* in fact came to control the life of the Cossacks—hiding and falsifying the figures of the payments due and of collections made. He assessed individual Cossacks on the basis of their actual catch rather than by merely prorating the fixed amount set by the government, and thus he pocketed the appreciable difference. He had become very wealthy and was in a position virtually to buy the acquiescence of the officers as well as to keep the rank and file in line. But his conflict with one of the *starshina*, Loginov, who wanted to be cut in on the large profits reaped by Borodin, precipitated the Cossacks' open rebellion against the *ataman's* authority. We need not dwell on the details of this long-drawn-out affair.[80] At first, the commission of investigation sent by the government sided with Borodin; a second team decided in favor of the rank and file. The Host was split into two factions—those loyal to the government, led by the *starshina*, and the discontented rank and file. The petitions of the latter were usually disregarded by the central government, especially as long as Count Z. Chernyshev remained at the head of the College of War.

The Iaik Cossacks had still other causes for discontent. To increase the revenues the government received from the Iaik Host, the fishermen were ordered to purchase state-owned salt at set prices. Salt was essential to preserve the catch, and forced purchase at high prices heavily burdened the Cossacks. As the war against Turkey dragged on, causing heavy losses in manpower, the College of War suggested the formation of an auxiliary "Moscow Legion" from the ranks of the smaller Cossack Hosts, each of which would furnish a set number of recruits for the legion (1769). The proposal was greeted with deep suspicion because it aroused the fear that through this indirect method the government would try to assimilate the Cossacks to the regular army, to impose *reguliarstvo*. It was a clear threat to the Cossacks' autonomous and traditional organization; the implied subjection to drilling, the use of unfamiliar weapons, the wearing of regular uniforms, and the shaving of beards and cutting of hair were anathema to a Cossack Host, whose members were mostly Old Believers. Finally, the government planned to control the Host's membership, to prevent escaped serfs from hiding in its ranks, and to keep accurate accounts for purposes of taxation and military service. To this end the Cossacks had to be registered, and the accession of new members became almost impossible.[81] The role of the Cossack assembly (*krug*) also was drastically reduced, to the benefit of the *ataman* and appointed officers.

In short, as the Petrine state threatened to eradicate most of their old privileges and traditions, the Cossacks' temper rose to the boiling point. With their petitions and requests disregarded in St. Petersburg (and even in Orenburg) and with the official commissions of investigation apparently siding with the *ataman* and the *starshina*, the Iaik Cossacks revolted. In 1772, provoked by the way General von Traubenberg was carrying out his investigation, they rioted.[82] They murdered Borodin, von Traubenberg, and several subaltern officers. The revolt was put down by a military detachment from Orenburg, but the tension remained.

The Iaik Host was prepared to follow any leader promising the return of the good old times, especially if he claimed to be the "legitimate" sovereign, Peter III. In due course such a pretender did appear—he was the Cossack Bogomolov. But Bogomolov did not have a chance to make much of a stir; he was seized and deported to Siberia (and died en route). Naturally, when Pugachev "revealed" himself as the true Peter III he immediately found support among the Iaik Cossacks. They not only were his first followers, but they also staffed his headquarters and provided him with his most loyal combat force and personal guard.[83]

While the deep involvement of the Iaik Cossacks with Pugachev may have been due in large part to the accident of their geographical location and to the particular troubles that immediately preceded Pugachev's appearance, there is no doubt that in general the Cossacks were a major factor in the revolt. The Don Cossacks, it is true, did not support Pugachev in the last phase of his revolt, when he was seeking their help after his flight from Kazan.[84] (They may have been reluctant to join someone whose success was then very much in doubt, but more important, their combativeness had been pretty much broken after *ataman* Efremov's attempt a few years earlier, and they were under close government surveillance.) But Pugachev himself had stemmed from their ranks, and in the earlier period of his career as a rebel (*buntovshchik*) he did find some support among them. The Iaik (Ural) and Volga Cossacks, of course, did follow him. What is even more interesting is the fact that all the Cossacks idealized his memory and his rebellion, weaving much of their folklore around it.[85] They exemplified the discontent and rebelliousness of a traditional group in the face of transformations wrought (or threatened) by a centralized absolute monarchy. Like the feudal revolts and rebellions in the name of regional particularism and traditional privileges in Western Europe, the Cossacks opposed the tide of rational modernization and the institutionalization of political authority. They regarded their relationship to the ruler as a special and personal one based on their voluntary service obligations; in return they expected the czar's protection of their religion, traditional social organization, and administrative autonomy. They followed the promises of a pretender and raised the standard of revolt in the hope of recapturing their previous special relationship and of securing the government's respect for their social and religious traditions.

As our brief survey of the difficulties experienced by the government with respect to the Cossacks, Bashkirs, and monastery peasants must have indicated, local administration left much to be desired in the eastern frontier regions. Inadequate local government was characteristic of the empire as a whole, but the deficiency was greater and fraught with more dangerous consequences in the east, where the population was sparse and diversified ethnically, the distances great, and the territory still open to incursions from the outside. We read with astonishment and almost disbelief that the Kazan *guberniia*, with six provinces and a population of about 2.5 million, was administered by only eighty regular officials.[86] The towns were sadly underpopulated, in most cases little more than walled-in villages, and their officials were ill-prepared to meet any serious challenge. They panicked and fled rather than take decisive measures, as seen in the numerous cases of *voevody* and other functionaries who deserted their posts at the first rumor of Pugachev's approach.[87] We might add that prior to and during the revolt the governors of Orenburg and Kazan (D. Volkov, I. Reinsdorp, and von Brandt) were of low caliber. Given these circumstances, the weak and inefficient response of the authorities to the first signs of the rebellion becomes understandable and its rapid spread comprehensible.

It is only fair to point out that the few and inadequately prepared officials had little military power they could rely on. The garrisons of provincial fortresses (with the exception of such centers as Orenburg and Tsaritsyn) were ridiculous both in number and in quality.[88] There is no need to insist; we have only to read the description of a small provincial garrison in the east as accurately and vividly drawn by Pushkin in *The Captain's Daughter*. In the east only a few landowners actually resided on their estates; the majority of the peasant serfs were supervised by unreliable and corrupt managers and a few government officials. ...

*   *   *

Without going into an account of the revolt itself, which would throw little light on its causes and background, we may, however, note a few of its characteristic features in an effort to understand better its dynamics and impact. The history of the revolt may be divided into three phases whose specific traits should be noted briefly.[89] The first period, the fall and winter of 1773–74, was characterized by the revolt of the Iaik Cossacks, who, with the assistance of the Bashkirs, attacked Orenburg, the seat of government authority in the region. The siege, which lasted several months, ended in failure; Pugachev could not take the city and was forced to withdraw into the Ural Mountains and the Bashkir region. There he remained until late spring, 1774, when the second phase of the revolt began. Having replenished his arsenal in the Ural factories, and expecting support from the peasants attached to factories and monasteries, Pugachev sallied forth westward from the Urals in the late spring or early summer of 1774. Most Bashkirs refused to follow him, and at first his support was limited to the Cossacks and some factory workers and peasants. But as he emerged from the Urals and turned toward the Volga he was well received by small towns, as well as by state and monastery peasants. He managed to capture Kazan bur failed to hold it. Forced to retreat, he first went north, then crossed to the right bank of the Volga and turned southward down the river toward the region of the Don Cossack Host. At this point, after Pugachev had crossed to the western shore of the great river, the serfs rose *en masse* in the adjoining regions. The uprising became general: landowning nobles were killed or put to flight, and their estates were burned; bands of serfs roamed the countryside almost to the gate of Nizhni Novgorod, striking fear and panic into the hearts of landowners in and around Moscow. This phase of the revolt had a flavor strongly reminiscent of the *Grande Peur* in France fifteen years later, except that in Russia the rising was sparked not by fear of bandits but by the actual forays of peasant gangs invoking the authority of the true Czar Peter III, Pugachev.

It has been argued that, had Pugachev properly understood the dynamics of the peasant uprising he helped to provoke, he would not have turned south but would instead have marched west; with the help of the widespread and spontaneous serf uprising he would have been able to conquer the center of Russia and even Moscow.[90] But like his Cossack forerunner in the seventeenth century, Stenka Razin, Pugachev was not interested in the fate of the peasants and preferred to recoup his forces by arousing the Don Cossacks (or perhaps merely to take refuge there). But he failed to capture Tsaritsyn; and in the manner typical of primitive rebellions his own Cossack lieutenants turned him over to the imperial troops who were pursuing him.[91]

We should note that, in the first place, Pugachev failed to hold any major urban center; his movement was confined to the open countryside, especially in the territory of Cossacks and natives. In the second place, we ought to keep in mind that the real serf and peasant revolt started only after Pugachev's defeat at Kazan; it was an anticlimax, even though it turned out to be the bloodiest phase of the rebellion as well as the greatest threat to the social status quo. The Cossacks thus were the permanent, solid core of the movement; the other groups and regions were involved only through the accidents and fortunes of Pugachev's struggle with the imperial army.

These facts raise the question about the nature of the revolt that has much agitated Russian and Soviet historiographers: Was it a "conscious" effort to change the social and political systems, or was it merely a spontaneous, violent outbreak of anger and discontent? The Soviets believe that it was a regular peasant war;[92] but this interpretation hardly seems justified in the light of what we have seen of the background and causes. At best it is a simplification which applies only to the last phase of the rebellion. The movement, it seems to me, was primarily a "frontier" and Cossack affair, and its leadership never understood the possibilities offered by the serf uprising and a direct move against Moscow. This fact may also help to explain why the Pugachev rebellion was the last large-scale peasant rebellion not limited to a locality.[93]

As pretender, Pugachev endeavored to project himself in the image of the ideal ruler. The folkloristic tradition has emphasized this image by providing the typical medieval validation: he was the real czar as long as he was successful; his very failure destroyed his claim and opened the way for a new pretender (there were several of them after 1774).[94] He could not be defeated in open combat, but, once his success had been questioned, his own closest followers turned against him, rejected him, and delivered him to those authorities whose success had proved their legitimacy.[95]

According to folk memory and contemporary legends (confirmed both by Pugachev and his followers at their interrogation), Pugachev appeared as the pretender-liberator. He was Christlike and saintly because he had meekly accepted his dethronement by his evil wife and her courtiers. He had not resisted his overthrow, but had left sadly to wander about the world. He had come to help the revolt, but he did not initiate it; the Cossacks and the people did that. The image, therefore, is that of a passive leader, strongly reminiscent, of course, of the image of the saintly meekness of the Kievan and medieval Russian ideals of kingship.[96] The pretender's wanderings, in truly holy fashion, took him to Jerusalem and Constantinople first; he then returned to Russia which he crisscrossed as a pilgrim.[97] Wandering about the Russian land he learned of its condition and needs; he helped his people through his counsel and prayers before he accepted again the leadership to restore rightful authority. But how did one know that he was the rightful czar? He had the imperial magic signs, like stigmata, on the chest and on the head. Pugachev uncovered them to prove his identity to the doubters. With a ceremonial that reminds one of the Muscovite and Byzantine tradition, he made himself awesome and difficult of access. As head of the movement, he acted primarily as ultimate judge, punishing and pardoning at will. The very arbitrariness of his actions was a sign of his regal sovereignty and nature.[98] He intervened only when called on to make a final decision or render a verdict of justice. Under the circumstances one may wonder how the people accounted for his failure. Interestingly enough, they did it in terms of God's law: Pugachev failed because he appeared before his time; he allowed himself to be tempted by human considerations (of pity and mercy) rather than abide by the will of God, Who had ordained that twenty years elapse between his dethronement and his return. In addition, he sinned by marrying a Cossack girl while his own lawful wife (whatever her crimes) was still alive; these acts of hubris predetermined his ultimate failure.[99]

Yet the image projected by Pugachev was not entirely medieval or traditional, as the legends and folklore might lead us to believe. There were also clearly elements of the modern Petrine notions of political authority. Like Peter the Great, the pretender had gone abroad to learn; like the first emperor, he was of foreign birth (here both positive and negative elements of the popular image of Peter I merge in a curious fashion). Pugachev tried to appear, in M. Cherniavsky's felicitous phrase, as "Sovereign Emperor."[100] The medals struck for him show him in neoclassical profile, in armor. Some presumed portraits make him look very much like Peter the Great, with the cat-like mustache and wild eyes. Finally, in some of his proclamations he had his name written in Latin (he was illiterate, of course); he was also alleged to have said that after he regained his throne he would make *Iaitskii gorodok* his "Petersburg."[101]

More significant than these externals were Pugachev's attempts at reproducing the St. Petersburg bureaucracy, the Petrine state. He established his own College of War (*Voennaia Kollegiia*) with quite extensive powers and functions. He created his own Count Chernyshev; he appointed to the rank of general, conferred titles, granted estates in the Baltic regions, and even gave away serfs.[102] He accepted and approved petitions for retirement from government service. Yet he also appointed a *dumnyi diak* (secretary of the czar's council in the seventeenth century) to act as his main secretary—an interesting amalgam of old and new titles similar to what was practiced even by the immediate successors of Peter the Great.[103] Particularly striking for someone who is alleged to have risen against the burdens of the state, Pugachev in his proclamations did not promise complete freedom from taxation and recruitment. He granted only temporary relief, similar to the gracious "mercies" dispensed by a new ruler upon his accession.[104]

We have here perhaps the main clue to Pugachev's and his followers' concept of the state. They believed that the basis of political organization of society was service to the state (sovereign) by commoner and noble alike. It was the notion which Peter Struve has aptly termed "liturgic state."[105] Thus all soldiers were changed into Cossacks—i.e., free, permanent military servicemen, and so were all other military personnel, even the nobles and officers who joined Pugachev's ranks (voluntarily or under duress). Symbolically, in pardoning a noble or officer who had been taken prisoner, Pugachev's first act was to order that the prisoner's hair be cut in Cossack fashion (paralleling the "shaving of the forehead" which signified conscription into the emperor's regular army). All peasants also should be servants of the state: they were to become state peasants (instead of serfs of private owners or of monasteries) and serve as Cossacks, i.e., militia. (Note, they were not to be given personal freedom.) The nobles in turn were no longer to be *pomeshchiki*, i.e., estate and serf owners, but were to revert to their previous status as the czar's servicemen on salary.[106]

Was there no concept of freedom in this movement? There was: freedom from the nobility, which implied the natural freedom to be what God had made one to be—a tiller of the soil, who was free to work and possess the land he had made productive, or cattle-raising nomads, who were free "like steppe animals."[107] Naturally, too, old religious practices were to be tolerated, for Pugachev "granted beards and the cross," i.e., the freedom to be an Old Believer. He talked about the nobles as traitors to himself and to the people, and of his intention to restore the natural direct bonds between himself and the people—there need not be any intermediaries, any "secular priesthood" of nobles. Pugachev's statements here are reminiscent, *mutatis mutandis*, of Ivan IV's missive from Aleksandrovskaia *sloboda* in which the awesome czar demanded the right to eliminate the boyars, who had interposed themselves between him and his loyal people, betraying both.

The ideal of Pugachev's followers was essentially a static, simple society where a just ruler guaranteed the welfare of all within the framework of a universal obligation to the sovereign. The ruler ought to be a father to his people, his children; and power should be personal and direct, not institutionalized and mediated by land- or serf owner.[108] Such a frame of mind may also account for the strong urge to take revenge on the nobles and officials, on their modern and evil way of life. This urge manifested itself with particular force, of course, in the last phase of the revolt: the serfs destroyed the estates of the nobility especially their most modern features (e.g., glass panes, windows, and mantlepieces), for these were symbols of the new, alien, secular civilization; there were also some instances of "Luddite" actions on the part of factory workers in the Urals.

Taking these features of the movement's ideology and symbolism as indications of its participants' basic attitudes and aspirations, it is quite clear that they felt disarray stemming from a sense of crisis of the old and traditional order.[109] Somehow they were aware that there could be no going back to the old forms, but neither could they accept the dynamic implications of the new. They were particularly frightened by apparent economic and social changes, and they rejected the individualistic dynamics implicit in them; they wished to recapture the old ideals of service and community in a hierarchy ordained by God. Most significantly, it seems to me, they were not able to come to terms with the functional organization and impersonal institutionalization of authority. In this inability they were not alone, nor the last, as the Decembrist movement and the history of the intelligentsia have shown. Pugachev and his followers needed a palpable sense of direct relationship with the source of sovereign power and ultimate justice on this earth. The Cossacks were, of course, most keenly aware of the loss of their special status and direct contact with the czar and his government; but so were the serfs and, in an inchoate way, some of the non-Russian natives as well. The movement was thus "reactionary" in the etymological sense, with its predominance of negative-passive ideological elements; at time it seemed a childlike desire to return to the quiet and security of the protective family.

Not surprisingly, in view of this childlike urge to return to the protective family, we detect on the part of the rebels a naïve desire to be loved by their elders, i.e., the true czar and his good boyars. Was this not the mirror image of the ambivalence the upper class felt, vis à vis the common people, which became noticeable at about the same time? Both the peasants and upper class dimly perceived that they had become alien to each other, that they had

ceased to be members of the same God-ordained, harmonious order. This realization may go a long way in explaining the excessive panic and fear that the
last phase of the rebellion aroused in the nobility of Moscow and St. Petersburg. Little wonder that the educated nobles reacted by trying to create a new
image of the peasant which would emphasize those very qualities that could
put their fears to rest. Instead of the view of the serf as an uncouth half-beast
who could be kept down only by force, we observe the emergence of the notion of the peasant as a child, a child who has to be protected against himself
and carefully guided into the new "civilization."[110] While this reaction was
clearly defensive, it also bespoke a subconscious and correct understanding of
the psychic mechanism that had driven the people to rebellion. The dim
awareness that for the peasant—as with children—feelings of justice and the
need for personified authority outweighed the possible advantages of rationalized and institutionalized power not only started a new trend in Russian literature but also helped to shape the basic attitudes of the elite: a feeling of ambivalence toward, and alienation from, the people, coupled with an almost
overpowering sense of social responsibility and moral guilt. These were to be
the driving forces in creating modern Russian culture with its double aspect of
guilt and distance with respect to both the state and the people.

Pushkin was perhaps the first to become fully aware of this ambiguity in
modern Russia's elite and its culture. He also was the first to give artistic expression to this new—post-Pugachev—relationship between the upper classes
and the people, a relationship he depicted with great psychological and historical insight and artistic felicity in *The Captain's Daughter*.[111] For our generation it is of course tempting to interpret his famous depiction—in Grinev's
dream—of the ambiguous relationship between the elite and the people in
Freudian terms, as a restatement of the Oedipal conflict. In such an interpretation the dream would express the feelings of young Grinev (representing
the westernized nobility) toward his castrating father (i.e., Pugachev), his
love-hate of the father who possesses the mother (i.e., the people).[112]

But may not another great Russian poet, Marina Tsvetaeva, have seen
deeper into Pushkin's meaning?[113] Instead of fastening on Grinev, who is the
concern of modern Freudians, she focuses on Pugachev. She notices his craving for Grinev's full, unquestioning love—as a father or perhaps an older
brother would want to be loved. Tsvetaeva's reading of the dream brings out
the sense of loss of the elite's affection that Pugachev—symbolizing the people—may have felt. Is Pugachev's love not the love of someone enchantingly
closer to nature, someone completely possessed by genuine feeling? Pushkin
speaks of Pugachev's magic (*char*), to which Grinev succumbs against his better judgment. Is this primitive, magical love not the saving force? Twice it
saves Grinev from the evils of nature and/or men. The ultimate tragedy of
Pugachev (the people) may have been that Grinev (elite as well as the people's
child) could not accept this free gift of love.[114] Was not the almost magical in-

tervention of the natural brother's gift of love an attempt to save the last representative of the old intelligentsia, Iurii Zhivago?

The rebellion of Pugachev was in truth the prologue to the history of modern Russian culture, and as such, it marked also the very beginning of the great Russian revolution of the twentieth century.

Notes

1. S. M. Troitskii, *Finansovaia politika russkogo absoliutizma v XVIII veke* (Moscow, 1966), p. 243.

2. J. T. Alexander, "The Russian Government and Pugachev's Revolt, 1773–1775" (Ph. D. diss., Indiana University, 1966), pp. 15–16.

3. Troitskii (*Finansovaia politika*, p. 215) gives the following figures:

	1719	1744	1762
Total pop. (in 1,000 souls)	15,578	18,206	23,236
Taxable male pop. (in 1,000 souls)	5,570	6,676	7,362

4. *Polnoe Sobranie Zakonov Rossiiskoi Imperii*, 1st ser. (St. Petersburg, 1830), no. 10,164, 20 December 1753 (hereafter cited *PSZ*).

5. *PSZ*, no. 15,447, 28 June 1782. The policy culminated in the privileges included in the Charters to the Nobility and to the Towns, *PSZ*, nos. 16,187 and 16,188, 21 April 1785.

6. Soviet historiography stresses increasing "feudal" exploitation and the abuses to which the serfs were subjected. But usually this led only to individual outbreaks and localized acts of disobedience or revenge. On the peasantry of the eighteenth century in general, a decent introduction in English is J. Blum, *Lord and Peasant in Russia from the Ninth to the Nineteenth Century* (Princeton: Princeton University Press, 1961), esp. chaps. 15–24; see also M. Confino, *Domaines et Seigneurs en Russie vers la fin du XVIIIe siecle—Étude de structures agraires et de mentalités économiques*, Collection historique de l'Institut d'Études slaves, no. 18 (Paris, 1963). The classical work is V. I. Semevskii, *Krest'iane v tsarstvovanie imperatritsy Ekateriny II*, 2 vols. (St. Petersburg, 1881–1901); the Soviet classic is N. L. Rubinshtein, *Sel'skoe khoziaistvo Rossii vo vtoroi polovine XVIII* v.: Istoriko-ekonomicheskii ocherk (Moscow, 1957).

7. The total sum collected by the state rose by 239 per cent, while the taxable population rose 131 per cent (Troitskii, *Finansovaia politika*, p. 219).

8. Troitskii, *Finansovaia politika*, p. 214.

9. *Ibid.*, p. 219.

10. Rubinshtein, *Sel'skoe khoziastvo Rossii*, pp. 355–56; for some judicious comments on Russian harvest yields see A. Kahan, "Natural Calamities and their Effect upon Food Supply in Russa," *Jahrbücher für Geschichte Osteuropas* 16, No. 3 (September, 1968): 353–77.

11. Rubinshtein, *Sel'skoe khoziastvo Rossii*, pp. 413–14.

12. The well-to-do nobles lived in the capitals or large cities surrounded by a crowd of domestic servants recruited from their serf peasantry. This represented in many cases a not insignificant drain of the productive rural population.

13. Confino, *Domaines et Seigneurs en Russie,* esp. chap. 1; see also M. T. Beliavskii, *Krest'ianskii vopros v Rossii nakanune vosstaniia E. I. Pugacheva: Formirovanie antikrepostnicheskoi mysli* (Moscow, 1965), pt. 4.

14. Rubinshtein, *Sel'skoe khoziastvo Rossii,* p. 156 (quoting calculations of Semevskii, *Krest'iane v tsarstvovanie Ekateriny II,* 1:49, 54). Possibly too, as the Soviets stress, peasants were becoming more involved in local trade (bringing their produce to nearby town markets).

15. Confino, *Domaines et Seigneurs en Russie,* pp. 198–201.

16. S. I. Tkhorzhevskii, *Pugachevshchina v pomeshchich'ei Rossii: Vosstanie na pravoi storone Volgi v iune—oktiabre 1774 g.* (Moscow, 1930), p. 36.

17. On the discussions at the Codification Commission of 1767 see Beliavskii, *Krest'ianskii vopros,* pts. 2 and 3; for a perceptive analysis of the nobility's economic attitudes see W. R. Augustine, "The Economic Attitudes and Opinions Expressed by the Russian Nobility in the Great Commission of 1767" (Ph.D. diss., Columbia University, 1969); and for a more superficial summary see P. Dukes, *Catherine the Great and the Russian Nobility: A Study Based on the Materials of the Legislative Commission of 1767* (New York: Cambridge University Press, 1967), chap. 3.

18. Augustine, "Economic Attitudes and Opinions," chaps. 2–3 and *passim;* Dukes, *Catherine the Great;* Beliavskii, *Krest'ianskii vopros,* pt. 2.

19. I. E. German, *Istoriia russkogo mezhevaniia,* 2d ed. (Moscow, 1910); L. V. Milov, *Issledovanie ob "Ekonomicheskikh primechaniiakh" k general'nomu mezhevaniiu: K istorii russkogo krest'ianstva i sel'skogo khoziaistva vtoroi poloviny XVIII v* (Moscow, 1965), chap. 1.

20. For example, the problem of "tilling soldiers" (*pakhotnye krest'iane*) in Tsentrarkhiv, *Pugachevshchina* (Materialy no istorii revoliutsionnogo dvizheniia v Rossii XVII i XVIII vv. pod obshchei redaktsii M. N. Pokrovskogo), vol. 2: *Iz sledstvennykh materialov i offitsial'noi perepiski* (Moscow-Leningrad, 1929), pp. 375–76; hereafter this document collection will be cited as *Pugachevshchina.*

21. N. N. Firsov, *Pugachevshchina: Opyt sotsial'no-psikhologicheskoi kharakteristiki* (St. Petersburg-Moscow, n.d.), p. 171; A. I. Dubasov, "Chuma i Pugachevshchina v. Shatskoi provintsii," *Istoricheskii Vestnik* 13 (1883): 113–35; see also R. E. McGrew, *Russia and the Cholera, 1823–1832* (Madison: University of Wisconsin Press, 1965), for a general background on epidemics, and Kahan, "Natural Calamities," for a tentative chronology of epidemics and crop failures.

22. P. Pekarskii, "Zhizn i literaturnaia perepiska P. I. Rychkova," *Sbornik stat'ei, chitannykh v otdelenii russkogo iazyka i slovesnosti imperatorskoi Akademii Nauk* 2, no. 1 (St. Petersburg, 1867): 136.

23. *PSZ,* no. 11,481; see also M. Raeff, "The Domestic Policies of Peter III and his Overthrow," *American Historical Review,* June, 1970.

24. An impression perhaps reinforced by the promulgation of the manifesto on the nobility's freedom from service; see *PSZ,* no. 11,444, 18 February 1762.

25. *PSZ,* no. 12,060, 26 February 1764.

26. P. Shehebal'skii, *Nachalo i kharakter Pugachevshchiny* (Moscow, 1865).

27. This was also an explanation given by Pugachev, *Pugachevshchina,* 2:194.

28. K. V. Sivkov, "Samozvanstvo v Rossii v poslednei treti XVIII v.," *Istoricheskie Zapiski* 31 (1950): 88–135.

29. K. V. Chistov, *Russkie narodnye sotsial'no-utopicheskie legendy XVII–XIX vv.* (Moscow, 1967), chap. 1; M. Cherniavsky, *Tsar and People—Studies in Russian Myths* (New Haven, Conn.: Yale University Press, 1961).

30. Shchebal'skii, *Nachalo i kharakter,* pp. 50–51.

31. Firsov, *Pugachevshchina,* p. 117; N. Dubrovin, *Pugachev i ego soobshchniki: Epizod iz istorii tsarstvovaniia Ekateriny II 1773–1774,* vol. 1 (St. Petersburg, 1884), pp. 160 ff.

32. Catherine II had tried to work out a new code of laws and to this end called together deputies to inform her on conditions and needs. In a way, this effort culminated in the Charters of 1785. But the very process of electing and convening the deputies in 1767 had set the popular mind aworking; it may have contributed to the restlessness and sense of expectation, as has been correctly noted by R. Portal, *L'Oural au XVIIIe siècle: Étude d'histoire économique et sociale,* Collection historique de l'Institut d'Études slaves, no. 14 (Paris, 1950), pp. 315, 319.

33. *PSZ,* no. 12,633. It is significant that permission for the nobles to petition the sovereign directly had to be clearly specified in the Charter of 1785.

34. See the table of land allotments compiled by Rubinshtein (*Sel'skoe khoziastvo Rossii,* pp. 434 ff.) for all of European Russia.

35. *Ibid.,* pp. 361–62.

36. Rubinshtein, *Sel'skoe khoziastvo Rossii,* pp. 156–58; see also A. I. Zaozerskii, "Buntovshchiki: Epizod iz istorii Pugachevskogo bunta," *"Veka"—Istoricheskii sbornik* 1 (1924): 115–16.

37. Zoazerskii, "Buntovshchiki"; E. S. Kogan, "Krest'iane penzenskoi votchiny A. B. Kurakina vo vremia dvizheniia Pugacheva," *Istoricheskie Zapiski* 37 (1951): 104–24.

38. A brief summary, although I do not share the interpretation, is found in V. V. Mavrodin, *Krest'ianskaia voina v Rossii v 1773–1775 godakh: Vosstanie Pugacheva,* vol. 1 (Leningrad, 1961), pp. 341–47; Semevskii, *Krest'iane v tsarstvovanie Ekateriny II,* vol. 1, chap. 12, esp. pp. 342–43.

39. T. P. Bondarevskaia, "Beglye krest'iane srednego Povolzh'ia v seredine XVIII v.," in *Krest'ianstvo i klassovaia bor'ba v feodal'noi Rossii: Sbornik statei pamiati Ivana Ivanovicha Smirnova,* Akademiia Nauk SSSR, Institut Istorii, Leningradskoe otdelenie, Trudy, vyp. 9 (Leningrad, 1967), p. 395, gives the following figures: from 1700 to the 1730s, 51.9 per cent of the escapees lived in their own households, compared with only 21 per cent from 1740 to the 1770s; hired help rose in the same periods from 20.9 per cent to 42.1 per cent.

40. T. Esper, "The Odnodvortsy and the Russian Nobility," *Slavonic and East European Review* 45, no. 104 (January, 1967): 124–34.

41. For a contemporary description see A. T. Bolotov, *Zapiski Andreia Timofeevicha Bolotova, 1773–1795* (St. Petersburg, 1873), vol. 3, pt. 16, chap. 141.

42. See Semevskii, *Krest'iane v tsarstvovanie Ekateriny II,* 2:721 ff., for a most comprehensive study of their economic situation.

43. F. I. Lappo, "Nakazy odnodvortsev kak istoricheskii istochnik," *Istoricheskie Zapiski* 35 (1950): 232–64; Sivkov, "Samozvanstvo v Rossii"; Mavrodin, *Krest'ianskaia voina,* 1:464–69.

44. V. V. Mavrodin, "Ob uchastii kolonistov Povolzh'ia v vosstanii Pugacheva," in *Krest'ianstvo i klassovaia bor'ba v feodal'noi Rossii,* pp. 400–413.

45. See *Pugachevshchina*, 2:71–73, for a description of the crop failure of 1773.

46. *Pugachevshchina*, 3:203–6.

47. G. G. Pisarevskii, *Vnutrennii rasporiadok v koloniiakh Povolzh'ia pri Ekaterine II* (Warsaw, 1914), pp. 1–2, 9–10.

48. See Mavrodin, *Krest'ianskaia voina*, 1:393–420, for a general discussion of discontent among monastery peasants. The classical account of their economic situation is in Semevskii, *Krest'iane v tsarstvovanie Ekateriny II*, vol. 2.

49. G. Plotnikov, "Dalmatovskii monastyr' v 1773–1774 g. ili v Pugachevskii bunt," *Chteniia obshchestva istorii i drevnostei rossiskikh pri Moskovskom Universitete* 28 (January-March, 1859), bk. 1, sec. 5, pp. 18 ff.; A. A. Kondrashenkov, *Ocherki istorii krest'ianskikh vosstanii v Zaural'e v XVIII v* (Kurgan, 1962), pp. 74–90.

50. Dubrovin, *Pugachev i ego soobshchniki*, vol. 1, and Shchebal'skii, *Nachalo i kharakter, passim.*

51. *PSZ*, no. 12,067, 27 February 1762.

52. Mavrodin, *Krest'ianskaia voina*, 1:420–21. See Semevskii, *Krest'iane v tsarstvovanie Ekateriny II*, vol. 2, for economic conditions; documentation is given in *Pugachevshchina*, 2:315, on relations among various groups of workers in the Urals and the Pugachev movement.

53. Portal, *L'Oural au XVIIIe siècle*, chap. 5, esp. pp. 231–58; A. A. Savich, *Ocherki istorii krest'ianskikh volnenii na Urale v XVIII–XX vv.* (Moscow, 1931), pp. 14, 16.

54. Portal, *L'Oural au XVIIIe siècle*, pp. 245–50; Savich, *Ocherki istorii krest'ianskikh volnenii*, p. 16.

55. Portal, *L'Oural au XVIIIe siècle*, chap. 6. The owners did not seem to be much interested in technological innovation, because they relied mainly on cheap labor. The situation is reminiscent of what we find in a "plantation" economy; see E. Genovese, *The Political Economy of Slavery* (New York: Pantheon Books, 1965).

56. The ascribed serfs tended to "vote" with their feet by taking advantage of Pugachev's approach in order to return to their villages. It was the *possessionnye* who had to make the decision of whether to join Pugachev or not; they had nowhere to go.

57. *Pugachevshchina*, 2:268–70. For a picturesque account see the historical novel by Stepan Zlobin, *Salavat Iulaev* (Moscow, 1941).

58. For example, *Pugachevshchina*, 1:202–4 (no. 250). See also *ibid.*, 2:316–17; A. I. Dmitriev-Mamonov, *Pugachevskii bunt v Zaural'e i Sibiri: Istoricheskii ocherk po ofitsial'nym dokumentam* (St. Petersburg, 1907), p. 65.

59. The numerous Soviet histories of the relevant constituent republids and autonomous regions provide many interesting facts and documents, whatever their interpretation. Of particular interest to us are: *Ocherki istorii Mordovskoi ASSR*, vol. 1 (Saransk, 1955); *Ocherki po istorii Bashkirskoi ASSR*, vol. 1 (Ufa, 1956), pt. 1; V. D. Dimitriev, *Istoriia Chuvashii XVIII veka: Do krest'ianskoi voiny 1773–1775 godov* (Cheboksary, 1959); the collection of documents *Materialy po istorii Bashkirskoi ASSR*, ed. N. V. Ustiugov, 4 vols. (Moscow, 1956), esp. vol. 4, pt. 2; and *Kazakhskorusskie otnosheniia v XVIII–XIX vekakh: Sbornik dokumentov i materialov* (Alma-Ata, 1964).

60. See the comprehensive memorandum of Colonel A. I. Svechin in *Pugachevshchina*, 2:3–40; see also Dimitriev, *Istoriia Chuvashii XVIII veka*, chap. 10.

61. They also seem to have been kept under particularly close surveillance because they were suspected of having contacts with the Turks. Perhaps, too, the revolt had negative effects on trade, which was one of the main occupations of the Kazan Tatars.

62. See *Sbornik imperatorskogo russkogo istoricheskogo obshchestva,* 148 vols. (St. Petersburg: Russian Imperial Historical Society, 1867–1916), vol. 115, where the *cahiers* of delegates of the natives are reprinted.

63. See, for example, *Materialy po istorii Bashkirskoi ASSR,* vol. 4, pt. 2, nos. 497 and 498; see also B. Nolde, *La Formation de l'Empire russe: Études, Notes et Documents,* 2 vols., Collection historique de l'Institut d'Études slaves, no. 15 (Paris, 1952–53) vol. 1, esp. pt. 2.

64. *Materialy po istorii Bashkirskoi ASSR,* vol. 4, pt. 2, *passim.*

65. The claim of Soviet historians that the rich chieftains, becoming involved in agriculture, played the government's game while the poor strata rose in revolt against both the chiefs and the government does not seem substantiated. The leaders of the Bashkir revolt, Salavat Iulaev, his father, and Kinzia Arslanov came from the ranks of the richest and most respected clan chiefs.

66. Nolde, *La Formation de l'Empira russe;* for a convenient summary see R. Portal, "Les Bashkirs et le gouvernement russe au XVIIIe s.," *Revue des Études slaves* 22, nos. 1–4 (1946): 82–104.

67. National rivalries were taken advantage of by both the government and Pugachev.

68. *Pugachevshchina,* 2:415–16. Failure to take Orenburg in a way predetermined the Bashkirs' eventual loss of confidence and interest in Pugachev's movement. They did not follow him outside their territory in the second phase of the revolt.

69. For a superficial account of these revolts, their causes and immediate consequences, see Alton S. Donnelly, *The Russian Conquest of Bashkiria, 1552–1740: A Case Study in Imperialism* (New Haven, Conn.: Yale University Press, 1968).

70. *Pugachevshchina,* 1:27–28. For a comprehensive discussion of the aspirations and "ideology" of the various groups involved in the Pugachev rebellion (especially good on the natives), see D. Peters, "Politische und gesellschaftliche Vorstellungen in der Aufstandsbewegung unter Führung Pugačevs, 1773–1775" (Inaugural diss., Freie Universität, Berlin, 1968).

71. Iu. A. Limonov, V. V. Mavrodin, and V. M. Paneiakh, *Pugachev i ego spodvizhniki* (Moscow-Leningrad, 1965); A. N. Usmanov, "Kinzia Arslanov: Vydaiushchiisia spodvizhnik Pugacheva," *Istoricheskie Zapiski* 71 (1962): 113–33. There is no place here for a discussion of the situation and role of other nomadic nationalities, especially the Kirghiz (Kazakhs) and Kalmyks. For an introduction see "The Kazakhs and Pugachev's revolt," *Central Asian Review* (London), 8, no. 3 (1960): 256–63; A. Chuloshnikov, "Kazakh-kirgizskie ordy i vosstanie Pugacheva, 1773–1774 g.," *Novyi Vostok* 25 (1929): 201–15; and the literature cited in note 59.

72. G. Stökl, *Die Enstehung des Kosakentums* (Munich, 1953); S. G. Svatikov, *Rossiia i Don, 1549–1917* (Belgrade, 1924); V. A. Golobutskii, *Zaporozhskoe kazachestvo* (Kiev, 1957).

73. Mazeppa's turning against Peter the Great forced part of the Dnieper Cossacks to go into exile in Turkey. The episode further split the Cossacks and cast an additional shadow of suspicion on them from the government's point of view. We shall leave the Ukrainian (Dnieper, Zaporog) Cossacks centered on the *Sich* (headquarters of the Dnieper Cossack Host) out of this account.

74. Svatikov, *Rossiia i Don,* pp. 210–16, 223; M. Raeff, "Russia's Imperial Policy and Prince G. A. Potemkin" [Chapter 11 of this volume], in *Statesmen and Statecraft*

of the Modern West, ed. G. Grob (Barre, Mass.: Barre Publishers, 1967), pp. 8–10.

75. Dubrovin, *Pugachev i ego soobshchniki*, 1:105–6.

76. Golobutskii, *Zaporozhskoe kazachestvo;* V. A. Miakotin, *Ocherki sotsial'noi istorii Ukrainy v XVII–XVIII vv.* (Prague, 1926).

77. Contrary to what Soviet historians are wont to claim, the loyalty of the *starshina* to the imperial government should not be taken for granted.

78. V. A. Golobutskii, "Gaidamatskoe dvizhenie na Zaporozh'e vo vremia 'Koliivshchiny' i krest'ianskoi voiny pod rukovodstvom E. I. Pugacheva," *Istoricheskie Zapiski* 55 (1956): 310–43. Soviet historiography sees this rebellion as a prologue to the Pugachev movement.

79. Pugachev himself was a Don Cossack; as a matter of fact he came from the same *stanitsa* (Cossack settlement) as Stenka Razin a century before him.

80. For the fullest traditional account see Dubrovin, *Pugachev i ego soobshchniki*, vol. 1; see also "Volnenie na Iaike pered Pugachevskim buntom: Zapiski kap. S. Mavrina, sostaviennaia na osnovanii doprosov kazakov v 1774," in *Pamiatniki Novoi Russkoi Istorii*, ed. V. Kashpirev, 3 vols. (St. Petersburg, n.d.), 2:250–94; I. G. Rozner, *Iaik pered burei* (Moscow, 1966).

81. Dubrovin, *Pugachev i ego soobshchniki*, 1:106.

82. Note the foreign name of von Traubenberg, and of quite a few officers and officials linked with the revolt. But there is no clear evidence of generalized xenophobia on the part of the rebels.

83. Some historians go as far as to claim that the Iaik Cossacks kept close surveillance on Pugachev, who in fact was their prisoner throughout the revolt. This seems a bit excessive in my opinion.

84. A. P. Pronshtein, *Don i Nizhnee Povolzh'e v period krestianskoi voiny, 1773–1775: Sbornik dokumentov* (Rostov-on-Don, 1961), esp. the editor's introduction.

85. I. I. Zheleznov, "Predaniia o Pugacheve," *Ural'tsy—Ocherki byta Ural'skikh kazakov*, 3d ed., vol. 3 (St. Petersburg, 1910), pp. 135–222; A. I. Lozanova, *Pesni i skazaniia o Razine i Pugacheve* (Leningrad, 1935).

86. Alexander, "The Russian Government and Pugachev's Revolt," p. 20.

87. Ia. K. Grot, ed., "P. S. Potemkin vo vremia pugachevshchiny," *Russkaia Starina*, July-December, 1870, p. 496.

88. Dmitriev-Mamonov (*Pugachevskii bunt v Zaural'e i Sibiri*, pp. 44–45) gives the following list of military personnel in Chelyabinsk: 1 poruchik (lieutenant), 4 corporals, 1 drummer-barber, 30 privates, 206 recruits, 6 retired officers, 7 retired non-commissioned officers, and 97 "retired recruits." The figures adduced by Dubasov ("Chuma i Pugachevshchina," p. 120) are no more impressive: in Shatsk there were 12 non-commissioned officers, 42 privates, 17 officers—and only 50 rifles! Incidentally, most of the soldiers were invalids. See also the memorandum from the College of War concerning garrisons in the eastern and southeastern regions in Dubrovin, *Pugachev i ego soobshchniki*, 1:377–86 (app. 3). The over-all total of military personnel for this vast and unprotected region was 27,779 men; the College proposed a reorganization which, among other things, involved the raising of that figure to 32,761 men.

89. A. Kizevetter, "K istorii krest'ianskikh dvizhenii v Rossii," *Krest'ianskaia Rossia* 8–9 (Prague, 1924): 3–26; see also R. Portal, "Pougatchev: Une révolution manquée," *Études d'Histoire moderne et contemporaine* 1 (1947): 68–98.

90. Well known is the memoir account by Bolotov, *Zapiski*, vol. 3, chaps. 177–78; see also "Perepiska Ekateriny II s Moskovskim glavnokomanduiushchim kn. M. N. Volkonskim," *Osmnadtsatyi Vek* (Moscow), 1 (1869): 79–183. The question remains open as to what Pugachev could have done even had he managed to enter Moscow. It is unlikely that the regime would have toppled (there was nothing to replace it with); at best there might have been a palace *coup* in favor of Grand Duke Paul, but this would not have changed the fate of either Pugachev or the Russian people.

91. E. J. Hobsbawm, *Primitive Rebels: Studies in Archaic Forms of Social Movement in the 19th and 20th Centuries* (New York: Frederick A. Praeger, 1959).

92. Some interesting and valid comments on the differences between the *Pugachevshchina* and the German Peasant War of the sixteenth century are made by Peters, "Politische und gesellschaftliche Vorstellungen."

93. Firsov, *Pugachevshchina*, p. 109; Mavrodin, *Krest'ianskaia voina*, 2: 22–25.

94. Sivkov, "Samozvanstvo v Rossii"; see also K. Bosl, *Frühformen der Gesellschaft im mittelalterlichen Europa* (Munich, 1964).

95. Hobsbawm, *Primitive Rebels*. Note the Christlike parallel of betrayal.

96. Cherniavsky, *Tsar and People;* G. Fedotov, *The Russian Religious Mind: Kievan Christianity* (Cambridge, Mass.: Harvard University Press, 1946), chap. 4.

97. *Pugachevshchina*, 2:188. In Pronshtein, *Don i Nizhnee Povolzh'e*, p. 83, mention is also made of Egypt. The legend is reminiscent of F. Tiutchev's famous stanza on Christ's wandering and blessing the Russian land ("Eti bednye selen'ia," 1855).

98. We are reminded of C. Schmitt's definition of sovereignty; see his "Soziologie des Souveränitätsbegriffs und politische Theologie," in *Erinnerungsgabe für Max Weber*, ed. M. Palyi, 2 vols. (Munich-Leipzig, 1923), 2:1–35.

99. *Pugachevshchina*, 2:109–10, 114; V. Sokolova, "Pesni i predaniia o krest'ianskikh vosstaniiakh Razina i Pugacheva," *Trudy Instituta Etnografi Akademii Nauk SSSR*, n.s., 20 (1953): 17–56.

100. Cherniavsky, *Tsar and People*, pp. 97–99.

101. *Pugachevshchina*, 2:111–12; R. V. Ovchinnikov, "Obzor pechatei na dokumentakh E. I. Pugacheva, ego voennoi kollegii i atamanov," in *Voprosy sotsial'no-ekonomicheskoi istorii i istochnikovedeniia perioda feodalizma v Rossii* (Moscow, 1961), pp. 328–35.

102. *Pugachevshchina*, 2:113. Volume 1 of this collection reproduces all the decrees and orders that were issued by Pugachev's College of War; see also *ibid.*, 3:7, and Mavrodin, *Krest'ianskaia voina*, 2:12.

103. *Pugachevshchina*, 2:107 and 1:136.

104. *Ibid.*, 3:110. Only at the very end of the revolt, on the last day of July, 1774, did Pugachev issue a proclamation virtually inviting the peasants to take the law into their own hands, to do whatever they wanted; see Ia. K. Grot, "Materialy dlia istorii Pugachevskogo bunta: Bumagi otnosiashchiesia k poslednemu periodu miatezha i poimke Pugacheva," *Zapiski imperatorskoi Akademii Nauk* 25 (1875), app. 4, p. 53.

105. *The Cambridge Economic History of Europe from the Decline of the Roman Empire*, vol. 1 (Cambridge, 1941), p. 419; for a discussion of this notion with respect to the "feudal" period of Russian history, see M. Szeftel's article in *Feudalism in History*, ed. R. Coulborn (Princeton: Princeton University Press, 1956).

106. *Pugachevshchina*, 2:135, 194.

107. Firsov, *op. cit.,* p. 127; *Pugachevshchina,* 1:28. Note also the traditional threats of dire punishment if they do not accept his "merciful grant" (R. V. Ovchinnikov and L. N. Slobodskikh, "Novye dokumenty o krest'ianskoi voine 1773–1775 g. v Rossii," *Istoricheskii Arkhiv,* 1956, no. 4, p. 131). The dissertation of Peters, "Politische und gesellschaftliche Vorstellungen," gives a detailed summary of the notions of state and power held by those who participated in the Pugachev movement.

108. *Pugachevshchina,* 1:74–75.

109. The same point was put somewhat differently in the seminar discussion of the present essay: The serfs, the Cossacks, and the *odnodvortsy* revolted ultimately in defense of their traditional closed system of social patterns and values. In their view the mortal threat to this system came from the "modern" (Petrine) state's going beyond its traditional (negative) function of dispensing security and justice by interfering with the form and content of men's traditional actions and appearance. They felt, in short, that the new state was attempting to change man's very being for the sake of a secular (evil) purpose. The noblemen (*pomeshchiki*) in their role as serf owners, also were threatening to break up the traditional patterns of peasant action and belief by interfering in their ways of tilling the soil, disrupting their family structure, by promoting a new, western and non-Russian, way of life. Religion having retained its traditional binding character for the Weltanschauung of the peasants, the revolt against innovation and modernization was most forcefully expressed by the Old Believers, who constituted a sizable minority of the peasants and an overwhelming majority of the Cossacks.

110. J.-L. Van Regemorter, "Deux images idéales de la paysannerie russe à la fin du XVIIIᵉ siècle," *Cahiers du Monde russe et soviétique* 9, no. 1 (1968): 5–19. One cannot help being struck by the parallel development in the United States after Nat Turner's rebellion.

111. Pushkin was also the first historian of the Pugachev rebellion. His *Istoriia Pugachevskogo Bunta* is valuable as a symptom and for the documentation included and appended therein; by today's standards and tastes it is pretty boring, being only what L. Febvre's school derides as *histoire évenementielle.*

112. A. Besançon, "Psychoanalysis: Auxiliary Science or Historical Method," *Journal of Contemporary History* 3, no. 2 (April, 1968): 153–54; *idem, Le tsarévitch immolé: La symbolique de la loi dans la culture russe* (Paris, 1967), pp. 164–69.

113. M. Tsvetaeva, "Pushkin i Pugachev," in *Moi Pushkin* (Moscow, 1967), pp. 105–60 (article was written in 1937).

114. James Baldwin echoes this same sentiment in *The Fire Next Time* when he points out that the only gift the downtrodden and the slave can bestow is the gift of love; and on our ability to accept love depends the creation of a meaningful relationship between the polar extremes of society, and of a livable civilization.

Bibliographic Note

The literature on the Pugachev rebellion is enormous. I make no pretense of having convered it fully. The most comprehensive bibliography that has come to my attention appears in the dissertation of D. Peters referred to earlier; it contains over five hundred items. The most up-to-date general history is a proposed three-volume work, of which the first two volumes have appeared, V. Mavrodin, *Krest'ianskaia voina v Rossii v*

1773–1775 godakh: Vosstanie Pugacheva (Leningrad, 1961–66). The first volume is a valuable (in spite of its bias) and detailed historiographical and bibliographical survey. A recent, brief account of the revolt itself is I. G. Rozner's *Kazachestvo v krest'ianskoi voine 1773–1775 gg.* (Lvov, 1966). A summary account of the revolt is contained in the recently published study of the government's reaction to the *Pugachevshchina*, John T. Alexander's *Autocratic Politics in a National Crisis: The Imperial Russian Government and Pugachev's Revolt, 1773–1775,* Russian and East European Series, vol. 38 (Bloomington: Indiana University Press, 1969).

FIFTEEN

State and Nobility
in the Ideology
of M. M. Shcherbatov

IN RUSSIA, MODERN POLITICAL thought made its appearance in the last third of the eighteenth century; the major stimulant for the debate was the "revolution" (Pushkin's definition) wrought by Peter the Great. Political thinking did not develop much earlier, except for an episodic manifestation in 1730, because it took educated Russian society almost half a century to assimilate the impact of Peter's reign. The "debate" of 1730 was not so much an expression of opposing ideas and concepts (there was an amazing degree of agreement on these), as an emotional reaction to a conflict in social interests. Of course, by the time of the last third of the eighteenth century, the "revolution" of Peter the Great had affected the entire country and created social and cultural conditions which in turn produced some very real problems that cried for solution.

The manner in which the problem was discussed, the terms of reference, and the methods used, the concrete reality which served as framework, all were to determine the contents, form, and dynamic potential of the first expressions of Russian political thought. For our illustration, or case study, let us take the ideas of Prince Mikhail Mikhailovich Shcherbatov (1733–90), who has the merits of having been a prolific writer, keenly interested in political problems, widely educated, and an active participant in the administrative, political, and scholarly life of his time.[1] His way of stating the central political issue of tradition and reason, and the practical consequences it entailed, apparently served as an inspiration to later political thinkers.[2]

There never had been any doubt in Prince Shcherbatov's mind that the nobility constituted the first and privileged class in Russia, and that this was as it should be. It was so evident to Shcherbatov that he rarely bothered to justify his conviction and naively took it for granted that everybody, unless completely blind and ignorant, shared his opinion. Talking about the nobility, its condition, merits, rights, and social role, Shcherbatov invariably used very high-sounding and emotional language, and with such passion that reasonable argument was often quite futile.[3] True, his attitude also reflected insecurity and self-consciousness. This was only too natural, for it was not long since the Russian nobleman had become fully conscious of his individual worth as a creative member of society. Moreover, since Peter the Great it had not been too clear how the nobility should be defined in Russia.

To justify the high rank and privileged position he advocated for the nobility, Shcherbatov stressed the nobleman's personal good qualities. In his mind there was no question that the nobleman was a person of honor and innate nobility of character (*blagorodnyi*), i.e., endowed from birth with noble qualities of mind and soul. For instance, he feared that degrading punishments would deprive noble children of "high-minded feelings and thoughts."[4] Shcherbatov was not so naive as to believe that every nobleman displayed these high qualities and virtues in his daily life. But even if individual noblemen, and this was particularly true of many in the provinces, did not display these features of nobility, they were nevertheless heirs of ancestors who had evidenced these virtues. The fatherland, Shcherbatov wrote, seemed to say to the young noble: "... you are born of virtuous ancestors; without yourself having done anything useful, you already have the distinguished title of nobleman; that is why more than anyone else you must show me your virtue and dedication."[5] Nobility was derived from virtuous, courageous, and noble qualities displayed by individuals in the service of the country.[6] These were the unusual individuals, those few truly active and creative figures in the life of a people. Their outstanding deeds and behavior had distinguished them from the mass of their fellow men. Their unusual moral and spiritual qualities singled them out as much from among the average individuals as physical traits. And, Shcherbatov claimed, as distinctive physical traits were passed on and inherited by later generations, so were moral qualities. Shcherbatov proclaimed at the twenty-second session of the Commission of 1767,

> There is no doubt that the first difference between conditions was due to nothing else than to a difference in virtue among some of the people; their successors in a similar way distinguished themselves from the others and rendered services to the society of which they were members; ... [this] led the people and the rulers ... to give the name and privileged status of nobility to those who had issued from such virtuous ancestors.[7]

This was Shcherbatov's rationale for recognizing nobility even in individuals who at a given moment did not display the virtues and noble qualities of their ancestors. He freely admitted that many noblemen of his day were far from

possessing the desirable noble qualities. Yet, he argued, they still had the potential for manifesting these qualities. At any rate, they had a much greater potential than did the average man. It was therefore more expedient to look for
the desirable qualities among the nobility and endeavor to bring them out
through education and proper treatment than to search for them among ordinary men with much less chance of success.[8]

Without question, to Shcherbatov's mind the ancestors' accomplishments,
heroic deeds, noble thoughts and passions, were the true foundation of the
nobility's privileged position in his own days. Yet, this was only a "passive"
foundation, a necessary but far from sufficient condition. To justify the claim
to nobility in the eighteenth century, the noble deeds and qualities of ancestors must have been carried on and perpetuated by later generations. "The
well-born [*blagorodnyi*] sees in his house and in his ancestors examples of love
for the fatherland and sovereign, examples which incite him to follow in the
ancestors' footsteps, to desire his own glory ... and he is ashamed of not being
the equal of his ancestors."[9] As a matter of fact, Russian noblemen have been
worthy continuators of their ancestors' deeds by virtue of their service to state
and monarch, and also because they have been the leaders in the country's educational, cultural, and moral development.[10] They were able to play this
leading role because, as a group, they took care of sending their children to
schools and gave them an education appropriate to their ancestors' example.[11]
Since Peter the Great, the nobility had eagerly promoted the Westernization
of Russia, it had adopted Western educational practices and programs, and
had developed to such an extent that it needed not feel ashamed before the
enlightened classes of Western Europe.[12] By the same token, the nobility had
helped to spread more knowledge, education, culture to all classes of society,
more particularly among merchants and artisans, but also among serfs.[13] In
short, the nobility was Russia's real hereditary leadership group. It had helped
Russia to attain and maintain a position of power and glory, and since Peter
the Great's times it had also fostered enlightenment and Westernization. This
leadership role, Shcherbatov believed, justified the nobles in claiming a monopoly over the possession of serfs and estates, as well as a large degree of participation in trade and industry. As a matter of fact, the economic activities of
the nobility were an additional aspect of their service and leadership roles.[14]

The Russian nobility, therefore, derived from the high deeds and accomplishments of ancestors, continued by their heirs and successors. By the same
token, Shcherbatov had to recognize that in exceptional cases, great contributions by contemporaries could serve as the source of nobility for new families.
Such ennoblements were to reward exceptionally meritorious services to the
state and had to be certified by letters patent signed by the Monarch, and registered by the assembly of nobles in one of the provinces.[15] Shcherbatov opposed this, but kept the door to noble status open to commoners on the basis
of promotion through the ranks (military or civilian). He felt that there were

enough nobles in Russia to take care of the country's social, cultural, and political needs if all members of the nobility did their duty. But he did not deny the role of selective rewards in ennoblement practices. And having granted the principle of state service as the origin of nobility, Shcherbatov found it difficult to stop mid-way and refuse further ennoblements as rewards for outstanding services to state and country. For instance, in recommending various measures for fighting the severe starvation that had gripped Russia in 1787, he proposed that the state encourage producers and merchants to turn over their surplus grain to the government at cost prices. As reward for a very large donation he recommended that the donor be given personal nobility or even, in cases of extraordinarily large donations, hereditary nobility.[16] True, this was an emergency suggestion, but it did indicate the profound roots of the notion that nobility was a reward for services to the community.

Shcherbatov did object to the mechanical and bureaucratic application of the rules of ennoblement provided for in the Table of Ranks, because they made it possible to attain nobility through patronage and protection of subaltern officials on whom depended promotion to those ranks which automatically entailed nobility.[17] But he could not reject completely the practice of ennoblement through regular promotion. He only wanted such promotions to come from the Monarch, as an expression of his own free and autocratic will and as the reward for truly outstanding services to the state, and not the outcome of intrigues, bribery, and shady deals.[18] Shcherbatov was well aware that the Table of Ranks had become such an essential part of Russian public and social life that it was impossible to advocate its outright abolition. Though he did not like it, he recognized the rationale behind Peter's legislation. He felt only that its intent had been perverted and misinterpreted by the great Emperor's successors. Peter, Shcherbatov believed (or pretended to believe), intended the Table of Ranks as an emergency measure, justified at a time when Russia was in the midst of a war for survival, and was short of adequate military and administrative leadership.[19] In the Table of Ranks, Peter only meant to say that those who had displayed meritorious qualities in the recent past should be ennobled; he did not say, nor did he intend to say, that this was a rule for the future as well.[20] Shcherbatov's argument was a grammatical quibble which today does not strike us as very convincing, but the fact that he should have resorted to it indicates that he was perhaps not quite convinced by his own argument. He was, after all, reluctant to condemn out of hand something that Peter the Great had done and that had served so well in modernizing Russia. In short, Shcherbatov's was a somewhat ineffective attempt at fighting off the bureaucratic routinization (*Veralltäglichung*) of the nobility's charisma, a routinization that had become such a prominent feature of the administrative and social life of eighteenth century Russia.[21] But it did not touch the core of the principle of service as a source of nobility.

More important was Shcherbatov's recognition that the original source of nobility was great deeds accomplished *in the service of the state*. It may be worth noting in passing that Shcherbatov tended to emphasize service to the state, the country, rather than the sovereign; when he spoke of the latter, it sounded like a verbal substitute for the former.[22] The Russian nobleman had always been a service man; the very title of nobleman compelled its holder to serve: "... [nobility] is a rank [*chin*] and a rank that compels hereditarily every holder to serve the fatherland."[23] According to Shcherbatov, this service was the source of all the moral and spiritual virtues of the nobleman, virtues that were displayed and manifested by every generation. These were the virtues of dedication to the common good, to the needs of the whole people, and the security of the state: "... the entire life of a nobly born youngster must be filled with constant teaching, admonition, and conversation or example that aim at instilling in his mind and heart those good seeds which, in time, should produce a fruit useful to his fatherland."[24]

The nobleman's dedication to service was selfless; it did not aim at promoting private interests or at satisfying any personal goals and whims. As a matter of fact, Shcherbatov maintained, this dedicated service was made possible only by sacrificing personal wealth, tranquility, and even happiness. It was an onerous burden, as the nobleman had to serve far away from home, at his own expense (salaries were inadequate), and had to make great sacrifices to educate his children in such a way that they could eventually serve effectively too.[25] Without service to the state there would be no real nobility, as there would be no occasion to manifest the qualities of high-mindedness, noble life, and dedication which were the hallmark of the well-born, the *blagorodnyi*.[26] Russian history, of course, had offered ample opportunity for the manifestation of this ideal of service. In Shcherbatov's own passionate words to the Commission of 1767:

> Tell me, respected deputies, tell me, have you heard from your fathers what services the nobility has rendered to all of Russia? In many places you can still see the ruins of destroyed temples, abandoned settlements—the results of the fury of the infidels! Who preserved your orthodox faith? Who freed you from the yoke and tortures of barbarians and foreigners if not the nobles? ...[27]

Besides saving Russia from the nomads of the steppes, liberating it from the Tartars, and preserving its national and religious integrity during the Times of Troubles, the nobility had, in more recent times, also labored hard at opening up Russia to modernization and Westernization and at securing the powerful international position it has enjoyed since the reign of Peter the Great.[28] All these great accomplishments were ample proof of the nobility's devotion and self-sacrifice to the common good, to the welfare and happiness of Russia, of the Russian state. "Who gave you a helping hand in your downfall, Russia? It was those loyal children, the Russian noblemen! Leaving all and sacrificing their lives, they freed you from foreign domination, they gave you your previous freedom."[29]

Continuous service to the state and monarch was the essential occupation of the nobleman. In spite of the fact that Shcherbatov did not want to see coercion and force applied to compel individual noblemen to enter service, he felt very strongly that a true member of the nobility must serve.[30] The more educated and enlightened the nobility, the more willing it would be to serve freely and to perform its true function in the state without compulsion.[31] According to Shcherbatov and in this he expressed but the common sentiment of his time and society, the nobleman lost caste and face if he did not enter state service, be it only for a while, upon completion of his education. State service was the primary social function and moral obligation of the nobleman; it justified his special position and adequately reflected his charismatic role.[32] The charisma, originally created by the accomplishments and high deeds of ancestors, was preserved and its virtue and valuable qualities displayed from generation to generation only through service. In this sense, Shcherbatov was a spirited advocate of the value of tradition and heredity.

We note the inseparable link that bound in Shcherbatov's mind the nobility to the state, much more so than the bond that tied the Western nobleman to his sovereign. In the latter case, the tie was personal, originating in the feudal hierarchy of personal loyalties and connections; in Russia, however, the nobleman's loyalty was to the much more abstract and global institutions of country and state. Servant of the state, the nobleman took part in the state's activities as a leader of the nation. This leadership role of the state had become much more dominant and conscious in the reign of Peter the Great. It was maintained at a high level thanks to the nobility's active and enthusiastic participation in cultural, economic, as well as diplomatic, military, and administrative affairs. Naturally, as we mentioned, education played a major part in preparing the nobility for this important function in the state. Shcherbatov, therefore, advocated all kinds of devices that would help raise the general cultural niveau of the nobility and separate it more sharply from the other classes. The special rights and privileges Shcherbatov demanded for the nobility were the means which enabled the nobility to fulfill its role in the state's survival and the development of its power and culture.[33] It is important to emphasize that the nobility played a role of leadership strictly at the behest and under the control of the state. There was no room for the nobility's independent initiative or autonomy. There could be more consultation of the nobility's desires and needs, more reliance on the information provided by noblemen on specific conditions in the provinces; it might also be desirable to have the nobility keep records and administer its own corporate concerns. But this was all that Shcherbatov was willing to leave to the nobility's free initiative; in all other respects, the state had the guiding and decisive voice.[34]

Again, we are struck by the fact that Shcherbatov made the nobility and its social role entirely dependent on the state, its will and policies; it was a traditional pattern.[35] Shcherbatov wanted to do nothing to change it. Even the charismatic element was based entirely on service to the state and the whole community, and its hereditary character only imposed the obligation on succeeding generations of noblemen to continue the pattern of service. The nobles were not truly free in their actions and patterns of behavior. They had to continue the tradition of service to justify their very existence, let alone special rights. In other words, Shcherbatov—like most Russians in the eighteenth century—firmly held to the belief that the nobleman's social role was to serve the state in its willful, rational (in the sense of goal-oriented) leadership function. In this sense, all Russians were the true followers of Peter the Great. From the point of view of strict social or political efficiency, the hereditary principle was not the best suited; it was therefore easily superseded by the concept of service reward as the most reasonable justification for social and economic privileges. The hereditary principle came into direct conflict with the principle of rationality which had become the dominant social and political ideal since Peter the Great. Shcherbatov shared the ambiguity of political thought which resulted from this conflict.

* * *

Socially and politically, eighteenth-century Russia was in a state of flux in which it was difficult to single out clear trends or consistent patterns of policy and behavior.[36] The only fixed point was the reign of Peter the Great with its reforms that had displaced traditional patterns and disrupted the old social balance. One's attitude towards Peter's legislation ultimately determined the meaning of one's political concepts and ideology, and Shcherbatov was no exception to this rule.

It is worth noting from the outset that Shcherbatov talked about the remote, pre-Petrine past of Russia in rather vague and general terms (in spite of the fact that he was the author of an important history of Russia from the origins to the seventeenth century). While he stressed the services rendered by the nobility to the Russian state in the past, he did not infer from it that this past should set a standard. More often than not, his references and illustrations from the remoter periods of Russian history had a rhetorical or demagogic flavor and were hardly ever used as serious argument or proof. In most cases, his illustrations referred to events since the accession of Peter the Great; and for Shcherbatov, Peter's legislation had all the rights of historical prescription. One quite definitely has the impression that the Muscovite period did not play a very significant role in Shcherbatov's thinking. Even though he was an historian, his political thinking was well-nigh completely present-minded.

There could be no question about Shcherbatov's admiration for Peter the Great.[37] Before his reign, Shcherbatov felt, Russia had been plunged in darkness, had barely been capable of maintaining her independence and integrity against enemy attacks, had been isolated and without political role in Europe.[38] Her political weakness was, of course, the direct consequence of the absence of any modern military establishment of the kind Peter the Great was to create. But even more important than Russia's political and military weakness was her cultural and social backwardness, her rude and brutal customs, the lack of enlightenment. In a sense, the Russians did not really exist, for "one can say, we [Russians] were born to sciences and culture in 1700. ..."[39] But most important and horrible of all was the absence of human dignity; the individual, even the most prominent bojar, was worthless and completely insecure in his person and property. Under such conditions, spiritual values and enlightenment could not develop.[40] It was Peter the Great who put an end to this situation and helped to turn Russia onto a path leading not only to the state's greater political power, but also to the development of culture and security, at least among the well-born. Peter the Great's initiative was still developing in the reign of Catherine II.

True enough, these transformations had been wrought by Peter quite forcefully, brutally and harshly. Had this been justified? Would Russia not have developed on her own in the right direction? Had there been no evidence in the seventeenth century, before the accession of Peter, of the impending change? Shcherbatov attempted to answer these questions several times, but most comprehensively and clearly he stated his position in a curious essay with the lengthy, but descriptive title, *"Primernoe vremjaischislitel'noe polozhenie, vo skol'ko by let, pri blagopoluchnejshikh obstojatel'stvakh, mogla Rossija sama soboju, bez samovlastija Petra Velikogo dojti do togo sostojanija, v kakom ona nyne est' v rassuzhdenii prosveshchenija i slavy."* In it Shcherbatov argued that had there been no Peter, lack of culture and inadequacies in the social and economic organization, the people's (including the nobility) ignorance and primitivity, the absence of individual initiative, intellectual curiosity and honor, would not have permitted Russia to attain the level of 1762 before 1892. And even then, one would have had to assume that during these 210 years Russia would have been completely safe from her neighbors, which could hardly have been expected. In other words, without Peter's dynamic drive and leadership, Russia would have made no striking progress; even the nobility would not have been educated, enlightened, and become the honorable and dedicated class it was.[41] One may ask in passing, what such an argument makes of Shcherbatov's notions about the hereditary transmission of noble virtues and qualities? But let us be kind to the passionate aristocrat and not test his logic further.

It is quite true that in his well-known pamphlet, "On the Corruption of Manners in Russia," Shcherbatov maintained that Peter's ways of changing

Russia had been too radical and brutal. This rude method had had deplorable consequences for Russian manners and morals at the end of the eighteenth century.[42] Yet, Shcherbatov did not deny the necessity of Peter's—or a similarly dynamic and commanding personality's—direct intervention to bring Russia out of her lethargic and backward state. One should also note in this connection that if the pamphlet praised the private morals of the pre-Petrine period, the Tsar's and bojars' simplicity of manners, and by contrast condemned the laxity and extravagance of the court of Catherine II, it did not claim that Russian culture and society had been more advanced before 1700.[43] Even if the present left too much to be desired, it did not mean that the past was an ideal worth returning to.

The nobility had played a major role in assisting Peter the Great in his task of reform and transformation. It was their devotion and faith that had made it a success.[44] The nobles were now the chief beneficiaries as well as continuators of the great Emperor's work. True, there were many evils and ills in Russia now, but most had come about because things did not develop as smoothly as Peter had hoped. Too often the weak and petty successors of the "fledglings from Peter's nest" had strayed from the high course he had set. His aim had been the right one, and his method of direct guidance and willful action the only possible approach.

Shcherbatov's notions of good government and healthy society can be gathered from his utopian novel, *Voyage to the Land of Ofir.*[45] The society of the Land of Ofir was Shcherbatov's ideal, but an ideal that reflected in many ways the Russia that had issued from the hands of Peter.[46] In effect, the Land of Ofir was a model of an *ordentlicher Polizeistaat,* such as an enlightened Prussian bureaucrat might have dreamt about.[47]

For the purposes of this article, I am not interested in the details of this society and the structure of its administration and government. I wish only to point out the principle and method that presided over the making of this utopia: Ofir was the result of the legislation of one great monarch (similar to Peter) who, respectful though he was of the basic principles of social organization, destroyed at one stroke of the pen the harmful patterns of the past and launched his country on a path of happiness and virtue. It was the exact counterpart of the *chiquenaude* of Descartes' divine mechanic. To maintain the country on the newly established path of virtue and happiness, the administration and society were thoroughly regulated in a mechanistic way, all aspects of life being constantly supervised. All decisions that affected more than the routine of everyday life had to be expressions of the state's leadership, imposed with the help of a devoted class of noble state servants.[48] Even the minutiae of dress, manner, tableware, etc., were carefully prescribed by rules and laws, mechanically arranged according to an hierarchic pattern.[49] Ofir looked much more like a modern rational, efficient, and public relations conscious business enterprise, than a living social organism.

Like so many social utopias, Ofir lacked flexibility and dynamism; it was a static society, organized on a functional caste basis. Once the good order had been put in motion, it remained forever the same. Basic change was avoided, and only minor "technical" adjustments were possible to take care of the natural wear and tear of the mechanism. In his lack of concern for growth and gradual change, his complete reliance on willful action (of a ruler or leader), Shcherbatov was a true child of the eighteenth century. His rationalistic enlightenment was more "radical" than "conservative" in its basic political implications. It was a natural attitude for Shcherbatov to take, as it reflected so well the recent social experience of Russia, the unhinging but positive work of Peter the Great. He felt that at the end of the eighteenth century, Russia again needed such a willful and dynamic leader to correct all the defects and ills that had been allowed to develop since Peter's death.[50]

Because Shcherbatov relied so heavily on willful leadership in political life, he was led to stress moral charisma in political leadership.[51] He firmly believed that a ruler, provided he had sufficient moral purity and sense of responsibility, would do the best job possible in organizing the social and political life of a country. The moral sense was so important because of Shcherbatov's fundamental conviction that a society, a social machine, needed rational and willful guidance and regulation to maximize the spiritual, economic, intellectual potential latent in the people. He was well aware, as Machiavelli had been, that an immoral absolute ruler, entrusted with the function of creative leadership, would corrupt his subjects and ruin his country. In support of this belief, Shcherbatov did not—and this is indicative of his eighteenth century radical rationalism—make appeal to the notion of Christian kingship. He did not look for support to the authority of medieval Russian Church writers, but rather drew on natural law and contract theories and recent Western examples. We see here again Shcherbatov's reluctance to make use of ideas, arguments, and realities of pre-Petrine Russia.

*   *   *

With Montesquieu Shcherbatov believed that the nobility was an essential element in a good monarchy, and that honor (Shcherbatov meant moral sense as much as ambition and thirst for glory) was the mainspring of the nobility's behavior and thought.[52] Such a quality was best developed in the family with its traditions of service, enlightenment, and dedication. At the same time, however, this tradition-oriented nobility had to play an active role in the rational, willful, transformation of the country, in the service of an efficiency-oriented institution; it had to act "rationally"—i.e., purposefully and efficiently—on grounds of abstract concepts of morality and state interests. In Western Europe, ideally at least, the nobleman was called to help out his sovereign or take an active part in the local and central administrations because he had displayed valuable traits in his private life or in the pursuit of his personal interests. But on the basis of eighteenth century Russia's situation, Shcherbatov reversed this order of things: The Russian nobleman acquired his good qualities, moral virtues, as a result of his service and active participation in the state's willful and creative social action. Deprived of this service function, the nobility became inconceivable to Shcherbatov as a social class with special rights and privileges. Thus Shcherbatov wanted that a "traditional" pattern of behavior and social organization serve "rational," willful, social construction. The Muscovite faith in the development of a way of life had been replaced by reliance on willful, purposeful creation.

Shcherbatov had also very little interest in and understanding for the negative or passive role of the state. The Western European tradition stressing the role of political institutions, as a means of defense and security *against* threats to the body social, did not, in the eighteenth century, seem to have penetrated very far into Russian consciousness. This may not be too surprising, for this tradition was not at its strongest in Western Europe, either. But it is somewhat incongruous to find the defender of a traditional and hereditary nobility advocate the same notions as the "radical" *Philosophes* or enlightened bureaucrats. In any event, in Shcherbatov's opinion, the state—i.e., the ruler with the help of the service nobility—had to "create," "make" society by giving it shape through rules and laws and by setting goals for the nation's cultural and social development. This was the lesson learned from Russia's experience with Peter the Great. In eighteenth century Russia, it was impossible to deny the positive role played by Peter, to ignore the fact that he had given a "body" and perhaps even a "soul" to the country, that he had brought civilization and culture to his backward and ignorant people. In so doing, Peter the Great had also helped bring into being a number of educated, enlightened state servants keenly conscious of their personal worth and dignity. Such individuals could not think of returning to Muscovite Russia, with its brutality, sloth, ignorance, and insecurity. They denied Muscovy and consequently had no feeling of historical continuity, "organic" development. Their outlook was voluntaristic and their "philosophy of history" a catastrophic one.

Shcherbatov's stress on the moral aspect of political leadership displaced a significant element of Western political thought: interest. The important thing to Shcherbatov was that the political leadership of state and nobility have a good moral purpose. Morality was an abstract notion that had general validity and could be found anywhere—at least potentially. It was not dependent on any specific stage of civilization, economic, social, cultural achievement, or on some natural conditions. This made it particularly attractive to a "new" country (and Russia was but recently Westernized and modernized), eager to break loose from the old conditions of backwardness, ignorance, barbarism. The moral precepts and notions could be derived from absolute value systems or abstract philosophical concepts, they did not depend on historical precedent, social routines, and particular interests.[53] It made gradualism and undirected historical evolution unnecessary. All this was made to appeal to *homines novi*, new in the cultural and social, if not necessarily chronological, sense. It was perfectly suited to stress the positive element of state action, the leadership function of political power (and of those who served it).[54]

In the struggle between tradition and reason that took place in many Russian minds in the eighteenth century, reason won out. The preference for direct, willful, planned action over blind faith in gradual development and historical evolution was unmistakable. Shcherbatov was only expressing a general feeling when he advocated reason and reserved a subordinate role to tradition in his own political thinking. It may very well be that this eighteenth century reaction (one still hesitates to call it a formed attitude, let alone ideology) was in more than one sense at the root of the weakness of true conservatism and true liberalism in Russian thought. The radicalism, the lack of consistency, shallowness, simple-mindedness, and paradoxality of Russian political thought have usually been ascribed to the general lag of Russian culture, the crudeness and "primitivity" of its social and economic organization, the borrowed character of its theoretical thought. These all played a part, no doubt. But was not the dilemma of tradition and reason a more immediate and basic reason for the state of political thinking in Russia? Russian writers rejected the traditions of their country's past for the sake of abstract (sometimes foreign) notions, direct action programs. There was good ground for it in Russia's own historical experience: Peter the Great stood at the opening of the modern period of Russian history, and—for better or for worse—he had been the prime mover, the first cause, and the creator of the only objective reality that the Russians knew. And Peter had been the embodiment of "reason," not in the Hegelian, but in Max Weber's more limited, yet more accurately descriptive sense of goal-directed and efficiency-minded action. Faced with the "reason" of the first Emperor, how could tradition maintain its own?[55]

The paradox of tradition and reason also helped raise the dilemma of means and ends—an equally important feature in the history of Russian political thought. It would appear that most Russian thinkers were particularly myopic with regard to the practical consequence of a discrepancy between ends and means. It was too often forgotten that authoritarian methods hardly lend themselves for the attainment of "liberal" ends. The naiveté, simplicity of much Russian political thought stemmed from this neglect. But at the source of this dilemma we find again the experience and attitude we have described in the case of Shcherbatov. Because Russia's past had been so dismal and because whatever good there was in Russia had been willfully created, there was no faith in the role of gradualism, historical experience, and "organic development."[56] Even advocates of moderate, gradualistic programs often believed that first a radical policy was necessary to blast open the path for change.

The eighteenth century had lacked (and the nineteenth largely inherited this lack) a sense of sympathy, respect, and humility towards the national past. It was Peter the Great who had been instrumental in destroying such feelings of sympathy and humility. He also had shown what positive political action could do. Whether they liked Peter's reforms or not, the Russians of the eighteenth century (and to a large extent this was also true in the nineteenth) could not escape the experience of a radical break with the past, a break which they experienced subjectively as having been almost total. The feeling that in Russia almost everything was owed to Peter, and almost nothing to Muscovy, was never fully overcome. Most acutely aware of this situation, the eighteenth century rejected tradition, denied the past, and accepted Peter's policies wholeheartedly not only as an historical event, but also as an ideal and method of social action. It set a style of thought, a "rational" way of looking at Russia's problems that lent a "radical" tone and "voluntaristic" slant to all expressions of political thought.

Notes

This article is dedicated to the late M. M. Karpovich.

1. For biographical data on Shcherbatov, see: V. Fursov, "Shcherbatov, Mikh. Mikh.," *Russkij Biograficheskij Slovar'*, Shchapov-Jushnevskij, (St. Petersburg, 1912), pp. 104–24; V. A. Miakotin, "Dvorjanskij publicist Ekaterininskoj epokhi" in *Iz istorii russkogo obshchestva*, (St. Petersburg, 1906), pp. 102–66; N. D. Chechulin, "Khronologija i spisok sochinenii kn. M. M. Shcherbatova," *Zhurnal Ministerstva Narodnogo Prosveshchenija* (1900), No. VIII, pp. 346–47.

2. Shcherbatov was a very versatile figure and has left a name in the history of literature, economic thought, historiography, social and political events. His ideology was far from being as simple as most writers have claimed ("reactionary aristocrat and defender of serfdom"). It would repay close analysis. In general, it seems fair to say that he advocated a curious blend of absolutism and aristocratic "constitutionalism" based on serfdom (though he condemned specific malpractices) and a rigid, "corporative" division of society. In a sense, he foreshadowed the so-called "Senatorial party" in the first decade of the reign of Alexander I. For Shcherbatov's contributions to historiography and economic thought, see (in addition to the works in note 1): P. N. Miljukov, *Glavnye techenija russkoj istoricheskoj mysli*, I. (2d ed.); (Moscow, 1898), Ch. II, sect. 2 and Ch. III, sect. 2; N. L. Rubinshtein, *Russkaja istoriografija* (Moscow-Leningrad, 1941), pp. 116–37 (bibl., p. 116); A. Pashkov, ed. *Istorija russkoj ekonomicheskoj mysli*, Vol. I, part 1 (Moscow, 1955), pp. 465–80 (bibl., p. 737).

3. D. V. Polenov, V. I. Sergeevich, N. D. Chechulin (eds.), *Istoricheskie svedenija o Ekaterininskoj komissii dlja sochinenija Proekta Novogo Ulozhenija*, *Sbornik Imperatorskogo Rossijskogo Istoricheskogo Obshchestva;* Vol. IV (1869) pp. 192–93 (24th session, 17 Sept. 1767). Hereafter, this source will be cited *Sbornik IRIO* and volume number. Cf. also *Sochinenija knjaz'ja M. M. Shcherbatova*, vol. I, I. P. Khrushchev, ed. (St. Petersburg, 1896), pp. 186–87, 219, 221.

4. *Sochinenija*, I, 19; cf. also *Sbornik IRIO*, VIII, 107.

5. *Sbornik IRIO*, IV, 150; also in *Sochinenija*, I, 57.

6. Incidentally, this coincided with the position taken by Catherine II in the *Nakaz,* Ch. XV, §§ 360, 361, 363.

7. *Sbornik IRIO,* IV, 150; also *Sochinenija,* I, 56.

8. "… it is possible that among plowmen we would find many Alexanders and Caesars …, but should we therefore search in the fields for Alexanders, Caesars, and Scipios at the risk of making thousands of mistakes?" *Sochinenija,* I, 237–38 ("Razmyshlenie o dvorjanstve").

9. M. M. Shcherbatov, *Neizdannye sochinenija* (Moscow, 1935), pp. 59–60 ("Zamechanija na Bol'shoj Nakaz Ekateriny II").

10. *Sbornik IRIO,* IV, 160; "Razmyshlenie o dvorjanstve," *Sochinenija,* I, 229.

11. "This name [of nobleman] compels them [noblemen] to serve with particular zeal their fatherland and sovereign, and to this end they endeavor to prepare themselves through education." *Sbornik IRIO,* VIII, 107; also *Sochinenija,* I, 114.

12. Behind the criticism of details and inadequacies, and along with proposals for improvement, we find expressions of Shcherbatov's positive evaluation of the progress accomplished in Russia in the eighteenth century in his essay "O sposobakh prepodavanija raznye nauki," *Sochinenija,* II (I. P. Khrushchev and A. G. Voronov, eds.) (St. Petersburg, 1898), pp. 439–602.

13. "Zamechanija na Bol'shoj Nakaz," *op. cit.,* p. 49; *Sbornik IRIO,* XXXVI, 311.

14. *Sbornik IRIO,* IV, 152 and *Sochinenija,* I, 61; also cf. *Sbornik IRIO,* VIII, 57–58. I am well aware that there was a very selfish side to Shcherbatov's argument. His defense of noble serf ownership monopoly has been a frequent subject of comment and analysis. And for purposes of the present article, it is not germane.

15. *Sbornik IRIO,* IV, 152; *Sbornik IRIO,* XXXII, 184; also *Sochinenija,* I, 15.

16. "Rassuzhdenie o nyneshmen v 1787 g. pochti povsemestnom golode v Rossii, o sposobakh onomu pomoch' i vpred predupredit' podobnoe neschastie," *Sochinenija,* I, 659–60.

17. *Sbornik IRIO,* IV, 151–52; also *Sochinenija,* I, 59.

18. *Sbornik IRIO,* IV, 299–300; also *Sochinenija,* I, 263. I realize, of course, that Shcherbatov had to take this position not to alienate completely a large segment of the existing nobility. Yet the fact that he had to bow to the idea of ennoblement through promotion and acquiesce to its rationale is significant in itself.

19. *Sbornik IRIO,* IV, 150; also *Sochinenija,* I, 55.

20. "Primechanija vernogo syna otechestva na dvorjanskie prava …," *Sochinenija,* I, 323–25.

21. Max Weber, *Wirtschaft und Gesellschaft,* (4. Aufl.) (Tübingen, 1956), pp. 144–46. All political and legal histories of eighteeth century Russia provide ample material for the bureaucratization of social and political institutions.

22. "Razmyshlenija o zakonodatel'stve voobshche," *Sochinenija,* I, 390.

23. "Primechanija vernogo syna otechestva na dvorjanskie prava na manifest," *Sochinenija,* I, 291.

24. "Razmyshlenie o dvorjanstve," *Sochinenija,* I, 226, also 225, 227.

25. "Razmyshlenie o dvorjanstve," *Sochinenija,* I, 247; "Zamechanija na Bol'shoj Nakaz," *op. cit.,* p. 59.

26. "Razmyshlenie o dvorjanstve," *Sochinenija,* I, 224.

27. *Sbornik IRIO,* XXXII, 489–90.

28. "Zamechanija na Bol'shoj Nakaz," *op. cit.,* p. 59.

29. *Sochinenija*, I, 88.

30. "The fatherland requires more the service that originates in love than the one [originating] in compulson ..." *Sbornik IRIO*, XXXVI, 20.

31. Thus, the compulsory measures of Peter the Great were no more necessary in Shcherbatov's time when the nobility had become quite enlightened as a class, though individual exceptions might still be found. For example, see *Sbornik IRIO*, IV, 150.

32. M. Weber, *op. cit.*, pp. 124, 140.

33. "Proekt o narodnom izuchenii," *Sochinenija*, I, 741, 742, 743.

34. "Primechanija vernogo syna ... na dvorjanskie prava ...," *Sochinenija*, I, 299; "Puteshestvie v zemlju Ofirskuju, g-na S ..., shvetskogo dvorjanina," *Sochinenija*, I, 751.

35. "Razmyshlenija o zakonodatel'stve voobshche," *Sochinenija*, I, 395.

36. S. V. Eshevskij, "O povrezhdenii nravov v Rossii (sochinenie kn. M. M. Shcherbatova)," *Sochinenija po russkoj istorii* (Moscow, 1900), p. 272.

37. See for example, the ode Shcherbatov composed on the accession of Elizabeth and which is actually a paean of praise for Peter, *Neizdannye Sochinenija*, p. 169; or his upbraiding of Nekljudov for implicitly disparaging Peter the Great in his address to Catherine II, "Otvet grazhdanina na rech' govorennuju E.I.V.—u. Ober-Prokurorom Senata Nekljudovym, po prichine torzhestva shvedskogo mira 179g, sentjabrja 5-go chisla," *Sochinenija*, II, 121. As an historian, Shcherbatov displayed great enthusiasm and energy in publishing the papers of Peter the Great and in ordering the files of the Emperor's private chancery.

38. "Primernoe vremjaischislitel'noe polozhenie ...," *Sochinenija*, II, 13–17.

39. "Razmyshlenie o dvorjanstve," *Sochinenija*, I, 250.

40. "Rassmotrenie o porokakh i samovlastii Petra Velikogo," *Sochinenija*, II, 40.

41. "Primernoe vremjaischislitel'noe polozhenie ...", *Sochinenija*, II, 20.

42. "O povrezhdenii nravov v Rossii," is printed in *Sochinenija*, II, 133–246. I used another edition that was more readily accessible to me at the time of writing, ninth fascicle of *Russkaja Zhizn'* (Moscow, 1908), to which all references will be made. Here, see pp. 21, 31.

43. *O povrezhdenii nravov*, pp. 12 ff, 21 ff.

44. "Zamechanija na Bol'shoj Nakaz ..." *Neizdannye sochinenija*, p. 19.

45. "Puteshestvie v zemlju Ofirskuju, g-na S ..., Shvetskogo dvorjanina" in *Sochinenija*, I, 749–1060. The work has remained incompleted. Besides the titles cited in note 1, the following studies deal at length with the "Voyage": N. D. Chechulin, "Russkij social'nyi roman XVIII, v." *Zhurnal Ministerstva Narodnogo Prosveshchenija*, 327 (Jan., 1900), pp. 115–66; A. A. Kizevetter, "Russkaja utopija XVIII v.," in *Istoricheskie ocherki* (Moscow, 1912), pp. 37–56.

46. Shcherbatov also used the novel to criticize specific failings of Catherine II's Russia and also to point out the errors and omissions in Peter's work. For example, it had been wrong to move the capital from its central location to the seashore; it would have been desirable to establish military settlements to support a professional militia; *Sochinenija*, pp. 796, 905.

47. For example, *Sochinenija*, I, 952, ff on the role of police supervision of all aspects of life on Ofir. It should be noted here that Shcherbatov had been a Free Mason and the Land of Ofir had many traits in common with the Masonic utopias of the period.

48. *Sochinenija*, I, 848, 901.

49. *Sochinenija,* I, 858, 861, 918.

50. Eshevskij, "O povrezhdenii nravov ...," *op. cit.,* p. 288.

51. *O povrezhdenii nravov,* pp. 84–85. For this reason, Shcherbatov also denied the complete determinism of "objective," impersonal forces, like climate. In opposition to Montesquieu he emphasized the role of moral individual leadership. Cf. "Zamechanija na Bol'shoj Nakaz," *Neizdannye sochinenija,* pp. 21, 32, 33, 38.

52. "Raznye rassuzhdenija o pravlenii," *Sochinenija,* I, 346.

53. "Rassuzhdenija o pravlenii," *Sochinenija,* I, 340.

54. "Rassuzhdenija o pravlenii," *Sochinenija,* I, 347; "Razmyshlenija o zakonodatel'stve voobshche," *Sochinenija,* I, 367–69. It is true that Shcherbatov, now and then, did point out the limiting factor of objective conditions, the value of selected historical precedents. But these *caveats* played a subordinate role in his ideology.

55. I need not emphasize that the preceding is an attempt at describing the subjective reactions of Russian thinkers in the eighteenth century. It does not imply any "objective," scholarly evaluation of Peter the Great's reign, nor an historical judgment on Muscovite Russia.

56. It may be observed that even the Slavophiles, and their various *epigoni,* did not really care for the "objective" historical past of Russia. For them the Russian past was a sort of Golden Age to which they wanted to return, it was a retrospective utopia. There were a few individual thinkers who tried to incorporate Russian history meaningfully and dynamically into their political thinking (Karamzin, Pushkin, Samarin, Chicherin, Struve, to mention the best known). But characteristically, in this respect, they had a very limited impact and almost no following.

SIXTEEN

Muscovy Looks West

THE RUSSIAN EPIC HERO, Ilia Muromets, sat paralysed for thirty years, unable to get up from his seat or use his hands. One day, when his parents had gone to the fields and left him sitting in front of his house, three pilgrims came up and asked him for a drink of water and food. When he told them that he could not get up and fetch it, they ordered him to stand up and to bring the water—and lo, behold, he did get up and draw water from the well. The pilgrims told him to drink the water and so he did, they then asked him how he felt. 'If there were a ring attached to the world,' he said, 'I would overturn the whole world.' The pilgrims ordered him to drink some more and this time Ilia Muromets felt his strength halved; the pilgrims went away and the young hero set forth from his house to do valiant battle for Prince Vladimir, the Beautiful Sun, of Kiev.

One is reminded of this story in connection with the stunning effect produced in Europe by the emergence of Russia as a leading military power following Peter I's victory over Charles XII at Poltava in 1709. Let us then take the epic as a literary conceit to guide us in understanding the dramatic appearance of a new political and military giant on the European stage.

Up to about the middle of the seventeenth century, with some rare and insignificant exceptions, 'medieval' Russia, or Muscovy, had existed in relative isolation from Central and Western Europe; even with its immediate neighbours, Poland and Sweden, there had hardly been much cultural and economic exchange. After the so-called Time of Troubles (1605–13), while licking the wounds inflicted by war, social anarchy, and economic collapse, Moscow had turned more xenophobic and isolationist. While Muscovy recovered from the worst effects of the Time of Troubles, it fell into permanent crisis—religious, dynastic, socio-economic, cultural—in the course of the second half of the seventeenth century. Muscovy was becoming progressively paralysed, unable to resolve the severe conflicts that were racking its body social and politic; at any rate unable to cope with the help of those traditional institutional and 'ideological' means which, in the fifteenth and sixteenth centuries, had enabled Moscow to assert its primacy over all Russian lands, build a powerful military and political organization, and develop a sophisticated religious culture.

Thus, by the last decade of the seventeenth century, Muscovy seemed to be a giant (for let us not forget that it was the largest compact territorial state in Europe) condemned to passivity and ossification. And there was no relief in sight, for traditionalist Muscovite society was not able to provide any viable alternatives; and its continuing existence appeared to be due less to its own vital energy than to its neighbours' weakness and disinterest.

In fact, however, there was a silent stirring, the water in the well was being refreshed by new underground streams, and soon it would become a miraculous draught to vivify the paralysed body of the Muscovite polity. Adumbrated first by Ivan IV (1533–84) and Boris Godunov (1598–1605), and pursued more consistently since the reign of Tsar Alexis (1645–76), the father of Peter I, Moscow's policy had been turning away from its traditional fixation on the East (and South-East), where it aimed at taking the place of the Mongol 'empire of the steppes'. Muscovy was now definitely seeing its main foreign policy tasks in the West (and South-West). This was partly due to the internal weakening of Poland and Moscow's growing involvement in the diplomatic and military affairs of East Central Europe. But in some measure it was also the result of the economic aggressiveness of Dutch and English merchants. Indeed, by way of Archangel, these enterprising traders were bringing western luxury and technical goods for the Kremlin's élite; in return they obtained Russian raw materials and eastern merchandise.

Russia's greater involvement in European wars required borrowing new techniques and tactics. The traditional mounted noble 'militia' that had been the backbone of the Tsar's military establishment had to give way to the so-called 'newly formed regiments'—units of professional soldiers, officered mainly by foreigners, and equipped with modern weapons. In short, a sizeable group of foreigners, settled for economic or military purposes, had become a fixed and significant element of Muscovy. Although the foreigners had to reside in a separate section (the foreign suburb—*nemetskaia sloboda*) of the capital, they took an active part in the daily life of Moscow. Increasingly, members of the Tsar's immediate entourage manifested curiosity for things West European, but they also endeavoured to acquire the cultural perquisites of a 'European' way of life. However, they did so cautiously and selectively, without abandoning their traditional and religious outlook and customs.

In paying greater attention to the West, the Muscovite state had also become more interested in what was happening in the European states—and vice versa, of course, Central and West European diplomats and rulers were becoming more curious about Muscovy. The Tsar's realm was seen not only as a possible ally in military and diplomatic schemes, but also as a land where western experiences and training might find useful and remunerative application. Many a German—or Dutch or Scottish—artisan, university graduate, or technician proved willing to settle (permanently or temporarily) in Moscow after failing to find a steady career in Europe. Many military men found employment in Moscow when circumstances forced them to leave their homeland (men like Patrick Gordon from Scotland or Franz Lefort from Geneva).

Moscow's curiosity for the happenings in the West led to the sending of embassies to the major European states. The ambassadors' reports quite clearly show not only their authors' bewilderment, but also their earnest efforts to inform themselves and to understand the diverse institutional, economic, social and cultural arrangements they observed on their mission. In addition to these embassies, the authorities in the Kremlin collected and 'abstracted' European gazettes, and summaries of the information thus gathered was circularized in print, in the so-called *Kuranty*.

West European intellectual achievements penetrated into Muscovy in a somewhat unexpected way. Political and ecclesiastical developments in the late sixteenth century had made possible infiltration of the Catholic Counter-Reformation into lands that had originally been exclusively Orthodox. To the Orthodox Church in the Ukraine, with its historical, spiritual, and intellectual centre at Kiev, it became obvious that to stem Catholic proselytism it was necessary to forge intellectual tools capable of countering Catholic arguments and educational efforts. This need led to a renaissance of theological and liturgical literature written by clergy from Kiev or the Ukraine in general. One of the consequences of this effort was the ritual reforms of Patriarch Nikon in the Russian Church and the resulting split with the Old Believers that destroyed the traditional religious-political consensus of the Muscovite polity; it was a significant factor of the paralysis of Moscow mentioned earlier.

Of particular significance from our perspective here was the Ukrainian and Belorussian Orthodox clergy's realization that they had to renew their homiletic and apologetic armoury with the implements fashioned in the West and which were so effectively used by their Catholic—primarily Jesuit—opponents. And so it was that the first East Slavic institution of 'higher ecclesiastic learning' was founded by Peter Mohyla, Metropolitan of Kiev, in 1632. This Academy became the centre for the intensive and modern training of the clerical élite, and it also stimulated the development of a network of schools in the Ukraine that were open to the laity as well. Furthermore, far from contenting itself with providing instruction in Kiev, the Academy arranged for more advanced study of its graduates at university centres in Western and Central Europe. In this way intellectual movements prevailing in Europe were assimilated by the best of the Ukrainian clergy in the course of the seventeenth century. Little wonder that these clergymen were highly regarded in the Eastern Slavic Orthodox world, in particular in Moscow.

The incorporation of the Ukraine into the Muscovite state in the mid-seventeenth century only intensified these ecclesiastical and intellectual contacts. By the late seventeenth century Kiev-trained clergy had established the Slavonic-Greek-Latin Academy in Moscow and such individuals as Epifanii Slavinetskii and Simeon Polotskii had become the dominant intellectual force in Moscow, participating in the education of the Tsar's children and of the younger generation of the Kremlin élite. We know now that even the clerks of the central government institutions of Moscow (*prikazy*), particularly the Office of Ambassadors (*posol'skii prikaz*—the 'foreign office') acquired some basic European intellectual-philosophical tools, not to speak of languages such as Latin, and were actively involved in the creation of a new secular and poetic literature that circulated in manuscript form among the élite.

Finally, such outstanding and influential individuals as the head of the Office of Ambassadors, A.L. Ordyn-Nashchokin, the Tsar's tutor Artamon Matveev, and others had been exposed, and to a large part had assimilated these Western intellectual currents by the end of Tsar Alexis' reign. By the late seventeenth century there was a significant minority of individuals in the capital—both native and foreign—who were interested in and capable of acquiring European models for intellectual as well as political reasons. What new source could now be tapped? It turned out to be the new political culture that had been taking shape in the West in the course of the seventeenth century, especially since the end of the Thirty Years War. It may be summarily defined as the administrative practices of the 'Well ordered police state' (*état policé, ordentlicher Policeystaat*); a reorientation of the purpose and character of government and specifically of administrative action. From having been conceived in the past in negative terms—defence against the outside enemy and maintenance of law for domestic security—government now acquired the positive function of organizing and disciplining society (or select sectors of it) for the purpose of maximizing productivity, so as to increase the power and prosperity of both state (monarch) and people.

To this end the numbers of administrative officers were increased and trained so as to transmute knowledge into action to shape social conduct and make it more productive. It provided a new ideal type or guide of action for the governments of Europe and resulted in the rise of modern, functionally organized administrations, the growth of codification, and the state's expanding involvement in economic, social and cultural pursuits. The socio-economic as well as intellectual and cultural progress of the eighteenth century (often subsumed under the categories of the Enlightenment and the agrarian and industrial revolutions) was certainly one of the major consequences of this intellectual and political reorientation of the West and Central European élites in the course of the seventeenth century. The easy transferability of this ideal type made it an attractive model to be borrowed and emulated. It offered an alternative to the impasse of crisis and ossification that bedevilled the Muscovite polity at the end of the 1680s.

To refer back to our literary conceit: Moscow was the paralysed budding hero, cameralism and the well ordered police state had refreshed the water of the family well, and implements for drawing the water were available in the new intellectual currents of western origin and the group of foreign and native personalities trained to make use of them. Only the miracle-making pilgrims were lacking. They made their appearance in the person of Peter I. The combination of his upbringing, personality and awareness of the need to find a way out of the impasse drove Peter to reorganize brusquely and ruthlessly the political and military machinery of Muscovy along lines suggested by the 'ideal type' of the well-ordered police state (specifically borrowing from the practices of Swedish, Prussian, Dutch and other cameralist administrations). The story is well known, even though the details and motivations in individual instances still need more research. But it is absolutely clear—whatever our interpretations and judgements—that Russia was forcibly dragged into Europe by Peter; and it arrived there as an energetic and powerful giant, ready to undertake new tasks and play a big role in the affairs of Europe. It soon became obvious that there was no way back to Muscovy—not only did Peter I move the capital to newly founded St. Petersburg which was rapidly rising out of the swamps of the Finnish Gulf, but he had definitely focused the interests and curiosity of the Russian élites on to 'Europe'. The first emperor instilled the best of his subjects with the intense desire and fervent hope of becoming members, in every respect, of the European community of thought, art, literature, science and social progress. The educated in Russia, whether nobles or commoners, were never to depart from this heritage, even to this day.

In conclusion, I would like to mention an aspect which, though well known, is often not given due attention in accounting for the particular nature of the process of Russia's Europeanization in the eighteenth century. ... It was the German *Aufklärung*, not the Anglo-French Enlightenment that came to Russia in the first half of the eighteenth century. The *Aufklärung* derived its inspiration not only from the rationalism of Descartes and Leibniz, but also from the emotionalism of Protestant Pietism; its interpretation of Natural Law stressed the duties and responsibilities of the individual rather than his rights, and always viewed him as an inseparable part and parcel of a community to which he should owe his primary allegiance. Last, but not least, the *Aufklärung* did not oppose religion and the Church (although it was at times critical of particular practices) and it readily acquiesced in the authority of the monarch or the secular powers.

This circumstance helps to explain the development of science in Russia, the religious-moralistic tone of the intelligentsia, the absence of doctrines of individual rights and codified legal guarantees. It also accounts for the revival

of spiritual religiosity and the enthusiastic reception of romanticism and ideal-
ist philosophy on the part of the élites in the late eighteenth and early nineteenth century. In a sense, both Russia's academic tradition and the philosophic inspiration of the educated and of the intelligentsia have their roots in
the heritage of seventeenth-century Pietism and *Naturphilosophie* mediated
through the 'Rosicrucian Enlightenment' and the *Aufklärung*.

It should also be remembered that the European scholars and technicians
who came to Russia to promote its Europeanization did not belong to the
avant-garde of western scientific and cultural achievements. Rather they were
the 'second stringers' who had not succeeded in making a career in the West
and were therefore willing to accept Peter's enticement to come to far away
and 'barbarous' Russia. What they brought, therefore, was not the most advanced knowledge and understanding, not the seminally dynamic ideas that
were beginning to have their impact in western Europe, but rather the routine
knowledge of their own student days. In short, in the early eighteenth century
they brought not the *contemporary* culture of the West but rather the cultural
achievements of the seventeenth century, particularly in their German garb.

This produced a *décalage*, a discrepancy of at least one generation, between
the newly 'westernized' Russian élite and the contemporary intellectual leadership of Europe. This fact changed the dynamics and specifics of Russia's acquisition of western ideas and knowledge. When, for example, the ideas of the
French Enlightenment began to penetrate into Russia in the second half of
the eighteenth century, they were transformed in the process of their assimilation by Russians who were steeped in the notions of the *Aufklärung*. For this
reason, too, the Russian Enlightenment always had a strong emotional, ethical and spiritual or religious component, so that its impact was to produce different conceptions of individualism, rights, law and of the role of the spiritual
and of authority, a greater concern for the community and for social solidarity—all traits we note in the classics of Russian social and political thought in
the late eighteenth and nineteenth centuries.

Quite obviously, this phenomenon of chronological *décalage* is an important feature in the process of cultural transfer and very relevant for the relationship between the so-called Third World and the modern West or the Soviet Union. In this sense, the history of the Europeanization of Russia may be
considered a paradigm for the process of all cultural transfer.

Be that as it may, Russia's arrival in Europe in the reign of Peter the Great
was not only relatively sudden, unforeseen and dramatic—it gave rise to panic
and to an uneasy sense of expectation of its future role, as A. Lortholary has so
well shown in his classic *Le mirage russe en France au 18e siècle* (Paris, 1951).
The epic hero had been well cured! As a terrified Karl Marx had pointed out,
the eighteenth century was the period of Russia's most dynamic expansion, an
expansion no longer directed to the East and South-East but to the West and
South-West: Peter I acquired the Baltic provinces, Elizabeth expanded her

hold on the Ukraine, Catherine II secured the northern littoral of the Black Sea, began to encroach on the Caucasus, and, as a result of the three partitions of Poland, she brought Russia's territorial boundaries into direct contact with Austria and Prussia—and that was not to be the end of it yet. Quite clearly, this expansion would not have been possible without the institutional machinery for which Peter I had laid the groundwork by importing the methods and organization of the European well-ordered police state as well as the intellectual baggage of the *Aufklärung*.

SEVENTEEN

The Enlightenment in Russia and Russian Thought in the Enlightenment

WITH THE REIGN of Peter the Great Russia entered the eighteenth century, but in his reign, too, 'Europe' moved into Muscovy.

Whether Peter's decision to put Russia into apprenticeship with 'Europe' was revolutionary or not, the fact remains that it did not occur without the country's being prepared for it in some measure. For almost three-quarters of a century before the accession of the great reformer, Moscow had received foreign travellers and residents from countries lying west of Poland.[1] The Foreign Quarter (*nemetskaya sloboda*) was of great importance in the formation of young Peter's outlook. It was here that he spent much of his time, that he was introduced to the pleasures of love and social intercourse, and that he became acquainted with Western technical and scientific expertise.

A few words about the nature of the foreign culture available through the *nemetskaya sloboda* at the end of the seventeenth century may be in order at this point. For all its importance in East European military and diplomatic affairs, Muscovy was still very much on the periphery of Western European consciousness; at best it was a frontier outpost, at worst the beginning of Asia. Only the most adventurous, those unable to find a suitable role for themselves in their homeland or in other Western countries, enrolled in the service of the tsars. Many of them were remarkable characters, but none belonged to what may be called the creative leadership of contemporary European culture. To the Russians they had little to offer beyond practical competence in a relatively narrow speciality. Their general knowledge of contemporary scientific, philosophic, and artistic culture was superficial and limited to what they would have picked up in their youth, i.e. about half a generation earlier. They transmitted slightly outdated factual, theoretical, and artistic knowledge, the kind of knowledge that was the common possession of Western society at large, not the most recent knowledge acquired by its creative and pioneering élite. Or to put it in slightly different terms—Muscovy was exposed to the widely accepted and vulgarized achievements of Western European culture, not to its *avant-garde* discoveries and speculations. There was nothing unusual about this situation: we can observe it in many places in our own days.

Another aspect of cultural contacts at the time of Peter's accession should be kept in mind. With a few relatively unimportant exceptions, the foreigners who contributed their skills and services to Muscovy came from Protestant lands: Holland, England and Scotland, German states. There were perfectly good reasons for this. In the first place the Russians viewed with the greatest suspicion all Catholics; this eliminated the neighbouring Poles and the Latin peoples. Secondly, the ravages of the Thirty Years War, as well as the political and confessional rivalries between the German principalities, limited greatly the opportunities available to the learned and skilled Germans; to a more limited extent this also applied to England and Scotland, which had both gone through long periods of civil and religious strife. Thirdly, Dutchmen and Englishmen had established and retained lively trade contacts with Russia since the sixteenth century, so that the ground was better prepared to attract craftsmen, traders, and technicians from Holland and Britain. In addition, we may also mention that Peter's military victories made available the knowledge and skills of Swedish prisoners of war; and here again we have Protestants whose cultural affiliations were with the Germanies and England. In short, only one group of European nations and men played an active role in first transmitting Western culture to Russia. This situation was to have a lasting effect, as we shall see.

Quite naturally, when Peter the Great adopted policies requiring the expansion of cultural and technical contacts with Western Europe, he addressed himself to the foreigners on the spot to help him contact and recruit newcomers. His own first travels abroad also took him primarily to Germany, Holland, and England, where he personally recruited technicians. Not that other parts of Europe remained completely outside the purview of Peter and his government. For example, a few young noblemen were sent to study in Spain and Venice; but for a variety of reasons their experience had less of an impact than that of students sent to northwestern Europe. Primarily it was a matter of numbers, for many more were sent to Holland and England than to Venice and Spain; but surely the less receptive atmosphere that prevailed in Russia for the Catholic and Mediterranean worlds played a role too.

We are, therefore, not dealing with a single 'Europe' or 'Western culture' which interested the Russians. They did not learn about the 'high' culture of the West European artistic and scientific élites, but they absorbed the applied technology and the 'consumer-oriented' popular culture. Furthermore, not all areas of 'Europe' were equally involved in influencing Russia directly. To be sure, some aspects were shared by all European countries at the time, e.g. the arts; but this was precisely an area of culture in which Russia did not become actively engaged until much later. The fact of several Europes from which one could draw inspiration did not escape the notice of Peter's countrymen. It found expression, for instance, in the opening sentences of a well-known tale of the time, *Povest o rossiyskom matrose Vasilii Koriotskom*, with a reference to Europe*s* (Evropii).[2]

As we survey the process by which Russia entered the eighteenth century, became part of 'Europe', we must keep in mind this basic fact of the existence of several Europes—in both the geographic and the cultural sense. The question then arises which of the 'Europes' had an impact and which ones did not, and why this should be so. A related question is that of the chronology of such impacts.

Conscious assimilation of European culture dates from the reign of Peter the Great in the sense that from this time on the Russian élites endeavoured to reshape Russia in the image of the West, rather than merely to use foreign inventions without transforming the traditional Muscovite pattern, as had been the case in the seventeenth century. As is well known, Peter's main interest, which he imparted to his collaborators, was in the domain of technology. He recruited engineers, shipwrights, architects, naval officers—and instructors in these fields. Concerned also with the development of the economic potential of Russia, especially its manufactures, Peter invited not only foreign industrialists and merchants, but also technicians and craftsmen in various fields such as metallurgy, textiles, glass, mining. Whatever contemporary theoretical, scientific, and philosophic knowledge did penetrate into Russia did so through the mediation of these specialists and had a distinctly subordinate role. The first schools established by Peter did not offer much beyond the pragmatic aspects of the major technical disciplines (mathematics, navigation, artillery). Even such a significant step as the establishment of the Academy of Sciences, largely explains the neglect with which his contributions were treated until the late nineteenth and early twentieth centuries. In opposition to the orientation prevailing at the Academy of Sciences, although suggested by the great speculative thinker Leibniz, was taken with only immediate practical aims in view.

But philosophy and theoretical science did come to Russia along with technology, for in the early eighteenth century the scientific revolution had progressed so far that even for limited practical applications a knowledge of the theoretical framework was required. We must, however, remember that the practitioners usually were somewhat behind the frontiers of speculation and experimentation, and whenever they gave expression to theoretical or philosophical considerations they were those of their mentors a generation earlier. For the history of Russia's cultural development it is also important to note that Leibniz and Christian Wolff were the most influential advisers on scholarly and academic matters in the first third of the eighteenth century. They helped recruit mainly German technicians, scientists, and professors who naturally were often their own followers and pupils. From the very beginning, therefore, in spite of the presence of a few pragmatic Englishmen, the scientific and philosophic orientation of those who came to work in Russia was that of Cartesian rationalism, rather than that of the empiricism of Bacon and Locke.

Towards the end of his life, Peter also became more interested in introducing the arts and social graces to his new capital St. Petersburg. He hired architects and artists to build up Petersburg and the suburban palaces and to organize lavish festivities at which proper etiquette was rigidly enforced. Although the model for the former was naturally Versailles, the chief artists were Italians or Germans trained in Italy.[3] This facet of the process of Europeanization needs further investigation, however. No satisfactory explanation has yet been given why so many Italian architects (e.g. Rastrelli, Quarenghi) and artists should have come to and settled in Russia. Some preliminary considerations may be offered: the French artistic guild had enough to do in Versailles and elsewhere, even during the difficult last years of Louis XIV—and the building boom resumed under the Regency (and kept up until the Revolution). If they left France at all, French artists went for shorter periods to less remote places, to Germany and Austria, for example. For their part, the Italians had influential schools and academies, a great tradition and reputation; but they could not easily find scope for their talents at home.

Thus from the very beginning of the eighteenth century, Russia took in several 'Europes'—the German scientific and philosophic, the Anglo-Dutch technical, and the Italian artistic. More significant than the diversity of geographic origins, however, were the implications that this selection had for the basic intellectual orientation of the early European influences.

The dominant conceptual framework of those foreigners who came to work and teach in Russia was provided by Cartesian rationalism and the philosophies of natural law as expounded and popularized by Pufendorf, Leibniz, and especially Christian Wolff.[4] This intellectual background suggests one reason why the Russians proved more receptive to Cartesian rationalism than to Newton's cosmology and Locke's epistemology. But it could not be the only reason, for after all the Russians were also in close contact with England, and many English or Scottish engineers and teachers (such as Farquharson and Bruce) worked and even settled in Russia in the reign of Peter the Great, as well as subsequently. A further factor in this easy receptivity may lie in the form in which it was presented by the German scholars of the day: Cartesianism seemed to conflict less with traditional Christian dogma and its cosmology. The duality of mind and matter appeared to preserve better traditional cosmological and ontological beliefs than the more radical effort at overcoming this duality by the English empiricists.[5] Another less obvious and even unconscious reason may stem from the fact that empiricism implies a respect for observable reality as the basis of both knowledge and action. Yet it was exactly the reality of Russia that Peter aimed at transforming, and in this aim both his Russian and foreign collaborators concurred. The rationalistic, perhaps abstract, but neat and comprehensive approach of Descartes and German natural-law philosophy could serve as basis for the construction of a new socio-political institutional system without as much regard for an empirical reality that was to be discarded.[6]

The role played by German universities in providing and training scholars and professionals for service in Russia served to anchor this intellectual tradition firmly and preserve its ascendancy in Russian academic and scientific life during the eighteenth century. It was quite natural that it should be so. The German scholars who came to Russia recommended that promising students be sent to those universities where they themselves had studied or taught, and quite naturally too they recommended their own friends and former colleagues for positions in Russia. Thus Peter's physician, Blumentrost, as President of the Academy, appealed to his Alma Mater (Halle) and his contacts there to find suitable candidates for posts at the Academy. While Leibniz himself did not come to Russia he recommended Christian Wolff who played a most active role in suggesting professors, members of the academy, and other professionals to the Russian government. This function was carried on by the scholars who were hired, as is amply demonstrated by their published correspondence with German academies, universities, and individual scholars.[7]

The best-known names—e.g. Mueller, Euler, Schloezer, Pallas, Stählin—were those of individuals connected with the major institution of learning and scholarship in eighteenth-century Russia: the Academy of Sciences. In spite of all efforts made by pre- and post-1917 scholarship to show the rapid Russification of the Academy, the fact remains that until almost the end of the century it was dominated, if not actually run, by German and German-trained scientists and scholars. Of course, in many instances—which grew more frequent as time wore on—a number of these German scholars settled in Russia for good and became partly Russified. Their children, too, followed often in their footsteps, but born and raised in Russia they were in fact bilingual and bicultural, so that in spite of their German names they may be counted among the Russian scholars. Yet even these Russo-German scientists usually received their advanced training in German universities (not until the middle of the nineteenth century was the entire academic training completed in Russia, although even then it was usually followed by a travelling fellowship to a German academy or university). In gauging the intellectual influence exercised by these scholars it should be kept in mind that the Academy's role extended beyond the narrow confines of its purely scientific work. For long periods in the eighteenth century its publications were the most important vehicle for the wide dissemination of general knowledge and cultural interests. Its members were called upon to work for the government (and to assist individual dignitaries) in planning and implementing in a variety of areas concerning all facets of the country's public life. Individual members of the Academy were also active in various educational and scientific institutions in the capital, for example the Corps of Cadets, the Imperial Free Economic Society, and the like. They thus had many opportunities to make an impact on Russian educated society in general, to popularize and maintain throughout the eighteenth century the basic philosophic conceptions and intellectual orientations which had taken shape in Germany in the late seventeenth century.

Of the many German universities that could provide well-trained scholars, scientists, and technicians and also serve to educate selected Russian students, only a few in fact did play this role to any significant degree. These were the universities of Halle, Marburg, Leipzig,[8] and at the very end of the century Göttingen.[9] Why these universities, particularly Halle, Marburg, and Leipzig? Professor E. Winter and his study group in Berlin have pointed out the main factor: Pietism.[10] The philosophical light of Pietism, Christian Wolff, whose role in staffing Russia with academicians we have noted earlier, was the major influence in Halle and later in Marburg. Leipzig, too, remained under strong pietist influence throughout the century.

We have also to consider what may at first glance appear as paradox. In modern estimation, the most significant intellectual achievements in Russia in the first half of the eighteenth century were the works of 'loners' whose importance and influence were recognized by their fellow-countrymen only very much later. The earliest modern Russian poet, Prince Antiokh Kantemir, something of a Renaissance man, was much influenced not only by French poetics (Boileau in particular), but also by the cosmology of Newton and the epistemological ideas of Locke.[11] Kantemir's contemporary, V. N. Tatishchev, too, displayed a strong empirical bent in his scholarly and scientific interests. A 'fledgling of Peter's nest', a pragmatic administrator, he tended to view all scientific and scholarly problems in terms of their usefulness for better administration and more effective economic development. His philosophical writings were, it is true, couched in fashionable German mould, but his research was carried on in the positivistic and empirical tradition of a Francis Bacon. Neither Kantemir's nor Tatishchev's philosophical ideas and scientific work made an immediate impact on Russian intellectual development. Kantemir's advocacy of Newton and Locke was ignored, while Tatishchev's manifold contributions to the study of geography, geology, history, climatology, etc. remained buried in his papers. Aside from the facts that Kantemir spent a large part of his adult life abroad (he died in Paris after a six-year assignment as ambassador in London) and that Tatishchev's cantankerous character limited his personal contacts with colleagues, their lack of influence in their own time may be explained by the fact that they did not share the prevailing intellectual orientation based on Cartesian rationalism and the natural-law philosophies taught by the Germans.[12]

An even more interesting illustration is provided by the career and reputation of the universal scientific and literary genius, M. V. Lomonosov. He himself was a product of German pietist schools (Marburg, Freiberg), in both science and literature. At first he followed in the footsteps of his mentors; for example, he translated the most popular and influential Wolffian textbook of physics into Russian. In the realm of literature he never went beyond this German influence, which may explain why this side of his genius found immediate resonance and recognition abroad as well as at home, and supported his reputation for a long time to come. But in his scientific work, especially chemistry, he freed himself from his teachers. In many ways his intuitions and inklings were of a very advanced nature and put in question many *idées reçues* of his time, especially Cartesian physics and Wolffian cosmology. This fact alone, apart from his bad personal relations with the German scholars at the Academy of Sciences, largely explains the neglect with which his contributions were treated until the late nineteenth and early twentieth centuries. In opposition to the orientation prevailing at the Academy of Sciences, Lomonosov was instrumental in organizing another institution of higher learning, the University of Moscow; but it did not come into its own until more than half a century after his death.[13]

What is the explanation for the profound influence exercised by the German academic—i.e. scholarly and scientific—orientation that lasted throughout the eighteenth century and even beyond? Some factors come to mind immediately. The late seventeenth and early eighteenth centuries witnessed a German intellectual and scholarly 'imperialistic drive' under the aegis of the pietist circles of Halle. For the sake of the reconstitution of Christian unity and the bringing together of Asia and Europe culturally as well as economically, the Pietists endeavoured to develop contacts and gain influence in Eastern European countries. As a little-explored and potentially valuable and powerful land, Russia was an obvious target. The Pietists' programme happened to dovetail with Peter's own plans for the modernization and economic development of Russia. He thus was happy to receive the merchants, technicians, and scholars trained at Halle who were recommended to him by Leibniz, Chr. Wolff, and his own physician Blumentrost, a graduate of Halle. On the other hand, the religious, political, and economic fragmentation of the German states drove many scholars and scientists to look for better opportunities in the unknown and promising empire of the tsars. Those who went first to Russia used their personal connections to draw in others and to help send Russians to Germany for study and training. Naturally, there was also the factor of proximity, for France and Italy were further away (and less penetrable to Protestant proselytism). As for the English and the Dutch, they had enough outlets for their energy in their own land or empire without seeking fortune else-where.

But on a deeper level, we must try to identify the reasons why the orienta-tion of Halle, as represented by the philosophy of Chr. Wolff and his pupils, was particularly congenial to the government and educated classes of Russia. In the first place was their sincere and complete acceptance of Christian doc-trine and the injunction to obey constituted authorities, an attitude most wel-come to a monarch jealous of his absolute power. No less significant a factor was the Wolffian interpretation of natural law. It stressed the conceptions of obligation and duty as the prerequisite of individual rights, in contrast to the 'possessive individualism' of the Hobbesian and Lockean tradition. It also gave priority to the community and to social institutions over and against the claims of the autonomous individual, as emphasized by the English and French notions of natural rights. Such an orientation, buttressed by a strong belief in a neo-stoicism which assigned a major role to human will and activity within the framework of generally valid universal moral laws, appealed to a service-oriented society dedicated to total change of traditional circum-stances. The doctrines taught by Wolff and his followers gave moral and philo-sophic sanction to the goal-directed, wilful, active state administration that Peter the Great had rooted in Russia.[14]

Wolff's original teaching at Halle and Marburg was carried on and further developed in Leipzig. This city served both Russia and 'Europe' as the main clearing-house of information pertaining to all fields of learning. In addition, its university remained a major centre of natural-law jurisprudence in the eighteenth century and was selected by the Russian government for advanced training of prospective officials. Its most famous Russian graduate was to be Alexander Radishchev, who drew much inspiration from the natural-law doc-trines of Leipzig jurists, and took good advantage of the opportunity it of-fered for becoming acquainted with pietist spiritualism, as well as with the most recent European philosophical literature. But Leipzig not only had a university, it was a publishing centre as well and its major periodical publica-tion, *Neue Zeitungen von gelehrten Sachen,* was a principal source of informa-tion for both Russians and Germans on what was going on in their respective countries. In Leipzig, too, the moralistic and sentimental literary circle around Gottsched maintained contacts with Russia. It played a significant role in preparing Russian literary taste for an easy acceptance of the *Sturm und Drang* and of English sentimentalism.[15] This continuing role of contacts with pietistically oriented universities and cultural centres should be kept in mind in any description of the gradual Westernization of Russian intellectual life.

From the social and economic points of view, Russia was closer to most German states than to the more advanced trading and manufacturing Holland and England or the immensely wealthy France. From the time of Peter I the Russian government was acutely aware of the necessity for developing the empire's potential resources. This had to be accomplished within an antiquated and unwieldy socio-institutional framework (e.g. lack of an entrepreneurial class) compelling reliance on state leadership and rational planning. Thus Russia seemed most suitable for the application of the precepts and practices of *Kameral- und Polizeiwissenschaften* which had been developed in response to similar circumstances in German lands. German-trained jurists, therefore, like Strube de Piermont, proved most influential in developing Russian legal and social doctrines; Justi and Bielefeldt influenced Catherine's political and economic outlook, while the Austrian enlightened cameralist Sonnenfels and the pedagogue Jankevich de Mirievo provided her with practical models for institutional reforms.

Naturally, many Germans in Russian service (although their number should not be exaggerated) contributed to preserve the intellectual orientations adopted in the beginning of the eighteenth century and to maintain active contacts and exchanges with German centres. To the extent that its members participated in Russian public life (not as extensively as is often believed) the nobility from the Baltic provinces also kept up the popularity and relevance of German ideas and scholarship. Finally, let us not forget the role of the German private tutor and of the teacher in boarding schools and corps of cadets (organized on the model of *Ritterakademien*) who were the main providers of Western culture and education to the majority of the Russian nobility in the eighteenth century. They were displaced only gradually, and never completely, by Frenchmen after 1789. Their teaching, based on an acceptance of the social and political *status quo*, emphasized the virtues of service, duty, and communal responsibility as opposed to individual rights.[16]

For lack of space we must leave out consideration of the influence of Italy (mainly in the arts), Spain, England, and Scandinavia.[17] We shall turn now to an examination of what at first glance may seem paradoxical within the context of French cultural influence, usually identified with that of the Enlightenment. That such an identification cannot be taken for granted, the preceding pages have tried to show, for the German *Aufklärung*, whose impact we have described, differed from the Anglo-French *lumières*.

On the surface French literary, artistic, and social models dominate the scene in Russia from the middle of the eighteenth century. But they do not inform the profounder and more basic aspects of the evolution of Russian culture and thought. Even when French philosophy and political thought provided inspiration to the Russians, the latter did not follow through their implications. We have noted that Descartes—by way of his German interpreters—contributed the basic framework of Russia speculative thought in the beginning of the eighteenth century. Yet the implications of Cartesian thought, exemplified by the scepticism of Bayle, the scientific empiricism of the *Encyclopédie*, the ironical cynicism of Voltaire, were ignored by the Russians, even though they had access to them. In spite of his popularity with Catherine

II and her court, Voltaire's ideas played only a small role in shaping the public mind and culture of the Russian educated élite.[18] Voltairianism became synonymous with mockery of the Church, but for this there was a healthy native tradition in the satirical tales of the seventeenth century, to which Voltaire only gave a more attractive and modern form.

Another telling example is provided by the reception of Montesquieu's ideas. Catherine II drew heavily on him in the compilation of her *Nakaz* and thus gave him *droit de cité* in Russia. Yet, as F. Taranovsky has convincingly demonstrated, Catherine not only disregarded many essential elements of the President's thought, she consciously chose to misinterpret him.[19] Rejecting Montesquieu's faith in the *corps intermédiaires* to preserve the nation's liberties, Catherine relied on an active bureaucracy to create the conditions of modern civilized life and thereby completely perverted the intentions as well as meaning of the *Spirit of the Laws*. Furthermore, when it came to practical institutional reforms, Catherine turned not to French models or writers (she talked to Diderot but pointedly refused to heed his advice), but to the Cameralists who were recommended by the German scholars in Russia, to some of her advisers (e.g. Sievers), and to Joseph II of Austria.[20] Even as moderate a reformer as the Physiocrat Mercier de la Rivière was poorly received in Russia when he came upon Catherine's invitation (in part, but only in part, his own arrogant vanity may have contributed to this reception).[21] His ideas proved too far removed from Russian reality and experience to have much impact, let alone application in Catherine's empire. It is true that in the discussions and labours of the Free Economic Society we detect a significant stream of Physiocracy, but it is much diluted with German Cameralism.

What is then left with respect to French influence? To be sure, French literature had a profound impact on Russian letters (as it did on all other European literatures), especially at the high tide of the popularity of neoclassicism. At Court and in the fashionable drawing-rooms of the richest dignitaries, French drama and novels were dominant. But even here we should exercise caution. This influence was never a monopoly. German critics and writers of the eighteenth century, Lessing, Gottsched, Gellert, Klopstock, and lastly Wieland, vied for popularity and influence with the French. As to 'second-rate' literature directed at a wide and not very sophisticated audience—the almanacs and journals for children, women, and the provincial nobility—they were full of selections translated or adapted from similar German publications.[22] Russian eighteenth-century literature is as much the product of German influence as it is a conscious imitation of French models (besides native tradition, and other Slavic literatures, of course). It is no accident that Lomonosov, Derzhavin, and Karamzin knew German before they learned French and that their first models and inspirations were German writers and critics (or classical works in German translation). Even English sentimental literature often came to Russia through German adaptations and translations. This circumstance may also explain the vogue and rapid assimilation of sentimental and pre-romantic literature which culminated in the extraordinary impact of Schiller's early works.[23] It also prepared the ground for the easy and rapid reception of German idealistic philosophy in the late eighteenth and early nineteenth centuries.

Our discussion leads us to the heart of the problem of influences and interconnections between West European culture and Russia in the eighteenth century. On an obvious and superficial level French influence appears in retrospect to have been so great because the Court and aristocracy aped French manners (and were satirized for it), because French novels and plays were much read for entertainment, and because Catherine II and her courtiers sang paeans of praise to the best-known French *philosophes*. After the outbreak of the French Revolution the writings of Voltaire, Diderot, Rousseau, etc. were blamed for the misdeeds of the revolutionaries; the impression was created that they had influenced Russian society much more than was actually the case. It is of course quite true that the French language became the vehicle for social intercourse at Court and in high society. In many instances, too, German and English ideas and works made their first appearance in French garb. The reason for this is not far to seek: French had become the universal language of polite society, so much so that even the German academic establishment frequently resorted to it in order to be read and appreciated by the upper classes. But to speak (and read) French is a far cry from absorbing the ideas of the *philosophes*. Russian readers, except a very few, did not have the sophistication and knowledge necessary to penetrate beneath the entertaining outward gloss to the barbed intellectual core of the literature of the French Enlightenment.[24]

Selection also took place in the case of German culture. The notions of natural law prepared the ground for the development of Russian philosophic and social theories.[25] Their greatest contribution was to set forth the moral and juridical foundations of the social bond and the primacy of duties towards the collective. The metaphysical and epistemological connotations were left out of consideration altogether by the Russians. As for Pietism, the specifically Protestant contents of its teachings and *Weltanschauung* proved to have no appeal in Russia. But Pietism reinforced the bent to individual mysticism and *kenosis* ever present in Russian orthodoxy and it helped to revive a deepening of personal religious life. The need for a deeper spiritual religious experience became strongly felt in the eighteenth century after Peter's and Prokopovich's *Spiritual Regulation (Dukhovny reglament)* had virtually deprived the established Church of its spiritual mission. Furthermore, Pietism propagated a social ethic which focused attention on the satisfaction of the physical and intellectual needs of man if he were to become a worthy and spiritually complete human being. In short, it represented a commitment to rational and socially oriented philanthropy. In view of the low material level and inadequate spiritual condition of the Russian people, such a commitment played a significant role in making the educated élite aware of the human condition of the serfs and of its duty towards them.

Another aspect of the process of selectivity among the foreign ideas available to Russia in the eighteenth century was the chronological dimension. Indeed, no one cultural complex was imported and absorbed *in toto* at one time. In any given period some specific elements of a foreign culture might appeal more strongly than others. As the Russian educated élite matured and acquired an ever wider range of 'Western' ideas and values, its receptivity grew while the focus of its interests changed. Following upon the uncritical and mechanical acceptance of the rationalist *Weltanschauung* of the early eighteenth century there came a period of adaptation of the foreign elements to Russian tradition. There also developed a greater capacity for an aesthetic appreciation and enjoyment of foreign literary and artistic creations. And it took still longer before the Russians understood and were able to make use of the dynamic creative elements at the core of foreign philosophies, ideologies, and values.

When the latter had become possible, the range of influences and choices had broadened as well. Let us illustrate this with one example: educational ideas and practices. The early educational efforts of Peter the Great aimed at giving the Russian service noblemen the outward manners and forms of Western gentlemen. This went together with an almost encyclopaedic factual and practical training, quite reminiscent of Rabelaisian pedagogy. To this end it was sufficient to ape the rigid curricula and harsh methods of education practised in the *Ritterakademien* and Jesuit schools. But there soon developed a need to absorb the basic intellectual elements of Western expertise, the dynamic sources, so to speak, of its progress, which was first done in the extracurricular activities of the Corps of Cadets (translations, dramatic performances, literary magazines, etc.). As time went on it was realized that Western education was not merely a matter of acquiring the external appurtenances of French or German courtiers or the practical skills of foreign officers. It was rather the formation of men who not only would fully appreciate and know the new culture but would also contribute to its creative process. Hence the desire to raise and educate receptive and intellectually creative individuals, such as were found in Western intellectual circles. As a result, by the beginning of the second half of the century, the Russians became interested in the educational ideas of Locke. While they still retained their negative stance with respect to his epistemological empiricism the Russians turned to Locke because of his focus on the human being who would result from a total education of the young child. But the Russians' interest—in part also aroused by Pietism—in the spiritual and psychological development of their youth arose at a time when another educational theorist had become popular in the West—Jean-Jacques Rousseau. Thus in Russia the adoption of Locke came at the same time as an infatuation with Rousseau's pedagogical ideas. The latter part of the eighteenth century witnessed a reorientation in educational theory and practice—best exemplified by the activities of Ivan Betskoy and the writings of Nikolay Novikov and Ivan Pnin—which combined an emphasis on knowledge with a concern for the spiritual and moral development of the child. Their aim was to create a new type of Russian, the 'true son of the fatherland', dedicated to the good—in a moral and spiritual, as well as political and social, sense.

Our example from the history of pedagogy has also shown that chronological discrepancies in the absorption of various foreign elements may create a dynamics significantly different from that of each element singly in its original intellectual constellation. Thus Locke's ideas received a very different tonality—emotional, moral, and spiritually passionate—by their being absorbed concurrently with Rousseau's. We find a similar situation with respect to the writings of the French *philosophes*, where both the elements of selectivity and of temporal discrepancy were present. A single instance may suffice: Alexander Radishchev. After the usual training in the Corps of Cadets Radishchev was sent to complete his studies at the University of Leipzig. There he studied natural-law jurisprudence which dominated the curriculum; a course of study which, along with the difficulties experienced by the Russian students in Leipzig, heightened his moral awareness and religious and spiritual concerns. At the same time Radishchev was also reading the most recent literature of the West. He became acquainted not so much with the founders of the French Enlightenment—Montesquieu, Voltaire, the Encyclopaedists—as with the second generation of *philosophes*. As has been well shown by G. Gurvitch, this later generation—Mably, Raynal, Helvétius, and of course Rousseau—had become aware of the social dimensions of individual rights, of the need to change the entire body of institutions if man was to have a freer development of his potential. Theirs was a more philanthropic, spiritual, moralistic, community-oriented, and in a way more radical, or utopian, bent of mind. For Radishchev the combination of German jurisprudence and Pietism and French radical Enlightenment proved to be a potent mixture. It became not only the foundation of his later thinking, but also provided the impetus for his fateful decision to broadcast openly his moral indignation at the conditions of the Russian serfs, a decision which led finally to his martyrdom and hallowed role in the revolutionary tradition of the nineteenth century. Indeed his famous *Journey from St. Petersburg to Moscow* echoes not so much the barbed but moderate criticism of Voltaire or the historical relativism of Montesquieu as the spiritual earnestness of the Pietists and the passionate commitment to the moral dimension in social relations that had been popularized by Rousseau and illustrated by Raynal. Finally, the mixture gave rise to Radishchev's belief in the possibility of complete institutional change on the basis of a true moral insight of all citizens and through the agency of an enlightened autocrat or state.

Perhaps the same phenomenon may also be illustrated from a different perspective. Russian absorption of the various elements of modern European culture took place over a period of time in discrete segments. During the first two-thirds of the eighteenth century these various elements were taken in separately and they coexisted on different planes without interpenetrating (e.g. the insulation of scholarship from the rest of Russian cultural life until the 1770s when it began to be incorporated into educational and institutional policy). Sooner or later, of course, these discrete and disjoined elements had to come together, since all facets of modern civilization are interrelated. It seems to be a general need of human civilization to formulate an all-embracing and creative *Weltanschauung* and not be content with a mechanical and inert assemblage of separate cultural elements. The urge for a broad interconnection and synthesis led to the discovery of implications that had lain dormant: for instance, the philanthropic, educational, and moralistic elements we have noted earlier, along with pietist spiritual precepts (and the Pugachev rebellion perhaps acting as catalyst), led to the discovery of the emotional and moral worth of the Russian peasant and of the élite's obligations to him.[26]

Awareness of their interconnections fostered deeper study and better understanding of each of the various elements, and made possible a greater degree of professionalism in all branches of knowledge. Various disciplines that heretofore had been viewed superficially as a necessary but external adornment of the educated Russian were beginning to be seriously studied for their own sake at the end of the eighteenth century. Juridical and scientific disciplines, as well as literature and the arts, were no longer seen as facile entertainment (or minimal skill for a career) but treated as activities with a significant philosophical and social dimension. Viewing the various fields of human endeavour in their interconnected totality enabled members of the Russian élite to endow them with a greater existential force or passion. It led to a fusion of their professional and artistic competence and interest in the emotional, moral pathos of their own experiences and ideals. The educated Russian gained a sense of purpose, of a humanly significant commitment that transcended the immediate task in hand. In this manner the Russians came to inject into the critical and analytical ideas of eighteenth-century Enlightenment an almost romantic passion, a moral concern. The ideas of the *philosophes* became radicalized existentially; intellectual activity ceased to be a mere play activity of the mind and became the serious commitment of 'the true sons of the fatherland'.

If our observations are correct, they may explain what seems at first glance somewhat strange: the immediate and total acceptance of romantic idealistic philosophies (and literature) while retaining a rationalistic and Enlightenment form of thought. The heady mixture received its fullest expression in the socialism of the first generation of the Russian intelligentsia in the 1840s (Alexander Herzen). But we see its first signs in the Decembrists who were the sons of the eighteenth century. It is in this sense that Russia made a belated, but very important contribution to the heritage of Western Enlightenment.

But did not the return current—from Russian culture to the West—manifest itself before the 1840s, in the eighteenth century? This is a most difficult question to answer as yet, because so little work has been done in this area. We can only make a few preliminary observations. The amount of information on Russia available in the West to an ever wider public was growing steadily and by the end of the eighteenth century it was far from being negligible. Russia had ceased to be a wondrous 'rude and barbarous kingdom', even though it remained on the periphery of Western civilization. In academic and literary circles there was available the latest information on discoveries and inventions in Russia thanks to the permanent contacts and exchanges between scholars of German origin active in Russia and German universities, academies, and scholarly publications. As for official news, Peter the Great had initiated the subsidizing of European 'public opinion makers', and in this respect no one was more brilliantly successful than Catherine II in her correspondence with the *philosophes*. The work of Lomonosov was known and often appreciated at its full value. Some Russian works of literature also became known in translation (Kantemir, Derzhavin, Karamzin).[27] As far as we can make out, however, from the spotty evidence brought to light so far, the West reacted with amusement rather than genuine interest, let alone understanding. It was an amusement mixed with condescending pride, as if to say 'look how well they have learned from us, how fast they are becoming civilized!'—the benign and patronizing praise of an older relative for the nice progress of a child, but of a child *tout de même*.[28]

With respect to politics, however, the impact made by this 'child' on the consciousness of Western Europe was significant indeed. On the most superficial level was the realization of the political and military potential of the huge empire. On an intellectual plane knowledge about Russia reinforced the sense of cultural and social relativism and expanded the horizon of the educated élite in the West. We know how much the sense of an expanded universe and of the infinite variety of human and natural phenomena contributed to the shaping of modern Western consciousness. The *philosophes* used this newly acquired awareness to promote their belief in progress, toleration, and liberty.

Finally, in a most direct and significant way Russia provided the *philosophes* with a great object-lesson. The reign of Peter the Great (as it was known and interpreted)[29] and the subsequent programme of Catherine II seemed to demonstrate that enlightened reason and wilful energy could transform society and lay the foundation for the improvement of the human race. If Peter and Catherine, in the true spirit of enlightened despotism, had indeed been able to Westernize Muscovite institutions and transform the Russian nobles into 'Europeans', i.e. civilized, cultured human beings, then the *philosophes'* belief in progress and man's capacity for self-improvement was fully vindicated. The success was not as complete as yet as one might wish; but Russia had shown the way.[30]

At the end of the eighteenth century the tsar's empire stood as a warning to conservatives, or as a promise to the radicals, of what rationalism at the service of autocratic power could accomplish. It is in this sense that the eighteenth century in Russia also turned into Russian influence on eighteenth-century Europe.

Notes

1. Not to mention the powerful influence that came by way of the Ukraine, especially through the mediation of the Kievan Graeco-Latin-Slavonic Academy. But it was mainly felt in ecclesiastical circles.

2. The phrase occurs, it is true, in a context identifying the European part of Russia, but the use of the plural—be it only to indicate an opposition between Russia and Europe—is significant enough. 'Povest o rossiyskom matrose Vasilii Koriotskom', in G. N. Moiseeva, ed., *Russkie povesti pervoy treti XVIII veka* (Moscow and Leningrad, 1965), 191–210.

3. Although Dutch models (and presumably architects) were used in planning the residential sections and quarters of St. Petersburg, Cf. E. Beletskaya, N. Krasheninnikova, L. Chernozubova, I. Ern, *'Obraztsovye' proekty v zhiloy zastroyke russkikh gorodov XVIII–XIX vv.* (Moscow, 1961), ch. 1. On artistic life see, among others, the interesting memoirs of the future President of the Academy of Fine Arts, Karl Stählin, *Aus den Papieren Jacob von Stählins, Ein biographischer Beitrag zur deutsch-russischen Kulturgeschichte des 18. Jahrhunderts* (Königsberg i. Pr. und Berlin, 1926).

4. We find this influence also in Feofan Prokopovich (especially in his *Pravda voli monarshey*). It remained a vital element in the curricula of the ecclesiastical schools throughout the eighteenth century and in this way affected also the clergy, and sons of clergy who went into government service and scholarship and literature.

5. See the suggestive observations of Robert Lenoble, *Esquisse d'une histoire de l'idée de Nature* (Paris, 1969), 2ᵉ partie, ch. 4.

6. This is not to deny Peter the Great's pragmatism. But he did frequently act as if he conceived himself in the role of a secular creator giving the well-known 'chiquenaude' to put the new social and institutional machine in motion.

7. For example, A. Juškević and E. Winter, *Die Berliner und die Petersburger Akademie der Wissenschaften im Briefwechsel Leonhard Eulers*, 2 vols. (Berlin, 1959–61); E. Winter, ed., *August Ludwig v. Schlözer und Russland* (Berlin, 1961).

8. Connections with Russia seem also to have been maintained by the universities of Greifswald and Königsberg—these are in the process of being studied by East German and Russian scholars.

9. Göttingen, founded in the middle of the eighteenth century, did not play a very influential role until the end of the century when Schlözer received the chair of statistics and political economy after leaving Russia. The heyday of Göttingen's role in the education of young Russians was in the first decade of the nineteenth century when it helped popularize a liberal cameralism in Russian economic thought.

10. M. Raeff, 'Les Slaves, les Allemands et les "Lumières"', *Canadian Slavic Studies*, i, no. 4 (1967), 521–51 and the literature cited therein.

11. Kantemir's cosmopolitan education was quite exceptional for a Russian in his time. See the interesting unpublished doctoral dissertation of V. Boss, 'Newton's influence in Eighteenth Century Russia' (Harvard University, 1962).

12. Of course national rivalries of the level of academic politics and influence played a role too, but their effects should not be exaggerated.

13. G. Mühlpfordt, 'Lomonosov und die Mitteldeutsche Aufklärung', *Studien zur Geschichte der russischen Literatur des 18. Jahrhunderts*, ii (Berlin, 1968), 135–231, and the same author's 'Leipzig als Brennpunkt der internationalen Wirkung Lomonosovs', ibid. iii (1968), 271–416.

14. Another aspect of this orientation was the church settlement on the Protestant model imposed by Peter and Feofan Prokopovich. Cf. also my book, *Origins of the Russian Intelligentsia* (New York, 1966), ch. 3.

15. G. Mühlpfordt, 'Leipzig als Brennpunkt der internationalen Wirkung Lomonosovs', *Studien zur Geschichte der russichen Literatur des 18. Jahrhunderts*, iii (Berlin, 1968).

16. The role of the ecclesiastical schools, especially in the Ukraine where they were attended also by the nobility, is a chapter in itself for which there is no space here. Suffice it to say that they too strongly emphasized the German natural-law and scholastic traditions.

17. The history of English influence has not been adequately studied as yet. For a very superficial and preliminary survey, strongly focused on *belles-lettres*, cf. Ernest G. Simmons's book *English Literature and Culture in Russia (1553–1840)* (Cambridge, Mass., 1935); cf. also the informative pioneering study by Iu. D. Levin, 'Angliyskaya prosvetitelskaya zhurnalistika v russkoy literature XVIII veka', *Epokha Prosveshcheniya, Iz istorii mezhdunarodnykh svyazey russkoy literatury* (Leningrad, 1967), pp. 3–109. In any event, the most significant impact came very late in the eighteenth century and bore its fruits only in the nineteenth.

18. This is not to deny the popularity of his novels as entertainment.

19. F. Taranovsky, 'Politicheskaya doktrina v Nakaze imperatritsy Ekateriny II', *Sbornik statey po istorii prava, posvyashchennykh Vladimirskomu-Budanovu* (Kiev, 1904), pp. 44–86.

20. Montesquieu's influence, however, was to be felt quite strongly in the nineteenth century, e.g. among the scholarly Decembrists.

21. V. Bilbasov, 'Merse de la River i N. I. Panin', *Istoricheskie monografii*, iv (St. Petersburg, 1901).

22. There obviously was also a non-Westernized popular literature circulating among townspeople, merchants, clergymen, and small noblemen. Unfortunately, there exists no study of this material.

23. Hans-Bernd Harder, *Schiller in Russland—Materialen zu einer Wirkungsgeschichte 1789–1814,* Frankfurter Beiträge zur Germanistik, Bd. iv (Bad Homburg, Berlin, Zürich, 1969), is the most comprehensive and recent survey.

24. This is still the case with the average Soviet reader of Western literature, mainly fiction—cf. the pertinent observations by Andrey Amalrik, *Will the Soviet Union Survive Until 1984?* (New York, 1970).

25. The scholastic and natural-law elements of the curriculum of ecclesiastical

schools and academies played an important role here too, especially if we remember that most members of the first generation of Russian academics and scholars had been graduates of such schools.

26. J. L. Van Regemorter, 'Deux images idéales de la paysannerie russe à la fin du XVIIIe siècle', *Cahiers du monde russe et soviétique,* ix, no. 1 (1968), 5–19.

27. Besides the articles of Mühlpfordt cited earlier and some other contributions in the same collection, a recent study illuminates this phenomenon on the English side. A. G. Cross, 'Arcticus and the *Bee* (1790–4): An Episode in Anglo-Russian Cultural Relations', *Oxford Slavonic Papers,* N.S. ii (1969), 62–76.

28. D. S. von Mohrenschildt, *Russia in the Intellectual Life of 18th Century France* (New York, 1936), and the more comprehensive and recent account of A. Lortholary, *Le mirage russe en France au XVIIIe siècle* (Paris, 1951).

29. The image was mainly the creation of Voltaire—cf. on this Lortholary, op. cit., E. F. Shmurlo, *Pëtr Veliky v otsenke sovremennikov i potomstva,* vyp. i, *XVIII vek* (St. Petersburg, 1912).

30. The critique of abbé Chappe d'Auteroche reads very much like genuine disappointment that things have not succeeded as completely as he had been made to believe, or had hoped. A similar attitude was to be displayed by the famous Marquis de Custine half a century later.

EIGHTEEN

The Well-Ordered Police State and the Development of Modernity in Seventeenth- and Eighteenth-Century Europe

An Attempt at a Comparative Approach

TRADITIONALLY, WESTERN HISTORIOGRAPHY traces the origins of the so-called modern world to the Enlightenment and the revolutionary waves, political and economic, at the end of the eighteenth century. These eighteenth-century origins are related to the rise of a new social class and its triumph over the *ancien régime* as a precondition for the unfolding of the two major aspects of modern civilization—capitalism and statism. But is this view not oversimple? We historians know all too well—and recent scholarship repeatedly reminds us of it—that the past is much more tenacious than public opinion imagines it to be. Little of the past is every fully lost, though its dynamic role may change and its forms be transmuted.

With respect to state policy and administration, the question arises whether the new ideas of the Enlightenment and the interests of a rising middle class helped to shape the actions of rulers and governments before the French Revolution. Was not the enlightened despotism (or "absolutism," as I would prefer to call it) such a response to intellectual and social pressures? But the very contradiction inherent in the notion of enlightened absolutism doomed the effort to failure and opened the way to the storm of revolution.[1] We may ask, therefore, whether older administrative practices, mental sets, and political traditions, as well as the leadership of established groups, were not more sig-

nificant than the demands of an emerging class and the rhetoric of a new ideology.

At the center of any consideration of the significance of the European historical heritage is the question of the roots of "modernity"—that is, the origins of "modernization" as a significant element of the social, economic, and
political dynamics of the last century and a half, at first in the West and, more
recently, elsewhere on our globe. Without pretending to offer a clear-cut, all-
encompassing, and unassailable definition of a phenomenon that has so many
facets, it is necessary to suggest at least a working descriptive definition to lend
some clarity and cohesion to our discussion and analysis. For heuristic purposes I would suggest the following as conveying the essence of what we call
"modern," as opposed to earlier, "traditional" European and non-European
patterns of culture: what may be detected in the second half of the seventeenth century—and what emerged into the open in the eighteenth in most of
Western and Central Europe—is society's conscious desire to maximize all its
resources and to use this new potential dynamically for the enlargement and
improvement of its way of life. The potential of resources includes not merely
material products and riches, but intellectual and cultural creations as well.[2]
But conscious action implies a goal, and such a goal must be related to a more
or less clear notion of the nature of human behavior and social relationships,
as well as a scale of ethical norms. This development, as I hope to suggest, had
its beginnings in the second half of the seventeenth century and reached its
full flowering by the middle of the eighteenth century. The absolute state provided the framework for public, political action, while rationalism gave the
philosophic underpinning. If this chronology proves indeed to be correct,
then the revolutionary convulsions of the last quarter of the eighteenth century were only aftereffects of the process, rather than its antecedent stimulus.

*   *   *

It is a historiographical cliché that, since the early sixteenth century, centralizing monarchical absolutism was the ascendant political system in Europe, a
system whose precursors were to be found in Burgundy, Tudor England, and
late Valois France, while its apogee was reached with Louis XIV. In our context, however, it is more important to note that the system reached an early
and full expression, albeit on a small scale, in German states after the Thirty
Years' War. A major factor was the success of the Reformation, which, in eliminating the Church as the main contestant for authority, enabled the prince to
become the sole source of all regulatory power in his domains. It may seem
ironic that an essentially "medieval" concern for the spiritual paved the way
for the prince's new secular power. Indeed the Reformation, by eliminating,
in Protestant lands, the traditional ecclesiastic institutions—while emphasizing the ethical concerns of the faith—encouraged the secular power to exer-

cise its authority fully in all domains of public and private life. Since the Church (i.e., the papacy) no longer offered religious guidance and moral control, the prince had to act so that the true Christian moral purpose of society be preserved and fostered. Not surprisingly, therefore, we encounter the first significant examples of the interventionist and regulatory *Polizeistaat* in the Protestant states of Germany, such as Saxony and Hessen, in the second half of the sixteenth century.[3] This political pattern, on the model of medieval town and gild controls, took somewhat longer to strike roots in Catholic states, not only in the large ones, such as France and Spain, but also in the smaller principalities of Italy and Germany, where control of public life was shared by the supranational Roman Church and its local institutions.

The Thirty Years' War reinforced the dynamics inherent in this political system. Not only did the ravages of war have to be repaired, but the military revolution of the mid-seventeenth century had created new demands:[4] the large-scale building of fortifications and strategic roads and the maintenance of permanent, regular armies that fell on the ruler (i.e., the state) instead of the feudal services and private entrepreneurs as of old.[5] In addition, though in a way difficult to assess specifically, the "baroque spirit" that had captivated most of Europe, even the more puritanical Protestant courts, in the wake of sixteenth-century Spain, involved great public displays which, in turn, required greater domestic productivity and livelier international trade.[6] The latter was, of course, enhanced by the new fashions and style of life made possible by the colonial expansion overseas.[7] In spite of the efforts at limiting its scope and effects, the urge to consume, and to consume conspicuously, was growing fast in seventeenth-century Europe.

These circumstances led the state (i.e., the prince and his administration) to act as pump primer in promoting and protecting the productive potential of society. There is no need to stress also the fact that this dynamic intensification of the state's role in the economic, social, and cultural domains was taking place in the context of a Europe divided politically and confessionally. Each state, large or small, endeavored to rely as much as possible on its own resources to provide the wherewith for its military, political, and court establishments in order to maximize its own power and avoid enhancing that of its neighbors.[8] The result was the set of policies that go under the names of cameralism and mercantilism, policies designed to accumulate monetary reserves and to achieve self-sufficiency through state subsidy, control, and protection.[9]

The theoretical justification of this conception of government presents an interesting blend of the spiritual and material, or secular, as befits Protestantism. The point of departure is the notion of the ruler's duty to safeguard the spiritual life of his subjects, to enable them to live the good Christian life and prepare themselves for salvation. This is nothing more than the medieval conception of life in society, for in this respect the Reformation marked a return to the spiritual traditions of the Middle Ages.[10] In another sense, however, focus on the spiritual also implied active concern for the material as its necessary precondition, and therein lay the modernity of the Reformation—the *vita activa* fully displaced the passive, ascetic ideal of the *vita contemplativa* as the desirable form of the most rewarding Christian way of life.[11]

Emphasis on the moral and material goals of administration came naturally to a ruler and his government that had to fight for survival on the international stage and at the same time try to benefit from the expanding imperial, cultural, and economic horizons. A strong independent government and a powerful ruler were believed to be the preconditions of the spiritual and material welfare of the subjects, and the latter's happiness was implicitly equated with the maximizing of the creative potential of the state in a God-pleasing manner. One should, therefore, not doubt the sincerity of the eudaemonistic argument that rulers and publicists set forth in the seventeenth century in advocating absolutism and the interventionist *Polizeistaat*. But it is equally important to remember that for seventeenth-century writers eudaemonism was not an end in itself, as it was going to become later, but only a means.[12] The subjects' welfare and prosperity would increase productivity and foster their creative energies and industriousness, which in turn would rebound to the benefit of the state and the ruler's power and provide the proper framework for a Christian way of life.[13] The full logical and practical implications of this outlook were drawn by Pietism—especially in A. H. Francke's educational and philanthropic institutions at Halle—which stressed the significance of the material world as the means for spiritual goals. Its impact on the administrative and economic policies of Prussia, Saxony, and others is well known.[14]

By the beginning of the eighteenth century the responsibility for this goal was thrust onto the person (i.e., the ruler) or single secular institution (i.e., the state) through the virtual elimination of all other institutions that the Middle Ages had developed to this same end—the Church, monastic orders, and fraternities.[15] As a result, the traditional mandate of government (i.e., rulership) shifted from the passive duty of preserving justice to the active, dynamic task of fostering the productive energies of society and providing the appropriate institutional framework for it.[16] Clearly ambiguity was built into the approach from the start, since it wavered between repressive controls and the encouragement of enterprise and initiative.

It seemed in fact to be an uneasy compromise between the passivity of traditionalism and the dynamism of modernity. It was the obligation of the ruler, while preserving harmony and justice (*suum cuique tribuere*), to initiate the necessary measures and regulations—the more so as the obligation coincided with the prevalent philosophic rationalism. As the Divine Maker has put into motion the well-regulated mechanism of nature and has kept it in operation by means of rational laws, so should the ruler enact the laws and regulations that shape society and keep it on the right path.[17] This is the conception that is at the root of the drive for centralization and uniformity, as well as of the excessive mania for regulation that we observe in the absolute monarchies of the later seventeenth century. Naturally, within the constricted framework of the middling and petty states of Germany, this centralism and regulatory bent easily led to the tyrannical control and supervision of every facet of public and economic life that may be observed in their legislative sources, the *Landes-und Polizeiordnungen*. But it is particularly important to stress that, as in the case of eudaemonism, the detailed and petty regulations were but means for the realization of the essential purpose: the maximizing of all the creative energies and potential resources of a stable and harmonious society so as to further the spiritual and political ends set by God through natural law.

It is not necessary to dwell on the well-researched problem of the relationship between absolute rulers and estates.[18] Their conflict, of course, dominated the political life of German states, as well as elsewhere, from the sixteenth century on. It would be fair, I think, to conclude that in the end the rulers triumphed, even though in many cases the estates retained some authority or subsequently reasserted their power in times of crisis. What is more significant in our context is that in many respects the rulers cooperated, or were brought to cooperate, with the representatives and functionaries of the estates, who thus contributed in significant ways to the regulatory and bureaucratic administration of the princes. The police ordinances of the latter half of the seventeenth century are noteworthy for the extent to which they rely on existing estate and corporative institutions and mechanisms to implement controls and regulations. Only a few new offices were created or officials appointed to enforce these controls and regulations. Essentially the task was delegated to existing functionaries, and, wherever possible, it was carried out with the help of corporations and other constituted bodies.[19] What was new is the greater degree of control and supervision exercised over the activities of these officials and institutions by the prince's councils and central offices. The officials became increasingly mere executors of the instructions and orders emanating from the center, which provided rational and comprehensive direction. Here, again, old institutional forms and means were used to achieve new, modernizing ends.

Quite clearly, the primary concern of the governments was to protect and foster the interests of those corporations and constituted bodies whose industry and productive potential were most beneficial. This did not mean the elimination of traditional social hierarchies and structures; quite the contrary. Yet it resulted in the government endeavoring to promote and favor all those members who worked in a way beneficial to the state's ultimate interests, as they were conceived in terms of the notions I have described. The state acted as arbiter—that is, as protector—of traditional useful bodies and as promoter of new interests. Cameralist police and mercantilist economic policies pursued exactly this same aim. If the peasantry had the short end of it, it was not only because of the ruler's desire to protect and placate "feudal interests"; it was mainly due to the conviction, based on prevailing experience, that there was a narrow range to the productive potential of the peasant, and the extent of this range did not depend primarily on the peasant's status.[20] It was sufficient to promote his security, it was felt, and to succor him in case of direst need. That is why the earlier regulations of agriculture and country life were limited in scope. It was only in the latter half of the eighteenth century, after it had been realized that agriculture, too, had a potential for dynamic expansion, that there developed more active legislation to promote the modernization of the countryside and agriculture.[21] We may conclude, paradoxically, that classes (in the Marxist sense of groups defined by their members' role and interest in the prevailing modes of production rather than by their social status and function) were the result of the encouragement and stimulation provided by the initiatives of the well-ordered *Polizeistaat*. By intervening in the daily activities of its subjects and by fostering the maximum utilization of all resources and creative energies, the absolutist state undermined the estate structure, on which it often relied in practice and promoted the dynamics of modernization and the formation of classes.

At the core of the system there was a profound contradiction between its fundamental aims and purposes, on the one hand, and the means it resorted to, on the other. First, there was ambiguity concerning the relative place and role held by the individual and by the group. Quite clearly, on the basis of a rationalist and mechanistic Weltanschauung, leadership must belong to the single person of the individual ruler.[22] Reliance on the individual would also be implied in the maximizing of all creative potentials, for they are the result of the creative efforts of individuals in their respective spheres of action. On the other hand, reliance on the existing corporations, estates, and institutions, and their functionaries, as well as a belief in the harmonious interaction and functioning of the several estates in the total economy of society, implies the subordination of the individual's interests and concerns to those of the group. It means stressing the duties of the individual rather than his rights, and it has for its effect the downgrading of the individual in favor of the community, as personalized by the ruler or materialized in the state.[23] While easily justifying sacrifices for the common weal, this point of view may also stifle those individuals and selfish drives that have frequently been at the origin of many creative innovations and have contributed to society's material and spiritual wealth.

In the second place, there is also an inbuilt contradiction in fostering individual creativity by means of centralized and directed controls. It was believed that such *dirigisme* would bring creativity to its highest pitch, while at the same time directing it into useful channels of innovation and dynamic progress. This was not to be, especially in view of the insistence on religious uniformity and sociocultural conformity. Again this approach proved particularly stifling in the petty states of Germany, though its disastrous implications became glaringly apparent in the case of France as well, when Louis XIV imposed religious uniformity by revoking the Edict of Nantes, or in the case of Russia's persecution of Old Believers.[24]

* * *

The application of a mechanistic view of the world to the sphere of government and the belief in voluntaristic state direction for maximizing the potential of society entailed active intervention and supervision on the part of prince and administrators. If government or ruler were to be initiators, they had to have a proper corps of assistants and a corpus of new administrative techniques. The traditional type of official was obviously ill suited to this end, as he operated on the basis of custom and *ad hoc* decisions in negative restraint rather than in constructive action.

Two features of the new administrative practice deserve to be mentioned here: routinization, in Max Weber's sense of the term, implied the separation of government activities from other public and private concerns, so as to lend to official acts more authority and free them as much as possible from personal relationships and influences by making them more "objective" and regular. It meant, in short, to endow the administration with the arcane aura of the distinct and objective, and hence the superior.[25] It also served to instill in the population the notion of the state as a separate, autonomous entity with its own—not merely the ruler's—goals, interests, and needs. Inasmuch as the administration was the source of the guidance, furtherance, and control of all potential energies, it had also a didactic function in familiarizing the people with its designs and goals. To our eyes, the minute and petty prescriptions for the operation of offices and clerkships to be found in many *Polizeiordnungen* and learned treatises of cameralist writers may seem naive or slightly ridiculous. But they are illustrative of the new concerns of government; the instruments of administration were coming to be as important as the ends they served or promoted, and they were acquiring a life of their own, becoming an end in themselves. The very routine of government operations threatened to swallow up the purpose for which it had been introduced, and the personnel of administration—the bureaucracy—was evolving into a separate class with its own specific interests, interests that were identified with those of the state rather than with those of a particular estate. The arrogance and self-righteousness of administrative power that reached the extreme degree we observe in the Russia of Peter the Great or the Austria of Joseph II take their roots in this development.

What has frequently been considered a particular manifestation of the brutal didacticism of Peter I of Russia, of his desire to civilize his society at one blow and to establish rigid and all-pervading state controls over all aspects of public and private life, was, in fact, nothing but a straight copying and translating of earlier German *Kanzleiordnungen*.[26] And Peter's rough and outspoken style has its match in the earthy language of the *roi sergeant*. The didactic success of *Kanzleiordnungen* in introducing a new administrative outlook and practice may be inferred from the fact that half a century later standard authors of treatises of administration did not need to go into as much detail as had Seckendorff, for the procedures had come to be taken for granted.[27] The process of assimilation was slower in Russia, as may be gathered from the detailed regulations and forms still prescribed by the imperial administration at the end of the eighteenth century.[28] In addition, the same formulas and rules were repeated each time a new institution was set up, although the basic pattern was supposed to have been set once and for all by the "General'nyi reglament" of Peter the Great.[29] The "enlightened" absolutism of Frederick II or Joseph II, which depended so much on administrative guidance and action, would have been inconceivable without this late seventeenth-century "rationalization" of chancery procedures. Even the notion of the abstract interest of the state taking precedence over the prince's private interests, which found expression in the well-known formula attributed to Frederick II that "the king is the first servant of the state," had its antecedents in the chancery and cameralist writings of the late seventeenth century.[30] Peter I's similar statements are but a more explicit and secular expression of sentiments that have their root in the Protestant notion of the prince's calling and Christian obligation to the welfare of his subjects. Of course there was much self-serving in this rhetoric, but its thrust is to be taken seriously. "L'état, c'est moi" did not mean only that "I am the state" but also that "the state is in me," that is, I am its fullest expression and its principal organ.[31]

An increasingly strong stress on the secular side of public life is an oft-noticed characteristic of cameralism and absolutism. The well-ordered police state was concerned with the promotion of rational organization of all public activity, including the ecclesiastic sphere. An interesting illustration may be found in the very beginning of the eighteenth century—long before the impact of the philosophes' writings—in the revised Church ordinance of the principality of Hessen, which, for the first time since the sixteenth century, concerned the proper policing of public worship. In specifying the order of admission to Holy Communion the ordinance stresses disregard of social and official rank. The reason given is the prevention of arguments and quarrels about precedence. But at the same time the ordinance states the government's belief in the equality of all subjects before God and the priority of public order, so that precedence should be based only on a person's proximity to the altar, with no consideration to status or rank.[32] This detail, though admittedly minor, is notable since we may infer that in earlier regulations it was taken for granted that precedence would be based on traditional status. The close similarity with Peter I's legislation in replacing traditional hierarchies by a more mechanical and rational "Table of Ranks" readily springs to mind.[33]

Similarly it was thought that the state should be concerned about educating its future citizens, especially its future administrators.[34] It is no accident that in view of their need for new parish clergy the Protestant princes took the initiative in creating universities in German lands. As a result, the sixteenth and especially the seventeenth centuries witnessed the emergence of the university-trained official as the principal adviser to the ruler.[35] While in Catholic countries the public role of the universities was on the decline, the Protestant universities were modernizing (*aggiornamento* would be the fitting word) their programs to provide training not only for their pastors but for their jurists, physicians, and scholars as well. In this manner, by the end of the seventeenth century many leading universities had become major avenues for the modernization of public life.[36] The high point of this development was the founding of the University of Halle—specifically the establishment of a chair in cameral studies—to prepare students for the *vita activa* in public affairs while imbuing them with the ethical and spiritual values of Pietism and with their responsibilities as leaders and teachers. The Pietist foundation in Halle stimulated the reform of other universities, particularly at Leipzig and Frankfurt an der Oder and paved the way for the new creation of Göttingen. All of these universities were to become important centers of natural law doctrines as expounded by Christian Thomasius and Christian Wolff and of the subsequent German *Aufklärung.*[37]

We note that this development in German intellectual life has a seventeenth-century origin; the university ordinances for Marburg, for instance, show an awareness of the need for professional training for state service.[38] If we compare the language of these Hessian university ordinances with that of later Russian edicts on education we detect an unmistakable similarity in tone. True, in the Russian case stress is on the development of "useful" noble subjects, as well as trained personnel, while at Marburg there still is an emphasis on the preparation of pastors. But we must not forget the secular functions of the Protestant minister, especially in the countryside. And we are again on familiar territory when we compare the Hessian ordinances with some of the proposals for reforming ecclesiastical schools and the training of priests in the reign of Catherine II.[39] The time lag should not surprise us in view of Russia's condition. We clearly are in the presence of a continuum in time for over a century and in space from the Rhine to the Volga, rather than of discrete periods and regions defined in terms of the spread of the ideas of the French Enlightenment.

Even a hasty perusal of collections of police ordinances indicates that the major elements of what we usually subsume under Enlightenment notions were, in the latter decades of the seventeenth century, being introduced pragmatically, in competition to the earlier regulatory and directive approaches. Thus, for instance, we note rational persuasion and appeal to individual initiative and self-interest in the Hessian regulations concerning reforestation and the planting of fruit trees.[40] Similar elements of freedom of individual activity as a prerequisite of individual self-development can be detected in legislation affecting such areas as health, military recruitment, and the regulation of trades and crafts. To be sure, in every case the political unit is rather limited, and it is still conceived as part of a system of separate and discrete units rather than as part of an all-European polity, or even humanity as a whole, as was the case in the second half of the eighteenth century.[41]

As a rule the German ordinances concerning the police (in the seventeenth- and eighteenth-century sense of the term, of course) relied for their implementation on existing corporate bodies and functionaries or on officials already in place. And if a new office was created, it was usually staffed by someone representing the corporate or constituted body most directly affected by the new regulation, as for example in the Hessian ordinances concerning the French Huguenot refugees: police and judiciary functions with respect to the refugees were to be taken care of in part by existing Hessian officials and in part by functionaries selected from among the French Huguenots themselves.[42] A very different situation obtained in Russia, especially with the regular police functions that had already been developed in Western and Central European states. Introducing modern administration and police, the Petrine state had to create new officials for the purpose. True, they were frequently drawn from the social group most directly affected by the legislation,[43] but it was a compulsory draft that transformed them into virtual state servants and made them responsible for the actions of their fellows. The paradoxical consequence was that there was, simultaneously, a delay in the formation of a professional bureaucracy for the local institutions and the prevention of the restructuring of social groups along self-governing, corporate principles.

In essence, Peter I and his successors were closely following the model offered to them by the police ordinances of the German states. But the interesting differences in the consequences and subsequent evolution stemmed from the means that were at the disposal of the Russian rulers. The explanation was not in the more impulsive, direct, and brutally coercive Russian ways. The main point is that the Russian sovereigns could not rely on those social resources that were available to their European models, largely as a result of sixteenth-century policies and development.[44] They had to create the social matrix, which already existed in the West, as well as the instruments, as did their models, in order to make their reforms stick. But in pursuing both ends they undermined the effective growth potential of each. In Central Europe the old estates were firmly set and could be put to use, even though in the final analysis the new policies and developments were to threaten their nature and very survival. But in Russia the old "estates," to the extent that they existed at all,[45] could not be used, and it was necessary to create a social matrix from which the ministers of the new administrative apparatus might be drawn. If the problem was not entirely clear to Peter I, it was to become quite obvious to his later successors.

* * *

The full practical formulation of the principal aspirations and thrust of what we are wont to call the well-ordered police state can be found not only in the words and deeds of such energetic rulers as Frederick William I of Prussia[46] but also in a treatise that was widely read and used by administrators throughout the eighteenth century. It is the first treatise on police (in the early eighteenth-century meaning of the term) by Nicolas de LaMare.[47] First it should be noted that de LaMare acknowledges fully the debt contemporary police notions and practices owed to medieval precedents. He sees a straight line of development in police legislation from the early Valois rulers to Louis XIV, and in a sense the well-ordered police state is for him little more than the medieval urban community writ large on a territorial scale. LaMare correctly underscored the atomized nature of the contemporary system of states with each state a self-contained, autarkical unit. But he also gave expression to the more modern, dynamic conceptions of government that had been introduced in the seventeenth century, pragmatically in France, more systematically in the German states. The purpose of all government is to maximize resources and unfold the potential of energies of a nation, and to this end the government should have concern for the general welfare, both spiritual and material, of the population. Police is the means by which this goal is best pursued.[48] But the implication clearly seems to be that where the pattern of traditional institutions has broken down or is nonexistent, the function of police is to create or re-create it; this was the voluntaristic implication and modern thrust to be derived from a reading of the *Traité de police*.

Catherine II of Russia was one of the treatise's readers.[49] It is interesting to note the way she approached the problem of a well-ordered police state and in what manner she differed in doing so from her imperial predecessor Peter I. Catherine II is frequently seen as one of the exemplars of enlightened absolutism, the enlightenment elements being inferred from the rhetoric of her famous instruction to the commission on legislation (1767) and her correspondence with Voltaire and Baron Grimm. But with equal justification, to my mind, she may be ranked among the great cameralist rulers, alongside the late seventeenth- and early eighteenth-century German princes from whom she stemmed, but with some interesting qualifications.[50] In her legislation we find the logical extension of a social policy paving the way for modernization while also displaying all the ambiguities of the *Polizeistaat* approach.

The well-known, but still inadequately studied, "Ustav blagochiniia" (1782), echoes the approach of an earlier century while also drawing on more recent German models.[51] Like its earlier sixteenth-century German antecedents, it has a strong moralistic bias indicating the ruler's awareness of a special responsibility for the spiritual well-being and progress of her subjects. In Catherine's statute there is a combination of moral obiter dicta and of modern Western European and scriptural precepts, a combination we find readily duplicated in the ordinances of Protestant princes in the age of Reformation. While conceivably some of the language of Catherine's didactic section—the so-called "Mirror"—may have indeed been derived from de LaMare, in this respect the latter also reflects an earlier tradition.[52] As a matter of fact, Catherine's "Mirror" is a worthy successor of the moral and didactic preambles and disquisitions to be found in the legislation of Peter I, and it would seem to indicate that neither ruler nor ruled in Russia had progressed very far since the early eighteenth century.

In the rather comprehensive articles of the "Ustav blagochiniia" concerning the policing of towns, Catherine followed cameralist ideas and the practice of seventeenth-century German ordinances.[53] The "Ustav blagochiniia," as it attempts to regulate and supervise all aspects of urban life, has the same comprehensiveness; it also exhibits the same intention to provide security and to maximize the creative potential of the urban population, so that it can play its assigned role in the total economy of the state. On the other hand, the Russian statute has an inordinately long section (almost one-half of the articles) detailing the punishments for every infraction of the rules. To enable the urban population to play its constructive role, Catherine attempted to lay the foundations of a gild system.[54] In so doing she followed German models, in particular by assigning urban police functions to the gilds, as did the administrative statute of Berlin of Frederick II. The towns and cities were to be subdivided into districts and *quartiers,* with a hierarchy of police functionaries for each and auxiliaries to be drawn from the local population. But here we encounter an essential difference: while for the setup in Berlin Frederick II relied on existing gild functionaries and the traditional system of corporate participation in the police, there were no such bodies in Russia.[55] The Russian police officials had to be drafted from the population in a way strongly reminiscent of the *sluzhba* (compulsory state service) practices of Muscovite and Petrine times that offered no counterpart advantages to those impressed and straightjacketed them in the rigid network of state service.[56] It also made the police very costly, while subjecting it to excessive bureaucratization and centralized state control.[57]

The reason for this approach is not far to seek, and it brings us to a second vital aspect of Catherine's legislation. It is precisely the corporate bodies and autonomous social institutions—Montesquieu's famous *corps intermédiaires*—that provided the essential framework for cameralism and police in Central and Western Europe and that were most conspicuously absent in Russia. Russian rulers, Peter I as well as Catherine II, were well aware of this absence. Peter I's heavy-handed efforts at forcing merchants to constitute corporations to perform the many services that the state demanded from them—for example, the Glavnyi Magistrat—resulted in failure. The most energetic and progressive urban elements withdrew and avoided the new institutions, while the administrative bodies of the cities were transformed into the reluctant agents of the bureaucracy, losing their spirit of enterprise and social autonomy.[58] Catherine II had, therefore, to return to the task; to implement her "Ustav blagochiniia," as well as to create the socio-institutional matrix for the modernization of Russia's economic and cultural life that she aimed for, she had to develop estates. This was the main thrust of her two charters of 1785, to the nobility and to the towns, as well as of the third charter, planned and drafted but never implemented, for the state peasants.[59] All of these legislative acts aimed at stimulating local administrative participation and responsibility by providing security and a corporate structure for the urban and noble sectors of society.[60]

In the short run, from the point of view I am considering, Catherine's legislation did have some success. It helped to promote the estate organization and participation on the local level and made possible the extension of *Polizeiordnung* to all urban centers as well as to some significant aspects of country life. But the ambiguity of the enterprise soon became apparent: the effort to create by the sovereign's fiat and legislation an estate structure capable of autonomous life foundered on the state's maintenance of direction and control.[61] This in turn meant handicapping the development of individual initiative and autonomous action on the part of estate institutions. And if this was indeed the case, the entire conception of both cameralism and enlightened absolutism—that is, the state's fostering of progress and modernization—was put in question. The equivocal results of this conception were fully experienced by Joseph II in his realm, for his imposition of a uniform and rational pattern provoked the resistance of those very constituted bodies whose creative energies he would have wanted to foster. In any event, and paradoxically perhaps, the interventionist and active policy of the cameralist *Polizeistaat* and enlightened absolutism, whether it relied on existing estate structures or tried to develop them, resulted in a greater awareness on the part of the members of society of the desirability of maximizing their own creative energies. This led to the transformation of traditional status solidarities into an emerging class-consciousness determined by individual self-interest and active economic and cultural involvement. In turn, it stimulated questioning of the legitimacy of absolutism and cameralism, while at the same time pushing society and its active members onto the road of modernity and individualism.[62]

* * *

As the preceding remarks have made clear, it is difficult to break up the web of administrative history into discrete, sharply defined periods: the web is seamless, and a specific pattern arises out of the immanent dynamics of ends and means set long before. Some key ideas that we associate with modernity and ascribe to the Enlightenment came into existence and reached practical significance long before the impact of the writings of the philosophes. Such, for example, is the notion of felicity. The eudaemonism of seventeenth-century cameralism and police contained *in nuce* this notion of general welfare and happiness, only at that time both welfare and happiness were considered to be the means for the attainment of the primary aim of any polity: the maximizing of potential energies to further the power, independence, and influence of the state. What may be called the "enlightenment amendment" to this conception was the transformation of felicity from a mere instrument of a transcendental political goal into an end to be achieved for its own sake. Furthermore—especially in France, less so in Germany whose *Aufklärung* retained much of the earlier communal outlook—the stress was put on the felicity of the individual, leading up to the Utilitarian slogan of the greatest happiness for the greatest number. This individualistic emphasis fostered a "possessive individualism" that gave priority to the pursuit of private material interest over the general welfare of the community. Politically it legitimized resistance to the claims of the state (or ruler) and fostered the resort to a new rhetoric. This rhetoric, in turn, generated attitudes that eventually endowed modernization with its contemporary dynamic force and transmuted it into a transcendent absolute that became a normative standard, similar to the abstract notions of justice embodied in modern codes of law.

In one respect, at least, the enlightened despots crowned the work begun by their cameralist predecessors. The quantity of ordinances had grown to such an extent that they threatened to stifle the proper operation of the very institutions they regulated. With the readjustments of borders and the expansion of economic units there was great need for regular and uniform procedures to facilitate a freer flow of goods and to provide security of persons and property.[63] Last, but not least, the individual's potential to maximize cultural and material resources—via inventions, art, and trade—had to be secured and firmly anchored.[64] This security should not depend on personal authority but on the interplay of social and economic relationships and the freely assumed responsibilities of members of society (or their organized bodies). Such a goal implied an effort at realizing the intellectual presuppositions on which the policies we have been concerned with were based: rational regularity and uniformity predicated on the uniformity of human nature, alongside a recognition of the variety of natural factors, such as climate, and the didactic lead of political power. This effort took the form of the codification of law, so as to provide a harmonious, regular, uniform, and stable legal framework within which the dynamic forces of modernity, which had been prodded into being by the *Polizeistaat,* might find their full scope and expression. The second half of the eighteenth century was the period of codification attempts par excellence on the European Continent—attempts that best exemplify the aspirations of both cameralist and enlightened absolutism.[65] Codification also aimed at routinizing the social conceptions of natural law doctrine that constituted the core of seventeenth-century absolutist cameralism and police: the priority of the obligations of members of society to the community (or the state). It meant emphasizing the individual's duties at the expense of his rights.[66] Further, one may see in the process of codification an example of the leadership role of the state, that is, of the political power.

We need not go into the history of the process of codification in various countries, a history that reveals still many gaps in our knowledge, particularly with respect to the antecedents of eighteenth-century codes and their debt to earlier practices and conceptions.[67] In any event, it is an incontrovertible fact that the successful codifications in Bavaria, Prussia, and Austria, and eventually the French Code Civil, played major roles in the process of modernization at the beginning of its most dynamic period. Franz Wieacker has rightly said that codification is a unique achievement of Western Europe, in fact of Continental Europe.[68] The factors of this achievement that Wieacker adduces should be extended to include the precursor role and basic contribution of the cameralist *Polizeistaat,* which made this kind of codification not only the passive response to necessity but a creative act, and as such a fundamental contribution to the eventual triumph of the spirit of modernity in the postrevolutionary era.

While professors of natural law jurisprudence at German universities proclaimed the individual's responsibility and obligations to the group, the practices of their rulers led to the disruption of group solidarities and the emergence of the selfish, interest-oriented person. The pursuit of exclusive personal advantage strengthened individualism, of course, but it also produced a greater alienation from the group. Individual creative enterprise becoming an end in itself, it had no limit except that of a confrontation with the other—hence alienation, in the sense of experiencing the other as adversary. This imposed a new function on the state and, in view of the disintegration of the estates, fostered the direct involvement of the government in keeping the conflicting selfish claims of individuals in their proper and socially tolerable bounds.[69] This need of the government to intervene to protect the communal solidarities threatened by the very forces it had promoted resulted in a directive and positively engaged state. Such a state could not be merely the "night watchman" of English nineteenth-century liberalism or remain the high justicer of medieval tradition: it was on the way to becoming the directive and interventionist welfare state of the late nineteenth century. And was it to be wondered if the state itself, no longer the ruler of society, became an end unto itself instead of being merely the means for the organization of security and welfare? Not only did the ruler become its first servant, but every citizen was put to serve the state's requirements of ongoing modernization. It was the last step in the conversion of the single individual from a creative force into an instrument of modernity for the benefit of the state.

What has been called "state socialism," and Frederick II its initiator, in fact had its roots in the cameralist and police administrations of seventeenth-century absolutism. As Georges Gurvitch has pointed out in an important, though sadly neglected, book, the seventeenth-century German emphasis on the communal component of natural law theories provided the basis for a doctrine of social rights that led the German states—as well as Bonapartist France and Russia—to take the initiative in introducing modern social legislation.[70] It surely contributed to make these Continental European countries receptive to state *dirigisme* in all walks of life. And if that is indeed the case, should not England's ideology of possessive individualism, and its nineteenth-century political triumph in Manchesterianism, be considered as an exception to the Western pattern of modernization?[71] Be this as it may, the Continental pattern of development may account for the particular strains accompanying modernization, since it assigns an ambiguous role to the political and intellectual leadership, a role inherited from cameralist absolutism but no longer to be contained in the contemporary industrial structure.

The general conclusion to be drawn from this account may not be anything more than to show once again that the web of human history is woven from the antinomies and paradoxes that stem from the discrepancy between ends and means: means devised to solve specific problems by one age become ends in themselves and thereby create problems whose very solution is limited by the terms set by the original intellectual framework. But in more specific terms, if the analysis has any validity, we must conclude that the practices and intellectual presuppositions of seventeenth-century absolutism, as manifested in cameralist and police legislation, proved more significant and came earlier than the ideas of the philosophes in giving dynamic impulse to the process of modernization. In endowing these earlier impulses with its own rhetoric, the Enlightenment appears only as a response to, not a precondition of, Europe's embarking on modernity.[72] True, the rhetoric itself became a powerful force in its own right—but that is another, and later, story.

Notes

1. For an insightful and subtle discussion of the dialectics of enlightened absolutism, see Leonard Krieger, *An Essay on the Theory of Enlightened Despotism* (Chicago, 1975).

2. For a sweeping survey of the transformation of the material potential, see Fernand Braudel, *Civilisation matérielle et capitalisme (XVᵉ–XVIIIᵉ siécles)* (Paris, 1967), and for France specifically, Ernest Labrousse *et al., Histoire économique et sociale de la*

France, 2 (Paris, 1970). There are also stimulating ideas to be gleaned in Douglass C. North and Robert Paul Thomas, *The Rise of the Western World: A New Economic History* (Cambridge, 1973).

3. Kurt Zielenziger, *Die alten deutschen Kameralisten: Ein Beitrag zur Geschichte der Nationalökonomie und zum Problem des Merkantilismus* (Jena, 1914). For a convenient repertory guide, see Erhard Dittrich, *Die deutschen und österreichischen Kameralisten* (Darmstadt, 1974); for a discussion of direct connection with Protestantism, see Franz Lütge, "Luthers Eingreifen in den Bauernkrieg in seinen sozialgeschichtlichen Voraussetzungen und Auswirkungen," in his *Studien zur Sozial- und Wirtschaftsgeschichte: Gesammelte Abhandlungen* (Stuttgart, 1963), 112–44, and, more specifically, Ludwig Zimmermann, *Der hessische Territorialstaat im Jahrhundert der Reformation,* 1 (Marburg, 1933–34).

4. On the vexed question of the ravages of the Thirty Years' War, see Wilhelm Abel, *Die Wüstungen des ausgehenden Mittelalters: Ein Beitrag zur Siedlungs- und Agrargeschichte Deutschlands* (2d ed.; Stuttgart, 1955); Günther Franz, *Der Dreissigjährige Krieg und das deutsche Volk (Untersuchungen zur Bevölkerungs- und Agrargeschichte)* (3d ed.; Stuttgart, 1961); Franz Lütge, "Die wirtschaftliche Lage Deutschlands vor Ausbruch des 30 jährigen Krieges," *Jahrbuch für Nationalökonomie,* 170 (1958): 43–99; Lütge, "Strukturelle und konjunkturelle Wandlungen in der deutschen Wirtschaft vor Ausbruch des 30 jährigen Krieges," in Bayerische Akademie, Philosophischhistorische Klasse, *Sitzungsberichte,* 5 (1958): and for a somewhat superficial summary, Henry Kamen, "The Economic Consequences of the Thirty Years' War," *Past and Present,* 39 (1968): 44–61.

5. Michael Roberts, "The Military Revolution, 1560–1660," in his *Essays in Swedish History* (Minneapolis, 1967), 195–225; Gerhard Oestreich, "Zur Heeresverfassung der deutschen Territorien von 1500 bis 1800," in his *Geist und Gestalt des frühmodernen Staates: Ausgewählte Aufsätze* (Berlin, 1969), 290–310.

6. Walter Hubatsch, "'Barock' als Epochenbezeichnung?" in Hubatch, ed., *Absolutismus* (Darmstadt, 1973), 268–87; see also the remarks in Carl Hinrichs, *Friedrich Wilhelm I, König in Preussen: Eine Biographie,* 1 (Hambrug, 1941; rpt., Darmstadt, 1968): bk. 2, ch. 3.

7. See, for example, J. H. Parry, "Transport and Trade Routes," and G. B. Masefield, "Crops and Livestock," in *The Cambridge Economic History of Europe,* 4, ed. E. E. Rich and C. H. Wilson (Cambridge, 1967), chs. 3–5.

8. Otto Hintze, "Machtpolitik und Regierungsverfassung," in his *Staat und Verfassung: Gesammelte Abhandlungen zur allgemeinen Verfassungsgeschichte,* ed. Gerhard Oestreich (2d ed.; Göttingen, 1962), 424–56.

9. The discussion concerning the nature of merchantilism and its relationship to cameralism does not seem close to being settled. I incline to the opinion that mercantilism, in the seventeenth century, is best seen as the trade and tariff policy of cameralism, which in turn is a more comprehensive system of national economy. On mercantilism, besides the classic work of Elie Heckscher, see the handy collection edited by D. C. Coleman, *Revisions in Mercantilism* (London, 1969), and Hermann Kellenbenz, "Probleme der Merkantilismusforschung," in XII^c Congrès des sciences historiques—Vienne 1965, *IV Rapports—Méthodologie et histoire contemporaine* (Vienna, 1965), 171–90. For the much-debated problem of the relationship that early modern economic policies bore to the formation of a territorial economic system, see Georg von

Below, "Der Untergang der mittelalterlichen Stadtwirtschaft: Über den Begriff der Territorialwirtschaft," in his *Probleme der Wirtschaftsgeschichte* (Tübingen, 1920), 501–620; Hans Spangenberg, *Territorialwirtschaft und Stadtwirtschaft* (Munich, 1932); and Franz Lütge, "Das 14/15. Jahrhundert in der Sozial- und Wirtschaftsgeschichte," in his *Studien zur Sozial- und Wirtschaftsgeschichte*, 281–335. For a discussion with specific reference to Russia, see Alexander Gerschenkron, *Europe in the Russian Mirror* (Cambridge, 1970). On cameralism as an economic system, see the still useful Albion W. Small, *The Cameralists* (Chicago, 1909); Anton Tautscher, *Staatswirtschaftslehre des Kameralismus* (Bern, 1947); and the bibliographic repertory of Magdalene Humpert, *Bibliographie der Kameralwissenschaften* (Cologne, 1937).

10. On the Renaissance as a "naturalistic" episode, see the suggestive points made by Robert Lenoble in *Mersenne ou la naissance du mécanisme* (Paris, 1943), introd., ch. 3.

11. The new concept of the proper *vita activa* is also related to the changing view of the pauper and beggar. See Wilbur K. Jordan, *Philanthropy in England, 1480–1660: A Study in the Changing Pattern of English Social Aspirations* (New York, 1959: rpt., New York, 1964); Jean-Pierre Gutton, *La Société et les pauvres: L'exemple de la généralité de Lyon, 1534–1789* (Paris, 1971); and his more recent summary of the problem on a European-wide scale, *La société et les pauvres en Europe (XVIͤ–XVIIIͤ siècles)* (Paris, 1974).

12. Kurt Wolzendorff, *Der Polizeibegriff des modernen Staates* (Breslau, 1918). The sixteenth-century roots are traced to Melanchthon by Ludwig Zimmermann: "Die 'Ordnung' ist daher Verwirklichung des gemeinen Nutzens. Für Melanchthon ist der *ordo politicus* geradezu gleichbedeutend mit *salus publica*. Er sieht die Geschichte im Sinne optimistischen Fortschritts"; and he concludes, "Der *gemeine nutz* wird das Bildungsideal religiös-sittlicher Erziehung, welche Kirche und Staat zu vollziehen haben. Der Staat ist ein *paedagogicum virtutis*, seine Politik richtet sich auf *foelicitatis progressum*, ihr letztes Ziel ist die ewige Seligkeit," *Der hessische Territorialstaat*, 1: 384, 386, italics in original. For a general summary of the eudaemonic intent in German law, see Walther Merk, *Der Gedanke des gemeinen Besten in der deutschen Staats- und Rechtsentwicklung* (Darmstadt, 1968).

13. The early eighteenth-century practitioner and publicist, Bernhardt von Rohr summarizes: "Wenn man erwäget, wie das Interesse des Herrn und die Glückseligkeit des Landes und seiner Untertanen genau miteinander vereint ... so dass dem Lendersherren unmöglich wohl sein kann, wenn nicht den Untertanen auch mit zugleich wohl ist." *Einleitung zur Staats-Klugheit, oder Vorstellung wie christliche und weise Regenten zur Beförderung ihrer eigenen und ihres Landes Glückseligkeit ihre Untertanen zu beherrschen pflegen* (Leipzig, 1717), 838, spelling and punctuation have been modernized.

14. Carl Hinrichs, *Preussentum und Pietismus: Der Pietismus in Brandenbrug-Preussen als religiös-soziale Reformbewegung* (Göttingen, 1971); Eduard Winter, *Halle als Ausgangspunkt der deutschen Russlandkunde im 18. Jahrhundert* (Berlin, 1953); Józef A. Gierowski, "Pietyzm na ziemiach Polskich do połowy XVIII wieku" (Pietism in Polish Lands to the Middle of the Eighteenth Century), *Sobótka* (St. John's Eve), 1972, no. 2, pp. 237–61.

15. *Mutatis mutandis,* this also applied to Catholic states. On the interesting consequences at the end of the eighteenth century in France, for example, see the fascinating

study of Maurice Agulhon, *Pénitents et Francs-Maçons de l'ancienne Provence* (Paris, 1968).

16. Besides the classic histories of medieval political thought by Otto von Gierke, R. W. and A. J. Carlyle, and Walter Ullmann, see the stimulating and penetrating remarks by Michel Villey, *La formation de la pensée juridique moderne* (Paris, 1968).

17. "Wie die Welt und das Naturgeschehen einem Vernunftschema eingegliedert wird, so bricht sich auch die Vorstellung Bahn, dass die wirtschaftlichen und sozialen Beziehungen des Menschen zu einander mit ihren Zielen und Zwecken restlos durch die Verstandeskraft begriffen und deshalb auch nach menschlichem Ermessen und Vernunfterwägungen gemeistert werden, menschlichen Willensäusserungen unbedingt dienstbar gemacht werden und untergeordnet werden können. Denn dies ist die stillschweigend angenommene Basis der merkantilistischen Wirtschaftspolitik: auch auf das Wirtschaftsleben wird das Geltungsgebiet der menschlichen Gesetzgebung ausgedehnt, wie auch der Kosmos Gesetzen gehorcht. ... Das Postulat jener Geistesrichtung, das Weltbild und seine Gestaltung durch die Vernunft lückenlos zu begreifen, *führt auch zwingend* zur logischen Konsequenz, diesen Ablauf durch vernunftmässige Willensäusserungen zu bezwingen und willkürlich zu verändern. ... Die ganze Wirtschaftspolitik des Zeitalters ist durchtränkt vom Glauben an die Allmacht eines staatlichen Willens." Luise Sommer, *Die österreichischen Kameralisten*, 1 (Vienna, 1920): 90–92, italics in original.

18. The literature on this question is immense. For German lands specifically, see F. L. Carsten, *Princes and Parliaments in Germany from the Fifteenth to the Eighteenth Century* (Oxford, 1959); Dietrich Gerhard, ed., *Ständische Vertretungen in Europa im 17. und 18. Jahrhundert* (Göttingen, 1969); Gerhard, "Regionalismus und ständisches Wesen als ein Grundthema europäischer Geschichte," *Historische Zeitschrift*, 1974 (1952): 303–37; and Helmut G. Koenigsberger, *Estates and Revolutions: Essays in Early Modern European History* (Ithaca, 1971).

19. Carl-August Agena, *Der Amtmann im 17. und 18. Jahrhundert: Ein Beitrag zur Geschichte des Richter- und Beamtentums* (Göttingen, 1972); Roland Mousnier, "État et commissaire: Recherches sur la création des intendants de province," in his *La plume, la faucille et le marteau* (Paris, 1970), 179–200; and the classic essays of Otto Hintze, "Die Wurzeln der Kreisverfassung in den Ländern des nordöstlichen Deutschlands" and "Der Commissarius und seine Bedeutung in der allgemeinen Verwaltungsgeschichte," both in his *Staat und Verfassung*, 186–215, 242–74, and "Der Ursprung des preussischen Landratamts in der Mark Brandenburg," in his *Regierung und Verwaltung: Gesammelte Abhandlungen zur Staats-, Rechts- und Sozialgeschichte Preussens,* ed. Gerhard Oestreich (Göttingen, 1967), 164–203.

20. For an example of an early rural *Polizeiordnung,* see "Landesordnung des Fürsten Christian I vom Jahre 1607," in *Mittheilungen des Vereins für anhältische Geschichte und Alterthumskunde,* vol. 2, pt. 7 (1880): 527–38. On the limits of agrarian growth potential, see the excellent little summary by Wilhelm Abel, *Massenarmut und Hungerkrisen im vorindustriellen Deutschland* (Göttingen, 1972).

21. André J. Bourde, *Agronomie et agronomes en France au XVIIIe siècle* (Paris, 1970); Guy Ferry and Jacques Mulliez, *L'état et la rénovation de l'agriculture au XVIIIe siècle* (Paris, 1970); Ambroise Jobert, *Magnats polonais et physiocrates français, 1767–1774* (Paris, 1941); Helen P. Liebel, *Enlightened Bureaucracy versus Enlightened Despotism in Baden, 1750–1792* (Philadelphia, 1965). As these studies, among many,

show, the impulse came from England—though Dutch models inspired some late seventeenth-century ordinances—but progress was slow because of the limitations of capital and resources.

22. The theoretician of this outlook, Christian Wolff, wrote: "On verra ainsi que la République ne sera heureuse que lorsque les affaires publiques seront dirigées par une *théorie certaine*. ... *Cette théorie se trouve dans le monde rationnel* qui comprend toutes les vérités universelles dont la philosophie, traitée avec une méthode scientifique, est la Description." *Le Philosophe-roi et le Roi-philosophe*, pt. 2: *La théorie des affaires publiques* (Berlin, 1740), 113, 121, italics in original. And his pragmatic follower Frederick II put it somewhat later in more telling words: "Un corps de lois parfaites ferait le chef d'oeuvre de l'esprit humain, dans ce qui regarde la politique du gouvernement; on y remarquerait une unité de dessein et des règles si exactes et si proportionnées, qu'un état conduit per ces lois ressemblerait à une montre dont tous les ressorts ont été faits pour un même but ... tout serait prévu, tout serait combiné, et rien ne serait sujet à des inconvénients; mais les choses parfaites ne sont pas du ressort de l'humanité." "Dissertation sur les raisons d'établir ou d'abroger les lois," in *Oeuvres complètes de Frédéric II roi de Prusse* (n.p., 1790), 7: 109, spelling modernized.

23. Fritz Valjavec, *Geschichte der abendländischen Aufklärung* (Vienna, 1961); Hans M. Wolff, *Die Weltanschauung der deutschen Aufklärung in geschichtlicher Entwicklung* (Bern, 1963).

24. Erich Haase, *Einführung in die Literatur des Refuge* (Berlin, 1959). On the Old Believers, see Gerschenkron, *Europe in the Russian Mirror*, and Robert E. Crummey, *The Old Believers and the World of Antichrist* (Madison, 1970).

25. Volker Press, *Calvinismus und Territorialstaat: Regierung und Zentralbehörden der Kurpfalz, 1559–1619* (Stuttgart, 1970), and for the Russian case, see the suggestive ideas of Michael Cherniavsky, "The Old Believers and the New Religion," *Slavic Review*, 15 (1966):1–39.

26. See, for instance, the *Kanzleiordnung* dated December 15, 1684, in C. G. Appel, ed., *Sammlung Fürstlich-hessischer Landesordnungen und Ausschreiben ...*, pt. 3: *1671–1729* (Cassel, 1770), no. 409; see also Veit Ludwig von Seckendorff, *Teutscher Fürstenstaat* (1656; rev. ed., Jena, 1737; rpt., Aalen, 1972), pt. 2, ch. 6. And see Horst Kraemer, *Der deutsche Kleinstaat des 17. Jahrhunderts im Spiegel von Seckendorffs 'Teutscher Fürstenstaat'* (Darmstadt, 1974).

27. For example, Christian A. Beck, *Versuch einer Staatspraxis oder Canzleiübung aus der Politik, dem Staat- und Völkerrechte* (Vienna, 1754). In contrast to Seckendorff, see any of the better-known treatises on *Polizeiwissenschaft* by Johann Heinrich Gottlob von Justi, Joachim Georg Darjes, and Joseph von Sonnenfels.

28. For example, order of A. A. Viazemskii, Sept. 13, 1784. Central State Archives of Old Charters in Moscow (hereafter TsGADA), *fond* 248, no. 6,570, fols. 8–12.

29. "General'nyi reglament" (General Regulation), Feb. 28, 1720 in *Polnoe sobranie zakonov Rossiiskoi imperii* (Complete Collection of Laws of the Russian Empire), 1st ser. (hereafter *PSZ*) (St. Petersburg, 1830), vol. 6, no. 3,534.

30. And, of course, the religious motivation dates back to the Reformation. Seckendorff, *Teutscher Fürstenstaat,* and von Rohr, *Einleitung zur Staats-Klugheit,* give good formulations. Their near contemporary, Jacob Döpler, still puts the religious motivation in almost medieval terms in *Treuer Herr / Treuer Knecht* (Leipzig, 1694).

31. Fritz Hartung, "L'état c'est moi," *Historische Zeitschrift*, 169 (1949): 1–30.

32. Church ordinance, Nov. 24, 1702, in Appel, *Sammlung Fürstlich-hessischer Landesordnungen*, no. 571. The ideas of religious toleration and the noninterference into basic Church matters by even the pious ruler are well developed by von Rohr, *Einleitung zur Staats-Klugheit*, 260–63.

33. "Tabel' o rangakh" (Table of Ranks), Jan. 24, 1722, in *PSZ*, vol. 6, no. 3,890.

34. For example, consider the creation of a *collegium illustre* in Tübingen, Marburg, and Cassel; and for the less well-known academic gymnasium at Zerbst, see Franz Kindscher, "Das hochfürstliche anhaltische akademische Gesammtgymnasium zu Zerbst unter Kannengiesser (1662–1680)," in *Mittheilungen des Vereins für anhältische Geschichte und Alterthumskunde*, vol. 6, pt. 2 (1892): 284–301.

35. Interesting data may be gleaned from the several essays collected in Günther Franz, ed., *Beamtentum und Pfarrertum, 1400–1800* (Limburg an der Lahn, 1972), and in Helmut Rössler and Günther Franz, eds., *Universität und Gelehrtenstand* (Limburg an der Lahn, 1970). For legal education at universities, see first of all histories of the major universities; see also Erich Döhring, *Geschichte der deutschen Rechtspflege* (Berlin, 1953), and Alfred de Curzon, *L'enseignement du droit français dans les universités de France aux XVIIe et XVIIIe siècles* (Paris, 1920).

36. For the situation in Hessen, see Wolfgang Metz, "Das Eindringen des Bürgertums in die hessische Zentralverwaltung," typescript (Göttingen, 1947).

37. Hans Maier, *Die ältere deutsche Staats- und Verwaltungslehre (Polizei-wissenschaft): Ein Beitrag zur Geschichte der politischen Wissenschaft in Deutschland)* (Neuwied, 1966); Notker Hammerstein, *Jus und Historie: Ein Beitrag zur Geschichte des historischen Denkens an deutschen Universitäten im späten 17. und im 18. Jahrhundert* (Göttingen, 1972).

38. University ordinance, 1684, in Appel, *Sammlung Fürstlich-hessischer Landesordnungen*, no. 410.

39. On Russian education in the eighteenth century, see in particular Mikhail F. Vladimirskii-Budanov, *Gosudarstvo i narodnoe obrazovanie v Rossii XVIII-go veka* (The State and Public Education in Eighteenth-Century Russia) (Yaroslavl, 1874), and Pavel N. Miliukov, *Ocherki po istorii russkoi kul'tury* (Essay on the History of Russian Culture), 3 (Paris, 1930). For ecclesiastical schools specifically, see Petr V. Znamenskii, *Dukhovnye shkoly v Rossii do reformy, 1808 g.* (Ecclesiastical Schools in Russia Prior to the Reforms of 1808) (Kazan, 1881). Catherine's notions for the education and role of the parish clergy are briefly discussed in my study, "The Empress and the Vinerian Professor," *Oxford Slavonic Papers*, n.s. 7 (Oxford, 1974): 18–41.

40. See especially the edicts of 1707, 1713, 1721, 1722, and 1724 on the planting of trees, in *Hessische Polizey Verordnungen die Hude, Gärten und Plantagen betreffend, 1647–1745* (n.d., n.p.), not paginated, a partly handwritten collection for didactic purposes.

41. A certain August Witzman writes around 1790: "Il faut pour ainsi dire considérer toute l'Europe comme une grande ville commerçante et les différents états comme autant de magasins de marchandises." Memorandum, n.d., Leningrad Section of Institute of History, Academy of Sciences of the USSR, Leningrad, *fond* 36, no. 451, fol. 160.

42. Hessian ordinances concerning Huguenot refugees, 1688 and Oct. 13, 1700, in Appel, *Sammlung Fürstlich-hessischer Landesordnungen*, nos. 437, 439, 531. These may be contrasted to the bureaucratic approach of Catherine in setting up a chancery

for the guardianship of foreign settlers. "Kantseliariia po opekunstvu inostrannykh kolonistov," July 22, 1763, in *PSZ,* vol. 16, no. 11,881.

43. For example, merchants were selected for membership in the Glavnyi Magistrat, a sort of city council. See "Reglament ili ustav Glavnogo Magistrata" (Regulation or Statute of the Main Magistracy), Jan. 16, 1721, in *PSZ,* vol. 6, no. 3,708.

44. Herman Rehm, "Die rechtliche Natur des Staatsdienstes," in Georg Hirth and Max Seydel, eds., *Annalen des deutschen Reiches,* vol. 17, nos. 10–12 (Munich, 1884): 565–792; Georg von Below, "Die Neuorganisation der Verwaltung in den deutschen Territorien des 16. Jahrhunderts," in his *Territorium und Stadt* (2d ed.; Munich, 1923), 194–208; Heinz Dollinger, *Studien zur Finanzreform Maximilians I von Bayern in den Jahren 1598–1618: Ein Beitrag zur Geschichte des Frühabsolutismus* (Göttingen, 1968).

45. On the vexed question of estates in Russia, see, for example, J. L. Keep, "The Moscovite Elite and the Approach to Pluralism," *Slavonic and East European Review,* 47 (1970): 201–31; Günther Stökl, "Gab es im Moskauer Staat Stände?" *Jahrbücher für Geschichte Osteuropas,* 11 (1963): 321–42; and, most impressively, Hans-Joachim Torke, *Die staatsbedingte Gesellschaft im Moskauer Reich: Zar und Zemlja in der altrussischen Herrschaftsverfassung, 1613–1689* (Leiden, 1974).

46. R. A. Dorwart, *The Administrative Reforms of Frederick William I of Prussia* (Cambridge, Mass., 1953); Dorwart, *The Prussian Welfare State before 1740* (Cambridge, Mass., 1971). For the broader context of the baroque world, see Hinrichs, *Friedrich Wilhelm I.*

47. Nicolas de LaMare, *Traité de police* (Paris, 1722; 2d ed., expanded, Amsterdam, 1729).

48. "J'ay ensuite montré que son [police] unique objet consiste à conduire l'homme à sa plus parfaite félicité dont il puisse jouir en cette vie. ... On y découvre en même temps combien cette Police que nous suivons a de conformité avec les Loix du Droit naturel et qui ont commencé d'être suivies dès le premier âge du monde. ... Les Loix ... ont la droite raison pour cause efficiente, le bonheur des Peuples, le bien et le repos de Etats pour fin. Les Loix n'ont pas seulement pour objet de punir les vices, mais encore d'exciter à la pratique de toutes les vertus." De LaMare, *Traité de police* (2d ed.), preface, pp. 4, 240. And note a later statement, derived from de LaMare, of much more sweeping import: "La police ... renferme l'universalité des soins relatifs à l'administration du bien public, le choix et l'emploi des moyens propres à le procurer, à l'accroitre, à le perfectionner. Elle est, on peut le dire, la science de gouverner les hommes et de leur faire du bien, la manière de les rendre, autant qu'il est possible, ce qu'ils doivent être pour l'intérêt général de la société." J. B. Ch. LaMaire, "La Police de Paris en 1770: Mémoire rédigé par les ordres de Mr. de Sartine," in A. Gazier, ed., *Mémoires de la société de l'histoire de Paris et de l'Ile de France,* 5 (Paris, 1879): 27–28.

49. Vladimir Grigor'ev, "Zertsalo upravy blagochiniia (epizod iz istorii Ustava blagochiniia 1782 g.)" (The Mirror of the Police Administration [An Episode from the History of the Police Statute]), *Russkii istoricheskii zhurnal* (Russian Historical Journal), 1917, nos. 3–4, pp. 73–103.

50. On Catherine's sources for her instruction, see Catherine II, *Nakaz imperatritsy Ekateriny II, dannyi kommissii o sochinenii proekta novogo ulozheniia* (The Instruction of Empress Catherine II to the Commission on the Compilation of a Proposed New Law Code), ed. N. D. Chechulin (St. Petersburg, 1907), and F. V. Taranovskii,

"Politicheskaia doktrina v nakaze imperatritsy Ekateriny II" (The Political Doctrine in the Instruction of Empress Catherine II), in M. N. Iasinskii, ed., *Sbornik stat'ei po istorii prava, posveshchennye M. F. Vladimirskomu-Budanovu* (Collection of Articles on the History of Law Dedicated to M. F. Vladimirskii-Budanov) (Kiev, 1904), 44–86.

51. "Ustav blagochiniia" (Statute on Police), Apr. 8, 1782, in *PSZ*, vol. 21, no. 15,379.

52. Article 41 of the "Statute on Police" (included in section D, "Instructions to the Police Administration") is generally called *zertsalo* (or "Mirror"), in imitation of the moral-didactic genre of the *Fürstenspiegel*. It contains general moral injunctions and rules of civilized behavior. Catherine's sources for this section are discussed by Grigor'ev, "Zertsalo upravy blagochiniia." In my opinion, Grigor'ev focuses too narrowly on possible verbatim borrowings from de LaMare's *Traité de police*.

53. Catherine also planned a police statute for the countryside (i.e., the state peasants). It was not implemented in full, though it affected some local legislation in the Ukraine. See "Proekt imperatritsy Ekateriny II ob ustroistve svobodnykh sel'skikh obyvatelei" (The Project of Empress Catherine II concerning the Administration of Free Rural Inhabitants), ed. V. I. Veshniakov, in *Sbornik imperatorskogo russkogo istoricheskogo obshchestva* (Collection of the Imperial Russian Historical Society), 20 (St. Petersburg, 1877): 447–98.

54. "Zhalovannaia gramota gorodam" (Charter Granted to the Towns), Apr. 21, 1785, in *PSZ*, vol. 22, no. 16, 188.

55. "O sochinenii reglamenta politsii" (On Drafting the Regulation for Police), Oct. 23, 1763, TsGADA, *fond* 248, bk. 3,411, no. 45, fol. 936–42. See also I. T. Tarasov, "Istoriia russkoi politsii i otnosheniia eia k iustitsii" (The History of the Russian Police and Its Relationship to Justice), *Iuridicheskii Vestnik* (Judicial Courier), 16 (1884): nos. 2–4, pp. 177–212, 383–411, 551–74.

56. "Ustav blagochiniia," section B.

57. For instance, implementing the Uprava Blagochiniia, the police administration, in Tula-Kaluga cost 27,728 rubles, 80 ½ kopecks, a very large sum for the time and for administrative expenses. "Report of Governor-General Mikhail Krechetnikov on the Kaluga, Tula, and Ryazan' Provinces, 1774–91: Report on the Establishment of Police Administrations in Tula and Kaluga," n.d., TsGADA, *razriad* 16, no. 729, pt. 2, fols. 10–11.

58. Aleksandr A. Kizevetter, *Posadskaia obshchina v Rossii XVIII stoletiia* (The Urban Commune in Eighteenth Century Russia) (Moscow, 1903).

59. "Zhalovannaia gramota dvorianstvu" (Charter Granted to the Nobility), Apr. 21, 1785, in *PSZ*, vol. 22, no. 16,187; "Zhalovannaia gramota gorodam"; "Proekt imperatritsy Ekateriny II ob ustoistve svobodnykh sel'skikh obyvatelei." A detailed analysis of the composition and sources of the charter to towns was made by Aleksandr A. Kizevetter, *Gorodovoe polozhenie Ekateriny II 1785 g. Opyt istoricheskogo kommentariia* (The Urban Statute of Catherine II in 1785: An Essay in Historical Commentary) (Moscow, 1909). For an original interpretation of Catherine's social legislation, see Dietrich Geyer, "Gesellschaft als staatliche Veranstaltung," *Jahrbücher für Geshichte Osteuropas*, 14 (1966): 21–50. I follow and illustrate further Professor Geyer's argument in "The Empress and the Vinerian Professor."

60. Robert E. Jones, *The Emancipation of the Russian Nobility, 1762–1785* (Princeton, 1973).

61. For the nobility the story has been told by Sergei A. Korf, *Dvorianstvo i ego soslovnoe upravlenie za stoletie 1762–1885 gg.* (The Nobility and Its Corporate Administration for the Century 1762–1855) (St. Petersburg, 1906).

62. The implicit model was England. But what seems to have been there an autonomous social development was the result of state policy on the Continent.

63. There were also the difficulties and confusions arising out of the coexistence of several systems of law, for example, Roman, German customary, and feudal laws. The situation was not dissimilar in France where there were two major types of law—*droit de coutume* and *droit écrit*—besides local variations. See the fascinating and subtle comparative analysis by John P. Dawson, *The Oracles of the Law* (Ann Arbor, 1968). The varieties of enforceable laws may be at the root of the requirement to exhaust normal juridical procedures in one system before appealing to the ruler and also of the distrust of "judge-made" law and decisions based on the moral judgment of the magistrate. For the latter, see, for example, Johann Friedrich Schram, *Richterlicher Gewissensspiegel* ... (Erfurt, 1729), preface.

64. On security of benefits of inventions and patents, see the interesting remarks in North and Thomas, *Rise of the Western World*.

65. And let us not forget the early efforts of Colbert in France. See Joseph van Kan, *Les efforts de codification en France* (Paris, 1929); André-Jean Arnaud, *Les origines doctrinales du Code civil français* (Paris, 1969); and the special issue, "Le droit au XVII^c siècle," of the journal *XVIIe siècle*, 1963, nos 58–59. To avoid misunderstanding, it should be observed that codification since the later seveenth century was not merely the collecting of ancient, existing laws as in the *coutumiers*, but also a systematic working over in order to bring about a new system of legal norms. The process was clearly illustrated in France, too, in the efforts of Chancelier d'Aguessau in the middle of the eighteenth century. Henri Regnault, *Les ordonnances civiles du chancelier Daguessau* (Paris, 1929–38); see also Dawson, *Oracles of the Law*.

66. Herein lies the root of the difference between the impact of natural law in Germany and its development in England and in France. Suggestive illustration is to be found in the recently published lectures of main authors of the Prussian and Austrian codification efforts in Hermann Conrad and Gerd Kleinheyer, eds., *Vorträge über Recht und Staat von Carl Gottlieb Svarez, 1746–1798* (Cologne, 1960), and in Hermann Conrad, ed., *Recht und Verfassung des Reiches in der Zeit Maria Theresias (Die Vorträge zum Unterricht des Erzherzogs Joseph)* (Cologne, 1964).

67. In addition to Villey, *La formation de la pensée juridique moderne;* Arnaud, *Les origines doctrinales du Code civil français;* von Kan, *Les efforts de codification en France;* and Dawson, *Oracles of the Law,* see Franz Wieacker, *Privatrechtsgeschichte der Neuzeit* (2d ed.; Göttingen, 1967). The literature on the codification in Prussia alone is boundless; for some interesting new interpretations, see Reinhart Kosellek, *Preussen zwischen Reform und Revolution* (Stuttgart, 1967); Hans-Uwe Heuer, *Allgemeines Landrecht und Klassenkampf* (Berlin, 1960); Günter Birtsch, "Zum konstitutionellen Charakter des preussischen Allgemeinen Landrechts von 1794," in Kurt Kluxen and W. J. Mommsen, eds., *Politische Ideologien und nationalstaatliche Ordnung: Festschrift für Theodor Schieder* (Munich, 1968), 97–115; Birtsch, "Gesetzgebung und Repräsentation im späten Absolutismus," *Historische Zeitschrift*, 208 (1969): 265–94; Hermann Conrad, *Die geistigen Grundlagen des Allgemeinen Landrechts für die preussischen Staaten von 1794* (Cologne, 1958); and Conrad, *Rechtsstaatliche*

Bestrebungen im Absolutismus Preussens und Österreichs am Ende des 18. Jahrhunderts (Cologne, 1961). As usual, the study by Wilhelm Dilthey repays reading. "Das allgemeine Landrecht," *Gesammelte Schriften,* 12 (Stuttgart, 1960): 131–207.

68. Codification is "die Unterwerfung des Richters und der Rechtsgenossen unter die Herrschaft eines lückenlosen Normensystems, das in widerspruchsfreier Folge vom einzelnen Rechtssatz, vom einzelnen Rechtsinstitut zu den obersten Begriffen und Grundsätzen aufsteigt. In diesem Sinne ist Kodifikation eine einzigartige, schwer errungene und schwer zu verteidigende Schöpfung der Rechtsgesittung auf dem west- und mitteleuropäischen Festland, und zunächst nur auf ihm: eine der charakteristischsten Bildungen des europäischen Geistes, in dem seine gesellschaftliche und ideengeschichtliche Eigenart mit besonderer Schärfe erscheint." Franz Wieacker, "Aufstieg, Blüte und Krisis der Kodifikationsidee," in *Festschrift für Gustav Boehmer* (Bonn, 1954), 34.

69. Mack Walker, *German Home Towns* (Ithaca, 1971).

70. Georges Gurvitch, *L'idée du droit social* (Paris, 1932).

71. C. B. Macpherson, *The Political Theory of Possessive Individualism: Hobbes to Locke* (Oxford, 1962); Hans Medick, *Naturzustand und Naturgeschichte der bürgerlichen Gesellschaft: Die Ursprünge der bürgerlichen Sozialtheorie als Geschichtsphilosophie und Sozialwissenschaft bei Samuel Pufendorf, John Locke und Adam Smith* (Göttingen, 1973). This contrast would have to be extended to include the United States and the Commonwealth countries (or their antecedents) in the nineteenth century.

72. The domination exercised by French literature and the psychological impact of the French Revolution (as well as of the "French interpretation" of the American Revolution) have tended to obscure the formative role played by earlier ethical and philosophical concepts going back to the sixteenth century. It also served to push into the background the impact of traditional political ideas and institutions, as well as the model provided by small republican states that were still significant in the eighteenth century. Besides the very rich material afforded by Arnaud, *Les origines doctrinales du Code civil français,* see in particular Franco Venturi, *Utopia and Reform in the Enlightenment* (Cambridge, 1971), and Venturi, *Settecento-riformatore: Da Muratori a Beccaria* (Turin, 1969). A suggestive interpretation of the American scene in terms of traditional political ideas and attitudes is Bernard Bailyn, *The Ideological Origins of the American Revolution* (Cambridge, Mass., 1971).

NINETEEN

Transfiguration and Modernization

The Paradoxes of Social Disciplining, Paedagogical Leadership, and the Enlightenment in 18th Century Russia

IN THIS PAPER I WISH to offer a few observations on some particular aspects of the concept of policing or disciplining (Sozialdisziplinierung) that are implicit in my interpretation of the Well Ordered Police State in the 18th century.[1] I shall base myself on the Russian experience which I am better acquainted with and which presents features that shed light on the dynamics of the process of "disciplining" society for the "modern" world.

It is a truism that, in a sense, social disciplining takes place everywhere and all the times. Is it anything but a form of what is called the process of socialisation every society inflicts on its young members? In so-called traditional societies (e.g. in all European societies before the onset of the "modern" period in the 16th century) socialisation and disciplining meant inculcating respect for tradition and the observation of specific ceremonial and behavioral forms; these were consciously instilled to the young through upbringing and education. But when a complex pattern of ways and values breaks down, there arises a need to create new social goals and norms, and the process of socialization and disciplining becomes so much more rational (zweckrational) and goal directed, requiring much effort in the application of will and reason to develop a new normative framework and ways of behavior. And in turn it means reshaping interpersonal relations and devising social institutions that can provide a framework for the new relationships. As this is a more conscious and rational process, education becomes more formal and institutionalized, making use of technological and intellectual innovations.

In Western and Central Europe the traditional norms and ways began to disintegrate as a result of developments which are usually considered to mark the end of the Middle Ages: the Reformation and the wars of religion, the impact of printing, the scientific discoveries and technical innovations, the geographic explorations, and, finally, the institutional political and economic changes associated with the early modern state and early capitalism.[2] These changes brought about the need to restructure interpersonal, political, intellectual and artistic patterns and devise new institutions and practices to root the new pattern of development.

A number of "instruments"—both traditional and new—were applied to this task. In the first place, the contents and methods of education and upbringing had to be transformed so as to promote those individual traits and socio-cultural norms most desirable in a changing world. The fortunate coincidence of the invention of printing and its rapid dissemination helped make the printed word the single most important and effective tool for the promotion of the new goals of socialization and disciplining. Upbringing was accompanied by an education designed to impart literacy, which in turn meant a vastly expanded role for formal schooling and requiring the redesigning of paedagogical methods as well as of the contents of education. Finally, to counteract the dangers deriving from social insecurity and cultural disorganisation in the wake of the abandonment of traditional norms and ways, and to provide a framework for redirecting the pattern of social values and goals, an institutional instrument was shaped in the form of the modern state—i.e. centralized, "rationally constructivist" (F. von Hayek) and formalistic (bureaucracies and codes).

*   *   *

Some of the instruments in this tool kit were inherited from the past (e.g. the Church, family, the personal authority of rulers and élites), but the use they were put to was quite new, "modern" we say. The major innovation was the belief in the practically limitless productive potential of man and the universe. The main social (political) goal became the maximization of productivity in the long run (what Gerschenkron has called a "high time horizon"). The expanded productivity of society, it was believed, would lead to more political and military power of individual states, and the material security of the population at large. The goal could be achieved by a proper taming of nature (thanks to the knowledge of its laws) and the will to organize society, so that all the energies of its members could be bent on expanding their creative potential in all domains and endeavors.

To this end particular stress had to be put on individual conscious effort and action; one could no longer rely on the undirected and uncontrolled activities of traditional sodalities. The reason and will of every individual had to be mobilized to engage in the common enterprise. Obviously, it was necessary to redefine the forms of interpersonal behavior and the norms of public and social conduct. In other words, developing new forms of civility or politeness was both a prerequisite and an aspect of successful assimilation and internalization of modern values; this was the purpose of Sozialdisziplinierung and enlightenment for knowledge, productivity, and cultural creativity.

With these general observations in mind (and I apologize for having detailed what was obvious to most of you) we can turn to the specific aspects of the Russian case.

Those sectors of Russian society that were involved in the public (political, economic, cultural) life of the country experienced the decline and ultimate breakup of the traditional patterns of social, religious, and political culture in the relatively short span of barely three quarters of a century; and what is more, they experienced them as a sudden and sharp break with the past.[3] The crisis of Muscovite traditionalism occurred in two stages. The first, in the second half of the 17th century, took the form of a profound religious split—the *Raskol*—that led to a crisis of identity and undermined the security offered by the traditional cultural and political consensus. Along with the Raskol came the penetration of Western philosophic and cultural models through the agency of educated clergy from the Ukraine. This further undermined the traditional sense of moral security and spiritual integrity, and it prepared the ground for the relatively easy reception by the Muscovite élite of Western scientific (or technical), artistic and intellectual innovations.

The second stage was much more tempestuous and radical in breaking down the traditionalism of the élite. We need not summarize Peter I's "revolution." Suffice it to say that it was inspired by the (ideal) model of the Well Ordered Police State and that it aimed at transforming the governing élites into "new men" equal in knowledge, accomplishments, and power to their counterparts in Western and Central Europe. Professor Meehan-Waters has perceptively noted that Peter's favorite feast day was the Feast of the Transfiguration—*Preobrazhenie* (note the name of his first and favorite guard regiment, *Preobrazhenskoe*). It is fair to say that Peter's aim was to initiate a process by which the Russian people (its élite sectors at any rate) would be "transfigured" (umgebildet) into contemporary Europeans and become active participants and producers in the civilization of the Western world. The Russians spent the entire 18th century to carry out the first emperor's program—and rather successfully if one is to judge not only by the military successes but also by the artistic and cultural creativity at the dawn of the 19th century. With some variations of accent, Peter's methods and tools were also used by subsequent generations of rulers and élites. It is precisely the chronol-

ogy of the process and selection of the means that help to account for some of
the paradoxical results of the Petrine revolution.

*   *   *

The institutional tools that Peter I imported from Central and Western Europe resulted in a far-reaching transformation of government, army, and society. But here I wish to recall some other instruments in his tool kit that were perhaps equally important, although they are often neglected in the general historical literature.

Not surprisingly the printed word proved one of the more significant tools in Peter's kit that helped lay the foundation of modern Russian culture. Printing had first come to Muscovy in the reign of Ivan IV, but it did not strike roots until the 17th century. But even then it was restricted to one printing press at the Patriarchate, and its quite limited production was almost exclusively of religious books, with the lion's share taken by primers and psalters. Realizing the significance of the mass distribution of the printed word—especially that of his own orders and regulations, as well as of useful technical knowledge, Peter simplified the alphabet and orthography to reach a larger audience. It is true, the reform tended to relegate the Church and its activities to a closed and self-sufficient realm; at the same time it facilitated the reception of foreign learning and literature by the majority of the upper classes.

Let us briefly summarise the evolution of 18th century Russian publishing as Professor G. Marker tells it with much quantitative detail on the basis of both published and archival sources.[4] While the Patriarch's palace retained its printing press (it was transferred to the Holy Synod in St. Petersburg after the creation of that institution), for all practical purposes it produced exclusively religious materials. Later on in the century a few printing presses were set up in diocesan centers, but they too produced only religious literature (in relatively small quantities). Over the century, however, the proportion of religious publications declined appreciably, but in absolute figures the print runs and titles of religious books increased quite significantly, showing the continuing need for this kind of literature. We shall return to this point later. It may also be mentioned that the basic primer which taught innumerable Russian children of all classes the first rudiments of reading and writing was based on scriptural texts and had perhaps the largest print run of any publication in the 18th century.

Central government institutions first entered the publishing field to disseminate laws and regulations. In the course of the first half of the 18th century they also played a dominant part in the publication and dissemination of didactic literature for the technical branches of the military services. Appropriately enough, in a country that was striving to become a well ordered police state, the flow of legislation did not abate after Peter's death; it reached torrential proportions under Catherine II, even though many decrees and *ad hoc* regulations circulated only in manuscript copies. In any event, reliance on the printed word grew throughout the 18th century leading us to suspect that the number of literate individuals increased too, probably including also quite a few peasants directly involved in the supervision of private estates or state peasant communities.

It was characteristic of the petrine didactic legacy that the major printing press for secular literature, including official and didactic publications, was set up under the management and authority of the Academy of Sciences. From the very beginnings of Russian secular publishing, therefore, an educational and scholarly institution was entrusted with the selection and production of books. Still more important, the Academy brought together or trained a corps of translators that made available Western works in Russian for dissemination among the educated élites. True, as Professor Marker's tabulations show, the production of the Academy press did not sell very well. As a consequence, to maintain itself, the Academy press had to rely on government subsidies and private patrons. By the middle of the century its commercial failure was evident, while its monopolistic position made thorough reform or reorganization impossible.

In view of the state's absolute monopoly over printing presses it is indeed notable that it also allowed educational institutions to enter the field. First, the Corps of Cadets (founded in 1731) and later the University of Moscow (founded in 1756), as well as some other privileged school establishments in St. Petersburg, received permission to maintain a printing press for which their staff and student body provided the main contributors and consumers. In their case, too, most of the publications consisted of translations of European classical and contemporary literature (including "philosophical" works). The school, and the presses dependent on them, provided the framework for an active and lively cultural life. Indeed, the first literary and intellectual circles (with their own codes of civility) arose within the walls of the schools for the élites and in conjunction with the publication possibilities afforded by their printing presses—for ex. the circle formed by literarily interested students of the Corps of Cadets and the one gathered at the University of Moscow under the patronage of its director, M. Kheraskov.

In 1783, both for financial and ideological reasons, with the former predominating according to Marker, Catherine II decided to give up the government monopoly and to authorise private printing presses. There instantly followed what may be called the "take off" for Russian publishing. Total privatization came only gradually—the weak economy and the absence of any assessment of the market, forced the presses to rely on government orders and individual patronage. Private presses still had to compete with several official ones, while censorship was tightened up at the end of the 1780s.

But the rapid expansion of private presses resulted in a serious split among the individuals and circles involved in publishing. Heretofore, the publication of non-specialized literature for the general public had been in the hands of dedicated intellectuals who, continuing the work of Peter I, believed that their main function and mission was to spread the "right values" (of modernization) by means of their literary and printing activities. Theirs was a didactic and "Kulturträger" function, and making profit was not their prime concern; and they often sacrificed potential earnings for the sake of producing "useful" literature, relying on their own means and on private or monarchical largesses to keep their enterprises going. This was true of even such a business minded publisher-intellectual as N. I. Novikov who in the final analysis failed commercially before being destroyed politically.

Successful printing presses, however, required men who would operate them for profit. This began to happen at the end of the 18th century when book sellers, book importers, as well as the printers themselves, entered the publishing field (not unexpectedly, most of the first non-noble and non-intellectual private publishers were German—immigrants or russified). Early on these publishers realized that profits depended on the defining and attracting a larger body of consumers. First in line were schools and their pupils for whom textbooks had to be produced. More important still, the *homines novi* in publishing discovered that light entertainment literature, regardless of its artistic or intellectual quality, had a potentially large consumer market. They began to publish, in ever growing quantities popular fiction, either translated or original. Predictably, this resulted in a split between the literature produced and promoted by the educated élites and the books for the semi-educated and frivolous, lazy readers who craved only for entertainment. Adventure and romance were the main ingredients of books published for profit, as they were to be of the reading matter printed in the 19th century for the urban and rural masses.[5] Thus the goal of Sozialdisziplinierung and "enlightenment" had as paradoxical outcome the emergence of "pulp literature" of entertainment. The very success of the tool precluded it from remaining in the hands of Kulturträger élite, and by ricochet created the conditions for the rise of a social group—the intelligentsia—whose aim will be to reject the modernizing state and to transvalue the values of the Aufklärung on which they had been weaned.

A major goal of Peter I's activities was to transform the traditional Russian élites' contentment with the God-given into individuals open to the innovative, bustling, and driving ways required by a production oriented society. Peter's efforts were directed at the ruling élites, the military nobility that also had to play a role in the civilian apparatus that the emperor was developing. In any event, Peter's policies aimed at separating the individual from his traditional ties—the clans and families in the case of the service nobles. He forced all into the service of the state and in so doing dealt with them as individual, atomized, and isolated units in the large military and civilian establishment that he was building along formalistic, bureaucratic lines. He wanted to make successful performance the criterion of advancement, not the belonging to a specific social group or family clan by virtue of birth. In other words, he wanted a service population of ambitious, enterprising and productive individuals who would find their reward in promotion and material remuneration by the ruler. As far as the service nobility—and a few individuals from other social groups—was concerned, Peter's aim was achieved, if not in his own lifetime then under his immediate successors. We need only recall the accomplishments of the imperial establishment in military, diplomatic, and cultural affairs. We should also note the amazing rapidity with which they developed a modern Russian culture modelled on Western examples and inspiration, and that gave manifest proof of the creative and productive potential of an ever growing number of Russians.

The individualism that Peter's reforms fostered and that his successors, by and large, secured, differed from what Western enlightenment understood by the term. Russian individualism did not appeal to the political and legal principles that we associate more specifically with the English paradigm. Moreover, Western individualism was rooted in and protected by corporate bodies and juridical persons that had power and authority in their own right. It was made for a pluralistic society whose constituent units served to check and balance conflicting interests without recourse to the ruler's arbitration or command. In Russia, on the other hand, and following the byzantine tradition, individualism meant only the possibility (or even the right) to have direct access to the ruler on a personal basis, disregarding the intervening links of social solidarities and institutions (i.e. the corps intermédiaires of Montesquieu).[6] As a consequence, enhancing the individual's active role in no way challenged or reduced the power of the sovereign, quite the contrary, the monarch's power seemed the best guarantee for personal security and increased material benefits.[7]

The reorientation of behavior patterns initiated in the reign of Peter I, first for the monarch's servitors (others will follow), had to be rooted and consolidated by dint of great effort: it required disciplining in the literal sense, threatening punishment and promising rewards, and systematic inculcation from an early age. Professor Pocock has noted the significance of new rules of manners and politeness in shaping an "enlightened" England.[8] Enlightenment in this context, Pocock observes, meant implanting a civility that curbed religious enthusiasm and the intolerant passions that had proven so harmful in the 17th century and that threatened the settlement of 1688. Albert Hirschman has further clarified the function of a new civility when he showed its relationship to the taming of uncontrolled passions by transforming them into manageable, selfish interests.[9] In the 16th century new codes of civility (we think of Castiglione's *Cortigiano* and Gracian's treatise) aimed at taming the energies of a military nobility and at directing their creative potential to the cultivation of the mind and of the arts. In the 17th century, on the other hand, *politesse* (honnêteté) endeavored to channel religious and individual passions into orderly discourse, reasonable emotions, and interpersonal relationships considerate of each individual's interests.

The new forms of *bon usage*, as practiced at Versailles and in Paris salons, served precisely to "police" behavior so as to make for "civilized" relation between individuals, while at the same time enhancing in orderly fashion each person's creative impulses and potential. It accounts for the formalism of the education dispensed in private schools and Ritterakademien. The same purpose was to be served by the publication of books on etiquette—the so-called mirrors for the young and well born. These mirrors of good conduct were brought to Russia and translated at the behest of Peter I and his successors, and they played a major role in fostering new forms of social intercourse—polite, civilized, respectful of the individual's public role and creativity. One of the first books to be translated into Russian and published on the order of Peter I was precisely such a mirror.[10] In the 1780s Catherine II prefaced the statute on civility (ustav blagochiniia) with a special instruction on public morality and behavior largely borrowed from de La Mare's *Traité de police*.

Not surprisingly, schooling turned out to be an essential element in implementing Peter's project of "transfiguring" Russian man—members of the noble service class in first line. The history of education under Peter I and his successors is well known and I have only a few observations to make here.

The goal of the westernized education was to internalize new values as well as to impart knowledge and inculcate forms of behavior. Internalization was rightly deemed crucial for the new norms of productivity, polite conduct, and civilized interpersonal relations to be operative and the political and social order maintained. Moral education and the inculcation of a number of prescriptive regulations were to provide a framework that made for orderliness, stability, and predictability in human intercourse, so as to enhance the educated man's spiritual and intellectual life as well. Within the framework of these prescriptions, social bonds would develop, solidarities based on common (higher?) interests formed—all for the benefit of the ongoing cultural and material progress of members of the imperial establishment.[11]

This was the origin of what was called in Russia the "*obshchestvo*"—best translated, I think, as "the civil society of the educated." In fulfilling the goal set by the state of acquiring the ideas, ways, and techniques of the Western European élites, this civil society also came to realize that a degree of autonomy was necessary to perform its public function adequately. By the end of the century the civil society was yearning for autonomy and privacy (Privatisierung) so as to be independent of the concerns and interests of the state. Only under this condition, the élite civil society felt, could the *Aufklärung* be properly internalized and effectively lived. The need of conflict or of "a parting of ways" had been laid. In the meantime, however, this civil society as part of the imperial officialdom had to provide the leaders and educators to bring about the "transfiguration" of Russian society Peter I had dreamed about.[12] Let us now turn to a closer examination of the values and forms Russian educated civil society absorbed in the course of the 18th century.

It is commonly held that during the late 18th century process of moving into the orbit of modern European civilization Russia acquired the ideas of the Western enlightenment. This is true only if we are clear about the meaning and contents of the enlightenment that Russia absorbed. For the present purposes I will deal only with some features of the process that, in my opinion, bear directly on social disciplining and its consequences.

In spite of a significant number of Catholics active in the Muscovite and Petrine establishments, their contribution to Russia's cultural and intellectual development in the 18th century was definitely overshadowed by that of the Protestants from Northern Europe.[13] We also should keep in mind the chronological discrepancy resulting from Russia's entering the world of modern Western intellectual and political culture only in the early 18th century. Thus the religious-scientific "baggage" the Russians took over was of late 17th century vintage rather than the avant garde of Anglo-French 18th century thought. Why did the Russians of the first half of the 18th century turn to the Protestant world of the 17th century for inspiration and to the German *Aufklärung* for emulation? On the political and institutional plane there was the attraction of the Lutheran churches' subservience to state control. But we may note that neither the Russian Church nor contemporary Catholicism offered significant threats to the state; they were (and had been for quite a while) firmly under secular control. It is also true that the Protestant world offered the model and inspiration for the most advanced (or "modern") and successful social and economic policies at the time. Sweden, Holland, and England, rather than France, Austria or Italy (not to speak of Spain) seemed worthy of emulation if the aim was to maximize the country's economic prosperity and military power.

There were, however, more weighty—though not always fully conscious—reasons for the Russian partiality towards ideas and mores rooted in contemporary Protestantism. First was the fact that the early wave of Westernization had come from the Ukraine. The Kiev theological academy that furnished the inspiration, as well as personnel, for this early intellectual Europeanization had been founded to counteract the proselytising efforts of the Counter Reformation, and in so doing had drawn much of its inspiration from the neo-scholasticism and the rhetorical and ethical teachings of the German Protestant universities. Furthermore, paradoxically perhaps, the *Raskol* (Old Believers' schism) had put the official Muscovite Church in opposition to the tradition of a literal reading and interpretation of the Scriptures and of the ritual. In so doing, however, the official Church removed itself from an active, dynamic involvement in the religious experiences and life of the faithful and left the field open to the individuals' search for a richer personal spiritual life. This trend was reinforced by Peter's (and his successors') limiting the Church's role to the performance of the ritual and in assisting the policing functions of the government. The result was to erode the pastoral and spiritual role of the clergy, especially with respect to the educated sectors of society.

In his stimulating study of Hegel's intellectual and socio-political background, Laurence Dickey has pointed to the renaissance of Alexandrine and Joachemite conceptions in shaping much Protestant thought in Germany in the second half of the 17th and the first half of the 18th centuries.[14] The notion of synergetism stressed the individual's ability to aim for the merging with Divinity by dint of his will power and efforts at changing himself and his environment.[15] It implied a *praxis pietatis* and the reconstruction of society to that end. An end which the Joachemite eschatological vision held forth as a realistic possibility. The "second reformers," among whom the Pietists were in the forefront, were totally imbued with this style of thinking and its behavioral consequences that meshed in with the presuppositions of the well ordered police state. We should remember at this point that the major elements of the Alexandrine theological tradition (e.g. Pelagianism) had always been present in Russian church and religious life (Byzantium having served as transmission belt). The Petrine establishment could readily mobilize this tradition, for, as we have seen, the aim was to "transfigure" Russian man to "reconstitute" society so as to maximize productivity and enhance progress. This was precisely the major thrust of the sermons and treatises of Peter's main religious helpmate, Archbishop Feofan Prokopovich (himself a product of the Kiev academy and Western universities). This orientation also dovetailed well with the teaching of the German natural law jurists, especially Pufendorf, who emphasised the *vita activa* and the individual's duties to the "good" community in preparation of the perfect City on the Hill. Not surprisingly Peter I had Pufendorf translated and Feofan frequently referred to his writings. Later on in the century this tendency was reinforced by the so-called Scottish enlightenment whose religious quality, as well as forward looking socio-economic ideas, have been noted by many scholars in recent times. The Scottish influence was markedly strong in Russia since several of its early jurists and publicists received their training at the universities of Glasgow and Edinburgh. And since the Scottish thinkers had also an impact on the Aufklärers of Kant's generation, the latter influenced in this sense their Russian pupils as well (a topic that still requires further investigation).

In spite of the alleged "secularization" of Russian public life in the 18th century, religious interests and concerns were not only not abandoned but even remained in the forefront of Russian culture. We observe that as literacy increased the number of religious books published and circulated increased as well. Not only did the presses of the Church establishment keep bringing out books of religious and spiritual contents but so did the private presses permitted after 1783. They published a number of translations or adaptations of 17th century German religious literature, in particular of the hermetic, rosicrucian, and mystical tradition. As the researches of Lauer, Rothe, and Levitsky show, religious inspiration played a major role in the poetry published and avidly read by the educated classes in Russia throughout the 18th century.[16] It contributed significantly to the revival of intense, mystically tinged piety and the early stirrings of "romanticism" at the end of the 18th century. The pietist tone in this literary as well as intellectual life in 18th century Russia is unmistakable.

We all know, of course, that Pietism laid great stress on Innerlichkeit—an orientation that converged with the need for society to internalize the new norms and ways that the Petrine revolution had introduced into Russian public life. Naturally, the focus of the process of internalization was the individual who had the prime constructive role in reconstituting society and "transfiguring" Russian man. Indeed, in accordance with Leibniz's philosophy that had become a major element in the thinking of the Russian élites (thanks to the paedagogic and intellectual leadership of Germans invited to the Academy of Sciences and schools), the relationship of the individual to the community was similar to that of the individual monad to the universal monad. In this perspective individualism acquired a positive significance for the realization of the establishment's social, economic, and cultural goals. Autocracy welcomed this individualism as long as it retained the "byzantine" character referred to earlier, and did not lead to the formation of corporations and other solidarities similar to those that were challenging the centralized and absolute monarchies in the West. The "true son of the fatherland" (like the good patriot of the Germanies) was an individual who developed all his material or spiritual creativity and practiced *praxis pietatis* for the greater benefit of "reconstituted" society in order to achieve maximum happiness and harmony on earth. The secular goal of the state and the spiritual concerns of the "enlightened" (aufgeklärter) individual coincided.

This explains the strongly felt need to develop the inner man. The state could only provide schooling in those secular subjects that would be useful in a material sense (this was Peter's emphasis), and that could also help develop the pupils' intellectual potential and bring them into direct contact with Western accomplishments. The narrowly artisanal and technical skills imparted by the Petrine schools were abandoned in favor of a broadly conceived general humanistic education. Such an education, pioneered in Russia by the Corps of Cadets, drew its inspiration, goals, and contents from the Ritterakademien and noble schools that had flowered in Central Europe at the end of the 17th century, and that embodied the tenets and values of the "second reformers" and Pietists as well.

In the last third of the 18th century, under the impact of all these trends and influences, Russia witnessed a blossoming of religious life outside the framework of the official Church, but in communion with it. Authors, thinkers, and officials turned to reading the German mystics (Boehme, Meister Eckhard, Arndt) whose works helped anchor firmly the "enlightened" (aufgeklärter) outlook and purposes of educated Russian civil society.[17] This same yearning manifested itself in the popularity of Utopias and utopian literature and the spread of masonic lodges. As had been the case in Central Europe, the masonic lodges were a focal point for the dissemination of the ideas of the *Aufklärung,* preeminently those with a strong religious component, and which rejected the materialist and radical formulations of late 18th century French *philosophes.* The masonic lodges thus provided an informal network for the enhancement and dissemination of German Aufklärung, including its "rosicrucian enlightenment" features. But they also made their own the secular (social, economic, and cultural) goals of the Petrine state. It explains that they could work in harmony with the state, at any rate as long as they restricted themselves to the promotion of the individual's spiritual and intellectual progress and personal engagement in bettering his fellow man. The relationship soured when it became apparent that the association of persons was developing into an "institution"—i.e. a corporate body pursuing its own goals, in its own fashion, and that might interpose itself between the individual subject and the ruler. The resulting rift provoked the brutal response of Catherine II that endowed the masonic leaders with the aura of martyrdom. It has led many historians to see the subsequent conflict between intelligentsia and state as a consequence of Russia embracing the enlightenment when, in fact, it was rather a conflict between two enlightenments for the loyalty of the educated sector or Russian society.

In the preceding pages I have argued that in Russia (and *mutatis mutandis* this was the case elsewhere as well) ideas of the *Aufklärung,* to which I could also associate those of J. J. Rousseau, not only furthered the "modernization"—economic, institutional, cultural—of the country and thus brought it into the mainstream of West European progress and development, but they also served to bring about a renaissance of religious concerns and spiritual life. They did so by giving a new vitality to the personal spiritual and intellectual creativity of those who, in ever larger number, were educated and disciplined into internalizing the values and goals of the well ordered police state. The paradox is in part explained by the fact that the Petrine reform removed the official church from the center of the public stage and made it into a decorative policing institution, thus leaving a void in the nation's spiritual and cultural life. This void was filled, not surprisingly, by the tradition harking back to the Alexandrine fathers and Joachemite theology which was melded into the social and ethical project of an active, production oriented Pietism. The result was a heightened commitment to promote the individual's spiritual inner life in the expectation that *praxis pietatis* would bring about the "transfiguration" of men as prodrome to a genuine synergetism. The imperial establishment welcomed such a belief and program, for it served to promote its own goal of a productive society and assisted it in disciplining the people to this end. It had not been expected that a successful implementation of this religious and secular project would lead to the emergence of a group of educated and spiritually committed individuals eager to be moral leaders and social activists. These men not only claimed the right to participate in public life but also the right to form autonomous corporate bodies to this end. This claim undermined the common project and led to the conflict between state and educated civil society that lay at the source of the Russian intelligentsia of the 19th century.

Notes

1. Marc Raeff: *The Well Ordered Police State—Social and Institutional Change through Law 1600–1800*. New Haven 1983.

2. J. H. Shennan: *The Origins of the Modern European State 1450–1725*. London 1974. Fernand Braudel: *Civilisation matérielle et capitalisme (XVe–XVIIIe siècle)*. Bd. 1, Paris 1967.

3. I shall focus exclusively on élite society. The history of the common people's involvement in the process of europeanization and enlightenment has been barely investigated.

4. Gary Marker: *Publishing, Printing, and the Origins of Intellectual Life in Russia, 1700–1800*. Princeton 1985. The discussion of printing is primarily based on this book.

5. Jeffrey Brooks: *When Russia Learned to Read—Literacy and Popular Literature, 1861–1917*. Princeton 1985.

6. Alexander Kazhdan, Giles Constable: *People and Power in Byzantium—An Introduction to Modern Byzantine Studies*. Washington 1982, esp. ch. I.

7. J. H. Shennan: *Liberty and Order in Early Modern Europe—The Subject and the State 1650–1800*. New York, London 1987.

8. John G. A. Pocock: "Clergy and Commerce. The conservative Enlightenment in England." In: *L'età dei lumi—Studi storici sul settecento europeo in onore di Franco Venturi*. Bd. 1, Napoli 1985, pp. 525–562.

9. Albert O. Hirschman: *The Passions and the Interests (Political Arguments for Capitalism before its Triumph)*. Princeton 1977.

10. *Iunosti chestnoe zertsalo ili pokazanie k zhiteiskomu obkhozhdeniiu*. St. Petersburg 1717 (and subsequent editions).

11. The Ustav blagochiniia (Statute of Civility), In: PSZ No. 15379 (18. April 1782); cf. Vl. Grigorev. "Zertsalo upravy blagochiniia (epizod iz istorii Ustava Blagochiniia 1782 g.)," *Russkii istoricheskii zhurnal* 3-4 (1917), S.73–103.

12. See E. V. Anisimov: *Rossiia v seredine XVIII veka—Bor'ba za nasledie Petra*. Moskva 1986, p. 206 on the educational policy of the Shuvalovs.

13. The major exception to this statement concerns architecture and music, and to some degree belles lettres. But the question deserves more searching study.

14. Laurence Dickey: *Hegel—Religion, Economics, and the Politics of the Spirit, 1770–1807.* Cambridge 1987.

15. Reinforced, of course, by the neo-stoicism of the late 16th and early 17th centuries. Cf. Gerhard Oestreich: *Geist und Gestalt des frühmodernen Staates. Ausgewählte Aufsätze.* Berlin 1969.

16. Hans Rothe: *Religion und Kultur in den Regionen des russischen Reiches im 18. Jahrhundert—Erster Versuch einer Grundlegung.* Opladen 1984. (Rheinisch-Westfälische Akademie der Wissenschaften. Geisteswissenschaften, Vorträge G 267). The recent studies by professors Lauer und Levitsky on masonic and spiritual poetry, respectively, have laid a solid factual base.

17. E. V. Beshenkovsky has reconstructed the library of Novikow at the time of his arrest and trial. The catalogue has not been published but from a perusal of the typescript it is clear that the importance of German religious and hermetic (as well as masonic) 17th century literature cannot be underestimated.

TWENTY

Literacy, Education, and the State in 17th–18th Century Europe

A PROBLEM THAT PREOCCUPIES the historian most particularly is that of change. In human affairs, as in nature, nothing remains stable for any length of time; all is in more or less rapid flux. It is with events, with those things that undergo or bring about change, that the historian deals. It is no accident that historical studies have seen their greatest development at the time of greatest historical change. The period of accelerated rates of change, of transformation in all realms, is the "modern period" of history—usually counted from the end of the Middle Ages and the beginnings of the Renaissance. Today, I wish to single out one perspective on the process of "modernization" that has characterized the last few centuries, a process that started in Western Europe in roughly the sixteenth century and has conquered the whole known globe.

In the eighteenth century, this process had acquired great dynamic force and had entered the consciousness of Western man. A central concern of that century was education—pedagogy—and one may ask the question, how come this was a central issue then (though its roots lay in the seventeenth)? And the further question arises: how was education related to what we call the rise of modernity, the process of "modernization"? It seems to me that education becomes a particularly critical problem and a major concern for societies, or civilizations, that have experienced—subjectively or objectively—a sharp break with the immediately preceding past. Old ways do not seem applicable any longer, and a conscious effort has to be made to prepare the next generation to deal with the new conditions and situations. A special task is therefore given society, that of disciplining and socializing the young without the benefit of former informal and traditional ways.

In the seventeenth and eighteenth centuries, the felt break with the previous principles and organization of society had been the result of changes that had occurred at the end of the Middle Ages. These were, on the one hand, the result of the Reformation, which broke the unity of Western Europe's ecclesiastical world and redefined and institutionally rearranged the role of the Church. On the other hand, the changes were also the outcome of the geographic discoveries of the fifteenth and sixteenth centuries that had altered the image of the world which had shaped the perceptions and values of medieval man. Closely related to the geographic discoveries was the scientific revolution of the early seventeenth century that had transformed the explanatory scheme of things that had predominated earlier and had constituted the base of the traditional process of socialization. There was a need to find new ways for reconstituting social bonds and patterns of behavior that had been seriously disrupted by all these developments. It marked the beginnings of a conscious effort to educate the young generation—educate them not only by imparting the new knowledge acquired about the world, but also by instilling new ways of acting and thinking in society as part of the process of upbringing. The effort was to have its high point and reach its goal in the course of the eighteenth century.

The Reformation, as you well know, encouraged the individual faithful to turn to the Scriptures in order to understand the basic propositions of their faith. Naturally, this precept could not be followed by everybody, and the majority of the population (still illiterate) was expected to follow the explanations and interpretations of ministers and pastors. Nevertheless, the key of Protestantism was the ideal goal of every believer being able to turn to the text of the Scriptures, to be literate to do so. To this end, Protestant churches and the political establishments that supported them encouraged the spread of literacy to as large a population as possible. The ordinances establishing and regulating Protestant churches included stipulations for the creation of schools and prescriptions for their curriculum. In the Germanies, in particular, we see the issuance of numerous *Kirchen- und Schulordnungen* throughout the sixteenth, seventeenth, and early eighteenth centuries, starting with that of Saxony—the first German state to make Lutheranism the state religion.[1] As a result a network of schools, in both the countryside and in the towns, arose and spread the rudiments of reading and writing through large segments of the population. Both church and state were interested in the success of this endeavor, for they believed that a firm anchoring in the faith would also enhance the stability of the social order and the security of the political establishment. The most striking illustration of this policy may be found, a bit later, in the Ordinance of 1686 issued by Charles XI of Sweden that made an examination in literacy the prerequisite for confirmation and made both secular and ecclesiastical local authorities responsible for its implementation.[2] This explains how Sweden attained almost complete literacy in the eighteenth century, way ahead of any other European state.

Since the Protestants had embarked on the course just outlined, the Catholic Church of Rome could not but follow suit if it wanted to preserve its position. The Catholic Counter-Reformation, therefore, also made education and a degree of literacy a goal of its reform program. The Council of Trent approved the notion of giving particular attention to the education of the young to safeguard them against the siren calls of Lutherans and other "heretics" and to inculcate obedience to the dogmas propounded by the Church of Rome. In the course of the late sixteenth and seventeenth centuries a number of monastic orders dedicated to the education and upbringing of the young were founded and spread rapidly throughout the Catholic world. The Jesuit order is the best known among them, but it was followed by the Piarists, the Brethren of the Christian Schools, and others, including special orders for the education of girls.[3]

A similar phenomenon may be observed in Eastern Europe, in particular in the Ukraine. A religious conflict and a sense of break in the religious tradition led to the establishment of schools. In the Ukraine, where there was a keen sense of threat of the Catholic Counter-Reformation, an advanced institution of religious learning was founded in Kiev by the Metropolitan Peter Mohyla (1632).[4] This was followed by a network of schools for both clergy and laity throughout the Ukrainian provinces. The example served as a model for Muscovy when the tsar's government decided that the country needed better preparation to cope with both Western influences and the effects of the schism of the Old Believers. As a matter of fact, the Old Believers, like the earlier Western Protestants, resorted to the authority of traditional liturgical texts to justify their rejection of the state Church and thus encouraged literacy among their followers. All these developments in Eastern Europe remained narrowly confined to the religious sphere until the eighteenth century and thus did not have as broad an import as in the West, where secular interests became associated with education and literacy early in the seventeenth century.

The trends I have just summarized dovetailed with the interests of the absolute centralized (or centralizing) states that were becoming more firmly entrenched on the political stage of Europe. Such states operated with the help of an officialdom (one hesitates to call them as yet bureaucracies) that acted according to set rules and regulations that had to be known by most subjects and that were fixed in writing. To make known and implement these rules and regulations they had to be broadcast not only orally but also in written (i.e. printed) form. The emerging "modern" states, therefore, needed a population among which literacy was widespread, if not universal. The need was particularly pressing, since the central authorities of these policies were trying to displace or supersede the traditional power exercised by landlords, village elders, guild leaders, and the like. However, they also endeavored to reach to the lower local levels that in the past had led an autonomous existence without direct interference, guidance, or control from the center.

Underlying this policy approach was the assumption of rational knowledge and the will to act on this knowledge on the part of both subjects and ruling elites (to the degree each was able to act). The education to be imparted to the majority of the population thus had to stress the possibilities of rational, factual knowledge that enabled one to follow the dictates of the laws of nature. But since the knowledge had to be translated into purposeful, organized, and regulated action, men's wills had to be attended to as well.

This explains the importance attached to the tenets of Stoic philosophy and the popularity of Neo-Stoicism in the first half of the seventeenth century.[5] Educating the will so as to have men act in accordance with the laws of nature and the rational commands of the authorities predicated upon them, such was the major aim of the upbringing imparted to all those destined to have an active role in the productive life of society. The benefits that would accrue to the military as well as economic aspects of public life are self-evident. Thus it was Neo-Stoicism that provided the philosophical and psychological underpinning to the military revolution of the seventeenth century, first introduced by the Prince of Orange in the Low Countries and then imitated by other military establishments, more particularly by the Elector of Brandenburg-Prussia. The revolution in military tactics required not only a disciplined army, but also soldiers who would be able to exercise some initiative and independence within the framework of the orders issued by their officers.[6] The same was true of economic activity: to apply one's will to implement regulations while also taking the initiative to profit from circumstances.

The scope of economic activities was enlarged by the awareness, on the part of the elites at any rate, of the greater potential inherent in nature than "medieval man" had suspected. The notion of a finite, limited universe (created for all times by a single act of God) was giving way to the realization that the potential inherent in nature is not limited, that it may be infinite, and that it depends on man's will to exploit it to his own advantage. Knowing the laws of nature and acting rationally and purposefully on that knowledge may lead to the improvement of man's condition and the greater prosperity of all society (and of the state in the first place). But such purposeful and rational action—on the basis of what can be discovered of the workings of nature—has to take place over a period of time. Man may have to postpone immediate, short term benefits for a greater advantage in the future. To this end he may have to bridle those instincts or passions that make him consume his production immediately, out of the irrational fear that there is no assurance of a tomorrow. The irrational impulse to consume immediately leads to conspicuous consumption, to show off for a moment rather than to husband one's "assets" for future benefits. It is thus the task of the elites to educate, discipline society to invest for the future by bridling their irrational impulse (passion) to consume immediately. In a fascinating essay Albert Hirschman has shown how literature and pedagogical practices in the seventeenth century aimed at controlling passions, at developing the individual's ability to bridle them in order to further his interests.[7] Anyone familiar with the writings of the French classical authors of the seventeenth century, in particular Corneille, knows that the conflict between passion, emotion, and interest based on reason is the key moral and psychological issue.[8]

In a similar sense, from a slightly different perspective, the late economic historian Alexander Gerschenkron has spoken of the discovery of the "high time horizon" in seventeenth and early eighteenth century economic thought.[9] In other words, it is necessary to plan and prepare for a future whose horizon is remote and high. One does not look only at what is under one's feet, available immediately, but one organizes and plans resources and activities to yield a benefit later on. The notion of a "high time horizon" involves both knowledge and will that have to be developed by proper education and upbringing. Taming passions to pursue selfish interests does not eliminate sources of friction and conflict with other members of society. This can easily lead to violence and anarchy—as the experiences of most European societies in the Wars of Religion, the English Civil War, and the Thirty Years' War have amply demonstrated. How is one going to plan without the assurance of some security, some predictability about the future? To be sure, political power may provide the basic elements of such stability and security. This explains the success of the absolutist centralized (usually monarchical) state in attaining monopoly of power and brute force—what Theodore Rabb has called the successful pursuit of stability in the seventeenth century.[10] But this external coercion may not be enough; there has to be an inner striving for controlling oneself as well as respecting the interests of others to insure security. The traditional, group-based ways of social discipline and control of public behavior were no longer effective or applicable in view of the new role acquired by the individual and his purposeful, autonomous sphere of action. J.A.G. Pocock has thus pointed out the transformation undergone by the rules of civility, of politeness in the second half of the seventeenth and early eighteenth centuries.[11] The essence of the new civility was the avoidance of violent confrontation—be it on matters of religion, be it on other, mundane matters. A civilized conduct restrains the individual's passions and feelings and acknowledges the other person as an equal interlocutor with whom one has to deal rationally and "peacefully". The emphasis is, therefore, on the individual and his rationality assisted by a developed will power—education and upbringing have to aim at furthering these traits.

These new attitudes and goals generated a whole literature to assist in the process of education and upbringing. It is called "mirrors for youth" and became the mainstay of the pedagogical efforts, first of German schools, but later spreading to other countries as well. It is characteristic of Peter the Great's policy of Europeanization that he ordered the translation of such a mirror as one of the first books published in the new script. The book not only listed the rules of behavior in public but also the basic principles of intellectual and moral development that had to be inculcated in the well-born young people of the Russian empire. Comparatively speaking, the *Mirror of the Honest* [i.e. well bred] *Youth* was a literary success and went through several editions in the course of the first half of the eighteenth century.[12]

The efforts of the "modern" states to inculcate the new ways and norms in their societies took the form of the regulations and laws issued by the central authorities. Predicated on the "high time horizon" outlook in matters economic, the so-called Well Ordered Police State wanted to guide and supervise all major activities of its people so as to maximize their productive potential, both material and cultural.[13] Naturally, increase in the productivity of society, increase in the quantity of goods produced, would benefit first the state (and ruler), enabling it to maintain an adequate military force to pursue an active foreign policy, but it also would in the long run increase the prosperity of all subjects. A wealthy society would pay more taxes and thus also enable the ruler (or government establishment) to manifest his power by symbolic and ostentatious displays. As we have noted earlier, the numerous rules and regulations, eventually codified, had to be disseminated as widely as possible, and to this end a literate population was desirable. For these reasons the Well Ordered Police State in the seventeenth and eighteenth centuries promoted the education of the population (without making it universal, as we shall see). Unlike the earlier school development sponsored by the churches, the Well Ordered Police State supported primarily institutions that stressed technical and practical knowledge and the development of those character traits most useful in a productive society. The practical disciplines included not only military architecture and engineering, but also manufacturing and agricultural techniques, as well as law, the sciences, and pedagogy for the governing elite.

* * *

Schools required textbooks and instructors needed guides and tractates. The new orientation both in contents and pedagogical approach found its most popular and best known expression in the writings of the Bohemian educator, Jan Amos Komensky (Comenius), more specifically in his widely read (and translated) *Orbis pictus*. It was the foundation of the approach and literature known in France (and practiced up to the 1930's) as *leçon de choses* that aimed at imparting to the young a concrete and rational knowledge of the natural world in which they lived. The example of Comenius was followed by many—most prominent among them were such German academic writers as E. Weigel and Christian Weise, whose tractates were also translated or adapted and disseminated in Eastern as well as Central Europe.[14] Needless to say that this education (and literature) took place in the vernacular, displacing the Latin that had been the language of instruction before. Among the elites that were to make use of this education in guiding the masses of the population we should not forget to include the clergy. Especially in the Protestant lands it was hoped that the pastors would be the leaders in introducing new techniques and in furthering the physical health as well as intellectual and moral development of their flocks. In this way moral precepts would be imparted alongside practical skills. Not surprisingly, the implementation of this goal left much to be desired, and in the best of circumstances proceeded but slowly. But a high degree of specialization and technical knowhow was rapidly spread among the members of the officialdom, thanks especially to the establishment of the so-called cameralist disciplines at the university. If need be, even new universities were created for that very same purpose, for example Göttingen, which in the mid-eighteenth century served to train the highly competent corps of government officials of Prussia. Somewhat earlier, a similar role had been played by the universities of Frankfurt on the Oder and Halle and the institutions associated with the Pietist Hermann Franke.[15] All these schools of higher learning also provided an important nucleus of modern administrators for countries further east, especially the Russian empire since the reign of Peter the Great, and served as models for the establishment of similar institutions there, as well.

In the period we are concerned with no government had the means—material or human—to set up a truly universal educational system encompassing the entire population, even all the youth. The primitive technology of transportation did not allow many to travel to schools at a distance. Yet, literacy and some schooling were clearly becoming an important avenue for material improvement and whatever social mobility the social system allowed. Not surprisingly, therefore, individuals and groups made efforts to provide schooling for their children on their proper initiative and at their own expense. The movement developed most in the urban setting, and it encompassed not only the wealthy patricians but also more humble guild members, tradesmen, and artisans. In most cases, such schools or school groups were neither officially licensed nor did they have a formal structure—in German they were called _Winkelschulen_ (i.e. schools behind the corner). Their existence is documented only sporadically and often indirectly, and for this reason their impact is hard to ascertain with any degree of accuracy. Recent studies for England and France, however, have shown that these local initiatives did bear fruit in a rapid increase of the number of literates in the second half of the eighteenth century.[16] Presumably something similar happened in Central Europe. It may also be surmised, from indirect evidence culled from memoirs and travelers' reports, that on a much smaller scale and in somewhat different form a similar trend was taking place in the Russian empire. The example set by the towns was followed, albeit sporadically and on a limited scale, by the more prosperous families in the villages.[17] By the end of the eighteenth century, the large minority of literate population in the major countries of Western and Central Europe provided a ready reservoir for a "modernizing" economy and society, a minority that was also aspiring in some measure to greater social mobility.

Obviously, the pressure for greater social mobility could become a threat to the stability of the existing social and political order, not to speak of its unforeseeable impact on the religious and moral consensus. The Churches worried that the spread of literacy among the common people might undermine their obedient belief in the dogmas of religion, stimulate a critical attitude, and make them amenable to the enticements of heretical ideas and denominations. To the state, the upward mobility appeared a danger for the existing distribution of power, and by stimulating conflicts might give rise to violence and disorder. Nor was the state unmindful of the possible depopulation of the countryside and the abandonment of physically difficult and financially unrewarding occupations on the part of those who had acquired the skills of literacy and claimed positions with a better status. The fear of losing manual labor, especially in agriculture, was all-pervasive throughout the eighteenth century in practically all countries. It was to stem "depopulation" (incidentally, and ironically, at a time when Europe's population was growing at an unprecedented rate) that the English government endeavored, unsuccessfully of course, to stem the migration to America, and the Continental powers made difficulties in allowing resettlement in Russia.

One way of coping with these perceived threats was to devise a school program that combines training in the necessary skills (of literacy) with a heavy dose of moral suasion. At the same time, the students should be accustomed to a proper work ethic and obedience by being involved as early as possible in productive labor. The idea was pioneered in the Austrian empire in Silesia, at Sagan by Ignaz Felbiger, and imitated in Prussia (after Silesia's conquest by Frederick II), in the core provinces of the Habsburg domains, and still later by Catherine II in the school reform drafted by Jankelevic de Mirievo, a former assistant to Felbiger.[18] In other words, the school was also turned into a workhouse where the young were brought up to accept obediently the status they had been born into and which, presumably, had been ordained for them by God. It is in this way, too, that the school system, combined with work in the put-out system of textile manufacturing, acted as a seedbed for the proto-industrialization process. As recent studies have shown, proto-industrialization was the necessary preparatory state for the full maturation of the industrial revolution.[19]

A further consequence of the proper conjunction of literacy and right moral values was the formation of loyalty to the existing political system. Adam Smith put this idea very pertinently in the following words:

The more they are instructed, the less liable they are to the delusions of enthusiasm and superstition, which, among ignorant nations, frequently occasion the most dreadful disorders. An instructed and intelligent people besides, are always more decent and orderly than an ignorant and stupid one. They feel themselves, each individually more respectable, and more likely to obtain the respect of their lawful superiors, and they are therefore more disposed to respect those superiors.[20]

* * *

Moreover, it is this kind of education that would permit fashioning a cohesive "nation", with a more or less uniform system of values—an ideal to which both the Well Ordered Police State and the philosophes of the Enlightenment were hoping to lead the people. This is what the *parlementaire* Rolland D'Erceville had in mind when he wrote:

L'uniformité dans l'enseignement peut seule opérer l'uniformité dans les coutumes et les moeurs ... [Une éducation commune] répand les mêmes principes et les mêmes lumières. Imbus dès l'enfance des mêmes vérités, les jeunes gens de toutes les provinces se dépouillent des préjugés de leur naissance, ils se formeront les mêmes idées de vertu et de justice ... Ces jeunes gens devenus les principaux d'entre les peuples demanderont eux mêmes des lois uniformes qui auraient offensé leurs pères, tous les intérêts particuliers seront effacés. Ils ne désireront conserver que les privilèges essentiels et utiles, ceux surtout qui pourront faciliter les occasions de donner au Roy des témoignages de leur amour et de leur fidelité et d'employer au service de leur patrie leurs biens aussi bien qu'ils lui sacrifient leur vie.[21]

The basic concept of the unitary national state is here stated long before the advent of the French Revolution that consecrated its triumph in Europe.

To bring about the transformation in outlook and behavior that was the aim of the educational practices we have surveyed it was not enough to make use of the rational and voluntaristic faculties of man. The new norms, values, and patterns of action had to be fully internalized so as to make them more or less natural and automatic. As Montesquieu noted, "Il y a de certaines vérités qu'il ne suffit pas de persuader, mais qu'il faut faire sentir". In other words, the affective side of man has to be engaged as well, the emotions—the "heart"—have to be put into the service of the "cerebral" purposes. The insight of Montesquieu was elaborated and applied to the upbringing of children by J.J. Rousseau (to some extent drawing on Locke's psychology) and put into practice by Basedow, Pestalozzi, and others in the latter part of the eighteenth century.

This insight also led to advocating—and putting into practice—more widespread educational opportunities for women. After all it was the mother who was the first to foster the emotional development of the child, so that the "enlightenment of her heart" was particularly crucial in raising the young generation of "modern" subjects. The notion of creating a new type of man was implicit in this belief. It found an explicit and graphic illustration in Peter the Great's aim at "transfiguring" (*preobrazovat'*) the traditional Muscovite man into a European, "modern," true son of the fatherland. Peter's frequent reference to the Transfiguration—note that his preferred regiment was the *Preobrazhenskii*—was not accidental and points to the main thrust of his aspirations. The same goal presides over the creation and curriculum of the Corps of Cadets (1731) and its subsequent transformation under Catherine II by I. I. Betskoi. It was Catherine, too, who extended Peter's pedagogic concerns to women by establishing the Smol'nyi Institut for girls of the nobility and richer urban families. Along the same line of wanting to "create a new breed of men", of transfiguring the traditional type of individual was the appeal of the moralistic journals and reviews that were so popular in the eighteenth century.[22] And it is no accident that the enlightened reformers in the late eighteenth century Russia turned their attention first to the reform of morals, to the reeducation of the emotional side of man. They did so in their dramatic, poetic, as well as discursive and publicistic works. Pride of place in their program was always given to pedagogy, the education of both mind and heart.[23]

The discovery and emphasis put on the "enlightenment of the heart" had a paradoxical consequence. Stress on the affective side of man's education resulted in turning to religion as a major force. Pietism had shown the way by combining education of mind and body (in developing useful skills) with constant religious practice. The goal was the synergetic union of man with the Godhead, and to this end mastery of the physical world had to be worked for in unison with spiritual improvement of the individual. This was the task and purpose of the *praxis pietatis* of the so-called Second Reformation (of which Wesleyan Methodism was the English manifestation).[24] It was the spirit that informed the Masonic lodges that devoted their energies to the betterment of man and society. Transferred to Russia—where its reception had been prepared by the policies of Peter the Great—it led to a religious emergence of the Russian intelligentsia, an "order of chivalry" dedicated to the moral improvement of the individual person and the material and social progress of the people.[25]

Our analysis and discussion has brought out a paradox—or antinomy—of a kind that is to be frequently encountered in human history. The original purpose of a set of actions, because of the manner it is carried out, often leads to quite an unexpected, if not outright contrary result. We have seen how literacy and "social disciplining" for the productive goals of the "modern", Well Ordered Police State have gone hand in hand. The process attained positive results—even when these fell short of original hopes and expectations—whenever society at large could be drawn into cooperation. This was the case in most of Western and Central Europe but not so in the case of Russia, where the heavy hand of autocracy did not allow for the full unfettering of the productive potential of society.

* * *

But we should note some even more telling paradoxes: schooling undertaken in the belief that it would promote stability and full acceptance of the existing order in fact stimulated the hankering for social mobility. This hankering threatened political peace and led the authorities to circumscribe the range and nature of education. Thus the school system was turned into an instrument for developing an obedient labor force submissive to the state. The second paradox was that the desire to internalize new norms, patterns of behavior, and conceptions of the world that rested on rational and factual insights led to a renewed emphasis on the affective, emotional components of man's psyche. In this way the rationalism of Enlightenment philosophy was transformed into the Enlightenment of the heart, and the latter brought about a return to religion and spirituality.

Finally, by promoting the literacy and education of ever larger numbers of its subjects without giving full scope for the application of their skills and recognition of their newly acquired intellectual and personal status, the state was creating its own grave-diggers. In this manner the royal policies of France and other Western European states helped the coalescence of a group of dissatisfied leaders, the radical philosophes, who played the crucial role in triggering the wave of revolutions that swept the Continent at the end of the eighteenth century. In Russia, on the other hand, the state's promotion of the "transfiguration" of Muscovite man into the Europeanized "true son of the fatherland" helped bring into being the intelligentsia that was to be its main adversary in the nineteenth century.

The final question that our examination of the pattern of education and of its relation to "modernization" raises is that of the possibility of planning and guiding fargoing transformations and developments in the body social. Not only is this endeavor fraught with many pitfalls if ends and means are not congruent, but can we ever know where change, once initiated, will lead? The specific trend in seventeenth and eighteenth century European history that we have examined, albeit cursorily, points to an answer in the negative. Should this not also be a warning for contemporary statesmen and politicians?

Notes

1. E. Sehling, *Die Kirchengesetzgebung unter Moritz von Sachsen 1544–49 und Georg von Anhalt* (Leipzig, 1899).

2. E. Johansson, "The History of Literacy in Sweden", in Harvey J. Graff ed., *Literacy and Social Development in the West: A Reader* (Cambridge, 1981), pp. 151–182.

3. R. Chartier, D. Julia, M.-M. Compère, *L'éducation en France du XVIe au XVIIIe s.* (Paris, 1976).

4. Cf. "The Kiev Mohyla Academy—Commemorating the 350th Anniversary of its Founding (1632)," *Harvard Ukrainian Studies*, VIII, No. 1/2 (June, 1984).

5. Günter Abel, *Stoizismus und frühe Neuzeit: Zur Entstehungsgeschichte modernen Denkens im Felde von Ethik und Politik* (Berlin, 1978).

6. Gerhard Oestreich, *Geist und Gestalt des frühmodernen Staates—Ausgewählte Aufsätze* (Berlin, 1969); Michael Roberts, *Essays in Swedish History* (Minneapolis, 1967).

7. Albert O. Hirschman, *The Passions and the Interests: Political Arguments for Capitalism before its Triumph* (Princeton, 1977).

8. Paul Bénichou, *Morales du grand siècle* (Paris, 1948).

9. Alexander Gerschenkron, "Time Horizon in Balzac and Others", *Proceedings of the American Philosophical Society*, 122 (1978), 75–91, and "Time Horizon in Russian Literature", *Slavic Review*, 34 (1975), 692–715.

10. Theodore K. Rabb, *The Struggle for Stability in Early Modern Europe* (Oxford, 1975).

11. John G. A. Pocock, "Clergy and Commerce. The Conservative Enlightenment in England," in *L'età dei lumi—Studi storici sul settecento europeo in onore di Franco Venturi*, I (Napoli, 1985), pp. 525–562.

12. *Iunosti chestnoe zertsalo ili pokazanie k zhiteiskomu obkhozhdeniiu* (St. Petersburg, 1717, and subsequent editions).

13. Marc Raeff, *The Well Ordered Police State: Social and Institutional Change through Law in the Germanies and Russia, 1600–1800* (New Haven, 1983).

14. Antoine Arnauld and Pierre Nicole, *La logique ou l'art de penser*, 1st ed., 1660; E. Weigel, *Kurtzer Entwurff der freudigen Kunst- und Tugend Lehre vor Trivial- und Kinder-Schulen*, Jena, 1662; Christian Weise, *Vertraute Gespräche wie der geliebten Jugend im Informations Wercke ... geraten seyn*, Leipzig, 1679.

15. Cf. Keith Tribe, "Cameralism and the Science of Government," *Journal of Modern History*, 56 (June, 1984), 263–84.

16. Chartier et al.; M.I. Clanchy, *From Memory to Written Record: England 1066–1307* (Cambridge, Mass., 1979).

17. *Zhurnal, ili zapiski zhizni i prikliuchenii Ivana Alekseevicha Tolchenova* (Moscow, 1974); N.V. Nechaev, *Gornozavodskie shkoly na Urale* (Moscow, 1956); indirect data is to be found in Gary Marker, *Publishing, Printing, and the Origins of Intellectual Life in Russia, 1700–1800* (Princeton, 1985).

18. James VanHorn Melton, *Absolutism and the Eighteenth Century Origins of Compulsory Schooling in Prussia and Austria* (Cambridge, forthcoming 1988).

19. Peter Kriedte, Hand Medick, Jürgen Schlumbohm, *Industrialisierung vor der Industrialisierung* (Göttingen, 1978) (English transl., Cambridge University Press).

20. Adam Smith, *The Wealth of Nations*, (N.Y., 1937), p. 740.

21. Cited in Chartier et al., p. 209.

22. Wolfgang Martens, *Die Botschaft der Tugend—Die Aufklärung im Spiegel der deutschen Moralischen Wochenschriften* (Stuttgart, 1968).

23. One thinks of the plays of D. Fon Vizin and the writings of A. Radishchev, I. Krylov, and the "masonic-pedagogic" publications of N.I. Novikov.

24. Laurence Dickey, *Hegel—Religion, Economics and the Politics of the Spirit, 1770–1807* (Cambridge, 1987).

25. Marc Raeff, *Origins of the Russian Intelligentsia—The Eighteenth Century Nobility* (New York, 1966).

Marc Raeff: A Bibliography (1946–1993)

Compiled by Molly Molloy
and Edward Kasinec

The first version of this bibliography appeared in *Russian Review* 41(4):454–471, October 1982. An updated version (compiled with the assistance of Elliot Isaac) appeared in *Imperial Russia, 1700–1917: State, Society, Opposition: Essays in Honor of Marc Raeff* (Northern Illinois University Press, 1988), pp. [289]–311. These articles are used with permission. Each item was examined and described *de visu*, as cited in the original publication. Slight changes have been made in this style to accommodate Westview's practices. Entries preceded by an asterisk also appear in the final section, "Reprints and Translations." This bibliography is a complete listing of Professor Raeff's publications through June 1993. Number 304 has recently been republished in Andrew Blane, ed., *Georges Florovsky: Russian Intellectual and Orthodox Churchman* (Crestwood, N.Y.: St. Vladimir's Seminary Press, 1993).

Abbreviations

AHR   *American Historical Review*
ASEER *American Slavic and East European Review*
BA   *Books Abroad*
CMRS *Cahiers du monde russe et soviétique*
CSP   *Canadian Slavonic Papers*
CSS/
    CASS *Canadian Slavic Studies/Canadian-American Slavic Studies*
CSSH *Comparative Studies in Society and History*
HUS   *Harvard Ukrainian Studies*
HT   *History Today*
JEH   *Journal of Economic History*
JGO   *Jahrbücher für Geschichte Osteuropas*
JMH   *Journal of Modern History*
JUS   *Journal of Ukrainian Studies*
LH   *Labor History*
NL   *New Leader*
NYT   *New York Times*

NYTM *New York Times Magazine*
NZh *Novyi zhurnal*
OSP *Oxford Slavonic Papers*
PC *Problems of Communism*
PNWQ *Pacific Northwest Quarterly*
PSQ *Political Science Quarterly*
RES *Revue des études slaves*
RH *Russian History*
RHMC *Revue d'histoire moderne et contemporaine*
RM *Russkaia mysl'*
RR *Russian Review*
SEEJ *Slavic and East European Journal*
SEER *Slavonic and East European Review*
SR *Slavic Review*
TLS *Times Literary Supplement*

1946

1. Review: "Na modnuiu temu: frantsuzskaia kniga o russkoi diplomatii." A review of: "C. de Grunwald: *Trois siècles de diplomatie russe*. Paris, 1945," *Novoe russkoe slovo*, 37(12,458):4, June 7.

1948

2. Review [pseudonym Mark Véart]: "On Russian Spirituality." A review of: "*A Treasury of Russian Spirituality*. Edited by G.P. Fedotov. New York: Sheed and Ward. 501 pp.," *NL*, 31(49):10, Dec. 4.

1949

*3. "An Early Theorist of Absolutism: Joseph of Volokolamsk," *ASEER*, 8(2):[77]–89, Apr. (See also no. 346)

1950

4. *The Peasant Commune in the Political Thinking of Russian Publicists: Laissez-faire Liberalism in the Reign of Alexander II*. Unpublished Ph.D. dissertation, Harvard University. 239 pp.

5. Review [pseudonym Mark Véart]: "A 16th Century Russian Despot." A review of: "Hans von Eckardt. *Ivan the Terrible*. Alfred A. Knopf," *NL*, 33(8):12, Feb. 25.

1951

6. "Russia After the Emancipation. Views of a Gentleman-Farmer," *SEER*, 29(73):470–485, June.

7. Review: "P. A. Zajončkovskij, ed., *Dnevnik D.A. Miljutina 1873–1875 (Diary of D.A. Miljutin 1873–1875)*, Volume I. Moscow: Gosudarstvennaja Ordena Lenina

Biblioteka SSSR imeni Lenina, Otdel rukopisej, 1947. 253 pp. 15 rubles," *ASEER*, 10(3):232–234, Oct.

1952

8. "Georges Samarin et le commune paysanne après 1861," *RES*, 29(1-4):[71]–81.
9. "A Reactionary Liberal: M.N. Katkov," *RR*, 11(3):157–167, July.
10. Review: "P.A. Zajončkovskij, ed. *Dnevnik D.A. Miljutina (Diary of D.A. Miljutin)*, Volume II, 1876–1877. Moscow: 1949. 290 pp. 15 rubles. Volume III, 1878–1880. Moscow: 1950. 324 pp. 12 rubles. Volume IV, 1881–1882. Moscow: 1950. 202 pp. 10 rubles. All published by Gosudarstvennaja Ordena Lenina Biblioteka SSSR imeni Lenina, Otdel rukopisej," *ASEER*, 11(3):241–243, Oct.

1953

11. "An American View of the Decembrist Revolt," *JMH*, 25(3):286–293, Sept.
12. "The Philosophical Views of Count M.M. Speransky," *SEER*, 31(77):[437]–451, June.
13. "The Political Views of Speranskij," *ASEER*, 12(1):[1]–21, Feb.

1954

14. Review: "V.V. Zenkovsky. *A History of Russian Philosophy*. 2 vols. George L. Kline, tr. New York: Columbia University Press, 1953. xiv + 947 pp. $15.00," *BA*, 28(2):227–228, Spring.

1955

15. Review: "Don Aminado. *Poezd na tret'em puti*. New York: Chekhov, 1954. 352 pp. $2.75," *BA*, 29(2):243, Spring.
16. Review: "Alexei Khomyakov. *Izbrannye sochineniia*. Nicholas Arseniev, ed. New York: Chekhov, 1955. 415 pp. $3.00," *BA*, 29(4):486, Autumn.
17. Review: "Horace G. Lunt, et al., eds. *Harvard Slavic Studies*, II. Cambridge: Harvard University Press, 1954. vi, 390 pp. $6.00," *BA*, 29(1):102, Winter.
18. Review: "Sergei Makovskii. *Portrety Sovremennikov*. New York: Chekhov, 1955. 415 pages. $3," *BA*, 29(4):487, Autumn.
19. Review: "Vladimir Nabokov. *Drugie berega*. New York: Chekhov, 1954. 269 pp., $2.25," *BA*, 29(3):307, Summer.
20. Review: "Georg von Rauch, *Russland: Staatliche Einheit und nationale Vielfalt. (Veröffentlichungen des Osteuropa-Instituts München, Band 5)*. München: Isar Verlag, 1953. 235 pp.," *ASEER*, 14(1):130–132, Feb.
21. Review: "Kniazhna Ol'ga Trubetskaia. *Kniaz' S.N. Trubetskoi—vospominaniia sestry*. New York: Chekhov, 1953. 271 pages. $2.25," *BA*, 29(3):366, Summer.
22. Review: "Martin Winkler, ed. *Slavische Geisteswelt. I: Russland*. Darmstadt: Holle, 1955. 367 pp. 14 dm.," *BA*, 29(4):439–440, Autumn.
23. Review: "V.S. Yanovsky. *Portativnoe bessmertie*. New York: Chekhov, 1953. 270 pages. $2.50," *BA*, 29(3):365–366, Summer.
24. Review: "Boris Zaitsev. *Chekhov: literaturnaia biografiia*. New York: Chekhov, 1954. 261 pp. $2.50," *BA*, 29(2):243, Spring.

1956

25. *Siberia and the Reforms of 1822.* Seattle: University of Washington Press. 210 pp. (*University of Washington Publications on Asia*)

26. Review: "Ivan Bunin. *O Chekhove (Nezakonchennaia rukopis').* New York: Chekhov, 1955. 412 pp. $3.00," *BA,* 30(3):289–290, Summer.

27. Review: "Nicolas Evreinov. *Istoriia russkogo teatra—s drevneishikh vremen do 1917 goda.* New York: Chekhov, 1955. 413 pp. $3.00," *BA,* 30(1):110, Winter.

28. Review: "Wilhelm Lettenbauer. *Russische Literaturgeschichte.* Frankfurt am Main: Humboldt, 1955. 431 pp. 16.50 dm.," *BA,* 30(4):464, Autumn.

29. Review: "A.M. Osorgina. *Istoriia russkoi literatury (S drevneishikh vremen do Pushkina).* Paris: YMCA Press, 1955, 266 pp.," *BA,* 30(4):464, Autumn.

30. Review: "Vladimir Seduro. *The Byelorussian Theater and Drama.* Edgar H. Lehrman, ed. New York: Research Program on the U.S.S.R., 1955. xxii, 516 pp.," *BA,* 30(2):226–227, Spring.

31. Review: "Sergei Shcherbatov. *Khudozhnik v ushedshei Rossii.* New York: Chekhov, 1955. 409 pp. $3.00," *BA,* 30(3):349–350, Summer.

32. Review: "Eugene Zamiatin. *Litsa.* New York: Chekhov, 1955. 285 pp. $2.50," *BA,* 30(2):241, Spring.

1957

33. "Education in the U.S.S.R.: Soviet System Declared Based on Slow Accumulation of Knowledge," *NYT,* 107(36,460):34, Wednesday, Nov. 20.

34. *Michael Speransky: Statesman of Imperial Russia, 1772–1839.* The Hague: Martinus Nijhoff. viii, 387 pp.

35. "The Russian Autocracy and Its Officials," *Harvard Slavic Studies, IV. Russian Thought and Politics.* Hugh McLean, Martin E. Malia, George Fischer, eds. Cambridge, Mass.: Harvard University Press. Pp. 77–91.

36. Review: "W.H. Bruford. *Anton Chekhov.* New Haven, Conn.: Yale University Press, 1957. 62 pp. $2.50," *BA,* 31(4):419, Autumn.

37. Review: "R.D. Charques. *A Short History of Russia.* New York: E.P. Dutton & Co., 1957. 284 pp., $3.95; Paul Sethe. *A Short History of Russia.* (Gateway Editions), Chicago: Henry Regnery Co., 1957. 192 pp., $1.25; C. Jay Smith, Jr. *The Russian Struggle for Power, 1914–1917: A Study of Russian Foreign Policy During the First World War.* New York: Philosophical Library, 1957. xv, 553 pp., $4.75," *SEEJ,* 15(3):220–221, Fall.

38. Review: "Walther Kirchner, ed. *Eine Reise durch Sibirien im achtzehnten Jahrhundert (Die Fahrt des Schweizer Doktors Jakob Fries). (Veröffentlichungen des Osteuropa-Instituts München,* Band X). München: Isar Verlag, 1955. 126 pp.," *ASEER,* 16(2):221–222, Apr.

39. Review: "*Littératures soviétiques. 1: Introduction aux littératures soviétiques: Contes et nouvelles.* Paris: Gallimard, 1956. 299 pp. 780 fr.," *BA,* 31(2):155, Spring.

40. Review: "Rudolf Neumann, *Ostpreussen, 1945–1955.* Frankfurt M. and Berlin: Alfred Metzner Verlag, 1955. 112 pp.," *ASEER,* 16(2):220–221, Apr.

41. Review: "V.S. Varshavsky. *Nezamechannoe pokolenie.* New York: Chekhov, 1956. 388 pp. $3.00," *BA,* 31(4):437, Autumn.

42. Review: "Velikii Kniaz' Gabriil Konstantinovich. *V Mramornom dvortse.* New York: Chekhov, 1955. 412 pp. $3.00," *BA,* 31(1):98, Winter.

1958

43. "Report on Russia's Big Red Schoolhouse," *NYTM*, 107(36,674, sec. 6):5, 37–40, June 22.

*44. "We Do Not Teach Them How to Think," *NYTM*, 107(36,527, sec. 6):7, 58–59, Jan. 26. (See also no. 347)

45. Review: "George Fischer. *Russian Liberalism*. [Cambridge, Massachusetts:] Harvard University Press, 1958. 240 pp. $4.50; Victor Leontovitsch. *Geschichte des Liberalismus in Russland*. Frankfurt am Main: Vittorio Klostermann, 1957. 426 pp. DM 34," *RR*, 17(4):307–310, Oct.

46. Review: "Hans Rosenberg. *Bureaucracy, Aristocracy, and Autocracy. The Prussian Experience 1660–1815*. Cambridge, Massachusetts, 1958. (*Harvard Historical Monographs*, XXXIV), ix, 247 pp.," *CSSH*, 1:396–399, 1958–1959.

47. Review: "Donald W. Treadgold. *The Great Siberian Migration: Government and Peasant in Resettlement from Emancipation to the First World War*. Princeton, New Jersey: Princeton Univ. Press, 1957. xiii, 278 pp., $5.00," *SEEJ*, 16(3):266–268, Fall.

1959

48. "Professors' Prose. Flight From Time," *Clark Scarlet*, 25(11):3–4.

*49. "Some Reflections on Russian Liberalism," *RR*, 18(3):218–230, July. (See also no. 348)

50. "Staatsdienst, Aussenpolitik, Ideologien. Die Rolle der Institutionen in der geistigen Entwicklung des Russischen Adels in 18 Jahrhundert," *JGO*, 7(2):[147]–181.

51. Review: "Robert F. Byrnes, *Bibliography of American Publications on East Central Europe, 1945–1957*. (*Slavic and East European Series*, XII.) [Bloomington:] Indiana Univ. Pubs., [1958]. xxx, 213 pp., $2.50," *SEEJ*, 17(New Series)(3):280–281, Fall.

52. Review: "Jaroslaw Iwaszkiewicz. *Der Höhenflug*. Kurt Harrer, tr. München: Langen/Müller, 1959. 114 pp. 6.80 dm," *BA*, 33(4):432, Autumn.

53. Review: "W.G.F. Jackson. *Seven Roads to Moscow*. New York: Philosophical Library, 1958. 334 pp. $7.50," *RR*, 18(4):348–349, Oct.

54. Review: "Gleb Struve. *Geschichte der Sowjetliteratur*. München: Isar, 1957. 595 pp. 38 dm," *BA*, 33(2):189, Spring.

55. Review: "Donald W. Treadgold. *The Great Siberian Migration: Government and Peasant in Resettlement from Emancipation to the First World War*. Princeton: Princeton University Press, 1957. xiii, 278 pp., $5.00," *JEH*, 19(2):323–325, June.

56. Review: "Mikhail Zetlin. *The Decembrists*. Tr. George Panin. Preface Michael M. Karpovich. New York: International Univ. Press [c.1958]. 349 pp., $5.00," *SEEJ*, 17(New Series)(3):303–304, Fall.

1960

57. "State and Nobility in the Ideology of M.M. Shcherbatov," *ASEER*, 19(3):[363]–379, Oct.

58. Review: "Hans Rogger. *National Consciousness in Eighteenth-Century Russia*.

Cambridge, Mass.: Harvard University Press, 1960. viii, 319 pp. (*Russian Research Center Studies*, 38)," *JGO*, 8(4):445–448.

1961

59. "Le climat politique et les projects de réforme dans les premières années du règne d'Alexandre Ier," *CMRS*, 11(4):415–433, Oct.-Dec.

60. Review: "M.M. Speranskii, *Proekty i zapiski*, edited by S.N. Valk. Moscow-Leningrad: Akademiia nauk, Institut istorii, Leningradskoe otdelenie, 1961. 244 pp. 75k.," *SR*, 20(4):706–707, Dec.

1962

61. "L'état, le gouvernement et la tradition politique en Russie Impériale avant 1861," *RHMC*, 9:[295]–307, Oct.-Dec.

*62. "Home, School, and Service in the Life of the 18th-Century Russian Nobleman," *SEER*, 40(95):295–307, June. (See also no. 349)

63. Review: "Jerome Blum. *Lord and Peasant in Russia from the Ninth to the Nineteenth Century*. Princeton: Princeton University Press, 1961. 656 pp. $12.50," *PSQ*, 77(2):307–310, June.

64. Review: "Michael Cherniavsky. *Tsar and People: Studies in Russian Myths*. New Haven and London: Yale University Press, 1961. xix + 258 pp. $6.00," *SR*, 21(2):344–346, June.

65. Review: "A Child of His Times." A review of: "Martin Malia: *Alexander Herzen and the Birth of Russian Socialism, 1812–55*. Harvard. 486 pp. $10.00," *NL*, 45(4):28–29, Feb. 19.

66. Review: "Anatole G. Mazour. *Russia: Tsarist and Communist*. Princeton, N.J.: D. Van Nostrand, 1962. x + 995 pp. $9.00," *SR*, 21(4):737–738, Dec.

1963

67. Editor. *Peter the Great—Reformer or Revolutionary?* Boston: D.C. Heath. xviii, 109 pp. (*Problems in European Civilization*)

68. Review: "*Eighteenth Century Russian Publications in the Library of Congress: A Catalog*. Prepared by Tatiana Fessenko. Washington, D.C. Government Printing Office, 1961. xvi + 157 pp. $1.00," *SR*, 22(1):185–186, Mar.

69. Review: "Horst Jablonowski and Werner Philipp (eds.), *Forschungen zur osteuropäischen Geschichte (Historische Veröffentlichungen des Osteuropa-Instituts an der Freien Universität Berlin)*. Vol. I[1954], II[1955], III[1956], IV[1956], V[1957], VI[1958], VII[1959], VIII[1962]. Wiesbaden: Otto Harrassowitz," *SR*, 22(4):[751]–753, Dec.

70. Review: "*Siberian Journey down the Amur to the Pacific, 1856–57*. Ed. by Charles Vevier. Madison: University of Wisconsin Press, 1962. ix, 370 pp. $6.00," *PNWQ*, 54(3):128, July.

71. Review: "Jacob Walkin. *The Rise of Democracy in Pre-Revolutionary Russia: Political and Social Institutions Under the Last Three Czars*. New York: Frederick A. Praeger, 1962. ix, 320 pp. $6.50," *SR*, 22(2):334–335, June.

1964

72. "The 150th Anniversary of the Campaign of 1812 in Soviet Historical Writing," *JGO*, 12(2):[247]–260, July.

*73. "Russia's Perception of Her Relationship with the West," *SR*, 23(1):[13]–19, Mar. (See also no. 349)

74. Review: "J.L.H. Keep. *The Rise of Social Democracy in Russia*. Oxford: Clarendon Press, 1963; Richard Kindersley. *The First Russian Revisionists; A Study of "Legal Marxism" in Russia*. Oxford: Clarendon Press, 1963; Arthur P. Mendel. *Dilemmas of Progress in Tsarist Russia—Legal Marxism and Legal Populism*. Cambridge, Massachusetts: Harvard University Press, 1963," *PC*, 13(4):48–50, July-Aug.

75. Review: "Hans Lemberg: *Die nationale Gedankenwelt der Dekabristen*. Köln, Graz: Herman Böhlau, 1963. viii, 168 pp. DM 16.50. (Kölner Historische Abhandlungen, Band 7)," *JGO*, 12(1):124–127, May.

76. Review: "Friedrich von Schubert. *Unter dem Doppeladler: Erinnerungen eines Deutschen in russischem Offiziersdienst, 1789–1814*. Edited by Erik Amburger. Stuttgart: K.F. Koehler Verlag, 1962. viii, 388 pp.," *SR*, 23(1):139–140, Mar.

77. Review: "Alexander Vucinich. *Science in Russian Culture: A History to 1860*. Stanford, Calif.: Stanford University Press, 1963. xvi, 463 pp. $10.00," *JMH*, 36(4):450–451, Dec.

1965

78. Review: "Horst Jablonowski and Werner Philipp, eds., *Forschungen zur osteuropäischen Geschichte*. Berlin and Wiesbaden: Otto Harrassowitz, 1963. 304 pp. (*Historische Veröffentlichungen des Osteuropa-Instituts an der Freien Universität Berlin*, Vol. IX)," *SR*, 24(1):130–131, Mar.

79. Review: "V.A. Maklakov. *The First State Duma (Contemporary Reminiscences)*. Bloomington: Indiana University Publications, 1964. 251 pp. $6.50," *RR*, 24(1):76–77, Jan.

80. Review: "André Mazon. *Deux russes écrivains français*. Paris: Didier, 1964. 427 pp. (*Études de littérature étrangère et comparée*, Vol. LI)," *SR*, 24(3):559–560, Sept.

81. Review: "Igor Smolitsch. *Geschichte der russischen Kirche, 1700–1917*. Vol. I. Leiden: E.J. Brill, 1964. lvii, 734 pp. 96 Dutch guilders. (*Studien zur Geschichte Osteuropas*, Vol. IX)," *SR*, 24(3):578–580, Sept.

1966

82. Editor. *The Decembrist Movement*. Englewood Cliffs, N.J.: Prentice-Hall. x, 180 pp. (*Russian Civilization Series*)

83. *Origins of the Russian Intelligentsia: The Eighteenth-Century Russian Nobility*. New York: Harcourt, Brace and World. 248 pp.

84. Editor. *Plans for Political Reform in Imperial Russia, 1730–1905*. Englewood Cliffs, N.J.: Prentice-Hall. xi, 159 pp. (*Russian Civilization Series*)

*85. Editor. *Russian Intellectual History: An Anthology*. With an introduction by Isaiah Berlin. (*The Harbrace Series in Russian Area Studies*) New York: Harcourt, Brace, and World. x, 404 pp. Also published: [Atlantic Highlands] N.J.: Humanities Press; Sussex: Harvester Press. (See also no. 350)

86. Review: "Mathias Bernath, Horst Jablonowski, and Werner Philipp, eds. *Forschungen zur osteuropäischen Geschichte*. Berlin and Wiesbaden: Otto Harrassowitz. (*Historische Veröffentlichungen des Osteuropa-Instituts an der Freien Universität Berlin*. Vol. X[1965]. 356 pp. XI[1966]). 175 pp.," *SR*, 25(4):688–691, Dec.

1967

87. "Filling the Gap Between Radishchev and the Decembrists," *SR*, 26(3):[395]–413, Sept.

*88. "La jeunesse russe à l'aube du XIXe siècle—André Turgenev et ses amis," *CMRS*, 8(4):[560]–586, Oct.-Dec. (See also no. 351)

89. "Les Slaves, les Allemands et les 'Lumières,'" *CASS*, 1(4):[521]–551, Winter.

*90. "The Style of Russia's Imperial Policy and Prince G.A. Potemkin," *Statesmen and Statecraft of the Modern West: Essays in Honor of Dwight E. Lee and H. Donaldson Jordan*. Gerald N. Grob, ed. Barre, Mass.: Barre Publishers. Pp. 1–51. (See also nos. 352–353)

91. Review: "Erik Amburger. *Geschichte der Behördenorganisation Russlands vom Peter dem Grossen bis 1917*. (*Studien zur Geschichte Osteuropas*, Number 10). Leiden: E.J. Brill, 1966. xxxii, 622 pp. 86 gl," *AHR*, 72(2):646–647, Jan.

92. Review: "Thornton Anderson. *Russian Political Thought: An Introduction*. Ithaca, N.Y.: Cornell University Press, 1967. xiii, 444 pp. $9.75," *AHR*, 73(2):541, Dec.

93. Review: "Martin Katz. *Mikhail N. Katkov: A Political Biography 1818–1887*. (*Studies in European History*, Number 6). The Hague: Mouton & Co., 1966. 195 pp. 24 gl.," *AHR*, 72(4):1450, July.

94. Review: "E. Lampert. *Sons Against Fathers: Studies in Russian Radicalism and Revolution*. Oxford: The Clarendon Press, 1965. x, 405 pp. 63 S.," *The Historian*, 29(3):471–473, May.

95. Review: "Vladen Georgievič Sirotkin. *Duel' dvuch diplomatij. Rossija i Francija v 1801–1812 gg. (Le Duel de deux Diplomaties. Russie et France en 1801–1812)*. Moscow: Izdat. Nauka, 1966. 206 pp. DM4," *JGO*, 15(3):442–443, Sept.

1968

96. "Correspondance," *Annales: Économies, Sociétés, Civilisations*, 23(5):1178–1179, Sept.-Oct. [Response to Michael Confino's review of *Origins of the Intelligentsia*, "Histoire et psychologie: A propos de la noblesse russe au XVIIIe siècle," *Annales: Économies, Sociétés, Civilisations*, 22(6):1163–1205, Nov.-Dec. 1967.]

97. "Introduction," Alexander Israel Wittenberg. *The Prime Imperatives: Priorities in Education*. Preface by George Polya. Toronto, Vancouver: Clarke, Irwin & Company Limited. Pp. xi–xiv.

98. Review: "I.A. Fedosov. *Iz istorii russkoj obščestvennoj mysli XVIII stoletija [A Contribution to the History of Russian Social Thought]. M.M. Ščerbatov*. Moscow: Izdat. Moskovskogo Universiteta, 1967. 258 pp. DM 6, 10," *JGO*, 16(1):150, Mar.

99. Review: "Robert E. MacMaster. *Danilevsky: A Russian Totalitarian Philosopher*. Cambridge, Mass.: Harvard University Press, 1967. ix, 368 pp. $7.95," *PSQ*, 83(1):107–109, Mar.

100. Review: "Hugh Seton-Watson. *The Russian Empire, 1801–1917*. Oxford: Clarendon Press, 1967. 813 pp. $10.00," *RR*, 27(1):88–90, Jan.

1969

101. *Michael Speransky—Statesman of Imperial Russia, 1772–1839.* The Hague: Martinus Nijhoff. 2d rev. ed. ix, 394 pp.

102. "Some Translations of Surveys and Sources in Russian History," *CSS*, 3(3):556–564, Fall.

103. Review: "François-Xavier Coquin. *La Sibérie—Peuplement et immigration paysanne au XIXe siècle.* Paris: Institut d'études slaves. Université de Paris. (*Collection historique*, No. XX). 1969. 789 pp. 60 F," *CSS*, 3(3):586–588, Fall.

104. Review: "Alton S. Donnelly. *The Russian Conquest of Bashkiria, 1552–1740: A Case Study in Imperialism* (*Yale Russian and East European Studies, 7*), New Haven and London: Yale University Press, 1968. x, 214 pp. $6.50. (Distributed in Canada by McGill-Queen's University Press, Montréal)," *CSS*, 3(4):750–752, Winter.

105. Review: "*Karlik favorita. Istorija žizni Ivana Andreeviča Jakubovskogo, karlika Svetlejšego Knjazja Platona Aleksandroviča Zubova, pisannaja im samym. Der Zwerg des Favoriten/ Die Lebensgeschichte Ivan Andreevič Jakubovskijs, des Zwerges des Fürsten Platon Aleksandrovič Zubov, von ihm selbst verfasst. S predisloviem i primečanijami grafa V.P. Zubova i poslesloviem Ditricha Gerchardta. Mit einem Vorwort und Anmerkungen von Valentin Graf Zubov sowie einem Nachwort von Dietrich Gerhardt.* Wilhelm Fink München 1968. 424 S. DM 68, (*Slavische Propyläen. Texte in Neu- und Nachdrucken* Band 32)," *JGO*, 17(1):112–113, Mar.

106. Review: "Forrestt A. Miller. *Dmitrii Miliutin and the Reform Era in Russia.* Nashville, Tenn.: Vanderbilt University Press, 1968. iv, 246 pp. $7.50," *CSS*, 3(2):429–431, Summer.

1970

107. "The Domestic Policies of Peter III and His Overthrow," *AHR*, 75(5):1289–1310, June.

108. "Pugachev's Rebellion," *Preconditions of Revolution in Early Modern Europe.* Edited with an introductin by Robert Forster and Jack P. Greene. Baltimore and London: The Johns Hopkins University Press. Pp. 161–202.

109. Review: "John T. Alexander. *Autocratic Politics in a National Crisis: The Imperial Russian Government and Pugachev Revolt, 1773–1775* (*Russian and East European Series,* vol. 38). Bloomington and London: Indiana University Press for the International Affairs Center, 1969. xii, 346 pp. $8.50," *SR*, 29(3):507–508, Sept.

110. Review: "Robert F. Byrnes. *Pobedonostsev: His Life and Thought.* Bloomington and London: Indiana University Press, 1968. xiii, 495 pp. $15.00," *PSQ*, 85(3):528–530, Sept.

111. Review: "James R. Gibson. *Feeding the Russian Fur Trade—Provisionment of the Okhotsk Seaboard and the Kamchatka Peninsula 1639–1856.* Madison: University of Wisconsin Press, 1969. xix, 337 pp. $15.00," *CSS*, 4(1):118–119, Spring.

112. Review: "Patricia Kennedy Grimsted. *The Foreign Ministers of Alexander I: Political Attitudes and the Conduct of Russian Diplomacy, 1801–1825.* (*Russian and East European Studies*). Berkeley and Los Angeles: University of California Press, 1969. xxvi, 367 pp. $9.50," *AHR*, 75(5):1493–1494, June.

113. Review: "Hans-Bernd Harder. *Schiller in Russland. Materialen zu einer Wirkungsgeschichte. 1789–1814.* Verlag Gehlen Bad Homburg v.d.H., Berlin, Zürich,

1969. 234 S. DM 30 (*Frankfurter Beiträge zur Germanistik*, Band 4)," *JGO*, 18(3):450–452, Sept.

114. Review: "Michael Jenkins. *Arakcheev: Grand Vizier of the Russian Empire*. New York: The Dial Press, 1969. 317 pp. $5.95," *CSS*, 4(1):119–120, Spring.

115. Review: "Miriam Kochan. *Life in Russia Under Catherine the Great*. (*European Life Series*, edited by Peter Quenell). London: B.T. Batsford Ltd. and New York: G.P. Putnam's Sons, 1969. ix, 182 pp. (Distributed in Canada by the Copp Clark Publishing Co., Toronto)," *CSS*, 4(3):619–620, Fall.

116. Review: "A. Walicki. *The Controversy over Capitalism. Studies in the Social Philosophy of the Russian Populists*. Oxford: Clarendon Press, 1969. 197 pp. 45 S. $7.25. (Distributed in Canada by Oxford University Press, Don Mills, Ontario)," *CSS*, 4(1):120–121, Spring.

1971

117. "Eighteenth- and Nineteenth-Century Russia," Norman F. Cantor. *Perspectives on the European Past: Conversations with Historians*. New York and London: The Macmillan Company and Collier-Macmillan Limited. Pp. 242–266 [Section II, Chapter 28].

118. *Imperial Russia 1682–1825: The Coming of Age of Modern Russia*. New York: Alfred A. Knopf. xi, 176 pp.

119. "Patterns of Russian Imperial Policy Toward the Nationalities," *Soviet Nationality Problems*. Edward Allworth, editor. New York; London: Columbia University Press. Pp. [22]–42.

120. "Random Notes on the Reign of Catherine II in the Light of Recent Literature," *JGO*, 19(4):[541]–556, Dec.

121. Review: "Mathias Bernath, Horst Jablonowski, and Werner Philipp, eds. *Forschungen zur osteuropäischen Geschichte*, vol. XV. (*Historische Veröffentlichungen des Osteuropa-Instituts an der Freien Universität Berlin*) Berlin and Wiesbaden: Otto Harrassowitz, 1970. 306 pp. DM 78," *SR*, 30(2):385–388, June.

122. Review: "Peter Yaklovlevich Chaadaev. *Philosophical Letters & Apology of a Madman*. Trans. and introd. Mary-Barbara Zeldin. Knoxville: The University of Tennessee Press, 1969. xi, 203 pp. $7.50; Raymond T. McNally. *The Major Works of Peter Chaadaev; A Translation and Commentary*. Introd. Richard Pipes. Notre Dame & London: University of Notre Dame Press, 1969. xix, 261 pp. $7.95," *CSS*, 5(1):129–130, June.

123. Review: "Peter K. Christoff. *The Third Heart: Some Intellectual-Ideological Currents and Cross Currents in Russia, 1800–1830*. (*Slavistic Printings and Reprintings*, 77). The Hague and Paris: Mouton, 1970. 130 pp. 34 Dutch guilders," *SR*, 302(2):393–394, June.

124. Review: "Robert O. Crummey. *The Old Believers and the World of Antichrist. The Vyg Community and the Russian State, 1694–1855*. Madison: The University of Wisconsin Press, 1970. xix, 258 pp. $10.00," *CSS*, 5(3):433–434, Fall.

125. Review: "Annelies Lauch. *Wissenschaft und kulturelle Beziehungen in der russischen Aufklärung—Zum Wirken H.L.Ch. Bacmeisters*. Deutsche Akademie der Wissenschaften zur Berlin. (*Veröffentlichungen des Instituts für Slawistik*, 51). (H.H.

Bielfeldt, Herausgeber). Berlin: Akademie-Verlag, 1969. 444 pp. (paper)," *CSS*, 5(3):435–436, Fall.

126. Review: "Norman E. Saul. *Russia and the Mediterranean, 1797–1807.* Chicago and London: The University of Chicago Press, 1970. xii, 268 pp., Sh. 79," *JGO*, 19(2):293–295, June.

1972

127. Editor. *Catherine the Great: A Profile.* New York: Hill and Wang. xiii + 331 pp. (*World Profiles.* Aida DiPace Donald, general editor)

128. "First Soviet-American Historical Colloquium," *SR*, 31(4):969–971, Dec.

129. Editor. *Peter the Great Changes Russia.* Lexington: D.C. Heath. xxiv, 199 pp. (*Problems in European Civilization,* John Ratte, ed.) [A new and revised edition of *Peter the Great: Reformer or Revolutionary?* Boston: D.C. Heath, 1963]

130. Review: "François-Xavier Coquin. *La grande commission législative, 1767–1768. Les Cahiers de doléances urbains (Province de Moscou).* Preface by Victor L. Tapié. *Publications de la Faculté des lettres et sciences humaines de Paris-Sorbonne.* (Série "Recherches," vol. 67) Paris and Louvain: Béatrice Nauwelaerts, 1972. ix, 258 pp.," *SR*, 31(3):663–664, Sept.

131. Review: "James Cracraft. *The Church Reform of Peter the Great.* Stanford, California: Stanford University Press, 1971. 336 pp.," *RR*, 31(1):77–79, Jan.

132. Review: "Revolution—Then." A review of: "Sam Dolgoff, editor and translator. *Bakunin on Anarchy: Selected Works by the Activist-Founder of World Anarchism.* Alfred A. Knopf; Leon Trotsky. *1905.* Translated by Anya Bostock. Random House," *Yale Review,* 61(4):625–628, Summer.

133. Review: "I.A. Fedosov, I.I. Astaf'ev, I.D. Koval'chenko, eds. *Istochnikovedenie istorii SSSR XIX–nachalo XXv.* Moscow. Izdatel'stvo Moskovskogo Universiteta (*Istoricheskii fakul'tet, Kafedra istorii SSSR—period kapitalizma*), 1970. 469 pp. 1 ruble 37 kopeks," *CASS*, 6(1):149–150, Spring.

134. Review: "N.M. Lisovskii, comp. *Russkaia periodicheskaia pechat' 1703–1900 gg. (Bibliografiia i graficheskiia tablitsy)* St. Petersburg 1895–Petrograd 1915. (Nachdruck by Zentral-Antiquariat der Deutschen Demokratischen Republik, Leipzig 1965) 267 pp. & Tables. $51.00; S.A. Vengerov, comp. *Russkiia knigi—s biograficheskimi dannymi ob avtorakh i perevodchikakh (1708–1893).* St. Petersburg, 1897–1899 (I. A-Babadzhanov; II. Babaev-Bogatyr'. III. Bogatyr'-Vavilov). (Nachdruck by Zentral-Antiquariat der Deutschen Demokratischen Republik, Leipzig, 1967). vii, 476 pp., iv, 472 pp. $81.00," *CASS*, 6(1):150–151, Spring.

135. Review: "K.A. Papmehl. *Freedom of Expression in Eighteenth Century Russia.* The Hague: Martinus Nijhoff, 1971. xvi, 166 pp. 26 Dutch guilders," *JGO*, 20(3):446–447, Sept.

1973

136. "The Enlightenment in Russia and Russian Thought in the Enlightenment," *The Eighteenth Century in Russia.* J.G. Garrard, editor. Oxford: Clarendon Press. Pp. [25]–47.

137. "Introduction," *Zhizn' i prikliucheniia Andreia Bolotova: opisannyie samim*

im dlia svoikh potomkov. Cambridge, Eng.: Oriental Research Partners. 3v. in 1. (*Memoir Series*) Pp. iii–[viii]. Reprint of the 1931 ed. published by Academia, Moskva.

138. Review: "*Forschungen zur osteuropäischen Geschichte (Werner Philipp zum 65. Geburtstag von seinen Schülern). (Historische Veröffentlichungen des Osteuropa Instituts an der Freien Universität Berlin).* Berlin: In Kommission bei Otto Harrassowitz Wiesbaden, 1973. 151 pp.," *CASS,* 7(4):545–546, Winter.

139. Review: "Joseph T. Fuhrmann et al. *Essays on Russian Intellectual History.* Foreword by James P. Hart. Introduction by Sidney Monas. Edited by Leon Borden Blair. (*The Walter Prescott Webb Memorial Lectures,* Number 5) Austin: University of Texas Press for the University of Texas at Arlington, 1971. 123 pp. $5.00," *AHR,* 78(2):464–465, Apr.

140. Review: "Helmut Grasshoff and Ulf Lehmann, eds. *Studien zur Geschichte der russischen Literatur des 18. Jahrhunderts.* 3 vols. (Deutsche Akademie der Wissenschaften zu Berlin. *Veröffentlichungen des Instituts für Slawistik,* Nr. 28. Herausgegeben von H.H. Bielfeldt). Berlin: Akademie Verlag, 1963–1968. 187 pp., 492 pp., 664 pp. 25, 46, 65 DM.; *A.N. Radiščev und Deutschland; Beiträge zur Literatur des ausgehenden 18. Jahrhunderts.* (*Sitzungsberichte der sächsischen Akademie der Wissenschaften zu Leipzig. Philologisch-historische Klasse,* Band 114, Heft 1) Berlin: Akademie Verlag, 1969. 132 pp. 9.50 DM," *CASS,* 7(1):118–119, Spring.

141. Review: "Friedhelm Berthold Kaiser. *Die russische Justizreform von 1864. Zur Geschichte der russischen Justiz von Katharina II bis 1917.* Leiden: E.J. Brill, 1972. 552 pp.," *RR,* 32(3):318–319, July.

142. Review: "Klaus Meyer. *Bibliographie zur osteuropäischen Geschichte. Verzeichnis der zwischen 1939 und 1964 veröffentlichten Literatur in westeuropäischen Sprachen zur osteuropäischen Geschichte bis 1945.* Unter Mitarbeit von J.H.L. Keep, K. Manfrass, A. Peetre. Herausgegeben von Werner Philipp. (*Bibliographische Mitteilungen des Osteuropa Instituts an der Freien Universität Berlin.* Heft 19). Berlin: Osteuropa Institut an der Freien Universität Berlin, 1972. xlix, 649 pp.," *CASS,* 7(4):544–545, Winter.

143. Review: "Tamara Talbot Rice. *Elizabeth: Empress of Russia.* New York and Washington: Praeger Publishers, 1970. xvi, 231 pp. $8.50," *CASS,* 7(1):122, Spring.

144. Review: "*La Russie et l'Europe XVe–XXe siècles.* Paris-Moscou: Bibliothèque Générale de l'École Pratique des Hautes Études-VIe Section, S.E.V.P.E.N., 1970. 326 pp.; *Au Siècle des Lumières.* Paris-Moscou: École Pratique des Hautes Études-Sorbonne-VIe Section: Sciences Économiques et Sociales; Institut d'Histoire Universelle de l'Académie des Sciences de l'U.R.S.S., 1970. 310 pp.," *CASS,* 7(1):120–121, Spring.

145. Review: "George L. Yaney. *The Systematization of Russian Government: Social Evolution in the Domestic Administration of Imperial Russia, 1711–1905.* Urbana, Chicago, London: University of Illinois Press, 1973. xvi, 430 pp. $13.50," *SR,* 33(2):345–347, June.

1974

146. "The Empress and the Vinerian Professor: Catherine II's Projects of Government Reform and Blackstone's *Commentaries,*" *OSP,* 7(New Series):[18]–41.

147. "Michael Cherniavsky," *JGO,* 22(Neue Folge)(1):159.

148. "Russia and the Soviet Union—II. A History of the Eighteenth Century," *Encyclopedia Britannica (Macropaedia)*. 15th ed. Chicago and other places, vol. 16, pp. 49–57.

149. Review: "Valentin Boss. *Newton and Russia: The Early Influence, 1698–1796.* (*Russian Research Center Studies*, 69) Cambridge, Mass.: Harvard University Press, 1972. xviii, 309 pp. $19.00," *AHR*, 79(1):196–197, Feb.

150. Review: "Peter K. Christoff. *An Introduction to Nineteenth-Century Russian Slavophilism*. Volume 2, I.V. Kireevskij. (*Slavistic Printings and Reprints*, 23/2). The Hague: Mouton, 1972. x, 406 pp. 68gls," *AHR*, 79(2):534–535, Apr.

151. Review: "Karp Emel'janovič Džedžula. *Rossija i Velikaja francuzskaja buržuaznaja revoljucija konca XVIII veka (Russia and the Great French Bourgeois Revolution at the End of the 18th Century)*. Kiev: Izdat. Kievskogo Universiteta, 1972. 449 pp. DM 14.70," *JGO*, 22(Neue Folge)(3):433–435.

152. Review: "Shmuel Galai. *The Liberation Movement in Russia, 1900–1905.* Cambridge at the University Press, 1973. x, 325 pp. $22.50," *The Historian*, 36(2):329, Feb.

153. Review: "Hans-Jürgen Krüger, editor. *Archivalische Fundstücke zu den russisch-deutschen Beziehungen. Erik Amburger zum 65. Geburtstag. Giessener Abhandlungen zur Agrar- und Wirtschaftsforschung des europäischen Ostens.* (*Osteuropa Studien der Hochschulen des Landes Hessen*. Reihe 1) Berlin: In Kommission bei Duncker & Humblot, 1973," *CASS*, 8(4):597, Winter.

154. Review: "Alexander V. Muller, translator and editor. *The Spiritual Regulations of Peter the Great.* (*Publications on Russia and Eastern Europe of the Institute for Comparative and Foreign Area Studies*, Number 3). Seattle and London: University of Washington Press, 1972. xxxviii, 150 pp. $10.00," *CASS*, 8(2):327–328, Summer.

155. Review: "S.O. Petrov, compiler. *Knyhy hraždans'koho druku vydani na Ukrajini XVIII–perša polovyna XIX stolittja: Kataloh (Books in Civil Type Published in the Ukraine in the Eighteenth and First Half of the Nineteenth Centuries: A Catalogue).* Xarkiv: Vydavnyctvo "Redakcijno-vydavnyčij viddil Knyžkovoji palaty URSR," 1971. 297 pp. 1400 copes," *Recenzija*, 5(1):25, Fall-Winter.

156. Review: "S. Frederick Starr. *Decentralization and Self-Government in Russia, 1830–1870.* Princeton, N.J.: Princeton University Press, 1972. xiii, 386 pp. $15.00," *American Political Science Review*, 68(1):332–333, Mar.

157. Review: "Robert C. Tucker. *Stalin as Revolutionary 1879–1929. A Study in History and Personality.* New York: W.W. Norton & Company, 1973. xx, 519 pp.; Stephen F. Cohen. *Bukharin and the Bolshevik Revolution. A Political Biography 1888–1938.* New York: Alfred A. Knopf, 1973. xix, 495 pp.," *NZh*, 115:267–271, June.

1975

*158. Review essay: "*Iz pod glyb i istoriia russkoi obshchestvennoi mysli,*" *NZh*, 119:[191]–203, June. (See also no. 354)

*159. "The Well-Ordered Police State and the Development of Modernity in Seventeenth- and Eighteenth-Century Europe: An Attempt at a Comparative Approach," *AHR*, 80(5):1221–1243, Dec. (See also no. 355)

160. Review: "G.R.V. Barratt. *Voices in Exile: The Decembrist Memoirs.* Montreal: McGill-Queen's University Press, 1974. xxi, 381 pp. $18.50.; Anatole G. Mazour.

Women in Exile: Wives of the Decembrists. Tallahassee, Florida: The Diplomatic Press, 1975. x, 134 pp. $15.00," *CSP,* 17(2&3):528–529, Summer and Fall.

161. Review: "Wolfgang Gesemann. *Die Endeckung der unteren Volksschichten durch die russische Literatur (Zur Dialektik eines literarischen Motivs von Kantemir bis Belinskij).* Wiesbaden: Otto Harrassowitz, 1972. 315s. (*Veröffentlichungen des Osteuropa-Instituts München,* Band 39)," *Zeitschrift für Slavische Philologie,* 38(1):197–201.

1976

162. "Imperical Russia: Peter I to Nicholas I," *An Introduction to Russian History.* Robert Auty and Dmitrii Obolensky, eds. With the editorial assistance of Anthony Kingsford. Cambridge: Cambridge University Press. Pp. 121–195. [Chapter 4]

163. "Introduction," S.G. Pushkarev. *Krest'ianskaia pozemel'noperedel'naia obshchina v Rossii.* Newtonville, Mass.: Oriental Research Partners. Pp. i–iv.

164. "Peter I," *The American Peoples Encyclopedia,* vol. 14:450–451. (Originally published in 1966)

165. "Russia's Autocracy and Paradoxes of Modernization," *Ost-West-Begegnung in Österreich. Festschrift für Eduard Winter zum 80. Geburtstag.* Herausgegeben von Gerhard Oberkofler und Eleonore Zlabinger. Wien-Köln-Graz: Böhlau Verlag. Pp. 275–283.

166. "Sergei Martynovich Troitskii, 1930–1976," *SR,* 35(3):595–596, Sept.

167. Review: "Adriano Cavanna. *La codificazione penale in Italia. Le origini lombarde.* Milano, A. Giuffré ed., 1975. (*Università degli Studi di Milano Facoltà di Giurisprudenza. Pubblicazioni dell'Istituto di Storia del Diritto Italiano,* 5), 317 pp., Trad. di Angelo Torre," *Rivista storica italiana,* 88(4):881–887, Dec.

168. Review: "Anton Denikin. *The Career of a Tsarist Officer: Memoirs, 1872–1916.* With an annotated translation by Margaret Patoski. Minneapolis: University of Minnesota Press, 1975. xxii, 333 pp. $17.95," *The Historian,* 38(4):752–753, Aug.

1977

169. "Uniformity, Diversity, and the Imperial Administration in the Reign of Catherine II," *Osteuropa in Geschichte und Gegenwart. Festschrift für Günther Stökl zum 60. Geburtstag.* Herausgegeben von Hans Lemberg, Peter Nitsche und Erwin Oberländer unter Mitwirkung von Manfred Alexander und Hans Hecker. Köln-Wien: Böhlau Verlag. Pp. 97–113.

170. "Zum Problem der Sowjetsprache und ihrer Rolle in der sowjetischen Geschichtswissenschaft," *Die Interdependenz von Geschichte und Politik in Osteuropa seit 1954-Protokoll der Historiker Fachtagung in Bad Wiessee 1976.* Stuttgart: Deutsche Gesellschaft für Osteuropakunde e.V. Pp. 26–31.

171. Review: "An Opening to the West." A review of: "Harold N. Ingle: *Nesselrode and the Russian Rapprochement with Britain, 1836–1844.* 196 pp. University of California Press. £8.20," *TLS,* 3904:8, June 7.

172. Review: "Wolfgang Knackstedt. *Moskau: Studien zur Geschichte einer mittelalterlichen Stadt. (Quellen und Studien zur Geschichte der östlichen Europa,* [vol. 8].) Wiesbaden: Franz Steiner Verlag, 1975. x, 285 pp. Maps. DM56, paper," *SR,* 36(4):[676]–677, Dec.

173. Review: "S.S. Landa. *Dukh revoliutsionnykh preobrazovanii ... Iz istorii formirovaniia ideologii i politicheskoi organizatsii Dekabristov, 1816–1825* [The spirit of revolutionary transformations ... from the history of the formation of the ideology and political organization of the Decembrists, 1816–1825]. Moscow: Izd-vo "Mysl'," 1975. 379 pp. 1.37 rubles," *RR*, 36(1):86–87, Jan.

174. Review: "The Rise of the Intelligentsia." A review of: "Nicholas V. Riasanovsky: *A Parting of Ways. Government and the Educated Public in Russia, 1801–1855.* 323 pp. Oxford: Clarendon Press. 12 pounds," *TLS*, 3930:839, July 8.

175. Review: "W.H. Roobol. *Tsereteli—A Democrat in the Russian Revolution: A Political Biography.* Translated from the Dutch by Philip Hyams and Lynne Richards. (*International Institute of Social History, Amsterdam, Studies in Social History,* 1). The Hague: Martinus Nijhoff, 1976, xii, 273 pp. Illus. 80 Dglds.," *SR*, 36(4):681–682, Dec.

176. Review: "*Russkaia religiozno-filosofskaia mysl' XX veka: sbornik statei.* Edited by N.P. Poltoratskii. (*Slavic Series,* 2). Pittsburgh: Department of Slavic Languages and Literatures, Faculty of Arts and Sciences, University of Pittsburgh, 1975. 413 pp. paper," *SR*, 36(1):132–133, Mar.

177. Review: "Jeremiah Schneiderman. *Sergei Zubatov and Revolutionary Marxism: The Struggle for the Working Class in Tsarist Russia.* Ithaca and London: Cornell University Press, 1976. 401 pp. $18.50," *LH*, 18(3):460–463, Summer.

178. Review: "Adam B. Ulam. *In the Name of the People: Prophets and Conspirators in Prerevolutionary Russia.* New York: The Viking Press, 1977. xii, 418 pp. $15.00," *PSQ*, 92(2):358–360, Summer.

179. Review: "Alexander Vucinich. *Social Thought in Tsarist Russia: The Quest for a General Science of Society, 1861–1917.* Chicago: University of Chicago Press, 1976. ix, 294 pp. $15.50," *CSP*, 19(2):223–225, June.

180. Review: "Analysing the Realm of a Russian Utopia." A review of: "A. Walicki: *The Slavophile Controversy,* 1975," *CASS*, 11(3):[431]–437, Fall.

1978

181. "Russian Intellectual History and Its Historiography: Critical Remarks," *Forschungen zur osteuropäischen Geschichte, "Werner Philipp zum 70. Geburtstag,"* 25:297–303.

182. Review: "O knige Alena Bezansona." A review of: "Alain Besançon: *Les origines intellectuelles du Léninisme.* Paris: Calmann-Lévi, 1977," *NZh*, 130:[219]–228, Mar.

183. Review: "Astrid von Borcke. *Die Ursprünge des Bolschewismus—Die Jakobinische Tradition in Russland und die Theorie der Revolutionären Diktatur.* Munich: Johannes Berchmans, 1977. 646 pp. DM 89," *RR*, 37(2):224, Apr.

184. Review: "*Landmarks: A Collection of Essays on the Russian Intelligentsia 1909: Berdyaev, Bulgakov, Gershenzon, Izgoev, Kistyakovsky, Struve, Frank.* Edited by Boris Shragin and Albert Todd. Translated by Marian Schwartz. New York: Katz Howard (200 East 84th Street, New York, N.Y. 10028), 1977. lx, 210 pp. $12.75," *SR*, 37(1):128–130, Mar.

185. Review: "What Became of the Liberal Tradition?—Comments on *Samosoznanie.*" A review of: "P. Litvinov, M. Meerson-Aksenov, and B. Shragin:

Samosoznanie: sbornik statei. New York: "Khronika," 1976. 320 pp. $9.00," *SR,* 37(1):[116]–119, Mar.

186. Review: "Intelligentsia et nationalisme ruthènes." A review of: "P.R. Magocsi: *The Shaping of a National Identity. Subcarpathian Rus'. 1848–1948.* Cambridge, Mass.: Harvard University Press, 1978. xiii, 640 pp.," *CMRS,* 19(4):451–452, Oct.-Dec.

187. Review: "George F. Putnam. *Russian Alternatives to Marxism: Christian Socialism and Idealistic Liberalism in Twentieth Century Russia.* Knoxville: University of Tennessee Press, 1977. xii, 233 pp.," *NZh,* 131:288–290, June.

188. Review: "N.V. Reviakina. *Problemy cheloveka v ital'ianskom gumanizme vtoroi poloviny XIV–pervoi poloviny XV v.* (*Problems of Man in Italian Humanism in the Second Half of the XIVth and the First Half of the XVth Centuries.*) Moscow: Nauka Publishing House, 1977. 272 pp. 1 ruble 14 kopecks; A.Kh. Gorfunkel'. *Gumanizm i naturfilosofiia ital'ianskogo Vozrozhdeniia.* (*Humanism and Natural Philosophy in the Italian Renaissance.*) Moscow: Mysl' Publishing House, 1977. 359 pp. 1 ruble 67 kopecks," *Renaissance Quarterly,* 31(3):373–378, Fall.

1979

189. Review essay: "The Bureaucratic Phenomena of Imperial Russia, 1700–1905," *AHR,* 84(2):399–411, Apr.

190. "Codification et droit en Russie impériale. Quelques remarques comparatives," *CMRS,* 20(1):5–13, Jan.-Mar.

191. Review: "Isaiah Berlin. *Russian Thinkers.* Edited by Henry Hardy and Aileen Kelly. Introduction by Aileen Kelly. New York. Viking Press, 1978. xxiv, 312 pp. $14.95," *SR,* 38(1):106–107, Mar.

192. Review: "*Russland, Deutschland, Amerika: Festschrift für Fritz T. Epstein zum 80. Geburtstag.* Edited by Alexander Fischer, Günter Moltmann, and Klaus Schwabe. (*Frankfurter Historische Abhandlungen,* vol. 17). Wiesbaden: Franz Steiner Verlag, 1978. xviii, 441 pp. DM 58, paper," *SR,* 38(3):485–486, Sept.

1980

193. "Catherine II, Empress of Russia (Catherine the Great)," *Academic American Encyclopedia,* vol. 4, pp. 209–210. Princeton, N.J.: Aretê Publishing Company.

194. "Russia/Union of Soviet Socialist Republics, history of," *Academic American Encyclopedia,* vol. 16, pp. 351–360. Princeton, N.J.: Aretê Publishing Company.

195. Review: "J.L. Black. *Citizens for the Fatherland: Education, Educators, and Pedagogical Ideals in Eighteenth Century Russia* (with a Translation of *Book on the Duties of Man and Citizen,* St. Petersburg 1783). (*East European Monographs,* no. 53). Boulder, Colo.: East European Quarterly, 1979. xiii, 273 pp. $16.50. Distributed by Columbia University Press," *RH,* 7(3):364.

196. Review: "John B. Dunlop. *The New Russian Revolutionaries.* Belmont, Mass.: Nordland Publishing Company, 1976. 344 pp. $18.50," *SR,* 39(1):124–125, Mar.

197. Review: "Manfred Hildermeier. *Die Sozialrevolutionäre Partei Russlands— Agrarsozialismus und Modernisierung im Zarenreich (1900–1914)* (*Beiträge zur Geschichte Osteuropas,* Dietrich Geyer and Hans Roos, editors, Band 11). Köln-Wien: Böhlau Verlag, 1978. xviii, 458 pp.," *CASS,* 14(4):560–561, Winter.

198. Review: "Was Peter All That Great?" A review of: "Robert K. Massie: *Peter the Great: His Life and His World*. New York: Alfred A. Knopf, 1980. 909 pp. $17.95," *New York Review of Books*, 28(4):49–50, Mar. 19.

199. Review: "James C. McClelland. *Autocrats and Academics: Education, Culture, and Society in Tsarist Russia*. Chicago: University of Chicago Press, 1979. xiv, 150 pp. $14.00," *RR*, 39(2):239–240, Apr.

200. Review: "*Russian Officialdom: The Bureaucratization of Russian Society from the Seventeenth to the Twentieth Century*. Edited by Walter McKenzie Pinter and Don Karl Rowney. Chapel Hill, N.C.: University of North Carolina Press, 1980. xviii + 396 pp. $20.00 hardcover, $12.00 paperback," *HUS*, 5(1):125–129, Mar.

201. Review: "*Russian Orthodoxy Under the Old Regime*. Edited by Robert L. Nichols and Theofanis G. Stavrou. Minneapolis: University of Minnesota Press, 1978. xi + 261 pp.," *CMRS*, 21(1):[123]–125, Jan.-Mar.

1981

202. "O tsarstvovanii Nikolaia I v svete noveishei istoriografii," *Russkii al'manakh*. [Edited by] Zinaida Shakhovskaia, Rene Gerra, and Evgenii Ternovskii. Paris: L'Almanach russe. Pp. 302–314.

203. Review: "Erik Amburger. *Ingermanland: Eine junge Provinz Russlands im Wirkungsbereich der Residenz und Weltstadt St. Petersburg–Leningrad*. 2 vols. (*Beiträge zur Geschichte Osteuropas*, vol. 13). Cologne and Vienna: Böhlau Verlag, 1980. xvi, 1947 pp., 16 pp. plates. Maps. DM 278," *SR*, 40(3):468–469, Fall.

204. Review: "Alex De Jonge. *Fire and Water: A Life of Peter the Great*. New York: Coward, McCann & Geoghegan, 1980. 279 pp. $12.95; Robert K. Massie. *Peter the Great: His Life and World*. New York: Alfred A. Knopf, 1980. xii, 909 pp. $17.95," *RR*, 40 (1): 58–60, Jan.

205. Review: "Harmut Klinger. *Konstantin Nikolaevič Bestužev-Rjumins Stellung in der russischen Historiographie und seine gesellschaftliche Tätigkeit. (Ein Beitrag zur russischen Geistesgeschichte des 19. Jahrhunderts*). Frankfurt/M: Peter D. Lang, 1980. 244 pp. SFr.45," *RR*, 40(3):342–343, June.

1982

206. "Beseda s istorikom Markom Raevym," *Vestnik russkogo khristianskogo dvizheniia*, 136(1/11):290–295. [K vykhodu v svet na frantsuzkom iazyke lektsii M. Raeva—*Comprendre l'Ancien Régime (Poniat' staryi rezhim)*, Seuil, 1981, 320 pp.]

*207. *Comprendre l'Ancien Régime russe: État et société en Russie impériale: Essai d'interprétation*. With a preface by Alain Besançon. Paris: Editions Du Seuil, 247 pp. (See also nos. 356–358)

208. "Intelligentsia i kruzhki v Peterburge v nachale XIX veka," *Obozrenie*, 1:10–18, Oct.

209. "Seventeenth-Century Europe in Eighteenth-Century Russia? (Pour prendre congé du dix-huitième siècle russe)," *SR*, 4(4):[611]–619, Winter; and "Reply," *SR*, 41(4):[634]–638, Winter.

210. "Some Remarks on the Pipes-Nove Exchange," *Russia*, 5-6:124–126.

211. "Voina 1812 goda i russkaia obshchestvennost' v tsarstvovanie Aleksandra pervogo," *RM*, 3438:10–11, Thursday, Nov. 11.

212. Review: "*Russia in the Age of Catherine the Great.* By Isabel de Madariaga. New Haven, Conn.: Yale University Press, 1981. Pp. xii + 698," *JMH,* 54(3):635–638, Sept.

213. Review: "J. Michael Hittle. *The Service City: State and Townsmen in Russia, 1600–1800.* Cambridge, Mass.: Harvard University Press, 1979. vii, 297 pp. $20.00," *LH,* 23(2):307–310, Spring.

214. Review: "Heinz Ischreyt, series editor. *Studien zur Geschichte der Kulturbeziehungen in Mittel- und Osteuropa* (Im Auftrage des Studienkreises für Kulturbeziehungen Mittel- und Osteuropas, herausgegeben von Heinz Ischreyt). Volume V: Heinz Ischreyt, general editor. Eva H. Balazs, Ludwig Hammermayer, Hans Wagern, Jerzy Wojtowics [sic], editors. *Beförderer der Aufklärung in Mittel- und Osteuropa (Freimaurer, Gesellschaften, Clubs).* Berlin: Verlag Ulrich Camen, 1979. 347 pp. Volume VI: Wolfgang Kessler, general editor. B.I. Krasnobaev, Gert Robel, Herbert Zeman, editors. *Reisen und Reisebeschreibungen im 18. und 19. Jahrhundert als Quellen der Kulturbeziehungsforschung.* Berlin: Verlag Ulrich Camen, 1980. 403 pp.," *RH,* 9(2-3):402–404.

215. Review: "*Russophilie und Konservatismus: Die russophile Literatur in der Deutschen Öffentlichkeit 1831–1852.* By Peter Jahn. Geschichte und Theorie der Politik. Unterreihe A: Geschichte, vol. 2. Stuttgart: Ernst Klett Verlag, 1980. viii, 333 pp.; *Das veränderte Russland: Studien zum deutschen Russlandverständnis im 18 Jahrhundert zwischen 1725 und 1762.* By Eckhard Matthes. Europäische Hochschulschriften. Series 3: Geschichte und ihre Hilfswissenschaften, vol. 135. Frankfurt/Main, Bern, and Cirencester: Peter D. Lang, 1981. 566 pp.," *SR,* 41(3):541–542, Fall.

216. Review: "*Rethinking Ukrainian History.* Edited by Ivan L. Rudnytsky. With the assistance of John-Paul Himka. Edmonton: The Canadian Institute of Ukrainian Studies and the University of Alberta (Distributed by the University of Toronto Press), 1981. x, 268 pp. $14.95 cloth; $9.95 paper," *HUS,* 6(1):100–103, Mar.

217. Review: "Orest Subtelny, *The Mazepists—Ukrainian Separatism in the Eighteenth Century.* viii, 280 pp. $20.00. *East European Monographs.* Boulder, Colo. Distributed by Columbia University Press, 1981," *HUS,* 6(3):415–417, Sept.

218. Review: "Alexander Yanov. *The Origins of Autocracy: Ivan the Terrible in Russian History.* Translated by Stephen Dunn. Berkeley: University of California Press, 1981. xvi, 339 pp. $19.95," *RR,* 41(4):474–476, Oct.

219. Review: "Dymitri Zlepko. *Der grosse Kosakenaufstand 1648 gegen die polnische Herrschaft. Die Rzeczpospolita und das Kosakentum in der ersten Phase des Aufstandes.* Veröffentlichungen des Osteuropa-Instituts München. Herausgeber: Georg Stadmüller. Band 49. Wiesbaden: Otto Harrassowitz, 1980. 132 pp. $19.50," *RH,* 9(1):129.

1983

220. "Academic Exchanges with the Soviet Union: Intellectual, Political, and Moral Dilemmas," *Proceedings. General Education Seminar. Columbia University.* Vol. 1: *Education Frontiers and the Cultural Tradition in the Contemporary University.* 1982–1983. Pp. 73–76.

221. "Na puti k revoliutsii v Rossii," *Obozrenie,* 4:30–31, Apr.

222. "The Russian Nobility in the Eighteenth and Nineteenth Centuries: Trends and Comparisons," *The Nobility in Russia and Eastern Europe.* Edited by Ivo Banac and Paul Bushkovitch. New Haven: Yale Concilium on International and Area Studies. (*Yale Russian and East European Publications,* 3). Pp. [99]–121.

223. *The Well-Ordered Police State: Social and Institutional Change Through Law in the Germanies and Russia, 1600–1800.* New Haven and London: Yale University Press. ix, 284 pp.

224. Review: "Richard Hellie, *Slavery in Russia 1450–1725.* Chicago & London. University of Chicago Press. 1982. xix–776 pp.," *LH,* 24(3):471–475, Summer.

225. Review: "*Russlands erste Nationalitäten: Das Zarenreich und die Völker der mittleren Wolga vom 16. bis 19. Jahrhundert.* By Andreas Kappeler. Cologne and Vienna: Böhlau Verlag, 1982. vii, 571 pp. Maps. DM 158," *SR,* 42(1):103–104, Spring.

226. Review: "Neil Weissman. *Reform in Tsarist Russia: The State Bureaucracy and Local Government, 1900–1914.* New Brunswick, N.J.: Rutgers University Press, 1981. xi, 292 pp. $19.50," *RH,* 10(1):109–111.

1984

*227. "Foreword," Alexander Davydoff. *Russian Sketches: Memoirs.* Introduction by John M. Dax. [Translated from the Russian by Olga Davydoff-Dax.] Tenafly, N.J.: Hermitage. Pp. 9–11. (See also no. 359)

228. "Proniknovenie zapadnykh idei v Rossiiu," *Obozrenie,* 11:33–37, Sept.

229. Review: "*Art and Culture in Nineteenth-century Russia.* Edited by Theofanis George Stavrou. Bloomington: Indiana University Press, 1983. xix, 268 pp. $27.50 £17.88," *SR,* 42(2):357–358, Summer.

230. Review: "Aileen Kelly. *Mikhail Bakunin: A Study in The Psychology and Politics of Utopianism.* Oxford (Clarendon Press). 1982. Pp. 320," *SR,* 43(4):678–679, Winter.

231. Review: "*Neopublikovannye proizvedeniia.* By V.O. Kliuchevskii. Moscow: Nauka, 1983. 416 pp. 2.20 rubles," *SR,* 42(2):[291]–292, Summer.

232. Review: "Heinz-Dietrich Löwe. *Antisemitismus und reaktionäre Utopie— Russischer Konservatismus im Kampf gegen den Wandel von Staat and Gesellschaft 1890–1917.* Hamburg: Hoffman und Campe Verlag, 1978. Reihe: Historische Perspektiven, Band 13. 304 pp. DM 58," *Studies in Contemporary Jewry.* Vol. 1. Edited by Jonathan Frankel. Bloomington: Published for the Institute for Contemporary Jewry, the Hebrew University of Jerusalem, by Indiana University Press. Pp. 496–500.

1985

233. "*Novyi Grad*' and Germany: A Chapter in the Intellectual History of the Russian Emigration of the 1930s," *Felder und Vorfelder russischer Geschichte: Studien zu Ehren von Peter Scheibert.* Herausgegeben von Inge Auerbach, Andreas Hillgruber und Gottfried Schramm. Freiburg im Breisgau: Rombach. Pp. 255–265.

234. "O pervoi russkoi emigratsii," *Obozrenie,* 16:29–33, Sept.

235. Review: "Franz Basler, *Die Deutsch-Russische Schule in Berlin 1931–1945: Geschichte und Auftrag.* Wiesbaden: Otto Harrassowitz, 1983. 98 pp. DM 20. Osteuropa-Institut an der Freien Universität Berlin. Slavistische Veröffentlichungen. Vol. 54," *JGO,* 33(Neue Folge)(2):312.

236. Review: "C.R. Bawden, *Shamans, Lamas and Evangelists—The English Missionaries in Siberia* (London: 1985)," TLS, 4279:381, Apr. 5.

237. Review: "Dietrich Beyrau, *Militär und Gesellschaft im vorrevolutionären Russland*. (*Beiträge zur Geschichte Osteuropas*, Band 15). Köln/Wien: Böhlau Verlag, 1984. x, 504 pp. DM 138,00," *CASS*, 19(1):65–67, Spring.

238. Review: "Mikhail Geller, *Mashina i vintiki* (London: Overseas Publications Exchange, 1985)," *Obozrenie*, 15:42–43, July.

239. Review: "*Religion and Rural Revolt*. Edited by Janos M. Bak and Gerhard Benecke. Manchester: Manchester University Press, 1984. x, 491 pp. £39.50," *CASS*, 19(2):239–240, Summer.

240. Review: "*The Image of Peter the Great in Russian History and Thought*. By Nicholas V. Riasanovsky. New York and Oxford: Oxford University Press, 1985. ix, 331 pp. Illustrations. $29.95," *SR*, 44(3):538–540, Fall.

241. Review: "Edward C. Thaden. *Russia's Western Borderlands, 1710–1870*. Assisted by Marianna Forster Thaden. Princeton: Princeton University Press, 1984. Pp. xi, 278," *AHR*, 90(5):1239–1240, Dec.

1986

242. "Dvesti let imperii: Popytka istoricheskogo analiza," *Obozrenie*, 19:10–16, Mar.

243. "Foreword," V.S. Yanovsky, *Elysian Fields: A Book of Memory*. DeKalb: Northern Illinois University Press. Pp. ix–xv.

244. "Foreword," and "Kliuchevskii—Historian of the Eighteenth Century," *CASS*, 20(3-4):[201]–202, and [383]–398, resp., Fall-Winter. Also editor of this special issue: "Kliuchevskii's Russia: Critical Studies."

*245. "Muscovy Looks West," *HT*, 36:16–21, Aug. (See also no. 360)

246. "Preface," Carol Leadenham, comp. *Guide to the Collections in the Hoover Institution Archives Relating to Imperial Russia, the Russian Revolutions and Civil War, and the First Emigrations*. Stanford, Calif.: Hoover Institution Press. (*Hoover Press Bibliographical Series*, no. 68) Pp. xi–xii.

247. "What is European History?" *HT*, 36:47–48, Jan.

248. Review: "Manfred Hildermeier, *Bürgertum und Stadt in Russland 1760–1870: Rechtliche Lage und soziale Struktur*. Köln, Wien: Böhlau Verlag, 1986. xix, 689 pp., 2 maps. DM 208,—Beiträge zur Geschichte Osteuropas. Vol. 16," *JGO*, 35 (Neue Folge)(2):258–261.

249. Review: "Westward the Course of Empire." A review of: "John L.H. Keep. *Soldiers of the Tsar: Army and Society in Russia 1462–1874*. 432 pp. Oxford: Clarendon Press. £35 019822575x; William C. Fuller, Jr. *Civil-Military Conflict in Imperial Russia 1881–1914*. 295 pp. Princeton University Press. £28.40 0691054525," *TLS*, 4339:601, May 30.

250. Review: "Jo Ann Ruckman. *The Moscow Business Elite: A Social and Cultural Portrait of Two Generations, 1840–1905*. DeKalb: Northern Illinois University Press. Pp. xiii, 275. $24.00," *AHR*, 91(1):152–153, Feb.

251. Review: "Peter Scheibert, *Lenin an der Macht—Das russische Volk in der Revolution 1918–1922*. Weinheim: Acta Humaniora, 1984. xx, 730 pp. DM 220,00," *CASS*, 20(1-2):186–187, Spring-Summer.

1987

252. "Introduction," *Russia in the Twentieth Century: The Catalog of the Bakhmeteff Archive of Russian and East European History and Culture.* Boston: G.K. Hall & Co. Pp. vii–ix.

253. "Letter to the Editor," *RR,* 46(2):[224], Apr. [This concerns Robert Himmer's "On the Origin and Significance of the Name 'Stalin,'" *RR,* 45(3):269–286, July 1986.]

254. "Russia from 1689 to 1825/55 [essay]," "Russia from 1689 to 1825/55 [bibliographical essay]," *Studying Russian and Soviet History.* Edited by Abraham Ascher. Boulder, Colo: Social Science Education Consortium. Pp. 21–31 and 87–92, resp.

255. "Russie—1796–1825" and "Spéransky, Michel—Mikhail Mikhailovitch," Jean Tulard, editor. *Dictionnaire Napoléon.* Paris: Fayard: Pp. 1485–1493 and 1587–1588, resp.

256. Review: "*Russia* by Edward Acton, xiii + 342 pp. (Longman, The Present and the Past Series, £17.50 hardback, £8.95 paperback)," *HT,* 37:53–54, Feb.

257. Review: "*No East or West.* By Paul B. Anderson. Edited by Donald E. Davis. Paris: YMCA Press, 1985. iii, 1975 pp. Photographs. Cloth," *SR,* 45(2):337, Summer.

258. Review: "Catherine Andreyev. *Vlasov and the Russian Liberation Movement—Soviet Realities and Emigre Theories.* Cambridge University Press, 1987; Jane Burbank. *Intelligentsia and Revolution—Russian Views of Bolshevism 1917–1922.* Oxford University Press, 1986; A.P. Stolypin. 'Na sluzhbe Rossii—Ocherki po istorii NTS'. Frankfurt, 'Posev,' 1986," *NZh,* 167:284–287, June.

259. Review: "*1905: la première revolution russe. Actes du colloque international organisé du 2 au 6 juin 1981.* Edited by François-Xavier Coquin and Céline Gervais-Francelle. Série internationale, no. 26. Collection historique de l'Institut d' études slaves, vol. 32. Paris: Publication de la Sorbonne, 1986. 568 pp. 280 F.," *SR,* 46(2):304–305, Summer.

260. Review: "*Aristocrats and Servitors: The Boyar Elite in Russia, 1613–1689.* By Robert O. Crummey. Princeton, N.J.: Princeton University Press, 1983. Pp. xvi + 315. $30.00," *JMH,* 58(1):378–380, Mar.

261. Review: "Druzhinin, N.M. *Izbrannye trudy: Revoliutsionnoe dvizhenie v XIX v.* Edited by S.S. Dmitriev. Moscow: Nauka, 1985. 485 pp. 3.40 rub.," *RR,* 46(4):[447]–448, Oct.

262. Review: "*A Radical Worker in Tsarist Russia: The Autobiography of Semën Ivanovich Kanatchikov.* Translated and edited by Reginald E. Zelnik. Stanford: Stanford University Press, 1986. 472 pp. $39.95," *LH,* 28(2):262–263, Spring.

263. Review: "Martin A. Miller. *The Russian Revolutionary Emigres 1825–1870.* Baltimore and London (The Johns Hopkins University Press), 1986. XII + 292 pages," *NZh,* 168–169:464–465, Sept.-Dec.

264. Review: "*The Ukrainian Impact on Russian Culture, 1750–1850.* By David Saunders. Canadian Library in Ukrainian Studies. Edmonton, Alberta: Canadian Institute of Ukrainian Studies, 1985. x, 415 pp. $14.95, paper. Distributed by the University of Toronto Press, Ontario, Toronto," *SR,* 45(4):767–768, Winter.

265. Review: "*Russian Studies.* By Leonard Schapiro. Edited by Ellen Dahrendorf. Introduction by Harry Willetts. Elisabeth Sifton Books. New York: Viking, 1986. 390 pp.," *SR,* 46(1):[132]–134, Spring.

266. Review: "*Na sluzhbe Rossii: ocherki po istorii NTS*. By A.P. Stolypin. Frankfurt a.M.: Possev, 1986. 302 pp. DM 33, paper," *SR*, 46(2):307–308, Summer.

267. Review: "Orest Subtelny, *Domination of Eastern Europe—Native Nobilities and Foreign Absolutism, 1500–1715*. Kingston and Montreal: McGill-Queen's University Press; Gloucester: Alan Sutton, 1986. xii, 270 pp.," *JUS*, 11(2):93–95, Winter.

268. Review: "Andrzej Walicki. *Legal Philosophies of Russian Liberalism*. Oxford (Clarendon Press), 1987, ix + 477 pages," *NZh*, 168-169:465–466, Sept.-Dec.

1988

269. "La culture russe et l'émigration," *Histoire de la littérature russe*. Volume 3: *Le XXe siècle*. Part 2: *La Révolution et les années vingt*. [Paris]: Fayard. Traduit de l'Anglais par Daria Olivier. Pp. [61]–96.

270. "L'émigration et la 'cité nouvelle'," *CMRS*, 29(3-4):[543]–552, July-Dec.

271. "Georgij Florovskij historien de la culture religieuse russe," *CMRS*, 29(3-4):[561]–565, July-Dec.

272. "Institutions of a Society in Exile: Russia Abroad, 1919–1939," *Rossiia/Russia*, 6:95–117.

273. "Literacy, Education, and the State in 17th–18th Century Europe." Transcription of a lecture given as the eighth annual Phi Alpha Theta distinguished lecture on history at the State University of New York at Albany on March 23, 1988. (Brochure) 12 pp.

274. "Marc Aldanov (1886–1957)," *Histoire de la littérature russe*. Volume 3: *Le XXe siècle*. Part 2: *La Révolution et les années vingt*. [Paris]: Fayard. Traduit de l'Anglais par Daria Olivier. Pp. 105–113.

275. "On the Heterogeneity of the Eighteenth Century in Russia," *Russia and the World of the Eighteenth Century*. Proceedings of the Third International Conference organized by the Study Group on Eighteenth-Century Russia and held at Indiana University at Bloomington, USA, September 1984. Edited by R.P. Bartlett, A.G. Cross, and Karen Rasmussen. Columbus, Ohio: Slavica Publishers, Inc., [c1986]. Pp. 666–681.

276. "Perspectives on the 18th Century in Russia," "*... aus der anmuthigen Gelehrsamkeit*": *Tübinger Studien zum 18. Jahrhundert. Dietrich Geyer zum 60. Geburtstag*. Herausgegeben von Eberhard Müller. Tübingen: Attempto Verlag. Pp. [169]–177.

277. "Pis'ma A.A. Kizevettera N.I. Astrovu, V.I. Vernadskomu, M.V. Vishniaku," *NZh*, 172-173:[462]–526, Sept.-Dec. [Includes introduction]

278. "Predislovie," Zh. Pavlova. *Imperatorskaia biblioteka Ermitazha. 1762–1917*. Tenafly, N.J.: Ermitazh. Pp. 9–11.

279. "Preface," *L'Émigration russe: revues et recueils, 1920–1980. Index général des articles*. Paris: Institut d'études slaves. (*Bibliotheque russe de l'Institut d'études slaves*, tome 81) Pp. vii–x.

280. "Werner Philipp on His Eightieth Birthday 13 March 1988," *JGO*, 36(Neue Folge)(1):[157]–158.

281. Review: "*Vlasov and the Russian Liberation Movement: Soviet Reality and Émigré Theories*. By Catherine Andreyev. Soviet and Eastern European Studies. Cambridge, London, New York, New Rochelle, Melbourne, and Sydney: Cambridge University Press, 1987. xiv, 251 pp. $34.50, cloth," *SR*, 47(1):131–133, Spring.

282. Review: "Anmartin Mikhal Broide [Brojde]. *A.V. Druzhnin—Zhizn' i tvorchestvo.* Copenhagen: Rosenkilde & Bagger, 1986. 553 pp.," *CASS,* 22(1-4):515–516, Spring-Summer-Fall-Winter.

283. Review: "Linda Frey and Marsha Frey. *Societies in Upheaval: Insurrections in France, Hungary, and Spain in the Early Eighteenth Century.* (Contributions to the Study of World History, number 6.) Westport, Conn.: Greenwood, 1987. Pp. xii, 142. $29.95; J.H. Shennan. *Liberty and Order in Early Modern Europe: The Subject and the State, 1650–1800.* (Studies in Modern History.) New York: Longman. 1986. pp. xii, 144. $10.95," *AHR,* 93(3):678–679, June.

284. Review: "*Time of Troubles. The Diary of Iurii Vladimirovich Got'e—Moscow—July 8, 1917 to July 23, 1922.* Translated, edited, and introduced by Terence Emmons. Princeton University Press, 1988. XIX + 513 pp.," *NZh,* 171:307–309, June.

285. Review: "R.H. Johnston. *'New Mecca, New Babylon'—Paris and the Russian Exiles, 1920–1945.* Kingston and Montreal (McGill-Queen's University Press) 1988. IX + 254 pp. Index & Bibliography," *NZh,* 170:318–319.

286. Review: "Walter Kirchner. *Die deutsche Industrie und die Industrialisierung Russlands 1815–1914.* St. Katharinen, F.R.G.: Scripta Mercaturae. 1986. Pp. 409. DM 58," *AHR,* 93(2):461–462, Apr.

287. Review: "John Doyle Klier. *Russia Gathers Her Jews: The Origins of the "Jewish Questions" in Russia, 1772–1825.* DeKalb: Northern Illinois University Press. 1986. pp. xxiv, 236," *AHR,* 93(1):195–196, Feb.

288. Review: "Russian Publishing and the Russian Intellectuals: An Enduring Pattern." A review of: "*Publishing, Printing and the Origins of Intellectual Life in Russia, 1700–1800,* by Gary Marker (Princeton: Princeton University Press, 1985), 312 pp. £17.60/$31.50," *Minerva,* 26(3):436–445, Autumn.

289. Review: "*The Muscovite Law Code (Ulozhenie) of 1649.* Part I: Text and translation. Transl. and ed. by Richard Hellie, Charles Schlacks [sic] Jr. Publisher, Irvine, California, 1988, XXXV + 425 pp.; *The Travel Diary of Peter Tolstoi—A Muscovite in Early Modern Europe.* Transl. by Max J. Okenfuss, Northern Illinois University Press, DeKalb, 1987. XXIX + 359 pp.; Ivan Pososhkov. *The Book of Poverty and Wealth.* Ed. and transl. by A.P. Vlasto and L.R. Lewitter. Intro. and comment. by L.R. Lewitter, Stanford University Press, 1987. X + 440 pp.," *NZh,* 172-173:589–592, Sept.-Dec.

290. Review: "Peter J. Potichnyj & Howard Aster, eds. *Ukrainian-Jewish Relations in Historical Perspective,* Edmonton (Canadian Institute of Ukrainian Studies), 1988. VII + 531 pp.," *NZh,* 171:305–307, June.

291. Review: "Th.G. Stavrou Editor. *Modern Greek Studies Yearbook.* Minneapolis, Minnesota (University of Minnesota), vols 1–3, 1985–1987," *NZh,* 170:317, Mar.

292. Review: "Vladimir Vodoff. *Naissance de la chrétienté russe. (La conversion du prince Vladimir de Kiev (988) et ses conséquences (XI–XIII siècles).* Paris, Fayard, 1988, 493 pp.," *NZh,* 172-173:587–589, Sept.-Dec.

293. Review: "*The Legal Philosophies of Russian Liberalism.* By Andrzej Walicki. New York: Clarendon Press of Oxford University Press, 1987. x, 477pp. $86.00, cloth," *SR,* 47(4):734–735, Winter.

1989

294. "Un empire comme les autres?" *CMRS,* 30(3-4):[321]–327, July-Dec.

295. "Historians and History in Emigration," *Survey,* 30(4)(Issue 131):[7]–21, June.

296. "Introduction" to "Boris Bakhmeteff, Ambassador to the United States from the Republic of Russia," *Foreign Visitors to Congress: Speeches and History.* Edited by Mary Lee Kerr. [Washington, D.C.]: United States Capitol Historical Society; Millwood, New York: Kraus International Publications. Volume 1: 1824–1956, pp. 81–82.

297. "Maloizvestnyi epizod vtoroi mirovoi voiny," *NZh*, 177:[255]–262, Dec.

298. "The Transformation of Muscovite into Imperial Culture (Public Lectures delivered at the Metropolitan Museum of Arts)," *Russian Literature and History: In Honour of Professor Ilya Serman.* Wolf Moskovich, Editor-in-Chief. Jerusalem: Hebrew University of Jerusalem, distributed by the Soviet Jewry Museum Foundation. Pp. 170–177.

299. Review: "E.V. Anisimov. *Rossiia v seredine XVIII veka—Bor'ba za nasledie Petra.* Moscow: Mysl', 1986. 239 pp. 1 rubel 60 kopeks; James F. Brennan. *Enlightened Despotism in Russia—The Reign of Elisabeth, 1741–1762.* New York–Berne–Frankfurt am Main–Paris: Peter Lang, 1987. 269 pp. $49.95," *RH*, 16(1):109–110, Spring.

300. Review: "Daniel Beauvois, editor. *Les Confins de l'ancienne Pologne-Ukraine-Lituanie-Biélorussie XVIe–XXe siècles.* Presses Universitaires de Lille 1988. Pp. 280," *Polish Review*, 34(2):173–175.

301. Review: "Dittmar Dahlmann. *Land und Freiheit: Machnovščina und Zapatismo als Beispiele agrarrevolutionärer Bewegungen.* (Studien zur modernen Geschichte, number 35.) Stuttgart: Steiner. 1986. Pp. 296. DM 68," *AHR*, 94(2):411, Apr.

302. Review: "*Novopokolentsy.* By Boris Prianishnikoff. Silver Spring, Maryland: n.p., 1986. vii, 296 pp. Photographs. Paper," *SR*, 48(2):305–306, Summer.

303. Review: "F. Thom. *Le moment Gorbatchev*, Paris, Hachette, 1989. 282 pages," *NZh*, 176:307–309, Sept.

1990

304. "Enticements and Rifts: Georges Florovsky as Historian of the Life of the Mind and the Life of the Church in Russia," *Modern Greek Studies Yearbook*, vol. 6, pp. 187–244. Edited by Theofanis G. Stavrou.

305. "Introduction," *Russia in the Age of the Enlightenment: Essays for Isabel de Madariaga.* Edited by Roger Bartlett and Janet M. Hartley. London: Macmillan, in association with the School of Slavonic and East European Studies, University of London, 1990. (*School of Slavonic and East European Studies 1990*) Pp. 1–6.

306. "Introduction," "Chronologie," "Bibliographie," Anatole Leroy-Beaulieu, *L'Empire des tsars et les Russes.* Paris: Robert Laffont, 1990. [Originally published: Paris: Hachette, 1881–1889, 3v.] (*Bouquins*) Pp.[I]–LXVII, [LXIX]–LXXX, [1361]–1369, resp.

307. "Pamiati B. Sapira," *NZh*, 178:350–351, Mar.

308. "Peter Scheibert 75 (May 3, 1990)," *JGO*, 38(Neue Folge)(1):[160].

309. "Préface," *L'Émigration russe en Europe: catalogue collectif des périodiques en langue russe 1855–1940.* Établi par Tatiana Ossorguine-Bakounine. 2è ed., rev. et complétée. Paris: Institut d'études slaves. (*Bibliothèque russe de l'Institut d'études slaves*, tome 40/1) Pp. [3]–5.

310. *Russia Abroad: A Cultural History of the Russian Emigration, 1919–1939.* New York; Oxford: Oxford University Press. 239 pp.

311. Review: "Consequences of *Glasnost*." A review of: "Walter Laqueur. *The Long Road to Freedom: Russia and Glasnost.* New York, Charles Scribner's Sons, 1989; Alec Nove. *Glasnost in Action: Cultural Renaissance in Russia.* Boston, MA, Unwin Hyman, 1989; Marquis de Custine. *Empire of the Czar: A Journey Through Eternal Russia.* Foreword by Daniel J. Boorstin. Introduction by George F. Kennan. New York, Doubleday, 1989," *Problems of Communism*, 39(2):105–108, Mar.-Apr.

312. Review: "W. Bruce Lincoln. *The Great Reforms—Autocracy, Bureaucracy and The Politics of Change in Imperial Russia,* DeKalb, Illinois (Northern Illinois University Press), 1990. XVII + 281 pages, Index, Bibl.," *NZh*, 181:360–363, Dec.

313. Review: "*Rossiia i revoliutsiia: russkaia religiozno-filosofskaia i natsional'no-politicheskaia mysl' XX veka.* By Nikolai Poltoratzky. Tenafly, N.J.: Hermitage, 1988. 352 pp. $17.50, paper," *SR*, 49(3):451–453, Fall.

314. Review: "Hugh Ragsdale. *Tsar Paul and the Question of Madness: An Essay in History and Psychology.* (Contributions to the Study of World History, number 13.) New York: Greenwood. 1988. Pp. xviii, 266. $39.95," *AHR*, 95(2):547–548, Apr.

315. Review: "Wladimir Vodoff. *Princes et Principautés Russes, Xe–XVIIe Siècles,* "Variorum," England, 348 pp.," *NZh*, 181:[354]–359, Dec.

316. Review: "D.A. Volkogonov. *Triumf i tragediia: Politicheskii portret I.V. Stalina.* V 2-kh knigakh, 4-kh chastiakh, M., APN, 1989; Evg. Anisimov. *Vremia petrovskikh reform.* L., Lenizdat, 1989," *NZh*, 180:[363]–373, Sept.

1991

317. "At the Origins of a Russian National Consciousness: Eighteenth Century Roots and Napoleonic Wars," *The History Teacher,* 25(1):[7]–18, Nov.

318. "La formazione di una coscienza nazionala russa," *L'età delle rivoluzioni.* Milan: Electa. (*Europa, 1700–1992: Storia di un' identità,* edited by Marco Guidi and Nanda Torcellan) Pp. 448–459.

319. "Introduction," Jakob Walter. *The Diary of a Napoleonic Foot Soldier.* Also editor of volume, and translator of six letters. New York: Doubleday. Translation [by Otto Springer] of *Denkwürdige Geschichtschreibung über die erlebte Millitäridienstzeit* [sic] *des Verfassers dieses Schreibens.* Pp. [xii]–xxx.

320. "Peter's Domestic Legacy: Transformation or Revolution," *Peter the Great Transforms Russia.* 3d ed. Edited and with an introduction by James Cracraft. Lexington, Mass.; Toronto: D.C. Heath and Co. (*Problems in European Civilization*) Pp. 286–301.

321. "Preface," *Catherine II's Charters of 1785 to the Nobility and the Towns.* Translated and edited by David Griffiths and George E. Munro. Bakersfield, Calif.: Charles Schlacks, Jr. (*The Laws of Russia,* Series II: *Imperial Russia,* volume 289: *April 21, 1785*) Pp. [ix]–xiii.

322. "Transfiguration and Modernization: The Paradoxes of Social Disciplining, Paedagogical Leadership, and the Enlightenment in 18th Century Russia," *Alteuropa—Ancien Régime—Frühe Neuzeit: Probleme und Methoden der Forschung.* Hans Erich Bödeker, Ernst Hinrichs, hrsg. Stuttgart-Bad Cannstatt: Frommann-Holzboog. (*Problemata,* 124) Pp. 99–115.

323. Review: "*Peter der Grosse.* By Erich Donnert. Leipzig: Koehler & Amelang, 1989. 355 pp. Plates. Cloth," *SR,* 50(1):[179], Spring.

324. Review: "*Threshold of a New World: Intellectuals and the Exile Experience, 1830–1848.* By Lloyd S. Kramer. Ithaca, N.Y.; and London: Cornell University Press, 1988. xii, 297 pp. Illustrations. Photographs. Tables. Cloth," *SR,* 50(4):1014–1015, Winter.

325. Review: "N.I. Pavlenko. *Petr Velikii.* M., Mysl', 1990, 592 str.," *NZh,* 182:380–382, Mar.

326. "In the Grand Manner." A review of: "Richard Pipes. *The Russian Revolution* (New York: Alfred A. Knopf, 1990). 944 pp., $40.00," *The National Interest,* 24:85–90, Summer.

327. Review: "R. Pipes. *The Russian Revolution,* New York, Alfred A. Knopf, 1990, XXIV + 944 pages," *NZh,* 182:375–380, Mar.

1992

328. "En guise de conclusion," *CMRS,* 34(1-2):[277]–284, Jan.-June.

329. "Le front populaire et la presse émigrée russe," *Russes, Slaves et Soviétiques: pages d'histoire offertes à Roger Portal.* Paris: Institut d'Études Slaves. (*Publications de la Sorbonne*) Pp. [415]–430.

330. "Introduction—M.P. Drahomanov's Political Thought," *Materiialy do istorii literatury i hromads'koi dumky: lystuvannia z amerikans'kykh arkhiviv 1857–1933.* Redaktory Bohdan Strumins'kyi i Marta Skorups'ka u spivpratsi z Edvardom Kasintsem i Nataleiu Livyts'koiu-Kholodnoiu. N'iu-Iork: Ukrainska vil'na akademiia nauk u Spoluchenykh Shtatakh Ameryky. (*Sources of modern history of the Ukraine,* vol. 3) Pp. 20–26.

331. "Legenden und Vorurteile," *Deutsche und Deutschland aus russischer Sicht: 18. Jahrhundert: Aufklärung.* Herausgegeben von Dagmar Herrmann; unter Mitarbeit von Karl-Heinz Korn. München: Wilhelm Fink Verlag. (*West-östliche Spiegelungen:* Reihe B; Bd. 2) Aus dem Englischen übertragen von Eva Neunzig. Pp. [53]–73.

332. "La noblesse et le discours politique sous le règne de Pierre le Grand," *CMRS,* 34(1-2):[33]–45, Jan.-June.

333. "Pis'ma M. Karpovicha G. Vernadskomu: publikatsiia, predislovie i kommentarii M. Raeva," *NZh,* 188:[259]–296, Sept.

334. "Ukraine and Imperial Russia: Intellectual and Political Encounters from the Seventeenth to the Nineteenth Century," *Ukraine and Russia in Their Historical Encounter.* Also one of the editors. Edmonton: Canadian Institute of Ukrainian Studies Press, University of Alberta. Pp.[69]–85.

335. Review: "*Science and Russian Culture in an Age of Revolutions: V.I. Vernadsky and His Scientific School, 1863–1945.* By Kendall E. Bailes. Indiana-Michigan Series in Russian and East European Studies. Edited by Alexander Rabinowitch and William G. Rosenberg. Bloomington: Indiana University Press, 1990. Pp. xii + 238. $29.50," *JMH,* 64(1):182–184, Mar.

336. Review: "S.A. Chibiriaev. *Velikii russkii reformator: Zhizn', deiatel'nost', politicheskie vzgliady M.M. Speranskogo* [The Great Russian Reformer: The Life, Work, and Political Views of M.M. Speranskii]. (Istoricheskie portrety.) Moscow: Nauka, 1989. Pp. 213. 1 r.," *AHR,* 97(2):582, Apr.

337. Review: "Andreas Kappeler (Hrsg.) *Die Russen. Ihr Nationalbewusstsein in*

Geschichte und Gegenwart. Markus Verlag Köln 1990. 22 pp. DM 48, Nationalitäten- und Regionalprobleme in Osteuropa. Vol. 5," *JGO,* 40(Neue Folge)(2):228–230.

338. Review: "Andreas Kappeler. *Russland als Vielvölkerreich. Entstehung, Geschichte, Zerfall.* Verlag C.H. Beck München 1992. 395 pp. Tables, Maps, Bibliography, Index. DM 58," *JGO,* 40(Neue Folge)(4):547–549.

339. Review: "Robert A. Karlowich. *We Fall and Rise: Russian-Language Newspapers in New York City, 1889–1914.* The Scarecrow Press. Metuchen, N.J. & London 1991. XXIII, 332 pp. $39.50," *JGO,* 40(Neue Folge)(4):580–581.

340. Review: "S.V. Mironenko. *Stranitsy tainoi istorii samoderzhaviia: Politicheskaia istoriia Rossii pervoi poloviny XIX stoletiia* [Pages from the Secret History of the Autocracy: A Political History of Russia in the First Half of the Nineteenth Century]. Moscow: Mysl', 1990. Pp. 235. 1 r.," *AHR,* 97(1):252–253, Feb.

341. Review: "*Russia Observed: Collected Essays on Russian and Soviet History.* By Richard Pipes. Boulder, San Francisco, and London: Westview Press, 1989. 240 pp. $34.95," *HUS,* 16(1/2):213–215, June.

342. Review: "*Tables de la revue russe Le Messager socialiste 1921–1963—Le Messager russe, recueil: 1964–1965.* [Publié par la Bibliothèque russe Tourguénev, la Bibliothèque de documentation internationale contemporaine et M. Alexandre Lande]. Préface d'André Liebich, Paris, 1992 (Institut d'études slaves—Bibliothèque russe de L'Institut d'études slaves, tome XC), XXIV + 391 pages. *Ukazateli zhurnala Sotsialisticheskii Vestnik 1921–1963—Sotsialisticheskii vestnik. Sbornik: 1964–1965,*" *NZh,* 189:383–386, Dec.

1993

343. "Hermann Aubin und die zeitgenössische Historiographie," *Forschungen zur osteuropäischen Geschichte,* Band 48. Berlin: Osteuropa-Institut; Wiesbaden: Harrassowitz. (*Historische Veröffentlichungen, Osteuropa-Institut an der Freien Universität Berlin;* Band 48) "Klaus Meyer zum 65. Geburtstag." Pp.[159]–166.

344. Review [M.R.]: "James E. Hassell. *Russian Refugees in France and the United States Between the World Wars.* Philadelphia 1991. VII, 96 pp. $20. Transactions of the American Philosophical Society. Vol. 81, Part 7," *JGO,* 41(Neue Folge) (1):[152]–153.

345. Review: "Marinus A. Wes. *Classics in Russia 1700–1855: Between Two Bronze Horsemen.* (Brill's Studies in Intellectual History, number 33.) New York: E.J. Brill, 1992. Pp. viii, 366. $94.50," *AHR,* 98(3):909–910, June.

Reprints and Translations

346. "An Early Theorist of Absolutism: Joseph of Volokolamsk," *Readings in Russian History,* Volume 1: *From Ancient Times to the Abolition of Serfdom.* Compiled by Sidney Harcave. New York: Thomas Y. Crowell Company, 1962. Pp. 177–187. (See also no. 3)

347. "Enseñemos a ponsar a nuestros alumnos," *La Educacion,* 10(3):47–48, Apr.-June 1958. (See also no. 44)

348. "Einige Überlegungen zum russischen Liberalismus," Lothar Gall, comp. *Liberalismus.* Köln: Kiepenheuer & Witsch, [1976]. Pp. [308]–318. [Translated by Anemone Bronecke.] (See also no. 49)

349. *The Structure of Russian History: Interpretive Essays*. By Michael Cherniavsky. New York: Random House, 1970. ["Home, school, and service ...", pp. 212–213; "Russia's Perception ...," pp. 261–266.] (See also nos. 62, 73)

350. Editor. *Russian Intellectual History: An Anthology*. With an introduction by Isaiah Berlin; sponsored by the Russian Institute of Columbia University. [Atlantic Highlands] N.J.: Humanities Press, 1978. x, 404 pp. (See also no. 85)

351. "Russian Youth on the Eve of Romanticism: Andrei I. Turgenev and His Circle," *Revolution and Politics in Russia: Essays in Memory of B.I. Nikolaevsky*. Ed. by Alexander and Janet Rabinowitch with Ladis K.D. Kristof. Bloomington-London: Indiana University Press for the International Affairs Center. (*Russian and East European Series*, vol. 4), 1972. Pp. 39–54. (See also no. 88)

352. "Der Stil der russischen Reichspolitik und Fürst G.A. Potemkin," *JGO*, 16(2):162–193, June 1968. (See also nos. 90, 353)

353. "In the Imperial Manner," *Catherine the Great: A Profile*. New York: Hill and Wang, 1972. xiii, 331 pp. (*World Profiles*. Aida DiPace Donald, general editor) Pp. 197–246. (See also nos. 90, 352)

354. Review essay: "*Iz pod glyb* and the History of Russian Social Thought," *Iz pod glyb: Sbornik statei* [From Under the Rubble: A Collection of Articles]. Paris: YMCA Press, 1974, 276 pp.," *RR*, 34(4):476–488, Oct. (See also no. 158)

355. "Der Wohlgeordnete Polizeistaat und die Entwicklung der Moderne im Europa des 17. und 18. Jahrhunderts und ein Versuch eines vergleichenden Ansatzes," Ernst Hinrichs, comp. *Absolutismus*. Frankfurt am Main: Suhrkamp, 1986. 398 pp. (Suhrkamp–TB Wissenschaft, 535) (See also no. 159)

356. *Understanding Imperial Russia*. Translated from the French by Arthur Goldhammer; foreword by John Keep. New York: Columbia University Press, 1984. xix, 248 pp. (See also nos. 207, 357–358)

357. *Poniat' dorevoliutsionnuiu Rossiiu: gosudarstvo i obshchestvo v Rossiiskoi imperii*. Translated from the French by Iaroslav Gorbanevskii and Natal'ia Diuzheva; with an introduction by Mikhail Heller. First Russian edition. London: Overseas Publications Interchange, 1990. 304 pp. (*Istoricheskaia biblioteka*, v. 4) (See also nos. 207, 356, 358)

358. *La Russia degli zar*. Translated (from the French) by Giovanni Ferrara. Bari: Editori Laterza, 1984. (*Storia et Societa*) xv, 240 pp. (See also nos. 207, 356–357)

359. "Préface," Alexandre Davydoff. *Images russes: souvenirs*. Traduit du russe par Olga Davydoff Dax; introduction par Jean Dax. Lausanne, Suisse: L'Age d'Homme, 1984. Pp. 7–9. (See also no. 227)

360. "Moscovy Looks West," *Russia and Europe*. Edited by Paul Dukes. London: Collins & Brown, 1991. "A *History Today* book." Pp. 59–68. (See also no. 245)

About the Book and Author

Marc Raeff is one of the truly outstanding scholars of Russian history. This volume offers a sampling of the best essays from his prolific, forty-year career; they span the history of Russia from the late seventeenth to the late nineteenth century. In these essays, Raeff considers the problems of imperial Russian politics and administration, analyzes Russia's intellectual and social history as it relates to the governance of the multiethnic empire, and places the institutional and intellectual history of Russia in the context of other Western and Central European developments.

Raeff's essays offer a sketch of the generation that came of age in the era of the Napoleonic Wars and the ensuing attempts at constitutional reform—the generation that laid the foundations of the modern Russian national consciousness. He explores modernization reform and liberalism in the second half of the nineteenth century, the acquisition and incorporation of Russia's multiethnic population, and the politics and administration of the reigns of Peter III and Catherine II. He examines how the Russian élites assimilated values from the Western and Central European Enlightenment and assesses the important intellectual and ideological effects the Enlightenment had on the nation. The volume concludes with a comparative look at the process of Westernization, focusing on issues of literacy, state leadership, and the role of the intelligentsia.

Many of these seminal essays are long out of print and hard to find. This timely volume makes Marc Raeff's insights readily available as Russia reemerges as a nation-state facing "new" challenges that are often deeply rooted in its past.

Marc Raeff, a preeminent force in Russian historical studies, is Bakhmeteff Professor Emeritus of Russian Studies at Columbia University.